THE COLLECTED WORKS OF DILGO KHYENTSE

VOLUME ONE

Enlightened Courage
The Heart of Compassion
Journey to Enlightenment

VOLUME TWO

The Excellent Path to Enlightenment
The Heart Treasure of the Enlightened Ones
The Hundred Verses of Advice
The Wheel of Investigation
The Wish-Fulfilling Jewel

VOLUME THREE

The Lamp That Dispels Darkness
Primordial Purity
Pure Appearance
Selected Verse
A Wondrous Ocean of Advice
Zurchungpa's Testament

THE COLLECTED WORKS OF
DILGO KHYENTSE

VOLUME THREE

Zurchungpa's Testament
A Wondrous Ocean of Advice for the
Practice of Retreat in Solitude
Pure Appearance
Primordial Purity
The Lamp That Dispels Darkness
Selected Verse

EDITED BY
Matthieu Ricard and Vivian Kurz

The Collected Works of Dilgo Khyentse
IS PUBLISHED IN COOPERATION WITH
SNOW LION PUBLICATIONS AND THE
NALANDA TRANSLATION COMMITTEE

SHAMBHALA · Boulder · 2010

Shambhala Publications, Inc.
4720 Walnut Street
Boulder, Colorado 80301
www.shambhala.com

9 8 7 6 5

Printed in the United States of America

⊗ This edition is printed on acid-free paper that meets the
American National Standards Institute z39.48 Standard.
♻ Shambhala Publications makes every effort to print on recycled paper.
For more information please visit www.shambhala.com.

Shambhala Publications is distributed worldwide by
Penguin Random House, Inc., and its subsidiaries.

Designed by Lora Zorian

LIBRARY OF CONGRESS CATALOGING-IN-PUBLICATION DATA

Rab-gsal-zla-ba, Dis-mgo Mkhyen-brtse, 1910–1991.
[Selections. English. 2010]
The collected works of Dilgo Khyentse / edited by
Matthieu Ricard and Vivian Kurz.—1st ed.
p. cm.
Includes bibliographical references and index.
ISBN 978-1-59030-592-8 (hardcover v. 1: alk. paper)
ISBN 978-1-59030-593-5 (hardcover v. 2: alk. paper)
ISBN 978-1-59030-627-7 (hardcover v. 3: alk. paper)
1. Spiritual life—Rñiṅ-ma-pa (Sect)
i. Ricard, Matthieu. ii. Kurz, Vivian. iii. Title.
BQ7662.6.R35 2010
294.3'444—dc22
2009038698

Dedicated to the flourishing
of the beneficial activities
of Dilgo Khyentse Yangsi Rinpoche,
Ugyen Tenzin Jigme Lhundrup

CONTENTS

CONTENTS

THE DALAI LAMA

REMEMBRANCE

DILGO KHYENTSE RINPOCHE is one of my most revered teachers. We first met propitiously in the Jokhang in Lhasa when I returned from my first pilgrimage to India. However, I did not really get to know him well until much later when we were both living in exile. I had clear indications in profound experiences and dreams that we had some special karmic connections, and as a result, I began to receive teachings from him. Characteristically for this great and warm-hearted man, he showed tremendous kindness to me by opening up his treasury of experience and knowledge and granting me empowerments, teachings, and transmissions.

Khyentse Rinpoche did not start out with a high rank in the religious hierarchy but became a great teacher by developing complete and authentic accomplishments. As an incarnation of the nineteenth-century Tibetan master Jamyang Khyentse Wangpo, he began even as a child to manifest the spiritual potential he had inherited from former lives. He received teachings from many masters, and instead of just leaving those teachings on the pages of his books, he actually put them into practice and gained direct experience of them.

At quite a young age, he chose the life of a hermit and devoted all his time to contemplating the teachings and gaining experience in their real meaning. He reached the very essence and vital point of meditation practice. As a result, he became a holder of the living tradition—the empowerments, transmissions, and pith instructions—of the eight principal spiritual lineages that flourished in Tibet and included both the sutra and tantra traditions.

Besides his many hidden qualities, he was manifestly a great scholar and practitioner. I particularly appreciated his deeply nonsectarian outlook. There existed in Tibet a number of different spiritual traditions, corresponding to different ways of practicing, each characterized by certain unique features: one aspect of the practice may be given more or less emphasis, or some important point of the teachings may be explained in a particular way. If we study these different traditions, we find that they complement one another. A nonsectarian approach is therefore very useful for one's own practice, as well as for helping to sustain the Buddhist teachings.

Despite his wide renown and large following, Khyentse Rinpoche always remained very gentle and humble. His deep spiritual experience was obvious, but he was never proud of his knowledge. This is something very remarkable. He was equally kind to all, regardless of social or economic standing, and he was never heard to say anything that would bring hurt or pain to others.

He worked tirelessly to preserve and spread the Buddha's teachings for the sake of all beings, saving and reproducing rare scriptures that had almost disappeared, restoring monasteries that had been destroyed, and above all teaching. Even in his old age, he was always ready at any time to give textual explanations, empowerments, and pith instructions to anyone who could become a genuine holder of the lineage. Everything he did was directed solely toward helping others and preserving the teachings. He also wrote a large number of treatises and commentaries.

Khyentse Rinpoche was a model for all other holders of the teachings. Not only should we admire his inconceivable knowledge, wisdom, and accomplishment, but more important, we should follow his example and emulate those qualities ourselves. That is the best way to fulfill our teacher's wishes, the best offering we can make to him. As Rinpoche's student, I would like to share with others my feeling that we are very fortunate to have met him and to have his teachings. What we received from him was priceless. Now, therefore, it is essential that we implement his teachings in our daily life, so that we become good students of a good lama.

Deep spiritual experiences, which seem to transcend logical explanation, are not easily expressed in words or transmitted by means of verbal explanation. They depend, rather, on the inspiration and blessings received from the spiritual lineage through one's teacher. This is why in Buddhism (and particularly Vajrayana Buddhism) the practice of Guru Yoga—"union with the teacher's nature"—is given such great importance. Since the practice of Guru Yoga is so important, the qualities of the teacher himself are extremely important too. The qualities necessary for an authentic teacher were described in great detail by the Buddha himself in many sutras and tantras. All of these qualities I found in Khyentse Rinpoche. It was a great privilege to have known him, and I am fortunate to revere him among my own precious teachers.

When the Buddhist teachings began to flourish in Tibet, the blessings of Guru Padmasambhava, who brought Buddhism to Tibet, were a very crucial factor. His prayers and his compassion established a special connection between him and Tibet. We are now living in an age in which, from a spiritual point of view, conditions have deteriorated. People are very intelligent and inventive; but the quality they often lack is true human goodness. Their intelligence is used in more and more destructive ways.

The Tibetans themselves have been going through a very difficult period, with the widespread destruction that Tibet and Tibetan Buddhism have suffered. And all over the world, all sorts of upheavals and misfortunes have arisen. At such difficult times, the blessings of Guru Padmasambhava are essential, and I feel that the same is true of Khyentse Rinpoche's blessing, since he had a very special connection with Guru Padmasambhava.

The year 2010 marks the one hundredth anniversary of Khyentse Rinpoche's birth in eastern Tibet. It gives me immense pleasure to know that to commemorate this event his teachings that have been previously translated into English are now being published as a complete collection. It will serve both as a reminder to those who met him and as a source of inspiration for those who did not.

With my prayers that my teacher's wisdom may permeate our minds, I would like to thank all those who have collaborated in this work—publishers, translators, and editors—for making his translated teachings available in these three volumes.

His Holiness the Fourteenth Dalai Lama
July 15, 2008

FOREWORD

THE YEAR 2010 MARKS the one hundredth anniversary of the birth of one of the greatest luminaries of Tibetan Buddhism in the twentieth century, Dilgo Khyentse Rinpoche (1910–1991). We are very pleased to commemorate this occasion with the publication of these volumes, in which are gathered all the main teachings given by Khyentse Rinpoche that have been translated into English.

I was brought up by Khyentse Rinpoche from the age of five and received every teaching he gave over twenty-five years. My first perception of him was that of a wonderfully loving grandfather. In fact, he was like my true father and mother in one person. Then, as I grew up, this perception gradually transformed into deep respect, confidence, and finally unchanging faith. Khyentse Rinpoche thus became my spiritual master. When I started studying the scriptures, I found in him all the qualities they described for an authentic and realized master. I now realize how fortunate I am to have met someone like him. My only aim is to be able to perpetuate his teachings and fulfill his wishes.

Khyentse Rinpoche was one of the finest examples of a spiritual teacher. He was a master of masters, and most twentieth-century Tibetan teachers received teachings from him, including His Holiness the Dalai Lama, who considers him one of his closest teachers.

Khyentse Rinpoche did his utmost to preserve the Tibetan Buddhist tradition and give teachings tirelessly, according to each person's need. He was concerned not only about the preservation of the Nyingma lineage but also about all the other major lineages of Tibetan Buddhism: Kadam, Sakya, Kagyu, Geluk, Kalachakra, Chö, Shije, and Jonang.

Because of his vast accomplishments, it seemed as if he lived numerous lives in one: he spent thirty years practicing in retreat; studied with
fifty great teachers and achieved unparalleled erudition; taught continuously several hours a day for over half a century; wrote twenty-five large
volumes of commentaries, arrangements for sadhana practices, songs of
realization, and pieces of advice, together with the texts of his own *termas,* or "revealed treasures"; and initiated and oversaw numerous major
projects to preserve and disseminate Buddhist tradition and culture.

Words do not suffice to express his qualities, and when I try to describe them, I wonder if people might think that I am exaggerating, even
though I am only touching on the most obvious ones.

Khyentse Rinpoche had a great transformative impact on people's
lives. After his death the strength of his presence, far from vanishing,
has become increasingly all-pervading. Although we unfortunately can't
meet him anymore, when we read his writings, we can experience the
profundity of his wisdom and the magnitude of his compassion.

I hope fervently that this collection will honor Khyentse Rinpoche's
legacy and bring to many English-language readers a treasure trove
of precious teachings that provide a profound inspiration to their lives
and reliable, wise, and compassionate guidance on the path to enlightenment.

SHECHEN RABJAM
Thegchog Gatsel Ling
Paro, Bhutan
May 2008

PREFACE TO *THE COLLECTED WORKS OF DILGO KHYENTSE*

ON THIS AUSPICIOUS OCCASION of the hundredth anniversary of the birth of Dilgo Khyentse Rinpoche, I feel fortunate to have a chance to participate in the publication of this special edition of commemorative volumes of his translated teachings.

For eleven continuous years while I was living with Khyentse Rinpoche as a disciple and attendant, I had the privilege and daunting responsibility of orally translating many of the teachings found in this volume. Over time transcripts were made available to qualified editors who worked on refining the manuscripts. Sharing these teachings through this collection gives all of us who participated in preparing them a gratifying sense of accomplishment.

When he first left Tibet as a refugee in 1959, Dilgo Khyentse Rinpoche lived for some time in the hill station of Kalimpong in West Bengal. Soon after his arrival, a few foreign students came to meet this extraordinary spiritual teacher and seek his guidance. Among them was John Driver (Könchog Pelgye), who was also one of the very few Westerners who met Dzongsar Khyentse Chökyi Lodrö, one of Khyentse Rinpoche's root teachers, who passed away in Sikkim in 1959. Others, such as Prince Peter of Greece, who was then living in Kalimpong, and a few European scholars also met Khyentse Rinpoche in these early years. Later, Gene Smith, arguably the most knowledgeable Western Tibetologist, also became very close to him and used to host him at his residence in New Delhi. Many other dedicated Western practitioners came to consider Khyentse Rinpoche as the main source of inspiration in their lives.

In the early 1960s Khyentse Rinpoche was invited to live in Bhutan, where he taught at the Simtokha School near Thimphu. For many years he gave extensive teachings, undertook intensive retreats, and performed ceremonies for peace in the country. Many disciples came to him for teachings and advice, and he became widely respected throughout the land.

During the years that followed, whenever Khyentse Rinpoche traveled to India and Nepal, more Western students began to study with him. Eventually, in 1976, Khyentse Rinpoche first visited Europe (at the invitation of Pema Wangyal Rinpoche) and the United States (at the invitation of Chögyam Trungpa Rinpoche). From then on, he visited Europe almost every year, particularly the south of France, where he taught countless disciples and bestowed instructions and empowerments on those who were engaged in the traditional three-year retreat practice. If we add up all the many times he spent at his seat in the Dordogne, Tashi Pelbar Ling, it would come to a full year of his life.

In the 1980s Rinpoche usually spent the spring and summer in Bhutan doing retreats, conducting *drupchen* ceremonies, or giving teachings to large crowds or to a small group of tulkus and disciples. During the fall and winter, he would teach tirelessly in various monasteries in Nepal and India. In addition to the main scheduled sessions of teachings that he gave almost daily, he would give more private instructions to the handful of foreigners who were present. Either Pema Wangyal Rinpoche or I would most often interpret for him in English on the spot, or translate his words later from recordings.

Over the years, some of these recorded live translations of teachings were transcribed, or retranslated carefully from the Tibetan. All the teachings included in this collection are from such oral teachings given to Western students at their request. These teachings are immensely precious. However, given the depth and breadth of Khyentse Rinpoche's teaching activities, these translations are but a drop in the ocean of all the oral teachings that were taped during the last fifteen years of his life. The recordings come to more than four hundred hours of tapes that are now carefully preserved in the Shechen Archives in Nepal and in other places where Khyentse Rinpoche taught.

The translated oral teachings convey the unique quality of Khyentse Rinpoche's oral exposition on the various stages of the Buddhist path from the perspective of meditative experience and actually putting the teachings into practice. They complement Khyentse Rinpoche's written commentaries, sadhanas, ritual arrangements, songs of realization, practice manuals, and spiritual treasures (termas)—his collected works, filling no fewer than twenty-five volumes of six hundred pages each, which were published in Tibetan in 1995 by Shechen Publications under the title *skyabs rje dil mgo mkhyen brtse rin po che'i bka' bum*. So far, only a very small percentage of these writings has been translated.

I have tried to arrange the oral teachings presented in this collection according to the progression of the Buddhist path and the nine vehicles. All but three of the texts included in the three volumes of collected works have been published before in various languages.

The collection begins with a condensed history of Khyentse Rinpoche's life story as a powerful source of inspiration (adapted from the book *Journey to Enlightenment*). It is followed by the teachings on mind training (*Enlightened Courage*) and a commentary on *The Thirty-seven Verses on the Practice of a Bodhisattva* (*The Heart of Compassion*), a practice that constitutes the life force of the Mahayana path.

The second volume begins with *The Excellent Path to Enlightenment*, a manual of instructions for the fundamental practice of *ngöndro*, which is also known as the "preliminary practice." According to Khyentse Rinpoche and other great teachers, this is the essential practice that will determine the quality of every other practice one might do later on. As Khyentse Rinpoche told us repeatedly, "Some consider the main practice profound, but it is the preliminary practices that we consider profound."

The next text, *The Wheel of Investigation*, is a commentary on a basic analysis of the body, speech, and mind, composed by Mipham Rinpoche. Soon after Khyentse Rinpoche was born, he was blessed by Mipham Rinpoche, and he often said that this meeting truly gave meaning to his life. As he wrote in his autobiography, "Whenever I teach or study the dharma, I still feel that the little understanding that I have achieved is due to the kindness of Mipham Rinpoche, who was Manjushri in person."

Following this is *The Wish-Fulfilling Jewel*, instructions for practicing guru yoga, "uniting with the guru's nature." This practice is the quintessence of all aspects of the path, in the beginning, the middle, and the end, and the deepest and most powerful way to progress and dispel obstacles.

After the guru yoga teachings are *The Heart Treasure of the Enlightened Ones* and *The Hundred Verses of Advice*. These are profound and direct instructions on how to practice the dharma of the vehicles of both the sutra and tantra, ranging from renouncing worldly activities, taking refuge, and developing bodhichitta, to transforming and freeing deluded thoughts and emotions and resting in the simplicity of pure awareness.

The third volume includes teaching on the development (*kyerim*) and completion (*dzogrim*) stages, and retreat practice that covers the various vehicles of Tibetan Buddhism. Two of the texts in this volume—*Pure Appearance* and *Primordial Purity*—were formerly restricted to students who have received pointing-out transmission, and are now being made available. It begins with *Zurchungpa's Testament*, Khyentse Rinpoche's explanation of the profound commentary written by his root teacher, Shechen Gyaltsap Rinpoche. The commentary is on the 580 short maxims organized into eighty chapters written by the famed eleventh-century Nyingma master Zurchung Sherab Trakpa.

This is followed by *A Wondrous Ocean of Advice for the Practice of Retreat in Solitude*. This short explanation of an inspiring text of Jigme Lingpa on doing contemplative retreat is published in this translation here for the first time. The next text, *Pure Appearance*, explains in detail the practice of the development stage of the Mantrayana and how to visualize wisdom deities, engage in mantra recitation, and purify the various stages of birth, death, and bardo.

Primordial Purity and *The Lamp That Dispels Darkness*, the last two texts in volume three, contain quintessential teachings on the ultimate nature of reality and of the mind.

Dilgo Khyentse Rinpoche studied poetic composition in his teens, and throughout his life he spontaneously wrote poetry including devotional songs, praises of sacred places, verses of advice, and letters in the form of poems. Only a few of his poems have been translated into English, and some of these are included in *Journey to Enlightenment* (in volume one) and at the end of volume three.

With this wonderful collection of teachings, students who sincerely wish to engage in serious practice of the nine vehicles of Tibetan Buddhism can find a complete array of instructions to inspire and guide them in a most authentic way. As the Buddha told his disciples before passing into *parinirvana*, "I shall come back in the form of scriptures." Since Khyentse Rinpoche is no longer present in this world in his physical form, these teachings are the true representative of his wisdom and compassion and the closest way to meet him as if in reality.

Matthieu Ricard
Shechen Monastery
Nepal
July 2008

ACKNOWLEDGMENTS

I WOULD LIKE TO EXPRESS my appreciation to the translators, publishers, and editors who have worked over the years on the texts included in *The Collected Works of Dilgo Khyentse*. I am grateful to Samuel Bercholz and the whole team at Shambhala Publications for enthusiastically embracing this project from the start.

The project, however, could not have progressed without the generosity of Jeff Cox and Sydney Piburn of Snow Lion, who gave us permission to reproduce the texts that they publish and distribute: *Enlightened Courage, Zurchungpa's Testament, The Wish-Fulfilling Jewel,* and *The Excellent Path to Enlightenment*.

Similarly, Larry Mermelstein allowed us to include two books that are published by the Nalanda/Vajravairochana Translation Committee: *Primordial Purity* and *Pure Appearance*. These teachings are of profound meaning, and their inclusion completes the comprehensive nature of this collection. Without the openheartedness of all these publishers, the *Collected Works* could never have come into existence.

Of course, it is only through the knowledge, hard work, and dedication of translators that these teachings are able to be shared with non-Tibetan-speaking readers. In particular, I would like to thank Matthieu Ricard, who translated ten of the thirteen texts and took most of the photographs included in these volumes. I am very grateful for his tireless efforts on behalf of the continuation of Dilgo Khyentse Rinpoche's lineage, including the publication of Rinpoche's complete collected works in Tibetan.

Almost all the commentaries and some of the root texts were translated by members of the Padmakara Translation Group: Wulstan Fletcher, Helena Blankleder, Stephen Gethin, and John Canti (who also edited all

ACKNOWLEDGMENTS

but three of Matthieu Ricard's translations). I am deeply appreciative of the accuracy, elegance, and polish of their distinguished work.

Equally, I would like to thank Erik Pema Kunsang, David Christensen, and Adam Pearcy, who translated the three root texts for the new commentaries included in volumes two and three, and who kindly gave us permission to use them. I am very grateful to Ani Jinba Palmo for translating two of the books included in this collection, as well as for her translation of Khyentse Rinpoche's autobiography, sections of which appear in *Journey to Enlightenment*. In addition, I am grateful to Erik Pema Kunsang and the Padmakara Translation Group for their help with many of the glossary definitions.

To all these very knowledgeable and talented translators, I extend my gratitude for their ongoing efforts to bring the teachings of Tibetan Buddhism into Western languages.

When I first had the idea of republishing these teachings as a collected work in honor of Khyentse Rinpoche's one hundredth anniversary, I mentioned it to Vivian Kurz. I extend my thanks to her for her dedication in diligently taking on the project from start to finish, through all its stages of creation and publication.

My appreciation goes to the whole staff of Shambhala Publications for their wise and patient input and hard work: Emily Bower, our in-house editor, for her sensitivity, guidance, and enthusiasm; Kendra Crossen for her careful and very intelligent handling of the texts; and Hazel Bercholz for her creative understanding of the power of images.

Finally, I am profoundly grateful to His Holiness the Dalai Lama for agreeing to share with us some of his own memories and feelings as a prelude to the first volume.

It is a great joy for us to present this collection. May its merit be dedicated to the benefit of all sentient beings, to the perpetuation of the Dharma, which is the source of all temporary and ultimate happiness, to the long life and compassionate activities of His Holiness the Dalai Lama and all the great holders of the Buddha's teachings, and especially to the flourishing of the beneficial activities of the reincarnation of Dilgo Khyentse Rinpoche, Yangsi Rinpoche, Ugyen Tenzin Jigme Lhundrup.

SHECHEN RABJAM
Shechen Monastery, Nepal
July 2008

ABOUT DILGO
KHYENTSE RINPOCHE

DILGO KHYENTSE RINPOCHE (1910–1991) was one of the last of the generation of great lamas who completed their education and training in Tibet. He was one of the principal lamas of the ancient Nyingmapa tradition, an outstanding upholder of the practice lineage who spent twenty-two years of his life meditating in retreat, accomplishing the fruits of the many teachings he had received.

He composed numerous poems, meditation texts, and commentaries, and was a tertön, a discoverer of "treasures" containing the profound instructions hidden by Padmasambhava. Not only was he one of the leading masters of the pith instructions of Dzogchen, the Great Perfection, he was also the holder of hundreds of lineages, which he sought, received, and taught throughout his life. In his generation he was the exemplary exponent of the Rime (nonsectarian) movement, renowned for his ability to transmit the teachings of each Buddhist lineage according to its own tradition. Indeed, there are few contemporary lamas who have not received teachings from him, and a great many, including His Holiness the Dalai Lama himself, who venerate him as one of their principal teachers.

Scholar, sage, and poet, teacher of teachers, Rinpoche never ceased to inspire all who encountered him through his monumental presence, his simplicity, dignity, and humor.

Khyentse Rinpoche was born in Denkhok Valley, in eastern Tibet, to a family descended from the royal lineage of the ninth-century king Trisong Detsen. His father was a minister to the king of Derge. When still in his mother's womb, he was recognized as an extraordinary incarnation by the illustrious Mipham Rinpoche, who later named the infant Tashi Paljor and bestowed a special blessing and Manjushri empowerment upon him.

Even as a little boy, Rinpoche manifested a strong desire to devote himself entirely to religious life. But his father had other ideas. His two elder sons had already left home to pursue monastic careers; one had been recognized as an incarnate lama and the other wanted to become a doctor. Rinpoche's father hoped that his youngest son would follow in his own footsteps, and he could not accept that he might also be a tulku, or incarnate lama, as had been indicated by several learned masters.

At the age of ten, the boy was taken ill with severe burns; he was bedridden for nearly a year. Knowledgeable lamas advised that unless he was allowed to embrace spiritual life, he would not live long. Yielding to everyone's entreaties, his father agreed that the child could follow his own wishes and aspirations in order to fulfill his destiny.

At the age of eleven, Rinpoche entered Shechen Monastery in Kham, eastern Tibet, one of the six principal monasteries of the Nyingmapa school. There, his root guru, Shechen Gyaltsap, enthroned him as an incarnation of the wisdom mind of the first Khyentse Rinpoche, Jamyang Khyentse Wangpo (1820–1892), the peerless lama who—along with the first Jamgön Kongtrul—set in motion a Buddhist renaissance throughout Tibet. All contemporary Tibetan masters draw inspiration and blessings from the Rime movement.

Khyentse means "wisdom and love." The Khyentse tulkus are incarnations of several key figures in the development of Tibetan Buddhism. These include King Trisong Detsen and Vimalamitra, who, along with Guru Rinpoche, brought tantric Buddhism to Tibet in the ninth century; the great Gampopa, disciple of Milarepa and founder of the Kagyu tradition; and Jigme Lingpa, who, in the eighteenth century, discovered the Longchen Nyingthig, the Heart Essence of the Vast Expanse.

At Shechen, Rinpoche spent much of his time studying and meditating with his root guru in a hermitage above the monastery. It was during this time that Shechen Gyaltsap gave him all the essential empowerments and instructions of the Nyingma tradition. Rinpoche also studied with many other great masters, including the renowned disciple of Patrul Rinpoche, Dzogchen Khenpo Shenga, who imparted to him his own major work, the *Thirteen Great Commentaries*. In all, he received extensive teachings and transmissions from more than fifty teachers.

Before Shechen Gyaltsap died, Khyentse Rinpoche promised his beloved master that he would unstintingly teach whoever asked him for Dharma. Then, from the ages of fifteen to twenty-eight, he spent most of his time meditating in silent retreat, living in isolated hermitages and caves, or sometimes simply under the shelter of overhanging rocks, in the mountainous countryside near his birthplace in Denkhok Valley.

Dilgo Khyentse Rinpoche later spent many years with Dzongsar Khyentse, Chökyi Lodrö (1896–1959), who was also an incarnation of the first Khyentse. After receiving from Chökyi Lodrö the many empowerments of the Rinchen Terdzö, the collection of "revealed treasures" (terma), Rinpoche told him he wished to spend the rest of his life in solitary meditation. But Khyentse Chökyi Lodrö's answer was, "The time has come for you to teach and transmit to others the countless precious teachings you have received." From then on, Rinpoche worked constantly for the benefit of beings with the tireless energy that is the hallmark of the Khyentse lineage.

After leaving Tibet, Khyentse Rinpoche spent much of his time traveling in the Himalayas, India, Southeast Asia, and the West, transmitting and explaining the teachings to his many disciples. He was often accompanied by his wife, Khandro Lhamo, and his grandson and spiritual heir, Rabjam Rinpoche.

Wherever he was, he would rise well before dawn to pray and meditate for several hours before embarking on a ceaseless series of activities until late into the night. He accomplished a tremendous daily workload with total serenity and apparent effortlessness. Whatever he was doing— and he was often giving his attention to several different tasks at the same time—seemed to make no difference to the flow of his view, meditation, and action. Both his teachings and his lifestyle combined into a harmonious whole all the different levels of the path. He made extensive offerings, and during his life offered a total of a million butter lamps. Wherever he went, he also supported many practitioners and people in need, in such a discreet way that very few people were aware of the extent of his charity.

Rinpoche held that building stupas and monasteries in sacred places helps to avert conflict, disease, and famine, promotes world peace, and furthers Buddhist values and practice. He was an indefatigable builder and restorer of stupas, monasteries, and temples in Bhutan, Tibet, India, and Nepal. In Bhutan, following predictions he had received for the peace of the country, he built several temples dedicated to Guru Padma-sambhava, as well as a number of large stupas, gradually becoming one of the most respected teachers of all the Bhutanese people from the royal family down. Rinpoche made three extended visits to Tibet in the 1980s, where he inaugurated the rebuilding of the original Shechen Monastery, destroyed during the Cultural Revolution; and he contributed in one way or another to the restoration of over two hundred temples and monasteries in Tibet, especially the monasteries of Samye, Mindroling, and Shechen. In India, too, he built a new stupa at Bodhgaya, the site of Shakyamuni Buddha's enlightenment beneath the bodhi tree, and initi-ated plans to construct stupas in each of the seven other great pilgrimage places sacred to Lord Buddha in northern India.

In Nepal, he transplanted the rich Shechen tradition to a new home—a magnificent monastery in front of the great stupa of Bodhnath. This became his principal seat, and it currently houses a large commu-nity of monks, led by their abbot, Rabjam Rinpoche. It was Khyentse Rinpoche's particular wish that this should be a place where the Buddhist teachings are continued in all their original purity, just as they were pre-viously studied and practiced in Tibet, and he invested enormous care in the education of the promising young lamas capable of continuing the tradition.

After the systematic destruction of books and libraries in Tibet, many works existed in only one or two copies. Rinpoche was involved for many years in publishing as much of Tibet's extraordinary heritage of Buddhist teaching as possible, a total of three hundred volumes, includ-ing the five treasures of Jamyang Kongtrul. Until the end of his life, Rin-poche was still seeking lineages he had not received, and transmitting to others those that he had. During his life, among countless other teach-ings, he twice transmitted the 108 volumes of the Kangyur and five times the 111 volumes of the Rinchen Terdzö.

He first visited the West in 1975, and thereafter made a number of visits, including three North American tours, and taught in many differ-ent countries, particularly in Dordogne, France, where people from all over the world were able to receive extensive teaching from him, and where several groups of students undertook the traditional three-year retreat program under his guidance.

Through his extensive enlightened activity, Khyentse Rinpoche un-sparingly devoted his entire life to the preservation and dissemination of the Buddha's teaching. What brought him the greatest satisfaction was to see people actually putting the teachings into practice and their lives being transformed by the blossoming of bodhichitta and compassion.

Even in the last years of his life, Khyentse Rinpoche's extraordinary energy and vigor were little affected by his advancing age. However, he began to show the first signs of ill health in early 1991 while teaching in Bodhgaya. Completing his program there nevertheless, he traveled to Dharamsala, where, without apparent difficulty, he spent a month transmitting a set of important Nyingmapa empowerments and transmissions to His Holiness the Dalai Lama, which the latter had been requesting for many years.

Back in Nepal, as spring advanced, it became obvious that his health was steadily deteriorating. He passed much of the time in silent prayer and meditation, setting aside only a few hours of the day to meet those who needed to see him. He decided to travel to Bhutan, to spend three and one half months in retreat opposite the "Tiger's Nest," Paro Taktsang, one of the most sacred places blessed by Padmasambhava.

After completing his own retreat, Rinpoche visited several of his disciples who were also in retreat. Shortly afterward, on September 27, 1991, he passed away. His reincarnation, Urgyen Jigme Tenzin Lhundrup, was recognized by Trulshik Rinpoche in 1995. He is being raised and educated under the guidance of Shechen Rabjam Rinpoche in Bhutan and Nepal.

Zurchung Sherab Trakpa (1014–1074).

ZURCHUNGPA'S TESTAMENT

A Commentary on Zurchung Sherab Trakpa's
Eighty Chapters of Personal Advice

Based on Shechen Gyaltsap's Annotated Edition

COMMENTARY BY DILGO KHYENTSE RINPOCHE

TRANSLATED FROM THE TIBETAN AND EDITED BY THE
PADMAKARA TRANSLATION GROUP

The Padmakara Translation Group gratefully acknowledges the generous support of the Tsadra Foundation in sponsoring the translation and preparation of this book.

Foreword

THE GREAT ELEVENTH-CENTURY Tibetan master Zurchung Sherab Trakpa was someone who, by practicing the Buddha's teachings throughout his life, attained the highest possible level of spiritual realization. Shortly before he left this world, he shared his extensive experience of Buddhist practice with his disciples in a series of instructions, the *Eighty Chapters of Personal Advice.* Beginning with basic topics such as faith, impermanence, and renunciation, these simple yet profound instructions cover the path of the three trainings—discipline, concentration, and wisdom—and culminate in the extraordinary view, meditation, and activity of the Great Perfection.

Our teacher Dilgo Khyentse Rinpoche, who was a living embodiment of the path that Zurchungpa describes, gave this teaching to a group of practitioners in retreat to use as an aid for their practice, basing his explanation on a commentary on Zurchungpa's text by his own teacher, Shechen Gyaltsap Rinpoche.

I am delighted that it will now be available to a wider public, and I am sure that all those who sincerely put this teaching into practice will derive enormous benefit, both for themselves and for anyone whom they encounter.

JIGME KHYENTSE
Dordogne, 2006

3

Translators' Introduction

A NOTABLE FEATURE of Tibetan Buddhist literature is the number of pithy and easily memorized texts that condense the classical teachings into practical instruction manuals. Often cryptic in style, they provide the practitioner with keys that serve as reminders opening up a complete range of teachings to be put into practice. Garab Dorje's *Hitting the Essence in Three Points*, Atisha's *Seven-Point Mind Training*, Gyalse Thogme's *Thirty-seven Practices of the Bodhisattva*, and Padampa Sangye's *Hundred Verses of Advice* are just a few examples of such works that have become important classics in their own right.

Less well known is Zurchung Sherab Trakpa's *Eighty Chapters of Personal Advice* (*zhal gdams brgyad bcu pa*). His advice is termed personal not only because it represents the distillation of a lifetime's experience of practice by a highly accomplished master, but also because it answers the needs of individual practitioners at different stages of the path. Each chapter deals with a particular topic and contains between three and thirty-four single-sentence instructions.

The Vajrayana teachings brought to Tibet by Padmasambhava, Vimalamitra, and other masters in the eighth century C.E. have come down to us by means of two kinds of lineal transmission: the short lineage of the treasures (*terma*), which were hidden by these great teachers and later rediscovered by the emanations of their disciples; and the long lineage of oral transmission (*kama*), in which the teachings have been transmitted from master to disciple until the present day. The early masters of this *kama* lineage belonged principally to four families, namely the So, Zur, Nub, and Nyak clans, and of these, the Zur family is noted for three outstanding masters: Zurpoche Shakya Jungne (the Great Zur), his uncle's grandson Zurchung Sherab Trakpa (the Little Zur), and Zur-chungpa's own son, Zur Dropukpa Sakya Senge. These three masters of the Zur lineage had such mastery over mind and matter that, to judge from His Holiness Dudjom Rinpoche's account in his *History of the Nyingma School*,[1] there was no distinction in their lives between the mi-raculous and the everyday. We read of them levitating, walking on water, flying through the air on the rays of the sun, passing through rock, lengthening a temple pillar that was too short, and performing numerous other feats. When, after a year-long retreat, Zurpoche performed a tantric dance, his foot sank up to the ankle in a rock. Zur-chungpa, prostrating to the footprint of his guru, left the imprint of his own topknot and dangling earrings.

Nowadays, with the abundant use of special effects in cinema and television playing to our fascination with the supernatural, it is all too easy for us to be dazzled by the Zur masters' superhuman lifestyles and to forget that their miraculous displays resulted from years of genuine spiritual endeavor. They were fully enlightened beings who had com-pletely transcended the feats they displayed. Their stories are intended to serve as inspirational models, and from reading them we can learn how to follow in their footsteps. In particular, Zurchungpa's life story teaches us two things: that he earned his extraordinary degree of spiri-tual attainment by carrying out every one of his teacher's instructions to the letter; and that everything he did, however spectacular, was simply a manifestation of his enlightened activity for the sake of beings. His flying through the air, for example, enabled him to travel long distances swiftly and thus give three sessions of teaching in one day, each in a remote location many tens of miles from the last. His sole purpose in this was to benefit beings and spread the teachings more expeditiously. And although such impressive feats undoubtedly inspired devotion in his disciples, enabling them to receive blessings and progress on the path, he never used them in order to become famous.

ZURCHUNG SHERAB TRAKPA (1014–1074)

Zurchung Sherab Trakpa was born to the accompaniment of wondrous signs. He learned to read and write in his seventh year, and in his ninth year he learned to chant the ritual of the peaceful and wrathful deities.

6

A disagreement with his fiancée in his thirteenth year upset him deeply, and he left home determined to meet Zurpoche Shakya Jungne and to devote his life to practicing the Dharma. When he arrived, Zurpoche asked him what clan he came from. Not daring to admit that he was the Guru's second cousin, Zurchungpa replied, "I am just a very small Zur (*zur chung*)." The name stuck. Despite the fact that he had only his wolf-skin coat to offer, he was accepted as a disciple by Zurpoche and immediately began studying. He underwent numerous austerities, at first refusing any material aid from his teacher, even though he was too poor to afford the supplies for copying books. Through his total devotion to Zurpoche, and by studying and practicing day and night in remote hermitages, he attained an extraordinary level of realization. Although he resolved to remain for twenty-four years in continuous retreat at the hermitage Zurpoche had given him at Mount Trak Gyawo, he was obliged for two main reasons to break his retreat after thirteen years, and was therefore prevented from actually attaining the rainbow light body—the ultimate accomplishment of the Great Perfection, where the practitioner's body dissolves into light. The first reason was that his attendant disturbed him during a long period of solitary practice: seeing that his master's mouth and nose were covered with cobwebs and thinking that he had passed away, he cried out loud and broke Zurchungpa's concentration. The second reason was that his active presence was required in order to ensure the preservation of the teachings.

Zurchungpa was famed and respected not only by Nyingmapas but also by followers of the New Tradition. On one occasion a geshe well versed in dialectics sent his student to challenge Zurchungpa to a debate. "Let this pillar be the topic of debate," he declared. Zurchungpa accepted by passing his hand through the pillar, to the astonishment of the student, who subsequently became his disciple. Not that Zurchungpa lacked the necessary dialectical skills to defeat his opponents. His debate with four others sent by another geshe was carried out more on their terms, but it was soon over: his replies to their questions left them with no hope of a rejoinder. They later became his four principal disciples.

The epoch of these three Zur masters was a golden age for the Mantrayana. At that time, these teachings were only given to carefully selected disciples, who then devoted themselves to intensive practice, following their teachers' instructions to the letter and thereby attaining the highest accomplishment. By the nineteenth century, these secret teachings were much more widely taught, to the extent that Patrul Rinpoche could write (in *The Words of My Perfect Teacher*), "In Tibet these days there cannot be a single lama, monk, layman, or laywoman who has never received an empowerment." As a result, the teachings began to lose their subtle force and directness, and the proportion of tantric practitioners who attained accomplishment declined over the centuries. Yet even as late as the mid-twentieth century, there were still a few who attained the rainbow light body, leaving behind no physical trace. And a considerable number of masters of the Great Perfection passed away to the accompaniment of sounds, light, earthquakes, and other remarkable phenomena, dissolving most of their bodies into light and leaving remains which, when cremated, yielded *ringsel* and other extraordinary relics. One such master was Shechen Gyaltsap Pema Gyurme Namgyal, on whose annotated edition of Zurchungpa's *Eighty Chapters* Dilgo Khyentse Rinpoche based his commentary.

SHECHEN GYALTSAP PEMA GYURME NAMGYAL (1871–1926)

Shechen Gyaltsap, also known as Jamyang Lodrö Gyamtso Drayang, the name by which he refers to himself in the colophon of the present text, was the heart-son of Ju Mipham Namgyal Rinpoche (1846–1912) and was largely responsible, with Khenchen Kunzang Pelden (c. 1870–c. 1940), for continuing Mipham Rinpoche's teaching tradition. He studied with the greatest teachers of his day, including Jamyang Khyentse Wangpo (1820–1892), from whom he received teachings on the present text, and Jamgön Kongtrul Lodrö Thaye (1813–1899). He was undoubtedly one of the most learned lamas of his time, and his collected writings fill thirteen volumes, which include an extensive commentary on Atisha's *Seven-Point Mind Training*, a detailed explanation of the preliminary practice, and a treatise on the nine vehicles. He was also one of the most accomplished practitioners. He once completed what was intended to be a three-year retreat in only three months and left the imprint of his foot in a rock at the entrance to his hermitage. It is said that when Shechen Gyaltsap's body was cremated, it vanished without a trace, and that where the smoke settled on the leaves in the surrounding countryside, crystal relics were found.

Shechen Gyaltsap Rinpoche was the first of Dilgo Khyentse Rinpoche's principal teachers, for it was he who recognized and enthroned him as the incarnation of Jamyang Khyentse Wangpo's mind. His many disciples included Jamyang Khyentse Wangpo's activity emanation, Dzongsar Khyentse Chökyi Lodrö (1896–1959), who was also one of Dilgo Khyentse Rinpoche's most important teachers.

Zurchungpa's *Eighty Chapters* of *Personal Advice*

The *Eighty Chapters* were Zurchungpa's last teaching, the testament he gave to his disciples before passing away. It is hardly surprising, then, that he concerns himself exclusively with practice, and although a few of his instructions assume some basic theoretical knowledge of such topics as the five aggregates, the eight consciousnesses, the ten actions, and so on, the emphasis is on how to put such knowledge into practice. There is little here that has not been written elsewhere, but that is not to say that Zurchungpa's text lacks originality. What is striking about his presentation of the Great Perfection is that while he often appears to repeat himself, he shifts slightly each time, lending contrast and perspective to the teaching and adapting his angle to the particular needs and intellectual capacities of his individual students.

The *Eighty Chapters* are divided into five main sections. The first of these is a short introductory section on faith and devotion, which are essential qualities for anyone who wishes to understand the teachings and put them into practice. This is particularly true in the Mantrayana, where realization depends on being open to the teacher's blessings. The bulk of the text comprises three main sections, each dealing with one of the Three Trainings, which encapsulate the whole of the Buddha's teaching—discipline, concentration, and wisdom. The training in discipline, for Zurchungpa, is not merely a question of observing lists of do's and don'ts. While these things are certainly important, for him the essential point is to create circumstances that will help inner realization to blossom and to avoid those that will hinder such realization. A sincere desire to get out of samsara, a constant awareness of impermanence, and a vigilant mind are more important to him than the wearing of monastic robes. The section on the training in concentration deals not so much

9

with how to concentrate, but rather with how to undistractedly keep in mind the view of the Great Perfection. And the realization of that view is the subject of the section on the training in wisdom. These are exceptionally profound instructions that need to be repeatedly heard from a qualified master. Some readers may find the later chapters difficult to understand, but those who have already received some "mind" teachings will hopefully be able to use these chapters as reminders that help to deepen their practice and understanding. The fifth and final section contains a single chapter summarizing the whole text.

On their own, even the most approachable instructions in the *Eighty Chapters* are not always immediately comprehensible. While it does not require a great deal of imagination to guess why "faith is like a wishing-gem," as we read in the second chapter, Zurchungpa's incitement in the forty-ninth chapter to "always strip naked" and to "commit suicide" calls for some explanation, as does "'slander the *yidam*" in chapter 20. This is why Shechen Gyaltsap Rinpoche intercalated the lines of Zurchungpa's original text with his own notes, usually in the form of a short sentence for each instruction. In some cases he merely inserted a qualifying word or phrase; in others he found it useful to add one or more paragraphs. He also included a structural outline based on the teachings that Jamyang Khyentse Wangpo had given him on this text and on a detailed commentary, which unfortunately we have been unable to identify. In our translation of Dilgo Khyentse Rinpoche's commentary, Zurchungpa's root text appears in bold typeface; Shechen Gyaltsap's introduction, notes, and structural outline in italics; and Khyentse Rinpoche's commentary in normal typeface. In the earlier sections, these different elements (root text, notes, and commentary) mostly appear separately, though they must be read together; in the later chapters, they are largely intermingled.

THE HISTORY OF THIS TEACHING

In the summer of 1986, Dilgo Khyentse Rinpoche made one of his regular visits to the Dordogne in France, during which he gave a series of teachings to the three-year retreatants at Chanteloube, who had just completed the preliminary practices and were starting the "main" practice of the sadhanas and mantra recitations. The teachings he gave therefore included numerous empowerments, along with the oral transmission of a number of important texts, including some by his root teacher, Shechen Gyaltsap Rinpoche. In particular he gave a detailed teaching on the latter's annotated edition of Zurchungpa's *Eighty Chapters of Personal Advice*, which he began by telling us, "While it is very important to receive empowerments to mature one's being, as we are engaged in practice it is also crucial to have the liberating instructions— the explanations on the practice. I will therefore give an explanation of these few pieces of spiritual advice."

We mention the background of this teaching not merely for historical interest but because it is important for readers to understand Khyentse Rinpoche's teaching within the context in which it was given. Zurchungpa's text contains profound instructions that will be difficult to put into practice effectively without first having received the necessary empowerments and blessings from a qualified teacher. Although times have changed and the Dzogchen teachings are given more openly than they were a thousand, or even fifty, years ago, it is certainly no less true that progress in the practice of Dzogchen depends exclusively on the blessings of the lama. Readers who wish to get the most out of Zurchungpa's advice need to use it hand-in-hand with the guidance of their own teacher.

Khyentse Rinpoche's manner of teaching consisted of reading the text—that is, Zurchungpa's root text and Shechen Gyaltsap's notes— interspersed with his own oral commentary. In some of the later chapters especially, he gave little or no commentary and read out the text on its own. Many of these sections consist of so-called pith instructions, seemingly simple phrases used by the enlightened masters of the Great Perfection to convey their profound realization to individual disciples, in quite specific situations. The words they used, often in relatively nontechnical language, were tools used as a support for transmitting ideas that completely transcended the literal meaning of the words themselves. The impact of these oral instructions is naturally lessened when they are confined to the printed page. And they are diluted even further in the process of being translated into English (with the syntactical constraints that translation implies and the possibility of errors in the interpretation of their stylistic peculiarities) by individuals whose spiritual realization could never begin to match that of the original authors.

Khyentse Rinpoche gave this teaching in Tibetan, and it was from recorded tapes that Matthieu Ricard subsequently made an oral translation for the benefit of the Chanteloube retreatants. The recording of this translation was then transcribed. Later the transcription was edited and a fresh translation was made of Shechen Gyaltsap's original text. Two editions were used. One was published by Dilgo Khyentse Rinpoche at Shechen Monastery in Nepal and was the edition he taught from. The other was a photocopy made by Matthieu Ricard of an original woodblock edition brought back in 1989 from Shechen Monastery in Tibet. Both editions contain mistakes, but since the Nepalese edition omits some words and even whole sentences present in the woodblock edition, we have generally taken the latter as the more reliable and have done our best to incorporate the corrections into our translation.

A text of this sort contains much repetition of technical terms such as "absolute nature" and "unborn." For stylistic reasons we have occasionally used synonyms for some of these words. These and other technical terms are briefly explained in the Glossary. A deeper understanding of many of them may be obtained by reading books dealing with the graded path (*lam rim*), in particular Jigme Lingpa's *Treasury of Precious Qualities*, Patrul Rinpoche's *The Words of My Perfect Teacher*, and Gampopa's *Jewel Ornament of Liberation*.

Many of the points that Khyentse Rinpoche mentions in his teaching would have been impossible to index satisfactorily, and we have therefore attempted to summarize them thematically in the outline on pages 15–22.

ACKNOWLEDGMENTS

The Padmakara Translation Group is deeply grateful to the following lamas who patiently gave their time to solving certain difficult points in the printed text: the late Kyabje Dilgo Khyentse Rinpoche, Taklung Tsetrul Pema Wangyal Rinpoche, Jigme Khyentse Rinpoche, Alak Zenkar Rinpoche, Lopon Nyima Dondrup, and Yangchen Chozom. We are especially indebted to Matthieu Ricard, without whose translation of the oral commentary the teaching in this book could never have been published. His translation was transcribed and edited by Stephen Gethin, who also revised the translation of the text with Helena Blankleder. Special thanks are due to Jill Heald, who entered the bulk of the handwritten transcript into a computer; to Jennifer Kane for her suggestions on the earlier chapters; and to Kali Martin and Anne Paniagua, who kindly read through the manuscript and suggested numerous improvements.

Thematic Outline of the Eighty Chapters

The following outline of chapters is included as a study aid. Please note that it is not a traditional outline composed by the Tibetan author but rather a thematic outline drawn up by the translators. Page numbers have been added for the reader's convenience.

peas), attachment to relatives, practicing while one has the chance, using one's wealth for the right purposes (the story of Anathapindaka, Milarepa's offering to Marpa), renunciation, keeping death in mind

5. Thirteen things that are very important   64

Realization, experiences, and compassion, the importance of the teacher, suitable disciples, giving up attachment, long-term vision (examples of Asanga and Ananda), devotion to the yidam and the Three Jewels (Songtsen Gampo and Lama Mipham), diligence, avoiding negative actions, dealing with discursive thoughts, compassion and bodhichitta, faith in the teachings, keeping one's vows and commitments, the unborn nature of the mind, secrecy in preserving the profound instructions

II. DISCIPLINE

6. Ten facts with regard to timeliness in the practice   80

Taking advantage of the continued presence of the Buddha's Doctrine, the exceptional chance of coming across the teachings, the chance of having the right qualities for practice, an exhortation to practice (don't listen to your relatives), generosity, dealing with difficulties in the practice, patience (the example of Jigme Lingpa, the rishi named Patient Words), the point of practicing correctly, remembering death and countering attachment, demons (obstacles to practice)

7. Thirteen instructions to put into practice   90

Remembering death as a spur to diligence (how precious the Dharma is, a king's offering in order to receive teaching), avoid seeing faults in the teacher (King Trisong Detsen's doubts), keeping harmony with other practitioners (practicing the teachings best suited to oneself, avoiding sectarianism), pleasing the teacher and avoiding upsetting him, keeping the precepts, the unborn nature of the ground-of-all, obstacles and distractions, the four boundless qualities, avoiding negative actions (mindfulness and vigilance), cultivating positive actions, understanding suffering (the value of hardships), diligence until enlightenment is reached, uniting the two accumulations

V. CONCLUSION

Colophons by Zurchungpa's disciple Khyungpo Yamarwa
and Shechen Gyaltsap

Part One

DILGO KHYENTSE RINPOCHE'S COMMENTARY
on Shechen Gyaltsap's Annotated Edition of
Zurchung Sherab Trakpa's
Eighty Chapters of Personal Advice

Introduction

AMONG THE MASTERS of the Nyingma tradition there are a number of great lamas that belonged to the Zur family, the most important being the Great Zur, Zurchen Shakya Jungne, and the Little Zur, Zurchung Sherab Trakpa. A third lama of the Zur family is sometimes referred to as the Middle Zur.

This text is a collection of pieces of advice written by Zurchung Sherab Trakpa. My root teacher, Shechen Gyaltsap Rinpoche, received the transmission from Jamyang Khyentse Wangpo, who also explained the text to him. Later, Shechen Gyaltsap wrote this annotated edition, interspersing Zurchung Sherab Trakpa's *Eighty Chapters of Personal Advice* with commentary in the form of notes.

THE TITLE

"An annotated edition of Zurchung Sherab Trakpa's precious oral instructions on the three trainings, *The Eighty Chapters of Personal Advice*, entitled *A Necklace of Jewels*." The subtitle is: "Pith instructions comprising the essence of the Pitakas in general and of *Epitome, Magic, and Mind* (in particular)." The latter refer to the three main tantras of the inner Mantrayana, namely the *Epitome of Essential Meaning*, the *Net of the Magical Display*, and the Eighteen Tantras of the Mind Section.[2]

A Necklace of Jewels is similar to Gampopa's *Four Themes*, one of the best-known teachings of the Kagyu tradition, composed of spiritual advice given according to the stages on the path. I shall explain all I know of it.

The most important thing when one is practicing in retreat is to develop a feeling of disillusionment with samsara so that one can progress on the path, and for this one needs to receive the pith instructions for the path. Here then are these instructions, set out clearly and concisely, for those who have been through the preliminary practice properly and are now doing the main practice.

THE TEXT

The text begins with homage:

NAMO RATNA GURU BHYA

NAMO means "homage" or "obeisance." RATNA is "jewel" or "rare and supreme."[3] GURU is "the Teacher." BHYA[4] indicates the action of paying homage. It therefore means:

I pay homage to the precious Teacher.

The text opens by saying:[5]

Bowing down to the teacher who is Vajrasattva in reality,
I shall thread a Necklace of Jewels,[6]
The Eighty Chapters of Personal Advice
Laid out in detail with a structural outline—
A treasury of gems of the three trainings.

This is a homage to Zurchung Sherab Trakpa, who was someone who had completely renounced wordly affairs and become a fully enlightened siddha. He was in no way different from Vajrasattva, so it is to him that homage is paid.

What do we mean by the three trainings? Whether we practice the sutras or tantras, we cannot avoid going through the trainings of discipline, concentration, and wisdom. As Jamgön Kongtrul Lodrö Thaye himself said when he wrote his vast treatise known as the *Treasury of Knowledge*, everything contained in this encyclopedia is included in the three trainings. The text we are studying now is like a treasury of jewels that condenses the most precious points of the three trainings. It includes many pieces of advice, arranged in eighty chapters. And in the same way that one makes a necklace by threading the jewels one after another, the author is now going to present this text in full.

The Buddha, having considered the various mental capacities of sentient beings,

As far as the Buddha himself is concerned, only the teachings of the ultimate meaning are necessary: he does not need to teach the expedient meaning. But as far as sentient beings are concerned, different kinds of teaching are necessary to suit their various mental capacities, whether modest, middling, or exceptional. Some beings have very vast minds; they can understand the most profound and vast teachings. Some have less open minds, and others are extremely narrow-minded. There are thus teachings for all levels—the Great Vehicle, the Basic Vehicle, and so forth—that the Buddha has taught according to beings' ability to understand and assimilate them. However elementary or essentialized such teachings may be, their purpose in all cases is to set beings on the path to liberation, and the final destination is the same irrespective of the point of departure.

Take the example of a mother feeding her baby. She starts by giving only milk, which is very easy for the newborn baby to take. If she were to give solid food, the infant would not even be able to swallow it, let alone digest it. But when the child grows a little bigger, he can start having slightly more solid food like the three white foods and the three sweet foods, yogurt, and so on. Then gradually, as he grows bigger, he is able to eat solid food of all kinds.

Similarly, the Buddha has given the teaching in stages covering the whole path of the sutras and tantras. He first gave the teachings for beings on the Shravaka level and the teachings for the Pratyekabuddhas. Then, for those beings who have a vaster mind he gave the Mahayana teachings. That is not to say that there are fundamental differences in the way the Buddha himself taught: his teaching can, rather, be likened to falling rain. When rain falls from the sky, it falls in exactly the same way over the whole land, but what the water becomes when it reaches the ground depends on the kind of container into which it falls. If it falls on a lake with very pure water, the rainwater will remain as it is, very pure and transparent. If it falls into a dirty pit or muddy pool, it will take on the color and appearance of the dirt or mud. In the same way, although the mind of the Buddha always expresses the ultimate truth, depending on the level of the beings receiving his teachings he set forth the absolute truth on a variety of levels, which we term "vehicles." This is why he

taught the various vehicles of the Dharma.

According to the Nyingma tradition there are nine such vehicles—three lesser vehicles, three intermediate ones, and three higher ones. More generally, we speak of three vehicles: that of the Shravakas, that of the Pratyekabuddhas, and that of the Bodhisattvas.

From these Deshek Gyawopa teased out the wool of the sutras and the tantras.

Deshek (*Sugata* in Sanskrit) means "a Buddha." *Gyawopa* means "the man who lives in Gyawo Trak," the name of Zurchungpa's mountain retreat. *Deshek Gyawopa* refers to Zurchung Sherab Trakpa, the teacher who is one with the Buddha, and means "the Sugata who dwells in Gyawo." What did he do? He carefully studied all the teachings of the sutras and tantras in the same way that one prepares wool for weaving by teasing it and fluffing it out, removing the bits of grass and other dirt in it.

He churned the milk of the Three Pitakas.

If you churn milk thoroughly for a long time, you get butter; by churning curd you obtain cheese and whey. In the same way, by going over the meaning of the instructions in the Three Pitakas—the Vinaya, Sutras, and Abhidharma—again and again, Deshek Gyawopa extracted the quintessence of the teachings, like butter from milk.

He drank the words of the learned ones like water.

The Dharma was originally introduced to Tibet from the supreme land of India. The great panditas from India were invited to Tibet, and together with the Tibetan translators they translated the scriptures from Sanskrit into Tibetan. According to the teachings of the Ancient Tradition, although the great panditas like the Abbot Shantarakshita and the great translators appeared in human form, they were not in any way ordinary people; they were fully realized beings. Translators like Vairotsana, Chogro Lui Gyaltsen, and Kawa Paltsek were emanations of Ananda and other close disciples of the Buddha who took rebirth in Tibet in order to spread the teachings. Guru Rinpoche himself used to say such-and-such a translator was the reincarnation of such-and-such an Indian pandita. So they were not like ordinary translators; they were not ordinary beings. They had full realization of the whole of the Dharma and their minds became inseparable from Guru Rinpoche's wisdom-mind. Thus it was that in the inconceivable, spontaneously accomplished temple of Samye, at the request of King Trisong Detsen, who turned all his wealth into gold and offered full measures of gold each time he requested the teaching, the great panditas headed by Guru Rinpoche and Vimalamitra, and the great translators headed by Vairotsana, translated the scriptures from Sanskrit into Tibetan. Through Guru Rinpoche's blessings, the works translated included not only well-known texts from India but also hitherto unknown teachings that had been kept as treasures by the dakinis. This is a special feature of the Nyingma tradition.

At a later period, the translator Ngok Loden Sherab[7] traveled to India, where he worked on a translation of the *Ornament of the Sutras*. In this he came across a passage where the word meaning "to be attached" occurs three times together. Wondering how he could translate the same word three times, he consulted Vairotsana's old translation and found that Vairotsana had translated it as referring to the three tenses, past, present, and future,[8] with the sense of "hesitation."[9] The passage actually meant "there is no hesitation in the past, present, or future." When he saw this, Loden Sherab became fully confident that the ancient translators were true Buddhas and praised them, saying,

> Vairotsana is like the sky,
> Ka and Chog are like the sun and moon,
> Rinchen Zangpo is like the morning star,
> And I myself am like a firefly.

He explained this as follows. Vairotsana's knowledge and wisdom are so vast that he is like the sky. Kawa Paltsek and Chogro Lui Gyaltsen are like the sun and the moon. Rinchen Zangpo,[10] who is without peer among all the translators of the New Translation tradition, is like the morning star, meaning Venus, which shines very brightly at dawn. And he himself, he said, had been given the title *lotsawa*,[11] but counted for no more than one of the fireflies one sees on a summer night.

Nowadays we can go to India very quickly and easily, but in the days of the great translators it was much more difficult. They had to travel on foot, carrying all their belongings on their backs and enduring the heat and numerous dangers on the way. Once they had arrived in India, in order to study with the panditas, translators had to obtain permission from the local kings, who in those days were very jealous and unwilling to let others study the precious teachings, employing guards to prevent these teachings from being taken away to Tibet.

Vairotsana, for instance, went to India for the first time at the age of thirteen, and we can read in his life story of the immense difficulties and hardships he had to go through to receive the teachings. The translators visited not only Bodhgaya but also all the great universities and seats of learning like Vikramashila and Nalanda, where there might have been five hundred or a thousand panditas. Very few of these panditas, however, were panditas of the Mahayana, and of these even more rare were panditas versed in the Secret Mantrayana. Moreover it was by no means easy for the translators to make inquiries in the local language to find out which panditas might be holders of the secret pith instructions. It was only through his own clairvoyance and the blessing and predictions of protectors such as Ekajati that Vairotsana was able to know which teachings to look for and find the panditas who held them. The translators of the New Translations also had to endure great hardships in order to receive the teachings, as we can see in the life story of the great translator Marpa, who traveled three times to India and four times to Nepal, each time carrying everything on his back.

He savored the realization and experience of former masters like salt.

Just as adding salt to food improves its taste, Zurchung Sherab Trakpa savored the pith instructions of the previous lineage masters, their profound wisdom and understanding, their experience and realization; and his hearing, reflecting, and meditating on the teachings was like adding salt to the teachings themselves.

Looking at appearances as in a mirror,

—meaning that he looked at the appearances of samsara and nirvana as if looking at reflections in a mirror, beautiful or ugly—

he saw that whatever one does there is nothing but suffering.

In the three worlds of samsara, whatever one does with one's body, speech, and mind, it is only the cause of suffering. This means that any samsaric action[12] is the cause of suffering. At present we can eat good food, wear nice clothes, and have a comfortable place to stay, and we feel this is quite a happy situation. But to obtain that, we have in fact done nothing but accumulate negative actions, which are the cause of future suffering. From the moment we are born from our mother's womb, we cannot but set off in the direction of death. Then, when we finally meet with death, even if we are very powerful, we cannot influence death; however rich we are, we cannot bribe death; however beautiful we are, we cannot seduce it. Look at the ordinary activities of beings in samsara: they are involved in protecting those who are dear to them, in getting the better of those who are not dear to them, in plowing fields and conducting business and trade. If you examine all these actions, they are all linked with negativity. There is hardly anything in them that is virtuous. Acting only in this negative way is like eating food mixed with poison: it may taste delicious at the time, but it will have deadly consequences.

Therefore,

He saw that the concerns of this world are to be given up.

He saw that it is better to completely give up all one's endless plans and projects that involve thinking, "If I do this or that, in the future I will be able to enjoy good food, have good clothes, and be in such-and-such a pleasurable situation."

He saw that besides accomplishing something meaningful for future lives, nothing is of any use.

Why? Because there is not a single being born who will not die. And there is not a single being who dies and does not take another rebirth.

When we leave this life, however rich we are, we cannot take even a handful of food. Though we may have many fine clothes, we cannot take a single thread of them. Even this body, which we have cherished so much, we will have to leave behind as a corpse. What we cannot avoid taking is the burden of our positive and negative actions. After we have crossed the threshold of death with this burden, the place in which we will find ourselves will not be somewhere pleasant and agreeable where we can feel comfortable and relaxed. It will be like coming to a huge plain, a place of complete desolation in which we do not know where we are or where we can go. We will be like a small child that is too young to walk, abandoned in the middle of a vast plain, where it will either die or be eaten by wild animals. Each and every one of us will end up in this situation, with this fear. But we remain blind to it. We cannot see it coming. We cannot see beyond this present life and spend our time complaining about our house, our food, and our possessions. We think that keeping our friends and getting rid of our enemies is the most important thing. But actually it only brings us harm. That is why the text continues,

> He saw that status and fame have to be thrown away like
> spit and snot.

Some individuals become very famous, and people say of them, "They are very learned, they are very powerful, they are very clever." But when death comes, it will be of no use to them. They will be obliged to give up all their fame and wealth, discarding it like snot without being able to ask themselves, "Should I keep it or should I throw it away?"

> He saw the need to rid himself of retinue and bustle—for it
> is hard to make everyone happy—and to meditate alone.

In ordinary life we are always having to concern ourselves with other people. If we have a family, wife, husband, and children, we are concerned with what will happen to them; we have to do everything to protect them, to ensure that they prosper. This involves endless activity, and in the process our entire human life runs its course. We never ask ourselves whether all this will be truly useful or whether it will do us harm in the future. We should now see that these things are, in fact, a disturbance, and just as we would wish to get rid of an enemy, we should want to get rid of these distracting conditions. If someone were to be hostile to our children or other members of our family, for example, we would think only of how to get rid of him, and even imagine using violence or killing him. But in truth there is no way one can subdue all one's enemies, and there is no end to the number of enemies one can have. The only way is to completely give up all these worldly concerns. One needs to go to a secluded place, a lonely mountain retreat, and turning one's thoughts inward, to work hard at putting the teachings into practice.

Deshek Gyawopa saw this, and he therefore went to the place known as Trak Gyawo, as we can read in the account of his life in the *History of the Nyingma School.*[13]

At Trak Gyawo he practiced intensively[14]

throughout his life, just as Milarepa did. As a result of his practice, he achieved realization for himself and for others, and opened the way for spreading the teachings of the Ancient Tradition, expressing his full realization in the form of spontaneous spiritual advice for beings of the future:

He himself made a living experience of these Eighty Chapters
of Personal Advice *on how to practice the whole of the Dharma.*

These are oral instructions that essentialize all the Buddha's own words and the commentaries on them, which are extremely vast and difficult to understand. They are presented in a way that is easy to assimilate, like food that a child can digest, and are given directly into our hands, in the form of eighty pieces of advice. They are not empty utterances, but instructions that he himself followed. As he said, the reason he was able to get out of samsara, the ocean of suffering, and attain the level of Vidyadhara, taking a place on the seat of enlightenment, was that he practiced instructions like these.

For those who fear birth and death, this is a practice for today.

There are two great sources of fear in samsara, the moment of birth and the moment of death. The suffering and fear experienced at these two times have to be faced completely alone; there is no one who can really help us. The only thing that can help alleviate those sufferings is the practice of the supreme Dharma. Nothing else can do so. But we do not know how to practice it: we have only become clever at doing worldly things. From an early age we have learned how to make things comfortable for ourselves and how to avoid being uncomfortable. This sort of attitude has resulted in a high degree of material achievement. We can fly through the sky in airplanes, and so on, and we have made life very easy from the material point of view. But actually we are just like children running after a rainbow. These things do not really help us. We need to turn our minds toward the Dharma by reflecting on these sufferings of birth and death. By doing so, we enter the path, first going through the preliminaries and then proceeding to the main practice. As we practice, we will gradually get a true taste of what it means to become disillusioned with worldly affairs and to progress on the path. This is something that will come with experience. But we must not postpone it, thinking, "I will do this practice next month or next year." If we have received a teaching today, it is today that we should start putting it into practice, for it is only from the moment we actually plant a seed that it will start to sprout.

He gave this as a spontaneous teaching, out of love, as direct heartfelt advice.

Deshek Gyawopa spoke these words for the sake of the many beings who would come in the future, so that if they were to hear this teaching and reflect and meditate on it, it might be of some help to them.

Parents who love their children give them all sorts of helpful advice, telling them what is right and what is wrong: "If you do this, you will get into trouble; if you do that, it will help you," or "If you associate with that sort of person, he will help you, but be careful not to go around with that other person, as he will trick you." The same is true for this extraordinary instruction by Deshek Gyawopa, which will aid us both in this life and in the next. If we fail to follow this advice, we will get into trouble and be harmed both in this life and in subsequent ones.

He gives this advice as if he were opening his heart, expressing his deepest, innermost thoughts for our benefit. It is like a final testament given to one's children as one is dying. Afterward the children will think,

"These were my parents' last words," and they will have all the more respect for what those words mean. Similarly, if we practice in accordance with the meaning of this, his final testament, it will greatly help us in the future. The way to do so is gradually, day after day, to reflect and meditate one by one on each of the pieces of advice in this series he has given us. Then they will be like flowers, which emerge as shoots in spring and grow day after day, finally coming into full bloom in summer.

> There are five topics. As we find in the scriptures:
>
>> Having cultivated firm devotion,
>> In the field of pure discipline
>> Sow the seed of concentration,
>> And see the harvest of wisdom ripen.

If we wish to practice the Dharma authentically but we do not have faith, however much we listen, reflect, and meditate, it will not bear fruit. Our practice will be without light, like the world before dawn when there is no sun.

We also need to use the field of pure discipline. To practice the Dharma, it is essential to have the solid foundation of the Pratimoksha, Bodhisattva, and Secret Mantrayana vows. Without these it is impossible to practice the Dharma, just as it is impossible to build a big house without having firm ground to build on.

Once we have this well-prepared field, we can plant in it the seeds of concentration from which experiences and realization will grow. We also have to take care of the field properly, to till the earth, spread manure, and water it; and the sun must shine on the field to warm it.

If all these conditions are brought together properly, then the crop of wisdom will grow without difficulty. And just as a good harvest brings wealth, with these three trainings, the trainings of discipline, concentration, and wisdom, it is certain we will attain liberation.

> Accordingly, there are the instructions on faith, the gateway.

When you want to enter a house, you go in through the door, not through the window. In the same way, faith is the door through which we should go in order to set out on the path of the Dharma. Then there are:

The instructions on discipline, the basis,

which shows the need for firm discipline in the practice. Discipline alone is not sufficient. We need to sow the seeds of concentration, so there follow

The instructions on concentration, the means,

which includes meditation on sustained calm and profound insight. These again have to be reinforced or permeated with wisdom:

The instructions on wisdom, the essence.

Wisdom is the essence of both discipline and concentration. Without it the path will not work in leading us to omniscience, that is, enlightenment.

The fifth section is

To conclude, a summary of the above.

This is the basic structure of Zurchungpa's *Eighty Chapters of Personal Advice.*

I

Faith

The first section, on faith, *has five chapters.*

I

Showing the importance of faith as a prerequisite

—without faith there is no way one can even begin to practice the Dharma—

and the fault in not having faith,

for without faith one is not a suitable vessel for the teachings.

Son, since it is a prerequisite for the whole of the Dharma, it is important to recognize the fault in not having faith and the virtues of having it.

Here Dharma means "that which will lead us to liberation from samsara and to ultimate omniscience and enlightenment." The word *Dharma* derives from a root that means "to correct." Just as when one makes a statue out of clay, first sculpting a rough form and then carefully correcting all the small defects to make a perfect representation, when we practice the Dharma, it corrects all our imperfections and brings all our good qualities to perfection.

Another meaning of Dharma is "to hold" or "to catch." For instance, when a fish is hooked, it cannot help being taken out of the sea and ending up on dry land. Once one has entered the door of the Dharma and been "hooked" by the Dharma, even if one does not practice very much, the blessing of the Dharma is such that one can only be benefited and drawn toward liberation. Of the many different kinds of activity, the Dharma, which is the activity aspect of the enlightened Buddha, is the most important. And when we take refuge in the Buddha, Dharma, and Sangha, the ultimate refuge is, in fact, the Dharma.

The Dharma has two aspects, transmission and realization—the teachings in the scriptures of the Tripitaka, which we can study, reflect upon, and practice; and the experiences and realization that grow out of such practice. These two aspects include all the Three Jewels. The Buddha is the one who expounds the Dharma; the Sangha consists of the companions on the path who accompany us in practicing the Dharma. Of all the different meanings of the word *dharma*,[15] the most important is this Jewel of the Dharma, the vast and profound teaching of the Buddha.

One might wonder whether the scriptures are the Jewel of the Dharma. They are not the ultimate realization,[16] but they are nevertheless the Jewel of the Dharma. This is because they are the support for that realization. Just as, on the physical plane, a statue or other image of our Teacher[17] inspires devotion when we look at it, and through generating devotion we receive blessings and can progress along the path, similarly the scriptural Dharma sustains our realization. This is why, when Lord Buddha passed into nirvana, he said that the Dharma would be his representative. Through studying the Dharma one can know what the Buddha himself is like and what the teaching is like; one can know the path to enlightenment. The Dharma is thus a likeness of the dharmakaya; it is the dharmakaya made visible.

In order for us to practice the Dharma, faith must come first. We need to know what are the drawbacks of not having faith and what are the qualities and benefits that come from having it. Faith, disillusionment with the world, and the desire to get out of samsara are not things that everyone has naturally, from the beginning. But they can be developed, for every sentient being has the tathagatagarbha, the buddha nature, within himself or herself. The presence of the buddha nature naturally helps all good qualities to grow, just as the presence of the sun in the sky naturally dispels darkness over the earth. It is this tathagatagarbha that is pointed out through the instructions of Mahamudra and the Great Perfection, and because of this buddha nature that we have within us, it is quite easy for faith, determination to be free, and so forth to arise on their own within our minds. To help these qualities grow in us, we need to receive teachings from our teacher, to follow him, and to reflect on the enlightened qualities we can see in him. As we do so, we will naturally understand the drawbacks of not having faith.

Now we may talk about faith, but unless we know what we mean by faith, it will merely be an empty word.

The essence of faith is to make one's being and the perfect Dharma inseparable.

When the Dharma and one's being have truly mingled, then there is perfect faith. Faith also implies aspiration, a sense of longing. When we long to become very rich, for example, we do everything necessary, undergo great hardship, and expend a lot of energy to achieve this goal. The same is true for wishing to become famous or to achieve any other worldly goal: if our aspiration and determination are strong enough, we will manage to achieve what we want. This is a very powerful quality. Similarly, with faith there is a strong motivation and wish to achieve something, and a natural understanding of the drawbacks of not having this sort of aspiration. When faith has become truly blended with one's mind and become part of it, then one's Dharma practice naturally becomes genuine and pure. This is what is meant by the "perfect Dharma."[18] This clear aspiration to practice the Dharma is what we call faith.

The etymology of the word faith *is: the aspiration to achieve one's goal.*

When we hear about all the qualities of the past Buddhas, the lives of the great teachers, and the realization they achieved, we may aspire to achieve such qualities ourselves and to set out on the path. This longing is what we call yearning faith. We may, for instance, think that the Dharma is something valuable and therefore start to learn Tibetan. As we gradually begin to understand the language, our longing to understand the teachings will grow more and more. This is the fruit of our aspiration. If we were to distinguish different kinds of faith,

> *The categories of faith are three: vivid faith, yearning faith,*
> *and confident faith.*

The first of these, vivid faith, is the natural interest and vivid joy we feel when we hear about the lives of Guru Rinpoche and the great siddhas, and the miracles they performed.

Yearning faith is the longing and hope we have when we then think, "If I practice the teachings, then in this life or at least in a future life I myself will achieve the level of Guru Rinpoche and the siddhas." We may also experience yearning faith when we hear of the qualities of Buddhafields such as the Pure Land of Bliss and aspire to be reborn there.

Confident faith is the confidence that gradually builds up when we have both vivid and yearning faith and we think, "If I practice these teachings, there is no doubt that I will be able to attain Buddhahood myself." It is the certainty that as in the past beings were able to gain realization through the Dharma, so it will be in the future. It is confidence in the truth of the teachings. It is confidence in death—in its fearfulness, imminence, and unpredictability—and in all the other aspects of the teachings.

There are six faults that come from not having faith.

If we do not have faith, we will not be suitable vessels for the teachings.

Without faith one is like a rock at the bottom of the
ocean—

the Dharma will not benefit one's being.

A rock on the bottom of the sea may remain there for thousands of years, but it never gets any softer. It stays as hard as ever. Similarly, if we do not have faith, the Dharma will never penetrate our being and benefit us.

One is like a boat without a boatman.

If the ferryman or boatman is absent, there is no way one will be able to cross a big river or lake. In the same way, without faith

> *one will not be able to cross to the other side of samsara.*

One is like a blind person who goes into a temple.

One is unable to see the precious relics and sacred objects, such as statues, that represent the Buddha's body, speech, and mind; and since he cannot see them, he cannot give rise to faith, respect, and devotion.

Similarly, if one has no faith,

> *one will be unable to understand the words and their significance.*[19]

One is like a burnt seed.

The sprout of enlightenment—devotion, diligence, and compassion—*will not grow.*

Without faith,

One is like a sheep stuck in a pen.

or like a sheep that has fallen into a steep-walled pit with no way to climb out:

> *there is no liberation from suffering* in the ocean of samsara.

One is like a maimed person who has landed on an island of gold.

Someone with no hands, even if he lands on an island filled with gold and precious jewels, is unable to bring anything back with him. Similarly, although in this life one may have obtained a precious human existence, met a spiritual teacher, and entered through the gateway of the Dharma, if one has no faith, one will not be able to reap any of the achievements or qualities of the path:

one will return empty-handed at the end of this precious
human life—

the freedoms and advantages will have been squandered.

2

The virtues of faith.

Son, there are six virtues of faith.

Faith is like a very fertile field.

When a fertile field has been well plowed and tilled, each grain the farmer sows, whether wheat, rice, or any other kind, will yield thousands more grains, and the farmer will become very prosperous. In the same way,

the whole crop of virtue will grow.

When one has faith, one will naturally feel a great longing to practice the Dharma, and through this one will be able to achieve all good qualities. As the Buddha said, faith is like a jewel or treasure. It is the root of all other trainings and practices.

Faith is like a wishing-gem.

It fulfills all one's own and others' desires.

Someone who finds a wishing-gem and places it on top of a victory banner will have all his wishes and prayers fulfilled. All the clothes, wealth, food, and valuable things he could want will be effortlessly provided, not only for him but for everyone else in the region who prays and makes wishes before that wishing-gem. Similarly, if we have faith, everything we desire to achieve in our Dharma practice, such as being able to listen to the teachings, to reflect on them, and to meditate on them, will be effortlessly granted, along with all the good qualities that arise from these.

Faith is like a king who enforces the law.

He makes himself and others happy.

As a result of faith, we naturally recognize that all happiness comes from observing the law of cause and effect, from acknowledging that negative actions lead to suffering and that positive actions lead to happiness. We develop mindfulness and vigilance, distinguishing between what is to be avoided and what is to be adopted, and we then become suitable vessels for the qualities of the Dharma. When a king enforces the laws he has decreed, there is peace throughout the kingdom and there are no quarrels, feuds, or bandits. Similarly, when we have faith, not only are we happy, we are able to make others happy too. The spiritual qualities that we gain from having faith will be perceived and shared by the people around us. And like a medicinal tree that heals anyone who touches it, our own faith will inspire others to endeavor in the Dharma and to seek liberation.

Faith is like someone who holds the stronghold of carefulness.

He will not be stained by defects, and he will gather qualities.

A temple or mansion that is built on the solid rock of a mountain is extremely safe and invulnerable to attack from hostile forces. Inside it feels very secure, and one can collect within it all sorts of valuable things. Similarly, if we have faith, we will gradually be able to gather and store safely the whole treasury of precious qualities of the Dharma, such as those of listening, reflecting, and meditating. Sakya Pandita said that if one studies one verse a day, one can gradually become very learned, like a bee gathering honey. Even though a bee has a tiny mouth, by collecting the nectar it is slowly able to amass a large quantity of honey. Likewise, by studying gradually with the mouth of faith we will be able to gather the qualities of the Dharma—disillusionment with the world and diligence directed toward liberation.

Faith is like a boat on a great river.

It will deliver one from the suffering of birth, old age, sickness, and death.

With a boat one can cross even a very wide river. One has little difficulty in safely carrying oneself across and transporting all sorts of goods
and valuables. In the same way, if we have faith, we can recognize the
defects of our condition in samsara, where we are afflicted by the sufferings of birth, old age, sickness, and death. Moreover, we gradually recognize that the only remedy for this is the Dharma, and through practicing
the Dharma we are able to free ourselves from these four root sufferings
of samsara.

When Buddha Shakyamuni's disciples encountered problems, the
Buddha used to explain how these difficulties had come about through
actions they had committed in their past lives. By this means, his disciples naturally began to understand the workings of the law of cause and
effect and the fact that nothing in samsara is beyond suffering. As a result, they rapidly attained the level of Arhat. Faith has the power to dispel any of these four main sufferings. To illustrate how it dispels the
suffering of old age, there is a story from ancient India about an old man
of ninety years who requested ordination from Lilavajra. Lilavajra told
him that since he was so old and did not even know how to read or
write, it was too late for him to take ordination and to begin the path of
Dharma in the usual way. But there was a special practice he could do,
and he gave him the empowerment and instructions on the sadhana of
White Manjushri. Because the old man had great faith and possessed the
appropriate karma, within seven days he had a vision of White Manjushri and attained the accomplishment of immortal life. It is said that to
this day he dwells in Payul Phakpachen. So through faith one can even
overcome the suffering of old age. One can equally alleviate the suffering
of sickness. By meditating on the Medicine Buddha and reciting his
dharani, one can purify the negative actions that are the cause of one's
illness and thus be cured of disease.

Faith is like an escort in a dangerous place.

It will free us from the fears of samsara and its lower realms.

Through faith we acquire confidence in the Dharma. We acknowledge the defects of samsara and we realize that the cause of our suffering
in samsara is our past negative actions, which in turn arise from afflictive
emotions. This leads us to exert ourselves in practicing the Dharma, and

as a result we are naturally freed from the lower realms. This is why it is very important to repeatedly generate faith in our minds.

3

The causes that nurture faith and its qualities.

Having recognized the fault in not having faith and the advantages of having it, we now have to see how to develop faith and make it grow. Faith is not something that beginners naturally have right from the start. It has to be developed through different causes and conditions.

> **Son, there are ten causes that give rise to faith.**
> **You need to know that there is no happiness in your**
> **present way of life and circle of friends.**

In all our previous lives until now we have constantly wandered in samsara. With our body, speech, and mind we have accumulated all sorts of negative actions. We have always clung to those dear to us and hated those we have perceived as enemies. We have been completely distracted by the eight ordinary concerns.

It is important to realize that all this has been pointless. As a result of it all, we find ourselves in our present condition: though we want to be happy, all we manage to achieve is suffering. However affectionate and well-intentioned our parents, relatives, and friends may be, if we listen to what they say, there is no way we will be led to practice the Dharma. They themselves have been caught in samsara for such a long time that the only advice they can give us is how to get the better of our enemies, how to plow the fields and grow crops, and how to get rich by doing business. They are friends leading us in quite the wrong direction. There is a saying:

> Don't ask your father's opinion,
> Don't discuss things with your mother,
> Tie your own nose rope around your head,
> Use the Dharma to get your head into the sun.[20]

The same is true of relationships with others: they are devoid of any happiness. This does not mean we suddenly have to regard all our friends as enemies. It is simply that we need to stop alternating between hatred for so-called enemies and excessive attachment to our friends. We should be free from attachment and hatred. We should feel only loving-kindness and compassion for those whom we perceive as enemies, and in the best case we should be able to introduce both friends and those who were formerly our enemies to the Dharma. Bear in mind that introducing beings to the Dharma is a way of repaying their kindness. It is said that even if one were to carry one's parents on one's shoulders all the way around the earth, one would still not be able to repay their kindness. So the best way to repay the kindness of beings, who have all been our parents, is to introduce them to the Dharma. To repay his mother's kindness, Buddha Shakyamuni went to the Heaven of the Thirty-three, where she had been reborn, and stayed there for the duration of the summer retreat,[21] expounding the Dharma. The teachings he gave there are recorded in the Kangyur in the *Sutra in Repayment of Kindness.*[22]

Where Shechen Gyaltsap's note says

Ultimately these are the cause of suffering,

he means that if we follow worldly ways, we may become quite successful, we may be rich and influential or have the command of a large army, but in order to achieve that we will have committed exclusively negative actions involving deceit, lies, and malice. These are the very cause of suffering, and it is for this reason that Lord Buddha and his followers left home and became renunciants. They lived in secluded hermitages and devoted their lives to practicing the Dharma, living on food given to them as alms and free from the negativity that comes from all the things one normally does to earn a living.

You need to have confidence in the law of cause and effect,

for it can never, ever fail.

The root of faith is confidence in the law of cause and effect. We should never think that small positive actions have no effect. Just as by collecting drops of water one can gradually fill a huge vessel, by reciting the six-syllable mantra a thousand times every day, for example, you will gradually accumulate a large number of recitations and acquire the excellent qualities associated with the mantra. On the other hand, never think there is no harm in doing a negative action, even a very small one. Even a tiny spark can burn a haystack as big as a mountain. Nor should we underestimate the power of a tiny negative thought. We might think, "I have not harmed anyone physically, I haven't spoken harshly. This is just a little thought; it is not that serious. It is not as if I had killed some-one. And anyway, I can purify it through confession." But as it is said, a thought of anger arising in the mind of a Bodhisattva for even a sixtieth of the time it takes to snap one's fingers is enough to make that Bodhi-sattva fall into the Hell of Ultimate Torment as many times as there are such instants of anger. We have to be constantly vigilant, watching what the mind is doing, looking to see whether our virtuous thoughts have increased, whether we can cultivate them further, and whether we need to apply the right antidote. We must be continuously aware of our good and bad thoughts, like children at school who are marked up or down depending on whether they have given the right or wrong answer.

There was once a brahmin in India called Ravi. In order to train his mind in virtue he made two piles of pebbles, one with white pebbles and one with black. Each time he had a bad thought or did something wrong he would put a black pebble aside. And each time he had a pure, virtuous thought he would put a white pebble aside. At the end of the day he counted these white and black pebbles. In the beginning he found he had almost only black ones, but by being mindful and applying the proper antidotes day after day, he reached a stage where half the pebbles were black and half were white. Gradually there came a day when he could hardly find any black pebbles; he had had only pure thoughts and actions during the day. This is how we can change our minds: because thoughts are compounded and conditioned, they can be changed. Thus even someone like a butcher can suddenly become deeply disillusioned with suffering, with samsara, and giving up all negative actions, enter the path of liberation and ultimately achieve enlightenment.

Then there is the story of the hunter Kyirawa Gonpo Dorje. In the beginning he was such a fanatical hunter that he would kill any animal within sight. Until he met Milarepa, his arrow never missed a single ani-mal that caught his eye. Then he met Milarepa and felt tremendous de-votion to him. He gave up everything and in a single lifetime was able to go to a pure realm.[23] Understanding the law of cause and effect is thus very important. It is what Buddha Shakyamuni taught when he first turned the Wheel of Dharma. He showed that suffering and the cause of suffering are what have to be discarded and that the path and the fruit of the path are what have to be achieved. To develop faith it is necessary to have confidence in the law of cause and effect. If we do so, our faith will necessarily lead to a result.

In ancient India there was a very learned Tirthika philosopher called Durdharsakala, whose knowledge of the ten branches of science was unrivaled. "No one in India is as learned as I am," he thought to himself, and he set out for the monastic university of Nalanda, where there were five hundred Buddhist panditas. So learned was he that when he engaged these Buddhist panditas in debate, he defeated most of them. He was on the point of defeating them all when the great pandita Aryadeva appeared and, sitting on a rock, took on Durdharsakala. In the debate that ensued, Durdharsakala was defeated. His punishment, as decreed by the local king, was to have both his hands cut off, and he was left to sit at the gates of Nalanda with a novice monk to feed him. From where he was sitting he could hear the Nalanda panditas reciting the Tripitaka. One day, as he listened, he realized that the passage being recited clearly concerned himself, for it was a prediction by the Buddha about a certain Tirthika sage who would come to Nalanda, be defeated in debate, and finally gain faith in the Dharma, becoming an active proponent of the teachings. He suddenly felt tremendous confidence in the truth of the Buddha's teachings. Asking the young novice attending him to bring him the volume of the Tripitaka and place it on his head, he made the following prayer: "If this prediction is true, then by the power of that truth may my hands be restored and may I be diligent in spreading and benefiting the Dharma. If it is not true, may I die here, right now." Through the blessings of the Buddha—for the prediction was true—as he uttered these words, he found his hands restored. Not only did he enter the path of the Buddhadharma, but he also went on to become famed as Lopön Pawo, one of the four most illustrious masters in the history of Indian Buddhism.[24] This story also appears in a work by Patrul Rinpoche on the benefits of reading the Mahayana sutras, which contains numerous examples showing clearly and simply how the law of cause and effect functions.

When we gain this sort of confidence in cause and effect, we will find it impossible to indulge in negative actions and quite natural to perform positive ones. Like a sick patient, once we are sure that a medicine is making us better, we will not hesitate to take it, however sour or bitter it may be.

You need to remember death and impermanence.

There is no certainty about when you will die.

Although one has this precious human body, it is utterly impermanent. There is no doubt we will lose it to death and resume wandering in samsara. For in samsara, all that is born will die, all that is gathered will be exhausted, all that comes together will be separated, and all that is high will fall down.

Yet the time of death is quite uncertain. Moreover, the circumstances that might bring death are unpredictable. When we consider how many of the people we have met in our life are already dead, or seriously sick or suffering, we can see clearly how impermanence works. This sort of reflection on death will induce us to go to a lonely place and devote our lives to spiritual practice. It is why Jetsun Milarepa himself went to a deserted place and spent his whole life in ascetic practice—because he was constantly aware of the suffering and imminence of death.

You need to remember that you will depart without your retinue or wealth.

When you die, you have to leave them all behind, so they are no use to you.

There was once a universal monarch named King Mandhata. As a universal monarch he had all the seven attributes of royalty and traveled through the sky on a cloud, preceded by a golden wheel, which gave him dominion over everywhere he went. King Mandhata ruled the four continents as well as the abodes of the Four Great Kings. He became so powerful that he ascended to the Heaven of the Thirty-three and shared the throne with Indra. But then it occurred to him that it would be nice if he could sit on that throne alone. As a result of this negative thought, he fell back to the lowest states of existence and became a common beggar with nothing at all. Just like him, however much wealth we may accumulate, there will be nothing we can take with us at death. Even if our fame spreads far and wide like the roar of a thousand dragons, it will not follow us through death, nor will it help us at all at the moment of death, however flattering it is now. Even if we become as rich as Vaishravana, we will not be able to take any of our wealth with us at the time of death. We will not even be able to take our own body with us. All these things we will have to leave behind. We will be taken out of the midst of all our wealth, fame, and power like a hair plucked out of a block of butter: it comes out alone without a single particle of butter sticking to it. This is true not only for ordinary beings and for universal monarchs like King Mandhata, but even for enlightened beings like the Buddha. He could fly through the sky accompanied by his whole following of Arhats, Shravakas, and Pratyekabuddhas, but now he has departed from this ordinary world, and apart from the account of his life and enlightenment there is nothing to be seen of him. Nor can we say to ourselves, "I'm not worried: when I die, I will go to a buddhafield," because this is not something that we can just predict or decide.

You need to bear in mind that you are powerless to choose your next rebirth.

There is no knowing where the force of your actions will take you.

Unless we have accumulated positive actions, there is no way we can go to the higher realms. And if we have committed negative actions, however powerful we may be, there will be no escaping their influence when we die. Like the body and its shadow, we can never separate from the result of our actions. The imprints of our positive and negative actions are like a huge burden on the shoulders of our consciousness, and as we enter the intermediate state this is the only thing that will not get left behind—it is certain to follow us. If we have spoken a single harsh word to someone, it will be there on our consciousness. If we have felt devotion for a single instant, it will be there on our consciousness. So if we have performed vast positive actions, we will be reborn in a Buddhafield, where we can meet the Buddha in person and receive teachings; or at the very least we will be reborn in the higher realms of samsara among gods or humans. But if negative actions predominate, then whether we like it or not, we will be thrown like a stone into the lower realms.

FAITH

The point is that we are blind to the existence of future lives. We spend most of our time endeavoring to become rich, attempting to get rid of anyone who prevents us from achieving our worldly ambitions, and trying to look after those dear to us. And when we succeed in these, we are really proud of ourselves and think, "What a clever person I am." But this will not help at all. We tend to think we are safe in our fortress, but this is not the case. We will have to go where our actions take us, and there is no certainty where we will be reborn. We are unaware that it all depends on our actions.

You need to remember how hard it is to obtain a fully endowed human body such as this.

It is difficult to bring together the freedoms and advantages and their multiple causes.

At present we have this human body, we have met a spiritual teacher, we have crossed the threshold of the Dharma, and we have received the teacher's instructions. So we have in our hands all the conditions that make it possible to achieve Buddhahood within a single lifetime. Truly this human existence is like a golden vessel. But if we do not put it to proper use, death could snatch it out of our hands at any moment, and who knows if in our next life we will meet the Buddha's teachings? Even if we happen to come into contact with the Buddhadharma in our next life, who knows whether we will be interested in it or whether we will be able to meet a spiritual friend? So it is now, when all the right conditions have come together, that we should make use of our human body. When people who are very sick manage to find a doctor—one, moreover, who has the right medicine—they do everything they can to continue receiving treatment, however difficult it may be for them. We are in the same situation. We have met the doctor, who is the spiritual teacher, and have received the medicine, his nectarlike instructions. We now have everything we need to practice. Rather than throwing away such an opportunity, we must make full use of it. Then, if we have practiced perfectly during our lives, the moment of death will consist of nothing other than recognizing the clear light of dharmakaya. If our practice has been of middling quality, we can confidently expect to be reborn in a Buddhafield, where we will be able to continue on the path. Failing that, we should at least have the confidence to be able to say to ourselves, "I have done this much practice, so I will certainly not be reborn in the lower realms."

It is not enough to simply have been born a human—this is not what is meant by a precious human life. There are billions of beings in this world who have a human body, but theirs is not the precious human body. What we call the precious human body is one endowed with the five individual advantages and the five circumstantial advantages. Beings without these are like people who have no eyes, nose, or tongue with which to see, hear, or taste. They have a useless human life.

In spring the farmers work late into the night plowing the fields, sowing seed, and tilling the soil, because it is the right moment, and if they miss it, they will not get a crop. For us too it is the right moment: we have these eight freedoms and ten advantages and we have met a spiritual teacher. We have gathered all the right conditions, so rather than falling prey to indolence and laziness we must seize this opportunity to practice the Dharma.

You need to bear in mind that the whole of samsara is suffering.

It is never anything other than the three kinds of suffering.

Why should we want to get out of samsara? Because when we examine samsara, we can see that nothing in any of the six realms is beyond suffering. Beings in the hells suffer from heat and cold; those in the preta realms from hunger and thirst; and animals suffer from being enslaved, from stupidity, and from being eaten by others. Human beings suffer from birth, old age, sickness, and death, from meeting enemies, from separating from loved ones, from encountering what they do not want, and from not getting what they do want. The asuras suffer from jealousy and from fighting with the gods. And the gods suffer from losing the perfect conditions they have enjoyed for so long. So there is not one of these six realms that transcends suffering. We in samsara should feel like a prisoner who has been thrown into jail and whose only thought with every passing hour is, "When can I get out? Will I be set free tonight? Tomorrow morning?" Once we realize the extent of the suffering in samsara, our only thought will be, "How can I find a way to get out of samsara? When can I manage to free myself? What is the quickest way to get rid of all the actions that make samsara go on and on?"

You need to see the immense qualities of the Three Jewels.

What can help us get out of samsara? It has to be something that is itself free from samsara. And this quality is only to be found in the Buddha, Dharma, and Sangha, which we know as the Three Jewels or the Three Precious Refuges. "Buddha" means someone who has rid himself of all defects and acquired all good qualities. He is like someone very rich and at the same time highly altruistic, who by virtue of his wealth can help an enormous number of people. As a result, if we feel even a single instant of faith in the Three Jewels or perform a single prostration toward them, they will naturally be there in front of us without our needing to invoke them. The blessings of the Three Jewels are so powerful that simply hearing their names can free us from the lower realms. And yet the chance to hear those names is still something very rare and precious, not to be had unless one has gained the appropriate merit. One might spend a billion gold coins, but one could never buy the opportunity to hear the names of the Three Jewels. If beings immersed in intense suffering—animals, hell beings, and even those who experience the unbearable agony of the Hell of Ultimate Torment—were to remember the names of the Three Jewels for a single instant, this would suffice for them to find themselves in that same moment in a Buddhafield. But such a thought never occurs to them. Why? Because they do not have the right merit for such a thought to arise in their minds; in their past lives they have never had any interest in practicing the Dharma. On the other hand, even small children born in a place where the Buddha came and taught have the good fortune to have a connection with him. From a very early age they know how to say, "I pay homage to the Teacher, to the Buddha, the Dharma, and the Sangha." Through this connection they are able to follow the path of the Dharma throughout their series of rebirths.

> It is certain that they forever protect us from the suffering of samsara.

Once one has been taken under the protection of the Three Jewels, samsara will recede further and further, and nirvana will come closer and closer. The wisdom minds of the buddhas are so filled with compassion that whoever makes a connection with them will eventually be set on the path to liberation. To take a present-day example, the Chinese have destroyed many temples and statues in Tibet, thus committing negative actions whose results they will have to experience as suffering. Yet the mere fact that they have seen those precious representations of the compassionate Buddha and have thus made a connection with him will eventually lead in some future life to their practicing Dharma and being liberated. The same is true for beings—even wild animals or birds—who hear the sound of the Dharma. Even if they do not understand anything, feel faith, or gain realization when they hear the scriptures of the Tripitaka being read, that sound is so full of blessings that those beings will find the gates of the lower realms closed and will be brought onto the path.

Now, who can show beings these great qualities of the Three Jewels and guide those who have understood these qualities along the path? It is the spiritual master.

You need to look at the lives and deeds of the Holy Beings.

The activities of their Body, Speech, and Mind are unstained by faults or defects.

When one meets a great scholar, out of admiration, one naturally feels like studying and becoming learned oneself. And when one meets a very accomplished being, one feels like practicing in order to become as realized as he is. Thus, meeting learned and accomplished beings creates a spontaneous desire to acquire the same qualities as they have. Look at the life of Jetsun Milarepa: his story—how he renounced the world, followed his teacher, and underwent much hardship to attain enlightenment—is well known even to non-Buddhists and is a universal source of admiration and respect. Similarly, anyone who reads about Guru Rinpoche's deeds— how he protected beings from the lower realms, establishing them on the path to liberation, and how he subdued all the negative forces in Tibet— feels like taking refuge in Guru Rinpoche.

Whatever we see of the physical aspect, the words, or the mind of a spiritual teacher will inspire us to practice the Dharma. Physically, he might be a perfect monk wearing the three monastic robes, and we will naturally feel joyful and think, "Here is someone who has given up all worldly affairs, who is free from all family ties, who has no family to support, who can spend all his life practicing the pure Dharma." We might hear the teachings or read the lives of great teachers such as Shabkar Tsogdruk Rangdrol—hearing how they renounced the world and stayed in mountain retreats—and we will naturally feel inspired to do the same and devote ourselves to Dharma practice.[25] As for the teacher's mind, when we receive teachings from him and reflect on their meaning, we will realize that the preliminary practice helps us develop disillusionment, determination to be free, and confidence; that the main practice leads to experiences and realization; that hearing the names of the Buddhas frees us from the lower realms; and that all these are due to the qualities of the teacher's enlightened mind, which has transmitted this understanding to us. The teacher is therefore like a stainless, perfectly pure jewel. Like the Norbu Jitaka gem whose radiance alone makes the turbid water in a muddy pool completely clear, a true spiritual master can turn everyone around him to virtue and to the authentic Dharma by the sheer radiance of his enlightened qualities.

You need to keep the company of excellent friends who abide by virtue.

Their good ways will naturally rub off on you, and faith and other virtuous qualities will increase.

Ideally we should be like a wounded animal, staying in solitary retreat without any companions. But if this is not possible, we should at least keep the company of friends with whom we have a pure connection, who are disciples of the same teacher, and who are inclined to virtue. Their presence will serve as a reminder if ever we find ourselves forgetting the Dharma. And they can help us clarify any doubts or questions we may have about the meaning of the teachings. When all the monks and nuns in a monastery are very mindful and careful in observing their vows, the atmosphere in the monastery is naturally harmonious. If we live with spiritual companions, their qualities will automatically rub off on us.

4

Counseling yourself with thirteen teachings on things to be regarded with distaste.[26]

Son, there are thirteen things to be abhorred.

Unless you turn your back on your fatherland, you will not vanquish the demon of pride.

As long as we stay in our native country there will be no end to disliking our enemies and being attached to our loved ones. In our own country, we meet people who are well disposed toward us and we become attached to them. This leads us to engage in all sorts of actions based on attachment. Then there are people who obstruct us and we think of them as enemies. It is impossible to avoid attachment and hatred. When we manage to get the better of our enemies, we feel very brave and successful. In our dealings with those we like, we indulge in attachment and busy ourselves with all sorts of different activities. When we are able to help others and show affection for those to whom we are attached, we feel we are good people. In either case, whether we are bravely subduing our enemies or virtuously helping others, we feel very proud of ourselves.

Wholeheartedly adopt foreign lands.

If you go somewhere where you do not know anyone, there is no cause for either attachment or hatred. In foreign countries you can wander indifferently. Even if you are an accomplished being, no one will know you; if you are a great scholar, nobody will recognize you. So there will be very few causes for distraction.

Unless you give up the activities of a household, you will never find the time to practice the Dharma.

When you are responsible for a household, you have to plow the fields or engage in commerce and look after the affairs of the house. You never have a chance to practice the Dharma. People in this situation may think or talk of practicing the Dharma but they are so busy they never have any leisure to actually do so, and their aspirations are merely words. That is why Shechen Gyaltsap adds,

Put aside the business of running a household.

In other words, you should drop all plans and projects for making your household more prosperous or for increasing it.

If you do not practice the moment faith arises, there will be no end to the jobs you have to do.

We have had the good fortune to meet a teacher and to receive some teachings, but this will not go on happening forever. When we have the chance to hear the teachings, reflect on them, and meditate, we should do so immediately because this opportunity may never come again. Otherwise, out of indolence and laziness we may think, "I have received all these precious instructions; I will definitely start putting them into practice in the future," and we will keep postponing our practice. When the hunter Kyirawa Gonpo Dorje met Milarepa, he felt great devotion and an ardent desire to practice the Dharma. He told Milarepa that he would return home just one last time to tell his family of his intention to practice the Dharma and then come back. Milarepa answered, "If you do that, you will probably change your mind. Start practicing now." And in his *Hundred Verses of Advice*, Padampa Sangye says, "People of Tingri, while you're thinking of it, practice straightaway." So

Cut through your indecision.

In other words, you should think, "Now that I am determined to practice the Dharma, I shall attend this teacher, I shall receive his instructions, and I shall put them into practice." This is something you have to decide by yourself and then actually implement.

Do not blame others for your own lack of faith.

If we do not feel much devotion, it is not because there is something wrong with one of our teachers or because our companions have affected us adversely. It is purely because of our own defects and wrong way of perceiving things. The teacher is placing in our hands all the means for achieving enlightenment, so we should see perfection in everything he does and says. If we think he is truly the Buddha, whatever he does is perfect. This sort of devotion will cause our impure perception, in which we see defects in the teacher, to give way to pure perception, in which we see his enlightened activities as they actually are. Unless we have faith, we will see defects in the teacher, as did Sunakshatra,[27] who declared that the Buddha's teachings were simply designed to fool beings, and Devadatta, who despite being the Buddha's cousin, spent his life trying to harm him. So examine your own mistakes and defects and:

Wind the nose rope around your head.

This refers to the rope Tibetans use to lead animals by the nose. In other words, mind your own mistakes.

**Unless you cast your possessions to the wind, you
will never exhaust your worldly ambitions.**

As long as we remain preoccupied with delicious food and comfortable clothes, wherever we are we will never be satisfied. However much we have, it will never be enough and we will always want more. On the other hand, if we can be content with just enough food to fill our stomachs and sufficient clothing to protect us from the cold, then, whether or not we live in pleasant surroundings, whether or not we have friends, we will be free to progress along the path to enlightenment, and that is more than enough.

*Whatever you have, use it to make offerings to the teacher and
to the Three Jewels.*

If you are wealthy, the best way to use your wealth is to serve the Sangha and to offer money for building temples and making objects that represent the Three Jewels.[28] You should also practice the three ways of pleasing the teacher. The best way to please him is through your own practice and accomplishment. The middling way is to do everything you can to serve him physically, verbally, and mentally. The least beneficial way to please him is to make material offerings.

Wealth is like an illusion, but if we offer it and use it for meritorious purposes, we will gather merit. Merit, too, is like an illusion, but it helps lead to enlightenment, for such merit never disappears. There was once a young country boy who was extremely poor. One day he saw the Buddha Vipashyin passing, begging for alms. He was suddenly filled with faith and wanted to offer him something, but because he was so poor he had nothing to offer except seven peas he was holding in his hand. With great devotion he threw the peas before the Buddha as an offering. Four of them fell in the Buddha's begging bowl, two touched his heart, and one fell on top of his head. As a result of the complete faith the boy had when he made this offering, he was later reborn as King Mandhata. Because of the four peas he had offered, he ruled the four continents. Because of the two peas that touched the Buddha's heart, he had dominion first over the realm of the Four Great Kings and later over the Heaven of the Thirty-three. And because of the pea that fell on the Buddha's head, he had the good fortune to share Indra's throne.

Everything depends on one's attitude. The boy's offering was very small but was made with a very pure attitude and therefore had a great result. On the other hand, an offering made simply with the intention of appearing important or gaining fame, or made with the competitive aim of being better than anyone else, will bring hardly any benefit, no matter how big it is. That is why we should have the same attitude to worldly possessions as Jigme Lingpa did: "Seeing all possessions and wealth as impermanent and without essence, seek the wealth of the seven noble riches." The seven noble riches are faith, discipline, a sense of shame in one's own eyes, a sense of decency in others' regard, and so forth. When we have them, all good qualities will grow from within. But if we accumulate a lot of wealth and hoard it greedily, we are simply creating the cause for rebirth as a preta.

Unless you distance yourself from your relatives, there will be no interruption in your attachment and aversion.

Stay far away from your relatives and friends, for when someone is good to you, it is very difficult to avoid becoming attached. Similarly, if someone wrongs you, it is difficult to avoid feeling aversion. This leads to all sorts of different activities. It is therefore important to stay away from them, like a wounded animal, which seeks an isolated place where it can recover from its wounds:

Always rely on solitude.

Unless you act now, you cannot be sure where you will go next.

At this moment we are truly at a crossroads, so now is the time to practice. We might think, "I will meet the teacher again next year and receive teachings, and I will practice then," but we cannot be sure that we will be able to do things as planned. We do not know what could happen even a short time from now.

Now, when all the favorable conditions have come together,
you should do anything to get free from samsara.

When one is thrown into jail by the authorities, one's only thought is, "How can I get out? Who can help me?" Similarly, when one is sick, one only thinks of finding a doctor and taking his medicine. One will do anything to get rid of one's predicament. So now that we have gathered the conditions for doing so, we should be constantly preoccupied with getting further and further away from samsara. We should be prepared to do anything to get even a millimeter further away from samsara.

Doing nothing now when you have the means, the prayers
you make for future lives are empty chatter.

You might say, "Right now I have to finish my work, for I have such-and-such business to attend to, but I'll pray that in a future life I will be a very good practitioner." But these are just meaningless words. Who knows what will happen in the next life? If we are caught up in so much attachment to friends in this life, then in the next life our attachment will be even greater. Attachment to our wealth and activities is the very cause for rebirth in the lower realms. And if we cannot get rid of animosity toward enemies, it will cause us to be reborn in the hells in the next life.

If you have the ability and you do not act, you are letting
yourself down.

When one has a garden that has been prepared for growing flowers and one does nothing about it, one is simply letting oneself down. Now, when it is possible for us to practice the Dharma, we should realize that this is an extremely rare and precious opportunity that should be used immediately, because things will change and it will not last forever.

Without lying to yourself, practice the Supreme Dharma.

If you think that being dishonest with yourself is all right, then that is fine. You might as well carry on with all your worldly activities—doing business and cheating others, crushing your enemies and promoting your friends. But if you think this is not actually the right way to benefit yourself, you will realize that you have only been harming and deceiving yourself. So instead,

take your own mind as a witness.

Jetsun Milarepa said, "The root of samaya is not to be ashamed of oneself." There is no way the mind can lie to itself. We know what we have been doing. We can easily see whether we have followed the teacher properly and whether we have put his instructions into practice or not. The mind can see the smallest things perfectly well—there is nothing it can hide from itself. If one has made a little progress or gained a few good qualities, the mind will know. But while it is very easy for one to know what is happening in one's own mind, it is difficult for others to judge from one's external appearance and behavior. So the only real witness to how you are thinking and acting should be your own mind.

**Forsake now what you will have to give up anyway,
and it will become meaningful.**

However much wealth you have accumulated, you will not take even a tiny bit of it with you through the door of death. All the delicious food you are always eating merely turns into excrement. Status and fame will have to be left behind when you die. But right now you can choose to give all these things up deliberately. You can give them away and devote yourself to practicing the Dharma. For when death comes, you will have to abandon them all anyway—against your will. Your friends and relatives will gather around weeping, and it will be tremendously hard to leave them. You will have to draw up your testament, leaving all your possessions behind. And on top of all that, you will not have acquired any spiritual qualities. So it would be far better to use your wealth to serve the Sangha, to make offerings to the teacher, and to offer it for worthy purposes.

At the time of the Buddha there was a householder called Anathapindaka who decided to give away all his land to build a vihara in which the Buddha and his disciples could stay. One day he was with the Buddha's disciple Shariputra marking out the ground for the vihara, and he noticed Shariputra smile. An Arhat does not smile without reason, so he asked Shariputra what had pleased him. Shariputra replied, "I have just seen that there is a palace already waiting for you in one of the Buddha-fields." That is how infallible the law of cause and effect is. At present Anathapindaka is in the Heaven of the Thirty-three enjoying the plea-sures of the gods. And as predicted by the Buddha, during this kalpa of a thousand Buddhas, Anathapindaka will come as a Bodhisattva, appear-ing as each Buddha's patron, building a vihara for him, and being reborn each time in a Buddhafield.

> *Whatever you have, your body and wealth, give it away for the Dharma.*

Jetsun Milarepa, for example, offered a big copper pot to Marpa, and through this offering he made the proper connection for becoming a fit vessel for the whole of Marpa's teaching.

> **Rather than concerning yourself with things you obviously cannot complete, concern yourself with making an experience of what you definitely can complete.**

Whatever you do, there are things that you will never be able to cope with. You might think of subduing enemies and manage to get the better of a few around you, but there is no end to those enemies. You could never subdue all the enemies on earth. Similarly, you may be attached to some people, but you could never be equally attached to all the sen-tient beings on this earth even though they have all been your parents. There is no end to ordinary attachment. But what you really can do at present is decide to practice the Dharma and devote all your energy to that. That is something manageable—something you can cope with. Therefore,

> *For the sake of the Dharma, be prepared for austerity and forbearance.*

> **Instead of preparing for next year—when you cannot be sure whether or not there will be a next year—prepare for death, which is certain to happen.**

How can we say, "Next year I shall do this or that, I shall conduct such-and-such business, I shall accomplish such-and-such a task"? You might just as well go to a dry riverbed, set a few nets, and put out lines and hooks in the expectation of catching some fish. That is why Shechen Gyaltsap notes,

> *Time is short; curtail your plans.*

Starting from this very moment, we should make a heartfelt aspiration to meet the teacher, to receive his teachings, to begin the preliminary practice, and, having completed it, to continue immediately with the main practice, going through the generation and perfection phases and the practices of the Great Perfection without pausing between one stage and the next. If we have the deep intention to practice like this, then everything will happen accordingly and there will be immeasurable benefits. Jigme Lingpa himself says in his teaching on the preliminary practice that those who complete the five stages of the preliminary practice without any major downfall are certain to take rebirth in the Copper-Colored Mountain.[29] But there is no time to lose, for we cannot be sure when death will come.

As you practice, food and clothing will take care of themselves, so do not have great hopes or fears.

If you begin by saying, "I want to practice, but first I must find somewhere nice to stay and buy food and provisions," this will only delay you. Once you decide to practice and start doing so, the blessings of the Three Jewels will take care of your most basic needs in terms of food and clothing. The Buddha himself declared that you will never find the bones of a Dharma practitioner who has died of hunger and cold. So,

> *For those who practice the Dharma it is very important to give*
> *up all concern for this life.*

The thirteen points in this chapter concern things for which we should feel distaste. What do we mean here by distaste? Like a jaundiced patient who has no appetite at all for greasy food, a genuine Dharma practitioner is said to be someone who is completely uninterested in possessions, achievement, fame, or glory in worldly life. Like someone thrown alive into a pit of fire, as *The Words of My Perfect Teacher* puts it, he has no desire at all for the things of this life.

5

Thirteen important points that show the unmistaken path.

Son, there are thirteen things that are very important.

If we observe these thirteen important points related to body, speech, and mind, we will have no difficulty practicing. The first one concerns the teacher:

His realization is like space, beyond all partiality.

Those whose realization has become as vast as the sky have no bias. They do not see samsara as something to be rejected, nor do they see the qualities of nirvana as something to be preferred and obtained. They have realized that all the afflictive emotions and the negative actions in samsara are by nature the kayas and wisdoms of the Buddhas.

In the causal vehicle of characteristics, absolute truth is considered to be that which has to be realized, while the phenomena of relative truth are considered as impure and to be rejected. But this sort of discrimination, this dual perception of pure and impure, of something to be obtained and something to be rejected, is not the correct view of the Secret Mantrayana. Why? The root of our wandering in samsara is the five gross aggregates. According to the Mantrayana, which distinguishes between the way things appear and the way things are, these aggregates, along with the elements, sense organs, and sense objects, may appear as our relative perceptions. But with regard to the way things are, the aggregates are the pure three seats—that is, they are by nature the five Dhyani Buddhas and their consorts, the eight male and female Bodhisattvas, and so on. When we fail to recognize this and cling to the gross aggregates, we give rise to the afflictive emotions. The aggregates thus become the cause for wandering in the three worlds of samsara. Mantrayana practitioners are able to dispel this deluded perception of the aggregates and so forth, and allow their true nature, the way it is, to appear clearly. They thus achieve the perception of infinite purity. Theirs is realization without any bias, in which there is no distinction between samsara as something to be rejected and nirvana as something to be preferred and obtained.

His experience is constant and level like the ocean.[30]

Realization comes through three stages: understanding, experiences, and realization. The first of these is theoretical understanding, which comes from learning the teachings. Of course it brings some benefit, but it is not very stable. It is like a patch sewn onto a piece of clothing: it can come off again. Although we have some theoretical understanding, it may not be very reliable in the face of different circumstances and might not help us cope with difficulties.

Experiences are like mist: they will fade away. Practitioners who spend their time practicing in seclusion are certain to have many different experiences, but these experiences are very unreliable. As it is said, experiences are like rainbows, but the great meditator who runs after them like a child will be deceived. We may occasionally have flashes of clairvoyance, seeing things we cannot ordinarily know. We may have signs of accomplishment, or predictions from the deity or the dakinis. But such experiences in most cases give rise to hope and expectation. They are none other than the tricks of demons: they simply cause obstacles.

When true realization dawns in one's mind, it is like the king of mountains, Mount Meru, which no wind can shake. This means that in a thousand good circumstances the mind does not become attached and in a thousand adverse circumstances the mind feels no aversion. It is said that for those who attain the level of Arhat it does not make the slightest difference whether on one side there is a beautiful person waving a sandalwood fan and on the other side a fearsome person threatening to kill them with an axe. They feel neither attachment to the one nor aversion to the other. This is the quality of realization one achieves through the so-called Lesser Vehicle, so how much vaster should the realization of the Great Vehicle be. And in the Great Perfection we speak of the "exhaustion of phenomena in the expanse of dharmakaya." "Exhaustion" here does not mean the extinction of phenomena but rather the exhaustion of all *deluded* perceptions. In that state, what is ordinarily perceived as suffering arises as perfect bliss, and all distinctions between good and bad have vanished. All circumstances, whether good or bad, thus become helpers, friends on the path.

> His compassion shines evenly, like the sun and the
> moon.[31]

When we have proper devotion and confidence in the Three Jewels and the teacher, their compassion is always present, like the sun and moon, which move constantly over the four continents. It is unthinkable that the sun and moon might ever stop shining, or that they might stop shining over one particular place. If your devotion to your root teacher and the Three Jewels is sound, you can be sure that they are watching over you with compassion constantly, day and night, through happiness and suffering.

> To a teacher who has these three qualities, it is very
> important to be respectful.

You should respect such a teacher with your body, speech, and mind. It is said that in the beginning one has to be skillful in finding the teacher, in the middle one has to be skillful in following him, and in the end one has to be skillful in putting his instructions into practice. Someone who succeeds in these three ways will travel the whole path without difficulty.

To enter the path of Dharma, we have to be properly prepared and very sure of what we are doing. In ordinary life, people who are about to start an important project, get married, or build a house begin by carefully considering the different elements of the situation. Similarly, if we want to practice the Dharma, we first have to find an authentic teacher, and for this we should not rely on how famous he is. Then, having found an authentic teacher, we have to follow him properly and practice his instructions. In following the teacher, it is said we should be like a belt that is imperceptible when worn; that is, we should never be a source of discomfort or disturbance for him. Like salt readily dissolving in water, we should be able to adapt to all circumstances and not be bothered by them. With our body, speech, and mind we should follow the teacher without causing trouble, doing whatever pleases him and never, even secretly, doing anything that might displease him. We should be like a swan or duck gliding between the lotus flowers, picking at the flowers and feeding, but without disturbing the surface of the water or making the water muddy. Like this, if we please the teacher throughout our life, then when death comes, our mind will readily become one with the teacher's mind in the same way that Jigme Lingpa merged his mind with Longchenpa's.

> As the teacher is the root of the path, follow him, pleasing him
> in the three ways.

He is the "root of the path" because without a spiritual teacher there is no way one can progress along the path. Of the three ways of pleasing the teacher, the best is to put his teachings into practice. He gives teaching not because he expects any sort of recognition, remuneration, power, or fame, but simply because he can see how beings are deluded in samsara and how they suffer on account of delusion. He gives instructions as a remedy for delusion, hoping that beings can thereby free themselves from ignorance. He does this out of sheer compassion, like parents who kindly advise their children to do certain things and warn them against doing other things, purely for their own good, hoping their children will lead happy lives. If the Buddha turned the Wheel of the Dharma three times, it was not because he was restless and had nothing better to do. Neither was it because he hoped to become famous. It was simply out of his intention to dispel the ignorance of beings and because he wished to set beings on the path to enlightenment. As a result of his kindness, we can now hear the names of the Three Jewels and read the teachings in the Three Pitakas that show what is positive and what is negative. Thanks to his kindness, the practice of Dharma is accessible to us.

> Do not do anything disrespectful, even in a dream.

It is said that if you dream you are committing a negative act like killing, lying, or stealing, even though it is a dream, when you wake up, you must regret what happened in the dream and confess it. Likewise, if you feel disrespect for the teacher, even in a dream, as soon as you wake up you should deeply regret it and confess. Remember, too, that the more you pray to the Three Jewels and to the teacher, the greater will be the blessings you receive.

It is very important to give instructions to disciples who are proper vessels.

Someone who has faith in the Three Jewels and the teacher, who is interested in hearing, reflecting, and meditating, and who is very diligent should be given the teachings without reserve, for this will bring great benefit. "Instructions" here refers to major instructions—the profound instructions that lead to liberation and enlightenment—and not to minor instructions for curing sickness, dispelling obstacles, and creating prosperity in this life. What then are the benefits that will come from giving such instructions to those who are suitable vessels?

They will hold the lineage and benefit themselves and others,
and the teachings and beings.

In the best case, disciples will become lineage holders, like the Seven Patriarchs who held Buddha Shakyamuni's teachings: they became equal to the Buddha himself and continued his activities, holding, expounding, and preserving the Dharma. Among Milarepa's disciples there were Gampopa, who was like the sun, and Rechungpa, who was like the moon, and eight who were able to go to the pure realms in their lifetime, in the very same body. These disciples were the true representatives of their teacher. It is through the kindness of such lineage holders, teachers who are fully enlightened holders of the teaching, that the different instructions of the eight great chariots can still be given and practiced today, despite the Buddha's having taught the Dharma over two thousand years ago.[32]

Do not be miserly with the teachings.

Someone who is truly concerned with the next life and interested in the Dharma should be shown all the texts and given all the instructions, without hiding anything. Of course, there is no need to reveal texts and instructions on black magic, since these can be harmful, but anything that is helpful for the disciple's practice should be given.

It is very important to give up attachment to things, externally and internally.

Practitioners who have full confidence in the Three Jewels need never worry about food and clothing. These will come their way anyway. When the sun shines in summer, it does not need to think about what it is doing—making the forests and meadows turn green, the flowers blossom, and fruits ripen, and warming everyone on the earth. It does all this naturally. Likewise, if you practice the Dharma sincerely, people will naturally be disposed toward you and will help you in your practice. Those who renounce the world and take ordination are naturally respected by their families and others, who are happy to support them. Those who are very learned do not have to talk about it; they easily win respect. And siddhas who have attained a high degree of accomplishment do not have to claim they are siddhas. Their accomplishment is evident and they are venerated for it. So we need not be preoccupied or obsessed with external necessities; they will come our way naturally. And in no event should we be attached to such things; otherwise we will be influenced by the eight ordinary concerns and be led into all sorts of activities in order to procure and keep them.

> *Remember the defects of attachment to the pleasures of the*
> *five senses.*

When we crave beautiful forms, we become like moths, which are attracted to light and get burnt by the flame. However much enjoyment we may derive from the pleasures of the senses, there will never come a time when we have had enough. The more we indulge in them, the more they become like honey smeared on a razor, cutting our tongues as we try to lick it off.

> The pleasures we desire will bring us ruin;
> They're like the kimba fruit, the Buddha said.[33]

So remembering these defects, give up desire as much as you possibly can.

> In practicing the instructions, it is very important to
> think in the long term.

In practicing the Dharma, the longer we maintain our diligence, the more good qualities will grow within us and the deeper our understanding of the Dharma will be. To really benefit from the teachings and develop good qualities, it is not enough to simply hear them. We have to be like the great teacher Vasubandhu: although he had developed the power of infallible memory and knew ninety-nine hundred thousand treatises by heart, he would still read them daily. He even used to recite them all night, seated in a large oil jar to protect himself from the wind. Jigme Lingpa said that truly diligent Dharma practitioners remain diligent even when they get old; they become less distracted and busy. This is a sign of a real practitioner, who has not been "touched by frost."[34]

Even if it takes very long, your days and life must be spent practicing. Jetsun Milarepa said, "Do not expect quick results; spend your time practicing—in a race with death." It makes no sense to think, "I have practiced for one year; will I obtain realization? I have practiced for three years; will I obtain realization?" Simply think, "If I die, that will be that, but until then I am going to practice." As you become more and more acquainted with the Dharma, your understanding will naturally become deeper and good qualities will grow. When the Dharma hits the mark, it becomes more and more effective.

It is said that Dharma practitioners start out with suffering and end up with happiness. When we start practicing, we have to go to a secluded place where we have very little food and must endure heat and cold. Moreover, the practice is difficult to begin with, there seems to be little progress, and we do not have any signs of experience or realization. But then, as we persevere in the practice and the Dharma gradually becomes part of us, our minds feel more and more confident and serene. In the beginning we are bound to have obstacles, but with time we will feel happier and happier in the practice.

With worldly activities it is just the opposite: everything is very pleasant to begin with, but the end is very painful. We may start off happy, with wealth, a comfortable existence, and all of life's pleasures. But in order to achieve that, we will have accumulated mainly negative actions and can therefore only end up suffering in this life and for many lives to come. This is why we must not view our Dharma practice in the short term. Never think, "I've practiced so hard for months and years, and I've still not had any result." Otherwise you will get discouraged when you have still not had any experiences after one, two, three, or more years. Take the example of Asanga. He meditated for twelve years, praying to Maitreya, and in all that time never had the slightest sign of accomplishment. Finally he had an experience of genuine and overwhelming compassion, and at that moment Maitreya appeared to him in person. "I've been praying to you all these years, and you never showed any sign of your presence," complained Asanga. Maitreya replied, "I have been next to you from the moment you began practicing, but on account of your obscuration you did not realize I was present." So,

> With regard to the Dharma, do not be impatient. You need to accompany the teacher for a long time.

To follow the teacher for a long time is of great value, and it is otherwise difficult to obtain all his qualities. Just as on a gold mountain all the trees, bushes, and flowers turn golden, if you follow the teacher like a shadow, you will become like Ananda: he never left the Buddha's side and eventually obtained all the qualities of his body, speech, and mind.[35] And just as all the gods and nagas take great care of the wishing-gem and make it their crown ornament—that is, they recognize its great value— you should never separate from your teacher even for an instant.

> Do not be skittish.

Do not be superficial and inconstant, thinking that following the teacher and receiving his teachings will make you famous or that receiving only a few words of instruction and making a "Dharma connection" will suffice.

> It is very important to develop fervent devotion to the yidam deity and the Three Jewels.

The essence of the Buddha's teachings is to be found in the Three Jewels and in the yidam deity, so you should have the intention to do the practices related to them, praying and reciting the mantras over a long period of time. If you do, the yidam will always be close to you, and you will receive blessings and eventually meet the deity face to face. In the *Mani Kabum*, Songtsen Gampo describes how to accomplish all the ordinary and supreme activities of pacifying, increasing, controlling, and fiercely subduing. He explains that for this one can do no better than to rely on Avalokiteshvara as one's yidam. He himself was able to meet

Avalokiteshvara as if shaking hands with him, and it is through Avalo-kiteshvara's blessings that the Land of Snows was protected and the Dharma introduced to Tibet. Similarly, Lama Mipham[36] practiced all his life on Manjushri as his peaceful yidam and on Yamantaka as his wrathful one, and through this practice his mind became united with the enlight-ened mind of Manjushri.[37]

All this depends on the strength of our devotion. The stronger our devotion, the greater the blessings. But to have no devotion is like hiding oneself in a house with all the doors and shutters closed. The sunlight will never get in. Without devotion, even if we spend all our time near the teacher, his blessings will never enter us. At the time of Lord Bud-dha, there were Tirthika teachers who spent some time in his presence and heard him teach, but since they had no faith they did not receive his blessings and could not attain enlightenment.

> *Without fervent devotion, blessings will not enter. At all times*
> *be diligent in taking refuge,*

because the root of all the Dharma is the refuge; it is the ultimate object of meditation of both the sutras and tantras.

It is very important to cultivate diligence in the practice of virtue.

It is said that if Buddha Shakyamuni could become a fully enlightened Buddha after accumulating merit and wisdom for three measureless kal-pas, it was from having brought the transcendent perfection of diligence to its ultimate point. He spent countless lives thus accumulating merit and in thirty-two of these was reborn as a universal monarch, each time accumulating boundless merit. As a result of this constant diligence, he finally became the Buddha, whom beings could know and meet. And it was with this sort of constant diligence that Jetsun Milarepa was able to reach the level of Vajradhara within a single lifetime.

> *Act like a beautiful woman whose hair has caught fire.*

A beautiful woman whose hair was on fire would not waste a second trying to put the fire out. With that sort of diligence there is nothing you would not be able to accomplish.

Do not fall under the influence of laziness,

Without applying yourself, you will never succeed at anything. If you are truly interested in listening, reflecting, and meditating, you should always be thinking, "There is so much to do, and no knowing when I might die," and you should not waste a single instant on distracting activities.

It is very important to steer clear of negative actions.

To do so you need to be very mindful and vigilant. Be aware of whether your actions are positive or negative. Once you know what has to be taken up and what has to be avoided, you must avoid even the minutest negative action. If you find you have committed a negative action physically, verbally, or mentally, you must acknowledge it immediately, confess, and repair the downfall. And if you see that you have done something positive, make a prayer: "May I do even more; may I increase in virtue."

Think of their fully ripened effect and avoid them as you would a speck of dust in your eye.

It is important to examine your actions very closely. Particularly with minor negative actions, we do not see what the result will be immediately, but it is certain that those actions will mature and that we will have to experience the result. Enlightened beings can see this very clearly. For them even the most minute negative action is like a speck of dust in one's eye—one has to get rid of it immediately. We ordinary beings, on the other hand, are unable to see the consequences of our actions. We are unaware of our minor deeds and lose track of them like an arrow shot into a thick forest. We act without understanding where our actions will lead. But if we had the vision of an enlightened being, we would see that even the minutest action has a result.

It is very important to rely on the absence of thoughts in your mind.

The root cause that makes us wander in samsara is the chaining of our thoughts, and it is said that discursive thought is the "great

73

ignorance" that makes us fall into the ocean of samsara. Unless we do something about it, this chaining of thoughts will go on and on forever. So it is very important to employ the correct remedy, and here the main remedy is to cultivate the state free from wandering thoughts.

Let the thoughts related to the five poisons dissolve by themselves.

For ordinary beings, thoughts related to the five poisons will keep on coming up in the mind. Nevertheless, we should not let these thoughts dominate us. Our approach to this can take different forms. In the Basic Vehicle one applies the appropriate antidotes for such thoughts. For example, the antidote for anger is to meditate on patience, the antidote for attachment is to meditate on disgust, and the antidote for ignorance is to meditate on the law of cause and effect and on interdependence, understanding how ignorance leads to samsara, and so on. In the Great Vehicle one investigates the five poisons and comes to the conclusion that they are like a dream or illusion: their ultimate nature is emptiness. Once one knows this, one cannot be influenced by them. In the Mantrayana one realizes that the basic nature of the five poisons is wisdom and, thus transformed, one uses them on the path of liberation and the path of skillful means.

In the postmeditation period, it is very important to rely on compassion and bodhichitta.

Whether we are practicing virtue or giving up negative actions, we should think that our sole purpose is to benefit sentient beings—all beings, without excluding a single one. As we realize the extent of beings' suffering and of our own inability to help them, we should develop the firm intention to do everything necessary to benefit them and dedicate all our physical, verbal, and mental actions to them. Otherwise, if we practice only with the self-centered intention to be comfortable in this life and to avoid being reborn in the lower realms in future lives, any virtuous practice we do will have very limited results. Unless we begin with the altruistic attitude and end by sharing the merit with all sentient beings so that they can attain enlightenment, our practice is not the genuine Mahayana. We may call it the "Great Vehicle," but there is nothing great about it. The root of the Great Vehicle is that for the preparation one generates bodhichitta, for the main practice one is free from concepts, and for the conclusion one dedicates the merit to all sentient beings. Without these three supreme methods it is impossible to practice the Mahayana. The principal practice of Bodhisattvas is to leave aside their own interests and consider others more important. We should follow their example.

> *This is the root of the Great Vehicle and is therefore indispensable.*
> *Train in considering others more important than yourself.*

The Buddha manifested countless times in this world as different Bodhisattvas. He did not do this in order to repeatedly win fame and glory, nor was it merely to have food and clothes. It was simply due to his universal compassion—his wish to help beings he saw snared by ignorance and to free them from their suffering.

It is very important to develop the conviction that the instructions are unmistaken.

When you receive authentic instruction, you should concentrate first on hearing it, then on reflecting on its meaning, and finally, through meditation, making it part of you. As you do so, you will gain the conviction that the instruction you have received is truly undeceiving and become confident of its excellence.

> *If you have no doubts, accomplishment will be swift in coming.*

The boundless benefits of putting the instructions into practice—meditating on the yidam, reciting the mantra, and so forth—are described in the relevant scriptures. Do not have any doubts about the truth of these, and you will swiftly achieve such qualities. But as long as you doubt and hesitate—wondering, "Does mantra recitation really have such power?" or "Can I really gain siddhi if I do the yidam practice?"—it will be impossible for you to achieve realization or accomplishment.

Furthermore, the root of attaining accomplishment is careful observance of the three vows: the Pratimoksha vows of the Basic Vehicle, the

Bodhisattva precepts of the Great Vehicle, and the samayas of the Vajra-yana. This is why Zurchungpa says,

It is very important to observe the vows and samayas.

This is the well-tilled, fertile field in which good crops naturally grow. Therefore,

> *Do not let your mind be stained by the downfalls and faults*
> *related to the three vows.*

The three vows refer to the outer vows of the Pratimoksha, the inner precepts of the Bodhisattvas, and the secret precepts of the vehicle of the Vidyadharas. As a lay practitioner, you might think you have never taken a Pratimoksha vow, but although you may not have been through the full Pratimoksha ritual, any Vajrayana empowerment you have received will have included Pratimoksha vows as an integral part of the empowerment. There is no empowerment in which one does not take the three vows, one after another. How do we receive the Pratimoksha vows in that case? Through the kindness of the teacher we give rise to deep disillusionment with samsaric affairs. This is already part of the Pratimoksha vow, the essence of which is to realize the sufferings and shortcomings of samsara and to develop a strong determination to be free.

In the same way, if you have received a Vajrayana empowerment, there is no way you cannot have taken the Bodhisattva vow, even if you did not go through the formal ritual. At the beginning of an empowerment the teacher says, "These teachings should be received and practiced for the sake of all beings, as numerous as the sky is vast." This is the essence of the Bodhisattva vow, arousing bodhichitta. Likewise for the samayas, the Vajrayana precepts: the empowerment introduces one to the realization that all forms are the deity, all sounds are the sound of the mantra, and all thoughts are the display of the absolute nature. For the body, we receive the vase empowerment with the image of the deity. For our speech, we repeat the mantra and receive the secret empowerment. For the mind, we receive the third empowerment with the deity's symbolic attributes. So in a Vajrayana empowerment all the Vajrayana vows are complete. We have all received Vajrayana empowerment,[38] so we have taken these three vows. It is therefore very important to keep them and to avoid all faults and downfalls related to them, as such faults and downfalls are extremely negative.

The essence of all these vows is summed up in this saying from the sutras:

> Abandon evildoing,
> Practice virtue well.

Give up all negative actions and you will be keeping the three vows. Cultivate positive actions and again you will be practicing the essence of the three vows.

However, if in performing positive actions—following the teacher, listening to his teachings, and putting them into practice—and in giving up negative actions you feel self-satisfied or proud and think, "What a good deed I've done," this sort of clinging is a great defect. You should always be completely free from clinging and see everything as a dream, as an illusion. Although you are following a teacher, in truth the absolute teacher is the dharmakaya, which is the nature of your own mind. The outer manifested teacher you are following at present is himself like a dream. His manifested body is not permanent, and he will again leave this world. The true inner dharmakaya teacher is never separate from you. So even if on the relative level you follow a teacher, practice, and do lots of positive actions, you must do so without any clinging, seeing all these as illusory by nature.

It is very important to establish the unborn nature of the mind.

As your mind and appearances are the display of the absolute nature, come to the clear conclusion that the nature of mind is unborn like space.

In short, all the infinite phenomena of samsara and nirvana are nothing else than the projection of one's own mind and are therefore an illusion. Nothing is truly existent and permanent. When you understand this, you will realize that everything is unborn like space, that its nature is emptiness. It is with this realization—that you yourself, the teacher, and all phenomena are like a dream and illusion—that you should practice the meditation on the wisdom deity and recite the mantra. And if you ever have a sign of accomplishment, even a vision of the yidam, you should continue to recognize its illusory nature and avoid the error of feeling attached or proud. To be conceited and think, "I have achieved a sign of accomplishment," is an obstacle, a demon. However high your realization may be, you must never be proud of any signs such as clairvoyance that you may experience, but must remain free from clinging and see their dreamlike nature. Otherwise, if you are attached to such things, it will be impossible for even the most basic qualities of the path to develop in your mind. As the great siddha Saraha said, "Wherever there is attachment, there will be a downfall." Even the husk of a sesame seed's worth of attachment will create great suffering in the mind. So if you have any result in your practice, you should simply think that it is the natural consequence of doing the practice and not be proud of it. As we read in *Parting from the Four Attachments*, the four-line teaching that Manjushri gave in a vision to the great Sakyapa teacher Jetsun Trakpa Gyaltsen:

As long as there is clinging, there is no view.

It is very important not to give the secret pith instructions to an improper vessel.

Profound teachings such as those of Mahamudra and the Great Perfection have to be given to a suitable disciple, for they are like the milk of the snow lioness, which can only be collected in a container made of gold or a similar precious substance. To worthy disciples, as has already been stated in this text, the teachings should be given and not concealed, for they will benefit them. But to give the teachings to someone who is not worthy is a pure waste, just as pouring the snow lioness's milk into an earthenware pot results in the pot's being broken and the milk's being wasted as well. The greater the extent to which the pith instructions are kept secret, the swifter the results in the practice. In ancient times in the supreme land of India, the Vinaya teachings were widely taught. But all the practices of the Secret Mantrayana were kept completely secret. In a gathering of a thousand panditas, no one would ever know which of them were practicing the Secret Mantrayana, who their yidams were, or what mantras they were reciting. It was only if one of them started flying through the sky or performing some other miracle that people would realize he had been practicing the Mantrayana. In Tibet, however, the Mantrayana teachings have gradually spread and are now known to everyone. As a result, the proportion of practitioners who actually attain accomplishment and realization is much smaller.

> *Divulging the secret teachings leads to criticism, so be careful:*
> *take pains to check the worthiness of the disciple.*

This is why the teacher should know how to recognize the disciple's potential. To someone worthy he should give all the instructions without holding anything back. But to disciples who do not have the appropriate qualities he should give teachings that will benefit them in accordance with their real capacity—first the teachings for beings of lesser capacity, then the teachings for those of middling capacity, and so on, thus gradually transforming them into suitable vessels. In your own practice, too, you should apply the same principle. Practice in accordance with your capacity and see everything as dream and illusion. If you do so, you will reap great benefit.

This was the first section from the *Eighty Chapters of Personal Advice*, the instruction on firm faith, the gateway.

In this section the immense qualities and importance of faith have been shown and expressed by teachers who were both very learned and highly accomplished and who were therefore able to condense the teachings into this essentialized instruction while retaining all their profound meaning.

II

Discipline

Instructions on the jewel-like superior training in discipline, the perfect foundation.

Just as it is impossible for the continents and mountains in the universe to exist without the ground as a foundation, in order to travel the path perfectly we need a perfectly pure foundation, namely the superior training in discipline.

There are eighteen chapters.

6

An instruction on timeliness in the practice.

If you practice the Dharma when the time is right, you can be sure that the practice will follow its proper course and that it will act as a marvelous method for perfecting experiences and realization.

Son, there are ten facts.[39]

If the continued existence of the Buddha's teaching and your having faith coincide, it is simply that you accumulated merit in past lives.

What is the relationship here between faith and the Buddha's teaching? It is that the Buddha's teaching is the right object of our faith. We have to distinguish between those objects that are worthy of our faith and those that are not. Worthy objects are the Three Jewels: the fully enlightened Buddha, the sublime Dharma, and the Sangha. Unworthy ones are worldly gods like Indra or Brahma, or spirits like *tsen* in whom people take refuge. Even if we take refuge in them sincerely, these unworthy objects do not have the power to protect us since they are not free from samsara themselves. Now, the Buddha may have taught, but if his teachings had not endured until the present day, we would have no teachings to receive and put into practice. While they continue to exist, you have the chance to hear and reflect upon the sublime Dharma. So if the teachings are present and you have confidence in them, it is a sign that you accumulated merit in your past lives.

> *Now that for once you have acquired the freedoms and*
> *advantages, do not squander them.*

If you do not have great diligence and you fail to make use of this present opportunity, there is no certainty that in your next life you will be reborn somewhere where the Buddha's teaching exists or that you will be interested in it and have faith. So you must not waste this opportunity by rendering this human life useless and empty. The most important thing for making use of such an opportunity is to have a keen interest in the Dharma. Unless you are interested, even though the teachings are there, you will never start practicing them. You will be like a dog presented with grass—it is not interested in eating it.

However, even if you are interested, there is a risk you will not get to the very heart of the teachings, so you need to follow an authentic teacher. A beggar goes to a rich man for alms, not to another beggar who has nothing to give.

> **If you are interested in the Dharma and meet a master**
> **who possesses the instructions, it is simply that the blind**
> **man has found the jewel.**

If a blind person were to find a wishing-gem in the dust on a path, it would be something to marvel at. All his wishes would be fulfilled and he would be able to fulfill the wishes of all beings. And in this life he would have food and clothes and be wealthy and prosperous. But to find the instructions of the Dharma is even more precious, for while the wishing-gem can give us all we want in this life, the Dharma can provide all we could wish for in this life and in all our future lives. Thus a faithful disciple who meets an authentic teacher has the means for attaining enlightenment in one lifetime.

> Later it will be hard to find such a teacher repeatedly, so stay
> with him for a long time without separating from him, like the
> eyes in your forehead.[40]

In general, wherever we go, day and night we take great care of our body, but we are especially careful about our eyes. We should have the same kind of concern for this precious human body and the teacher's instructions, and stay with the teacher over a long period of time, for it will be very difficult to find such an opportunity again.

**If faith, diligence, and wisdom coincide in a body free
of defects, it is simply that these good qualities are the
karmic result of having trained in the Dharma.**

Once we have this precious human body, which is free from the eight intrusive circumstances and the eight incompatible propensities, we should make use of it to practice the Dharma. At the same time, if we have faith, diligence, and wisdom, we have the three qualities required for entering the Vajrayana. In the Vajrayana, which is the highest and most profound of all the vehicles, the teacher first guides disciples who have faith by means of the ten outer empowerments that benefit. Then, to disciples who also possess diligence, he gives the five inner empowerments that confer ability. To disciples who additionally possess keen wisdom, he bestows the three profound secret empowerments. These three qualities are equally necessary in the Sutrayana: without faith it is impossible to progress along the path; without diligence there will be no result in the practice even if one starts to listen, reflect, and meditate; and without keen intelligence and wisdom one will never get the vital point of the teachings, however much effort one makes. If you have these three, it is a sign that in your past lives you have already trained in the Dharma and developed such qualities. So

Be diligent in the methods for making these three grow.

Ordinary beings' minds are utterly fickle, quaking like kusha grass, which bends in whichever direction the wind blows. You must therefore be very diligent, following the example of the great sages of the past who continuously applied themselves to increasing their faith, diligence, and wisdom. Otherwise you will be unable to prevent yourself from falling back and will be carried away in the ocean of suffering. This is why the root text says,

> If your being born in samsara coincides with relatives scolding you,[41] it is simply that you are being exhorted to practice.

Decide for yourself and practice the Dharma.

However well-meaning your relatives and friends may be, their advice and pleas will only greatly increase your attachment and involvement in samsara—and it is because of your afflictive emotions and past actions that you were in samsara in the first place. This is why listening to all their propositions will hinder your practice. You must make your own decision. If you really want to practice the Dharma correctly, the only person who can give you proper advice is a spiritual teacher; the only advice you can really rely on is the Buddha's teachings. While there is nothing the teacher says that does not accord with the Buddha's teachings, any advice our parents and family may give us, though of course motivated by love and affection, is based on ignorance, for they are still enveloped in the gloom of samsara. Unfortunately they can only tell us how important it is to protect our kin and get rid of those who might harm us; how courageous we will be if we get the better of our enemies; and how proud they will be if we succeed in this. So you must make a definite decision not to follow the advice of anyone but your teacher and remain like a drop of mercury in the dust, which stays perfectly clean and does not mix with the dust around it.

> If your having things and your being delighted to give them away coincide with a beggar, it is simply that generosity is coming to perfection.

In order to practice generosity, when you have things like food, clothes, money, and so on, you should be eager to offer them to the Buddhas or give them to beggars. Then, if you meet a beggar, all the favorable conditions for an act of generosity will be present. You should take advantage of these three occurring together and give away as much as you can without being influenced by niggardliness. If you think, "I won't give now; I'll give later," or "This beggar doesn't look desperate enough; I'll give to one who is more in need," you will never manage to be generous. Look at the bees, who gather so much honey and store it, only to have it taken away in the end by someone else. And mice, who spend their time hoarding grains that are then taken by others. Look at the many immensely rich people in this world who still never think of making an offering to the Three Jewels or giving to the needy.[42] Their wealth is piled up for no purpose; it is a complete waste. Someone who is very poor who offers just a single butter lamp with a pure intention will have inconceivably greater merit when he dies than an apparently rich person who is unable to give anything away or make offerings. Therefore,

Without being trussed by the knot of miserliness, give away impartially.

Do not be selective in your generosity, thinking that it is better to give to one cause than to another. All forms of offering and giving are equally good. You should not imagine that making an offering to the Buddha is something very superior and dignified while giving to a beggar is very limited ("He will just eat what I give him, and that will be the end of it"). The Buddha himself became a Buddha by perfecting generosity and giving to the needy. It was because he was so generous that great compassion and wisdom grew in him. So there is no difference between making offerings to the Buddha and giving to the poor. In fact we should consider all the beings we meet, beggars and so on, as teachers showing us the path and helping us fulfill our wish to attain enlightenment. We should make offerings to them and give without discrimination.

If, when you are practicing, the dam of suffering bursts, it is simply that you are purifying your negative actions.

Rejoice and give up wrong views.

If you spend your whole life practicing alone in a mountain retreat, you will certainly have plenty of difficulties. You will fall sick, experience pain, and encounter many adverse circumstances. At such times do not think, "Although I am practicing the Dharma, I have nothing but trouble. The Dharma cannot be so great. I have followed a teacher and done so much practice, and yet hard times still befall me." Such thoughts are wrong views. You should realize that through the blessing and power of the practice, by experiencing sickness and other difficulties now, you are purifying and ridding yourself of negative actions you committed in past lives that would have led to rebirth in the hells and other lower realms in future lives. By purifying them now while you have the chance, you will later go from bliss to bliss. So do not think, "I don't deserve this illness, these obstacles, these negative influences." Realize instead that through the teacher's kindness and the power of the practice you can completely purify yourself of all your past negative actions. Experience your difficulties as the blessings of the Three Jewels. Furthermore, bear in mind that many, many beings are suffering in a similar way. Make a wish that the suffering you yourself are experiencing may take the place of all other beings' suffering, thinking, "May their suffering be exhausted in mine." So when you do experience such difficulties, you should be very happy and avoid having adverse thoughts like, "Why are such terrible things happening to me? The Guru and the Three Jewels don't care for me; they have no compassion; the practice doesn't help."

> If people are hostile toward a Dharma practitioner who has done nothing wrong, it is simply that they are setting him on the path of patience.

Avoid grudges and ill will; keep in mind the benefits of patience.

As Kunkhyen Jigme Lingpa said:

An enemy repaying your good with bad makes you progress in your practice.
His unjust accusations are a whip that steers you toward virtue.
He's the teacher who destroys all your attachment and desires.
Look at his great kindness that you never can repay!

If someone criticizes or blames you even though you have not done anything wrong, do not get upset and angry or try to get even. Instead be grateful: regard it as an opportunity to purify your own actions from the past when you yourself blamed others. Don the armor of patience, reflecting on this verse:

> No evil is there similar to anger,
> No austerity to be compared to patience.
> Steep yourself, therefore, in patience,
> In various ways, insistently.[43]

Jigme Lingpa himself said that although many people accused and criticized him unreasonably, he always prayed, "May these people become my disciples in a future life so that I can benefit them." And indeed in his future lives he manifested as Do Khyentse Yeshe Dorje and as Jamyang Khyentse Wangpo.[44]

Here is a story that illustrates the benefits of patience. In one of his previous lives as a Bodhisattva, the Buddha was the rishi Patient Words. Although he was the brother of a king, he had long since forsaken worldly life and taken to a life of solitude and meditation in the forest. One day the king and his retinue of queens went into the forest for a picnic. The king fell asleep, and while he was sleeping, the queens wandered off and came across the rishi, Patient Words. When the king awoke and found that everyone had gone, he set out to look for his queens and eventually found them seated before the rishi listening to him teach. In a fury the king drew his sword and asked, "Who are you?"

"They call me Patient Words," replied the rishi.

"Let's see how patient you really are," cried the king, and with his sword he started cutting the rishi to pieces, slicing off his arms and legs. He was at the point of cutting off the rishi's head when the latter spoke:

"As you cut me up bit by bit, I vow that in a future life, when I attain enlightenment, one by one I will slice away all your afflictive emotions." Thereupon the king cut off the rishi's head. From the rishi's body, instead of blood, there flowed milk. The king suddenly realized that this was not an ordinary being he had killed, but a siddha.

"Who was this rishi?" he asked. When he learned that it was his very own brother who had become a great rishi by meditating in the forest, he felt deep remorse. He took the body of the rishi back to his capital, held an enormous offering ceremony, and constructed a stupa in which the relics were enshrined. When the rishi became the Buddha Shakyamuni, by the power of his prayer in that previous life the king became one of the first five disciples who received the Buddha's teaching at Varanasi. So a Bodhisattva is someone who takes refuge thinking, "May the harm that others cause me create a connection through which they may attain happiness."

If we achieve some results from our practice and find ourselves being respected by people, we must never be conceited or proud that our activities are increasing. See everything as a dream, as an illusion, and avoid getting attached to wealth and possessions, otherwise you will fall back into samsara and end up having nothing at all.

> **If your having consummate faith coincides with applying the instructions, it is simply that you have come to the end of karma.**

The instructions are something we have to put into practice. Merely reading the doctor's prescription will never cure our illness. Our teacher's instructions are meant to be used when we encounter obstacles and difficulties. We should use them correctly and not miss the point. Just as the best way to kill someone is to stab him in the heart—he will not even survive one hour—if you apply the instructions correctly and hit the vital point, even one month of practice will be effective in dispelling your afflictive emotions and actions. Otherwise, however much you study and listen to the teachings, the instructions and your own being will go different ways. Unless you gain stability in your practice so that you really overwhelm your ego-clinging and afflictive emotions, any so-called advanced practice you do will be pointless, no more than an impressive-sounding name. But if you practice properly now,

> *In the future you will not be reborn in samsara.*

Like a hooked fish pulled out of the water, you will have been hooked by the compassion of the Buddhas. If in this life you are diligent and practice in the right way, even if you do not attain full realization, you will be reborn in a place where you can come across the teachings, meet the teacher, and continue to progress. The greater the connection you make with the Dharma in this way, the more you will benefit. It was through practicing the Dharma that all the sages in the past attained their level of realization.

The whole of the Dharma should serve as the antidote to attachment and aversion.

Otherwise doing a lot of practice will only increase your pride; spending a long time in a cave or secluded place will just be a way to pile up possessions, and you will become an evil spirit. The practice will not have acted as an antidote to your attachment and aversion; it will not have been genuine Dharma.

If your own fear of death coincides with other people's dying, it is simply that the time has come to turn your mind away from samsara.

Once the Lord Buddha came across four strong men trying to split a huge rock blocking the road. However hard they tried, they were unable to move it. Using his miraculous power the Buddha tossed the rock into the air with his toe, and when it landed again, he reduced it to gravel by pointing his finger at it. Everyone was amazed and said, "Surely there is no one in the world more powerful than you."

"Yes," replied the Buddha, "there is someone much stronger than me."

"Who can that person be?" they asked.

"When I pass into nirvana, I shall meet the Lord of Death. He is far more powerful than I am."

It is very important to constantly bear in mind that we are going to die, and that we will have to endure all the pain of dying. This does not apply only to us. Think how many people have died in the past month. And consider *how* they have died: some have died old, others have died young, and in all sorts of different circumstances. Where are all those people now—in which of the six realms have they ended up? Some of them must now be enduring the most terrible suffering. And we are bound to experience those very same sufferings too. When we reflect on all the torments that will befall us, it seems that nothing in this worldly life is of much benefit to us.

Do not be attached to happiness and comfort in this life.

However delicious the food is that we eat, it all turns into excrement. However beautiful the clothes we wear, they are only covering what is under the skin—foul components like flesh, blood, and lymph. So what is the point of dressing one's body up in brocades? This life is as fleeting as a cloud in the sky; it can vanish at any moment. No one can say how long they will live. And if they do live a certain amount of time, no one can say whether they will be happy and satisfied all their life. Nothing is certain—neither the circumstances of our death nor those of our life, so we should have no attachment to the things of this life. The only way to use our lives properly is to practice the Dharma, and to do so when we are young and our bodies and minds are in their prime. We might think, "For the next twenty years, or perhaps a bit less, I shall earn and save enough money to be able to stop working, and then I'll practice the Dharma." But who knows when we might die; who knows if in the meantime we might change our minds? This is why the root text says,

> **If you think you will finish your projects for this life first and after that practice a bit of Dharma, this is simply the demon's delaying tactics.**
>
> *It is very important not to fall under the influence of such a demon.*

What we call a demon is not something with goggling eyes, a gaping mouth, sharp teeth, and a terrifying look. The real demon is our predilection for worldly activities, our attachment to friends and relatives, our aversion to enemies, and the fact that we are completely dominated by the eight ordinary concerns, together with the circumstances—both good and bad—that can make us stray from the Dharma. It is said that favorable circumstances are more difficult to deal with and use on the path because they are more distracting and make us forget the Dharma. So when we have everything we need—money, status, a comfortable home, food, and clothes—we should not be attached to these but view them as illusory, as things that appear in a dream.

Undesirable circumstances are relatively easier to deal with. It is relatively easier to meditate on patience when someone gets very angry with us or threatens us, and to practice when we are sick, because these are causes of suffering and suffering naturally reminds us of the Dharma. But when we are happy, when things are going well, these good circumstances have a tendency to blend very comfortably with our minds, like massage oil, which spreads easily over the body. When we enjoy good times, attachment rests easily on the mind and becomes part of our feelings. And once we are attached to good circumstances, the demon of the sons of the gods has arrived. Of the four demons, this is the one that creates pride: we become infatuated with success, fame, and riches. It is very difficult to rid the mind of such pride.

7

Thirteen instructions to put into practice.

Son, there are thirteen instructions.

As a spur to diligence in the practice, consider your own death and others'.

The time of death is uncertain, so give up all this life's pointless activities and projects.

For the Dharma, you need strong determination and diligence. Even if your life is at stake, the Dharma is something you must never give up. Just as one uses spurs to make a horse go faster, the main spur to diligence is to reflect on death. Think how many people in the world spend their time trying to defeat those they consider as enemies. They spend years and years fighting, and often die before they reach victory. For them the end result is rebirth in the hell realms. Others spend their time looking after the interests of their relatives and friends, but many die before being successful. And because of the attachment they have, they are reborn as pretas. If we were able to know precisely when we will die, we would be able to plan our lives and calculate exactly what we would do and when. But this is not the case. Some people die when they are going from one place to another. Others die when they are still in their mother's womb. Some die young, others die very old after going through all sorts of difficulties, illnesses, and all the sufferings of old age. There is no certainty at all about when we will die. And worldly activities are really very unimportant. So if you think you will complete all your ordinary projects first and practice the Dharma after that, you are not only wasting your time, but you also cannot be sure you will ever practice. It is said, "Worldly activities are like children's games. If we abandon them, there will be nothing more to do. If we continue them, they will never end." Moreover, it is important to realize how valuable the Dharma is and to realize that if you have had the chance in your present life to hear the teachings and reflect on them, this is only the result of your having accumulated merit in your past lives.

Just how precious and rare it is to receive the Dharma is illustrated in some of the former lives of the Buddha. In several of these lives he was reborn as a king in a place where there was no one teaching the Dharma. So great was the king's longing to receive teaching that he erected a high throne in front of his palace and offered his entire kingdom to anyone who would come and expound the Dharma. On one occasion, a rishi arrived and said he was willing to teach, but it would not be enough for the king to offer his kingdom: he should be ready to give his own life. The king replied that he would happily do so. The rishi therefore told him to make an offering of a thousand lamps by piercing a thousand holes in his body, placing a wick and some clarified butter in each hole. Without hesitating, the king proceeded to do so and lit all the lamps. The rishi mounted the throne and gave a single verse of teaching:

Abandon evildoing,
Practice virtue well,
Subdue your mind:
This is the Buddha's teaching.

Afterward the rishi asked the king whether he had any regrets. The king replied, "I am filled with joy at having received this teaching." He was profoundly grateful and felt no pain at all. At that moment all the gods appeared in the sky and praised the king's determination to receive teaching. Through the blessing of his complete sincerity and joy in hearing the teaching and his total absence of regret in sacrificing himself, all his wounds were miraculously healed.

The king was required to undergo similar ordeals in other lives, like piercing his body with a thousand nails or jumping into a pit of fire. On each occasion, he did so without the slightest hesitation, and each time, on account of his joy at receiving instruction, he was completely cured.

All this shows just how precious it is to receive the teachings. We will always manage somehow to find food and clothing, but the Dharma is much more rare and precious, so it is important to have a deep respect for it.

> **If you want to cultivate extraordinary respect, examine the teacher's outer and inner qualities.**

For us the teacher is the source of all good qualities and accomplishments. So you should examine him carefully to see the perfection in all his outer and inner qualities, and take them as examples to be followed. But in so doing, you must never have wrong thoughts or distorted views:

> *Avoid thinking of defects.*

If you think the teacher has done something that seems not quite perfect, you should realize that this is simply your own deluded way of perceiving him, as was the case for the monk Sunakshatra, who thought the Buddha only gave teachings in order to fool people. Even if you see a minute defect, realize that it is your own wrong perception: rid your mind of such thoughts and cultivate pure perception. As Shechen Gyaltsap's note says:

> *Seeing faults reflects your own impure perception.*

When Guru Rinpoche came to Samye, although he was a fully enlightened Buddha and displayed many marvelous deeds and miracles, there were still evil ministers who had wrong thoughts about him. They doubted his qualities and tried to obstruct his activities. Even King Trisong Detsen was prey to such doubts. Having received instructions from Guru Rinpoche, he went to Yamalung and meditated in a cave, practicing the sadhana of Amitayus. Through the blessings of this practice, Amitayus appeared in the sky before him and bestowed the empowerment from his own long-life vase: the king received the blessing for attaining immortality. He then returned to Samye riding a horse and arrived just as Guru Rinpoche was bestowing the empowerment of long life. The Guru was at the point of dispensing the long-life nectar when one of the evil ministers whispered to the king, "Who knows whether the liquor has been mixed with poison?" For a second the king hesitated, wondering whether it was true, and as a result the auspicious connection that would have secured the blessing he had received earlier was broken. This shows how important it is not to have wrong thoughts or doubts when there is actually nothing wrong.

> **If you want your conduct to concord with all, do not obstruct the efforts of others.**

It is very important to maintain perfect harmony and good relations with all your Dharma companions, brothers, and sisters. You should be like a belt for them, like something one wears all the time but does not feel. You should be very adaptable, like salt, which readily dissolves in any kind of water, clear or muddy. Relating to the teacher alone will not do; you must be able to cope with other people. Otherwise, you will cause your samaya to deteriorate and upset the teacher. In everything you do, act in accordance with the Dharma and behave harmoniously with everyone. You can never become a genuine practitioner by relating poorly to people—upsetting everyone and acting contrary to their wishes.

Furthermore, of the Dharma's nine vehicles, practice the one that can truly help you in accordance with your present capacity and condition. Never dismiss the so-called lesser vehicles, thinking that they are too low for you. Each vehicle has teachings that can help us according to our capacity. So you should receive and examine the teachings of the Shravaka Vehicle properly, seeing the truth in them and practicing them as much as possible. Similarly, in the Bodhisattva and Mantra vehicles you should learn whatever is beneficial for you and practice them as well as you are able. Thus, do not discriminate against lower vehicles or long to practice the so-called advanced teachings. Realizing that these teachings do not contradict each other, practice them in such a way that they truly help you to progress. Then everything will arise as teaching. The Buddha gave all the various teachings out of compassion, and they are all imbued with his wisdom: there is not a single word in them that can harm beings. Each one has the virtue of leading beings to liberation and enlightenment. So do not be sectarian and think, "Our teachings are far superior to those of other schools and philosophical traditions."

As all the vehicles are true in their own terms, do not have
rigid opinions about paths or philosophical schools.

While we should never think that our own tradition is best and other
traditions are inferior, there is no harm in genuine discussion and debate
that is free of attachment and animosity, if it helps to clarify minor misunderstandings or incorrect interpretations in our own view. Likewise,
misinterpretations of others' views can be corrected by discussions between learned siddhas.[45]

So as never to upset the teacher, practice hard.

It is very important not to upset the teacher or his other disciples. To
have adverse views and act out of tune or disrespectfully with the
teacher and those around him is not the way to please him, however
much you might think you are practicing his teachings. Be fully determined to carry out the teacher's instructions exactly. Once you have received them, be diligent in practicing them as much as you can. If you
do so,

You will acquire all good qualities without exception.

If there were a mountain of solid gold, all the birds—big and small—
nesting on that mountain would naturally become golden in color. In
the same way, if you stay with a spiritual teacher for a long time, his
good qualities will naturally bring about a change in you, and you will
acquire those same qualities. And if the teacher is pleased with your
practice, accomplishment will be swift, since the yidam, dakinis, and protectors are none other than the teacher's display.

If you want to attain accomplishment quickly, keep the
Pratimoksha and Bodhisattva **vows and** Vajrayana
samayas without letting them degenerate.

It is important to know what is permitted and what is not, to observe
the precepts in accordance with your capacity,[46] and to be one-pointed
in trying not to transgress them. When a king's subjects observe his laws
carefully, the king is satisfied and his reign is peaceful: it is easy to run

the kingdom and everyone benefits. In the same way, if we rely on the Buddha's words and the teacher's instructions, our ten negative actions and afflictive emotions will naturally decrease.

> All the precepts boil down to giving up the ten negative actions
> and the five poisons as they are ordinarily experienced.[47]

So be diligent and single-minded in getting rid of these five afflictive emotions. As long as you do not do so, they will be the root of your wandering in samsara, and you will be swept away as if by a big river, taken wherever the water carries you without being able to get to the bank. In the three worlds of samsara, the main sufferings are the four rivers of birth, old age, sickness, and death. Under their influence there is no freedom to practice. The crucial point you need to know is that to stop the flow of these four rivers, one has to listen to the teachings.

**If you want to halt the four rivers, you must ascertain
the unborn nature of the ground-of-all.**

The root of our wandering in the three worlds of samsara and the source of all actions and afflictive emotions is the erroneous perception of production where there is no production. We hold the unproduced ground to be produced, and this erroneous belief is the cause of our delusion. So we need to ascertain its unborn nature, to establish its empty nature.

When we speak of the "ground-of-all,"[48] it can refer to two things. One is the support of all the afflictive emotions and of the imprints of our actions. This is the deluded ground-of-all, which we have to be rid of. The other ground-of-all is the primordial ground from which both samsara and nirvana arise. It is the sugatagarbha or buddha-nature present in every sentient being. It is what the Prayer of Samantabhadra refers to when it says, "There is one ground." This is what we are talking about here. When you recognize this ground, you will know the absolute nature beyond origin, and you will thus realize that for all phenomena there is no coming into existence, no existing, and no ceasing to exist. Once you realize the unborn nature of the ground, you will no longer be swept away by the current of the four great rivers of suffering.

> *When you have understood the unborn nature of the*
> *ground-of-all, the continuous flow of birth and death will cease*

and you will see the end of samsara. In the best case, you can put an end to samsaric rebirth in this very lifetime. And if not, through these precious instructions you should at least be able to free yourself from samsara within three lifetimes. In particular, those who practice the Mantrayana will in one life and one body attain the indestructible union body.[49]

If you want no obstacles to your accomplishing enlightenment, leave behind the distractions of this life.

For those who are able to practice diligently and one-pointedly it is possible to attain Buddhahood in a single lifetime. However, there are bound to be obstacles: outer obstacles, such as dangers related to the five elements (water, fire, wind, and so on); inner obstacles that cause physical illness, such as disorders of phlegm, bile, or energy; and secret obstacles caused by one's thoughts. These obstacles arise from attachment to the things of this life. If one has no attachment, it is impossible for such obstacles to occur. So it is very important to leave behind all the distractions of this life.

> *Trying to help others without having the ability is yet another*
> *distraction.*

Unless you have fully realized the unborn, absolute nature yourself, to think of helping others will simply distract you and act as an obstacle to your own practice.

> *Do not try to benefit others when you yourself are not ready.*

A Bodhisattva who has truly realized the ultimate, unborn nature of phenomena does not think of his own welfare for even an instant. There is never a moment when he is not concerned with the welfare of others. But if you have not realized the absolute nature, what you may call benefiting others will merely be making you more busy. In fact, you will simply be creating more difficulties for yourself. There is a saying:

Free yourself with realization,
Liberate others with compassion.

So if you really wish to benefit others, the first step is to attain realization yourself. You must first mature your own mind; otherwise you will be incapable of helping others. Giving other people water is impossible unless you have a jug with water in it. If it is empty, you might make the gesture of pouring, but no water will come out. To take another example, when one lights a set of butter lamps using a lamp that is already lit, the latter must be full and burning with a bright flame in order to light the others. You therefore need to have the genuine wish to help others and, with that attitude, to be diligent in the practice so that experience and realization can grow. This is why the root text says:

If you want to benefit others effortlessly, meditate on the four boundless qualities.

To truly benefit others, you must have the precious bodhichitta fully developed in your being. Once you have it, you do not need to think of helping others or to make a deliberate effort to do so. It just happens naturally. The main thing that helps us develop the precious bodhichitta is to meditate on the four boundless qualities: love, the wish that all beings may be happy and have the causes of happiness; compassion, the wish that all beings may be free from suffering and the causes of suffering; sympathetic joy, the wish that all beings who are happy may remain so and become even happier; and impartiality, the wish that happiness may come to each and every sentient being without distinction, whether they are close to us or strangers. We call these four qualities "boundless" for four reasons. First, their benefits are boundless. Second, the number of beings to whom we should direct them is boundless, for sentient beings are as numerous as the sky is vast. Third, the qualities of enlightenment, which is the result obtained from meditating on them, are boundless. Fourth, the attitude we have when cultivating these four is boundless. Just as seed sown in a field that is properly tilled, watered, manured, and exposed to the sun will naturally produce a good crop, if you meditate sincerely and deeply on these four boundless qualities, the precious bodhichitta will certainly take birth in your being. Once you have trained your mind and experienced bodhichitta, even if you do not gather a lot of disciples and put on a performance of benefiting them, whatever you do directly or indirectly will naturally help others. So always keep in mind that the best way to benefit others is to meditate on the four boundless qualities.

> *If you train in bodhichitta, nothing you do will exclude others'*
> *welfare.*

Someone who has such compassion is not only immune to harm from violent people and destructive spirits; he can, moreover, set them on the path to liberation.

If you are fearful of the three lower realms in your
future lives, steer clear of the ten negative actions.

It is important to be convinced that you will have future lives in which you can expect heat and cold in the hells, hunger and thirst among the pretas, and enslavement and slaughter in the animal realms. If you want to avert these miserable states, you have to avoid the ten unvirtuous actions and find antidotes for the five poisons in this life. If you can counteract anger, you will not be reborn in the hells. If you can counteract attachment, you will not be reborn among the pretas. If you can counteract bewilderment, you will not be reborn as an animal. Whether you avoid negative actions and cultivate positive ones is entirely in your hands. If you are able to do so, there is no way you will be reborn in the lower realms. But if you are not careful, and you indulge in all the negative actions while failing to cultivate positive ones, then, when you die, you will fall helplessly into the lower realms like a stone thrown into an abyss. So

> *Be careful, all the time.*[50]

An ordinary being's mind is like a restless monkey. To tie this monkey so that it does not wander too far, we need to apply mindfulness (remembering what we have to do and what we have to avoid) and vigilance (keeping watch over our thoughts, words, and deeds). With mindfulness and vigilance, we will be aware of any unwholesome thoughts that arise and so be able to come up with the antidote to prevent them from growing. As a result, we will be happy—even in this life. And if we have love and compassion, we will naturally be able to help others; in making others happy we will find our kindness returned and will be safe from harmful spirits and other nonhumans. With regard to future lives, if we have cultivated love, compassion, sympathetic joy, and impartiality in an ordinary way, we will be reborn in the celestial realms, like Indra's Heaven of the Thirty-three. And if we have cultivated the four boundless qualities with the aim of bringing all beings to Buddhahood, we will eventually attain full enlightenment.

> **If you want to be happy in this and future lives, be diligent in performing the ten positive actions.**

The ten positive actions can be applied on different levels. While it is highly positive to refrain from negative actions, it is even more powerful to perform additional positive acts that are the opposite of the negative ones. Not only should we refrain from killing, for example, but in addition we should protect life by saving animals from being slaughtered. As well as refraining from stealing, we should give generously, and so on. To practice in this way, you have to become convinced of the truth of the law of cause and effect. Having gained this conviction, cultivate even the tiniest positive actions and avoid even the minutest negative actions. In this way you will gradually progress upward through the different vehicles of the Shravakas, Pratyekabuddhas, and Bodhisattvas. Never think that the need to avoid negative actions and cultivate positive ones is a feature of the Basic Vehicle and that there is no such need in the Great Vehicle or in the Vajrayana. To do so is a fundamental error, which is why Shechen Gyaltsap's note says,

> *Now, when you have the choice, do not confuse what is to be adopted with what is to be avoided.*

While you have in your hands the freedom to act and you know which actions are negative, you should not err in the decisions you make and the way you behave.

> **If you want your mind to engage in the Dharma, you must experience the hardship of suffering.**

To turn our minds to the Dharma we first have to realize for ourselves just what suffering in samsara implies. Unless we have a taste of samsaric suffering, our minds will never turn to the Dharma. Once we know what suffering is about, we will naturally try to find a way to be free from it. So we should understand the suffering inherent in samsara by studying the detailed explanations on the preliminary practice. Moreover, we need to be aware that by engaging in negative actions we are buying suffering in future lives. So we should be mindful, vigilant, and careful, and confess and repair our previous negative actions.

Beginners should also understand that when they start practicing the Dharma there is bound to be some difficulty. Trying to blend one's mind with the Dharma *is* difficult, but this is a very worthwhile kind of difficulty. There is a saying: "In experiencing difficulty one achieves something rare." It is only through great hardship that one can gain unique and worthwhile achievements. Buddha Shakyamuni, for instance, had to go through great difficulties accumulating merit over a period of three measureless kalpas, even though he himself said that the Great Vehicle was the vehicle for beings of superior capacity. And if the Vajrayana is said to be the path for attaining Buddhahood in a single lifetime, that is not to say that it is an easy path. Look at the hardships Jetsun Milarepa went through. For twelve years he meditated diligently, sitting on the bare ground in the cave of White Rock with neither a bite to eat nor a stitch of clothing. Without that sort of effort, the supreme accomplishment will never come on its own.

Reflect on the pointlessness of weary toil and develop deep
determination. There has never been a spiritual path that is easy.

Look at the trouble and difficulty ordinary people go through in governing a country, for instance. They make such enormous efforts and yet it is all entirely pointless. If they were to make the same effort for a single day practicing the Dharma, that would bring them so much closer to liberation. But they have been wandering in samsara for so long that their minds automatically go in the wrong direction. Their natural inclination is to take life, to steal, and to do all sorts of other negative actions, such as harming old people. They have never turned their minds toward the Dharma, let alone practiced it. This is why it takes many months and years of practice for us to develop a peaceful, happy mind. Because we still have so many wrong habits from previous lives, we do not gain peace and happiness easily. So with the momentous goal of attaining liberation in mind, turn your thoughts away from samsara and put your efforts one-pointedly into practicing the Dharma.

> **If you want to turn away from samsara, strive for**
> **unsurpassable enlightenment.**

We need to remain diligent all along the path. Even if we have reached the level of Arhat as a Shravaka or Pratyekabuddha, we still have further to go to attain complete Buddhahood. "Unsurpassable enlightenment" refers to the ultimate result of the Great Vehicle, so this is what we should be seeking. And when Zurchungpa says "strive," he means that we should think of being diligent for our entire life. It is no use thinking that it is a question of practicing for only a few months or years. We are heavily obscured by our afflictive emotions, so we have to practice diligently and one-pointedly until we have completely removed all our obscurations.

> *It is important to recognize the benefits of liberation and*
> *enlightenment according to the three vehicles.*

To gain even a few of the qualities of liberation and enlightenment is to obtain something very precious. Bear in mind that realizing even a fraction of the Buddha's enlightened qualities brings immense benefit, whereas engaging in even a little worldly activity causes great harm. If you practice the teachings of the three vehicles in their entirety, you will acquire all their respective qualities and understand that these teachings are not contradictory. And as a result you will attain the three kayas— the dharmakaya, sambhogakaya, and nirmanakaya.

> **If you want to obtain the result, the three kayas, unite**
> **the two accumulations.**

The two accumulations are the accumulation of merit—with concepts—and the accumulation of wisdom—without concepts. The former comprises the first five transcendent perfections—generosity, discipline, patience, diligence, and concentration—while the latter comprises the sixth perfection, transcendent wisdom. By diligently accumulating merit and wisdom together you will attain Buddhahood.

This will cause the stains veiling the three kayas to be removed.

The perfect buddha-nature is in fact present within us, but it is obscured by afflictive emotions and by karmic and conceptual obscurations. We can remove these, as we have seen, by turning the mind toward the Dharma and cultivating the four boundless qualities.

8

Showing how to recognize what is not true practice: five things that are useless.

Son, there are five things that are useless.[51]

These five refer to what is not true Dharma: if you follow them, they will lead to your ruin.

No need to say you are interested in the Dharma if you have not turned your mind away from samsara.

Unless you feel deep down that samsara is a pit of burning coals, there is no point in saying, "I am practicing the Dharma, I am meditating, I am deep in samadhi." Without that profound conviction, you can only go in the opposite direction to the Dharma. Even if your practice leads to your gaining a good reputation, it will be completely in vain.

If everything you do is for this life alone, you will not accomplish the Dharma.

With this sort of attitude it is impossible to practice the Dharma properly. You will simply get involved in things like protecting your relatives and friends and getting rid of your enemies; your life will run counter to the Dharma. Dharma and worldly activities are like fire and water. If you practice the Dharma genuinely, you cannot help giving up worldly activities. On the other hand, if you devote yourself to worldly activities, you will never be able to practice the Dharma properly. So cultivate a deep desire to abandon the things of this world and a strong determination to practice Dharma.

> *To practice the genuine Dharma, you have to counter attachment to samsaric perceptions.*

The root of our repeatedly taking birth in samsara is the alternating desire and loathing we have for the objects of the five senses—forms, tastes, smells, sounds, and physical sensations—together with the perceptions our eight consciousnesses hold of these sense objects. When we feel attachment or, conversely, aversion to the experiences of the five senses, we sow the seed for rebirth in samsara. It all starts with attachment. If we had no attachment, there would be no reason for aversion. Because we are strongly attached to ourselves and to what is ours—our friends and relatives, our belongings, and so on—we feel aversion to anyone who might harm us or anything that is ours. But without attachment in the first place, there would be no aversion. Once attachment and aversion are present, however, we feel well disposed to those who are good to us and we want to retaliate when people hurt us. This leads to a multitude of actions, which are the activities of samsara. Once our minds are dominated by attachment and aversion, any intention to practice the Dharma is eclipsed, so it is important to gain realization of emptiness.

> **No need to meditate on emptiness if you have not countered attachment to the things you perceive.**

Meditation on emptiness implies a state like space. There is no occasion for thoughts like "I," "mine," "my body," "my mind," "my name," or "my belongings." This sort of clinging has no place in meditation on emptiness. So if you have thoughts like "my possessions" and so on, there is no way your meditation and practice can be genuine.

> *One meditates on emptiness in order to release one's clinging, believing that things truly exist.*

A genuine practitioner does not have this attachment to relatives and possessions, neither does he feel any aversion for enemies.

Unless you are free from this, emptiness is no more than a word;

it is quite useless.

No need to practice meditation if you do not turn your mind away from desire.

To say "I meditate" and at the same time still have an ordinary mind with desire and attachment will give no result.

Great meditators who end up sidetracked by village ceremonies risk dying as ordinary men.

Practitioners who have meditated in mountain retreats for a few years are often taken by ordinary folk to be very advanced meditators, and many of them begin to believe the fools who speak of them as great meditators who have reached a high level of realization. They start accepting offerings and reverence from people, and they grow rich. They end up spending their time going from one village ceremony to another and behaving in a completely worldly way. This is no use at all.

No need for fine words if you have not assimilated the meaning yourself.[52]

If you want to practice the Bodhisattva path, whatever you do—be it a single prostration, one circumambulation, or just one recitation of the *mani*—you must do it for the sake of all sentient beings, with the wish that they all attain enlightenment. This is the true practice. On the other hand, practicing without such an attitude, mainly to become rich and happy and to achieve greatness in this life, while saying nice things and speaking as if one were a great Bodhisattva working for the benefit of others, is pointless.

There are many who are fooled by smart talk about the view, so hit the crucial point of the natural state.

To say things like "Everything is void," "There is no such thing as good or bad, virtue or evil," "All perceptions are spontaneously liberated as they arise," or "Afflictive emotions are liberated as they arise," without having true confidence in such a view and stability in one's practice, is known as merely carrying the view on one's lips. This is why Guru Rinpoche said to King Trisong Detsen, "My view is like space, but conduct must never slip toward the view, for if it does, it will be a wholly black, demonic view." He said that the view should be as high as possible but that one's conduct should comply with the most basic teachings. So it is important to get to the crucial point and master the true nature of things through your own experience and not merely in words. And regarding this, there is

No need to apply the instructions if you do not have devotion.

If you have great devotion, seeing the teacher as the Buddha himself, and maintain a lofty inner view while keeping your external conduct completely down to earth, all the qualities of experience and realization will grow effortlessly. Experiences and realization in fact come through the spontaneous devotion you have to your teacher, so when they occur, they are truly due to the teacher's kindness.

Any experiences, realization, or good qualities that occur depend on the teacher's blessing: without devotion the blessings can never possibly penetrate.

When Atisha was in Tibet, some people said to him, "Give us your blessing!" "Give me your devotion," replied Atisha. If you have devotion, you will receive the blessings; without it you can never do so.

9

Showing how to practice with determination and the great armor of diligence: five things one needs to do.

To accomplish the Dharma you should be ready to give your body and life a hundred times over. That is the sort of determination and courage it takes. If you practice sincerely even for a month, you will see some progress. But without determination, diligence, and energy you will not get much benefit.

Son, there are five things you need to do.

You need to have fervent devotion to the teacher, for then the blessings of the lineage will automatically rub off on you.

The first thing that illuminates the virtuous path[53] is devotion. If your devotion is such that you see your teacher as the Buddha in person, all the blessings of the lineage masters from Samantabhadra down to your own root teacher will enter you as naturally as water flowing down a slope, without your needing to seek or fabricate them.

The practice of the Secret Mantrayana is the path of devotion and blessings.

In the mantrayana one perceives all forms as the deity, all sounds as mantra, and all thoughts as the display of the absolute nature. The path for achieving this depends on receiving the teacher's blessings, and those in turn depend on devotion. The more you feel devotion, the more your confidence in the practice of Dharma will grow.

The root and lineage teachers are of one essence.

Many spiritual teachers have appeared in the past. Some were learned scholars, others were accomplished siddhas; some were monks, others were yogins; some appeared as deities like Vajrasattva, others appeared as dakinis like Lekyi Wangmo.[54] But whatever form they have taken, they are not different from one another in the way that ordinary beings are different. Their essential nature is exactly the same. They are in fact the display of a single teacher. The teachers from whom we ourselves have received teachings actually manifest the infinite array of tantric deities— the one hundred peaceful and wrathful deities, and so on. Just as space contains all the planets and other celestial bodies without overflowing, and the whole universe with its mountains and continents fits without difficulty into the infinite expanse of emptiness that is the absolute state of dharmakaya, so likewise all the Buddhas and lineage teachers are included in our own teacher. If we have firm devotion to our teacher, we will naturally receive the blessings of all the Buddhas:

> *See the teacher as the Dharmakaya Buddha. That way the blessings of all the Buddhas will enter you.*

> **You need to accumulate exceptional merit, for then everything you wish for will work.**

By putting into practice everything the teacher says, you will please him. And if you go through all the stages of the practice, such as the five sections of the preliminary practice and the offering of the seven branches, you will accumulate merit and thereby easily accomplish everything you aspire to in the Dharma.

> *The wishes of someone who has merit will be accomplished.*

If you practice the Dharma properly, you will accumulate great merit and become like those with very good fortune: they have all the money they need to do whatever they want, they befriend influential people, and so on. It is merit that gives them the fortune to have all their wishes fulfilled. So if you have a great store of merit, to begin with you will always be reborn in the higher realms as a human or celestial being, and ultimately you will attain Buddhahood.

> *At all times offer the seven branches, backed by bodhichitta.*

Of the many ways to accumulate merit, one of the quickest and most condensed is the offering of the seven branches. It includes all the methods for gathering merit and purifying obscurations—in short, for gladdening the Buddhas. And since we claim to practice the Great Vehicle, we must dedicate this and everything we do to the enlightenment of sentient beings without straying into thinking of our own welfare.

> *That way you will necessarily acquire a good heart.*

If you have prepared your mind in this way, rendering it fit with mindfulness and vigilance so that negative thoughts do not occur and good thoughts grow, you will certainly develop extraordinary concentration:

> You need to make your mind fit, for then extraordinary
> concentration will be born in your mind.

To make a lamp burn brightly, without flickering, one puts it inside a glass lantern to protect it from the wind. Similarly, to develop deep concentration we have to prepare the mind and still our thoughts with devotion and a correct attitude.

> *It is important to train perfectly in making the body and mind fit.*

Through practice your body and mind will become fully trained and adaptable. As a sign of this, you may experience clairvoyance or be able to remain in meditation for days without feeling hungry or thirsty, and so forth.

> You need to cultivate extraordinary concentration, for
> then the afflictive emotions will be overwhelmed.

When a lion roars, all the other animals naturally cower and flee. Likewise, when we develop genuine concentration, the afflictive emotions automatically diminish and shrink away. How do we achieve this? Ordinary people's minds are constantly ruffled by a multitude of thoughts. Unless we still these thoughts, it is very difficult to get rid of afflictive emotions. So first we need to stabilize our minds through the practice of sustained calm. Having tamed our wild thoughts and afflictive emotions with sustained calm, we then eradicate them through the practice of profound insight. In this way concentration will grow.

Sustained calm is like a glass lantern protecting the flame inside from the wind. It quiets our thoughts and stops the mind from running after external objects. However, we cannot gain freedom from samsara with sustained calm alone. We need to extend it with profound insight. When we practice sustained calm, we will have the experiences of bliss, clarity, and absence of thoughts. If we cling to these experiences, desiring them and feeling a sense of achievement and pride when they happen, we will not progress. Profound insight completely frees us from clinging to the experiences of sustained calm. We therefore need to unite these two practices. When we do so,

> *Sustained calm crushes the afflictive emotions, profound insight eradicates their seeds.*

Unless we unite sustained calm and profound insight in this way, we will never succeed in realizing deep concentration.

You need to be free of afflictive emotions, for then you will quickly attain enlightenment.

On one occasion Padampa Sangye was asked, "Do negative actions tinge us once we have realized emptiness?" He replied that once we have realized emptiness, there is no reason for committing any negative action.

What do we mean by Buddhahood, or *sangye* in Tibetan? The first syllable, *sang*, implies waking up from the deep sleep of ignorance. Ignorance pervades all the eighty-four thousand afflictive emotions. Buddhahood is awakening out of all these afflictive emotions, which obscure the buddha nature—present and unchanging in every single sentient being—just as the clouds in the sky obscure the sun, so that we cannot see it. The reason it is possible for us to attain Buddhahood is precisely because we all have the buddha-nature present within ourselves. Even a tiny insect on a blade of grass has it. So the path is simply a question of gradually unveiling our innate Buddhahood by practicing sustained calm and profound insight. It is not a search for something different from what we already have.

> *Besides your own mind divested of obscurations, there is no other enlightenment to be sought.*

10

Identifying counterfeit Dharma.

We may appear to be practicing the Dharma, but if it is not genuinely Dharma, our practice can lead us to the hells and the other lower realms. To say we are practicing the Dharma will simply be a lie.

Son, there are five things that become lies.

As long as you delight in the things of this world, saying you are afraid of birth and death becomes a lie.

People who are so totally involved in worldly affairs that they carry on working day and night in order to become rich, powerful, and famous, to look after their relatives and friends, and to get rid of anyone who gets in their way are telling a big lie when they say, "I am afraid of death."

Unless you are truly free from attachment, it is impossible to gain liberation from birth and death.

The way to achieve freedom from attachment is the Dharma, so without practicing the Dharma there is no way you can be liberated from birth and death.

Unless you are afraid of birth and death, going for refuge becomes a lie.

When people are in difficulty, they seek protection. If they have broken the law, they ask to be pardoned. Why? Because they are afraid. In the same way, someone who wants to get out of the cycle of birth and death goes for refuge in the Three Jewels out of fear. So to say "I take refuge" without actually being afraid is to tell a lie. We might say, "I take refuge," or "Look on me with compassion," or "Teacher, you know everything; I am in your hands." But if we make such utterances simply on our lips without having a deep inner faith and without having realized the defects of samsara, our devout words may impress ordinary folk, but they certainly will not convince enlightened beings.

The words alone will not help.

Unless you are rid of desire, saying you are a great meditator becomes a lie.

Although we speak of the Mantrayana as being the vehicle in which the object of desire is used as the path, it is still necessary to be free of attachment to that object. As long as you have attachment, the Mantrayana will not work, and you are lying to yourself if you think you will be able to attain enlightenment without giving up attachment. People who do not completely and purposefully give up all concern for friends, relatives, enemies, growing crops, building houses, and so on, and who at the same time think they are great meditators, end up as the old hermits one hears about, who merely accumulate things in their hermitages. If you really are a great meditator, you will know that

> The end of all gathering is dispersing.
> The end of all living is dying.
> The end of all meeting is parting.
> The end of all rising is falling.

When you come to die, you will have to leave all your possessions behind; they will be of no use to you then. Neither should you be concerned with any external good qualities you might have such as a pleasing appearance or skill with words:

> *Attachment to anything, inside or out, is a cage imprisoning you.*

Just as a bird in a bamboo cage can never get out, a mind caught by desire and attachment has no opportunity to escape onto the path of liberation.

> *Whether one is shackled with a golden chain or bound with a rope, it is the same*

—one is immobilized, one cannot move one's legs. The Dharma is like gold, but if we do not practice it properly, it will tie us down in the same way as an ordinary rope. To practice genuinely we need to be deeply convinced about the law of cause and effect with regard to our actions.

> **Unless you have understood the law of karma, saying you have realized the view becomes a lie.**

Without understanding the principle of karmic cause and effect, any Dharma practice you do will simply be a semblance of the real thing. As it is said, one's view should be as high as the sky, but one's conduct must be finer than flour. When you find yourself at the point of committing even a very minor negative action, you should not dare to do it because you know it will cause future suffering. And if you have the opportunity to perform even a tiny positive action, you should eagerly do so, knowing that it will help you accumulate merit and progress toward liberation. On the other hand, it will not help at all to think that negative actions do not matter because they can be purified by confession or because according to your lofty view there is no such thing as positive or negative, good or bad. A practitioner who has truly realized the empty nature of everything naturally has a much clearer understanding of interdependence and is convinced that actions inevitably produce effects. Saying one has realized the view without having understood the law of cause and effect is a lie, and so is saying that there is no need to avoid negative actions and undertake positive ones. This is why Shechen Gyaltsap notes,

> You have to master the essential point that emptiness manifests
> as cause and effect.

The more complete one's realization of emptiness becomes, the more clearly one sees the infallible relationship of cause and effect in relative truth.

> **Unless you have abandoned the abyss of existence, saying
> you are a Buddha becomes a lie.**
>
> *Without getting rid of the cause, the five poisonous emotions,
> you will never close off the abyss of samsara, their result. So be
> diligent in applying the antidote, the three trainings.*

II

*Practicing over a long period with determination, the armor of
diligence,*[55] *and daring.*

It is important to keep up our determination under all circumstances. Obstacles should make us practice even harder. Even if we become seriously ill, we should put yet more effort into listening, reflecting, and meditating, and not let illness defeat us. Similarly, if we run out of food, we should continue with even greater diligence. As long as we are motivated in this way, everything will work out. So practice with devotion, great diligence, and wisdom.

> Son, there are five things that are true.
>
> It is true to say that without meditating one will never become a Buddha.
>
> *If you do not put the path into practice, even the Buddha catching you with his hand cannot help you.*

Just as it is impossible to buy anything without money or make anything without materials and tools, there is no way to attain enlightenment without practicing. Unless you practice properly, purifying your past negative actions and avoiding further downfalls, it is no good imagining that the Buddha will catch you with his hand and prevent your falling into the lower realms. It is true that no one in this world has greater compassion, wisdom, and ability than the Three Jewels, whose blessings are omnipresent. But if you do not have devotion and do not practice, you will not be open to the Buddha's blessings, and even if he holds you in his hands, he will not be able to help you. When King Trisong Detsen's daughter, Lhacham Pemasel, was dying, the King put her on Guru Rinpoche's lap, but even then the Guru said it would be impossible to save her from death. It takes more than simply being held in a Buddha's hands. Indeed,

> *This very universe rests on the palm of the Buddha Vairochana-Himasagara.*

We already dwell in the hands of the Buddha Vairochana-Himasagara, but despite this we are still in samsara. Resting on the universal Buddha Mahavairochana's two hands—folded in the meditation posture—is a jeweled alms bowl. In it is a great lake of nectar on which grows a lotus. Its twenty-five flowers are tiered one above the other from the alms bowl up to the Buddha's crown protuberance, and in one of these our whole universe is contained.[56] So we are there too, always dwelling in the hands of the universal Buddha, and yet that is still not enough.

Why does it not help? Because we have accumulated all kinds of negative actions and afflictive emotions.

> **It is true to say that if you do not break the samaya, you will not go to hell.**

Whatever you do, if you have not broken the samaya, you will not fall into the lower realms. There is a story about a disciple of the supreme physician, Gampopa. He was one of Gampopa's monks but later he gave up monastic ordination, married, and had many children. He made his living rearing pigs and over many years slaughtered a large number of them. One day he fell sick and was at the point of death. His wife summoned a Kadampa geshe who lived nearby to come and give him some last advice. "You have sinned greatly," the geshe told him, "now it is time to confess and repair your negative actions before you die. You must put your trust in the Three Jewels."

"What are the Three Jewels?" the dying man asked. "Are they outside or inside?"

"The Three Jewels are the Buddha, the Dharma, and the Sangha and they are outside," replied the geshe. Taking a statue of the Buddha he told him, "This statue is the Jewel of the Buddha." He then proceeded in similar vein to give an explanation of the Dharma and the Sangha.

"The Three Jewels are not outside, they are inside," said the sick man, "and the precious Gampopa told me they are present within one's mind; they are the nature of the mind. I have no need of your Three Jewels outside." At this the geshe became very upset and left. The old man then died, and when his body was taken to the cemetery and cremated, rainbows appeared everywhere and *ringsel* relics were found in the ashes. On hearing of this, Gampopa said, "The reason for this is that the old man never stopped practicing the essential instructions I gave him on Mahamudra. Although he committed many negative actions like giving up the robes and killing pigs, he maintained the flow of blessings from the practice I gave him, and he was therefore not stained by his negative actions and could attain a certain degree of realization at the time of death." So it is very important to preserve the samaya bond between oneself and the teacher.

> *Always take your own mind as witness and never part from mindfulness and vigilance.*

Jigme Gyalwai Nyugu had a disciple who was the head of a group of hunters. When they went hunting wild yaks, he used to be content with just the tails of the animals they killed. Having loaded the tails onto his horse, he would look to the east. If he saw a cloud there, he would fold his hands together and say, "My teacher Jigme Gyalwai Nyugu, who is Chenrezig in person, is up there." The younger hunters used to scoff, "You can see how devoted he is to Jigme Gyalwai Nyugu from the way he kills all those animals." On his deathbed he told them, "Jigme Gyalwai Nyugu has come in person; I have met him." He prayed with great devotion and then said, "Now Apu[57] will take me to Zangdopelri[58] and guide me there. There is nothing to worry about."

This story shows how powerful devotion can be in purifying all one's obscurations. Faith and devotion are like a universal medicine. Even though Jigme Gyalwai Nyugu's disciple had committed many negative actions like killing wild yaks, because of his faith and pure samaya with his teacher he was able to attain liberation.

> **It is true to say that if you separate skillful means and wisdom, you will fall to the Shravaka level.**

"Skillful means" refers here to compassion; "wisdom" is the understanding of emptiness. Unless you have genuine bodhichitta and keep in mind that everything you do is for the enlightenment of all beings, simply saying "I am a follower of the Great Vehicle" or "I am a Bodhisattva" or "I am a Vidyadhara" will not be of much use, nor will it be true. On the other hand, if you constantly have the genuine wish to benefit others, even if you do not say very much or do anything very spectacular, you will surely be on the path of the Great Vehicle.

> *One who trains in the Great Vehicle must never separate skillful means and wisdom.*

How does one cultivate the skillful means of great compassion? All sentient beings without exception want to be happy, yet they fail to see that the cause of happiness is cultivating positive actions. They do not want to suffer, yet they do not realize that negative actions result in suffering. When we think of all these beings, who without exception have been our kind parents, and we see that out of ignorance they do the exact opposite of what would produce happiness, we feel enormous compassion for them. That is what is called the skillful means of great compassion.

The wisdom of emptiness involves seeing that all beings are ensnared by ignorance and deciding to perform positive actions with one's body, speech, and mind (for example, respectively prostrating and circumambulating, reciting prayers and mantras, and meditating on compassion), dedicating all the resulting merit for the sake of all beings—all this without any attachment.

If you can permeate the skillful means of compassion with the wisdom of emptiness, uniting the two, you will naturally be acting in accordance with what we call the six transcendent perfections.

Train in the path of the six transcendent perfections.

Whatever you do in practicing the Dharma revolves around view, meditation, and action. Of these, the view is of paramount importance. When you are traveling through a country, you have to know where to go, which form of transport to use, what the hazards are, and which routes are the safest. Similarly, on the path to enlightenment, you must have a clear view, understanding how to travel the path. Action is a companion for the view but should never conflict with it. The view itself may be as high as you wish: it should be the attitude of the Great Vehicle and the view of the Great Perfection. But as far as your conduct is concerned, unless your view is completely stable, your actions should never be on the same level as the view. It is wrong to adopt lofty conduct on the basis of there being no such thing as the result of an action, no such thing as cause and effect, no such thing as good and bad. Keeping your actions very down to earth will never interfere with the loftiness of your view. But if your conduct is on a higher level than your view, this will constitute a real obstacle.

It is true to say that if you do not know how to unite
view and conduct, you are on the wrong path.

As one traverses the nine vehicles, the view becomes increasingly advanced. The Shravaka's view, for instance, asserts the existence of indivisible particles and indivisible instants of consciousness. As a result of this view, Shravakas are unable to let go of their firm belief in the true existence of the material world. Although they have methods for purifying the obscurations of afflictive emotions, they are unable to purify the conceptual obscurations. Bodhisattvas, on the other hand, do not have the belief in the true existence of phenomena, and on this basis they accumulate merit and wisdom on a vast scale, infusing everything with the wish to help others. As a result, their view is much vaster than that of the Shravakas. Nevertheless, in the Sutrayana there is still the dualistic notion of samsara as something to be rejected and nirvana as something to be attained. There is no such dualistic concept for someone who has entered the Vajrayana and has full realization of emptiness, of the view of the inherent union of purity and evenness. When we have realized this, we are on the swift path to enlightenment. This is why it is important that the view should be as high as possible. But our conduct should match our capacity. In other words, our actions should suit the moment. For this, practitioners have to look inward and ask themselves whether what they are doing is appropriate to their level or not. If we are unable to judge our own capacity, we risk taking the wrong path.

> Take heed that the view does not slide toward action, and that action does not slide toward the view.

Ultimately the view is not something to be sought outside: it has to be found within. So the text continues,

It is true to say that the mind is by nature perfectly pure and clear, unstained by defects.

When we speak of mind, the aware mind—with its many ceaseless thoughts—is not the ultimate mind. But once these thoughts have cleared away, there is left the true, ultimate mind whose essential nature is empty, whose natural expression is luminosity, and whose manifestation is all-pervading compassion.[59] This natural state of the mind, when realized, is like the sun in a cloudless sky dispelling darkness all over the earth. Until we realize this natural state of mind, our determination to be free, our compassion, and our contentment with what we have will all remain limited in scope.

This nature of mind is not something that some beings have and others do not. Even ordinary beings completely caught up in delusion have it. Even tiny insects have it. It is simply that they have failed to recognize it. The recognition of this natural state of mind constitutes the perfectly pure view completely free from any stains or defects. As it is said of the perfect view of the Middle Way, "I have no postulate, there is no flaw in my view." Once all the clingings to samsara and nirvana have dissolved into the absolute expanse, one reaches the emptiness possessed of everything sublime, the view beyond all postulates of existence and nonexistence, and so forth. Kunkhyen Longchen Rabjam describes this as the ultimate view, the great purity and evenness. "Great purity" refers to the fact that there is no fundamental difference between samsara and nirvana; they are both, from the very beginning, the infinitely pure state of emptiness. "Great evenness" refers to the equality of all phenomena. It is pervaded by the unchanging great bliss, which is not the ordinary bliss obtained from the pleasures of the senses, like delicious food and so on, but the unchanging bliss that is the natural condition of the Buddha's enlightened mind.

This supreme great bliss is ever present in the Buddha's mind, so even if we were to look there, we would never find such a thing as suffering in his mind. Bodhisattvas who have realized this all-encompassing emptiness are completely free from expectation and apprehension. If someone is standing by their side with a sandalwood fan wafting a cool, sandal-scented breeze over them, they do not feel elated or attached to this. If someone insults them or blames them without cause, they do not feel any ill will. Even if someone threatens to chop off their head with a sword, as in the story of the rishi Patient Words, they feel neither fear nor anger. All this is the result of their having fully realized emptiness. But the emptiness they realize is not a mere blank, in which there is nothing at all. Its natural quality is clarity. The true view is the inherent union of emptiness and clarity.

This realization of emptiness completely destroys all the afflictive emotions. And it is not only the full realization of emptiness that has such power. According to Aryadeva, merely thinking just once that phenomena might possibly be empty—merely doubting their solid reality—is sufficient to tear the afflictive emotions to pieces. We ourselves may be quite a long way from realizing emptiness, but we can approach it by watching the nature of the mind and ascertaining its empty nature. That is what we call the path.

Mind is intrinsically radiant and has never been contaminated by adventitious impurities, so its natural expression is the great purity. This is the very reason exerting oneself on the path is meaningful.

If it were intrinsically impure, there would be no transforming it into something pure, and there would therefore be no point in striving on the path.

That very nature has never been fundamentally changed. It has always been there, and revealing it is known as the supreme accomplishment of Mahamudra, the ultimate goal. The reason Bodhisattvas have to accumulate merit and wisdom for three measureless kalpas is that they still have not recognized this Mahamudra. Otherwise there would be no need to continue. We keep going because that is the way to progress and to recognize the Mahamudra. Those who practice the three trainings on the path of the Shravakas and Pratyekabuddhas gain only partial realization of the ultimate emptiness, but this is already sufficient to rid themselves completely of afflictive emotions. Thus, striving on the path is worthwhile, because it brings us closer and closer to realizing emptiness. Without diligence, we will never realize emptiness.

Our efforts are also meaningful because we all have this buddha-nature; it is fundamental to us. If the mind were not primordially pure, it would be quite impossible to make it pure, just as it is impossible to extract gold from ordinary rock, however much one breaks it up and tries to melt and refine it. But just as refining gold ore by washing, melting, and beating it will eventually produce gold, striving on the path will unveil the nature of enlightenment, which has been with us from the very beginning. This is precisely why we can attain enlightenment. If that perfectly pure absolute nature were not already present within us, there would be no way to create it by exerting ourselves on the path. Indeed, it is said in the Vajrayana that if one did not have the ground empowerment from the beginning, there would be no way to attain enlightenment. Unless the ground empowerment were present in the disciple's being, empowerment would not do any good. One cannot empower a grain of rice to be a grain of wheat. Giving empowerment to a pea or grain of buckwheat and telling it that it is now a grain of rice will not turn it into a grain of rice. But if it is already a grain of rice, then naturally it will grow and develop into a crop of rice.

In the same way, the view, meditation, and action related to the absolute nature are present within one's being. By unveiling this absolute nature through practice one can actualize Buddhahood. We all have the buddha-nature. Now we need to recognize it through practice, like making fire by striking steel and flint in the presence of tinder. We can attain Buddhahood because its nature is intrinsic to us. It is important to understand this and put it into practice.

12

Son, there are five things that are pointless:

You might do them, but the result will be wrong.

These refer to certain things we might do that do not liberate us from samsara or lead us to ultimate enlightenment. Like worldly activities, they produce the wrong result, the opposite of what we wish to achieve.

There is no point in following a master who does not have the nectar of the teachings.

It is important to check first whether he is authentic.

If the teacher himself does not possess the nectar of the teachings, even if you follow him very faithfully, there will be no result. All the effort you put into listening, reflecting, and meditating will be wasted because he cannot give you what he himself does not have. Conversely:

There is no point in accepting a disciple who is not a proper vessel.

If an authentic teacher pours the nectar of the teachings into an improper vessel, it is a waste for everyone. The teacher has given the teaching, but the disciple is unable to make use of it. It is wasted, like nectar poured into a broken or leaking pot so that it spills on the ground. Someone who is not a proper vessel may stay with the teacher and follow him like his shadow, but he will derive no benefit from the teaching and may even develop adverse views, like the monk Sunakshatra. He spent twelve years with the Buddha and learned the whole Tripitaka by heart, but because he had wrong views, he saw faults in the teachings and in the Buddha himself, and was subsequently born as a preta in a nearby garden.

> *Even if he follows you like your shadow, do not give him instruction. It will benefit neither you nor him.*

There is no point in making a connection with someone who will not keep the samaya.

The samaya is the very life of the teaching and of one's relationship with the teacher, so there is no point in making a connection with someone who will not keep pure samaya. Inasmuch as someone who cannot keep the samaya is not a proper vessel, the teacher, especially, should avoid making a connection with such a person.

> *The fault of his breaking the samaya will rub off on you, and he will not benefit either.*

Breaches of samaya can obscure us in two ways: first, they obscure the samaya breaker; second, they obscure anyone who associates with a samaya breaker. In the latter case, even if we have not committed any fault ourselves, simply associating or living with samaya breakers causes us to become obscured by their stain, just as a frog with contagious skin sores infects all the frogs in the same pond and a drop of sour milk makes fresh milk also turn sour. So making connections with those who have broken the samaya helps neither us nor them.

There is no point in performing positive actions that are mixed with negative ones.

For example, killing animals to earn money to build a temple or make representations of the Buddhas' body, speech, and mind,[60] or selling meat and liquor in order to sponsor the Sangha is tantamount to accumulating negative actions for the sake of the Three Jewels. It is quite contrary to the Dharma and does not help at all.

> *The preparation and conclusion must not be mixed with negative action.*

Anyone—a sponsor, for example—who performs a positive action should begin by having the pure intention to help the Dharma and to benefit all sentient beings. The beneficial act itself should be devoid of any negative deed, such as taking life or cheating other people in order to accomplish the so-called positive action. And after having performed a very virtuous deed like sponsoring the Sangha, one should not feel proud or look down on those who have not managed to do as much. Thus, to be genuinely positive, the action must be free from negativity in its preparation, main part, and conclusion. Otherwise, if white and black deeds are mixed, the positive action will be spoiled in the same way as delicious food is spoiled by mixing it with something unpalatable.

> *It is the nature of mixed actions that they mature as happiness and suffering separately.*

In other words, if an action consists of positive and negative deeds mixed together, one will experience both happiness and suffering in turn.

There is no point in knowing the teachings if you do not act accordingly.

If you know the teachings of the Dharma but do not practice them, they will be no more than empty words. Devadatta, for example, knew the whole of the *Avatamsaka Sutra* by heart, but he did not apply it to his conduct or integrate it with his mind. This is why the note says,

> *It is important, rather, to integrate everything you know with your being and to put it into practice.*

Whatever you have heard and learned, do not leave it as empty words. Incorporate it into your mind so that your mind blends with the teachings. Then the teachings will act as a remedy for your afflictive emotions, and that is the point of the practice.

13

Putting the instructions into practice over a long period with determination, armor,[61] and daring.

It is said that with a single line of instruction one can attain complete Buddhahood. So even if you have not received many different teachings, you should greatly value any instruction. You should be prepared to give your life and all you have to receive it and practice it diligently, donning the armor of forbearance in the face of cold and heat, hunger and thirst, so that you can stay in isolated mountain retreats and devote your whole life to practice. And when you meet with obstacles or adverse circumstances, you should muster all your strength and apply yourself with even greater effort. If you do so over a long period of time, it is certain that your practice will bear fruit.

> **Son, there are eight instructions.**
>
> **As you practice, cross the pass of attachment and aversion.**
>
> *Begin by falling upon those bandits, the eight ordinary concerns.*

The greater our diligence in listening, reflecting, and meditating on the teachings, the more we will deepen our realization and free ourselves from the fetters of attachment and aversion. To practice the Dharma, we have to be free from the eight ordinary concerns—pleasure and pain, fame and obscurity, and so on. In particular, we should never practice with the idea of becoming famous, nor should we be attached to any recognition we may gain from doing a lot of practice. Our minds should be completely rid of these eight ordinary concerns.

> **When you are studying the texts, don the armor of forbearance.**
>
> *Earnestly put up with physical hardships and your inner fears regarding the profound meaning.*

It is very difficult in the beginning to study all the various scriptures thoroughly and to put them into practice correctly. As ordinary people, our minds are full of afflictive emotions and are stained by past actions, which contradict what the Dharma teaches. Nevertheless, as we follow the teachings, our afflictive emotions and actions will gradually start to diminish. So it is important to put on the armor of forbearance, practicing with uninterrupted effort day and night. Even ordinary people do not mind going a whole day with nothing to eat or drink in order to attain mundane goals, making a lot of effort and undergoing great hardship. But in pursuing their worldly activities, they are involved in negative actions and are sowing the seeds of future suffering, so it is all for the wrong purpose. How much more meaningful it is to undergo similar difficulties—even for a day—for the sake of the Dharma, for it will purify our obscurations from the past and help us progress toward liberation. This is one kind of patience—putting up with difficulties in the practice. Another kind is to have the patience to accept the profound meaning. Mahamudra and the Great Perfection contain the highest teachings on the absolute nature and on emptiness, which are difficult for beginners to understand and accept. Indeed, some people feel afraid when they first hear the teachings on emptiness. Have the strength and openness of mind to accept these advanced and profound teachings, remembering that it was by practicing the teachings on this view as vast as space that all the great enlightened beings of the past attained realization.

**When you are staying in sacred sites and secluded places,
do not let your mind hanker after food and wealth.**

Once you have received the teachings and diligently studied them, you need to integrate them with your mind by practicing in a secluded place, where there are few people and where your practice will not be disrupted by ordinary distractions. Your mind should be constantly on the watch, recalling what is the correct way to practice and then checking whether you are indeed practicing correctly. If you do something with your body, speech, or mind that is contrary to the teachings, you should confess it, repair it, and promise not to commit it again. If you do something that accords with the teachings, rejoice and dedicate the merit, thinking, "Through this may my obscurations be cleared away and may I eventually be able to benefit other beings."

What you must avoid doing, however, is thinking about the food you eat and worrying whether in the future you will have any food at all. It is particularly important to be content with what you have. It is said, "Those who know contentment have true wealth at their door." Be satisfied with having enough food to sustain you and enough clothing to protect you from the cold. Someone who is content with having just enough can adapt to any conditions and accepts things more easily. This is why

It is important to have few desires and be content with what you have.

Otherwise there will be no end to your desires, just as there is no end to a dog's appetite. One can feed a dog a large meal, but as soon as it has finished, it starts sniffing around for more. We are the same. We can eat a delicious meal and still want more. We can have all the clothes we need but still want to buy more. And there is no end to how much money we can have: if we have a million, we want two million; if we have two million, we want three. Unless we know how to be satisfied with what we have, our desires can never be fulfilled. A Dharma practitioner should be someone who knows how to have enough. Once you know how to be content in this way, you will realize that this is itself the greatest wealth one can have.

When you want the profound teachings, follow a master well versed in them.

The highest teachings, such as those of the Great Perfection, are the most profound and quintessential teachings in Buddhism. If we wish to practice them, we have to rely on a teacher who has a real knowledge of these teachings. Students who follow someone overconfident, who explains such teachings in order to show off without really being certain of the genuine view, meditation, and action, will find it hard to understand the true meaning and even harder to put it into practice, let alone obtain the proper result. So for the teachings of the Great Perfection, we need a teacher who has a complete knowledge of the view, meditation, and action of the Great Perfection and who has directly experienced and realized these himself. Only a teacher who is qualified in this way can impart similar knowledge to the disciple.

Do not relegate the instructions to superficial knowledge: clear up all your doubts about them.

It is said, "Do not leave the instructions on the bookshelf." If you do so, and you let them remain superficial, theoretical items of knowledge, they will not help you to give up worldly activities or to feel the urge to free yourself from samsara. They will not lead you to practice genuinely, and there will be no growth in your experience or realization. So you must first be diligent in listening to the teachings. Then, having received them, go over the instructions point by point, and clear up any doubts you have concerning their meaning. Finally, integrate them and make them a direct inner experience. Having done this, go to a secluded place and make a firm commitment: "From now until I attain enlightenment I shall do nothing but put these instructions into practice."

When you meet a truly knowledgeable master, do all you can to please him and never upset him.

By doing so, you will gain all the qualities of his knowledge.

If you are able to please your teacher through your practice, you will make progress on the path. Look at Tilopa, who made Naropa undergo twenty-five great hardships, and at Father Marpa, who had Milarepa build the nine-storied tower several times. Because Naropa and Milarepa were convinced that their teachers were fully enlightened Buddhas, they did not have a single doubt. They followed their masters' instructions to the letter, and for this reason they were able to attain enlightenment themselves. If your teacher asks you to do something that you think is too burdensome or beyond your ability—even though it accords with the Dharma—and you fail to implement his advice, it will be an obstacle to your practice and will prevent your obtaining the qualities of realization. You should be like a skillful minister who knows how to fulfill the king's wishes. To always please the teacher with your practice and conduct is the best way to make progress on the path to liberation and the most certain way to attain realization. By always doing as the teacher says, you will gain the same qualities as he has, just as good-quality clay in a flawless mold produces an image identical to the original.

Always be careful in your behavior.

Constantly apply mindfulness, vigilance, and carefulness in your physical, verbal, and mental actions, doing only what accords with the teacher's instructions. Never upset the teacher. Receive his teachings like a swan feeding off the various waterweeds and flowers in a lake without disturbing the water. It is important to know how to follow the teacher, listen to the teachings, and relate with the people around him, receiving what you need without causing any trouble.

**When the Dharma gets difficult, stamp on your faint-
heartedness.**

For the sake of the Dharma, you should be ready to risk your life and body. Never think, when the teacher tells you to do something, "I dare not do this," or "It is too difficult for me." The Buddha himself said that even a bee could attain Buddhahood if it had faith, diligence, and compassion. So

> *With no concern for body and life, serve the Teacher and act
> with one taste*

without distinguishing between pleasant and unpleasant or wishing you could be left to lead a quiet, comfortable life somewhere.

**When your family disowns you, cut all attachment in
your mind.**

When you follow a teacher and receive teachings from him, your relatives may try to discourage you, saying, "It is not good to give up all worldly affairs; in the future you will fall on hard times." Though they may not be very happy that you are practicing the Dharma, reflect as follows: "They are caught up in the activities of samsara; they do not realize the benefits of liberation. I have encountered the Dharma, and this might be my only chance. Now that I have this opportunity, I shall practice whether they like it or not." In this way you should sever the ties of attachment in your mind.

> *Treat friends and enemies equally and let attachment and
> aversion be liberated by themselves.*

It is said,

> No evil is there similar to anger.[62]

Falling under the influence of anger constitutes a real obstacle on the path to liberation. It is therefore important to cultivate great patience with regard to those who harm us and to arouse bodhichitta, wishing that they may attain enlightenment. Similarly, excessive attachment to those who are dear to us will simply draw us into an endless series of activities in caring for them, and our Dharma practice will go to waste. So reflect on the fact that enemies have been your friends or relatives in past lives and cultivate love for them. Those who are dear to you have been your enemies in past lives; excessive attachment to them will only prevent your encountering the teachings and receiving instruction, and then your practice will be spoiled. This is why it is important that all the ties of attachment and aversion are loosened.

When you are straying into ordinary thoughts, bring your consciousness back to the essence.

If the mind strays onto the object, afflictive emotions will grow, so tether them with the rope of faith, diligence, mindfulness, and vigilance.

When you encounter external circumstances, whether favorable or adverse, turn your mind inward and apply mindfulness so that you are not influenced by your habitual tendencies. Otherwise, each time you give in to attachment and are seduced by beautiful forms, fragrant scents, or sweet melodies, your afflictive emotions will grow. You will be going in exactly the opposite direction to the Dharma. So instead, develop great faith in the teachings, cultivate a yearning to practice them, and apply yourself diligently day and night. Remember clearly what you should and should not be doing. Keep an eye on what your body, speech, and mind are doing, tethering them with the rope of vigilance. In this way you will tame the wild elephant that is your mind. Maintain your practice year after year, generating ever greater diligence and constantly checking your progress and experience. In this way, the realization of Mahamudra and the Great Perfection will enter your being, and when that happens, all your deluded perceptions will be liberated by themselves.

Develop determination and endurance. Use the antidote of primal wisdom to let deluded thoughts be liberated by themselves. This is a crucial point.

I4

How to practice by applying whatever is necessary in the particular situation.

In this present age, beings have very short lives and a multitude of wild thoughts and gross afflictive emotions. We compound this by frittering away our lives in superficial, theoretical study. But the essence of the Dharma is to actually practice it and achieve inner realization. Before we can practice, therefore, we have to prepare ourselves with all the favorable conditions, just as someone who wants to travel somewhere begins by securing all the provisions and other things he will need on the journey.

Son, there are thirty-four pieces of advice.

If you are distracted outwardly by crowds and bustle, your virtuous activities will be dispersed.

When our minds are distracted by different enjoyable experiences like going out with our friends, dancing, singing, drinking, and attending big public events, our practice becomes dispersed. It is not enough, however, to live alone in a retreat hut.

If you are distracted inwardly by thoughts, afflictive emotions will rise up.

If inwardly we have a lot of wild thoughts and we are constantly recollecting all the samsara-oriented things we habitually did in the past, thinking of all sorts of things that might happen in the future, and letting our minds be disturbed by our likes and dislikes in the present, we will give rise to many afflictive emotions and fall under the influence of all these thoughts. We will wander and be distracted from our practice.

If you are otherwise distracted by your own magical powers and giving blessings, your own life will be threatened.

Coming in between outer and inner distractions, it may happen that, after spending a long time practicing, we attain a relative degree of realization, so that people begin to think we have great powers, can perform feats of magic, and can give great blessings. If we become involved in practicing magic and so forth, in the end we create conditions that can harm our lives. Also, if people think we have great powers or realization, they will pay respect to us and serve us. This too can be a major source of distraction, ultimately affecting our lives and our very liberation.

For this reason,

As they are a source of obstacles, give up distractions.

However wealthy you are, even if you are as rich as Vaishravana, the god of wealth, with whole houses full of clothes, enormous estates, and lots of money, none of these things will help you one little bit when you die. So it is important to think to yourself, "Life is running away. I do not have time to get involved in all these activities. I only want to practice the Dharma."

When you are struck by death's poison, nothing will be of any use:

There is no time to tarry: quickly, meditate!

Do not be concerned with how you live

in this life, subduing enemies and protecting your kin;

be concerned with how you will die.

As Dharma practitioners, our job is not to defeat enemies and protect friends, but to find out how to rid ourselves of all our defects, prevent afflictive emotions from arising, and seek the quickest way to enlightenment. We should not concern ourselves with the ordinary things that may happen to us in this life, constantly thinking, "How can I become the bravest general and conquer as many countries as possible?" or "How can I become as rich as possible?" Rather, we should give up all such preoccupations and focus on what is going to happen to us at death and in the intermediate state—like someone who is seriously ill and knows he is going to die very soon: he does not go on making elaborate plans for the future.

Take the example of a young maiden's bangles.

When a young woman with three brass bangles on her wrists tries to wash her hands, the bangles jangle together unpleasantly. It is much easier and quieter for her to wash her hands if she removes them first. Similarly, if we try to practice in a place—even a so-called retreat center—where there are a lot of people, one person may start talking to another, who talks to a third person, and so on ad infinitum. It is much easier to stay completely alone with no one to talk to and no cause for distraction.

Practice alone without the luxury of attendants.

Otherwise you might think, "These people are helping me; I have to do something for them in return." Or you may find yourself being unhappy about the way they do things for you. If you stay completely on your own, there will be no cause for distraction and you will not need anything.

If you really must have companions, they should themselves possess the qualities of Dharma so that they help you progress. But companions whose main preoccupations are worldly activities, distractions, and even negative actions will cause you to stray from the Dharma, and you will no longer be able to benefit from practicing in a secluded place. Therefore,

In particular, avoid bad company.

As attachment to family is your own mind's

deluded perception, cast it aside.

If on account of excessive attachment you are unable to sever ties with your relatives, you will be prevented from practicing the Dharma. You will not be able to achieve anything. It is important to realize that attachment to relatives and hatred for enemies are deluded perceptions. They are no different from the horses, chariots, and other things that someone who has taken a psychedelic drug experiences as hallucinations, which can neither harm nor benefit him. But when we attach too much importance to the delusions of ordinary life, we get caught up in them. The remedy for this is:

Do not indulge

in physical activities, talking, and thinking:

Too much of these gives rise to adverse circumstances.

Instead of spending your time with distracting activities like playing sports, attending public events, and working with all sorts of machines, devote your energies to doing prostrations and performing the various yogic exercises. And since the mouth is said to be the storehouse of afflictive emotions, rather than chatting carelessly and endlessly about everything that is happening all over the world, take a vow of silence and recite only mantras and prayers. As for your mind, as long as you follow your thoughts, there will be no end to them. Indulging in excessive activities of this sort with your body, speech, and mind leads to adverse circumstances.

There is no need to be concerned with trying to please people:

You will be much happier having no one for company.[63]

We might feel that we need someone to support our practice and provide for our needs, but this can be another source of distraction, for we then feel obliged to keep our sponsors happy, giving them small presents and flattering them. In the process, we are diverted into wanting to become rich and receiving offerings that are stained by wrong attitudes. So rather than remaining in a place with lots of people to distract you, stay alone, be diligent in the practice, and be content with the little you have. Then you will have no obstacles to your practice. You will find contentment in this life and finally attain ultimate bliss, enlightenment.

Thus attachment and aversion will not arise:

With no one to keep you company, there is no attachment or aversion.

Since sentient beings' desires are never satisfied,

It is impossible to make *everyone* happy—*even the Buddha could not do so*—so stop trying to please people.

Even when Lord Buddha was alive, there were non-Buddhist teachers who criticized him, who were not satisfied with his teachings, found fault with them, and developed wrong views. So if the Buddha was not able to keep everyone happy, how can we ordinary beings ever hope to do so? Give up being concerned with trying to keep people happy: it will simply interrupt your practice.

> *Here is a metaphor for being without thoughts related to attachment and aversion:*
>
> **Stay alone like a corpse.**

A corpse carried to the graveyard is not impressed or pleased by being given fine clothes or having nice things said about it. Neither does it feel cold if it has no clothes or get angry if one insults or scolds it. You should be like that, completely indifferent to good or bad conditions, to pleasant or unpleasant words, to being treated well or not.

> *Avoiding the abodes of attachment and aversion, and thus being free from clinging and desire,*
>
> **Do not enter a pit of thorns: stay in a place where you will be happy.**

In places with a lot of people, one thought or word leads to another, and we build up a constant stream of attachment and aversion. Such places are like a pit of thorns. Instead, you should stay somewhere pleasant where there are no such causes for attachment and aversion, and where you will remain in a happy frame of mind.

> *Until now you have surrendered your bodies and lives to attachment and aversion.*

From time without beginning we have been wandering in samsara. Countless times in our innumerable rebirths, our attachment has led us to give up our lives trying to fulfill our desires. Countless times our hatred has caused us to lose our lives trying to vanquish our enemies. If we were to collect all the tears we have shed in despair at not achieving our goals, they would more than fill the biggest oceans on this earth. And yet nothing of all this has brought us the slightest benefit.

Enough with the past; now stop such surrender.

Instead, make a promise that whatever difficulties you encounter, whether you are hungry or cold, you will give up ordinary activities and devote yourself to practicing the Dharma.

Now surrender your body and life to the Dharma.

Since all beings are endowed with the buddha-nature

(they suffer because they have not recognized that buddha-nature),

Do not consider people as enemies and friends; maintain primal wisdom.

Rather than holding on to the concepts of enemies and friends, which lead to our performing all sorts of karmic actions, regard them as helpers on the path to liberation. Better still, view everything from the point of view of wisdom.

Apply yourself eagerly to sameness.

Be assiduous in realizing the sameness of samsara and nirvana, of friends and enemies, of good and bad.

Do not look to fame *or to experiencing any others of the eight ordinary concerns;* **watch your own mind.**

That will be much more helpful.

Practice the ascetic discipline of guarding the mind.

There is no need for any other so-called ascetic practice.

Unless you are diligent *in this,* **you will go down.**

Even a single instant of negative thought creates the cause for being thrown into the lower realms.

Until now we have led ordinary lives spent mainly in trying to extend our possessions, build houses, run businesses, and raise families. We have worked very hard at these things, and yet they have not brought us much benefit. So now we should put our efforts into transforming our minds. Unless we do so, we will fall under the influence of all the different afflictive emotions that arise in the mind, and their destructive power is very great. As it is said, a single thought of anger arising in the mind of a Bodhisattva will completely destroy all the merit he has accumulated in three kalpas and cause him to be reborn in the hell realm for twenty intermediate kalpas.

Throughout the beginningless series of our lives, we have believed in the existence of things that do not exist. We have postulated the existence of an "I" where there is no "I" and of friends and enemies where there are no such things as friends and enemies.

From time without beginning, your belief in the reality of things has fettered you in samsara. So now

Give up your wandering ways of the past.

There is no need to be concerned about the past. Irrespective of where you were reborn previously, the main thing at present is that you have not been born in one of the three lower realms. It is now time to give up all your wandering in samsara.

It is important to know that

Of the seven noble riches, the foremost, the source of them all, is being content.

Arhats, Pratyekabuddhas, and Bodhisattvas have no need for ordinary riches such as gold, silver, and jewels. Their wealth is much more meaningful, for they have faith, discipline, generosity, learning, a sense of shame in their own eyes, a sense of decency in others' regard, and wisdom. With these, at each instant they come closer and closer to liberation. It is very important to have these seven noble riches. If you lack faith, wisdom, and so forth, you should cultivate them. As far as the Dharma and these seven noble riches are concerned, you should never be satisfied: never think, after doing a little practice, that you have exerted yourself enough. But as far as ordinary wealth and possessions are concerned, you should be easily satisfied.

Go to the island in the ocean that has the riches you desire.

If you know how to be content, you will be truly rich, like the merchants in ancient times who used to sail to jewel islands to gather all the precious things there.

Without the capacity to be content, even a king is no better off than a beggar,

because even if we are as a rich as Vaishravana, our wants never cease; we never think we have enough, and, like beggars, we are always looking for more. Instead,

Be satisfied with simply enough food and other necessities to stay alive.

If you reach this island, you will never return.

Once you reach the island of liberation and ultimate omniscience, you will never fall back into samsara. Those who have reached the sublime Bodhisattva levels and have little clinging to food and other things do not need gross material food. They are able to sustain themselves on the nourishment of concentration.

If you have property, give it to your father.

Get rid of all your belongings and give them to your parents and relatives without thinking of keeping or storing them. However, "father" here refers rather to one's spiritual father, the teacher.

If you please your teacher by offering him everything you have, he will give you all the profound instructions,

for it is said that to offer a single drop of oil to anoint the teacher's body has greater merit than making boundless offerings to a thousand Buddhas. This is because it is the teacher himself who is able at this moment to establish you and all beings on the path of enlightenment; he is the most sublime of all objects of offering. So if you please him, he will give you all the instructions without holding anything back, as was the case with Marpa: he was so pleased by Milarepa's total dedication and diligence that he gave him the complete oral transmission.

If you make your old father happy, he will give you his heartfelt advice.

In an ordinary situation, when children are respectful and loving toward their father, he teaches them everything he knows so that they can be successful in the world, achieve their goals, look after their family, overcome difficulties, and so forth. Similarly,

The teacher too

Speaks to his son straight from the heart.

When the teacher is pleased with our conduct and practice, he will teach us how to defeat our enemies—not ordinary enemies, but our archenemies, afflictive emotions. He will teach us how to progress on each stage of the path to enlightenment, for he himself has made the same journey, and he therefore knows the path and has the necessary experience. Even a single word or sentence spoken by the teacher is of immense benefit. For the time being, it will give us joy and contentment; ultimately, it will bring us the bliss of enlightenment.

To a suitable vessel he gives the instructions in their entirety.

But to give the complete instructions to an unsuitable vessel would be wasting them, for the lineage would then be broken.

The disciple should guard them like his own heart and put them into practice

with one-pointed diligence.

When one comes across a wish-fulfilling jewel, there is no need to feel miserly, for it will freely grant everything one wishes or prays for—

food, clothes, riches, whatever one wants. Likewise the teacher and his instructions will provide everything you need to attain liberation. So:

Once you have found a gem, do not throw it away.

Turn *the mind* **back** *from the deluded perceptions that are* samsara **and correct yourself.**[64]

Most activities in samsara are like children's games or the antics of a madman, so it is important to realize this and turn the mind away from such activities. If you happen to fall back into ordinary delusion, you must correct yourself immediately and return to the mind that is free from deluded perceptions.

Travel the highway to enlightenment.

Do not take the side roads of delusion: keep to the main highway, on which it is very pleasant to travel.

When your vajra brothers and sisters are assembled, think of yourself as the least important of them all.

When you are with them, hold them in high esteem and humbly consider your own qualities to be very few in comparison.

When your brothers and sisters are all together, listen to what they say and carry it out.

If you fear *your practice* **is being scattered, fence it in**

with mindfulness and vigilance, without which ordinary beings inevitably lapse into delusion and their practice becomes completely dispersed. Therefore,

Rely on mindfulness and vigilance and never be without them,

otherwise you will destroy the path to liberation.

If you fear you are running after *the objects of the six senses,* **hold yourself with the hook:**

Employ the watchman that is mindfulness.

Someone who has been captured with a hook has no option but to go wherever he is led. In the same way, if we catch hold of our mind—which risks being distracted by the objects of the six senses—with the hook of mindfulness, and with vigilance and carefulness, this will be of enormous benefit. We should use this watchman to constantly check how many positive or negative thoughts and actions we produce during the day. When we are able to control our minds through mindfulness, everything that appears in samsara and nirvana becomes an aid in our practice and serves to confirm the meaning of the teachings. All appearances are understood as being dharmakaya. We perceive everything in its natural purity, and there is nothing we can call impure:

> Know that all perceptions are dharmakaya, and with that
> confidence—as though you had landed on an island of gold and
> jewels,

where you would not find ordinary stones even if you looked—

Make your view stand firmly on its own.

When we have confidence in our view and meditation, we can cope with any kind of circumstance and deal with any emotion that arises, since the effective antidote is always at hand.

> Do not be ashamed in front of the deity, the teacher, or your
> own mind.

Observe discipline without hypocrisy.

The reason for practicing the Dharma is not so that others will have a good opinion of you. You should never practice in order to impress the yidam deity or the teacher or anyone else. Practice, rather, in such a way that you are never ashamed of yourself and can confidently say, "This is how I have practiced: my practice has not been tainted with negative actions or the eight ordinary concerns. I have practiced well." You know what goes on in your own mind, so make sure you are not uncomfortable with yourself. Then you will be able to conduct yourself according to the holy Dharma, observing the vows of the Basic Vehicle, the Great Vehicle, and the Mantrayana without hypocrisy. But if one moment you pretend to be a strict holder of the Vinaya and the next moment you let everything drop, this will not help.

Give generously and impartially,

and stop expecting anything in return or any karmic reward.

Do not think, "If I give a hundred now, I will get back one thousand tomorrow." And do not make distinctions, thinking, "I will only give to the sublime objects of refuge and not to ordinary beings—they are only ordinary, so they will not help me." Whoever they may be, good or bad, high or low, give generously.

Patiently bear with adversity,

providing help in return for harm.

If people harm you, instead of retaliating angrily, make a wish that your connection with them will enable you in the future to bring them onto the path to liberation. Cultivating patience in response to their harming you helps you deal with all kinds of difficulties and adverse circumstances.

In particular, difficulties you may have when studying or practicing—sickness, aches and pains, hunger and thirst, and so on—are the result of negative actions you committed in the past. By experiencing them now, you are purifying these negative actions, so be joyful at having such an opportunity. On top of that, make a wish: "May all similar sufferings that other beings are experiencing be gathered into mine; may this suffering of mine replace theirs; may all their suffering thereby be exhausted." And practice the exchange, sending all your happiness and well-being to all beings.[65]

Put up with suffering when you are listening and reflecting:

readily accept such things as illness, pain, hunger, and thirst
that you endure for the sake of the Dharma, and take others'
suffering upon yourself.

However, even if you are diligent in listening and reflecting and you meditate for a long period of time, you must never think these will bring you renown. Even if you do become famous, do not indulge in expectation or attachment:

> Do not cast your meditation into the mouth of fame
>
> *with hopes, and so on, of distinction and renown.*
>
> Your conduct should be such that you are not carried away by the demons
>
> *of the eight ordinary concerns. It is important to match it with your progress.*

We need to carefully assess our level of experience and realization, and to match our conduct with that level. When we are beginners, for example, we should behave like bees, going from flower to flower to feed on the nectar. Then, when we have gathered a sufficient amount of teaching, we should proceed to the next stage, reflecting on the teachings we have received and experiencing them in order to extract their quintessence, just as we would churn milk to make butter. Finally, at the third stage, we should gain the ability to free ourselves from the afflictive emotions fettering us. On the other hand, if we fail to properly assess our level of realization, thinking that we are highly realized and can do exactly as we please, drinking alcohol, indulging in sex, and eating lots of meat, we will be going in a direction quite the opposite to the Dharma.[66] Of course, if we truly have a high level of realization, whatever we do will directly benefit beings. So we need to be timely in our conduct. Mixing up our conduct and our level of realization will bring us no benefit.

According to the instructions of the Great Perfection, in the beginning one should be like a bee going from flower to flower searching for nectar. In the middle, one should go to an isolated retreat to practice the teachings, like a wounded wild animal that looks for a lonely, uninhabited spot in which to stay until its wounds are healed. In the end, having gained complete confidence in one's practice, one will be like a lion sleeping in a cemetery.

> *If you chase after the things you perceive, the demons that are the five poisonous thoughts will arise and*
>
> You will be beguiled by the demon of appearances.

You should understand that everything you perceive, beautiful or ugly, pleasant or unpleasant, is the display of primordial wisdom. As long as you do not lapse into being attracted to beautiful things and disgusted by ugly things, the mind will not be caught by outer phenomena.

> *It is important, therefore, that the mind does not chase after the object.*

15

Six instructions for warding off defects.

Son, do not discredit the house of your forefathers.[67]

Where our parents and ancestors have set us an example in conducting themselves perfectly and so on, we should adopt the same ways. Otherwise we will bring shame on our family name. Similarly,

> *Do not bring shame on your own root teacher,*

from whom you received so many instructions,

> *nor on the teachers of the lineage.*

Do not taint your siblings and relatives.[68]

> *Avoid conflicts that prevent you from keeping the samaya with your brothers and sisters—those who have the same teacher as you and those* in general *who have entered the Vajrayana.*

Do not throw dust on other relatives, close or distant.

"Other relatives" refers not only to blood relations but also to those with whom we have a connection through the Dharma—in other words, all other practitioners. So

> *Never speak harshly to others who practice the Dharma,*

for among them there might be beings who are very learned or highly realized. It is important to recognize that practitioners from other

Dharma traditions also have good qualities—qualities that we ourselves need to develop. Instead of disparaging them, try to follow their example. So never criticize those who follow other traditions, whether Sakyapa, Kagyupa, Nyingmapa, Gelugpa, or any other.

> **Without paying taxes to the king, you cannot hope to be his subject.**[69]

When a king's subjects please him, he rules the country well, benefiting his subjects and bringing peace to the land. It is likewise when one pleases one's spiritual teacher. On the other hand,

> *If you do not please the teacher, his compassion and blessings will not flow.*

With regard to the teacher, we first have to check whether he is a qualified master. Then, having made a spiritual connection with him and begun to follow him, we need to please him in three ways: the best way is by practicing his instructions; the second is by serving him with our body, speech, and mind; and the least effective is by offering him material gifts. However, if the teacher is displeased by our conduct, we will not receive his blessings, and without the Guru's blessings success in the practice is impossible. When Jetsun Milarepa was undergoing all those hardships building the nine-story tower, Marpa was so severe with him that his consort, Dakmema, took pity on him. Seeing that Milarepa had still not received any instructions from the master, she gave him a valuable turquoise and sent him to Marpa's principal disciple, Ngoktön Chökyi Dorje, with a forged letter asking him to give Milarepa instruction and let him practice. On reading the letter, Ngoktön Chökyi Dorje put Milarepa in retreat. After seven days, he came to Milarepa to check whether he had gained any realization and was astonished to find that Milarepa, who was obviously a very diligent practitioner, had made no progress. He left him in retreat for another week or so, at the end of which he again asked Milarepa if he had had any signs of realization. When Milarepa replied, "No," he could not believe it and recognized that something must be wrong. Milarepa then explained that, since Marpa had not given him any instructions even though he had been with him such a long time, Marpa's consort, Dakmema, had sent him with the turquoise and the letter in the hope that Ngoktön Chökyi Dorje would teach him. "Now I understand," said Ngoktön Chökyi Dorje. "With the instructions I have given you, it is impossible not to have some sign of realization within a week. The fact that you have not done so is simply because you have not received your teacher's permission." As this story shows, without the teacher's blessings any practice we do will be quite sterile.

Do not race downhill

toward negative actions,

otherwise you will find yourself tumbling into the lower states of existence, like a huge boulder rolling faster and faster down the mountainside.

Do not be clever in wrong ways

such as craft and pretense.

One's respect and devotion to the teacher should be completely genuine and sincere, right down to the marrow of one's bones. Always be free from any kind of deceit, not only with regard to the teacher but in everything you do.

16

An instruction on ten good and bad situations that do no harm—if one can cope with them.

Son, there are ten things that do no harm.

Here "if you can cope" implies a choice: if you can cope, take it on; if you cannot cope, do not take it on.[70]

If you put a heavy load on a horse or elephant, it can bear it. Similarly, if from among the Greater and Lesser Vehicles you choose the Great Perfection, you are making the right choice—provided you can handle it. But if you do not have the necessary prerequisites, like determination to be free, disillusionment with samsara, and acceptance by a qualified master, you must not overconfidently embark on the Great Perfection, for this will be harmful.

> *"Do no harm" means: if a particular situation does no harm,*
> *use it; if it is harmful, don't.*

People who are careful about their health, for example, avoid eating even small quantities of food that disagrees with them. Similarly, it is important to avoid anything that goes against the teacher's instructions, and to be able to put up with difficulties, hardship, and fatigue in order to accomplish anything that accords with those instructions.

> *So when you are able to take all adverse situations on the path*
> *without their affecting you adversely,*

> If you can cope with the place, there is no harm in staying
> in your own country.

> If you can cope with those with whom you are connected,

> *and do not develop attachment to friends and hatred for enemies,*

> there is no harm in not leaving your family.

> If you can cope with the question of clothing,

> *and have completely given up such things as worrying about*
> *how attractive you are or being embarrassed,*

> there is no harm even in going naked.

> If you can cope with the problem of attachment and
> aversion

> *and are able to take joy and sorrow on the path as one even taste,*

> however you conduct yourself outwardly, if inwardly you
> have confidence in the absolute nature, you will not come
> to any harm.

> *When you realize your own mind as being the teacher, all notions*
> *of difference are liberated by themselves. Thus,*

> If you know how to handle the teacher, there is no harm
> in discontinuing respect.

When one realizes that one's own mind is the teacher, such distinctions as "My teacher is good and dwells in dharmakaya; I am inferior and dwell in samsara" are liberated by themselves. If, by avoiding such duality and getting rid of the concept of being separate, you can handle the teacher's instructions properly, you will naturally benefit disciples and Dharma brothers and sisters, and there will be no harm in discontinuing your efforts in things such as respect.[71]

When one uses reasoning to analyze samsara and nirvana, one finds that they are concepts. They do not have the slightest bit of true existence. They are simply the display or natural expression of the absolute nature. So

> *In realizing that there are no such things as the names of*
> *samsara and nirvana and that everything one perceives is self-arisen*
> *primal wisdom,*
>
> If you can cope with the ocean of suffering that is
> samsara, even if you do not practice, you will not come to
> any harm.
>
> If you can cope with the lower realms
>
> *by liberating the mind and appearances into the absolute nature,*
> *so that there is no trace of the habitual tendencies* accumulated
> over such a long time in the past—at this level of realization,
>
> even if you perform negative actions, you will not come
> to any harm.

Put briefly, there are ten negative actions. You should avoid all of them, and on top of that you should save lives[72] and carry out other actions that help others, thereby performing the ten extraordinary positive actions. Nevertheless, at a high level of realization,

> *If it is for the sake of others, whatever one does is permissible.*
>
> *The absolute nature is free from effort and activity;*
> *The essential nature appears in different ways*

Yet the natural expression is free and nondual.
When you know your own mind to be samsara and nirvana,
Beyond the observance of all samayas to be kept,

you can cope with the hells, and there is no harm in not keeping the samayas even if you have entered the door of the secret mantras.[73]

If you are confident in the view

that is beyond intellect and free from activity, and recognize that activities are delusion,

there is no harm in taking things easy and sleeping.

When we realize that all our activities are delusion and we seal everything with the awareness beyond the intellect, we gain the confidence of the view. We no longer feel the need to put our energies into worldly activities but simply remain in meditation.

If you can cope with the problem of residence

and are not attached to the quality of your dwelling

—if you make no distinction between a splendid mansion with lots of rooms and windows and fine things inside (to which its owner would normally be very attached) and a hovel that provides no more than protection from the wind and rain—

it does not matter where you live.

If you can cope with the problem of food

and are free from dualistic concepts of food being good or bad, pure or polluted,[74]

it does not matter what you eat.

If you can cope with the problem of the body

and have severed the ties of self-love,

even if you do not steer clear of contagious diseases, you will come to no harm.

17

Examining and deriding one's own faults and those of Dharma practitioners in general:

Son, there are eighteen objects of derision.

These are, in general, derisory behavior, erroneous practices, foolishness, and breaches of samaya; and there are eight things that prevent such faults from occurring.

It is important to be aware of our own faults. We should recognize them by comparing our own conduct with that of our teacher and Dharma companions, and by constantly checking whether our actions are positive or negative. Derisory behavior is behavior that is so completely wrong that one simply feels like laughing at it, as one would at a children's game. Erroneous practices include those of certain ascetics who, for instance, sit under the midday sun surrounded by four fires at the four cardinal points: they almost die of heat believing that they are thereby purifying themselves. An example of foolishness is someone who has understood nothing of the teaching but thinks he has understood it and even tries to teach others. Together with breaches of samaya, these all need to be avoided. There are eight things that help do so.

Someone good-natured who is competent to guide one;

Someone with a good nature—meaning someone open-minded, diligent, intelligent, and not distracted—is fully able to guide us and lead us along the path, taking us through all the various stages on the path of liberation.

A good friend who is clever at leading one;

By "good friend" we mean someone who is careful not to lapse into committing negative actions, who knows how to act in accordance with the Dharma, and who is diligent in following the path to liberation.

A concern for future lives that stems from remembering death;

The most important way for us to keep the Dharma in mind is to think of the imminence and inevitability of death. This will spur us to be diligent and one-pointed in listening, reflecting, and meditating.

Careful avoidance of negative deeds stemming from the conviction that happiness and suffering are the result of actions;

If we are unhappy now, it is simply because we have harmed others in past lives or earlier in this life. And if we are happy and content now, this is the result of our having helped others. Once we realize the inevitability of this law of cause and effect, we will hesitate to do negative actions; should we happen to commit negative deeds, we will appreciate the need to confess and purify them. And when we do anything positive, we will dedicate it for the benefit of all beings.

A sense of shame in one's own eyes;

We need to feel a sense of shame with regard to ourselves, thinking, "I have followed such great teachers and practiced the sadhanas of the wisdom deities: how can I now have negative thoughts, words, and deeds? How can I behave like this when I have received all those teachings?"

A sense of decency in others' regard;

We should also feel a sense of shame at others' opinion of us: "What will the teachers and wisdom deities think of me?" For we must remember that when we do things contrary to or other than the Dharma, all the Buddhas and Bodhisattvas of the three times and ten directions, with their perfect omniscience, can see them clearly.

Great determination;

Once we know how to practice the Dharma, we should not waste a single moment but should practice day and night. As Jetsun Milarepa said, "Do not hope for swift realization; practice until you die."

*Reliability, as in someone whose word can be trusted and who
does not break his promise.*

*From the eight faults that are the opposite of these come derisory
behavior and the rest.*

Someone old who sees people siding with their relatives and friends
and trying to defeat their enemies is inclined to laugh just as he would
at a children's game, because he can see that all these things are so child-
ish and vain—they do not lead to anything truly worthwhile or important. Similarly, whether we are practicing the Dharma or simply engaged
in ordinary activities, without the eight conditions mentioned above,
whatever we do is an object of derision.

*An object of derision here is an object of scornful laughter or of
contempt, something to be ashamed of both from the conventional
point of view and from that of the holy Dharma.*

Now, to explain these eighteen objects of derision, the first three concern
faith.

In the beginning when faith is born,

and one feels devotion to the teacher and the Three Jewels,

one is ready to leap in the air.

*When one receives the teachings, one does all sorts of things
such as tearing one's hair out and weeping.*

Some people become so elated that they do all sorts of strange things,
instead of listening properly, reflecting calmly, and sitting quietly in their
Dharma robes with their eyes focused in front of their nose.

**Later, torn by doubts, one fills desolate valleys with
one's footprints**

—meaning that one spends one's time going from place to place asking
different teachers this and that.

Without having cleared up one's doubts about the instructions,
one grows hesitant and wanders all over the place.

Instead, you should find a qualified teacher and trustworthy spiritual companions to help you clear up all your doubts.

In the end, having completely lost faith, one becomes a mooring stone on the bottom of hell.

Once one starts to think that the teacher is not acting in the right way or one develops other wrong views of the teacher, one becomes like a stone that has sunk down to the deepest of the hells.

In the end one develops wrong views with regard to the Dharma and the teacher.

These are the three faults in not having firm faith.

The next three concern the teacher.

In the the beginning, having found the master, one talks about all the teachings he has transmitted.

When we first meet the teacher, we entrust everything, our entire being,[75] to him. Then when we start to receive teachings, instead of keeping them for the purposes of our own practice, we repeat all the secret instructions to others, telling them how profound they are:

Having entrusted body and soul to him, one proclaims the secret teachings for all to hear, saying, "These are the most profound of my teacher's words."

Later, one tires of the master and criticizes him.

One regrets everything one offered before

—the material offerings one made and the effort one put into following him—

and one spreads rumors, claiming he has hidden defects.

In the end, one abandons the teacher and considers him as one's greatest enemy.

One makes new acquaintances and follows other teachers.

These are the three faults of following the teacher in the wrong way.

In the beginning, when one achieves a degree of concentration, one thinks, "There is no practitioner as good as I am."

Priding oneself on some small experience one has in sustained calm,

such as a flash of clairvoyance or paranormal insight, one thinks this is a sign of advanced realization. When one becomes infatuated with oneself in this way,

one gets the idea there is no greater meditator or better practitioner than oneself.

Later, one gets tired of meditating and resembles an inmate in an open prison.[76]

We feel as if we were in prison doing practice, though without any great hardship, since we can let the time pass and sleep when we feel like it. At the same time, with this sense of imprisonment, we feel that our practice is not really leading anywhere:

In the hermitage one becomes bored during the day and fearful at night; at sunset one is glad to eat and sleep.

In the end, one gives up meditation and loiters in the villages.

If one does not integrate the Dharma with one's being and merely puts on a facade of Dharma, one ends up performing village ceremonies or working as a hired laborer, a servant, and so forth.

These are the three faults of failing to go through the practice properly.

In the beginning when experiences occur, one brags about them

like someone deranged

who thinks he can achieve great things but has nothing on which to base his confidence.

One is contemptuous of relative truth.

We do not follow the tradition, because we have our own ideas concerning relative truth and the need for the methods and practices that belong to the relative level.

Later one gives up meditation and, as an expert in letters, takes to giving teachings.

Like someone who shows others the way when he himself has no idea which road to take, one explains the teachings to others without having any understanding or realization oneself.

If we ourselves do not know the path and have not reached the dry land of liberation, we cannot know all the dangers on the way. We cannot say, for example, "Here it is muddy; in that place there is a risk of fog; further on, the path becomes dangerous." Without any true experience of the path, how can we guide others?

In the end, when one abandons one's body, one dies in a completely ordinary state.

Like an ordinary being, one dies without having really set out on the path.

These are the three faults of not obtaining any stability in the experience of the practice.

Next, unless we have clarified our view by following a realized teacher, receiving teachings from him, and clearing up all our doubts with him,

In the beginning, one develops but a faint conviction in one's realization of the view.

*Having merely gained a vague and general understanding, one
prides oneself on one's superb realization.*

As a result of one's pride,

One looks down on others

and ends up lapsing into distracting activities like frequenting crowded
places, setting up a business, and engaging in all sorts of worldly activities.

**Later, torn by doubts, one lies about one's knowledge
and questions others.**

*Pretending to be knowledgeable when in fact one knows nothing,
one pesters others with questions.*

**In the end, far from having the view, one is completely
dominated by errors and obscurations.**

*Having fallen under the influence of eternalistic and nihilistic
views like those of the Tirthikas, one never realizes the great evenness,
the union state free from elaboration.*

*These are the three faults of not gaining the confidence of genuine
realization.*

**When the result is lost in error, the windows of liberation
are shuttered.**

*By failing to unite skillful means and wisdom, one misses the
crucial point of the path and closes the door to nirvana, the result.*

**By blocking the windows of liberation, one will never
interrupt the stream of birth and death.**

*Because of one's belief that everything that appears is real and
the notion of one's body and mind as "I," one is fettered by karma
and afflictive emotions, and there is no liberation.*

As a result,

**Unless one interrupts the stream of birth and death, one
is powerless to choose where one will be reborn.**

On account of one's actions and afflictive emotions, one cannot but take rebirth in existence.

These are the three faults or objects of derision where the result is utterly wrong.

They are derisory because sublime, realized beings who see us making such mistakes cannot help laughing.

Therefore, recognize these faults that come from not blending your mind and the Dharma, identifying them just as you would a criminal or thief, and do your best to avoid them.

18

Clarifying errors and obscurations: fifteen ways in which the practice goes wrong.[77]

When we fail to go straight to the vital point of the practice, we make mistakes and the practice goes wrong.

Having turned away from the holy Dharma, one follows ordinary, worldly ways while retaining the appearance of Buddhadharma.

This is what we call "wrong dharma." The word "dharma" or "way" can be used both for the worldly path taken by ordinary people and for the spiritual path trodden by those who seek liberation. What we call a wrong path is that of someone who has the appearance of a spiritual practitioner but whose mind is dominated by ordinary concerns.

Son, there are fifteen ways in which the practice goes wrong.

The first of these is:

The view rushes into uncertainty.

Without having ascertained or directly experienced the view, we wrongly believe we have reached a high level of realization and start to seek celebrity, bearing out the saying that fools run after fame. We have only a superficial understanding but no sound realization, and we completely miss the crucial point of the view, which is the very root of attaining enlightenment. Instead of inner realization

one repeats others' words,

such as the sayings of scholar-siddhas that describe the view,

without having transformed one's own being.

The meditation gets lost in idiot meditation.

Unless we have clarified all our doubts and uncertainties concerning how to meditate, we may become complacent with only a vague, beginner's experience of sustained calm.

Without profound insight one does not destroy the foundation,
afflictive emotions: experiences and realization cannot take birth.

It is necessary to combine sustained calm with the view of profound insight, of emptiness, where there is no clinging. Otherwise, without profound insight, we can only crush the afflictive emotions somewhat, but we cannot eradicate them, and even if we spend many years in a mountain retreat, our practice will not give rise to meditative experiences and realization.

As a result of having failed to realize the view,

The action strays into wild, inappropriate conduct.

Acting in ways contrary to the Dharma, one behaves like a
madman.

Without having gained firm confidence in the view, we engage in improperly considered actions, adopting a sham of Mantrayana conduct and thinking it is all right to drink beer, eat lots of meat, womanize, and so on. We fail to recognize the right time and the right way to act, and so end up behaving like a mad person. This is because

One has not recognized the crucial point of accumulation
and purification.

We think that as we progress toward realizing the absolute nature we no longer need to accumulate merit and wisdom and to purify our obscurations. In fact, the vaster our realization of the absolute nature becomes, the more clearly we understand the need for these two. It is said that even when we reach the stage where there is no difference between the meditation and postmeditation, we must still engage in practices that require effort. We still have to continue practicing in four sessions and so on, because our view may be as high as the sky but our conduct must be down to earth and as fine as flour.

The samaya gets lost in being undervalued.

We apply a measure to the samaya, thinking that we will keep the samaya up to a certain point beyond which there is no need to observe the minor details. But it is wrong to imagine that keeping the samaya is easy, that one need only keep the root samayas and that the branch samayas do not matter and can be overlooked.

> *Without knowing the precepts to be observed, one disdains the samaya, thinking there is no harm in spoiling it up to a point.*

The master is treated as one of one's own.

> *Thinking of him as an uncle,[78] one fails to develop faith or respect.*

Instead of seeing the teacher as the Buddha in person, we have the same feelings for him as we do for our family and friends. We feel affection for him but we do not see him as a true Buddha. As a result, his blessings cannot enter us.

The disciple attends teachings unwillingly.

> *If you listen to keep others happy or for fear of people criticizing, you will never understand the teachings.*

We attend the teachings unwillingly, without any real motivation save that of being concerned about other people's opinions of us (if we do not attend, they might think that we are not interested). Or we may fear that if we do not attend the teachings, people will criticize us or the teacher will be upset. We may also attend because we have heard that the teacher is very famous, and our attendance becomes more an indispensable social event. In either case, we are not deeply concerned with listening to the teachings, reflecting on them, and putting them into practice.

The practice is left for when one has the leisure.

By falling under the power of sleep and indolence, one will never obtain the result.

We practice the Dharma when we are in a happy frame of mind and our body is relaxed and comfortable, but at other times we drop it. However, Jetsun Milarepa said, "There's a long way to go, so practice without alternating between periods of being energetic and tense and of being loose and relaxed." For if we keep taking up the practice and then dropping it like this, we will not obtain the result—experience and realization.

One's experiences are ghost sightings.

Like a clairvoyant, one sees spirits and thinks of them more and more.

We become one of those people who can see nonhumans—ghosts, spirits, celestial beings, and the like—and instead of pursuing realization of the view and experiences in the practice, we lapse into thinking we are seeing ghosts and claiming that the dakinis have given us various predictions and so forth; we finally become obsessed by all these spirits and celestial beings. Such things are of little value in gaining realization, and when we become proud of them, they act as obstacles and are the sign of the demon. As the saying goes, "Obstacles are the sign of the demon; increase and decrease are the signs of meditative experiences." For it is the nature of experiences that they come and go.

The result of the practice is the achievement of worldly fame.

The attachment and aversion of the eight ordinary concerns increase, and one is no different from ordinary people.

Instead of undoing the fetters of the afflictive emotions in our minds and giving birth to the wisdom of no-self, which is gained through sustained calm and profound insight, we err into running after worldly fame. We think, "I have spent years in solitary retreat. I have realized the Great Perfection. I have completely destroyed the eight ordinary concerns." And when we let others believe this, we start to gather a large following of disciples and to accept offerings and respect. This leads to many faults and takes us further and further away from the Dharma, while the eight ordinary concerns increase more and more.

One receives the instructions inauthentically.

Without serving the teacher or putting the teachings into
practice, one relies merely on having the texts and receiving the
transmission. Thus one does not throw oneself with real diligence into
experiencing the practice.[79]

We receive teachings but only superficially and not as suitable vessels who will be able to practice them in the right way and subsequently become holders of the teachings. At the same time, it may happen that a teacher who has only received the transmission of the text but has no proper experience of the practice gives the profound instructions to anyone who helps him or serves him, without considering whether that person is a suitable vessel who will practice and be able to hold the teachings. In this case he cannot transmit anything valuable to the disciple, and the latter will never develop a sound understanding of the view, meditation, and action.

Having obtained a human body in Jambudvipa,[80] one returns empty-handed,

like coming back empty-handed from an island of jewels.

Beings in this world of Jambudvipa have an exceptional opportunity to accumulate merit and wisdom and to purify their obscurations. If we do not use this privileged human existence to practice the Dharma or if we use it to practice the wrong way, we will be led to the lower realms. As the peerless Dagpo Rinpoche[81] said, if one does not get the crucial point of the teachings, even if one practices, the Dharma itself becomes the cause for falling into the lower realms. Similarly, for someone who travels to an island full of jewels and then comes away again without having taken any, all the difficulties he has gone through—sailing the ship, escaping from sea monsters, and so on—will have been in vain.

> From the bed of a Dharma practitioner they remove the corpse
> of an ordinary person.[82] There was no point in obtaining a human
> body.

Whether we have touched the true point of the Dharma or not is something we will know when we die. If we have no fear or anguish at the moment of death and are able to take the Dharma along the path—that is, to realize the dharmakaya—this is a sign that we have arrived at the essential point of the practice. But if, on the other hand, our "practice" has been the pursuit of exclusively worldly interests, we will die and leave a corpse in the same manner as any ordinary person. We will not have used this human existence to practice in accordance with the teachings: obtaining it will have been meaningless.

At death, one dies with regrets.

While we are alive, we might think that we have understood the view, that we are meditating on emptiness, that we are practicing the Great Perfection. But as it is said, "It is when practitioners have to face situations that their hidden faults show up," and in the face of death our shortcomings will become all too clear. If we have not gained confidence in our practice, we will feel great remorse when we come to die, and that remorse will not help us.

> At that time, even if you regret, you will have run out of means.

There will be no way to escape, for even if, stricken with remorse, you now start to think of practicing the Dharma properly, there will be no time to do so.

The Dharma practitioner is betrayed by his own name.

A practitioner who is truly worthy of the name is someone who has assimilated the teachings. But there is otherwise no benefit at all in simply being known as a hermit who has spent many years in retreat or as an erudite scholar of whom people say, "He has received many teachings and studied a lot."

> Unless you have truly practiced the Dharma, being called a practitioner does not help. If you have not transformed your being by practicing the three trainings and you act contrary to the Dharma, though you may be called a "spiritual friend," you will have become a counselor in evil.[83]

One listens to empty sounds.

> Like listening to a melodious song of praise, nothing will come from listening to the dry leaves of flattery and praise. One risks pointlessly wasting one's human life.

Someone who is reputed to be a realized being or Dharma practitioner but has not actually reached such a level belies his reputation. He is an impostor. People may say of us, "He is a highly realized being, he is a great meditator," but if we listen to such sweet-sounding praises and conceitedly believe them, we become impostors, for these are but empty names that we do not merit, and we risk seeing our lives run their course in vain.

> If one acts contrary to the Dharma,

then despite adopting the appearance of a Dharma practitioner, spending many years in retreat, being reputed to have a high degree of realization, or being proud of one's learning,

After death, one cannot but go to the hells.

What then is the principal cause for these fifteen ways in which the practice goes wrong? It is that instead of being concerned with future lives we are only interested in achieving fame and status in this life. So it is important to recognize these faults within ourselves so that we can then apply the correct antidotes. Just as we would identify a thief in order to punish him, we must recognize our own defects so that we can correct them. As the Kadampa teachers used to say, "Recognize your own faults; do not go looking for others' defects." This is how we should avoid these fifteen wrong paths.

> *The root and source of all these is attachment and clinging to the things of this life, so recognize them as faults and get rid of them.*

19

> *Showing, by means of twenty-six kinds of folly, where indulging in negative actions will lead.*

These twenty-six kinds of folly are a sign that we are not acting skillfully in accordance with the Dharma. Instead of eagerly practicing the Dharma, which entails meaningful enthusiasm, we readily throw ourselves into worldly activities and negative actions, with misplaced enthusiasm.

> *Taking twenty-six examples of folly in ordinary life,*
>
> **Son, there are twenty-six kinds of folly** *in the holy Dharma.*
>
> **It is foolish not to fear an army whose arrival is inevitable,**
>
> *that is, to have no fear of death.*

To not be afraid when a huge army is about to invade one's country and to think, "I'll manage; I'm not afraid to give my life; I shall send them packing on my own" is very rash and stupid. The point of this metaphor is that, of all our enemies, the most deadly is death itself, and the only thing that will help us combat death is to practice the Dharma. So to indulge in worldly activities instead of practicing the Dharma and to still pretend we are not afraid of death is thoroughly foolish.

> **It is foolish not to repay a debt you have definitely incurred,**
>
> *that is, not to purify your karmic debts, negative actions, and obscurations.*

> When you borrow a lot of money, you have to gradually pay it back, a little bit each year. But if you were to suddenly

find yourself having to pay it back all at once, you would be left destitute. It is the same with all the negative actions you have done with your body, speech, and mind throughout your past lives. They are like a letter of debt, and if you do nothing about it and do not gradually purify all your obscurations and negative actions in order to pay it off, it will drag you down to the lower realms of samsara.

It is foolish to run toward an enemy who will surely take you captive,

that is, to cling to samsara unafraid.

If you run toward an enemy, it is quite certain that you will be captured, imprisoned, tortured, and dismembered. Likewise, if you fail to recognize that samsara is exclusively a place of difficulty and suffering, where one can only be the loser in the face of enemies such as birth, old age, sickness, and death, and instead of being afraid of these enemies you perceive them as pleasurable and are even attached to them, you are very foolish.

It is foolish to enjoy carrying a greater load than you can bear,

that is, to not shy away from the ripened effect of negative actions.

When you go somewhere carrying a load on your back, it is important to make sure it is a reasonable weight, one that you can easily carry a long way. To think, "I can carry a mountain" is thoroughly foolish. But it is no less stupid to act without steering clear of negative actions, ignoring the fact that they will inevitably lead you to the lower realms in your future lives.

It is foolish to be eager to go somewhere unpleasant.

Only an idiot would gladly go somewhere dry and barren rather than to a region where food is naturally plentiful and clothing easy to obtain. Likewise it is utterly stupid *to take pleasure in doing negative actions.*

Even a very minor negative action will have serious consequences far into the future that one can scarcely imagine, as described by Nagarjuna in his *Letter to a Friend*:

> For one whole day on earth three hundred darts
> Might strike you hard and cause you grievous pain,
> But that could never illustrate or match
> A fraction of the smallest pain in hell.[84]

The hell realms are nothing other than the result of one's own negative actions. If we ignore this and happily go on committing negative deeds—taking life, telling lies, fooling and cheating people, and so on—we are being thoroughly stupid.

It is foolish to leap into an abyss where you are certain to die.

Nobody but a mad person would jump over the edge of a cliff with a sheer drop of several thousand meters into the jaws of certain death. Yet people in this world do things thinking only of fame and renown, or go to war with their minds full of hatred, thereby creating the causes for their future rebirth in the hells. Similarly, they greedily amass wealth and hoard it for themselves, neither giving to those in need nor making offerings to the Three Jewels: thus they create the causes for rebirth as pretas. They have no faith in the Buddha's teachings and ignore the law by which positive and negative actions give corresponding effects: their stupidity and lack of discernment cause rebirth in the animal realm. All these negative actions must be avoided, for to indulge in them is

to jump into the three lower realms,

ignoring the enormous harm that will result.

It is foolish to sow buckwheat and hope to grow barley,

that is, to hope that negative actions will result in happiness.

Someone who tills a field and sows buckwheat seed in it expecting to harvest a crop of barley the following year can only be a fool. But we are no better. We spend this life pursuing honors and fame, building up wealth and property, and thinking how to get rid of our opponents and how to protect and favor our family and friends. To achieve all this, we throw ourselves into performing the ten negative actions such as killing and cheating others. When we are successful in these, we imagine we have attained greatness and we pride ourselves on the result, thinking this is something to be happy about. Yet we have only managed to build up a pile of negative actions that will bring us enormous suffering.

It is foolish to expect the sun to shine into a north-facing cave.

If you go to a cave that faces north expecting to enjoy yourself sunbathing, then you are going to have a long wait.[85] It is equally stupid

to expect the teacher's blessings to happen when you have no devotion.

The teacher is a true Buddha. His compassion and blessings make no distinction between one being and another. But just as we cannot expect the sunlight to enter a house when all the doors are closed and the windows shuttered, we cannot hope to receive the teacher's blessings if we lack devotion and close ourselves to those blessings.

It is foolish to place your hope and trust in someone who is obviously going to deceive you,

that is, to be attached to the good things of this life.

Right now we are being fooled by the things we hanker after, like comfortable clothes, delicious food, and fame and renown. But they are no better than children's toys or the mimicking antics of a monkey. It is important to realize they are tricking us and to not be distracted by them or crave them. Otherwise, if we pursue ordinary pleasures like dancing, singing, gambling, recounting stories, and listening to others' gossip, we are wasting the opportunity we have to determine our future lives.

It is foolish for someone of humble origins to vie with one of royal blood,

like a common subject contending with a prince; that is, to hope to develop noble qualities when one is just an ordinary person.

One would never consider someone from a very humble family to have the same rank as a prince, however much he might try to act like him or rival him. In the same way, someone very ordinary who pretends he is a realized being but has none of the extraordinary qualities of supreme beings—such as having purified obscurations, attained perfection in study, reflection, and meditation, and overcome worldly distractions—cannot hope to develop those qualities.

It is foolish to hope to be rich when you possess nothing,

that is, to hope to be other people's master when you have no qualities yourself.

Someone who hopes to become wealthy without running a business and working hard will never get rich. Likewise, you can never expect to become a teacher and gain other people's admiration and respect if you have not acquired the necessary good qualities that come from practicing the Dharma.

It is foolish for a cripple to try to ride a horse,

that is, to make a promise you cannot keep.

A person with a broken leg who mounts a wild horse in the hope of having a pleasant ride will inevitably be thrown. It is equally foolish to promise yourself or anyone else that you will carry out a big task when you are unable to do so. Not only will you not complete the task, it will also bring shame on you.

It is foolish to say you have completed a task without having done any work,

that is, to disdain skillful means when you have not realized the natural state.

Unless you have gone through all the stages of the practice, to say, "I have realized the natural state; I have gained sound experience and realization" is just foolish prattling. You may think it is unnecessary to accumulate merit, to purify yourself, to have the determination to be free, to wish to get out of samsara, and to be content with little, but until you have truly realized the wisdom of no-self, such disregard for the methods of the practice is as foolish as a person with no legs thinking he will be able to walk great distances.

> It is foolish, when you have still not recovered from an illness, to get fed up with the doctor and to take a liking to someone who has prepared a vial of poison,
>
> *that is, to have no respect for the doctor who cures the disease of the five poisons while relishing the company of those who indulge in negative actions.*

Whether you are suffering from a phlegm disorder or an energy imbalance, you should undergo the full treatment and do everything the doctor says until your illness is cured. However difficult that may be, however unpleasant the taste of the medicine, or however painful the treatment, it is all for your own good. But if you are unable to endure the treatment and you do whatever you like—even happily taking things that are dangerous for you—you will end up causing your own death.

Likewise, if you do not want to take the medicine for the sickness of the five poisons by following the teachings expounded by the Buddha and, instead, you prefer to keep the company of people who indulge in negative actions and take you hunting and whoring, you will destroy yourself.

> It is foolish for a merchant with nothing to sell to be a hearty eater,
>
> *that is, to teach others when you have not realized the meaning yourself.*

A big merchant who abandons his business and does nothing but spend his time eating will soon exhaust his wealth and find himself destitute. In the same way, to want to teach others the Dharma when you have not attained liberation yourself is pure folly. You will not be able to benefit them if you have neither acquired a sound understanding of the teachings nor gained any realization through practice. Like a wooden mill,[86] you will make a lot of noise but produce nothing useful.

> *It is foolish to run off without listening to your father's advice,*
> *that is, to take the wrong direction without listening to the*
> *teacher's instructions.*

If we ignore the advice of our father who tells us, "This is how you should proceed if you want to succeed, overcome adversity, and protect your own interests," and we do not follow right ways even in worldly terms, but act rashly, get drunk, and do all sorts of mischief, we are surely being very foolish. The same is true if we do not do as our teacher says when he tells us, "If you practice in this way, if you avoid this and adopt that, then you will progress toward enlightenment."

> **It is foolish for a daughter to ignore her mother's advice,**

for if mother and daughter quarrel, it will be to her detriment for a long time afterward. Likewise, it is foolish

> *to prefer the pleasures of the senses in this life to what is beneficial*
> *for future lives.*
> **It is foolish, having left the house naked and then found**
> **clothes, to return home again without them;**
> *that is, having learned the Dharma, to get rich instead of*
> *practicing.*

Having found the clothes of Dharma, we do not wear them—we do not study and meditate, but return to worldly activities like doing business and trying to become wealthy. This is a great waste.

> **It is foolish to take off your boots when there is no river;**
> *that is, to interrupt the practice of Dharma when you do not have*
> *the confidence of realization.*

Apart from when you have to ford a river, if you take off your boots, you will simply hurt your feet on the stones. Similarly, if you stop practicing the Dharma before gaining sound realization, you will only do yourself harm. This also applies to interrupting other people's practice in an untimely manner, when you do not have realization yourself. For example, you might say to them, "You should practice Mahamudra or the Great Perfection. There is no point in doing prostrations, in purifying your obscurations, or in accumulating merit." Or you might tell someone who is practicing to study, and someone who is studying to stop wasting their life learning things and to practice instead.

> **It is foolish to drink salty water that will never quench your thirst,**
>
> *that is, to have desires and never know contentment.*

The more one drinks salty water, the thirstier one gets. Likewise, if you indulge your thirst for sensual pleasures, you will never have enough. As it is said, desire is like a hungry dog that is never satiated.

> **It is foolish to be oblivious of the inside when the outside has collapsed;**
>
> *your body is old, yet your mind is still full of attachment and aversion.*

It is the height of folly to remain inside a house unaware that it is deteriorating and needs urgent repairs—with the roof about to fall in and the walls collapsing. It is the same with our body: we do not realize that it is aging year after year, that it is slowly breaking down. And yet inside we have more attachment and aversion than ever, and we give no thought to our future lives.

> **It is foolish to be clever at counseling others while giving yourself the wrong advice.**
>
> *You do not practice what you preach.*

Some people are very good at giving other people advice. Their words are like rays of sunshine, helping people all over the country, and yet they do not know how to conduct their own lives properly. Similarly, if you teach others the Dharma but do not know how to apply it yourself, what you say is in contradiction to what you do.

It is foolish to scale a fortress without a ladder.

It would be unthinkable to try and enter a fortress with very high walls without using a ladder to reach the top of the wall. Likewise it is stupid

> *to boast of heading for liberation without completing the two accumulations.*

> **It is foolish for children to not want to do a job they will definitely have to do;**

> *that is, for beginners to put off virtuous activities until later.*

Some people, instead of trying to learn something, to improve themselves, and to develop good qualities, waste their time like children playing useless games. Beginners in the Dharma are equally foolish if they remain idle and carefree instead of being diligent in practices such as accumulating merit, performing prostrations, making offerings, and practicing the generation and perfection phases.

> **It is foolish not to be worried about crossing an unfordable river,**

> *that is, to be unconcerned by birth, old age, sickness, and death.*

If you were to arrive on the bank of a big river where there was no ford and you did not have a boat or other means for crossing the river, it would be ridiculous not to be worried about how you were going to get across. It would be similarly absurd not to be concerned about the four great rivers of birth, old age, sickness, and death, which are inherent to the samsaric condition and are unavoidable. If you do not use the Dharma to prepare yourself to face death and these other sufferings, and you simply get carried away by worldly activities, you are deluding yourself.

It is foolish to look elsewhere when *the Buddha's wisdom* is already within you.

You are like someone who has a wish-fulfilling gem but does not know it and puts all his effort into doing business, farming the land, and so on, in the hope of becoming wealthy.

The above can all be summarized as five faults:

1. *hankering after the things of this life;*
2. *wanting to have the result without the cause,* that is, without accumulating merit and wisdom;
3. *not listening to the words of the teacher,* that is, his instructions, and being a Dharma practitioner only in name;
4. *pledging yourself to the holy Dharma but then following ordinary ways* that incorporate attachment and aversion; and
5. *not practicing what you preach,* in other words, speaking in terms of the Dharma and acting in contradiction to the Dharma.

20

Nine pieces of personal advice for softening one's being.[87]

What do we mean by personal advice?

This is personal advice because it consists of oral instructions spoken directly—advice to be kept in the heart.

It is the well-intentioned advice, backed by experience, that a father gives his children. If they follow it, they are likely to succeed in whatever they do. Likewise, if we follow our teacher's instructions, we can obtain the ordinary and supreme accomplishments. As the great siddha Saraha said,

When the teacher's words enter your heart,
It is like seeing you have a treasure in the palm of your hand.

Son, there are nine pieces of personal advice.

The first one is

If you want to compete, take on the Buddha.

Look at the Capable One's life and train yourself following in his footsteps.

If you must compete with someone, vie with the Buddha. Take the example of Buddha Shakyamuni, who accumulated merit and wisdom over three measureless kalpas and, in order to receive teachings, gave his own limbs, his body, his kingdom, and his queen and children. He underwent incredible hardships such as piercing his body with a thousand nails. You should think, "I must do likewise." Once you have this intention to match the Buddha, to do as he did, although you may not be able to act on such a vast scale now, you will definitely be able gradually to progress toward Buddhahood.

If you want to backbite, slander the yidam.

People are fond of saying all sorts of things about others behind their backs, mentioning their names again and again. Instead of slandering others in this way, "slander" the yidam: utter his name repeatedly by reciting his mantra all the time.

All the time, without fail, be diligent in the approach and accomplishment practices,

murmuring his name day and night in the continuous recitation of the mantra. If you constantly recite the *mani*, the mantra of Avalokiteshvara, it is as though you were continuously calling him by his name—"He who is endowed with the Jewel and the Lotus"—and there is no doubt that you will receive his guidance and blessings.

If you have to be mean, be so with the instructions.[88]

In ordinary life there are some who greedily hoard wealth, filling their coffers with diamonds and gold. They check regularly to see how much they have and think only of how they might acquire more. We should have the same sort of meanness and interest in the practice of the generation and perfection phases, constantly wondering how we can improve our practice while at the same time keeping these gems hidden away in the treasury of our minds.

> *If you keep them secret and practice them, blessings, experience, and realization will swiftly come.*
>
> **If you are going to be unkind, be unkind to your negative actions.**
>
> *Do not look back at negative actions and friends who act negatively.*[89]

Someone unkind may seem very pleasant and well spoken the first time we meet him, but gradually his bad character will emerge and we will start to quarrel and fight. It is the same with negative actions and acquaintances who indulge in negative actions. Do not stay with them as you would do with your friends. Avoid them as much as possible by applying the antidote.

> **By all means be munificent—with the teacher.**

Give unsparingly, particularly in making offerings to the teacher, to whom you should feel able to offer all your wealth and possessions, and even your own body.

> *It is more beneficial than making offerings to the Buddhas of the three times.*

The best kind of offering is that of our practice and realization. And though we may be unable to completely realize the Buddha's intentions through our practice, if we can at least have a good heart and help others, this will also fulfill the Buddha's wishes.

> **If you want to give someone the cold shoulder, make it samsara.**

After a quarrel, we may turn our back on the other person. But our real quarrel should be with samsara.

Investigate your mind minutely.

If you find any flaws in your mind, get rid of them, and nurture any good qualities you have, like respect, devotion, and confidence in the law of cause and effect—in short,

> *Be diligent in the methods that will prevent your taking birth in samsara in the future.*

If you are going to enumerate faults, list your own defects.

Look inward and find fault with yourself: "I'm not meditating correctly; I'm not studying properly. . . ." This is a good way to spur one's diligence.

> *Depart from the land of your hidden defects.*

Bid farewell to your laziness, lack of diligence, and other faults. This also implies giving everything you own, your wealth and possessions, to other people and going somewhere else to live.

When you have the victory, give it to others.

Give everything you have unstintingly to others. As Milarepa said, "If you do something good for others, they will regard you as a celestial being." If you forget your own selfish motives and consider others more important, being kind to them and treating them with compassion, in the long term it can only help you.

> *Ultimately it will be for your own good.*

As for the sutras and tantras, tease them out like wool.

To make woolen cloth one first has to wash the wool and then tease it out into separate fibers before spinning it into yarn for weaving. If the wool is teased out properly, it is easy to make the yarn. Likewise,

> *Seeking the teachings impartially and integrating them with your mind, correct your practice and your own mind. This is very important.*

21

Nine pieces of heartfelt advice for keeping a low profile.

Son, there are nine pieces of heartfelt advice.

Be a child of the mountains.

Being in a place where there are a lot of distractions leads to much attachment, to arguments, and to likes and dislikes. One's meditation becomes dispersed. On the other hand,

> *For the great meditator who never leaves the mountains, good qualities grow day by day, month by month.*

And there is a saying: "Be the child of the mountains; drape yourself in mist."

Eat the food of famine-time.

Do not let food, clothes, and conversation get the upper hand.[90]

If you need lavish helpings of food or an unusual diet, you will have to spend much time and effort to get these, and this again will be a cause for distraction. Remember that whether or not the food you eat is delicious, it all ends up as excrement. Be content to make do with enough food, however plain, to take the edge off your hunger and sustain your body. The same applies to clothing and conversation: you should have little care for special clothes and reduce worldly conversation to a minimum.

Do the things that please the enemy.

If you do not cast your ordinary ways to the wind, you will never destroy the castle of desire and hatred.

If you do not resist or compete with your enemies and do not become attached to your friends,[91] any enemy you have will be delighted and think, "This guy's a pushover. He isn't even trying to contend with me. I shall easily get the better of him." By casting away all hopes of becoming rich in this life, of becoming a governor or someone powerful, you will be free from the eight ordinary concerns and you will destroy the citadel of attachment and aversion.

Wear clothes that no one wants.

Without any attachment it is easy to practice.

Dress yourself in clothes that are sufficient to protect you from the cold and wind, without caring whether they look nice. If you use clothes that have been thrown away because nobody wants them, you will not need to worry how you use them: they will simply serve to protect you from the cold. But having to find beautiful, expensive clothes will simply involve you in unnecessary effort and cause further distraction.

Flee the crowds, alone.

As with the example given earlier of the young maiden who removes the bangles from her wrists in order to make less noise when she washes her hands, if we get away from being surrounded by lots of people, our meditation will not be broken up by useless chatter.

> *Your virtuous activities will presently increase, there will be no obstacles, and you will get food and provisions as well.*

Be without a handle for your relations,

that is, a handle by which they can take hold of you and pull you. If you are caught by ordinary attachment to home life, you will be preoccupied with becoming a rich and influential householder. So

> *Unless you give up your longing and affection* for your relatives and friends, *you will not be able to cut the ties*

that keep you bound to them. Therefore,

> *Do not let people take your nose rope.*[92]

Your attachment makes you like an animal with a rope through its nose: people can make it go wherever they want. As long as you do not leave that rope in the hands of others you will be free to make your own decisions, particularly for practicing the Dharma.

Tie your fickleness down with a rope.

The human mind, like water, goes wherever it is led, so tether your mind with the rope of mindfulness.

People have fickle minds; they listen to everything other people say. They change their minds all the time and are unable to concentrate on anything or make firm decisions. If you tell them to study, they rush off to find a book and start studying. Then if you tell them to practice, they immediately stop studying and start practicing instead. And if you tell them to go and work and engage in ordinary activities, they immediately go and do that. But they will never achieve anything by acting this way.

The human mind is the same, constantly wavering and changing direction, like grass on a mountain pass, which bends as the wind blows. It is like water, which goes wherever you channel it: if you dig a ditch or break the earth in front of floodwater, it immediately flows along the channel you have made for it. So instead of letting the mind go wherever it likes, you should tether it with the rope of mindfulness, just as one ties up a horse with a halter to prevent it from wandering off. Concentrate your mind one-pointedly on the Dharma instead of giving in to its whims and letting it do whatever occurs to it.

Abandon havens of delight.

Some places, such as beautiful gardens, may seem very delightful: everyone is dancing and singing or talking, and one feels thoroughly at ease. But this is where one's attachment and aversion will grow. Therefore,

> *Do not be attached to the pleasures of samsara. If you do not forsake them, you will never stop the constant stream of negative actions, misery, and bad talk.*

Focus your mind on space.

It is important to thoroughly familiarize yourself with the two kinds of no-self.

Space is something one cannot take hold of. It is free of preference and partiality. It has no limits or dimensions. It cannot be defined; there is nothing in it that one can grasp. You should aspire to practicing like that, free from conceptual elaboration, and to realizing the two kinds of no-self, the no-self of the individual and that of phenomena. It is very important to get used to this meditation and to gain experience in it over a long period of time.

22

Instructions, through five beatitudes, on taking good and bad circumstances equally.

Son, there are five beatitudes.

Blessed are they who recognize samsara for what it is: a poisonous tree of suffering.

Having recognized that its very nature is suffering, they avoid it.

Samsara is like a poisonous plant. Enjoying it and indulging in samsaric actions will bring us ruin, just as eating a poisonous plant, attractive and delicious though it may be, will make one very ill and even kill one. Once we recognize it as being poisonous, we avoid taking it even though its leaves or flowers or fruit look beautiful; and thus we stay healthy. Likewise, once we recognize that there is nothing but suffering in samsaric activities, we will no longer be attracted to them. Instead, we will recoil and avoid them.

Blessed are they who see those that give rise to afflictive emotions as spiritual friends.

When they see an enemy, for example, he is a master making them develop patience.

What makes afflictive emotions arise in our minds is attachment to those we like and aversion to those we do not like. But if instead of hating those we consider enemies we think of helping them, and instead of being attached to friends and relatives we simply regard them as illusions or as people we meet in a dream, we will free ourselves of the notions of friends and enemies; we will feel relaxed and happy. When you see enemies, people who might harm you, try and develop patience. Regard them, moreover, as friends helping you to progress on the path. If they actually do harm you, think that this is retribution for negative actions you did in the past and that you are thus purifying yourself of those actions. When you are able to do this and bear such circumstances patiently, your enemies become teachers helping you to develop the precious bodhichitta.

> **Blessed are they who correctly view the master who has trained in the three wisdoms.**
>
> *By seeing the teacher as the Buddha and his instructions as nectar, they will be set on the path to lasting liberation.*

When you see a sublime master—sublime from having perfected wisdom through hearing, wisdom through reflection, and wisdom through meditation—you should realize that to emulate this teacher in the way he acts, speaks, and thinks will bring you happiness in this life and future lives. Seeing him as the Buddha in person, you must never tire of drinking the nectar of his teachings. In this way you will truly be set on the path to liberation.

> **Blessed are they who see everything—outer and inner things and circumstances—as being without origin.[93]**
>
> *By doing so they will realize the wisdom mind of the Buddha.*

When you see that external phenomena (forms, smells, sounds, tastes, and tangible things) and your inner reactions to them (attachment to those that are pleasurable, aversion to those that are not) have never come into existence, do not truly exist in the moment, and will not go anywhere when they cease to exist, you will realize the void nature of all these external and inner phenomena. At that time it will be impossible for your mind to be deceived by external perceptions. You will be free from the impulse to accept some things and reject others, and you will easily realize the Buddha's wisdom.

> **Blessed are they who postpone all activities and set out on the unmistaken path.**

Such people understand that all the busy activities of body, speech, and mind are completely unnecessary and decide to drop them since they will soon be dead. They then set their minds to one-pointedly practicing the supreme Dharma, the unmistaken path to liberation, for the duration of this life. Such people are very close to liberation and are not distracted by ordinary activities.

> In short, if they give up all the activities of this life and put the perfect instructions into practice, the sun of happiness is certain to rise in their minds.

23

Avoiding the twenty causes of breaking the samaya, the samaya being a distinguishing point between sutra and tantra.[94]

Son, there are twenty things that lead to breaches of samaya.

Apart from in exceptional circumstances,

To be *deliberately*[95] **secretive about your teacher while extolling your own virtues leads to a breach of samaya.**

There might, on occasion, be an important reason for concealing the identity of our teacher, but if we do so simply because the teacher is a very humble person, or a wandering hermit, or because he is not a very learned scholar, and we extol our own qualities, boasting about the different teachings we have received and now hold, this will lead to a breach of samaya, as will showing contempt for our teacher.

> *Unless it is* specifically in order *to get rid of* afflictive emotions or to acquire disillusionment with samsara and determination to be free, for anyone[96] to view an erudite scholar and an uneducated person as equals leads to a breach of samaya.

> **Competition,** *with self-seeking and hostile motives,* **between patrons and disciples leads to a breach of samaya.**

For example, a disciple who sees that the teacher has a generous patron might try and attract the patron's support, thereby diverting the patron's support away from the teacher.

To have the intention of offering *the teacher your wealth,*
property, and so forth that are yours to dispose of[97] **and to put**
off doing so leads to a breach of samaya.

You might start by thinking, "I will offer my teacher a hundred dol-
lars," and then think, "Maybe fifty will do." To reduce an offering in this
way, to delay making it, or to regret it afterward causes the samaya to
degenerate and also exhausts your good fortune.

Receiving as many teachings as you can possibly hear
without considering whether or not there are conflicts and suchlike
in the lineage **leads to a breach of samaya.**

Before receiving a teaching from a teacher, we should check whether
the lineage or anything connected with the teacher has been stained by
breaches of samaya in the past, because if this is the case, even if we
practice that teaching, it will not give rise to the common and supreme
accomplishments. If we simply take it for granted that there has been no
breach of samaya and that everything is pure and correct, we will be
stained by samaya breaches ourselves. Whatever our connection with
such stained lineages, our own good fortune will diminish: even in ordinary terms we will become poor, and so on.

An alternative version appears in the Commentary:[98] *"To*
receive the teachings unworthily . . ." Any teachings you receive
must be with the prior approval of the teacher.

If we receive teachings against the teacher's wish, or without first
checking whether he has agreed, or we use various means to oblige the
teacher to give us teachings without being sure whether he considers
those teachings suitable for us, this will lead to a breach of samaya.

When the time is not ripe, using pressure or complaint

To insist on getting the instructions leads to a breach
of samaya.

The teacher knows the disciple's capacity and therefore the most suitable teaching to give. So if we use different means such as cunning and

insistence to get teachings against the teacher's wishes, we will cause our samaya to degenerate.

> *Using lies and cunning* to deceive your teacher and fellow disciples, whom you should consider as your father and as your brothers and sisters, leads to a breach of samaya.

> To put the blame on the master for wrong *that is not your own doing* leads to a breach of samaya.

It may somehow happen that a fault or something wrong is associated with us even though we have not really done it ourselves. But if we claim that the teacher or our Dharma friends are responsible, we will cause our samaya to degenerate.

> *In a spirit of competition,* to treat the master as a rival leads to a breach of samaya.

One might, for example, vie with one's teacher or Dharma brothers and sisters with the wrong kind of motivation, thinking, "Let's see if I am as learned as they are," or try to compete with them in terms of spiritual accomplishment.

> To abuse the master's confidence, *divulging secrets he has entrusted you with or keeping your own defects secret from the teacher,* leads to a breach of samaya.

If the teacher entrusts us with secret instructions and tells us not to disclose them to anyone else until we have practiced them and obtained signs of accomplishment and realization, and we then spread them to other people like wealthy patrons who come and make large offerings, we are breaking the samaya. This is also the case if we try to hide our own defects from the teacher.

> To scorn his kindness, *rather than repaying it when you are able,* leads to a breach of samaya.

When we are in a position to do so, we should not fail to repay our teacher's kindness. On the other hand, if we do not see that any progress we have made in the practice is entirely due to his kindness, and instead we scorn his kindness and think, "It is because I am so diligent and perfect that I have all these qualities," our samaya will degenerate.

> **To be intent on looking after your own interests** *by being utterly self-centered, self-seeking, and proud* **leads to a breach of samaya.**

When we are following the teacher and serving him, if we behave too selfishly, the teacher and the other disciples will get tired of us. Likewise, if we are very proud, this too will upset the teacher. Instead we should maintain a humble position and be free of pride.

> **To steal instructions and books**—*writing them down secretly without asking your teacher or fellow disciples or, worse still, obtaining them by actually stealing the texts*—**leads to a breach of samaya.**

Someone who copies secret instructions without permission or, even worse, actually steals books or notes is breaking the samaya, particularly if he also gives them to others. Furthermore, the instructions in question will bring them no benefit.

> **To secretly enumerate the master's faults**—*the hidden defects of the teacher and his retinue*—**leads to a breach of samaya.**

If it happens that the teacher or some of the people in his retinue have defects or hidden faults and we tell others about them behind their backs, we are breaking the samaya.

> **To block another's aspiration,** *discouraging someone who has faith,* **leads to a breach of samaya.**

If you frustrate the wishes of someone who wholeheartedly wishes to practice the Dharma or who has no desire to achieve anything in samsara, you will cause your samaya to degenerate.

> **To make an outer show of the inner practices,** *performing the secret activities prematurely,* **leads to a breach of samaya.**

If the time is ripe and we are completely free from the ties of afflictive emotions, practicing the secret activities of the Mantrayana will enhance our practice. But performing these activities without the teacher's permission or authority and without our having gained complete confidence and stability in the view, meditation, and action will cause our samaya to degenerate. This applies also to making an outward show of the Mantrayana's inner practices.

> **To be jealous of vajra brothers and sisters**—*one's general brothers and sisters and closest vajra siblings*[99]—and to act in such a way that one is always in conflict with everyone else **leads to a breach of samaya.**
>
> **To act indiscriminately without a teacher or instructions,** *practicing just as one pleases without having obtained the teachings or, if you have obtained them, without approval,* **leads to a breach of samaya.**

Practicing teachings we have not received or, even if we have received them, practicing them without proper permission from the teacher—thus engaging in a version of the teachings we have made up ourselves—leads to our spoiling the samaya.

> **To masquerade as a teacher,** *giving clever explanations of one's own invention with no aural lineage and without knowing anything oneself,* **leads to a breach of samaya.**

This refers to someone who is ignorant and has none of the qualities obtained through hearing the teachings, reflecting on them, and putting them into practice. He has not received the instructions through a genuine lineage but pretends to teach others, giving them instructions he has made up himself.

> *If the Buddha taught that one should not, with animosity or attachment, look down on even the Tirthikas, this is no less applicable in the case of the others. For this reason,*
>
> **To criticize teachings and those who practice them leads to a breach of samaya.**

It is not proper to criticize other religions, or even the lower Buddhist vehicles, in a hostile or petty way, thinking that the teachings we have received are much more advanced. If it is wrong to criticize those who have false, non-Buddhist views, one need hardly mention how wrong it is to criticize other views included within the Buddha's teaching. So rather than speak ill of other teachings and practitioners, which would cause a breach of samaya, we should have pure perception with regard to all of them.

> To exhibit[100] the instructions to unsuitable vessels, *giving the secret teachings literally[101] to those in the lesser vehicles and the like,* leads to a breach of samaya.

Those who practice the lesser vehicles may not have the necessary openness of mind to accept the teachings of the Great Vehicle—the profound teachings on the view of emptiness and so on—and they may not be fit vessels for these teachings. Therefore, openly disclosing these teachings to them without first checking whether they have the capacity can lead to spoiling their practice and cause our own samaya to degenerate.

> *Furthermore, having learned the different categories of root and branch samayas that have to be kept, the causes that lead to their degenerating, the disadvantages of their degenerating, and the benefits of keeping them, you should maintain constant diligence with mindfulness and carefulness.*

There are many different categories of samaya—the root samayas of body, speech, and mind, the twenty-five branch samayas, and so forth. If we transgress the samaya by having wrong views concerning the teacher, for example, or by doubting the teachings of the Secret Mantrayana, we create the causes for suffering in this life and in future lives. We therefore need to know the causes of breaking the samayas and the difficulties that will result, as well as the benefits of keeping them. If we guard the samaya as well as we protect our own eyes, all the accomplishments will come without any effort. So it is necessary at all times to remind ourselves exactly what we should do and what we should avoid, remaining constantly watchful and concerned as to whether we are actually conducting ourselves accordingly.

This completes these instructions, which are like a mother who guides and cares for her child, giving him good advice and teaching him the right way to behave. Through them a faithful vessel will be inspired to practice the Dharma and, relying on the superior training in discipline in accordance with the general pitakas, will keep it as the basis of his practice and thereby transform his being.

This was the second section from the *Eighty Chapters of Personal Advice*, the instruction on perfect discipline, the basis.

Concentration

Instructions on the superior training of the mind, the perfect means.

Of the three trainings—discipline, concentration, and wisdom—this section deals with concentration.

It contains seventeen chapters.

24

Showing how the four blessings help one's meditation.

The combination of the teacher's blessings, the student's devotion, and the profundity of the instructions makes experience grow swiftly.

If we want to progress on the path to liberation, we have to benefit from the teacher's blessings. Without them, no amount of learning, power, or wealth will ever help us reach liberation. However, unless we have such fervent devotion that we see the teacher as the Buddha himself, we will not receive his blessings. It is said,[102]

> Unless the sun of devotion shines
> On the snow peak of the teacher's four kayas,
> The stream of his blessings will never flow.
> So earnestly arouse devotion in your mind.

Moreover, we need the profound instructions, and to obtain them we should be prepared to give everything we have, even our lives. Through these three things—the teacher's blessings, the devotion that enables us to receive them, and the instructions, which we should value greatly—experience will grow swiftly. In the best case we will progress by fulfilling the teacher's wishes and by practicing, in the middling case by serving him with our body, speech, and mind, and in the least ideal case by making material offerings to him.

Son, there are four practices that confer blessing.

What are these four kinds of blessing?

> *When you know your mind to be the absolute nature, all objects are liberated in the absolute nature and you will be unaffected by external circumstances.*

The teacher's blessings will show us the nature of our mind, though this is something we already have inherently. When we achieve stable recognition of this absolute nature, all outer phenomena, which normally give rise to emotions such as attachment and aversion, will reinforce our practice rather than harm it. They will become helpers for our practice. The mind will no longer be deceived by external circumstances, and as a result our concentration and our realization of the view, meditation, and action will swiftly grow.

> This is **the blessing of yourself, as exemplified by the sole of a shoe.**

If you cover the soles of your feet with leather, the result will be the same as if you were to cover the whole earth with leather: you will not hurt your feet on things like thorns and stones. This is like blessing yourself.

Having received this "blessing of yourself," in the same way that one can transform iron into copper and then into gold by alchemy, you will realize that all phenomena are the naturally arisen primal wisdom. This realization will be unstained by ordinary concepts associated with the adventitious obscurations that veil this primal wisdom.

Once all phenomena are recognized as the naturally arisen primal wisdom, they are beyond adventitious conceptual characteristics.

This is **the blessing of perceptions, as exemplified by a mountain torrent in spate.**

A torrent in spate running down the mountainside carries away all the rocks and trees and other things in the valley. Likewise if all outer phenomena become helpers enhancing one's practice, then the blessings that come from perceiving things in such a way sweep away all the afflictive emotions from one's nature.

With one-pointed concentration, there is no interruption in the flow.

A great river is something that never ceases; it is never exhausted; it flows continuously. One will be able to reach the level of the yoga that is like a flowing river—meaning the practice will never have any interruption. Likewise, if one can maintain concentration day and night,

This is **the blessing of the mind, as exemplified by the middle of a great river.**

Karma and afflictive emotions will not be able to interrupt this continuous flow of concentration.

Like the black jackal, whose eyes see as well by night as by day, one is introduced to the nonduality of perceiver and perceived.

Having been introduced to the absolute nature, which is free from a subject that perceives and an object that is perceived,

This is **the blessing** of the realization **of nonduality, as exemplified by a jackal.**

Now, by recognizing that appearances are the mind, the mind is empty, emptiness is nondual, and nonduality is self-liberating, one clears away all misconceptions about the outer, inner, secret, and absolute.

In the process of recognizing the nature of one's mind, the natural state of mind, we begin by saying, "Outer appearances are the mind." In other words, whether we perceive outer phenomena as pure or impure, in both cases they are the projection or product of our own minds. Outer objects are not inherently pure or impure. Next, when we turn inward and examine the mind carefully, we cannot find any color, shape, or location for this mind: it is what we term "empty." Yet these two—outer phenomena that appear and mind that is empty—are not two separate things like the two horns of a goat. They are united: the mind appears as the perceptions of phenomena yet it is empty; it is empty yet it appears. Moreover, the realization of this intrinsically nondual nature of appearance and mind is itself free from grasping at the notion of nonduality. It is important to know how to let this natural liberation of nonduality take place: if we cling to the concept of emptiness, we have to liberate that clinging to emptiness; if on the other hand we cling to appearance, we should let that clinging dissolve. In this way, we should dispel all misunderstandings and doubts about the realization of the different levels of emptiness: outer emptiness, inner emptiness, secret emptiness, and absolute emptiness.

> However, this alone is not much help if you have not liberated
> your own mind into the absolute nature, just as ice, despite being
> water, does not function as water unless you melt it. So it is
> important to meditate with intense devotion.

The result of dispelling all misconceptions and doubts is that everything is liberated in the absolute nature. But unless you can free this mind, which has attachment and aversion, in the absolute nature, it will not help simply to think, "Appearance is empty, emptiness and appearances are one." Your mind will be like ice. Although the ice that forms when water freezes in winter is essentially water, it does not behave like water. Until you melt it, it is hard and sharp; water is soft and fluid. Ice can support the weight of objects; water penetrates and always flows down to the lowest point. So it is important to meditate with intense devotion to the teacher. If you have fervent devotion, the blessings will enter, and it will be easy to travel the path to liberation.

> Although a yogi currently on the path has truly realized the
> absolute nature of his mind, he has not yet liberated all phenomena

in the absolute nature, and so qualities such as the twelve hundred
qualities do not manifestly appear. Nevertheless, through gradual
habituation to that realization, all phenomena are liberated or
dissolved into the absolute nature, and at that time all the
qualities up to the level of ultimate Buddhahood become manifest.

As a result of the teacher's introduction, a yogi currently on the path realizes that the buddha-nature is something that is truly within him. With the confidence of that direct realization of the ultimate nature of the mind, all subjective perceptions are liberated into the space of the absolute nature and the yogi actualizes what is called "liberating whatever arises as great wisdom." Someone who has seen the truth[103] gains twelve hundred qualities such as the ability in one instant to have a vision of one hundred Buddhas, to enter into and arise from one hundred concentrations, to turn one hundred wheels of the Dharma, and so on. These qualities are not manifest at present because one is obscured by the net of the body, but as the power of the view of emptiness increases, they become clearer and clearer.

This is why it is taught that while we are ordinary beings, as at
present, our realization can both increase and decline. From the
attainment of the first level onwards, realization increases but
does not decline. On the level of Buddhahood it does neither.

We who are now on the path fluctuate in our practice. Our realization is not stable, and our practice increases and declines alternately. When you make some progress and realization and experiences are on the rise, do not be influenced by pride and conceit. When your practice declines, do not be discouraged and think, "I will never learn to meditate." Eventually the alternation of growth and decline becomes exhausted and, having completed the paths of accumulating and joining, one reaches the path of seeing. From that point onwards and until the tenth level one's realization of emptiness becomes vaster but it does not decline. Finally when one reaches the ultimate level, the level of Buddhahood, it does not increase either. At that point there is no decline, for there are no defects, neither is there any increase, for the development of qualities has reached its culmination.

25

Showing, by means of illustrations, how using things as the path helps the meditation.

The understanding of the absolute nature is something that has to be practiced with one-pointed concentration. How we practice will now be explained by means of illustrations.

Son, there are four instructions for using things as the path.

As it is said in the Six Prerequisites for Concentration:

> *On account of material possessions one suffers.*
> *To own nothing is supreme bliss.*
> *By abandoning all its food,*[104]
> *The pelican becomes ever happier.*

For someone engaged in a life of contemplation, possessions and material things are simply a disturbance, a cause of difficulties. To have no possessions is supreme bliss. When we have nothing, we have no enemies. We are happy because we do not have the problem of first acquiring wealth, then protecting it and trying to increase it. As we find in the saying:

> Base your mind on the Dharma.
> Base your Dharma on a humble life.
> Base your humble life on the thought of death.
> Base your death on an empty, barren hollow.[105]

So if we give up all possessions, practice becomes very easy and we will find sublime happiness, like the pelican. The pelican can collect a lot of fish in its bill, but it is prey to being chased by other birds that try to make it give up its catch. It does not get a moment's peace until it surrenders the fish to its pursuers. But once it has done so, it is much happier. Similarly, when we have no possessions, we are free to remain comfortably at ease. On the other hand, with possessions we become preoccupied with having more, and we worry that we might lose them to enemies and thieves.

Accordingly,

Make freedom from attachment the path, as exemplified by the pelican carrying fish.

Now, in order to actually progress on the path we have to be free from afflictive emotions, for it is afflictive emotions that bind us in ignorance.

Since afflictive emotions can arise as primal wisdom,

Make the five poisons the path, as exemplified by the recitation of mantras over poison.

This does not refer to the ordinary emotions as they normally present themselves. It refers to finding their true nature, the ultimate nature of wisdom in the depth of these afflictive emotions. Once wisdom has truly arisen within us and we recognize the empty nature of the afflictive emotions, they cannot harm us, just as when an accomplished yogi recites a mantra over poisoned food, the poison is rendered harmless. When we recognize the empty nature of the afflictive emotions, they are liberated as wisdom and we can use them as the path. If we experience afflictive emotions in the ordinary way, they can only bind us down in samsara. But if we can recognize these emotions as wisdom, they will become helpers in our practice.

Now afflictive emotions arise in the mind by means of the eight consciousnesses.

If we recognize the eight consciousnesses as unborn, we cut the root of existence, the notion of a self.

This idea of a self, the thought of "I," is the very root of samsara. It is this that has to be cut. When a tree is cut at the roots, there is no need to cut the branches, leaves, and flowers: they all fall at the same time and dry up. At present we have not been able to realize that the eight consciousnesses are unborn and we have therefore been unable to cut the belief in an "I" at the root. But once we know how to get rid of this notion of an "I," then whatever happens to us—suffering, happiness, attachment, or revulsion—it will all help our practice progress:

193

Make the unborn nature of the eight consciousnesses the path, as exemplified by cutting a fruit tree at the roots.

The unborn absolute nature is completely empty, like space, unstained by relative phenomena such as the notions of permanence or nihilism that constitute wrong views. The view of this absolute, spacelike nature is unblemished by such extremes, like the lotus flower, which grows above the surface of the lake and is unstained by mud:

As the unborn absolute nature is unaffected by relative phenomena,

Make the great purity the path, as exemplified by the lotus growing from the mud.

26

Showing by means of illustrations how knowledge helps the meditation.

Son, here are instructions on four things to be known.

If you are to meditate with one-pointed concentration, you need to know clearly what you have to meditate on.

All phenomena in samsara and nirvana are devoid of true existence.

At present we perceive samsara as something we have to reject and nirvana as something we have to attain. Now, while this is correct according to relative truth, according to absolute truth the nature of the afflictive emotions and actions that we are supposed to reject is nothing other than emptiness, and the nature of the kayas and wisdoms we have to achieve is also nothing other than emptiness. When we realize the dharmakaya, which is free from true existence, we will know that all perceptions are similar to a dream or an illusion and we will no longer crave these phenomena. As it is said, "While there is attachment, there is no view."[106] And absence of attachment is the supreme view.

Know freedom from attachment, as illustrated by the magician,

for a magician knows that the things he has created do not exist truly and he is therefore not attached to them.

When you ascertain the nature of all phenomena, everything comes down to the truth of emptiness. The entities of samsara that have to be rejected are emptiness; the qualities of nirvana that have to be attained are emptiness. Their emptiness is not of different kinds: phenomena have the same all-pervading nature, the one taste in multiplicity, the sole essence. Therefore,

> *As phenomena and their nature are not two separate things,*
>
> **Know indivisibility, as illustrated by sandalwood or the musk deer.**

Sandalwood cannot be separated from its fragrance, nor the musk deer from its smell. It is in this same way that you should recognize the essential indivisibility of samsara and nirvana.

> *Since there is no relying on conditioned phenomena with characteristics,*
>
> **Know that relatives deceive, as illustrated by being let down by a friend.**

One cannot rely on the conditioned things of samsara like fame, wealth, rank, and so forth. There are no relative phenomena in samsara and nirvana on which one can depend. It is important to know this. If, for example, you are traveling to a distant land in the company of a friend who then somehow lets you down, you will realize you can no longer trust that friend. In the same way you should know that attachment to relatives and friends is simply a cause of deception. Free yourself from clinging and do not rely on such things.

> *Since the absolute nature has been present in you from the beginning,*
>
> **Know inseparability, as illustrated by a sesame seed or the flame of a lamp.**

The absolute nature has been constantly present within you since the very beginning. It is not something that you have been given by the teacher's blessings, like a gift. Nor is it something that has been changed from something else, like a square of woolen cloth that is dyed a different color. It has not been newly fabricated. Rather, it is like the oil in a sesame seed: despite the sesame seed's tiny size, there is always oil present in it. Or like the flame of a lamp: whatever the size of the flame, the light it gives out is naturally part of it. In the same way, you should know that none of the qualities of nirvana is ever separate from your essential nature.

> *When one knows this, the bonds of belief in true existence and dualistic concepts are loosened by themselves, and immaculate wisdom is born in one's mind.*

27

Showing by means of illustrations how the crucial instructions help the meditation.

Son, there are four crucial instructions.

Although the creative power of the empty absolute nature appears multifariously, from the moment phenomena manifest they have no inherent existence: appearance and emptiness are united.

Because everything is by nature empty, infinite manifestations can arise: from the natural creative potential of emptiness all the phenomena of samsara and nirvana can manifest as an infinite display. Although all these manifestations arise, it is not as if they are permanent when they are there and impermanent when they are no longer there. Everything arises as in a dream or like a magical illusion. It is like a rainbow, which, though it appears clearly in the sky, is not solid. It is apparent yet empty. But its emptiness and its appearance are not two separate aspects. It is not that the rainbow being present is one aspect and its being empty is another. The rainbow is simultaneously apparent and empty, and there is no other emptiness than the rainbow itself. The same is true for all the phenomena of samsara and nirvana: they are empty from the very moment they appear.

> **You need the crucial instruction that shows how to make a clear-cut decision regarding the unobstructed nature of appearances, as illustrated by a clean silver mirror.**[107]

Take the example of a mirror. If you take a silver mirror and polish it thoroughly, many images will arise on its surface. But though they appear clearly on the surface, they are not in the mirror nor are they sticking to the mirror's surface. We cannot say that they are inside the mirror or outside. How then do they arise? It is simply the conjuction of there being, say, someone's face in the front of the mirror and the mirror being there. As a result of these different conditions, an image appears. Now, anyone can understand that, although all sorts of images appear in a mirror, they do not exist in any solid way. But we have to understand that the same is also true for all the infinite manifestations of samsara and nirvana. The emptiness and the manifestation are indivisible: the emptiness cannot be separated from the manifestation. When we speak of emptiness and appearance, this does not mean that there are two things in the same way that we talk about the two horns of an animal. It means that there is no emptiness besides the manifestation and there is no manifestation besides emptiness. Once we are free from clinging to this sort of duality, our concepts of existence and nonexistence will naturally fall apart. It is important to have a clear understanding—free of doubts—of this unimpeded manifestation.

> *When one is not bound by clinging to what is not two as being two, phenomenal characteristics are freed by themselves.*

> **You need the crucial instruction on not being bound by characteristics, as illustrated by a prisoner who has been released.**

A prisoner who has just been set free is very concerned not to do anything wrong that might put him back in jail again. We should be similarly mindful and vigilant so that we are not bound by concepts of existence, nonexistence, eternalism, or nihilism; otherwise, we will be seriously tied down by ignorance.

What is the crucial point here? It is to know the meaning of the unborn nature of the mind. The mind does not have a color, shape, location, or any other characteristics. So although there is nothing solid and no characteristics on which to meditate, once you have gained stability and confidence in the realization of the unborn nature of mind, do not stray into distraction and wander from that recognition even for an instant. Simply remain in the state of nongrasping, which is free from mental activity.

*Although there is not even an atom to meditate upon with regard
to the unborn nature of your own mind, do not be distracted for
an instant. Be free from mental activity and conceptualization:*

**This is the crucial instruction you need on not being
distracted from the unborn nature, as illustrated by shooting
an arrow straight at the target.**

By aiming an arrow very straight, one is certain to hit the target.
Likewise, when the realization of the unborn nature is aimed at the target of grasping at a self, it is impossible for it not to hit the mark.

*With the realization of the triple space, do not move from the
inseparability of the absolute space and awareness.*

There are three spaces: the outer space, the blue sky, which is like an
ornament;[108] the inner space, which is the nature of the mind; and the
space in between, the space in the eye channels that connects the outer
and inner spaces. When these three spaces are blended together, one
realizes the inherent union of the empty aspect, the absolute expanse,
and the clarity aspect, one's awareness. Do not waver from that understanding.

**You need the crucial instruction on resting in one-pointed
concentration, as illustrated by an ophthalmic surgeon.[109]**

When people with an eye disease that is making them go blind find
a doctor who can treat them, they listen carefully to the doctor and do
everything necessary for the treatment to succeed. As a result of the
treatment, their eyes open and they can see the mountains and all the
other beautiful things in the universe. If we listen in the same way, with
one-pointed attention, to our teacher's instructions and practice them
exactly as he tells us, one day our eyes will open and we will see the
absolute nature just as it is. All the deluded perceptions of samsara and
nirvana will clear by themselves, for they are, after all, groundless by
nature, unborn and empty. Then all our dualistic concepts of existence,
nonexistence, and so forth will naturally fall apart.

By this means deluded perceptions, being groundless, are cleared away and phenomenal characteristics fall apart by themselves.

28

Personal advice on how to cut conceptual constructs regarding mental and extramental phenomena.

Son, there are four "cuts."[110]

Whatever dualistic thoughts arise, there are none that are anything other than the absolute nature.

Cut the stream of the arising of dualistic thoughts and the following after them, taking the example of a tortoise placed on a silver platter.

Of the many thoughts that arise in our minds, good or bad, none of them move away and separate from the absolute nature for even a moment. They are like a tortoise placed on a silver platter: it finds the feeling of the smooth silver surface underneath it so pleasurable that it does not move at all. So if we never depart from the absolute nature, even when thoughts arise in our mind, there will be no way they can chain together and give rise to delusion. Normally, when we think of something in the past, it leads to another thought, which again leads to the next thought, and we project into the future, creating an uninterrupted chain of deluded thoughts with each thought triggering the next. If we follow such chains of thoughts, they will never stop. But if, whenever a thought arises, we remain in the absolute nature without wavering, the flow of these thoughts will naturally cease.

Whatever appears, nothing has moved from the absolute nature.

Decide that nothing is extraneous to the absolute nature, taking the example of gold jewelry.

Once we know how to remain in the absolute nature, the manifold thoughts that arise in the mind are no different from gold jewelry. One can make all sorts of things out of gold, such as earrings, bracelets, and necklaces, but although they have a variety of different shapes, they are all made of gold. Likewise, if we are able to not move from the absolute nature, however many thoughts we might have, they never depart from the recognition of the absolute nature. A yogi for whom this is the case never departs from that realization, whatever he does with his body, speech, and mind. All his actions arise as the outer display or ornament of wisdom. All the signs one would expect from meditating on a deity come spontaneously without his actually doing any formal practice. The result of mantra recitation is obtained without his having to do a large number of recitations. In this way everything is included in the recognition that nothing is ever extraneous to the absolute nature.

In that state one does not become excited at pleasant events or depressed by unpleasant ones. Everything,

> The whole variety of joys and sorrows, is one within the state
> of awareness.

**Decide on its indivisibility, taking the example of
molasses and its sweet taste.**

We usually think of molasses as one thing and sweetness as another, and we therefore have two names and concepts for these. But in fact it is impossible to separate the sweetness from the molasses itself. If we reach a similar clear-cut understanding that all phenomena in samsara and nirvana, all happiness and suffering, are included in the absolute nature, then

> All of samsara and nirvana arises from the creative display of the
> spontaneous primal wisdom.

**Decide that it is naturally manifesting awareness, taking the
example of the moon in the sky and its reflection in water.**

When the moon shines on a lake, it is reflected on the water and the moon appears in its reflection exactly as it appears in the sky. Similarly, when we have a glimpse of awareness, it is what we call the illustrative wisdom: it is an image of the actual wisdom, something that we can point to as an example of it. Even though it is only a glimpse, it is still of the same nature as the absolute wisdom, a true likeness of it. Through the recognition of this illustrative wisdom, one is led to the recognition of the absolute wisdom,[111] which is like the moon in the sky. Both arise by themselves, and we should understand clearly that there is no basic difference between the illustrative wisdom and the ultimate awareness or absolute wisdom. It is, rather, a question of one's realization becoming vaster, of one becoming more skilled in one's recognition. Just as there is no difference in nature between the moon seen in the water and the moon seen in the sky, so it is with the illustrative wisdom and the absolute wisdom.

29

Showing how dealing properly with samsara and nirvana helps the meditation.

Son, there are four views.

The essential nature being union, its display is arrayed as an ornament.

View thoughts and appearances as the ornament of the absolute nature, taking the example of a rainbow adorning the sky.

As we have already seen, the essential nature is the intrinsic union of emptiness and appearance. All the infinite manifestations of samsara and nirvana arise spontaneously as the creativity of the absolute nature. They arise as its ornament and not as something different and separate from the absolute nature or as something that interferes with it. When a rainbow appears in the sky, beautiful and multicolored, the sky is empty but the rainbow appears in it like an ornament. Similarly, for a yogi who has realized the wisdom of the absolute nature, all manifestations appear as its ornaments. All thoughts appear as ornaments of the absolute nature, and there is nothing, no meditational defect such as dullness or excitement, that can obstruct it.

> *When one knows thoughts to be the absolute nature, attachment and aversion are put to death,*

and one no longer accumulates karma.

View thoughts as the absolute nature, taking the example of tempering and honing a sword.

With a sword that has been tempered and carefully sharpened, one can cut the toughest branches and even the trunk of a tree. Similarly, if the mind is tempered with the absolute nature, any thoughts that arise will be severed by themselves. As a result,

There are no traces accumulated as habitual tendencies,

and the tendencies of good and bad karma will not be perpetuated.

View thoughts as leaving no trace, taking the example of birds flying in the sky.

With a bird that flies all over the sky, this way and that, it is impossible to point out exactly where it has flown, for it leaves no trace of its flight. For a yogi, too, the many various thoughts, good or bad, that arise in his mind leave no trace because as soon as they arise they immediately dissolve in the absolute nature. Thoughts related to attachment, aversion, and bewilderment may well arise in his mind, but since they dissolve as soon as they arise, they do not leave any trace. As a result, they do not lead to the accumulation of karma and suffering. Good thoughts also, like faith, devotion, and compassion, may arise but immediately dissolve in the absolute nature and therefore do not lead to pride or attachment developing in the mind.

Phenomena are freed in the absolute nature.

View existence as untrue, taking the example of waking from a dream.

In a dream one dreams of all sorts of things good and bad; but when one wakes up, there is nothing left of them. Just so, the whole display of the universe and beings continues to manifest infinitely; but once we have realized the absolute nature, we do not cling to notions such as good and bad, and we view all these manifestations as being without any solid existence.

30

Explaining the actual method of resting in meditation.

Son, there are four kinds of meditation.

Bringing together everything that favors concentration and
mastering the crucial point of how to rest in meditation, diligently

Meditate with increasing habituation, taking the example of the waxing moon.

In order for the realization of this absolute nature to dawn, we need to gather favorable conditions—to be free from conditions that break up the meditation and from distraction and grasping. Unless they are free from distraction, beginners who try to meditate will not benefit much. Moreover it is important to find the right balance between being too tense and too relaxed. If we are too tense, we will suffer from disturbances of the subtle energies and the mind will become unbalanced. If we are too relaxed, we will lapse into ordinary states of mind. So we have to be well versed in the various methods of meditation. At the same time we need to have great diligence. If we try to realize the absolute nature day after day, our realization will gradually become vaster and more stable, like the waxing moon, which grows fuller each day between the first and fifteenth days of the lunar month.

This is the view of the Prajnaparamita (the Mother of the
Victorious Ones), the sphere of the inexpressible, inconceivable,
supreme primal wisdom.

The wisdom that we realize cannot be described. The more our realization grows, the more the qualities associated with it—spontaneous devotion and compassion—will bloom. And the emptiness aspect of this absolute nature is what we call the Mother of the Victorious Ones, that is, Prajnaparamita, who is the mother of all the Shravakas, Pratyekabuddhas, Bodhisattvas, and Buddhas.

Meditate on thoughts and appearances as the inexpressible great bliss, taking the example of having your mouth full of water.

When one's mouth is full of water, even if one wants to say, "PHAT,"[112] one cannot possibly do so. Similarly, when we realize the absolute nature, although the phenomena of samsara and nirvana are still experienced, it is impossible to express them in words. This is why Zur-chungpa says, "Meditate on great bliss."

> **Meditate that fame and the like—**
>
> *that is, the thoughts of the eight ordinary concerns—*
>
> **are not ultimately true, taking the example of mist, which does not truly exist.**

When the sky is full of mist in the morning, it seems as if there is something veiling the sun, but in fact there is nothing one can catch hold of, and the mist does not affect the actual sky behind it. Similarly, practitioners who have realized the absolute nature are not affected by the eight ordinary concerns: they do not crave fame and glory, and even if they happen to get these, it does not make them proud. If they are criticized or blamed, they do not get depressed. Such things do not affect their minds. They are completely free from ordinary worldly concerns, and they see everything as in a dream, as an illusion. So they meditate seeing fame and related manifestations as impure—in the sense of irrelevant—like mist, which has no true existence.

> **Meditate on the uncontrived nature as empty, taking the example of water and bubbles;**
>
> *the nature of the mind is empty like space.*

In a river there may be many eddies and bubbles, but they are never something other than the water in the river. They are formed from water, they remain no different from water, and they again dissolve back into the water. So, too, with all the manifestations and experiences that arise as the creativity of awareness: they never change into anything different from the absolute nature. The absolute nature is always present within them, like the empty space that is always present inside a bamboo stem.

31

Showing how conduct[113] should be endowed with experience and realization.

Son, there are four kinds of conduct.

**In your conduct, turn your back on worldly ways;
consider the examples of a bride and a madman.**

*In other words, make sure you are conscientious and considerate
of others' opinions, like an anxious newly wed bride; do not act
contrary to the Dharma like a madman who does whatever occurs
to him.*

When a newly wed bride arrives in her new home, she is very conscientious, well behaved, and concerned to create a good impression.[114] We practitioners should be just as careful in everything we do, and if we do things contrary to the Dharma, we should feel thoroughly ashamed, knowing that we are in the presence of the infinite Buddhas. At the same time, we must avoid the extreme of behaving like a madman, who does whatever comes into his mind and never stops to think, "This is not the right way to behave."

In your conduct, *the multifarious phenomenal perceptions*
**should not move from the absolute nature: take the example
of fish in the ocean.**

Wherever they go, fish in the ocean always remain in it, for there is no end to the ocean. In the same way, the manifold appearances of samsara and nirvana should be perceived as never having been extraneous to the absolute nature.

In your conduct, whatever appears—*the five poisonous
emotions and so forth*—**should be primal wisdom: take the
example of fire raging through a forest.**

In a forest fire, the stronger the wind, the further the fire spreads; the more wood it reaches, the more the fire blazes. And while the afflictive emotions bind an ordinary person, for a yogi any thoughts that arise in his mind simply fuel his realization, which grows even stronger and clearer, because he experiences whatever appears as the display of wisdom.

**In your conduct, the many should have the single
taste**—*phenomena and their nature or appearance and emptiness*

being inseparable: **take the example of salt dissolving in water.**

The absolute nature and relative phenomena are indivisible, as are appearance and emptiness, just as when salt dissolves in water, the saltiness and the water are completely inseparable. Thus, when relative conditioned phenomena dissolve into the absolute nature and they blend in one taste, all deluded thoughts vanish and can no longer arise.

32

Showing different kinds of experience.

Son, there are four kinds of experience.

When we try to preserve the recognition of the absolute nature in this way, we will have various experiences. The first of these is:

The experience of no clinging to thoughts, as illustrated by a small child and a mirror:

although there are perceptions, there is no clinging.

Experiences *will* arise. If we did not have experiences on the path, we would be on the wrong path. But although they arise, we must be completely free of clinging to them, like a small baby in front of a mirror. Whatever the baby does, the mirror will reflect it. But the baby does not cling to it as being good or bad. Likewise, someone who is completely free from clinging is not caught by notions of good and bad.

The experience of wisdom taking birth where it has not previously arisen, as illustrated by a poor woman finding treasure:

experience and realization are newly born.

When a new experience or realization of wisdom arises in the mind, we should be joyful, and the joy we feel should inspire us to even greater diligence in the practice. It is just as when a woman who is destitute finds treasure buried underground. She is overjoyed, knowing that for seven generations to come there will be no need to worry about being poor, and she therefore takes great care of the treasure she has found.

> The experience of neither apprehension nor esteem, as
> illustrated by a swallow *entering the nest* and a lion:
>
> *one has gained decisive confidence.*

At one point we will gain a sense of certainty and confidence from having a clear idea of where we are on the path, of how antidotes work on the emotions, and of the view of emptiness. We will find that we have no hesitation, like a swallow coming to the nest. Before building its nest, the swallow looks carefully for a good site free from possible dangers. But once it has built the nest, it flies straight to it, without any hesitation. Likewise, having carefully built up our meditation, we will reach a point where we have no hesitation and we immediately recognize the nature of our experiences. Like the lion, the king of animals, which has no fear of other animals wherever it goes, a yogi has no apprehension, whatever experiences arise in his mind. At the same time, he is not proud or infatuated with his experiences. Neither does he esteem experiences, nor is he apprehensive about them.

> The experience of being unafraid of philosophical views,
> as illustrated by the lion who is not scared of the fox:
>
> *there is no fear of the view and action of lower vehicles.*

When we have realized the absolute nature, we will not be tied by the views and conduct of the lower vehicles. Like the lion, which is never afraid of the fox however much it barks, someone who has full realization of the Great Perfection is not affected by the numerous teachings on the view, meditation, and action of the gradual vehicles; they do not make him hesitate.

33

The signs that arise from experience.

Son, there are four kinds of signs.

When experience and realization bloom within, this is

the sign of awareness shining within, as illustrated by a butter lamp inside a vase.

When a butter lamp is placed in a vase, it is protected from the wind and therefore burns very steadily and brightly. Similarly, when clear awareness fills one's inner space, karma and afflictive emotions are immediately dispelled.

> *For this there are four ways in which objects of knowledge are*
> *freed in their own nature.*

Once we have realized the absolute nature, all concepts are dispelled within that same absolute nature.

> *They are self-freeing, like iron cutting iron.*

Just as iron can be cut by iron but not by wood, when the ultimate nature of the subject and object acts as the antidote for the same subject and object, all duality naturally dissolves.

> *Appearances and the mind being inseparable, they are freed*
> *through one single thing, like fire lighting a fire.*

When there are many different afflictive emotions occurring in the mind, there is no need to search for a separate antidote for each one. The absolute nature serves as the antidote for them all, like fire lighting a fire. Once one has realized that mind and appearances are inseparable, the more firewood one adds, the stronger the fire blazes.

> *By knowing one's own nature, they are freed into the*
> *fundamental reality, like space mixing with space.*

Inside a vase there is space, and that space is basically the same as the space outside. When the vase is broken with a hammer, the space inside and the vast space outside blend as one and become indistinguishable.

> *Appearances are recognized as being manifestations of the mind,*
> *like a mother and child meeting.*

Once we have recognized that all outer phenomena are simply the self-manifestation of our own awareness or absolute nature, outer conditioned phenomena cannot deceive our inner absolute nature. This recognition that outer phenomena are our own projections is like a mother and child meeting: between them there is certain recognition, without hesitation or mistake.

> *When there is no effort,* this is

> **The sign of the mind not getting involved in the pleasures of the senses, as illustrated by a king seated on his throne.**

A king who has complete dominion over his kingdom has no need to actively increase his authority, nor to involve himself in the day-to-day running of the state. Similarly, when we have confidence in the absolute nature, we will not be lured by attractions and sensory experiences outside. The mind will not run after objects of desire. This is a sign of stability.

> *When one curtails one's plans because there is no time to waste, or decides clearly that all phenomena are unborn,* this is

> **the sign of focusing the mind on the unborn nature, as illustrated by a sick person and a cemetery.**

There are two examples here, reminding us that although we may have this sort of realization, we must never feel complacent with regard to impermanence and death, and we must be decided about the unborn nature of phenomena.

The first example is that of someone who is terminally ill and knows that there is little time left before the final journey to the cemetery. Such a person does not feel like wasting time. The second example (pointing to the realization that all phenomena are unborn) is that of the sick person's corpse being carried to the cemetery. Just as one does not need to take care of a corpse as one did of the living person, once we have realized the absolute nature we do not need to pay special attention to "what is to be rejected"—afflictive emotions and so forth. We do not need any other antidote for them than the realization of the unborn nature. Other, ordinary antidotes become irrelevant.

If we are free from *both the things to be rejected and the antidotes* to be applied, we will gain the confidence of a hawk. When a hawk sees a pigeon flying quietly through the forest, it does not hesitate for a second in swooping down on its prey. Likewise, if we have the confidence of having gone beyond both the things to be rejected and the need for anti-dotes, we will overwhelm the afflictive emotions without hesitation. This is

> **the sign of having stamped on the afflictive emotions, as illustrated by the pigeon and the hawk.**

> ### 34
>
> *Showing that without experience and realization, one is powerless not to be reborn in samsara.*
>
> **Son, there are four instructions related to optical illusions,**
>
> *with examples of being fooled by illusions.*

If you press your eye with a finger while looking at the moon, you will see two moons, but of course there has never been more than one moon. Similarly, neither the world outside nor your own body, your name, or your mind has ever existed in any true way. Yet you assume they exist truly, and therefore you cling to them.

> **As in the example of perceiving a mirage as water,**
>
> *believing there is something when there is nothing,*
>
> **if you do not know that the pleasures of the senses are a delusion, you will wander.**

Because we have been accustomed for so long to believing the true existence of things, we err. We are like wild animals on a vast plain in hot weather who see a mirage in the distance. Believing it is water, they run toward it, only to find as they approach that there is nothing there. In the same way, if we do not realize that all the desirable things of samsara related to form, feeling, smell, and taste are nothing other than delusions, we cling to them and wander. We cling to things that appear very beautiful or pleasant and feel averse to things we cannot bear. As a result of being thus deluded by our perceptions, we get involved in all sorts of different activities.

We also cling to things that we believe to be other than what they are:

> As in the example of perceiving a rope as a snake,
>
> *thinking it is, even though it is not,*
>
> if you do not know that you are being fooled, you will wander.

When one cannot see very well, one may mistake a rope for a snake and get a terrible fright—simply because one has not looked at the rope properly. It is the same with the various desirable experiences we can have. Because we believe that they truly exist, we go to a great deal of trouble to fulfill our desires. Instead of recognizing the benefits of following a teacher and practicing the Dharma, we are fooled by our perceptions and so we wander endlessly in samsara.

> As in the example of the parrot eating poison *(and, by thus imitating the peacock, causing its own death),*
>
> *if you behave as if you have attained realization even though you have not and*
>
> you cling to things thinking that they truly exist, you will wander.

If we have not achieved the full realization of emptiness that allows us to use emotions as the path, and if we try to perform activities that are the domain of realized beings, we will go astray. Take the example of the peacock and the parrot. The peacock can eat poisonous berries, and doing so only makes its plumage more brilliant. But if a parrot tries to do the same, it dies. Similarly, if we try to imitate the great siddhas in enjoying desirable experiences, it will only tie us further to samsara, because we still have the concept that the object of desire truly exists. Rather than enhancing our practice and serving to transform our afflictive emotions into wisdom, it will simply result in our being obscured by our afflictive emotions and actions.

> *Believing in existence where there is no existence, one is helplessly confused by attachment and aversion.*

As in the example of the child and the empty fist

tricking it into thinking it contains a treat,[115]

if you are fooled by your perceptions, you will wander in samsara.

There are no phenomena that exist truly. Yet we postulate the existence of phenomena and cling to them. Once we are caught by such delusions, clinging enters our being and we become helplessly attracted to things we like and repelled by things we dislike. Thus we are fooled by the perceptions of the senses, like a small child who is approached by someone pretending he has something in his hand. The child holds out his hand happily, expecting to receive a gift, only to cry with disappointment when the person opens his hand and there is nothing in it. Just so are we fooled by our senses, and this is how we wander in samsara. This is why we need to recognize that all phenomena have no true existence at all.

35

Son, there are ten ways of failing the Buddhas

in one's commitment, which must accord with one's level.

It is important that our conduct accords with our level of realization. If you are a great siddha, you can act accordingly. If not, you should act according to your level. But if you do not have a high degree of realization and you behave as if you did, you will end up betraying the Buddhas in ten ways. As we said earlier, if the conduct follows the view too closely, the view will become demonic.

> *The way to avoid failing in your commitment is to take the Buddhas of the three times as your witnesses; for the fault in breaking a promise knows no bounds, whereas if you do not break it, inconceivable good qualities will be yours: you will become the foremost child of all the Buddhas of the past, present, and future. Therefore, within each six-hour period of the day take a reckoning, and if you have broken your promise, make your confession and renew the promise with a firm vow.*

In order not to be caught in this way by your actions and afflictive emotions, take the Buddhas of the past, present, and future as your witnesses. The Buddhas, who have the eye of wisdom, know that if you experience delusion in an ordinary way, it is impossible to attain liberation and enlightenment. We fall under the power of delusion because we fail to recognize that phenomena have no inherent existence. If we make a promise not to fall into delusion and we then break that promise, there will be boundless negative consequences. If we manage to keep that promise, we will gain inconceivable qualities and become the foremost child of all the Victorious Ones. Since the path shown by the Enlightened Ones is without mistake, if we follow it properly, we too will be treading the right path without mistake. You must therefore be mindful, conscious of the good and bad elements within you, and take stock of your faults and qualities. If you find that you have transgressed the samaya, regret your mistake, confess it, and repair the samaya, promising not to commit the same mistake again. If you find, on examining yourself in this way, that you have not transgressed the samaya, rejoice and dedicate that source of good to all sentient beings.

> *Recognizing that all happiness and suffering is the manifestation of your own previous actions,*
>
> Even if the whole world rises up in enmity against you, do not stray from the absolute nature. If you do, you will be betraying the Buddhas of the three times.

It is important to realize that all the happiness and suffering, joy and sorrow you are experiencing now have not been decided for you by gods such as Indra, Brahma, and Vishnu, nor have they come about on their own. They are the natural result of your own past actions. So make a promise that even if the whole world rises up as your enemy, you will not wander from the absolute nature. Then, even if someone appears to threaten your life, if you can remain in equanimity within the recognition of the absolute nature, that enemy will be unable to harm you. But if you fall into delusion, thinking that enemies exist truly, and as a result you react by trying to defeat them and to protect others who arouse attachment in you, then you will surely be betraying the Buddhas of the past, present, and future.

Be mindful at all times of what is right and what is not; and be vigilant as to whether you are actually acting accordingly. Mindfulness and vigilance will then be your teachers.

> *Constantly supported by mindfulness and vigilance,*

> **Whatever you do, do not wander from the continuum of the unborn absolute nature. If you do, you will be betraying the Buddhas of the three times.**

In terms of the relative truth, you should accumulate merit in accordance with the unfailing interdependence of cause and effect, while knowing that these are like a dream or illusion. At the same time, in your meditation, you should never move from the understanding of the empty nature, dharmata.

> *Whatever happens to you, apply the antidote, refresh yourself with faith, assimilate the instructions, be unhypocritical in discipline, and have confidence in the law of actions and their results. By these means,*

> **Even if your life is at stake, never lose sight of the Dharma. If you do, you will be betraying the Buddhas of the three times.**

Whatever circumstances occur, whether they are good things like praise, fame, comfort, and wealth or bad things like criticism, injury, and sickness, do not be influenced by believing that these circumstances truly exist. Use the antidote on them. Remember that suffering is the result of your past deeds and make a wish that with your own suffering you may be able to take others' sufferings upon yourself. If you become wealthy or encounter other favorable situations, regard these as though they were a dream or an illusion and enjoy them without being attached. If you can do this, the antidote will have been efficient.

All these circumstances should also help to revive or increase your faith in the Three Jewels and your devotion to the teacher, like rekindling a fire. At the same time you should recognize the value of the instructions more deeply, practice discipline without hypocrisy, and have a firm conviction as to how the law of cause and effect operates. This should lead you to resolve never to lose sight of the Dharma, that is, never to lapse into negative actions, even if it costs you your life.

> *Keeping in mind the related benefits and risks, and remembering* your teacher's *kindness,*
>
> **Do not spoil even an atom's worth of your samaya with the sublime teacher. If you do, you will be betraying the Buddhas of the three times.**

In ordinary life, a merchant who conducts his business may gain an enormous profit, but there is also a risk involved, especially if his methods are slightly irregular. He may lose everything or end up in trouble with the law. For us Dharma practitioners, too, there are great benefits and great risks—related to our root teacher. If we practice in accordance with what he tells us, there is no doubt that we will derive the greatest benefit and achieve all the qualities of liberation and ultimate omniscience. But our relationship with the teacher also entails great risk: if we do not practice according to his instructions but behave hypocritically, pretending to do as he says in his presence and doing the opposite behind his back, we risk falling into the vajra hell.

> *Remembering death and reflecting on the defects of samsara,*
>
> **Rather than now accomplishing fame** *and other goals related to the eight ordinary concerns* **in this life, put all your efforts into the task of training in the mind** *turned toward enlightenment.* **If you involve yourself in the affairs of this life and are not diligent in the mind training, you will be betraying the Buddhas of the three times.**

What should we do in order to practice wholly in accordance with the Dharma and avoid anything that goes against it? We must remember death—the certainty that death will come and the unpredictability of when it will come. We also need to bear in mind the shortcomings of samsara and how any inclination to samsaric activities simply perpetuates suffering in samsara. Reflect as follows: "Today I have this human body with its freedoms and advantages. I have met a spiritual teacher and crossed the threshold of the Dharma. I have been lucky enough to receive the instructions that can bring Buddhahood in one lifetime, so I must practice them. Otherwise, if I indulge in activities that are motivated by the eight ordinary concerns, I will be fooling myself." So instead of thinking that fame and other ordinary concerns are important, make every effort to train single-mindedly in bodhichitta, purifying the two obscurations with the intention of benefiting the whole infinity of sentient beings. On the other hand, if you are diligent only in the affairs of this life, if you do not cultivate mindfulness of what is right and what is wrong, and if you are not constantly vigilant in checking whether you are acting, speaking, or thinking accordingly, you will be transgressing the precepts of the Buddhas of the past, present, and future and betraying them.

As it is said in all the sutras and tantras,

See the noble teachers as Vajrasattva in person and have devotion.

In terms of qualities and accomplishment, the teacher is truly the equal of all the Buddhas. But in terms of kindness, he is far kinder. Bearing this in mind, we should be full of respect and devotion throughout the six periods of the day and night and deeply determined to do whatever the teacher says.

If you do not, you will be betraying the Buddhas of the three times.

Recognizing that everything that appears is the mind, that the mind itself is empty, and that the inseparable union of clarity and emptiness is primal wisdom,

Know that everything outside and inside is the mind, and do not have attachment or aversion. If you do, you will be betraying the Buddhas of the three times.

We speak of the deluded perceptions of samsara where everything is seen as impure, and, linked to these, the afflictive emotions and the workings of karma. We also speak of nirvana and the pure phenomena of the kayas and wisdoms. But who made these two, the impurity of samsara and the purity of nirvana? It is the mind. If we look at the basic nature of this mind and ask ourselves what it is like—what is its shape, color, or locality—it is impossible to find any. It is nothing but emptiness. At the same time, it is not a a blank nothingness like the emptiness of an empty pot. The mind also has the power to know everything. This is the mind's clarity aspect. In truth, the mind is clarity and emptiness united, and the inseparable union of clarity and emptiness is what we call nondual wisdom.

All the outer objects, the universe and beings, and the inner subject that knows these, that conceives of subject and object and creates the notions of enemies and friends—all these are the mind. If we do not know that they are all the projections of the mind and we fail to recognize the mind's empty nature, we will be fooled by the various emotions such as attachment and aversion that grow in the mind. We must therefore understand that the whole manifestation of samsara and nirvana is nothing but the play of the mind and that the nature of this mind is emptiness. Its essential nature is unborn emptiness and its natural expression is clarity, the faculty of knowing. When we know this, we are no longer alienated; we are not influenced by attraction to the desirable and aversion to the undesirable. But when we fall under the power of attraction and aversion, we betray the Buddhas of the three times.

> *Acknowledging beings as your mothers, remembering their kindness, and wishing to repay that kindness,*
>
> **Cultivate great compassion and work for the sake of sentient beings. If you *depart from bodhichitta and* strive for your own sake alone, you will be betraying the Buddhas of the three times.**

Practicing the Dharma just for your own benefit is of little use. You should practice for the sake of all sentient beings, who are as numerous as the sky is vast. Acknowledge that all beings have been your parents and feel the same love and gratitude for them as you do for your actual parents in this life. Think how kind they have been to you, giving you life and then providing you with everything you needed, such as food, clothes, and affection. We can see how strong parents' love is for their children: even the most cruel animals like hawks and wolves, who eat nothing but flesh and blood, manifestly love their young. It is important to realize what a debt of gratitude every sentient being owes its parents.

How can we repay this kindness? The best way to do so is through the Dharma, recognizing that all phenomena are like a dream or an illusion. Look at yourself and see if you are able to avoid even a single negative action and to undertake a single positive action. If you make it your concern to do more and more positive actions and fewer and fewer negative ones, and on top of that you have bodhichitta, the wish to benefit others, then you will truly be practicing the Great Vehicle. On the other hand, if you transgress bodhichitta, if you fail to recognize that all beings have been your kind parents and as a result you are preoccupied only with fulfilling your own selfish goals, you will betray the Buddhas of the three times, for you will actually be behaving in complete contradiction to what they have taught.

> All dualistic concepts *on account of clinging to everything outside and inside as truly existing* are the work of demons, so know that there is no duality of subject and object. If you fail to do so, you will be betraying the Buddhas of the three times.

Where does the delusion that makes us go counter to the Buddhas' teachings come from? It comes from the mistaken belief that the universe and the beings in it truly exist. As a consequence of this dualistic clinging, we become very pleased with things like success, fame, praise, and gain, and get very upset by loss, criticism, and obscurity. For us the eight worldly concerns are all-important. At the root of this is the duality of the inner subject, the grasping mind, and the outer object that is grasped. Because of this grasping relationship between subject and object we are attracted to things that are pleasant and desirable and feel averse to anything that harms us, people's criticism, and so forth. Thus we divide the whole world into pleasant and unpleasant, and we do everything we can to keep the one and get rid of the other. It is this duality that makes us fall into deluded ways of acting, and it is these that are the work of the demon. What do we mean by "demon"? It is anything that obstructs the path of liberation from samsara and prevents one from attaining ultimate omniscience. The antidote for this is to recognize all the phenomena of samsara and nirvana as the nondual wisdom of awareness and emptiness. If we fail to recognize this nonduality, we betray the Buddhas of the three times.

With this body as a support, be careful—

that is, maintain mindfulness in the four kinds of conduct, guarding the body and so forth—

as you seek the fruit of Buddhahood. If you fail to do so, you will be betraying the Buddhas of the three times.

At present you have this human existence, which is free from the eight unfavorable conditions and endowed with the ten advantages—the five individual advantages and the five circumstantial ones. With this human body as a support, there is no path in the Dharma's nine vehicles—those of the Shravakas, Pratyekabuddhas, and Bodhisattvas and the six vehicles of the Vajrayana—that cannot be practiced. Each of these paths, if practiced, leads to a corresponding result. It is like finding a wish-fulfilling jewel that grants every wish or prayer one makes. Were one to be in possession of a wish-fulfilling jewel, it would be foolish not to make use of it. Similarly, now that we have this human body we should be one-pointed in using it to practice the supreme Dharma in every one of our four kinds of activity—eating, sleeping, walking, and sitting. In all these we need to constantly examine our minds, watching like a spy and checking whether we are acting in a negative or positive way. At the same time we have to remember clearly what is positive and what is negative—what we have to undertake and what we need to avoid. This mindfulness is the most extraordinary form of protection. So do not waste this opportunity by being careless. Use mindfulness to maintain control over your body, speech, and mind so that you are not influenced by worldly concerns. To be mindful of what is right and wrong and vigilant as to whether one is behaving accordingly is the basis of Dharma practice. Not to be mindful and vigilant is shameful, for it is betraying the Buddhas of the three times.

36

Using instructions to meditate without distraction,

for the practice has to be done with full concentration.

Son, there are four ways not to be distracted.

Master the crucial point of the methods for settling in
concentration, following the examples given in the Six Prerequisites
for Concentration.[116]

As the first step in training the mind we need to pacify the mind, protecting it from excessive activity. This is achieved through the practice of sustained calm, which acts like a glass lantern protecting the lamp's flame from the wind. This practice makes the mind more tranquil so that it is less prone to being carried away by attachment and hatred. It is therefore important to become skilled in the crucial point of letting the mind rest in concentration. This entails avoiding any sorts of extreme. If you are too tense in trying to control the mind, your concentration will tire and your enthusiasm for the practice will wane. On the other hand, if you relax too much, you will simply stray into an ordinary state. For this reason it is said:

> Tauten at times,
> Ease off at others:
> Here is a crucial point in the view.

Do not be distracted from the expanse of the mind free
of grasping, like a straight arrow.

There are four ways of meditating that concern practitioners who do this sort of practice in mountain retreats. Regarding the first of these, in our ordinary state we conceive of phenomena and consciousness as truly existing. As long as we have such concepts, we are certain to accumulate karma in samsara. If, on the other hand, we are able to recognize the unborn nature of the mind and be free from these concepts and fixations, and if we remain without straying in the expanse of the mind that is free of grasping, this is very powerful, like a perfectly straight arrow, which flies directly to the center of the target.

Without any mental grasping at the unborn nature,

Do not be distracted from the absolute space, which is
free from thoughts, like a *champion* **athlete**

or like a painter of sacred art mixing his colors.

At all times we should be aware of the unborn nature of the mind. However, we must never cling to this unborn nature; we must remain completely free. The point is to remain in the absolute nature, where there is no such thing as a meditator, an object of meditation, or an act of meditating. As long as one still has these sorts of notions and concepts, even if one has a reputation as a "great meditator," one's meditation will not be in any way superior to the worldly concentrations.[117] So we must not stray from the absolute space, which is free from thoughts. "Thoughts" here refers to the constant alternation of likes and dislikes, being pleased with favorable situations and upset by unfavorable ones. Train in this total concentration like a champion athlete training with bow and arrow or with the sword. If he drops his mindfulness and vigilance and is distracted even for an instant, he will be struck by his opponent's weapon. A painter, too, has to be mindful and attentive when preparing his paints, mixing the pigments with the right base and diluting it correctly so that the paint spreads easily on the canvas and produces the fine lines, details, and delicate shades that will please the eye.

As no phenomena are extraneous to the absolute nature,

Do not be distracted from *their being indivisible, or from*
the expanse of evenness, like a hooked fish.

As no relative phenomena ever depart from the absolute nature, they are naturally inseparable from it. Their not being two things is also called "the great evenness." It is important to know how to never wander from this expanse of evenness. Just as a hooked fish is certain to be hauled out of the water onto dry land, if we have constant mindfulness, we will definitely be taken out of the ocean of samsara.

With the view free from extreme beliefs and your meditation free
from intellectual fabrication,

Do not be distracted from the state beyond all thought,
as if you were removing a thorn.

The root of liberation from samsara is having the correct view, and the correct view is the view that is free from the different extremes. If one clings to the appearance aspect, one falls into the extreme of eternalism; if one clings to the emptiness aspect, one falls into that of nihilism. We have to be free from clinging to either of these extremes of existence and nonexistence. This cannot be achieved by intellectual fabrication. The absolute nature can only be recognized by direct experience. It is not a question of trying to isolate an empty aspect of the mind and to fix one's mind on it, or of isolating a clarity aspect of the mind and clinging to that. This sort of intellectual manipulation will never bring us to Buddhahood. Our meditation must therefore be free from the work of the intellect.

Do not be distracted from this state beyond all thought. And although there is no particular deity to meditate upon, no visualization details or attributes that you have to remember, no object for the mind to concentrate on, at the same time there must be no wandering, no lack of mindfulness. The close mindfulness and vigilance needed here are the same as those of someone trying to pull a thorn out of his skin—very carefully, without hurting himself. The real meditation is to simply remain in the absolute nature without obscuring the mind with all sort of intellectual constructs.

37

Meditation using the instructions on the method of "resting."[118]

Son, there are four instructions on the method.

To let go of the subject inside that apprehends the objects of the six consciousnesses—

We are talking here about the six sensory experiences—seeing forms, hearing sounds, smelling odors, tasting flavors, and feeling things.[119] When we perceive an object, our reaction is to cling to what we perceive. For example when we see a form, the object, the eye and the consciousness interact and we think, "This is beautiful; I need it," or "That is ugly; I don't want it." We thus have an infinite number of such thoughts—of good and unpleasant tastes, fragrant and offensive smells, pleasant and unpleasant tactile sensations, and so on. All these lead to actions, and that is how the wheel of samsara is set in motion.

How should we let go of these clingings? By establishing the empty nature of the perceiving consciousness. Once we establish the empty nature of the mind, it is not that we cease to see objects, but rather that the sight of them no longer gives rise to clinging. Therefore, we no longer experience the attraction and aversion that lead to delusion. Free of these clingings, we should remain in meditative equipoise, which only one's self-awareness can experience. It is a state that is completely limpid and empty, like a vast open space, quite free from the stains of fixation. This is

> **The instruction on the state of mind devoid of all ordinary perception and thought, like a dry skull,**

which has no eyes, ears, and tongue, and therefore has no ordinary perceptions.

> *Now for the actual instruction on the method of "resting,"*
> *which is sixfold:*

It is said that in meditation an object on which one makes an effort to focus is the prison of the view, so

> (1) *Leave things effortlessly in the expanse free from references.*

In meditation, in which the yogi's concentration is like the flow of a river, the natural state unfolds. Through it we may have a glimpse of the absolute nature, and even though this glimpse is not full realization, we will be sure that it is not something we have fabricated and that this nature has been ours since the very beginning. Once you have recognized the absolute nature, remain in it without modifying it in any way:

> (2) *Leave everything without contrivance in the uncompounded*
> *absolute space.*

If we do not remain in that state of simplicity but make all sorts of fabrications, these will obscure our recognition of the absolute nature. Constantly stirring water with a stick will never make the mud settle and allow the water to become clear. But if the water is left as it is without being agitated, gradually all the mud particles will sink to the bottom, leaving the water perfectly pure, clear, and transparent. We should do the same with the mind, leaving it in its natural state without interfering, without stirring it up with fabrications.

> (3) *Though everything arises in your own mind, leave it without any notion of "I" or self.*

It is important to realize that all the phenomena of samsara and nirvana appear as projections of your own mind, like the various reflections that appear in a mirror. At the same time you must remain completely free of any concept of a self. When the phenomena of samsara and nirvana appear in the mind, you should not grasp at them, thinking, "This is my mind," or "This is the object," or "I have perceived that object as beautiful (or ugly)." All perceptions should be left as they are without entertaining any notion of "I" or self.

> (4) *Leave everything without conceptualization in the uncontrived expanse.*

The absolute nature is what we call the uncontrived state. This primordial, uncontrived nature is not a state that is blind to forms, deaf to sounds, and so on. On the other hand, it is completely free from attachment to what is called beautiful and from aversion to what is called ugly. This means that it is free from the notions of subject and object and the clingings associated with these notions:

> (5) *Leave things just as they are in the expanse free of subject and object.*
>
> (6) *Leave things in the ineffable unborn expanse.*

By "unborn" we mean that this absolute nature is not something that has come into existence at one point and may cease to exist at another. It is completely beyond coming into existence and ceasing to exist. And it is not something distant, that you have to search for far away: it is present within the basic nature of your mind. How is this? If you do not prolong the past thought and do not encourage a future thought to arise, if you look between the past thought and the future thought that has not yet come and watch the nature of the present moment, you can recognize the primordial uncontrived nature of the mind, which has always been within you. This is the wisdom free from thought, which is between the thoughts. It is liberation itself. When one is able to see this vivid state, this is what we call profound insight, which is clear awareness.

> **The instruction on the mind that, watching, sees nothing, like someone who has eaten poison.**

> *The example is that of the falling lines that appear to the eyes of someone who has eaten a poisonous plant. Its meaning is that by recognizing that the apparent objects of the six consciousnesses are devoid of reality one reverses the belief in true existence.*

People, and even animals, that eat the fruit or seeds of the plant known in Tibet as *thang trom* experience all sorts of hallucinations. All about them they see scorpions, donkeys, and all sorts of terrifying beasts. Also, people who suffer from phlegm disorders experience visual aberrations and see lines and dots and so on. All these are pure hallucinations, deluded perceptions of things that have never truly existed. But our ordinary way of perceiving the six sensory experiences is no less deluded. We need to recognize them as delusions, as devoid of any solid existence. Once we do so, we will be free from our belief in the true reality of phenomena.

> *The actual instruction concerns the primordial unborn nature and comprises six points:*

> *(1) The absolute nature is primordially unstained by clinging.*

This primordial nature is like the lotus flower, which grows out of the mud but is not dirtied by it. Just as the lotus flower, with its beautifully colored petals enclosing the anther and the nectar inside, is unsullied by the mud, the primordial nature with all its qualities is completely unstained by the dualistic clinging to subject and object.

> *(2) The realization is naturally free from craving.*

It is free from the strong attachment to the eight ordinary concerns. But that freedom from attachment is not achieved by applying a remedy: craving dissolves by itself, naturally.

(3) The way of arising is spontaneous and free from grasping.

It is something that happens on its own, unlike contrived meditation in which one makes an effort to maintain sustained calm and to prevent deluded thoughts from arising in the mind. It is the wisdom realization of the absolute nature arising spontaneously without trying to contrive it or trying to control the mind.

(4) The experience is naturally present and not something that is made.

The wisdom of the absolute nature is always present and has been since the beginning. It is not something that has been made. And the experience of the recognition of that natural presence is devoid of any clinging to the recognition itself.

(5) The natural state is, from the very beginning, unborn and entirely devoid of self.

The recognition of the natural presence is not something to be sought outside. It is the natural manifestation of what is within us. Therefore,

(6) The display arises spontaneously and is not something to be sought.

If we adulterate appearances with our clinging, delusion will never cease. Therefore,

For outer appearances not to be spoiled by inner clinging, there is

The instruction on the mind free from judgments, like an infant.

Sometimes we think, "Today my meditation went well. I managed to remain in the natural state." At other times we get depressed because we have been unable to keep our mind under control. It is important to be free of these sorts of judgment where we value certain states and not others. We should be like tiny infants. Babies do not feel attachment if

226

something beautiful is put in front of them, nor do they think of feeling afraid if they are about to be killed by a butcher wielding a sword. They do not esteem good, they do not distrust bad.

The actual instruction:

(1) The absolute nature is the uncontrived mind.

The uncontrived mind is the Buddha's mind. If we look at the uncontrived nature of the mind, we will reach a state that is free from discursive thoughts:

(2) The view is the mind without thoughts.

It is the wisdom free from dualistic distinctions such as getting excited about good experiences and feeling uncomfortable about bad experiences:

(3) The primal wisdom is the mind without concepts.

It is the wisdom of the nondual mind.

(4) The meditation is the undistracted mind.

Although there is no particular object on which to focus, at the same time the mind should not wander.

(5) The essential nature of the mind is unwavering.

When our recognition of that nature becomes quite steady, it does not waver, like a mountain that is never moved by the wind. This is known as "leaving as-it-is like a mountain."[120]

(6) The samaya of the mind is the knowledge that nothing transcends the mind,

for none of the phenomena that exist in samsara and nirvana ever pass outside this absolute nature. When we realize that they are all the display of the nature of the mind, this is the true samaya of the mind.

(7) The activity of the mind is not to give up

—not to give up mindfulness in our actions, both in the meditation period and the postmeditation period, until we attain complete and firm realization of the absolute nature. Only then will the meditation be free from the defects of excitement and drowsiness.

For leaving the consciousness just as it is, relaxed in its own state, there is:

> **The instruction on leaving the mind as it is, as if stunned, like someone whose heart has been removed.**

> *The example is that of someone whose heart has been taken out: there is no hope of revival, and the continuous stream of thoughts is cut. The instruction on "leaving as it is, as if stunned"*[121] *is that by leaving everything as it is in the uncontrived natural state— without a subject that leaves, without an owner, as if stunned—one will settle at ease, free of grasping and effort, in the arising of the multifarious phenomena.*

If one removes the heart from someone's chest, there is no hope of his remaining alive. Likewise when one has permeated all one's perceptions with the view of the absolute nature, delusion has no hope of staying. "Leaving everything as it is" means that one does not apply all sorts of fabrications: one leaves things as they are in the mountainlike view. But it is not that there is a subject that leaves and something that is left. There is no question of taking possession of the state of meditation and thinking, "This is my meditation" or "This is your meditation." "As if stunned" implies that there is no owner. It is a neutral state in which there is a complete absence of grasping. With all the myriads of perceptions that arise in the mind, there is no fixation or clinging to these perceptions. They are just left in a completely relaxed state.

> *In this natural state of the inseparability of the two truths, leave things in uncontrived simplicity, a state of clear, empty awareness that is not produced by effort through different causes and conditions.*

In short, the manifested aspect, which is the infinite display of phenomena arising interdependently in accordance with the laws of causal-ity, is relative truth. And the fact that all these phenomena are permeated with the emptiness endowed with all supreme qualities is the absolute truth. The true nature is the essential unity of these two truths, relative and absolute. It is not a state that is produced artificially by means of different causes and conditions. It is something that is recognized by remaining in the great evenness, directly recognized through the blessings of the teacher. It is clear, empty awareness free from effort and not made to happen by a combination of causes and conditions. In that state there is no subject who meditates, no act of meditation, and no object of meditation: these three concepts are entirely absent.

38

The instruction on how to rest in the natural flow.

Son, there are four ways to stay.

Stay without thought in the clarity that is not acquired and can *never* be lost,

for the Buddha's wisdom has been present within you from the very beginning.

What do we mean by the wisdom of the Buddha? It is the indivisible union of clarity and emptiness, the absolute nature that is uncompounded and uncreated, the nature of the primal wisdom. That primal wisdom, which is the essence of Buddhahood, has always been present in our minds, but in our present deluded condition it is obscured, like the sun obscured by clouds. However, from the point of view of that nature itself, there has never been any obscuration, just as from the sun's point of view the sun has never been obscured. Once this view of the absolute nature has been realized, it cannot be lost again, for it has always been there. Neither is it something that has to be looked for or acquired, because one has always had it. It is free from discursive thoughts.

Stay without thinking in the bliss that is not to be evoked and cannot slip away,

for the mind from the very beginning is not caught and is not fettered.

In truth, the mind, since the very beginning, has never been caught or tied. It is the primordial state of enlightenment, which has never been bound or fettered. It is not something that one can lose, nor does one need to evoke it.

> **Stay in vivid clarity, undistracted in the state beyond distraction,**
>
> *for distracting objects have never been extraneous to the absolute nature.*

Since even the objects of distraction remain within the absolute nature, it is impossible to stray from the absolute nature. This is the true undistracted state.

> *How does one stay like that? There are six ways to be without contrivance:*
>
> *(1) If you look for mind, it is empty.*

At present, because we do not investigate things properly, we happily take them for granted and assume that the mind actually exists. After all, the mind seems so powerful. With all its past, present, and future thoughts it manages to accumulate so much karma. And yet, if we start to look for the mind, it is impossible to find it anywhere—not in any part of the body nor anywhere else. Neither is it possible to attribute to it any color or shape. If you look for the mind, you will only find emptiness.

Nevertheless, despite its empty nature, the mind does not stop producing thoughts. These thoughts must be recognized as being the mind's natural activity, its creativity, like the light constantly given out by the flame of a lamp. The reason we fall into delusion is that we fail to recognize that all these thoughts are, in fact, nothing other than the display of the absolute nature. So you must not think that true meditation is an absence of thoughts, a calm state of extinction in which nothing arises at all. If your idea is to prevent thoughts from arising, you will simply not realize the absolute nature:

> *(2) Block it and you will spoil it.*
>
> *(3) Contrive it and you will adulterate it.*

If you try to fabricate this absolute nature, which has been there from the beginning, you will simply be mixing it with impurity, staining it with defects.

(4) Meditate and you will be bound.

In any purposeful meditation, where you have the concepts of a meditator and a meditation, you will be tied down by the very act of meditating.

(5) Look at it and it will disappear.

When you look at the nature of the mind, "there is no mind," as it says in the *Prajnaparamita Sutras*. You cannot find it; it vanishes, because there is no true existence to be found in it.

(6) Effort will obscure it.

Therefore, do not seek, do not block, do not contrive, do not meditate, do not look, do not make effort: leave it just as it naturally is.

There being nothing in the mind for it to act on, nor anything to do through the path of action, nor anything that is accomplished,

Remain unhurried, with nothing to do, perfectly poised,[122]

the practice neither overtaut nor slack, like the string of a bent bow.

You should not say, "This is what I will meditate on," for there is nothing—no definite object with characteristics—that you have to realize. This is because the nature of mind is uncompounded and empty. It is not produced by any action, for it is primordially present. Simply remain in the recognition of this nature, watching it directly. Your practice should not alternate between sometimes being too tense and at other times being too relaxed. It should be even, like a bowstring, which is equally taut along its whole length, not tighter at one point and looser at another.

39

Unobstructed natural arising, the crucial point of the mind.

In order to preserve the absolute nature, we should not try to modify the mind or to block it.

Son, there are six crucial points of the mind to be
understood.

*Awareness, the fourth moment beyond the three—that directly
experienced, uncontrived state that is not adulterated by the notions
of subject and object—is the simplicity of the dharmakaya. So
recognize the mind with this instruction—the natural dissolution of
concepts:*

Relaxation is the crucial point of the mind, exemplified
by someone who has completed a task.

What we call the fourth moment is that in which one does not follow
the past thought, one does not invite future thoughts, and one is not at
present distracted by anything. It is the fourth aspect of time that transcends those three moments. If you look into awareness, there is no object to hold on to, neither any mind that clings. It is unstained by the
concept of subject and object. That direct experience is the natural dharmakaya state. With the spontaneous mindfulness of the absolute nature,
as if the dharmakaya were looking at itself, one is neither narrowly concentrated as in the effortful mindfulness of sustained calm nor distract-
edly ordinary. This is the instruction for naturally dissolving concepts.

Recognizing the mind in this way, one reaches a state similar to that
of someone who has successfully completed an enormous task and is
now utterly relaxed and calm, not busying himself in any way. Likewise,
when the mind sees its own nature, it is relaxed and does not make any
deliberate effort.

*Being free from the clinging to the true existence of things, one
has no concerns, thinking of things as good or bad:*

Freedom from concern is the crucial point of the mind,
exemplified by someone who has recovered from an
illness.

It is important to be free from clinging to the true existence of things.
Otherwise the mind will make distinctions—between good experiences
and bad ones, such as afflictive emotions and suffering. You should reach
the state in which the mind is unconcerned by good and bad thoughts,
like someone who has caught a disease and, having now recovered from
it, is no longer concerned about that disease.

As there is not a single thing that has not been pure and perfect since the very beginning, be free of the dualistic fixation of blocking some things and encouraging others.

Freedom from hesitation is the crucial point of the mind, exemplified by a madman jumping off a cliff.

There is not a single thing that is not by nature as primordially pure and perfect as a Buddha, so we should be free of different fixations such as stopping some things and accomplishing others. A Buddha is someone who has cleared away all obscurations and therefore does not need to prevent afflictive emotions and so on, which are no longer present in him. Similarly, he has all the qualities of the kayas and wisdoms, which are expressed naturally like the rays emitted by the sun, and so he does not need to deliberately accomplish or create these qualities. The crucial point, therefore, is to be free of concepts and to not evaluate one's meditation by wondering whether or not one is meditating correctly. Rather we should be like a mad person jumping off a precipice—without any hesitation.

Everything that appears is liberated as primal wisdom, so the view is free from duality, the meditation is free from fixation, the action is free from effort, and the result is free from aspiration.

Freedom from expectation and apprehension is the crucial point of the mind, exemplified by one's *having* met a person one had been looking for.

At this time, everything that arises through the six senses—visual, auditory, olfactory, gustatory, and so forth—will be understood as being the display of wisdom and will therefore be liberated in its own wisdom nature. The view will be free from clinging to the duality of subject and object. The meditation will be free from fixation such as concepts of existence, nonexistence, and the rest. The action will be completely spontaneous, with no efforts or goals such as cultivating generosity, contriving discipline, and so on. The result will be free from any expectation of achieving a result in the future, for our own awareness—this natural state of the present moment, the dharmakaya within ourself, the fresh state of Buddhahood that we hold in our hand—is not something to be obtained sometime in the future. So the mind should be relaxed, entertaining neither hopes nor fears, just as when we have met an old friend we had been looking for—we feel fully satisfied and do not need to search any further.

Uttering the specific language of Ati overawes those in the lesser vehicles.

Freedom from fear is the crucial point of the mind, exemplified by a lion walking among other savage beasts.

All these terms—freedom from hope and doubt, primordial simplicity, and so on—are the language of Ati, the Great Perfection, and they might alarm those with narrow minds who are following lesser vehicles. Just as the lion, when it comes upon other wild animals, has nothing to fear, the crucial point in the practice of the Great Perfection is that one is fully confident and has no fear of other views.

The natural state is naturally radiant; no veils obscure it.

Clarity with absence of thoughts is the crucial point of the mind, exemplified by the flame of a lamp filled with sesame oil,

which shines very brightly.

40

Showing that the view, meditation, action, and result are innate and not extraneous.

Son, there are four things you need not seek.

Since the wisdom of the absolute nature free of intellect dwells in you innately, there is no need to look for it anew using one-sided views that are the product of the intellect.

Having the view that has no dualistic fixation, do not seek one that has; take the example of the sun: it does not have to look for its rays.

Similarly, this view devoid of dualistic fixation is like the natural radiance of the sun.

> *Regarding the uncontrived natural flow, there is no need to meditate on it with dualistic fixation as if it were something new for you.*

> Having the meditation that has no object on which to focus, do not seek one that has; take the example of a wish-fulfilling gem: it does not have to look for the things one wants.

If you simply rest in the uncontrived natural flow, you do not need to look for new ways of meditating, applying the methods of sustained calm and so forth. Simply by being what it is, a wish-fulfilling gem is able to fulfill the wishes of everyone in the country, bringing wealth to the poor and so on. Likewise, there is no need to transform a meditation without supports into one with supports.

> *Since things to be rejected and antidotes—afflictive emotions and primal wisdom, for instance—have the same taste, there is no duality of deed and doer, so*

> Having the action free of adoption and rejection, do not seek one to adopt and reject; take the example of a person: he does not have to look for himself.

By achieving the even taste in which there is no need to get rid of afflictive emotions and apply antidotes or look for wisdom, you should realize this evenness in which there is no action involving rejection and adoption. Just as there is no need for a person to look for himself, follow the action in which there is nothing to give up and nothing to adopt.

> *The result, the primordial state of Buddhahood, dwells within you, so*

> Having the result free of hope and fear, do not look for one with hope and fear; take the example of a monarch: he does not have to reassert his royalty—

> *a king presiding on his throne depends on no one else.*

The result, primordial Buddhahood, is within you and does not need to depend on anything else, just as a king seated on his throne does not depend on others to rule his kingdom. He is master and is answerable to no one. Neither does he need to be afraid of another equally powerful king: both are confident in their own power and dignity. In the same way, the result implies complete confidence, without a trace of expectation or apprehension. So you do not need to look for a state in which hopes and doubts are still present.

> *Thus, since all phenomena in samsara and nirvana are by nature inseparable, do not move from the* inconceivable *evenness of the absolute nature that is beyond hope and fear, concept and effort.*

> *These chapters on the superior training of the mind have been arranged in a different order in the* Commentary *as follows. After the thirtieth chapter come chapters thirty-six to thirty-nine, at which point one jumps to chapter seventy-seven in the section on the training in wisdom. Next, one returns to chapters thirty-one to thirty-five, followed by chapter forty. Here, however, I have followed the exact order of the root text.*

Although in the Commentary the chapters have been rearranged in the logical order of the subjects they deal with, in this present annotated edition, for the sake of clarity, the order has been kept as it is in the root text.

> *To sum up, I have used these chapters to give an explanation to suit readers' individual capacities, so that relying on the superior training in concentration according to the* Prajnaparamita, *the* Epitome, *and the* Magical Display, *they practice the view and meditation on the path in much the same way as one brings up a small child—in stages—combining skillful means and wisdom like a bird flying in the sky. This completes the instruction.*

The different subjects have been expounded in order according to the *Prajnaparamita Sutras;* the *Epitome of Essential Meaning,* which is the *Gathering of the Great Assembly;*[123] and the *Net of the Magical Display of Peaceful and Wrathful Deities.* Relying on these three main sections, we should practice the view, meditation, and action on the path in the same way as one gradually brings up a child. In doing so, we need always to combine skillful means and wisdom, just as a bird needs both its wings to fly in the sky. All this has been explained to suit the different capacities of beings, some of whom are more intelligent than others.

> This was the third section from the Eighty Chapters of Personal Advice, the instruction on one-pointed concentration, the means.

Wisdom

Instructions on the superior training of wisdom, the perfect essence.

"Wisdom" here refers to the wisdom of no-self, which we have to realize.

There are thirty-eight chapters.

41

Twelve points that explain the view.

The realization referred to in the Later Mind Section is like a slash with a very sharp blade: with the wisdom devoid of the three concepts, all afflictive emotions and discursive thoughts are severed at the root. The way this happens is that since all phenomena of the ground, path, and result—samsara and nirvana—arise as the play of one's own unborn mind, they are free from ontological extremes, from good and bad, like space. The mind is by nature unborn, its display is unobstructed, its essential characteristic is absence of duality, and so on. In introducing this, the All-Accomplishing King *states,*

> Because all things are subsumed in the root, the mind,
> It is the root that has to be taught.

The Great Perfection is divided into the Mind Section, Expanse Section, and Section of the Pith Instructions. The Mind Section has eighteen subsections, divided into what are known as earlier and later,[124] referring to the order in which they were given. The explanation here follows the later teachings. These are said to be like a very sharp sword. In what way? In our present condition, we believe that subject, object, and action truly exist. It is these three concepts that we have to cut through, using the sharp blade of this instruction, which slices the root of all the afflictive emotions and deluded thoughts. When one cuts a tree at the root, everything—the trunk, branches, leaves, flowers, and fruit—falls to the ground at the same time. Similarly, if we cut ignorance at the root, the whole delusion of samsara will be instantly felled.

How do we cut through delusion? From the point of view of the way things appear, the ground—that is, our present condition when we start on the path—can be considered as impure, the path as a mixture of pure and impure, and the result as perfectly pure. But from the point of view of the way things are, there are no such things as pure and impure. What appears as impurity is simply an adventitious, temporary obscuration that has no existence of its own. But fundamentally there is nothing that has ever become anything other than what it has always been, primordially pure. The difference lies in whether or not this primordially pure nature is obscured. From its own point of view, the nature has not become worse when impurity is perceived; neither has it improved when purity is seen at the time of the result. It is like space, which can contain all the different universes, continents, mountains, and so forth and yet is not affected in any way by these things: it is not made better by things being beautiful, nor made worse by things being ugly. Similarly, all the different phenomena of the ground, path, and result arise as the display of one's mind, not affected by concepts such as good and bad. By nature the mind is unborn, its display is infinite and unobstructed, and its characteristic is the union of clarity and emptiness. This is how the nature of the mind is introduced, as being unborn, unobstructed, and free of duality. As it is said in the *All-Accomplishing King*, one of the Mind Section tantras, everything can be brought back to the mind, because the root of delusion and nondelusion is to be found in the mind itself. It is this mind that will now be explained.

Son, there are twelve points.

The unborn ultimate nature of your own mind is **not concealed anywhere,** *and yet* **nobody can see it** *as a concrete object with characteristics.*

An ordinary being who uses the conditioned intellect to search for the unborn nature of the mind, the dharmakaya, will find that there is nothing to be seen. It is impossible to assign any characteristic to this nature of the mind in the same way that one attributes combustion and heat to fire or a tendency to stay at the bottom of its container to water.

Though it has **never stopped being** *yours* **since the very beginning,** *hitherto you have* **not recognized it** *as your nature.*

In fact there is nothing to be seen, nothing to be sought, because the mind has been with you from the beginning. It has not been with you sometimes and separate from you at other times. Like your shadow, it always accompanies you. The only problem is that you have not recognized the nature of mind, like a pauper who is unaware that he is in possesion of a precious gem.

Since nothing exists as such inherently, **when things are examined, nothing is seen.** *However, when unexamined, they seem to exist: thus all the phenomena of samsara and nirvana* **appear in every possible way,** *unobstructedly.*

In terms of relative truth, we happily take it for granted that things exist and therefore believe in their existence. But as soon as we examine them in depth, everything collapses; we cannot find anything that truly exists. And yet they all—the deluded phenomena of samsara and the wisdom phenomena of nirvana—arise as an infinite display of the mind, appearing in every possible way, unobstructedly.

Though in fact there is nothing, deluded appearances **appear in all their variety,** *but since they do not intrinsically exist in any way,* **there is nothing real.**

In truth these are all deluded appearances. They appear but they do not truly exist, for though they manifest in one way or another, their ultimate nature is not something that one can seize with one's hand or touch with one's finger. Once we have realized the unborn absolute nature, we see that all these phenomena never separate from that nature and therefore have no true existence even though they appear. But they still arise multifariously, and even though from the point of view of the absolute nature they are nonexistent, when we perceive them in a deluded way we perpetuate karma.

> Though you have wandered for kalpas *in existence,*
> you have never lost or been parted *from the buddha-nature,*
> *sugatagarbha.*

Even though we have wandered in samsara for kalpas and kalpas, we have never once been parted from the essence of enlightenment. You might think that one is cut off from the buddha-nature when one is in samsara and reunited with it when one attains nirvana, but there has never been any separation.

> Though *the ultimate nature* appears *in* a variety of ways *as samsara and nirvana,* there has *never* been any change *in what it is.*

The absolute nature pervades the whole of samsara and nirvana. Even deluded phenomena occur within the absolute nature, but it is not tainted by them. In other words, deluded phenomena do not occur outside the absolute nature, and yet the absolute nature does not intrinsically contain delusion. It is unchanging and has never been stained or limited, even when we are deluded, for despite delusion not happening outside the absolute nature, when it is dispelled and we realize the absolute nature, the latter does not grow better in any way; it remains as it has always been.

> Without having *as much as* a part of the *minutest* atom[125] *of solid existence,* it pervades everything *like space.*
>
> Within emptiness, *which is like space,* the various *phenomena that arise through the interdependent process of cause and effect* appear *unobstructedly.*

In this emptiness, which is like space, relative phenomena manifest interdependently, with causes giving rise to effects, so that negative actions lead inevitably to suffering and positive actions lead inevitably to happiness.

> *The mind is like an unbroken horse: if you are tense and agitated,*
> *you cannot control it; if you relax, you can control it. Therefore,*
> **When it is not held or tied, it stays wherever it is.**

We can never understand the nature of the mind through intense effort but only by relaxing, just as breaking a wild horse requires that one approach it gently and treat it kindly rather than running after it and trying to use force. So do not try to catch hold of the nature of the mind, just leave it as it is.

> *By uniting sustained calm and profound insight,* **one travels**
> **through the space** *of the absolute nature* **unsupported,** *like*
> *a soaring garuda.*

A garuda launching itself into space from the top of a cliff does so without the slightest apprehension: it does not need anything to support it as it soars into the sky. Likewise, with sustained calm and profound insight united we can fly unsupported in the space of the absolute nature.

> *From the absolute nature that is not anything, anything can*
> *arise, so*
> **everything possible is accomplished without effort.**

This absolute nature has no characteristics whatsoever. Neither is there any solidity to it that makes it existent, nor is it nonexistent in the sense of being a blank void. And it is precisely for this reason, its being devoid of all characteristics, that it can manifest in every way possible; in other words, everything possible is effortlessly accomplished.

> **Without** *the mind's having color, shape,* **form, or**
> **characteristics, whichever way one views it** *and meditates*
> *on it, in that way* **it appears.**

The mind, too, is intrinsically devoid of characteristics. We cannot say that it has a color, a shape, a form, and so on. Because of this it, too, can appear in every possible way. Whichever way one looks at it or meditates upon it, in that way it appears. It is this very fact that everything is empty that allows the whole multiplicity of phenomena to manifest.

> To sum up, this is an introduction to the nature of the mind.
> As it is unborn, there is no real basis to it that can be found. As
> its display is unobstructed, unlimited, and infinite, it arises in
> various ways, manifesting as suffering, happiness, and neutral
> states. As it is ultimately free of duality, there is nothing to cling
> to as true, as existing or not existing; one cannot ascribe any
> solid existence to it. When the conceptual mind is liberated in
> its essence, nothing ever moves from the dharmata.

42

> Twelve kinds of confidence confirming the view.
>
> From having seen the ultimate truth in its full nakedness, the
> mind is free of doubt.

Once we have seen the dharmata, we no longer have the slightest doubt or hesitation. We do not need to ask ourselves, "Is this really the absolute nature?"

> Son, there are twelve kinds of confidence:
>
> The confidence that just as the whole of existence is
> created and destroyed in space, everything in samsara and nirvana
> is one and the same in thatness and therefore has no intrinsic
> nature.

It is in space that in the beginning the universe and beings are formed as a result of karma, it is in space that in the end they all dissolve and vanish, and it is in space that they remain in the meanwhile. Similarly, everything in samsara and nirvana is of one taste within the absolute nature. Once we know this, we gain the clear conviction that everything is devoid of true existence.

The confidence that since the root *of all things*—both delusory and pure—is subsumed in the mind, Buddhahood is not *to be sought* elsewhere than in the mind.

The confidence that since the mind *by nature* has no birth *and no cessation,* it is uncompounded.

The confidence that since everything that appears is delusory, in truth enemies and friends do not exist *inherently as different entities.*

Everything we perceive is like an illusion conjured up by a magician. Simply by blowing a spell onto a table or other prop, the magician can make horses, chariots, and even an entire army appear, but there are no horses or chariots there: it is all an illusion. Similarly, when we gain the conviction that everything we perceive is an illusion—for though it appears, it does not truly exist—we will see that friends and enemies, too, are not truly existent.

The confidence that since all actions *based on delusion* are suffering—*that is, they are the cause of suffering*—in truth, *in terms of the ultimate nature,* there is nothing to be done—

no action to be performed and therefore no suffering to be experienced.

The confidence that since *the unborn absolute space* is the nature of all *phenomena, the nature* is nondual.

The confidence that there is no traveling *the path,* for realizing *the unborn nature of your mind* is Buddhahood—

Buddhahood is simply realizing what you actually have.

The confidence that the mind cannot be troubled by attachment and aversion, for everything that appears is untrue *like a magical illusion.*

The confidence that *although mind and appearances are many* and multifarious, *they have one taste* in being the display of the mind, *and that therefore the thoughts related to the five poisons such as* attachment and aversion are *intrinsically* unborn.

The confidence that objects *such as friends and enemies*
that arouse *afflictive emotions, apart from simply being labels
assigned by the ordinary mind, do not have any essential existence
of their own; they* all dissolve in the mind.

The objects that make afflictive emotions grow, namely enemies and
friends, are simply labels created by the mind. They do not exist on their
own. There is no such thing as an enemy that remains one's enemy all
one's life and throughout one's series of lives. Neither is there such a
thing as a friend who has been a friend from the very beginning and will
remain a friend forever. "Friend" and "enemy" are just labels that the
mind attaches to the relevant objects. Once we know that these notions
have no true existence, we will become confident that they dissolve
within the mind.

The confidence that as *the nature of mind,* emptiness, is
the source of everything *in samsara and nirvana,* it is the
Absolute Space—the Mother, Prajnaparamita.

The confidence that *the natural state of the mind* is the great
immensity, *for, like space,* it is the place where everything
dwells.

This is confidence in the vastness of the nature of the mind. Just as
space can accommodate the whole universe—the mountains, continents,
and so forth, the nature of the mind is so vast that it can accommodate
the whole of phenomena.

43

An instruction on seeing the absolute nature in nine ways.

Son, there are nine things *that, as a yogi on the path,* one sees.

One sees that everything *in samsara and nirvana* is empty.

One sees that the root *of all phenomena* is the mind.

If one has not recognized the nature of mind, the mind is the root of
delusion; if one does recognize it, it is the root of enlightenment.

One sees that the nature *of one's own mind* is unborn.

One sees that *since the seventeen kinds of perception and so forth are unobstructed in the way they arise,* one's situation is unpredictable.

The mind displays in different ways depending on different circumstances. There are seventeen major ways in which it manifests: six correspond to the six realms, two to eternalism and nihilism, and nine to the nine vehicles.

One sees that the nature *of all phenomena* is devoid of true existence.

One sees that *despite the multifariousness of appearances and perceptions,* the natural state *of the absolute space* does not change.

Phenomena never waver from the wisdom of the dharmakaya, so although the way they appear may differ, the way the expanse of the absolute nature is never changes.

One sees that *since it is spontaneously arisen and free of causes and conditions,* the way-it-is is devoid of duality,

because in the nature of mind there is no division into subject and object.

One sees that *while it displays multifariously because of conditions,* the ground nature itself does not tend toward any particular direction.

One sees that the fundamental nature is devoid of concepts, *for there are no thoughts of ontological extremes such as existence and nonexistence.*

44

Seeing seven aspects of sublimity.

The meditator is free, for his mind has no owner and no responsibility.

Son, there are seven sublime things.

To be free from intellectual meditation is the sublime "leaving things as they are":[126]

Do not try to fixate on existence and nonexistence, appearance and emptiness, and so on.

To be free of *the ordinary mind's dualistic* references *with regard to the absolute nature, which is beyond all reference,* is the sublime reference.

Neither thought nor no-thought transcends the intellect, and intellectual activity obscures freedom from intellect; thus,

Not to meditate on absence of thoughts is the sublime absence of thought.

Whether one has thoughts or remains in a state where there are no thoughts, one is still within the domain of the intellect. But trying to stop conceptual thoughts is not the solution, because the state free from the intellect remains obscured by intellectual fabrication. We need to be in a state that is beyond elaborations and concepts, free from thought, and, at the same time, without intentional meditation. This is the sublime absence of thought as opposed to a relative, limited, and artificial absence of thought.

Not to use any *object of knowledge* as a support is the sublime support.[127]

Not to meditate on anything, *such as the union of appearances and emptiness,* the union of clarity and emptiness, or the union of emptiness and awareness, *making it a mental object,* is the sublime meditation.

To remain undistracted, with no *deliberate* attempt to stop the movements *of the mind and mental factors,* is the sublime concentration.[128]

The sublime concentration is one in which the movements of the mind flow freely without obstruction, without any attempt to block them. One does not try to stop the mind and its functions, but at the same time one is never distracted from the recognition of its nature.

> **When the mind is not involved with any** *of the objects of*
> *the eight consciousnesses,* **seeing forms, scenting odors, tasting,**
> **and so on, this is the sublime absorption.**[129]

> *In short, all these amount to leaving things as they are,*
> *unadulterated by dualistic fixation and contrivance.*

45

An instruction on perceiving in a nondualistic way but without
denying the experiences of *the six sense organs being distinct*
and different.

Son, there are six wisdom sense organs

that arise from certainty concerning the absolute nature.

When one knows that perceived forms are unborn, one does not grasp
at them, and therefore

One sees the forms of mind's projection with the wisdom
eye.

One understands the meaning of emptiness—*the absolute*
nature—**with the wisdom ear.**

One senses *the nature* **as unborn with the wisdom nose.**

One tastes *multifariousness* **in a nondualistic way with the**
wisdom tongue.

One touches *the truth,* **the absolute nature, with the wisdom**
body.[130]

One knows that all that arises as the **mind's projection arises in**
the *unborn* **nature of the mind with the wisdom mind.**

46

Using the above modes of perception to perceive in a nondualistic
way without denying things being distinct and different.

If your own mind is free in the absolute nature, everything that appears outside arises as the absolute nature.

When one has recognized the nature of mind and there is no clinging to any of the phenomena of samsara and nirvana, all outer phenomena arise as the display of that nature, as ornaments to it, and they thus enhance the realization of the absolute nature. They are realized as manifestations of the absolute nature and therefore do not obstruct its recognition. So here, instead of six delusory objects, we shall consider six wisdom objects.

Son, there are six wisdom objects.

The absolute nature **seen as clarity and emptiness inseparable is the wisdom form.**

If one has the direct experience of seeing the absolute nature as the nondual, intrinsic union of clarity and emptiness, this is what we call wisdom form.

Sound understood as spontaneously arisen, *like the voice heard in an echo that does not belong to anyone,* **is the wisdom sound.**

The voice you hear in an echo is not really somebody's voice, even though you hear it as a voice. It is simply a reflection; the echo has not actually been created by anyone. So when sound is perceived as the echolike resonance of emptiness, this is the wisdom sound.

The *teacher's* **instruction imbibed to satiety is the wisdom fragrance.**

It is the teacher's instructions that enable us to realize the absolute nature, so we should carefully savor even a single one of them again and again, listening to it, reflecting upon it, and then meditating on it over and over. When we delight in the teacher's instruction like this, that delight is the wisdom fragrance.

The experience of *all phenomena* **as unborn is the wisdom flavor.**

When, without any notion of subject and object, we directly experience all the phenomena of samsara and nirvana as being unborn, we experience the wisdom flavor. It is the true flavor of the meaning of the teachings and not merely of the words.

> The great bliss—*the absolute nature*—touched is the wisdom texture.

Within the absolute nature there is nothing but purity. It is impossible to find even a trace of impurity. There is therefore no suffering. Neither is there a cause of suffering such as an afflictive emotion or action. There is only the great bliss, which, when we attain it, is the object of the wisdom sense of touch.

> The recognition *of the natural state, the dharmata,* is the wisdom phenomenon.[131]

The dharmata is something that has to be recognized, but in a nondualistic way and not as an object that is recognized by a subject. It can only be realized by Awareness.[132] This recognition is the "object" of the wisdom mind.

47

Upon investigation, things are seen to be nonexistent in six ways.

On a relative level, the phenomena of samsara and nirvana appear and seem to exist, but if we examine them properly, we find that they have no true existence. There are six ways of perceiving this nonexistence.

> Son, there are six authentic experiences.[133]
>
> *Since all phenomena have no true existence as such,*
>
> To not see them at all is authentic sight.

Relative phenomena appear momentarily like a rainbow forming in the sky: in truth they have no intrinsic, permanent existence. And since they do not exist, there is nothing to see. To see that there is nothing to see is what is known as "the great seeing," or "authentic sight." Seeing the absolute nature is sight without a seer, an object seen, or an act of seeing. Nevertheless, we give this realization of the true nature of phenomena the name "sight."

> *Since there is no duality of a hearer and something to be heard regarding the absolute nature,*
>
> **To not hear anything is authentic hearing.**
>
> *There being in fact no duality of someone who senses and something to be sensed,*
>
> **To not sense anything is the authentic perception.**

In truth, in the absolute view, meditation, and action there is no object or action. One is beyond all such concepts. So the authentic perception is absence of perception with regard to the whole of phenomena, from form up to omniscience.

> *Similarly,*
>
> **To not taste anything is the authentic taste.**

If we experience happiness, pleasure, suffering, or pain, it is because the experience is tinged with clinging. But here we are talking about the experience that is a nonexperience, the supreme experience.[134]

> **Not mentally touching anything,** *true or false or whatever,*
> **is the authentic contact.**

This is contact where the mind does not touch either the supposed truth of nirvana or the supposed falsity of samsara.

> **Not being aware of any** *characteristics in the whole of*
> *phenomena* **is the authentic awareness.**

This is awareness that does not take the conditioned characteristics of phenomena as its object.

48

Explaining six kinds of effortlessness, there being nothing
in the absolute nature to adopt or reject.

There is nothing to obtain through purposeful effort, so

If one knows how to leave all phenomena without deliberate
action, one is liberated in the basic natural state:

Son, there are six declarations on effortlessness.

Because in the space of one's unborn mind there is not the duality
of a viewer and something to be viewed, **one settles in the**
view *without contrivance or modification, affirmation or negation,*
and one's mind remains **in total rest without any concept of**
vastness or constraint.

When we stay in the view of natural simplicity without trying to
modify what we feel is bad by transforming it into something good or
to prevent some things and accomplish others, the mind will rest in the
infinite expanse of the absolute nature without any feeling of congestion
or obstruction.

The meditation is the utter peace *of the absolute nature,*
radiance from the depth, *free of grasping and devoid of rough*
edges—thoughts related to outer and inner phenomena.

Within the absolute nature there is nothing to meditate on and no
action of meditating. We are simply dealing with the spontaneous radiance of wisdom deep within. Like a flame, wisdom is inherently luminous. At the same time, it throws light on other things, yet remains free
from clinging to them. The meditation is a state devoid of the spikes of
thoughts related to outer and inner phenomena. It is the utter peace of
the absolute nature.

The action, *uncontrived and natural,* **is joyful spontaneity,**
without *the effort of* **adoption** *or abstention.*

In this kind of action there is nothing that has to be specially grasped or achieved, nothing one has to try to get rid of. It is natural and effortless, acted out in accord with a spontaneous joy.

> *Since the mode of being of things is actualized,* **there is no hope** *of achieving* **the result or fear** *of not achieving it;* **there is** **all-pervading peace:** *dualistic concepts of subject and object dissolve by themselves.*

Once one has realized the nature of things, one no longer hopes to attain Buddhahood, neither is one apprehensive that one might not obtain it. One simply remains in the even state of all-pervading peace in which all notions of subject and object have been freed in their own sphere.

> **It is the universal evenness** *in the continuum of the absolute nature: things are* **beyond all distinctions of quality or magnitude.**

In the absolute nature all relative phenomena, whatever they are, are the same. There is no good or bad, large or small. Only a universal evenness, with no difference either between meditation and postmeditation.

> **It is the utmost ease where the mind has no sorrow,**
>
> *for samsara, without being rejected, is primordially free, beyond suffering.*

There is no need to reject samsara. It is all nothing but wisdom, so one is free from the torments of conditioned existence. There is only the utmost ease.

49

An instruction on sixteen metaphoric practices.

Son, there are sixteen metaphoric practices.

Once the absolute nature is actualized, all the various phenomena become its symbols.

Always strip *the awareness* **naked** *so that it is unobscured by* *characteristics.*

This is what we need to realize, awareness divested of all obscurations related to characteristics of conditioned things.

Always perform the great ablution *of emptiness as the* *antidote for the belief in substantial existence and for clinging to* *true existence.*

It is the realization of emptiness that is the principal antidote for our belief in solid reality and our clinging to true existence.

Take the sun and the moon—*emptiness and compassion***—in** **your hand.**

By holding the sun and the moon in our two hands we would dispel the darkness of the whole world. Similarly, when we realize the emptiness of phenomena and when, within that emptiness, there arises spontaneous compassion, the union of these two is the culmination of the Bodhisattva path.

Whirl the wheel *of view and meditation.*

Whirling the wheel of the view and meditation directly cuts through all deluded perception and confusion.[135]

Gaze in the *magical* **mirror** *of your mind.*

If you look at yourself in a clear mirror, you can see all the blemishes on your face and can then try to remove them. Likewise, by looking in the mirror of the mind, you can see all the delusion that has occurred in it and thus remove that delusion.

Cure the sickness caused by the poison *of the* five *afflictive* *emotions.*

Untie the rope binding you—*that of the three poisons or* the notions *of subject and object.*

Flee *the company of evildoers: they are like* **savage beasts of prey.**

Keeping the company of negative friends who hold incorrect views is likely to make you stray off the path to liberation, so you should stay well away from them.

> *Having recognized the spontaneously arisen primal wisdom,*
> **reside in the crystal vase** *of awareness—emptiness and clarity*
> *inseparable.*

Once we have recognized self-cognizing primal wisdom, all the vital points of the practice are contained within the vase of empty, clear awareness.

> **Climb the jewel stairs** *from the bottom to the top,*
> *practicing the ten Dharma activities*[136] *and so on with faith,*
> *diligence, mindfulness, vigilance, and carefulness.*

With these five[137] we cannot but accomplish the activities of the sublime Dharma and we will not do any negative actions. So climb the steps of the ten Dharma activities, such as reading and writing, for whatever we undertake of the ten activities will lead to our accumulating an inconceivable store of merit and naturally acquiring excellent qualities.

> **Cut the tree** *of belief in a self* **at the root.**
>
> **Sleep in the openness of space,** *uncircumscribed awareness.*

Rest in the immensity of space, in the state of evenness, which has no edge or limit.

> *Let your own thought-movements* **commit suicide.**

"Commit suicide" refers to the fact that the movements of deluded thought destroy themselves—that is, they dissolve by themselves—in the realization of the absolute nature.

> **Hasten to the golden isle** *where everything that appears*
> *and is perceived arises as the absolute nature.*

Just as one would never find ordinary stones on a golden island, once one has realized the absolute nature, everything that appears to the six senses arises as an ornament for the absolute nature and cannot cause that realization to decline.

> **Anoint your body with the balm** *of concentration to allay*
> *the fever of desire and hatred.*

Anointing the body of a feverish patient with camphor or some other medicinal substance rapidly brings down the patient's temperature. Similarly, the cooling balm of concentration naturally causes the fever of attachment and aversion to abate.

> **Pick sky flowers:** *in truth they do not exist; phenomena are*
> *but names.*

All phenomena—pillars, vases, mountains, and the rest—are simply names given to perceptions, the manifestations of things that do not exist, like the two moons one sees if one presses a finger on one's eye when looking at the moon. Through the interdependence of cause and effect, relative phenomena appear but they have no true existence, like a sky flower. When we speak of a sky flower, it is only a name: it has neither shape nor scent. You cannot pick it with your hands, neither can you make a garland with it.

50

> *There being nothing to adopt or reject, the view is free of*
> *affirmation or negation.*

As there is no clinging to the notions of good and bad, there is nothing to reject and nothing to adopt.

> **Son, there are five views.**
>
> *All thoughts that arise are the unborn absolute nature, so*
>
> **Do not get angry at thoughts.**

The primal wisdom of no-thought is not to be meditated on separately.

When one remains in the natural flow of the absolute nature, various thoughts may pass one after another through the past, present, and future but in truth they are never born, they never remain, and they never cease. They never leave the realm of the unborn absolute nature. With regard to thoughts, therefore, there is nothing to be angry at. Simply see them as the ornament of the absolute nature. Besides recognizing the absolute nature and seeing thoughts as its ornament, there is no wisdom of no-thought that has to be meditated on separately.

Primal wisdom or dharmata is not to be sought on some far shore rid of afflictive emotions and thoughts, so

Do not be attached to the absolute nature.

As long as you have attachment you create the cause for wandering in samsara.

It is important to realize that wisdom and the afflictive emotions are not two separate things, like a piece of gold and stains on it. The very nature of desire, hatred, and the other afflictive emotions is wisdom. So wisdom is not some distant land to be reached, leaving the afflictive emotions behind. It is simply a question of dwelling in the recognition of the absolute nature. But if, in doing so, the thought occurs to you that you have achieved the perfect view, you may fall into the error of attachment; as it is said, "While there is attachment, there is no view,"[138] and attachment is the cause of samsara.[139]

Knowing all phenomena to be equal,

Do not be proud of *your* concentration—

do not feel conceited or self-satisfied, priding yourself on your concentration being free from distraction and delusion.

Everything unwanted and all wrong thoughts are a display of your own mind, so

Do not be resentful of anything wrong.[140]

Undesirable circumstances such as suffering and sickness, and wrong thoughts like desire and attachment, are, all of them, simply the display of your own mind, so you should recognize their nature rather than trying to get rid of them. Here "resentful" of wrong thoughts means that when they arise, you should not begrudge them and be obsessed with feeling you have to get the better of them.

Since you yourself possess the spontaneously arisen primal wisdom,

Do not be confused with regard to wisdom:

Recognize it.

The self-arisen wisdom is not something you have to look for far away. It is present within you. If you recognize this wisdom that you have, you are no longer obscured by confusion.

51

Explaining ten aspects of complete confidence in the natural state.

Since all the dualistic perceptions of happiness, suffering, and so forth are freed in the absolute space, one cannot be benefited or harmed by anything:

Son, there are ten aspects to complete confidence.

Ordinary beings have the concepts of suffering and happiness: suffering is something they wish to get rid of; happiness and pleasure are something they want to keep. But for someone in whom everything has dissolved in the absolute space, happiness brings no benefit, suffering does no harm. The complete confidence one gains from remaining in such a state of evenness can cope with ten kinds of situations.

The self-arisen primal wisdom or bodhichitta has no cause or conditions and is therefore unchanging in the past, present, and future.

Everything possible[141] may pour down like rain,

but bodhichitta, the kingly doer-of-all, will never get wet or stained.

The self-arisen wisdom, which is also called bodhichitta, is not something that has been fabricated, a new product created by the conjunction of causes and conditions. It never has changed, never changes, and never will change. The absolute nature remains what it is, perfectly pure, at all times. Even if it appears obscured for impure beings at the start of the path, it has never actually been obscured. If it seems to be a mixture of pure and impure during the course of the path, it in fact always remains pure. And at the time of the result, perfect enlightenment, it is simply the same ground nature made evident and not something new that was not there before. So even though all the hallucinations that make up existence fall like rain from the sky, it cannot affect one's confidence: the kinglike bodhichitta that is the doer-of-everything will never be stained or dampened.

> *Similarly,*
>
> **The three worlds may overflow, gushing forth like a river** cascading over a cliff,
>
> *but it*—the kingly bodhichitta—*will not be carried away.*
>
> **Even though the six mental states—the five poisons and** miserliness—**may blaze like fire,**
>
> *it*—the absolute nature—*will not be consumed.*
>
> **The one thousand million worlds may be buffeted as if by the wind,**
>
> *but it will remain unmoved.*

The universe of a thousand million worlds may shake as if buffeted by the wind, but the realization of the nature will remain unmoved, like a mighty mountain. As it is said, leaving things as they are is the measure of the perfect, mountainlike view.

> **The three poisons may gather like darkness,**
>
> *but it will not grope in confusion.*

The three poisons may obscure everything, but they cannot obscure wisdom, which is inherently luminous and radiant from within.

The thousand million worlds may be filled by the sun,

but this will never illuminate the primal wisdom.

The sun may spread throughout the universe of a thousand million worlds, but this could never make wisdom brighter than it already is and has always been.

Whole continents may be plunged into darkness,

but the nature can never be eclipsed by ignorance.

Birth and death may be distinct,

but it cannot die.

Birth and death might appear different, but in truth there is no such thing as birth and death.

One may have karmic tendencies,

but from the very beginning the nature has never been affected,
so there is nothing to discard now.

There is no need to get rid of habitual tendencies that come from having accumulated positive and negative actions, because they only exist from the point of view of the way things appear. From the point of view of the way things are, there have never been any habitual tendencies to stain the absolute nature, so there is no need to discard them now.

Phenomenal existence may be turned upside down,

but the nature will not be destroyed or separated.

As the "Prayer of Samantabhadra" says, "Even when the three worlds are destroyed, there is no fear." Neither is there attachment.

These are the vajra words on the wisdom—the total confidence
and conviction—that cannot be crushed by anything.

52

An instruction that matches examples and their meanings to show how the absolute nature permeates everything.

These various examples give a general idea of the absolute nature.

Son, there are four examples and their meanings.

Take the example of a Sugata's body: whichever way one looks at it, it is beautiful. *Similarly,* **everything** *a realized being* **does, since it is permeated with the** *realization of the* **unborn nature, is bliss,** *for he does not have ordinary attachment and aversion.*

Whether one looks at a Sugata's face or any other part of his body, one never feels one has looked enough. It is an example of ultimate beauty. Similarly, those for whom everything is backed by the realization of the unborn nature no longer have ordinary attachment and aversion, and such persons can therefore act like enlightened beings: whatever they do is bliss. Since they have fully realized the absolute nature, there is no question of telling them, "This is the right thing to do; that is something you should not do." They have no concepts or limits, so they can act as they wish. Everything they do will be nothing but bliss.

Take the example of a smile and a scowl: two expressions but no more than *one* **face.** *Similarly,* **everything that appears, everything that exists—***all the manifestation of samsara or nirvana***—does so within the unborn absolute nature.**

Samsara and nirvana are like two expressions on the same face, one dark and sullen, the other light and smiling. But, whatever the expression, we are not talking about a different face. It is not degraded when smeared with the dirt of samsara, neither is it improved when the dirt of samsara is washed off. Samsara and nirvana remain within the expanse of the absolute nature in the same way that the universe with its different continents all appear in space.

Take the example of a blind person: it makes no difference whether one smiles at him or not. *Similarly, since everything that arises unobstructedly from the unborn absolute space is inseparable from it and has the same taste,* **in the absolute nature there is nothing to be adopted or rejected.**

If you smile at blind people, they do not think, "That person is happy with me." If you frown at them, they do not think, "He is upset with me." It is the same with phenomena: they are all of one taste, intrinsically one, appearing in an unobstructed way from the expanse of the unborn while remaining inseparable from it. For this reason, in the absolute nature there is nothing to adopt and nothing to give up.

Take the example of the trunk of a plantain tree: it has no core.[142] *Similarly,* **phenomenal existence has no essence,**

for when examined using such logical arguments as "Neither one nor many,"[143] *there is nothing to be found.*

The plantain tree is hollow inside: it has no solid core. It is also said that it is without essence, in the sense that it bears fruit only once. If you analyze phenomena with the aim of determining their ultimate nature, using the "neither one nor many" argument, you will find they have no true existence. Phenomenal existence is devoid of essence: it is emptiness endowed with supreme qualities.

53

When the four ontological extremes dissolve by themselves, it is shown that phenomena are the mind's projections and do not have to be abandoned.

Son, there are four dissolutions of extremes.

As regards all the phenomena of samsara and nirvana,

In the absolute truth they are unborn, so they are beyond the extreme of existence.

Although samsara and nirvana appear, in truth they are devoid of solid existence, of any existing entity. One cannot, therefore, say that they exist.

In relative truth,

the appearance aspect that is the interdependent gathering of causes and conditions,

they are unceasing, so they are beyond the extreme of nonexistence.

This empty nature, the lack of intrinsic existence in phenomena, does not imply a blank naught in which there is nothing at all, as we find in the view of the nihilists. According to relative truth, all phenomena arise as a result of the interdependent conjunction of causes and conditions. This enables us to explain not only how samsara is formed but also how it is possible to progress toward nirvana. There is no contradiction between the absolute nature and its infinite display and, because of this, one is free from the extreme of *existence* and that of *nonexistence*.

Ultimately, the two truths, or appearance and emptiness, do not exist as distinct phenomena: *there is no basis for such distinctions, they are inseparable—in other words,* they are not two, so they are beyond the extreme of both existence and nonexistence.

One cannot say that the two truths are distinct or that appearance and emptiness are distinct, because if one examines the relative truth in depth, one arrives at the absolute truth, and it is within the absolute truth that the relative truth appears as its display. They are actually indistinguishable, they cannot be separated, and they are thus not two. In this way one must be free from the extreme of *both existence and nonexistence*.

Intellectually apprehended, "neither" arises as "both," so phenomena are beyond the extreme of neither existence nor nonexistence.[144]

One might, then, cling to the opposite notion and have an intellectual concept that phenomena neither exist nor do not exist. So one must be free of this extreme as well, the extreme of *neither existence nor nonexistence*.

Regarding this, there are four faults that occur if one asserts that the two truths are one and the same:

Ultimately we must be free of all kinds of ontological extremes and postulates. The two truths are neither two distinct things nor a single entity; they are beyond any concept of being one or two. To those who cling to the concept of a single entity and say that the two truths are one and the same, excluding even the possibility of its having two aspects, it can be shown that there are four faults in such an argument:

(1) it would follow that ordinary beings who see compounded phenomena could see the absolute truth;

If there were no difference whatsoever between absolute truth and relative truth, this would mean that since ordinary beings can perceive the relative truth they must also be able to see the absolute truth. This is not the case.

(2) it would follow that the absolute truth could be an objective condition for afflictive emotions arising;

Relative phenomena are the causes for afflictive emotions arising, so if relative and absolute were the same, absolute truth would also be a cause for the arising of afflictive emotions. This is not the case.

(3) it would follow that there was no distinction between relative and absolute;

If they were the same, there would be no way to recognize absolute truth as distinct from relative truth, and this too is not correct.

(4) it would follow that the absolute truth would not depend on listening to the teachings and reflecting on them.

To experience the relative truth one does not need to practice the Dharma or gain any experience in it, so if the two truths were exactly the same, one would also be able to realize the absolute truth without listening to the teachings, reflecting on them, and meditating: such things would be unnecessary.

> *And there are four faults that occur if one asserts that they are different,*

One might argue, on the other hand, that the relative truth and absolute truth are essentially separate and distinct. Such an argument also has four faults.

> *for it would then follow that:*
>
> *(1) the mind that had realized the absolute could not dispel the belief that relative phenomena truly exist;*

If relative and absolute were completely separate and unrelated, realizing the absolute truth would not help to dispel our clinging to relative phenomena as truly existent. But in fact when one realizes the absolute truth, the belief in the true existence of relative phenomena is simultaneously dispelled.

> *(2) absolute truth would not be the ultimate nature of relative phenomena;*

If they were separate things, the ultimate nature of relative truth could never be absolute truth. But in reality, when we examine the nature of relative truth, we arrive at absolute truth.

> *(3) the absence of intrinsic existence in relative phenomena would not be the absolute truth;*

The fact that the phenomena of relative truth have no true existence of their own *is* the ultimate truth. So we speak of absolute truth in relation to relative truth. If they were completely separate entities, we could not describe absolute truth in these terms.

> *(4) sublime beings would see them separately and would be bound and liberated at one and the same time.*

Seeing relative phenomena means being in a state of ignorance, while understanding absolute truth means being free. If, then, the two truths were separate, enlightened beings would see both separately; they would be at the same time enslaved in relative truth and liberated in absolute truth.

> In our tradition there are none of these faults because we make no assertions at all about the two truths being either single or different. We establish two truths in relation to the conditions, deluded or nondeluded, of a single mind: in the deluded state the absolute truth does not appear to the relative, deluded mind, while in the nondeluded state the delusory relative does not appear to the mind that has realized the absolute truth. Thus the two truths are like light and darkness. On the one hand, they have one and the same nature but different aspects; on the other hand, their differences disallow their being one and the same. Both of these are explained in the Commentary.

None of the above faults is to be found in our own tradition because we do not subscribe to the views that see the two truths either as a single entity or as two distinct entities. All we are saying here is that the relative and absolute truth are related to the condition of a single mind that is either deluded or nondeluded. When it is deluded, this is the relative truth, and the ultimate nature of things does not arise in the deluded mind. When the undeluded absolute truth is realized, the delusory perceptions of relative truth do not arise. In this way relative and absolute truths are like darkness and light. One cannot have darkness and light at the same time. Likewise, relative truth and absolute truth, though fundamentally of the same nature, are simply two aspects, one obscured and the other enlightened, each excluding the other. When the light manifests, darkness disappears. When darkness is present, there is no light. This is explained in the Commentary.

54

Four ultimate aspects that decisively establish the ultimate path.

Son, there are four ultimates.

Having recognized all outer and inner phenomena to be
the play of your own mind,

like the things that appear in a dream,

to know that the mind is empty and immaterial is the
ultimate reach of the view.

As exemplified by a person in a magical illusion,

While not blocking the five senses, to be free from notions
of subject and object is the ultimate reach of meditation.

The illusions of people, soldiers, horses, and so forth that a magician
creates are simply the result of his casting a spell or reciting some mantras, and the magician himself is not attached to the things he has projected. So to be free from any clinging to subject and object, while not
blocking the perceptions of the five senses, is the ultimate reach of meditation.

*As exemplified by the accumulation of merit and wisdom by a
great emanation,*

To know how to act uniting view and action is the
ultimate reach of action.

Bodhisattvas work for the benefit of beings, make offerings, and so
forth, and thus they accumulate great merit. At the same time they
know that everything is like a dream and like an illusion. Although they
are accumulating merit, they do not have any clinging and they know
the illusory, void nature of that merit; thus, they accumulate wisdom.
This is the ultimate reach of action, the ability to unite view and action.

As exemplified by an illusory being enjoying riches in a dream,

To be free of the belief that there is any truth in
phenomenal existence is the ultimate reach of experience
and realization.

However much wealth the illusory being may enjoy in the dream,
when he wakes up, there is nothing left. Similarly, to have no clinging

to the universe and beings as truly existing is the ultimate reach of meditative experience and realization.

55

An instruction on the five dharmakaya aspects of the mind, with illustrations.

Son, there are five dharmakaya aspects of the mind,

the unobstructed, all-pervading primal wisdom or absolute nature, emptiness and clarity inseparable.

The primal wisdom that is empty and radiant, unobstructed and all-encompassing, can also be called the absolute nature. It pervades the whole of samsara and nirvana, and at the same time it knows itself. This is the dharmakaya of the mind, and it has five aspects.

The unmoving dharmakaya,

the absence of movement in the absolute nature, the naked state of awareness and emptiness inseparable,

illustrated by the oceanic deep—

it is very difficult to fathom; at the same time it is utterly still.

The unchanging dharmakaya,

the absolute nature in which there is no change,

illustrated by Mount Meru.

In the middle of the great ocean stands Mount Meru, made of five kinds of precious jewels. Neither the wind nor the waves of the ocean can shake it. Similarly, when a yogi rests in the meditation of the absolute nature without wavering, this is what we call dharmakaya.

The uninterrupted dharmakaya,

the continuous state of the absolute nature or radiant clarity,

illustrated by a great river.

A great, continuously flowing river has its origins in the ocean, being fed by the rain, and ends up flowing back into the ocean. In the same way that the river flows in an uninterrupted cycle, there is no interruption in the absolute nature.

> **The undimming dharmakaya,**
>
> *the primal wisdom that neither grows brighter nor grows dimmer,*
>
> **illustrated by the sun,**

never changing, always shining and emitting rays of light.

> **The thought-free dharmakaya,**
>
> *clear awareness devoid of thought,*
>
> **illustrated by the reflection of the moon in water.**

The moon's reflection on water appears without obstruction and seems to shine very brightly, yet it is simply the appearance of something that does not exist. There is no such thing as a moon in the water. Likewise, when one recognizes that thoughts have no true existence, one recognizes awareness, and this is dharmakaya.

56

An instruction using the symbolic language of the secret mantras.

Son, there are six primal wisdoms related to the mind.

The fresh nature just as it is, **unadulterated** *by thoughts, is* **free of the duality** *of subject and object; it* **is the wisdom of coalescence.**

With this first wisdom, dualistic notions are liberated as soon as one recognizes their nondual nature.

> *The mind* **neither reaching out** *toward the object* **nor withdrawing, there is the wisdom of one taste** *with regard to the manifold perceptions and thoughts.*

Here, the mind neither reaches out to phenomena outside nor with-
draws inside. It is the state of wisdom in which the outer perceptions of
the six senses such as forms, sounds, smells, and tastes and the inner
thoughts concerning the past, present, and future are all blended in one
taste. All these things manifest in different ways. Ordinary beings alternate between positive and negative thoughts regarding them, but in
truth they are never anything other than being one taste in the absolute
nature. This wisdom, in which one is not scattered outward nor withdrawn inward, is all-penetrating and unobstructed. It is the knowledge
that outer and inner perceptions are one within the nature of mind.

> **With no adoption or rejection** *with regard to anything*
> *in samsara and nirvana,* **there is the wisdom with no hope**
> **or fear.**

Within our own buddha-nature we naturally have all the qualities of
nirvana, so we do not need to look for them and take possession of them
outside. Neither do we need to get rid of anything, because the obscurations that are temporarily veiling our realization of the absolute nature
are not inherent to that absolute nature. So with this third wisdom,
doubts are completely absent: there is no wondering, "Will I be able to
achieve all those qualities?" or "Will I succeed in getting rid of all these
defects?"

> **Putting the seal** *of the unborn absolute nature* **on the**
> **perceptions** *of the multifarious phenomena,* **there is the**
> **spontaneously arisen wisdom.**

Just as placing a yellow filter in front of a source of light makes everything look yellow, the self-arisen wisdom permeates and colors all the
various manifestations of conditioned phenomena with the absolute nature. Once we have put the seal of the absolute nature on everything,
however many relative phenomena arise they will not harm our realization of ultimate reality.

> *The nature of mind beyond all ontological extremes,* **the**
> **union of appearances and emptiness, of awareness and**
> **emptiness, is the wisdom of union.**

The eight consciousnesses and their objects having been empty from the very beginning, there is outer emptiness and inner emptiness: this is the wisdom of emptiness.

57

Introducing the nature of the mind.

Son, there are seven ways in which the nature of the mind is introduced.

The Great Space *says:*

Its nature is not definitely any one thing:
Whichever way one looks at it, in that way it appears.

Even a single object, on account of one's own mind, appears in various ways. For this reason, the outer object is devoid of intrinsic existence, and thus,

The object is introduced as being the mind's projection.

As explained in the *Tantra of the Great Space,* which is one of the tantras of the Great Perfection, one cannot define the mind as having any one definite nature. How it appears depends on how one looks at it. It is because of the mind that any one object can be perceived in different ways. This demonstrates that outer phenomena have no intrinsic existence and so introduces the fact that an object's appearance is a projection of the mind.

The multifarious manifesting aspects of one's own mind arise unobstructedly like reflections: their nature is never anything other than emptiness. Thus,

The mind's projection is introduced as a reflection.

The mind projects appearances in many ways. To someone who has done many positive actions, everything will appear as the blissful Buddhafield of Amitabha, where all is perfect. On the other hand, someone who has mainly committed negative actions will perceive everything as a hell realm, where all is suffering. All these various phenomena appear unobstructedly like reflections; their nature is never anything other than empty. This is the introduction to the mind's projection as being a re-flection: it appears but there is nothing one can catch hold of.

> *The appearances of spontaneously arisen primal wisdom arise without bias,*

The self-arisen wisdom does not manifest in one particular direction and not in the other. It pervades everything,

> *and thus,*

> **Appearances are introduced as infinite.**

> *By means of the pith instruction of the triple space,*[145]

> **The consciousness is introduced as being without support.**

> *By realizing the nature of one's own mind,*

> **Awareness is introduced as being self-cognizing.**[146]

Awareness is self-cognizing: it is not an awareness of objects outside like forms, sounds, smells, and the other objects of the six senses.

> *The objects that appear to the eight consciousnesses have never in fact come into existence, so*

> **The object is introduced as being unborn.**

> *The ultimate unborn nature is devoid of dualistic characteristics, so*

> **The unborn is introduced as being free of conceptual constructions.**

58

> *Placing a seal by introducing the ultimate nature of things that appear.*

> **Son, there are six ways of introducing the ultimate nature of everything that arises,**

> *everything being one in the absolute nature so that there is nothing to be adopted or rejected—*

no distinction between samsara as something to be rejected and nirvana as something to be attained.

> *From the creativity of the nature of one's own mind the*
> *seventeen kinds of perceptions and appearances—the six kinds of*
> *perceptions of the beings in the six realms, the two Tirthika views*
> *of eternalism and nihilism, and the nine different viewpoints of*
> *the nine vehicles—arise indeterminately, so*
>
> **Do not value existence**
>
> *by considering anything to be truly existent.*

The whole range of different ways of perceiving things can be summarized into seventeen kinds: six for the beings of the six realms, who each perceive things in their own way; two for the Tirthikas—the eternalists (who believe in the *atman*, or a permanent, intrinsically existent, and unchanging creator), and the nihilists (who deny that beings take rebirth in a continuous series of lives, reject the law of karma, and do not accept that samsara is essentially imperfect); and nine for the nine vehicles, which each have different viewpoints. And yet none of these perceptions and appearances are truly existent, so we should not cherish the notion of their so-called existence. Neither should we feel proud if we have realized that they are nonexistent.

> *Everything is the play of the absolute nature, so since you*
> *perceive things, good and bad,*
>
> **Do not prize nonexistence.**
>
> *Since phenomena do not fall into ontological extremes,*
>
> **Do not reconcile them in** *a conceptual* **inseparability** of
> existence and nonexistence.

While not falling into the extremes of existence and nonexistence, you should not conceptualize phenomena as not being either of these two, for their existence and nonexistence have been indivisible from the very beginning. Neither should you divide things up:

Do not differentiate things *as good or bad.*

Do not conceive of anything *as existent, nonexistent, or whatever by intellectual analysis.*

Avoid applying intellectual analysis to the absolute nature and thinking, "Is it existent, is it nonexistent . . . ?"

Do not be distracted from the radiant deep—*ultimate reality.*

59

Introducing the ultimate nature of things that appear.

Son, there are eight introductions.

The mind is perfectly clear, *like space, uncompounded awareness.*

The movements *of thoughts* **subside by themselves** *like ripples subsiding back into the water.*

Thoughts are leveled instantly, *the protuberance-like thoughts born from circumstances subsiding naturally the moment they arise.*

Different thoughts may arise on account of good circumstances that make us feel attached or proud, or of bad circumstances that make us feel depressed. They should all be left to dissolve naturally.

Awareness is naturally pure, *for it is* naturally *unobscured by the eight consciousnesses.*

It is not perceptible, *for there is nothing that one can grasp with certainty and say, "This is it."*

The object is naturally empty, *because what appears has no intrinsic existence.*

Like a dream, **it is there but it does not exist.**

Like the moon reflected in water, **it does not exist and yet it is there.**

60

Nine sayings introducing the unborn nature of things that appear.

Phenomena lack true origin, they are deceptive appearances: without considering them to be real, without clinging to their existence,

Son, the unborn nature is introduced in nine ways.

Since the very beginning, none of the phenomena of samsara and nirvana have ever been born as anything that truly exists. Their existence is false, like that of a dream or an illusion.

All phenomena that arise interdependently, when investigated with reasoning directed at their ultimate status, have no inherent birth, so

What is seemingly **born is unborn,** *like the horses and oxen in a magical illusion.*

"What is born" refers to all the phenomena that arise through interdependent production. If we carefully examine their true nature, we will find that they are unborn and therefore do not have any intrinsic existence. They are like the horses and oxen created by a skillful magician.

What *is uncompounded and* **has not been born** *through causes and conditions is* **unborn,** *like space.*

"What has not been born" refers to uncompounded phenomena like space that have not been created through causes and conditions. One might think that such phenomena exist in some way even though uncompounded, but they have no true existence either.

Compounded phenomena do not exist as such, so

What will never be born is unborn, *like the son of a barren woman.*

Since compounded phenomena are all nonexistent by nature, they never will be born. Thus, they are unborn in the same way that the son of a barren woman is unborn.

Forms and suchlike have no intrinsic existence, so

What appears is unborn, *like a dream.*

There is nothing that can produce emptiness, so

Emptiness is unborn, *like the horn of a rabbit.*

There is no such thing as a rabbit's horn, so there could never be a cause for its coming into existence. The same is true of emptiness.

Since it cannot be grasped with certainty—one cannot say, "This is it"—

Awareness is unborn, *like the eight consciousnesses of a person in an illusion.*

A person created by a magician does not have any of the eight consciousnesses. It is therefore impossible to apprehend its eight consciousnesses. So it is with awareness.

Since the unborn—or emptiness—is not one-sided, it has the potential to appear in every possible way:

The unborn appears, *like an optical illusion.*

One should not fall into the extreme of nihilism, taking only the side of emptiness and the unborn. Emptiness also has the ability to manifest in infinite ways, and we therefore speak of the manifestation of the unborn that is like a mirage. There is nothing there and yet it appears.

Since it is beyond intellectual investigation and has been unborn from the very beginning,

The unborn is primordially nonexistent, *like space, which has always been so.*[147]

When we speak of the unborn, this is not a mental fabrication, a label that we attach to things that we then call "unborn." It is beyond the realm of the intellect, primordially unborn like space, which has always been empty and is not something that suddenly became empty.

The unborn is not affected by the concepts of the eight extremes—
existence, nonexistence, and so forth—just as one cannot say,
"Space is this (or that),"[148] *so*

The unborn is free from extremes.

We cannot say that space exists, because there is nothing one can take hold of. Neither can we say that it does not exist, because there is something that we see that we call space.[149] In the same way, what we call the unborn is free of all concepts and extremes.

61

An instruction with four similes introducing the ultimate
nature of things that appear.

Son, there are four similes,

conventional examples used to signify the absolute nature.

All phenomena arise from the state of inseparability of mind's triple
space—the space above us, the space of the mind, and that of
the absolute nature; *there they dwell and into it they dissolve; they*
have never moved from it. So all intellectual assertions of tenets such
as "they exist" or "they do not exist" are reduced to nothing. There-
fore,

Taking the example of a mountain, *which is unmoved by*
circumstances, by the wind, rain, and so on, **stamp your**
being with the view free from assertions.

Since there is neither meditation nor anything to be meditated
upon, there is no intentional movement:

Taking the example of a king seated on his throne, stamp
your being with the meditation free of effort.

Once you have the view, you need to cultivate it through meditation. But in this case there is no meditating nor anything to meditate on. It is meditation devoid of subject and object, which does not involve any effort, in the same way that a king governs his kingdom and brings happi-

ness to his people naturally by sitting on his throne, without any particular effort on his part.

> *Everything is the play of the absolute nature, and no* conditioned
> *phenomena are excluded, so*

**Taking the example of someone who has arrived on
a golden island**—even if they look for ordinary stones there,
they will never find any—**stamp your being with the action
free from dualistic perception,**

> *where there is nothing to adopt and nothing to abandon.*

> *In the absolute nature, the basic way of being, which is naked
> and all-penetrating, freedom and nonfreedom are meaningless: there
> is no other so-called result to be sought.*

**Taking the example of a knot in a snake, stamp your
being with the sole result in which there is freedom from
hope and fear.**

When a snake makes a knot in its body as it coils itself, it can undo
that knot by itself without anyone else's help. In the same way, delusion
naturally subsides by itself.

62

> *Five instructions on the ultimate nature of appearances.*

Son, there are five instructions.

> *Ultimately, objects of knowledge, subject and object, are not born
> from causes and conditions; they do not depend on anything else;
> they are not the product of alteration,* for example, by trans-
> forming bad into good; *they are intrinsically unborn from the very
> beginning. Therefore,*

Know that form and the consciousness of it are unborn.

Without clinging, be aware of what you perceive, *the objects
of the eight consciousnesses.*

Remain without being distracted by the eight *ordinary* concerns—*praise, criticism, and so forth.*

With the view able to stand up to circumstances, the meditation immune to distraction, the action resistant to going off course, and with confidence in the result,

Remain without the consciousness being carried away by circumstances.

When we are resting in the view, it should not be disturbed by any situations, happy or unhappy, that may occur. And even if we have to be somewhere with a lot of distractions or a great many people, or we have to work, we should still be able to remain undistracted in meditation. Neither should we let our action be influenced by afflictive emotions and the results of our past actions. As for the result, we should have the firm conviction that it has been present within us since the very beginning.

Seal the mind

with the realization that your own mind is unborn,

and has always been from the very beginning, for it possesses the buddha-nature.

63

The view of the one absolute nature without distinct aspects.

Son, there are five experiences of wisdom

that indicate that one has gone to the heart of the view and meditation.

The Six Points of Meditation *states,*

> Whatever dualistic thoughts may arise,
> If you recognize that very thought as the absolute nature,
> There is no need to meditate on any other dharmadhatu.

Accordingly,

Thoughts—good or bad—**are the absolute nature,**

they dissolve in the absolute nature devoid of dualistic thoughts of subject and object.

All the **characteristics** *of both samsara and nirvana* **are freed by themselves** in the nondual expanse of evenness.

Looking directly confirms *the recognition of the absolute nature in all perceptions, like meeting an old acquaintance.*

When one meets someone one knows, even if they are in the middle of a crowd of a thousand people, one recognizes them immediately. Similarly, once one is familiar with the absolute nature, one recognizes the absolute nature in everything that arises; one's recognition is confirmed by looking directly at one's perceptions.

Deluded **clinging** *to friends, enemies, and so forth* **stops by itself.**

One naturally gives up one's desire to achieve one's own selfish aims and to avoid helping others.

The duality *of blocking impure perceptions and developing pure perceptions* **vanishes by itself.**

All dualistic desires to block impure perceptions—those of ordinary beings—and to develop the pure perceptions of the Buddhas, Bodhisattvas, Pratyekabuddhas, and the Shravaka Arhats vanish by themselves.

64

A brief explanation of the way in which the indivisible absolute nature arises.

Son, there are four ways in which the nondual absolute nature arises.

The absolute nature is the sole essence, for it is not divided into good and bad:

In the absolute nature, *the fundamental view of* the great
evenness, there is no good or bad; this is the all-penetrating
primal wisdom.

By dwelling naturally without seeking anything—*which is
the meditation of the all-penetrating wisdom*—one remains in
the state without conceptual constructs.

Not adulterating or fabricating—*which is the spontaneous action*
with no goals or purposeful deeds—is the great impartiality.

The result of actualizing the absolute nature is that, as the ultimate
nature of the mind arises spontaneously, primal wisdom
unfolds in the expanse.

65

Six ways in which the indivisible absolute nature arises.

Son, there are six ways in which the nondual absolute
nature arises.

Since *the nature of mind, which is spontaneously arisen primal
wisdom,* arises in the state of simplicity free of contrivance
from the very beginning, it is fresh.[150]

Since everything is complete within the mind, it is
spontaneous.

Since there is no blocking or encouraging, it is great primal
wisdom.

It is great wisdom because when the natural presence of the infinite display of phenomena arises, it is beyond trying to prevent or accomplish
it.

Since there is no *dualistic* division into concepts such as
samsara and nirvana, *good and bad,* it is the nondual vajra.

Since mind is Buddha from the very beginning *without
depending on causes and conditions,* it is the self-born vajra.

Since it is not caught by enemies *or by good or bad circumstances,* it is the great evenness.

66

Four ways in which indivisible absolute nature arises.

Son, there are four ways of arising without duality.

With the mind's concepts of past, present, and future severed, and the mind left in the natural flow,

It is clear and uncontrived, the natural radiance devoid of thoughts,

like an immaculate crystal.

Without any concepts whatsoever, it is the mirror of awareness,

like an untarnished mirror.[151]

It is the realization of the radiant primal wisdom, self-cognizing awareness, *like* a wishing-gem *that naturally produces everything one could desire.*

In the spontaneously arisen primal wisdom, there is no "other-elimination,"[152] so

Everything arising by itself, it is the unpremeditated wisdom.

67

Some instructions on the indivisible absolute nature.

Within absolute nature there is no division into good and bad, happiness and suffering.

Son, there are four instructions.

The absolute nature has no bias, so

In completely pervading all ten directions it is the great pervasion.

There is no direction associated with the absolute nature. One cannot say that it dwells more in the south or in the east or north or west. It is all-encompassing. That is why it is called the great pervasion.

> Since it is without an outer gate and inner sanctum—*or periphery and center*—it is the bodhichitta free of partiality.

> As anything arises *from that bodhichitta*, it is the great unpredictability.

One cannot classify it and put it in a definite category, because from the enlightened mind anything can happen, and one cannot predict that this or that will occur.

> Since it is neither lit nor dimmed *by circumstances, the absolute nature* is the *perfectly* pure enlightened state.

68

An instruction on seeing the unborn absolute nature by means of eight kinds of natural dissolution.

Son, there are eight kinds of natural dissolution.[153]

When one knows that the objects that appear have no true existence, one's belief in true existence naturally dissolves: the moment one rests with the mind undeluded in the direct perception of the absolute nature—seen directly, not merely apprehended intellectually—*everything that arises as the object of the six consciousnesses is ascertained as being appearance and emptiness inseparable, like a magical illusion or a dream. Thus,*

Forms seen by the eye—*whether beautiful or ugly—***dissolve as they are seen.**

How does this happen?

They dissolve in the sphere of the unborn, *which is the intrinsic nature of both object and consciousness.*

As both the object and the consciousness that perceives it are intrinsically unborn, forms dissolve in the expanse of the unborn.

In the same way, **sounds heard by the ear**—*pleasant, unpleasant,* **words of praise, words of criticism,** *and so forth*—**fade away as they are heard; they fade away in the expanse of the unborn.**

Odors smelled by the nose—*fragrant, foul, and so on*—**dissolve as they smelled; they fade away in the sphere of the unborn.**

Tastes savored by the tongue—*sweet, sour, and so on*—**dissolve as they are tasted; they fade away in the expanse of the unborn.**

Sensations felt through contact **by the body**—*smooth, rough, and so on*—**dissolve as they are felt; they fade away in the expanse of the unborn.**

Perceptions too—*the seventeen kinds of perceptions*[154] *and others*—**dissolve by themselves; they fade away in the sphere of the unborn,** *appearance and emptiness inseparable.*[155]

Words uttered, names, and categories—*whether of the Dharma or not*—**dissolve by themselves; they dissolve in the expanse of the unborn,** *sound and emptiness inseparable.*

Thoughts too—*whether virtuous or not*—**are free in themselves; they dissolve into the sphere of the unborn,** *naturally pure awareness.*

69

Seeing how having the four stainless things prevents one going astray.

Son, there are four things that are stainless.

To recognize the unborn *absolute nature* **in everything that appears,** *the whole of phenomenal existence, illustrated by the eight similes of illusion,* **is the stainless wisdom of the view.**

Using the eight similes of illusion—a dream, a magic show, a mirage, a city of gandharvas, a flash of lightning, and so on—one realizes the unborn absolute nature in everything that appears, the universe and the beings in it. This is the stainless view.

Taking the unborn *nature* as the path *at all times* is the stainless path *of meditation.*

When one settles in the natural flow, in the unborn nature, an incapacity to express this nature is the stainless experience.

Not to stray from the unborn nature into ordinary thoughts *related to past, present, and future* is the stainless result.

70

Showing that the practitioner's insight will not find anything else other than the unborn nature.

Son, there are five things you will not find.

When one investigates using the "neither one nor many" reasoning,

There is no finding an object outside as something that truly exists:

things are like the bits of hair that appear to someone with an ophthalmic condition.

There is an eye condition that makes one see hairs in the air in front of one. Although the hairs appear to the patient, they do not exist.

Since there is neither a seeker nor anything to be sought,

There is no finding a mind inside.

That would be like space looking for space.

There is nothing to actually look for nor a subject that can look. Within this state of nonduality we will never find anything we can call a mind, just as if we try to find space there is nothing to be found.

When the body is divided and subdivided into its limbs, digits, and so forth, there is nothing left to call a body, so

There is no finding a body in between.

It is like the core of the plantain tree, for the plantain tree is hollow inside.

As there exists neither a place in which to circle nor anyone to go around in it,[156]

There is no finding the sentient being you do not want to be.

There is no samsara in which to go round and round, neither any beings to go round in it. None of this duality exists since there is nothing whatsoever that truly exists. So you will never find any being that exists in any solid way.

Beings are like a crowd in a dream.

Say you have a dream in which there is a great gathering. The people in it do not exist outside the dream; they all appear inside it, the dream of a single person. You can dream of all sorts of things—that nice things happen to you, or that someone kills you—but nothing has actually happened. And yet none of it is separate from you.

Apart from your own unborn mind, there exists no other Buddha, so

There is no finding the Buddha you would like to be.

The Buddha is not to be sought outside yourself.

71

How there is nothing to be found by someone on the path besides the absolute nature.

Son, there are five instances where there is nothing to be found.

From the beginning, the nature of all phenomena, outer and inner, has never been anything but emptiness. **Whatever appears** *as an object outside* **is an appearance of something that does not exist.** *So even if you look for it,* **you will never find it** *in the past, present, or future:* **there is nothing to be found.**

Outer phenomena like the universe and beings and inner phenomena such as the eight consciousnesses have never been beyond the sphere of emptiness. They are like the two moons you see when you press one eye with your finger while looking at the moon: they are simply appearances of things that do not exist. So even if one looks for them, one never finds them. One never has found them and one never will.

> Awareness, *your own mind inside,* is awareness and emptiness inseparable, so you will not find it: there is nothing to be found.

It is the same with the inner mind, which holds on to outer things as truly existing entities. If you search for the nature of the mind, as it is actually the awareness nature, you will only find awareness and emptiness in union. You will not find any shape or color to this awareness.

> The body *composed of the six elements*—earth, water, fire, wind, space, and consciousness—has no essence, so you will not find it: there is nothing to be found.

For if you separate the skin, bones, blood, body cavities, and so on, they all divide up into their corresponding elements.

> *Deluded* beings *also* are, *in truth,* unborn, so you will not find them: there is nothing to be found.

Although all these things do not exist, they appear and are perceived by beings in a deluded way—with clinging to subject and object, with attachment and aversion. This deluded way of seeing things is like the perception of someone with jaundice for whom a brilliantly white conch is yellow. In fact, all things are unborn like a rainbow in the sky: they have never truly come into existence; they do not exist in any way at present; and they will never cease to exist, for if they have never been born, how could they ever cease? Thus one cannot find any so-called universe; one cannot find any so-called beings. They are all unborn.

> *As for* the undeluded Buddha state, it is your own mind, so you will not find it *anywhere else:* there is nothing to be found.

One might wonder whether there is a Buddha, an undeluded being, besides the mind. In truth the essence of Buddhahood has never been separate from us, so the Buddha too is not to be found elsewhere, outside. This buddha-nature is none other than the profound, clear, and nondual primal wisdom. But even though it is within you, if you try to look for it, you will never find it as something that has form, color, or any other characteristic.

72

A detailed explanation of how the absolute nature arises nondually,

that is, without notions of subject and object. This absolute nature dwelling forever within us is the primordial, continuous simplicity of the mind that has never been altered.

Son, there are five things to take as the path, *leaving the mind without contrivance in its own state* of primordial simplicity.

There is nothing whatsoever to focus on regarding the absolute nature, so

Do not conceive of its being anything.

As regards the absolute nature, there is nothing with a shape and color to meditate on as one does in the practice of sustained calm, where one concentrates on a small object or on a Buddha image. The nature of mind is devoid of any characteristics, so here one does not conceive of it as this or that.

Do not indulge in any object *outside—forms, sounds, and suchlike,*

distinguishing between beautiful and ugly, clinging to the one and feeling disgust for the other.

Mind is the Buddha, right now, so

Do not entertain any hope whatsoever—*such as a desire to obtain the qualities of the path and the result.*

Buddhahood is something that is already present, it has always been there. The result of the five paths is simply the recognition of the buddha nature that we already have. Once we recognize this fundamental nature, there is no need to look for any extra, separate qualities associated with the result, enlightenment—just as when we see the sun, we do not have to look for its rays. So do not feel that enlightenment is something far, far away that you might obtain in the distant future and that your present condition is different. The nature of mind is the Buddha at this very moment, so there is no need to wonder hopefully, "How can I obtain this result?"

> *Nothing that you perceive, suffering or bliss, afflictive emotions*
> *or primal wisdom, is extraneous to your own mind, so*
>
> **Do not regard anything as a defect.**

In our present condition, which is samsara, we experience a lot of suffering. But if we were to examine this suffering, we would find that it is nothing but emptiness; and emptiness is pervaded by the supreme, unchanging great bliss. From the point of view of the way it is, suffering is nothing other than the wisdom of great bliss. From the point of view of the way it appears, suffering is suffering, and it appears thus because we have misconstrued our perception of the great unchanging bliss. Similarly, from the point of view of the way things appear to ordinary deluded beings, the five afflictive emotions experienced in a deluded way are the very cause of being bound in samsara. But if we realize their true nature directly, we will find that the nature of hatred is mirrorlike wisdom, that pride has the nature of the great evenness, that ignorance is the wisdom of the absolute expanse, that attachment is all-distinguishing wisdom, and that the nature of jealousy is all-accomplishing wisdom. In the same way, we will see that outer phenomena are nothing other than the play of the absolute nature. Inner thoughts and emotions are also the play of the absolute nature. Their nature is the wisdom of the great purity and great evenness, so they must not be seen as defects or as enemies that we have to get rid of.

> *Give up thinking about past, present, and future, mulling over*
> *one's memories, and so on:*
>
> **"Force"**[157]—*meaning leave*—**the mind into its natural state.**

289

If we continue to nourish our past habits, one thought will lead to another in a continuous chain of delusion. We will remember our enemies and think, "They have wronged me in such-and-such a way, now I must retaliate." We will think of those to whom we are attached and give rise to even more attachment. This is something we must avoid. Nor should we give rise to all sorts of ideas for the future, thinking, "If I do that, I will earn a good living and lead a comfortable life. . . ." In short, do not recollect the past or make projects for the future; in the present do not be affected by dullness and distraction. In this manner, give up the train of thoughts—past, present, and future—and simply watch the mind as it is, without change. This is the wisdom of seeing the very face of simplicity. It is present within us, always with us. There is nothing more to obtain.

73

An instruction on how the way-it-is endowed with triple emptiness arises by itself.

Son, emptiness is threefold,

the fundamental nature of all phenomena, for which from the very beginning there is no birth, no cessation, and no dwelling.

What do we mean by the threefold voidness? In general, what is the cause for the appearance of deluded phenomena? As it says in the *Guhya-garbha Tantra*, the buddha-nature has been deluded because of thoughts and actions:

> *Emaho,* this wondrous reality
> Is the secret of all the perfect Buddhas.
> Within the unborn everything is born;
> In birth itself there is no birth.
>
> *Emaho,* this wondrous reality
> Is the secret of all the perfect Buddhas.
> Within no-cessation everything ceases;
> In cessation itself there is no cessation.
>
> *Emaho,* this wondrous reality
> Is the secret of all the perfect Buddhas.

Within nondwelling everything dwells;
In dwelling itself there is no dwelling.

Emaho, this wondrous reality
Is the secret of all the perfect Buddhas.
Within nondiscernment everything is discerned;
In discernment itself there is no discerning.

Emaho, this wondrous reality
Is the secret of the all the perfect Buddhas.
Within there being no coming and going, everything comes
and goes;
In coming and going itself there is no coming and going.

When we say *Emaho* ("Wonder"), it is the wonder or surprise that comes from realizing the unborn nature. Phenomena have never been born in the past, they do not dwell in the present, and they will never cease in the future. They neither come nor go. This is the real meaning of the absolute truth, the primordial nature.

The threefold emptiness refers to emptiness of the past, present, and future. It is emptiness that has always been, since the very beginning. It is not a new emptiness produced by emptying something. If one were to make a pot out of clay and then break it with a hammer, one could not say one has made the pot become unborn or unproduced. That would be an artificial way of making something unproduced. But in the case of phenomena, they are naturally unborn:

Being intrinsically unborn from the beginning,

Phenomena outside are not born: they are empty.

Just as outer phenomena are empty, unborn, so too is the mind that perceives them:

Mind being without foundation or root,

The mind inside is empty: it is not born.

The aggregates "in between" are empty: they do not dwell.

Form that appears is like foam;

Foam looks like something that has been produced on the surface of the sea, but it is soon dispersed by the breeze.

feeling experienced is like the plantain tree;

The plantain grows one year but dies the next; it does not propagate. There is nothing permanent either about feelings: happiness turns into unhappiness, youth into old age, and so on. And even now, like the plantain, feelings have no essence.

perception is like a mirage;

It perceives the characteristics of pleasant or unpleasant feelings. But it is like the water one sees as a mirage in the middle of a plain when the earth becomes hot with the sun.

conditioning factors are like the plantain;

When feeling and perception come together, there arise conditioning factors;[158] these comprise the impulse to acquire what is pleasant and get rid of what is not. But these too are like the plantain, without any core or essence.

consciousness is like a magical illusion.

Consciousness is what is aware of these feelings, perceptions, and conditioning factors. But it is like an illusion: it has no truth, either now, or in the past, or in the future.

These five aggregates are the basis of all the manifested phenomena of samsara and nirvana. And yet if we investigate them, we will come to the conclusion that they are nothing other than emptiness.

74

Sealing phenomenal existence by taking groundlessness as the path.

By putting the seal of emptiness on all phenomena, the universe and beings, we will not fall into delusion.

**Son, there are three things to take as
the path.**

Take as the path the absence of any ground *acting as a
support for,* **or root** *that gives rise to, anything in samsara and
nirvana.*

If you thoroughly investigate the different elements of samsara and
nirvana, you will find they are devoid of any solid basis for being born
or root from which to be born. It is as impossible for them to come into
existence as it is to make a knot in the sky.

Stay without giving importance to things—*as true or
untrue, to be hoped for or feared, and so on.*

As a result of believing that phenomena are solid and real, we try to
get pleasant things like fame, praise, and enjoyable sensations, and we
try to avoid unpleasant things like criticism. Such clingings arise only
because of temporary conditions coming together, and they do not actually exist on their own. So you should not give any importance to things
you hope to achieve and things you are afraid of experiencing.

Apply the seal *of the unborn to phenomenal existence.*

Why? Because if you do so, it will be impossible for you to experience
delusion.

75

Severing ties—outer, inner, and in-between.

When outer phenomena (forms, smells, and so on), inner phenomena
(the consciousness that perceives form, the consciousness that perceives
sound, and the rest of the eight consciousnesses) and the sense organs in
between (the eye, ear, tongue, and so on) come together, this connection
makes us cling to anything that is beautiful, melodious, or sweet and
reject anything that is the opposite of those. In other words, as long as
they are connected, they give rise to delusion. So it is important to break
this connection:

If you do not cut outer and inner ties before putting the
instructions into practice, the practice will degenerate into a mere
attempt to impress others—a hypocritical facade.

Son, there are four ties to be severed.

Sever outer ties *such as distracting circumstances—crowds*
and bustle.

What do we mean by severing outer ties? If we stay in a place where
there are many people and much activity, we can easily be distracted by
good circumstances—people praising us, being of service to us, and so
forth. Unless we cut such ties, it will be very difficult for us to gain any
genuine experience of sustained calm and profound insight.

Sever inner ties *such as enemies and friends—objects that*
arouse attachment and aversion.

It is also important to cut through our attachment to those we like
and our hatred for those we dislike. See enemies as your kindest parents,
who have helped you throughout your series of lives. Develop great love
for them, compassion, and bodhichitta. As for the few selected beings to
whom you are attached, bear in mind that your attachment will make
you postpone your Dharma practice and stray from the path.

Sever "in-between" ties *such as the things you cling to*
that concern this life—

anything, such as the performance of village ceremonies, that involves
your trying to become wealthy, famous, or powerful in this life.
These three ties, then, correspond to the world outside, the mind
inside, and the body, the way we act.

Moreover, having first gained a deep conviction concerning the
teachings you have heard, having then cut through your intellectual
doubts and having ultimately destroyed misconceptions regarding
the view, meditation, and action,

Rely constantly on lonely places.[159]

To begin with, you should perfect your learning by gaining a clear understanding of the unborn, nondwelling, and unceasing nature of phenomena. Then, once you are convinced of this, inwardly you will have no hesitation or doubt; you will not continue to wonder whether or not the mind is empty. Realizing this point is what we call the view. Experiencing the view again and again is meditation. And acting without letting the view and meditation lapse into the ordinary condition is proper action. So, ultimately, cut through all the many misconceptions that arise with regard to the view, meditation, and action of the nine vehicles and acquire all their qualities, always relying on a secluded place to practice.

76

This chapter has two parts: (i) the eight activities to be performed and (ii) how the teacher remedies faults in one's meditation and confers happiness and blessings.

i) The eight activities to be performed.

As we have seen, when we are in meditation, we need to realize that phenomena are unborn, nondwelling, and unceasing. But when we arise from meditation, there are eight activities we need to undertake.

Son, there are eight activities to be performed.

At times such as the beginning of a practice, meditate on

The three protections—*outer, inner, and secret.*

In order to practice we need to get rid of all outer and inner distractions and find an isolated place in which to meditate one-pointedly. Then, when we begin the practice, we must meditate on the three protections. The outer protection is the visualization of the protection tent that guards us against interruptions and obstacle makers. The inner protection is the use of various medicines that remedy disorders related to the channels, energies, and essence, the five elements, and so forth. The secret protection is the realization of the unborn, nondwelling, and unceasing nature of the mind that protects us from falling into delusion.

Make provision, *gathering everything you will need in order to practice.*

You should make sure that you have everything you will need for doing the practice, and in the right amount. If you have collected all sorts of things that are unnecessary for the practice, that shows you do not know how to be satisfied with little. On the other hand, if you try to practice with nothing, you will not have what you need to keep yourself alive and in good health, and this will constitute an obstacle to your continuing to practice. Try and find the right balance between being distracted because you have too many things and not having the strength to practice because you do not have enough—enough food to keep hunger at bay and remain healthy, and enough clothing to protect you from the cold. All these things should be prepared beforehand. Deciding you need different things once you have started the practice will create obstacles and lead to difficulties.

Simplify—*that is, remain in the natural state: leave your body, speech, and mind just as they are,* and always have been.

And make offerings *to the teacher and the Three Jewels.*

From within that state offer all you have, making the outer, inner, and secret offerings to the teacher and the Three Jewels, for it is thanks to their kindness that you have all your current happiness, well-being, and possessions.

Regarding the actions you have committed in the past, **confess your negative actions** *with the four powers.*

Before you started following the Dharma, you accumulated a multitude of negative actions, for at that time you did not have the teachings to help you avoid such actions. These negative actions will hinder you on the path, so you must now purify them using the four powers: the power of regret, the power of the support, the power of the antidote, and the power of resolution.

And pray *that experience and realization may be born in your being.*

Pray fervently and one-pointedly as follows: "May experience and realization arise where they have not yet come to be; and where they have arisen, may they not diminish but grow and flourish more and more."

Sit **on a comfortable seat** *in a secluded place,*

so that you are not distracted as you meditate,[160]

And **perform the yogic exercises,**[161] *controlling body and speech.*

It is important to adopt the correct posture related to the body and speech. Regarding the body, it is impossible to develop perfect concentration if one is lying carelessly or sitting in an unbalanced posture, leaning to either side or forward or backward. This is why we need to adopt the seven-point posture of Vairochana, for with it concentration will naturally increase. It is said that when Lord Buddha was meditating in the forest, the monkeys came and imitated him, sitting in the same perfect posture. As a result, their channels were straightened and, despite their having no understanding, this allowed the wisdom energy to increase naturally so that they began to have a glimpse of emptiness. So this is why physical posture is so important. The body contains channels and the mind is associated with the energies that flow through the channels. When the impure karmic energy associated with the deluded mind flows through impure channels, it gives rise to the three poisons—attachment, aversion, and bewilderment. If the karmic energy that creates these three poisons is purified, this allows the wisdom energy to arise. And when one's channels, energies, and essence become wisdom channels, wisdom energy, and wisdom essence, one obtains supreme concentration, perfect recollection, and confidence.

ii) How the teacher remedies faults in one's meditation and confers happiness and blessings.

To remedy the various problems—errors, obstacles, and the like—that can occur during meditation, it is important to follow the advice of a qualified teacher who is himself thoroughly experienced. By clearing up such problems and receiving the blessings of that secret treasure, the Guru's heart, one can easily travel the authentic path.

In the Commentary, this section appears after the seventy-ninth chapter, but here we shall follow the order in the original text.

Visualize *your root teacher* seated on a *lotus and moon* throne *on the crown of your head.* Begin by *arousing bodhichitta and* performing the seven branches.

Consider your root teacher seated on a lotus and moon disk above your head and arouse bodhichitta, thinking that whatever practice you are going to do physically, verbally, and mentally will be dedicated to the ultimate enlightenment of all sentient beings. Then in order to complete the accumulation of merit and wisdom do the seven-branch offering, which is likened to preparing a fertile field for planting crops: the prostrations and offerings correspond to tilling the ground, and confession to removing weeds and stones.

Next examine samsara.

Reflect on the nature of impermanence, suffering, and so on.

In order to prepare the ground for the growth of experience and realization, reflect on the fact that from the very bottom of the hells to the pinnacle of existence there is nothing in samsara that escapes suffering. However high one's position, however great one's wealth and fame, these things are impermanent: they change every moment and are no less fleeting than a rainbow in the sky. And even if you have a comfortable situation for the time being, it has mostly been obtained by accumulating negative actions, to others' detriment. In doing so you have been buying your own future suffering. So reflecting on this again and again, you should develop a strong wish to get out of samsara.

Then recall the intermediate states.

There are six intermediate states. In the natural intermediate state one recognizes the absolute nature that one had not recognized, like an orphan meeting its mother.

By "intermediate state" is meant a condition in which one is uncertain what will happen. Our present ordinary condition, the fact of dwelling in samsara, is what we call the natural intermediate state. In order to dispel the delusion of this natural intermediate state, we need to recognize everything as the absolute nature, the primordial simplicity of the natural state that we have hitherto failed to recognize. For that we need the teacher's instructions. Wandering in the delusion of samsara, we are like a child who has lost his parents wandering aimlessly with no one to protect him, feeling hungry and cold, in danger of falling sick. But when we meet with a qualified teacher, receive the teachings of the Great Vehicle, put them into practice, and finally have the experience of recognizing the absolute nature, the tremendous joy and relief we feel is like that of the lost child if he were suddenly to meet his mother. We should practice until we have that experience of the absolute nature manifesting like the mother we had lost.

> In the intermediate state between birth and death one recognizes
> the primal wisdom as if one held up a torch in a dark cave.

The intermediate state between birth and death lasts from the moment one is born until one dies. In order to destroy the delusory perceptions of this intermediate state, we need to recognize the wisdom free from all delusion. This is like being cured of jaundice and seeing the whiteness of a conch as it has always been, or like lighting a torch in the darkness: even if it is in a place that has been in total darkness for thousands of years, the moment one lights the torch all that darkness will immediately be dispelled.

> In the intermediate state of dream one recognizes everything that
> appears as the mind, just as on an island of sages one would not
> find other beings even if one looked.

When we fall asleep, the consciousness dissolves into the consciousness of the ground of all and we experience deep sleep. From this state, dreams manifest. We might dream that we become immensely rich, but when we wake up, we have not even a single needle and thread. We might dream that we have been installed on Indra's throne, but we wake up only to find ourselves on our bed. All these dreams, whether good or bad, are simply the product of the subtle karmic energy that moves the mind. They are projections of our own mind and nothing else. Just as one would never find any other kind of people on an island of sages even if one looked, one will never find any dream appearances that are truly existent, that are anything other than projections of the mind.

> *In the intermediate state of concentration one makes clear*
> *what is not clear, like a model looking in a mirror.*

The intermediate state of concentration is the period between entering meditation and rising from it into the postmeditation period. It is important during this intermediate state to get rid of all mistakes in our concentration and to make clear what is not clear. This requires the attentiveness of a young woman looking in the mirror, examining her face carefully for blemishes so that she can remove them. Without a mirror she will never find those blemishes, even though they are on her own face. Similarly, for us the mirror of mindfulness is indispensable. Otherwise if we rise out of meditation and fall into delusion in our postmeditational conduct, the benefit we gained through meditation will be lost. So, like the beautiful woman looking in the mirror, during meditation we must check whether or not we are straying into dullness or distraction, and during the postmeditation period we must watch whether we are losing control, even in the middle of acting very quickly.

> *In the intermediate state of becoming, one connects with one's*
> *remaining stock of positive actions, like inserting a pipe into a*
> *broken irrigation channel.*

Between death and the next rebirth we have a mental body, which is tossed about like a feather by the wind of karma, moving constantly from place to place. If in the life we have just left we started practicing the Dharma and gained some experience and realization but did not attain ultimate realization, it is now, in this intermediate state of becoming, that we must make a connection so that we can meet a teacher again and continue our progress on the path. The instruction we need in order to get rid of the delusion of this intermediate state—the bridge between the moment of death when the perceptions of this life fade away and the moment of rebirth when the perceptions of the next life appear—is like a pipe or canal joining a source of water to an unirrigated field.

In the intermediate state of the radiant absolute nature, primal
wisdom appears all-penetrating, like a shooting star in the sky.

At death all the senses, elements, and so on dissolve into radiant light, after which they again arise from it. This luminosity is the intermediate state that comes between the delusion of this life and the delusion that arises in the intermediate state between this life and the next. If we manage to recognize the luminosity, we will realize the undeluded wisdom that is all-penetrating, and which even a mountain cannot obstruct. It arises like a shooting star appearing brightly in space for a short instant, so in order to recognize it and attain liberation in its arising, we need to receive the teacher's pith instructions.

The crucial points on these—the methods for attaining
liberation in the six intermediate states—*are condensed in*
the teacher's pith instructions. Put them into practice.

77

Using seven concentrations to meditate.

Son, there are seven concentrations *in which one does not*
move away from the view and meditation.

In order to cut the stream of birth, death, and the intermediate state, we need to be diligent in concentration. First we must acquire the correct view and gain complete conviction in it. Then we have to repeatedly make an inner experience of the view by means of what we call meditation, and this meditation must be free from faults such as dullness and distraction. In this way we will reach a stage where the view and meditation are united. If we do not have the correct view, however hard we try to meditate we will encounter problems and make mistakes. If, on the other hand, our view is perfectly sound, our meditation will naturally follow suit. But unless we observe constant self-control in a place where there are no distractions, our meditation will be dissipated by external conditions. To help us avoid straying from meditation, there are seven concentrations.

The concentration of the emptiness of the inner,

that is, the consciousnesses of the sense organs, the eye being devoid of eye-ness, and so forth.

The eye organ is what sees forms outside. The eye consciousness is what, on seeing forms, thinks of them as being beautiful or ugly and accordingly clings to them or rejects them. Form is the object of the eye organ to which it appears. If we think of what we see as truly existing, then clinging to beautiful things and aversion to ugly things arise. But if instead we recognize that the object, the sense organ, and the consciousness are all three devoid of true reality and we realize their emptiness, we will recognize the inner consciousness as empty, for it does not dwell outside, inside, or in between.

The concentration of the emptiness of the outer,

that is, the six objects, form being devoid of form-ness, and so forth.

Recognition of the emptiness of forms outside is what we call the concentration of the emptiness of outer phenomena, for outer phenomena— the whole universe and beings—are completely impermanent. Not only will they be destroyed at the end of the kalpa, but with the passing of the seasons, and even with every second that goes by, nothing remains the same. This is equally true for the thoughts inside us. Past, present, and future thoughts seem to follow one another, but, when analyzed using Madhyamika reasoning, they can be seen to possess not even a particle's worth of existence. So when we realize that things outside are empty and things inside are empty, all of our afflictive emotions will be naturally and completely destroyed.

Regarding compounded phenomena there is

The concentration of the emptiness of both inner and outer,

compounded phenomena, the container and contents,[162] *or* phenomena outside and the mind inside.

And regarding uncompounded phenomena there is

The concentration of the emptiness of the *uncompounded* **absolute.**

Then there is

The concentration of the lion's imposing demeanor,

which overawes deluded perceptions.

The lion is the king of animals, feared by all other animals, large and small. In the same way, one's recognition of the emptiness of all phenomena will overawe all deluded perceptions, all clinging to subject and object, all attachment and aversion.

The concentration of clear wisdom,

that is, the recognition of *the natural state free from the duality of subject and object.*

When one destroys even the most subtle concepts and notions of subject and object, one arrives at the way things truly are. But this state of emptiness is not empty like an empty pot or void space. It is filled with the clarity of awareness. By attaining sound realization of this concentration of clear wisdom, one is able to destroy an entire mountain of negative actions and obscurations.

The vajralike concentration,

which cannot be overcome by afflictive emotions and ignorance, nor separated from us, is

indestructible and inseparable.

78

Six preparatory branches of the practice.

Son, there are six preparatory practices.

The six practices described here are called in Tibetan *jorwa druk*, but they are not the same as the well-known six-limbed yoga of the Kalachakra tradition.[163]

Sit on a comfortable seat,

as is proper for practicing concentration.

If you do not sit properly in the correct posture and on a seat that is perfectly comfortable for the purposes of meditation, your concentration will be constantly disrupted. This is why it is important to adopt the seven-point posture of Vairochana, to avoid pointless chitchat, and to keep the mind from being excessively withdrawn or excessively dissipated in following external phenomena.

Then visualize the channels *and wheels*[164] *in the body,* *the container.*

As a support for concentration, use your own body, which is formed from the growth of the different channels. Within these channels the energies flow, carrying the essence. The object of the practice is to bring about the cessation of the impure channels, energies, and essence, which are permeated with ignorance, and to let the wisdom channels, energy, and essence become manifest. The three main channels are the *uma* in the center, the *roma* on the right, and the *kyangma* on the left. There are also the five wheels: the wheel of great bliss in the crown of the head, the wheel of enjoyment in the throat center, the wheel of dharmas in the heart center, the wheel of manifestation in the navel center, and the bliss-preserving wheel in the secret center. Visualize these one by one. This is the meditation on the "outer fence of voidness" of the body.[165]

Expel the *poisonous* **energies** *that are contained.*

The channels are like a path on which the energies travel. The impure karmic energies associated with delusion are mixed with the three poisons—attachment, aversion, and bewilderment—and as they flow through the channels, the afflictive emotions grow stronger and stronger. We therefore need to dispel these impure energies related to delusion, for if the energies can be purified, the qualities of wisdom will naturally increase. To do this, make a vajra fist with each hand and expel the poisonous energies, first through the left nostril to expel the energy associated with attachment, then through the right nostril to expel the energy associated with aversion, and finally through both nostrils together to expel the energy associated with bewilderment. Do this three times, or in greater detail nine times. This is like cleaning a vessel very thoroughly.

> Perform the *physical* yogic exercises, *filling with the upper and lower energies and dispelling obstacles.*

There are two kinds of energy, or *prana*, referred to here. The upper prana, which passes through one's nostrils and mouth, is the prana associated with great bliss, the skillful means aspect. The lower prana, which passes through the lower doors, is that connected with emptiness, the wisdom aspect. To train these two pranas there are four steps. The first is to inhale. The second is to fill the "vase," pressing the upper prana down and bringing the lower prana up so that they meet together in the region below the navel center. Hold the breath in this way as long as you can. When you cannot hold it any longer, take a small additional breath and turn the prana three times on either side and three times in the middle, below the navel. This is the third step. Fourth, expel the prana, shooting it out like an arrow.

While you are trying to train the prana like this, various obstacles and problems may occur, so in order to dispel these you should go through the different yogic exercises, or *trulkhor*. If you do this practice over a long period of time, the channels will be straightened, the energies will be purified, and the door to the manifestation of wisdom opened.

> Rid yourself of other *pointless thoughts,* mental turbidity.

To take an example, the mind is like a crippled person, the energy like a blind horse. Unless the horse is controlled by its crippled rider, it will take the latter anywhere it likes—that is, the mind will be overpowered by wild thoughts. But once the cripple can control the horse, everything will come under control. So it is important to give up unnecessary wandering thoughts, all those thoughts related to attachment and aversion that we constantly follow and perpetuate, rendering the mind turbid like water in a muddy pool that has been stirred. Holding the breath in the "vase" exercise helps reduce these meaningless thoughts.

Bring the mind into the one-pointed concentration *of bliss, clarity, voidness, and the like.*

Having dispelled the thoughts and purified one's channels, energies, and essence, when one rests without wavering in the empty nature of the mind, three different experiences may occur: experiences of bliss, clarity, or voidness, which correspond to the nirmanakaya, sambhoga-kaya, and dharmakaya, respectively. However, if these experiences are tinged with clinging, the bliss will lead to rebirth in the world of desire; the clarity, to rebirth in the world of form; and the absence of thought, to rebirth in the world of formlessness. So while these three experiences will, and indeed must, occur as a normal result of progress on the path, when they occur, you must not have the slightest clinging to them but permeate them with the realization that they are completely empty. Realize that they are simply manifestations of your own mind. Even if you reach a stage where you are able to stay in unwavering concentration for days and days without even feeling hungry or thirsty, you must never feel proud or pleased with yourself. Stay free of clinging and pride, pray with fervent devotion to the teacher, and practice diligently. That way, you will easily develop these various kinds of concentration. As it is said, everything can be accomplished with a little hardship. But if one remains idle and indifferent, it is difficult to achieve anything. So in order to cultivate these experiences of bliss, clarity, and voidness you should bring everything into one-pointed concentration.

79

The five-limbed main practice of the yogi on the path.

Son, there are five branches in the main practice,

branches for practicing the actual path.

The practice of these various concentrations is like a journey on a road. The road changes all the time, sometimes ascending, at other times descending. One moment it is straight, the next it is winding. One will thus encounter different aspects of the path, branches such as sustained calm and profound insight, or the generation and perfection phases. Here we shall consider five main branches of the actual path.

> **Drop** *ordinary* **activities, put them off**—*such things as business and farming the land: there will never come a time when they are finished.*

All these ordinary activities are like children's games. If we continue them, they will never end. But if we abandon them, that is the end of them. And however successful one may be at such activities, they are completely pointless, for they are no exception when it comes to the four ends:

> The end of all gathering is dispersing.
> The end of all living is dying.
> The end of all meeting is parting.
> The end of all rising is falling.

The more you become involved in such distracting activities, the longer you will continue to postpone the practice of Dharma. So rather than putting things off until later, make an effort now to practice the concentration that will bring bliss, clarity, and absence of thoughts.

> *Once you leave them aside, virtuous activities will blossom and*
>
> **Your body, speech, and mind will be extremely happy.**

You will feel completely relaxed and blissful, like a smooth, level plain with no rocks or rough features. In this serene state, this well-prepared ground, concentration will easily grow:

> *As a result, inner concentration will grow and various experiences occur:*
>
> **The mirror of awareness will shine within.**

Concentration, or the realization of wisdom, is supported by the body, which is why one needs to straighten the channels, purify the energies, and free oneself of discursive thoughts. By doing so, it is certain that the experiences and realization of the path will come. If your mind is free from dullness and distraction, you will realize your own nature, as when you see your face in a clear mirror.

At that time the Sugatas will bestow their splendor.

In other words, you will acquire the thirty-two major and eighty minor marks of a Perfect Buddha, one by one.

> *The Buddhas, Bodhisattvas, and Vidyadharas will bless you, the guardians of virtue*[166] *will protect you, and because of the majesty you will have gained, hindrances, negative forces, and obstacle makers will be unable to do you any harm.*

Gradually you will be able to meet all the Buddhas, Bodhisattvas, and Vidyadharas dwelling in the Buddhafields and receive their blessings and instructions so that all obstacles and problems on the path are cleared. Just as a son who takes care of his family's fields, tilling the soil and producing a good harvest, will greatly please his parents, so too by keeping your body, speech, and mind in tune with the Dharma and persevering on the path for the sake of all sentient beings, you will gladden all the Buddhas and Bodhisattvas and they will shower blessings upon you. You will be able to reach Buddhafields like Tushita and Dumataka and other celestial fields. And you will be protected by all those who abide by virtue—Buddhas, Bodhisattvas, and the various protectors. You will obtain the majesty of the Buddhas and Bodhisattvas, with all their blessings, so that no hindrances, negative forces, or obstacle makers will be able to do you any harm.

It will be impossible for conditioned thoughts *such as the five or three poisonous emotions* to arise.

Why are the afflictive emotions called poisons? Just as swallowing poison can have mortal results, if you harbor these afflictive emotions in your mind, they will kill any chance of liberation and you will continue to wander in samsara. However, close examination of these poisons will reveal that they are nothing other than conditioned thoughts. As such, they are unborn, nondwelling, and unceasing. If you realize their empty nature, afflictive emotions will be unable to rear up in your mind.

> *In short, if you give up all ordinary activities, by practicing the profound path with no conflict between your mind and the three trainings you will temporarily and ultimately master infinite qualities, accomplishing your own and others' welfare according to your wishes.*

All our different activities are projections of the mind, created by our thoughts. If you follow these deluded thoughts, there will be no end to your mind being upset by delusion, just as when the wind blows over the surface of a lake, the crystal clarity of the water is masked by ripples. It is therefore important to control the mind by applying the view, meditation, and action, both in meditation and in postmeditation, for major situations and minor ones. If you can do this and do nothing that goes against the practice of the three trainings of discipline, concentration, and wisdom, ultimately you will attain omniscient Buddhahood; and in the meanwhile you will be reborn in the higher realms of samsara as a human or celestial being. While you are on the path, you will be unfettered by afflictive emotions. Without any selfish hopes of attaining the peace of nirvana alone, you will constantly keep the vow of bodhichitta in mind to bring all sentient beings to the essence of enlightenment. By thus accomplishing both your own and others' aims, you will naturally make the inconceivable qualities of perfect Buddhahood a reality.

> *These chapters on the superior training in wisdom have been arranged in a different order in the Commentary, which explains the text as follows. After the forty-second chapter it jumps straight to chapter 48. It then continues from chapter 50 to 54. After that come chapters 63 and 69. Next, chapters 43 to 47, after which come chapters 68, 70, 71, 49, and and 55 to 59. Then chapters 60 to 67, leaving out chapter 63, which came earlier. Next, chapters 72 to 79, omitting chapter 77, which came in the section on the training of the mind. Here, however, I have followed the order in the root text.*

> *To sum up, by using these chapters to realize the meaning of the Later Mind Section of the Great Perfection, one achieves certainty through "clearly distinguishing," and complete confidence. As if*

vanquishing an adversary with a razor-sharp blade, this is the path that eradicates samsara and establishes the unborn nature with certainty.

Of the three sections of Atiyoga, the Great Perfection, namely the Mind, Space, and Pith Instruction sections, we have here followed mainly the Mind Section. These instructions for clearly distinguishing between the ordinary mind and awareness and for acquiring complete confidence in awareness alone are like a sharp sword that routs the legions of samsara, cutting samsara at the root and establishing its unborn nature.

This concludes the instruction on this section, which I have explained to suit those with keen intelligence.

This was the fourth section from the *Eighty Chapters of Personal Advice*, the instruction on stainless wisdom, the essence.

V

Conclusion

80

A concluding instruction on examining the disciple and how the disciple should practice.

These teachings will not help disciples who hear them unless they are going to put them into practice. It is therefore important to check first whether the disciple is a suitable vessel.

Son, there are three points in conclusion.

In the first place, these instructions should not be given to people who are not suitable vessels. Not only will such people derive no benefit from them, but the profound instructions, whose purpose is to free one from the bonds of afflictive emotions, will themselves be wasted. So the teacher must identify any faults in the disciple.

i) The defects of disciples to whom the instructions should not be given.

Recognize defects in disciples who might be liberated by these profound instructions:

do not give the instructions to improper vessels who are not interested in the Dharma and only indulge in worldly activities, **whose natural disposition is unsuitable,**

being bad-tempered, ungrateful, and so on—unable to acknowledge and return kindness,

who are inconstant *and have fickle minds,*

who find fault *in their own teacher,* **in the Dharma, and in individuals,** who lack pure perception and have no respect and devotion,

and who, *having received the profound instructions,* **will not put them into practice.**

Even if you do give them the instructions, you will not do them any good, and divulging the secret teachings will result in criticism and retribution.

ii) Suitable vessels to whom the teachings may be given.

To those who are good-natured—*who acknowledge what is done for them, are grateful for kindness, and so on,* and are prepared to give their lives, their body, speech, and mind to repay their teacher's kindness—

who are stable—*their faith,* diligence, *and suchlike never change*—

who have very pure perception *with regard to the Dharma, people, and so forth.*

and who, not content with merely hearing the teachings, **are assiduous in the practice,** *accomplishing what they have heard,*

to them you can give the instructions.

By doing so you will ensure that they hold the lineage of the teachings and serve the doctrine, fulfilling the aims of many—attaining realization for *themselves and* benefiting *others.*

iii) As for how disciples who are suitable vessels should put the instructions they have been given into practice,

They should see the teacher as the Buddha.

As a result they will receive the blessings of the lineage.

Such suitable disciples see the teacher as the Buddha himself, considering him as the true embodiment of the knowledge, love, and ability of all the Buddhas of the past, present, and future. And because of their devotion they will receive the blessings of all the lineage teachers from Samantabhadra down to their own root teacher.

They should keep the instructions in their hearts,

for the view, meditation, and action of the Mantrayana are exceedingly profound.

> *If they are able to keep them secret and to practice them, the two accomplishments,* common and supreme, *will come without effort.*

> **Befriending solitude,** *far from crowds and bustle* that make it hard to develop stable concentration, **they should practice.**

> **As a result, experience and realization will bloom and they will become the snow lion's cubs.**

The true signs of accomplishment are that one becomes controlled and peaceful, completely free from afflictive emotions. Along with these, such accomplishments as the various forms of perfect recollection and clairvoyance will come naturally. As meditative experiences and realization increase, one becomes fearless, like a snow lion cub, which has no fear of other, ordinary animals.

> *This completes the explanation of the instructions on how to recognize suitable disciples and on how to give rise to excellent qualities in one's being.*

> **This was the fifth section from the** *Eighty Chapters of Personal Advice*, **the instruction on the vessel and a related teaching.**

Colophon

This is the essence of the heart of Deshek Gyawopa, the
Lord who attained the summit of the view.[167]

These instructions are the essence of the heart of Zurchung Sherab
Trakpa, who brought to full realization the view of the Great Perfection
and was known as the Sugata (indicating that he had attained Buddhahood) of Gyawo—the name of the mountain hermitage in which he
lived and practiced.

It covers the Three Pitakas and follows the texts of
Epitome, Magic, and *Mind.*

These texts are the *Epitome of Essential Meaning* (referring to the Great
Gathering);[168] the *Net of the Magical Display*, related to the *Guhyagarbha
Tantra;* and the Eighteen Tantras of the Mind Section, which is the first
of the three sections of Atiyoga.

It is an instruction that within a single lifetime liberates those
with faith, diligence, and wisdom who practice one-pointedly.

Written down by Zurchungpa's disciple Khyungpo
Yamarwa exactly as the Lord spoke it, it is the culmination and
quintessence of his profound teachings.[169]

The Eighty Chapters of Personal Advice
By the glorious heruka, Zurchungpa—
Great victory banner of the teaching, the glorious heruka
  come in human form—

314

Who bestows the fruit of complete liberation
On all who hear his name or even think of him,
Is the sublime and extraordinary jewel of the Ancient Translation
    lineage,
A treasure of the profound tantras, commentaries, and pith
    instructions,
An event as rare in the three times as the udumbara lotus
That I have come upon through no effort of my own.
Such is my delight and joy at my good fortune in being able
    to receive these teachings and reflect on them *that I have*
    written these notes.
If I have made the slightest error therein (and any of these notes
    contradicts the words and meanings of the teachings of
    the Victorious Ones),
I confess it to the teacher and supreme deities.
Through the merit may the great enlightenment be swiftly
    attained by all sentient beings, especially those who have
    made a connection with this teaching.
In all our lives may we never be parted from the sublime tradition
    of the glorious Zur,
May we hear the teachings, reflect on them, and put them
    into practice, bearing aloft the victory banner of this
    teaching,
And by correctly holding, preserving, and spreading it
May we achieve both aims—our own and others'—and may we
    all attain ultimate Buddhahood.

Using as a basis the text and structural outline transmitted to
me by the Vajradhara Khyentse Wangpo (who had received these
teachings through both the direct and long lineages),[170] *I, the*
kusali Jamyang Lodrö Gyamtso Drayang,[171] *wrote these few notes to*
make it clearer, thinking that they might be useful for people of
limited intellect like myself. They follow the explanation given in the
detailed commentary The Lamp of Shining Jewels. *I wrote them*
at Demchok Tashi Gempel[172] *at an auspicious time in the month*
of Kartika[173] *in the Wood Mouse Year (1924). As a result of this, long*
may the sublime doctrine of the secret and ultimate essence
endure.
　　Sarwada mangalam bhavantu.

Part Two

ZURCHUNG SHERAB TRAKPA'S
EIGHTY CHAPTERS OF PERSONAL ADVICE

I

Faith

I

Son, since it is a prerequisite for the whole of the Dharma,
It is important to recognize the fault in not having faith
And the virtues of having it.
There are six faults that come from not having faith.
Without faith one is like a rock at the bottom of the ocean.
One is like a boat without a boatman.
One is like a blind person who goes into a temple.
One is like a burnt seed.
One is like a sheep stuck in a pen.
One is like a maimed person who has landed on an island
of gold.

2

Son, there are six virtues of faith.
Faith is like a very fertile field.
Faith is like a wishing-gem.
Faith is like a king who enforces the law.
Faith is like someone who holds the stronghold of carefulness.
Faith is like a boat on a great river.
Faith is like an escort in a dangerous place.

3

Son, there are ten causes that give rise to faith.

You need to know that there is no happiness in your present
way of life and circle of friends.

You need to have confidence in the law of cause and effect.

You need to remember death and impermanence.

You need to remember that you will depart without your
retinue or wealth.

You need to bear in mind that you are powerless to choose
your next rebirth.

You need to remember how hard it is to obtain a fully
endowed human body such as this.

You need to bear in mind that the whole of samsara is
suffering.

You need to see the immense qualities of the Three Jewels.

You need to look at the lives and deeds of the Holy Beings.

You need to keep the company of excellent friends who abide
by virtue.

4

Son, there are thirteen things to be abhorred.

Unless you turn your back on your fatherland, you will not
vanquish the demon of pride.

Unless you give up the activities of a household, you will never
find the time to practice the Dharma.

If you do not practice the moment faith arises, there will be no
end to the jobs you have to do.

Do not blame others for your own lack of faith.

Unless you cast your possessions to the wind, you will never
exhaust your worldly ambitions.

Unless you distance yourself from your relatives, there will be
no interruption in your attachment and aversion.

Unless you act now, you cannot be sure where you will go next.

Doing nothing now when you have the means, the prayers
you make for future lives are empty chatter.

Without lying to yourself, practice the Supreme Dharma.

Forsake now what you will have to give up anyway, and it will
become meaningful.

Rather than concerning yourself with things you obviously
cannot complete, concern yourself with making an
experience of what you definitely can complete.

Instead of preparing for next year—when you cannot be sure
whether or not there will be a next year—prepare for death,
which is certain to happen.

As you practice, food and clothing will take care of themselves,
so do not have great hopes or fears.

5

Son, there are thirteen things that are very important.

To a teacher who has the three qualities, it is very important
to be respectful.

It is very important to give instructions to disciples who are
proper vessels.

It is very important to give up attachment to things, externally
and internally.

In practicing the instructions, it is very important to think in
the long term.

It is very important to develop fervent devotion to the yidam
deity and the Three Jewels.

It is very important to cultivate diligence in the practice of
virtue.

It is very important to steer clear of negative actions.

It is very important to rely on the absence of thoughts in your
mind.

In the postmeditation period, it is very important to rely on
compassion and bodhichitta.

It is very important to develop the conviction that the
instructions are unmistaken.

It is very important to observe the vows and samayas.

It is very important to establish the unborn nature of the mind.

It is very important not to give the secret pith instructions to
an improper vessel.

This was the first section from the *Eighty Chapters of Personal Advice*, the
instruction on firm faith, the gateway.

Discipline

6

Son, there are ten facts.

If the continued existence of the Buddha's teaching and your
   having faith coincide, it is simply that you accumulated
   merit in past lives.

If you are interested in the Dharma and meet a master who
   possesses the instructions, it is simply that the blind man
   has found the jewel.

If faith, diligence, and wisdom coincide in a body free of
   defects, it is simply that these good qualities are the karmic
   result of having trained in the Dharma.

If your being born in samsara coincides with relatives scolding
   you, it is simply that you are being exhorted to practice.

If your having things and your being delighted to give them
   away coincide with a beggar, it is simply that generosity is
   coming to perfection.

If, when you are practicing, the dam of suffering bursts, it is
   simply that you are purifying your negative actions.

If people are hostile toward a Dharma practitioner who has
   done nothing wrong, it is simply that they are setting him
   on the path of patience.

If your having consummate faith coincides with applying the

instructions, it is simply that you have come to the end of karma.

If your own fear of death coincides with other people dying, it is simply that the time has come to turn your mind away from samsara.

If you think you will finish your projects for this life first and after that practice a bit of Dharma, this is simply the demon's delaying tactics.

7

Son, there are thirteen instructions.

As a spur to diligence in the practice, consider your own death and others'.

If you want to cultivate extraordinary respect, examine the teacher's outer and inner qualities.

If you want your conduct to concord with all, do not obstruct the efforts of others.

So as never to upset the teacher, practice hard.

If you want to attain accomplishment quickly, keep the vows and samayas without letting them degenerate.

If you want to halt the four rivers, you must ascertain the unborn nature of the ground-of-all.

If you want no obstacles to your accomplishing enlightenment, leave behind the distractions of this life.

If you want to benefit others effortlessly, meditate on the four boundless qualities.

If you are fearful of the three lower realms in your future lives, steer clear of the ten negative actions.

If you want to be happy in this and future lives, be diligent in performing the ten positive actions.

If you want your mind to engage in the Dharma, you must experience the hardship of suffering.

If you want to turn away from samsara, strive for unsurpassable enlightenment.

If you want to obtain the result, the three kayas, unite the two accumulations.

8

Son, there are five things that are useless.

No need to say you are interested in the Dharma if you have
not turned your mind away from samsara.

No need to meditate on emptiness if you have not countered
attachment to the things you perceive.

No need to practice meditation if you do not turn your mind
away from desire.

No need for fine words if you have not assimilated the
meaning yourself.

No need to apply the instructions if you do not have devotion.

9

Son, there are five things you need to do.

You need to have fervent devotion to the teacher, for then the
blessings of the lineage will automatically rub off on you.

You need to accumulate exceptional merit, for then everything
you wish for will work.

You need to make your mind fit, for then extraordinary
concentration will be born in your mind.

You need to cultivate extraordinary concentration, for then the
afflictive emotions will be overwhelmed.

You need to be free of afflictive emotions, for then you will
quickly attain enlightenment.

10

Son, there are five things that become lies.

As long as you delight in the things of this world, saying you
are afraid of birth and death becomes a lie.

Unless you are afraid of birth and death, going for refuge
becomes a lie.

Unless you are rid of desire, saying you are a great meditator
becomes a lie.

Unless you have understood the law of karma, saying you have
realized the view becomes a lie.

Unless you have abandoned the abyss of existence, saying you
are a Buddha becomes a lie.

11

Son, there are five things that are true.

It is true to say that without meditating one will never become a Buddha.

It is true to say that if you do not break the samaya, you will not go to hell.

It is true to say that if you separate skillful means and wisdom, you will fall to the Shravaka level.

It is true to say that if you do not know how to unite view and conduct, you are on the wrong path.

It is true to say that the mind is by nature perfectly pure and clear, unstained by defects.

12

Son, there are five things that are pointless.

There is no point in following a master who does not have the nectar of the teachings.

There is no point in accepting a disciple who is not a proper vessel.

There is no point in making a connection with someone who will not keep the samaya.

There is no point in performing positive actions that are mixed with negative ones.

There is no point in knowing the teachings if you do not act accordingly.

13

Son, there are eight instructions.

As you practice, cross the pass of attachment and aversion.

When you are studying the texts, don the armor of forbearance.

When you are staying in sacred sites and secluded places, do not let your mind hanker after food and wealth.

When you want the profound teachings, follow a master well versed in them.

When you meet a truly knowledgeable master, do all you can to please him and never upset him.

When the Dharma gets difficult, stamp on your faint-
heartedness.
When your family disowns you, cut all attachment in your
mind.
When you are straying into ordinary thoughts, bring your
consciousness back to the essence.

14

Son, there are thirty-four pieces of advice.
As they are a source of obstacles, give up distractions.
There is no time to tarry: quickly, meditate!
Do not be concerned with how you live; be concerned with
how you will die.
Practice alone without the luxury of attendants.
Deluded perception—cast it aside.
Do not indulge: too much activity gives rise to adverse
circumstances.
You will be much happier having no one for company.
With no one to keep you company, there is no attachment or
aversion.
It is impossible to make everyone happy, so stop trying to
please people.
Stay alone like a corpse.
Do not enter a pit of thorns: stay in a place where you will be
happy.
Enough with the past, now stop surrendering.
Do not consider people as enemies and friends; maintain
primal wisdom.
Do not look to fame; watch your own mind.
Unless you are diligent, you will go down.
Give up your wandering ways of the past.
Go to the island in the ocean that has the riches you desire.
If you reach this island, you will never return.
Give your property to your father.
If you make your old father happy, he will give you his
heartfelt advice.
He'll speak to his son straight from the heart.

Once you have found a gem, do not throw it away.
Turn back and correct yourself.
When your brothers and sisters are all together, listen to what
    they say and carry it out.
If you fear being scattered, fence yourself in.
If you fear you are running away, hold yourself with the hook.
Make your view stand firmly on its own.
Observe discipline without hypocrisy.
Give generously and impartially.
Patiently bear with adversity.
Put up with suffering when you are listening and reflecting.
Do not cast your meditation into the mouth of fame.
Your conduct should be such that you are not carried away by
    the demons.
You will be beguiled by the demon of appearances.

15

Son, do not discredit the house of your forefathers.
Do not taint your siblings and relatives.
Do not throw dust on other relatives, close or distant.
Without paying taxes to the king, you cannot hope to be his
    subject.
Do not race downhill.
Do not be clever in wrong ways.

16

Son, there are ten things that do no harm.
If you can cope with the place, there is no harm in staying in
    your own country.
If you can cope with those with whom you are connected,
    there is no harm in not leaving your family.
If you can cope with the question of clothing, there is no harm
    even in going naked.
If you can cope with the problem of attachment and aversion,
    however you conduct yourself outwardly, you will not
    come to any harm.

If you know how to handle the teacher, there is no harm in
    discontinuing respect.
If you can cope with samsara, you will not come to any harm
    even if you do not practice.
If you can cope with the lower realms, you will not come to
    any harm even if you perform negative actions.
If you can cope with the hells, there is no harm in not keeping
    the samayas even if you have entered the door of the secret
    mantras.
If you are confident in the view, there is no harm in taking
    things easy and sleeping.
If you can cope with the problem of residence, it does not
    matter where you live.
If you can cope with the problem of food, it does not matter
    what you eat.
If you can cope with the problem of the body, even if you do
    not steer clear of contagious diseases, you will come to no
    harm.

17

Son, there are eighteen objects of derision.
In the beginning when faith is born, one is ready to leap in
the air.
Later, torn by doubts, one fills desolate valleys with one's
    footprints.
In the end, having completely lost faith, one becomes a
    mooring stone on the bottom of hell.
In the beginning, having found the master, one talks about all
    the teachings he has transmitted.
Later, one tires of the master and criticizes him.
In the end, one abandons the teacher and considers him as
    one's greatest enemy.
In the beginning, when one achieves a degree of concentration,
    one thinks, "There is no practitioner as good as I am."
Later, one gets tired of meditating and resembles an inmate in
    an open prison.

In the end, one gives up meditation and loiters in the villages.
In the beginning when experiences occur, one brags about
  them.
Later one gives up meditation and, as an expert in letters, takes
  to giving teachings.
In the end when one abandons one's body, one dies in a
  completely ordinary state.
In the beginning, one develops but a faint conviction in one's
  realization of the view.
Later, torn by doubts, one lies about one's knowledge and
  questions others.
In the end, far from having the view, one is completely
  dominated by errors and obscurations.
When the result is lost in error, the windows of liberation are
  shuttered.
By blocking the windows of liberation, one will never interrupt
  the stream of birth and death.
Unless one interrupts the stream of birth and death, one is
  powerless to choose where one will be reborn.

18

Son, there are fifteen ways in which the practice goes wrong.
The view rushes into uncertainty.
The meditation gets lost in idiot meditation.
The action strays into wild, inappropriate conduct.
The samaya gets lost in being undervalued.
The master is treated as one of one's own.
The disciple attends teachings unwillingly.
The practice is left for when one has the leisure.
One's experiences are ghost sightings.
The result is the achievement of worldly fame.
One receives the instructions inauthentically.
Having obtained a human body in Jambudvipa, one returns
  empty-handed.
At death, one dies with regrets.
The Dharma practitioner is betrayed by his own name.
One listens to empty sounds.
After death, one cannot but go to the hells.

19

Son, there are twenty-six kinds of folly.

It is foolish not to fear an army whose arrival is inevitable.

It is foolish not to repay a debt you have definitely incurred.

It is foolish to run toward an enemy who will surely take you captive.

It is foolish to enjoy carrying a greater load than you can bear.

It is foolish to be eager to go somewhere unpleasant.

It is foolish to leap into an abyss where you are certain to die.

It is foolish to sow buckwheat and hope to grow barley.

It is foolish to expect the sun to shine into a north-facing cave.

It is foolish to place your hope and trust in someone who is obviously going to deceive you.

It is foolish for someone of humble origins to vie with one of royal blood.

It is foolish to hope to be rich when you possess nothing.

It is foolish for a cripple to try to ride a horse.

It is foolish to say you have completed a task without having done any work.

It is foolish, when you have still not recovered from an illness, to get fed up with the doctor and to take a liking to someone who has prepared a vial of poison.

It is foolish for a merchant with nothing to sell to be a hearty eater.

It is foolish to run off without listening to your father's advice.

It is foolish for a daughter to ignore her mother's advice.

It is foolish, having left the house naked and then found clothes, to return home again without them.

It is foolish to take off your boots when there is no river.

It is foolish to drink salty water that will never quench your thirst.

It is foolish to be oblivious of the inside when the outside has collapsed.

It is foolish to be clever at counseling others while giving yourself the wrong advice.

It is foolish to scale a fortress without a ladder.

It is foolish for children to not want to do a job they will definitely have to do.

It is foolish not to be worried about crossing an unfordable
river.
It is foolish to look elsewhere for something that is already
within you.

20

Son, there are nine pieces of personal advice.
If you want to compete, take on the Buddha.
If you want to backbite, slander the yidam.
If you have to be mean, be so with the instructions.
If you are going to be unkind, be unkind to your negative
actions.
By all means be munificent—with the teacher.
If you want to give someone the cold shoulder, make it
samsara.
If you are going to enumerate faults, list your own defects.
When you have the victory, give it to others.
As for the sutras and tantras, tease them out like wool.

21

Son, there are nine pieces of heartfelt advice.
Be a child of the mountains.
Eat the food of famine-time.
Do the things that please the enemy.
Wear clothes that no one wants.
Flee the crowds, alone.
Be without a handle for your relations.
Tie your fickleness down with a rope.
Abandon havens of delight.
Focus your mind on space.

22

Son, there are five beatitudes.
Blessed are they who recognize samsara for what it is: a
poisonous tree of suffering.

Blessed are they who see those that give rise to afflictive
emotions as spiritual friends.
Blessed are they who correctly view the master who has
trained in the three wisdoms.
Blessed are they who see everything—outer and inner things
and circumstances—as being without origin.
Blessed are they who postpone all activities and set out on the
unmistaken path.

23

Son, there are twenty things that lead to breaches of samaya.
To be secretive about your teacher while extolling your own
virtues leads to a breach of samaya.
To view an erudite scholar and an uneducated person as equals
leads to a breach of samaya.
Competition between patrons and disciples leads to a breach
of samaya.
To have the intention of offering and to put off doing so leads
to a breach of samaya.
Receiving as many teachings as you can possibly hear leads to
a breach of samaya.
To insist on getting the instructions leads to a breach of
samaya.
To deceive your teacher and fellow disciples leads to a breach
of samaya.
To blame the master for wrong leads to a breach of samaya.
To treat the master as a rival leads to a breach of samaya.
To abuse the master's confidence leads to a breach of samaya.
To scorn his kindness leads to a breach of samaya.
To be intent on looking after your own interests leads to a
breach of samaya.
To steal instructions and books leads to a breach of samaya.
To secretly enumerate the master's faults leads to a breach of
samaya.
To block another's aspiration leads to a breach of samaya.
To make an outer show of the inner practices leads to a breach
of samaya.

To be jealous of vajra brothers and sisters leads to a breach of samaya.

To act indiscriminately without a teacher or instructions leads to a breach of samaya.

To masquerade as a teacher leads to a breach of samaya.

To criticize teachings and those who practice them leads to a breach of samaya.

To exhibit the instructions to unsuitable vessels leads to a breach of samaya.

This was the second section from the *Eighty Chapters of Personal Advice*, the instruction on perfect discipline, the basis.

Concentration

24

Son, there are four practices that confer blessing.
The blessing of yourself, as exemplified by the sole of a shoe.
The blessing of perceptions, as exemplified by a mountain
    torrent in spate.
The blessing of the mind, as exemplified by the middle of a
    great river.
The blessing of nonduality, as exemplified by a jackal.

25

Son, there are four instructions for using things as the path.
Make freedom from attachment the path, as exemplified by the
    pelican carrying fish.
Make the five poisons the path, as exemplified by the recitation
    of mantras over poison.
Make the unborn nature of the eight consciousnesses the path,
    as exemplified by cutting a fruit tree at the roots.
Make the great purity the path, as exemplified by the lotus
    growing from the mud.

26

Son, here are instructions on four things to be known.
Know freedom from attachment, as illustrated by the
    magician.

Know indivisibility, as illustrated by sandalwood or the musk
    deer.
Know that relatives deceive, as illustrated by being let down
    by a friend.
Know inseparability, as illustrated by a sesame seed or the
    flame of a lamp.

27

Son, there are four crucial instructions.
You need the crucial instruction that shows how to make a
    clear-cut decision regarding the unobstructed nature of
    appearances, as illustrated by a clean silver mirror.
You need the crucial instruction on not being bound by
    characteristics, as illustrated by a prisoner who has been
    released.
You need the crucial instruction on not being distracted from
    the unborn nature, as illustrated by shooting an arrow
    straight at the target.
You need the crucial instruction on resting in one-pointed
    concentration, as illustrated by an ophthalmic surgeon.

28

Son, there are four "cuts."
Cut the stream of the arising of dualistic thoughts and the
    following after them, taking the example of a tortoise
    placed on a silver platter.
Decide that nothing is extraneous to the absolute nature,
    taking the example of gold jewelry.
Decide on its indivisibility, taking the example of molasses and
    its sweet taste.
Decide that it is naturally manifesting awareness, taking the
    example of the moon in the sky and its reflection in water.

29

Son, there are four views.
View thoughts and appearances as the ornament of the

absolute nature, taking the example of a rainbow adorning
the sky.

View thoughts as the absolute nature, taking the example of
tempering and honing a sword.

View thoughts as leaving no trace, taking the example of birds
flying in the sky.

View existence as untrue, taking the example of waking from
a dream.

30

Son, there are four kinds of meditation.

Meditate with increasing habituation, taking the example of
the waxing moon.

Meditate on thoughts and appearances as the inexpressible
great bliss, taking the example of having your mouth full of
water.

Meditate that fame and the like are not ultimately true, taking
the example of mist, which does not truly exist.

Meditate on the uncontrived nature as empty, taking the
example of water and bubbles.

31

Son, there are four kinds of conduct.

In your conduct, turn your back on worldly ways: consider the
examples of a bride and a madman.

In your conduct, do not move from the absolute nature: take
the example of fish in the ocean.

In your conduct, whatever appears should be primal wisdom:
take the example of fire raging through a forest.

In your conduct, the many should have the single taste: take
the example of salt dissolving in water.

32

Son, there are four kinds of experience.

The experience of no clinging to thoughts, as illustrated by a
small child and a mirror.

The experience of wisdom taking birth where it has not
   previously arisen, as illustrated by a poor woman finding
   treasure.
The experience of neither apprehension nor esteem, as
   illustrated by a swallow and a lion.
The experience of being unafraid of philosophical views, as
   illustrated by the lion who is not scared of the fox.

33

Son, there are four kinds of signs.
The sign of awareness shining within, as illustrated by a butter
   lamp inside a vase.
The sign of the mind not getting involved in the pleasures of
   the senses, as illustrated by a king seated on his throne.
The sign of focusing the mind on the unborn nature, as
   illustrated by a sick person and a cemetery.
The sign of having stamped on the afflictive emotions, as
   illustrated by the pigeon and the hawk.

34

Son, there are four instructions related to optical illusions.
As in the example of perceiving a mirage as water, if you do
   not know that the pleasures of the senses are a delusion,
   you will wander.
As in the example of perceiving a rope as a snake, if you do
   not know that you are being fooled, you will wander.
As in the example of the parrot eating poison, if you cling to
   things thinking that they truly exist, you will wander.
As in the example of the child and the empty fist, if you are
   fooled by your perceptions, you will wander in samsara.

35

Son, there are ten ways of failing the Buddhas.
Even if the whole world rises up in enmity against you, do not
   stray from the absolute nature. If you do, you will be
   betraying the Buddhas of the three times.

Whatever you do, do not wander from the continuum of the unborn absolute nature. If you do, you will be betraying the Buddhas of the three times.

Even if your life is at stake, never lose sight of the Dharma. If you do, you will be betraying the Buddhas of the three times.

Do not spoil even an atom's worth of your samaya with the sublime teacher. If you do, you will be betraying the Buddhas of the three times.

Rather than now accomplishing fame in this life, put all your efforts into the task of training the mind. If you involve yourself in the affairs of this life and are not diligent in the mind training, you will be betraying the Buddhas of the three times.

See the noble teachers as Vajrasattva in person and have devotion. If you do not, you will be betraying the Buddhas of the three times.

Know that everything outside and inside is the mind, and do not have attachment or aversion. If you do, you will be betraying the Buddhas of the three times.

Cultivate great compassion and work for the sake of sentient beings. If you strive for your own sake alone, you will be betraying the Buddhas of the three times.

All dualistic concepts are the work of demons, so know that there is no duality of subject and object. If you fail to do so, you will be betraying the Buddhas of the three times.

With this body as a support, be careful as you seek the fruit of Buddhahood. If you fail to do so, you will be betraying the Buddhas of the three times.

36

Son, there are four ways not to be distracted.

Do not be distracted from the expanse of the mind free of grasping, like a straight arrow.

Do not be distracted from the absolute space, which is free from thoughts, like an athlete.

Do not be distracted from the expanse of evenness, like a hooked fish.

Do not be distracted from the state beyond all thought, as if
you were removing a thorn.

37

Son, there are four instructions on the method.
The instruction on the state of mind devoid of all ordinary
perception and thought, like a dry skull.
The instruction on the mind that, watching, sees nothing, like
someone who has eaten poison.
The instruction on the mind free from judgments, like an
infant.
The instruction on leaving the mind as it is, as if stunned, like
someone whose heart has been removed.

38

Son, there are four ways to stay.
Stay without thought in the clarity that is not acquired and
cannot be lost.
Stay without thinking in the bliss that is not to be evoked and
cannot slip away.
Stay in vivid clarity, undistracted in the state beyond
distraction.
Remain unhurried, with nothing to do, perfectly poised.

39

Son, there are six crucial points of the mind to be understood.
Relaxation is the crucial point of the mind, exemplified by
someone who has completed a task.
Freedom from concern is the crucial point of the mind,
exemplified by someone who has recovered from an illness.
Freedom from hesitation is the crucial point of the mind,
exemplified by a madman jumping off a cliff.
Freedom from expectation and apprehension is the crucial
point of the mind, exemplified by one's meeting a person
one had been looking for.

Freedom from fear is the crucial point of the mind, exemplified
by a lion walking among other savage beasts.
Clarity with absence of thoughts is the crucial point of the
mind, exemplified by the flame of a lamp filled with sesame
oil.

40

Son, there are four things you need not seek.
Having the view that has no dualistic fixation, do not seek one
that has; take the example of the sun: it does not have to
look for its rays.
Having the meditation that has no object on which to focus,
do not seek one that has; take the example of a wish-
fulfilling gem: it does not have to look for the things one
wants.
Having the action free of adoption and rejection, do not seek
one to adopt and reject; take the example of a person: he
does not have to look for himself.
Having the result free of hope and fear, do not look for one
with hope and fear; take the example of a monarch: he does
not have to reassert his royalty.

This was the third section from the *Eighty Chapters of Personal Advice*, the
instruction on one-pointed concentration, the means.

IV

Wisdom

41

Son, there are twelve points.
Not concealed anywhere, the mind is invisible.
From the beginning never separate from you, it has not been
 recognized.
Invisible when examined, things appear in every possible way.
They appear multifariously, yet they are not real things.
Despite kalpas of wandering, it has never been lost or
 separated.
Though it appears in multifarious ways, it has never changed.
There is not an atom to it, yet it pervades everything.
Within emptiness, all sorts of things appear.
When it is not held or tied, it stays wherever it is.
Unsupported, one moves through space.
Without any effort, everything is accomplished.
With neither form nor characteristics, it appears as it is viewed.

42

Son, there are twelve kinds of confidence.
The confidence that the whole of existence is one and the same
 in space and therefore has no intrinsic nature.
The confidence that since the root is subsumed in the mind,
 Buddhahood is not elsewhere.

The confidence that since the mind has no birth, it is
uncompounded.
The confidence that since everything that appears is delusory,
in truth enemies and friends do not exist.
The confidence that since all actions are suffering, in truth
there is nothing to be done.
The confidence that since it is the nature of everything, it is
nondual.
The confidence that there is no traveling, for realization is
Buddhahood.
The confidence that the mind cannot be troubled by
attachment and aversion, for everything that appears is
untrue.
The confidence that attachment and aversion are unborn.
The confidence that objects that arouse all dissolve in the
mind.
The confidence that as it is the source of everything, it is the
Absolute Space—the Mother.
The confidence that it is the great immensity, it is the place
where everything dwells.

43

Son, there are nine things one sees.
One sees that everything is empty.
One sees that the root is the mind.
One sees that the nature is unborn.
One sees that one's situation is unpredictable.
One sees that the nature is devoid of true existence.
One sees that the natural state does not change.
One sees that the way-it-is is devoid of duality.
One sees that the ground nature itself does not tend toward
any particular direction.
One sees that the fundamental nature is devoid of concepts.

44

Son, there are seven sublime things.
To be free from intellectual meditation is the sublime "leaving
things as they are."

To be free of references is the sublime reference.
Not to meditate on absence of thoughts is the sublime absence
of thought.
Not to use anything as a support is the sublime support.
Not to meditate on anything is the sublime meditation.
To remain undistracted, with no attempt to stop movements,
is the sublime concentration.
When the mind is not involved with anything, this is the
sublime absorption.

45

Son, there are six wisdom sense organs.
The wisdom eye, which sees the forms of mind's projection.
The wisdom ear, which understands the meaning of
emptiness.
The wisdom nose, which senses the unborn.
The wisdom tongue, which tastes in a nondualistic way.
The wisdom body, which touches the absolute nature.
The wisdom mind, which recognizes the mind's projection as
arising in the nature of the mind.

46

Son, there are six wisdom objects.
The absolute nature seen as clarity and emptiness inseparable
is the wisdom form.
Sound understood as spontaneously arisen is the wisdom
sound.
The instruction imbibed to satiety is the wisdom fragrance.
The experience of the object as unborn is the wisdom flavor.
The great bliss touched is the wisdom texture.
Recognition is the wisdom phenomenon.

47

Son, there are six authentic experiences.
To not see at all is authentic sight.

To not hear anything is authentic hearing.
To not sense anything is the authentic perception.
To not taste anything is the authentic taste.
Not mentally touching anything is the authentic contact.
Not being aware of anything is the authentic awareness.

48

Son, there are six declarations on effortlessness.
One settles in the view in total rest, without any concept of
  vastness or constraint.
The meditation is the utter peace, radiance from the depth.
The action is joyful spontaneity, without adoption.
The result is all-pervading peace, where there is no hope or
  fear.
It is the universal evenness beyond all distinctions of quality or
  magnitude.
It is the utmost ease where the mind has no sorrow.

49

Son, there are sixteen metaphoric practices.
Always strip naked.
Always perform the great ablution.
Take the sun and the moon in your hand.
Whirl the wheel.
Gaze in the mirror.
Cure the sickness caused by the poisons.
Untie the rope binding you.
Flee from the midst of savage beasts of prey.
Reside in the crystal vase.
Climb the jewel stairs.
Cut the tree at the root.
Sleep in the openness of space.
Commit suicide.
Hasten to the golden isle.
Anoint your body with balm.
Pick sky flowers.

50

Son, there are five views.
Do not get angry at thoughts.
Do not be attached to the absolute nature.
Do not be proud of concentration.
Do not be resentful of anything wrong.
Do not be confused with regard to wisdom.

51

Son, there are ten aspects to complete confidence.
Everything possible may pour down like rain.
The three worlds may overflow like a river.
The six mental states may blaze like fire.
The one thousand million worlds may be buffeted as if by the
    wind.
The three poisons may gather like darkness.
The thousand million worlds may be filled by the sun.
Whole continents may be plunged into darkness.
Birth and death may be distinct.
One may have karmic tendencies.
Phenomenal existence may be turned upside down.

52

Son, there are four examples and their meanings.
Take the example of a Sugata's body: whichever way one looks
    at it, it is beautiful. Similarly, everything one does, if it is
    permeated with the unborn nature, is bliss.
Take the example of a smile and a scowl: two expressions but
    no more than a face. Similarly, everything that appears,
    everything that exists, does so within the unborn absolute
    nature.
Take the example of a blind person: it makes no difference
    whether one smiles at him or not. Similarly, in the absolute
    nature there is nothing to be adopted or rejected.
Take the example of the trunk of a plantain tree: it has no core.
    Similarly, phenomenal existence has no essence.

53

Son, there are four dissolutions of extremes.
In the absolute truth, phenomena are unborn, so they are
    beyond the extreme of existence.
In relative truth, they are unceasing, so they are beyond the
    extreme of nonexistence.
Not existing as distinct phenomena, they are not two, so they
    are beyond the extreme of both existence and nonexistence.
"Neither" arises as "both," so phenomena are beyond the
    extreme of neither existence nor nonexistence.

54

Son, there are four ultimates.
Having recognized all outer and inner phenomena to be your
    own mind, to know that the mind is empty and immaterial
    is the ultimate reach of the view.
While not blocking the five senses, to be free from notions of
    subject and object is the ultimate reach of meditation.
To know how to act uniting view and action is the ultimate
    reach of action.
To be free of the belief that there is any truth in phenomenal
    existence is the ultimate reach of experience and realization.

55

Son, there are five dharmakaya aspects of the mind.
The unmoving dharmakaya, illustrated by the oceanic deep.
The unchanging dharmakaya, illustrated by Mount Meru.
The uninterrupted dharmakaya, illustrated by a great river.
The undimming dharmakaya, illustrated by the sun.
The thought-free dharmakaya, illustrated by the reflection of
    the moon in water.

56

Son, there are six primal wisdoms related to the mind.
The fresh nature, unadulterated, free of the duality is the
    wisdom of coalescence.

Neither reaching out nor withdrawing, there is the wisdom of
  one taste.
With no adoption or rejection, there is the wisdom with no
  hope or fear.
Putting the seal on perceptions, there is the spontaneously
  arisen wisdom.
The union of appearances and emptiness, of awareness and
  emptiness, is the wisdom of union.
There is outer emptiness and inner emptiness: this is the
  wisdom of emptiness.

57

Son, there are seven ways in which the nature of the mind is
  introduced.
The object is introduced as being the mind's projection.
The mind's projection is introduced as a reflection.
Appearances are introduced as infinite.
The consciousness is introduced as being without support.
Awareness is introduced as being self-cognizing.
The object is introduced as being unborn.
The unborn is introduced as being free of conceptual
  constructions.

58

Son, there are six ways of introducing the ultimate nature of
  everything that arises.
Do not value existence.
Do not prize nonexistence.
Do not reconcile them in inseparability.
Do not differentiate things.
Do not conceive of anything.
Do not be distracted from the radiant deep.

59

Son, there are eight introductions.
The mind is perfectly clear.

Movements subside by themselves.
Thoughts are leveled instantly.
Awareness is naturally pure.
It is not perceptible.
The object is naturally empty.
It is there but it does not exist.
It does not exist and yet it is there.

60

Son, the unborn nature is introduced in nine ways.
What is born is unborn.
What has not been born is unborn.
What will never be born is unborn.
What appears is unborn.
Emptiness is unborn.
Awareness is unborn.
The unborn appears.
The unborn is primordially nonexistent.
The unborn is free from extremes.

61

Son, there are four similes.
Taking the example of a mountain, stamp your being with the
  view free from assertions.
Taking the example of a king seated on his throne, stamp your
  being with the meditation free of effort.
Taking the example of someone who has arrived on a golden
  island, stamp your being with the action free from dualistic
  perception.
Taking the example of a knot in a snake, stamp your being with
  the sole result in which there is freedom from hope and
  fear.

62

Son, there are five instructions.
Know that form and consciousness are unborn.

Without clinging, be aware of what you perceive.
Remain without being distracted by the eight concerns.
Remain without the consciousness being carried away by
    circumstances.
Seal the mind.

63

Son, there are five experiences of wisdom.
Thoughts are the absolute nature.
Characteristics are freed by themselves.
Looking directly confirms.
Clinging stops by itself.
Duality vanishes by itself.

64

Son, there are four ways in which the nondual absolute nature
    arises.
In the absolute nature, there is no good or bad; this is the all-
    penetrating primal wisdom.
By dwelling naturally without seeking anything, one remains
    in the state without conceptual constructs.
Not adulterating or fabricating is the great impartiality.
As the ultimate nature of the mind arises spontaneously,
    primal wisdom unfolds in the expanse.

65

Son, there are six ways in which the nondual absolute nature
    arises.
Since it arises in the state free of contrivance from the very
    beginning, it is fresh.
Since everything is complete within the mind, it is
    spontaneous.
Since there is no blocking or encouraging, it is great primal
    wisdom.
Since there is no division into samsara and nirvana, it is the
    nondual vajra.

Since mind is Buddha from the very beginning, it is the self-
born vajra.
Since it is not caught by enemies, it is the great evenness.

66

Son, there are four ways of arising without duality.
It is clear and uncontrived, the natural radiance devoid of
thoughts.
Without any concepts whatsoever, it is the mirror of
awareness.
It is the self-cognizing awareness, a wishing-gem.
Everything arising by itself, it is the unpremeditated wisdom.

67

Son, there are four instructions.
In completely pervading all ten directions, it is the great
pervasion.
Since it is without an outer gate and inner sanctum, it is the
bodhichitta free of partiality.
As anything arises, it is the great unpredictability.
Since it is neither lit nor dimmed, it is the pure enlightened
state.

68

Son, there are eight kinds of natural dissolution.
Forms seen by the eye dissolve as they are seen; they dissolve
in the sphere of the unborn.
Sounds heard by the ear fade away as they are heard; they fade
away in the expanse of the unborn.
Odors smelled by the nose dissolve as they are smelt; they fade
away in the sphere of the unborn.
Tastes savored by the tongue dissolve as they are tasted; they
fade away in the expanse of the unborn.
Sensations felt by the body dissolve as they are felt; they fade
away in the expanse of the unborn.

Perceptions too dissolve by themselves; they fade away in the
sphere of the unborn.
Words uttered dissolve by themselves; they dissolve in the
expanse of the unborn.
Thoughts too are free in themselves; they dissolve into the
sphere of the unborn.

69

Son, there are four things that are stainless.
To recognize the unborn in everything that appears is the
stainless wisdom of the view.
Taking the unborn as the path is the stainless path.
In the unborn nature, an incapacity to express is the stainless
experience.
Not to stray from the unborn nature into ordinary thoughts is
the stainless result.

70

Son, there are five things you will not find.
There is no finding an object outside.
There is no finding a mind inside.
There is no finding a body in between.
There is no finding the sentient being you do not want to be.
There is no finding the Buddha you would like to be.

71

Son, there are five instances where there is nothing to be
found.
Whatever appears is an appearance of something that does not
exist. You will never find it: there is nothing to be found.
Awareness is awareness and emptiness inseparable, so you will
not find it: there is nothing to be found.
The body has no essence, so you will not find it: there is
nothing to be found.
Beings are unborn, so you will not find them: there is nothing
to be found.

The undeluded Buddha state is your own mind, so you will
   not find it: there is nothing to be found.

72

Son, there are five things to take as the path.
Do not conceive of anything.
Do not indulge in any object.
Do not entertain any hope whatsoever.
Do not regard anything as a defect.
"Force" the mind into its natural state.

73

Son, emptiness is threefold.
Phenomena outside are not born: they are empty.
The mind inside is empty: it is not born.
The aggregates "in between" are empty: they do not dwell.

74

Son, there are three things to take as the path.
Take as the path the absence of any ground or root.
Stay without giving importance to things.
Apply the seal.

75

Son, there are four ties to be severed.
Sever outer ties.
Sever inner ties.
Sever "in-between" ties.
Rely constantly on lonely places.

76

Son, there are eight activities to be performed.
The three protections.

Making provision.
Simplifying.
Making offerings.
Confessing negative actions.
Prayer.
Sitting on a comfortable seat.
Performing the yogic exercises.

Visualize the teacher seated on a throne.
Begin by performing the seven branches.
Next examine samsara.
Then recall the intermediate states.

77

Son, there are seven concentrations.
The concentration of the emptiness of the inner.
The concentration of the emptiness of the outer.
The concentration of the emptiness of both inner and outer.
The concentration of the emptiness of the absolute.
The concentration of the lion's imposing demeanor.
The concentration of clear wisdom.
The vajralike concentration.

78

Son, there are six preparatory practices.
Sit on a comfortable seat.
Next, visualize the channels.
Expel the energies.
Perform the yogic exercises.
Rid yourself of other mental turbidity.
Bring the mind into one-pointed concentration.

79

Son, there are five branches in the main practice.
Drop activities, put them off.
Your body, speech, and mind will be extremely happy.

The mirror of awareness will shine within.
The Sugatas will bestow their splendor.
It will be impossible for conditioned thoughts to arise.

This was the fourth section from the *Eighty Chapters of Personal Advice*, the instruction on stainless wisdom, the essence.

V

Conclusion

80

Son, there are three points in conclusion.

Recognize defects in disciples who might be liberated by these
profound instructions: do not give the instructions to
improper vessels whose natural disposition is unsuitable,
who are inconstant, who find fault in the Dharma and in
individuals, and who will not put the instructions into
practice.

To those who are good-natured, whose minds are stable, who
have very pure perception, and who are assiduous in the
practice—to them you can give the instructions.

They should see the teacher as the Buddha. They should keep
the instructions in their hearts. Befriending solitude, they
should practice. As a result, experience and realization will
bloom and they will become the snow lion's cubs.

This was the fifth section from the *Eighty Chapters of Personal Advice*, the
on the vessel and a related teaching.

This is the essence of the heart of Deshek Gyawopa, the Lord
who attained the summit of the view.

It covers the Three Pitakas and follows the texts of *Epitome*,
Magic, and *Mind*.

It is an instruction that within a single lifetime liberates those with faith, diligence, and wisdom.

Written down by Khyungpo Yamarwa exactly as the Lord spoke it, it is the culmination and quintessence of his profound teachings.

Shechen Gyaltsap Pema
Gyurmed Namgyal (1871–1926).

Part Three

SHECHEN GYALTSAP RINPOCHE'S
A NECKLACE OF JEWELS

An annotated edition of
Zurchung Sherab Trakpa's
precious instructions on
the three trainings,
Eighty Chapters of Personal Advice

Pith instructions comprising
the essence of the Pitakas in
general and the three
inner tantra sections:
Epitome, Magic, and Mind

Introduction

NAMO RATNA GURU BHYA

I pay homage to the precious Teacher.

Bowing down to the teacher who is Vajrasattva in reality,
I shall thread a Necklace of Jewels,
The Eighty Chapters of Personal Advice
Laid out in detail with a structural outline—
A treasury of gems of the three trainings.

The Buddha, having considered the various mental capacities of
*   sentient beings,*
Taught the various vehicles of the Dharma.
From these Deshek Gyawopa teased out the wool of the sutras and
*   the tantras.*
He churned the milk of the Three Pitakas.
He drank the words of the learned ones like water.
He savored the realization and experience of former masters like salt.
Looking at appearances as in a mirror,
He saw that whatever one does there is nothing but suffering.
He saw that the concerns of this world are to be given up.
He saw that besides accomplishing something meaningful for future
*   lives, nothing is of any use.*
He saw that status and fame have to be thrown away like spit and
*   snot.*
He saw the need to rid himself of retinue and bustle—for it is hard
*   to make everyone happy—and to meditate alone.*
At Trak Gyawo he practiced intensively.

He himself made a living experience of these Eighty Chapters of
     Personal Advice *on how to practice the whole of the Dharma.*
For those who fear birth and death, this is a practice for today.
*He gave this as a spontaneous teaching, out of love, as direct heartfelt
     advice.*

There are five topics. As we find in the scriptures:

> *Having cultivated firm devotion,*
> *In the field of pure discipline*
> *Sow the seed of concentration,*
> *And see the harvest of wisdom ripen.*

> *Accordingly, there are the instructions on faith, the gateway;*
> *The instructions on discipline, the basis;*
> *The instructions on concentration, the means;*
> *The instructions on wisdom, the essence;*
> *And to conclude, a summary of the above.*

I

Faith

This first section has five chapters.[174]

I

Showing the importance of faith as a prerequisite and the fault in not having faith.

Son, since it is a prerequisite for the whole of the Dharma, it is important to recognize the fault in not having faith and the virtues of having it.

The essence of faith is to make one's being and the perfect Dharma inseparable. The etymology of the word "faith" is: the aspiration to achieve one's goal. The categories of faith are three: vivid faith, yearning faith, and confident faith.

There are six faults that come from not having faith.

Without faith one is like a rock at the bottom of the ocean—*the Dharma will not benefit one's being.*

One is like a boat without a boatman—*one will not be able to cross to the other side of samsara.*

One is like a blind person who goes into a temple—*one will be unable to understand the words and their significance.*

One is like a burnt seed—*the sprout of enlightenment will not grow.*

One is like a sheep stuck in a pen—*there is no liberation from suffering.*

One is like a maimed person who has landed on an island of gold—*one will return empty-handed at the end of this precious human life.*

2

The virtues of faith.

Son, there are six virtues of faith.

Faith is like a very fertile field—*the whole crop of virtue will grow.*

Faith is like a wishing-gem—*it fulfills all one's own and others' desires.*

Faith is like a king who enforces the law—*he makes himself and others happy.*

Faith is like someone who holds the stronghold of carefulness—*he will not be stained by defects and he will gather qualities.*

Faith is like a boat on a great river—*it will deliver one from the suffering of birth, old age, sickness, and death.*

Faith is like an escort in a dangerous place—*it will free us from the fears of samsara and its lower realms.*

3

The causes that nurture faith and its qualities.

Son, there are ten causes that give rise to faith.

You need to know that there is no happiness in your present way of life and circle of friends. *Ultimately these are the cause of suffering.*

You need to have confidence in the law of cause and effect, *for it can never, ever fail.*

You need to remember death and impermanence. *There is no certainty about when you will die.*

You need to remember that you will depart without your retinue or wealth. *When you die, you have to leave them all behind, so they are no use to you.*

You need to bear in mind that you are powerless to choose your next rebirth. *There is no knowing where the force of your actions will take you.*

You need to remember how hard it is to obtain a fully endowed human body such as this. *It is difficult to bring together the freedoms and advantages and their multiple causes.*

You need to bear in mind that the whole of samsara is suffering. *It is never anything other than the three kinds of suffering.*

You need to see the immense qualities of the Three Jewels. *It is certain that they forever protect us from the suffering of samsara.*

You need to look at the lives and deeds of the Holy Beings. *The activities of their Body, Speech, and Mind are unstained by faults or defects.*

You need to keep the company of excellent friends who abide by virtue. *Their good ways will naturally rub off on you, and faith and other virtuous qualities will increase.*

4

Counseling yourself with thirteen teachings on things to be regarded with distaste.

Son, there are thirteen things to be abhorred.

Unless you turn your back on your fatherland, you will not vanquish the demon of pride. *Wholeheartedly adopt foreign lands.*

Unless you give up the activities of a household, you will never find the time to practice the Dharma. *Put aside the business of running a household.*

If you do not practice the moment faith arises, there will be no end to the jobs you have to do. *Cut through your indecision.*

Do not blame others for your own lack of faith. *Wind the nose rope around your head.*

Unless you cast your possessions to the wind, you will never exhaust your worldly ambitions. *Whatever you have, use it to make offerings to the teacher and to the Three Jewels.*

Unless you distance yourself from your relatives, there will be no interruption in your attachment and aversion. *Always rely on solitude.*

Unless you act now, you cannot be sure where you will go next. *Now, when all the favorable conditions have come together, you should do anything to get free from samsara.*

Doing nothing now when you have the means, the prayers you make for future lives are empty chatter. *If you have the ability and you do not act, you are letting yourself down.*

Without lying to yourself, practice the Supreme Dharma. *Take your own mind as a witness.*

Forsake now what you will have to give up anyway, and it will become meaningful. *Whatever you have, your body and wealth, give it away for the Dharma.*

Rather than concerning yourself with things you obviously cannot complete, concern yourself with making an experience of what you definitely can complete. *For the sake of the Dharma, be prepared for austerity and forbearance.*

Instead of preparing for next year—when you cannot be sure whether or not there will be a next year—prepare for death, which is certain to happen. *Time is short; curtail your plans.*

As you practice, food and clothing will take care of themselves, so do not have great hopes or fears. *For those who practice the Dharma it is very important to give up all concern for this life.*

5

Thirteen important points that show the unmistaken path.

Son, there are thirteen things that are very important.

His realization is like space, beyond all partiality. His experience is constant and level like the ocean. His compassion shines evenly, like the sun and the moon. To a teacher who has these three qualities, it is very important to be respectful. *As the teacher is the root of the path, follow him, pleasing him in the three ways. Do not do anything disrespectful, even in a dream.*

It is very important to give instructions to disciples who are proper vessels. *They will hold the lineage and benefit themselves and others, and the teachings and beings. Do not be miserly with the teachings.*

It is very important to give up attachment to things, externally and internally. *Remember the defects of attachment to the pleasures of the five senses.*

In practicing the instructions, it is very important to think in the long-term. *With regard to the Dharma, do not be impatient. You need to accompany the teacher for a long time. Do not be skittish.*

It is very important to develop fervent devotion to the yidam deity and the Three Jewels. *Without fervent devotion, blessings will not enter. At all times be diligent in taking refuge.*

It is very important to cultivate diligence in the practice of virtue. *Act like a beautiful woman whose hair has caught fire. Do not fall under the influence of laziness.*

It is very important to steer clear of negative actions. *Think of their fully ripened effect and avoid them as you would a speck of dust in your eye.*

It is very important to rely on the absence of thoughts in your mind. *Let the thoughts related to the five poisons dissolve by themselves.*

In the postmeditation period, it is very important to rely on compassion and bodhichitta. *This is the root of the Great Vehicle and is therefore indispensable. Train in considering others more important than yourself.*

It is very important to develop the conviction that the instructions are unmistaken. *If you have no doubts, accomplishment will be swift in coming.*

It is very important to observe the vows and samayas. *Do not let your mind be stained by the downfalls and faults related to the three vows.*

It is very important to establish the unborn nature of the mind. *As your mind and appearances are the display of the absolute nature, come to the clear conclusion that the nature of mind is unborn like space.*

It is very important not to give the secret pith instructions to an improper vessel. *Divulging the secret teachings leads to criticism, so be careful: take pains to check the worthiness of the disciple.*

This was the first section from the *Eighty Chapters of Personal Advice,* the instruction on firm faith, the gateway.

II

Discipline

The eighteen chapters that follow comprise the instructions on the jewel-like superior training in discipline, the perfect foundation.

6

An instruction on timeliness in the practice.

Son, there are ten facts.

If the continued existence of the Buddha's teaching and your having faith coincide, it is simply that you accumulated merit in past lives. *Now that for once you have acquired the freedoms and advantages, do not squander them.*

If you are interested in the Dharma and meet a master who possesses the instructions, it is simply that the blind man has found the jewel. *Later it will be hard to find such a teacher repeatedly, so stay with him for a long time without separating from him, like the eyes in your forehead.*

If faith, diligence, and wisdom coincide in a body free of defects, it is simply that these good qualities are the karmic result of having trained in the Dharma. *Be diligent in the methods for making these three grow.*

If your being born in samsara coincides with relatives scolding you, it is simply that you are being exhorted to practice. *Decide for yourself and practice the Dharma.*

If your having things and your being delighted to give them away coincide with a beggar, it is simply that generosity is coming to perfection. *Without being trussed by the knot of miserliness, give away impartially.*

If, when you are practicing, the dam of suffering bursts, it is simply that you are purifying your negative actions. *Rejoice and give up wrong views.*

If people are hostile toward a Dharma practitioner who has done nothing wrong, it is simply that they are setting him on the path of patience. *Avoid grudges and ill will; keep in mind the benefits of patience.*

If your having consummate faith coincides with applying the instructions, it is simply that you have come to the end of karma. *In the future you will not be reborn in samsara. The whole of the Dharma should serve as the antidote to attachment and aversion.*

If your own fear of death coincides with other people's dying, it is simply that the time has come to turn your mind away from samsara. *Do not be attached to happiness and comfort in this life.*

If you think you will finish your projects for this life first and after that practice a bit of Dharma, this is simply the demon's delaying tactics. *It is very important not to fall under the influence of such a demon.*

7

Thirteen instructions to put into practice.

Son, there are thirteen instructions.

As a spur to diligence in the practice, consider your own death and others'. *The time of death is uncertain, so give up all this life's pointless activities and projects.*

If you want to cultivate extraordinary respect, examine the teacher's outer and inner qualities. *Avoid thinking of defects. Seeing faults reflects your own impure perception.*

If you want your conduct to concord with all, do not obstruct the efforts of others. *As all the vehicles are true in their own terms, do not have rigid opinions about paths or philosophical schools.*

So as never to upset the teacher, practice hard. *You will acquire all good qualities without exception.*

If you want to attain accomplishment quickly, keep the vows and samayas without letting them degenerate. *All the precepts boil down to giving up the ten negative actions and the five poisons as they are ordinarily experienced.*

If you want to halt the four rivers, you must ascertain the unborn nature of the ground-of-all. *When you have understood the unborn nature of the ground-of-all, the continuous flow of birth and death will cease.*

If you want no obstacles to your accomplishing enlightenment, leave behind the distractions of this life. *Trying to help others without having the ability is yet another distraction. Do not try to benefit others when you yourself are not ready.*

If you want to benefit others effortlessly, meditate on the four boundless qualities. *If you train in bodhichitta, nothing you do will exclude others' welfare.*

If you are fearful of the three lower realms in your future lives, steer clear of the ten negative actions. *Be careful, all the time.*

If you want to be happy in this and future lives, be diligent in performing the ten positive actions. *Now, when you have the choice, do not confuse what is to be adopted with what is to be avoided.*

If you want your mind to engage in the Dharma, you must experience the hardship of suffering. *Reflect on the pointlessness of weary toil and develop deep determination. There has never been a spiritual path that is easy.*

If you want to turn away from samsara, strive for unsurpassable enlightenment. *It is important to recognize the benefits of liberation and enlightenment according to the three vehicles.*

If you want to obtain the result, the three kayas, unite the two accumulations. *This will cause the stains veiling the three kayas to be removed.*

8

Showing how to recognize what is not true practice: five things that are useless.

Son, there are five things that are useless.

No need to say you are interested in the Dharma if you have not turned your mind away from samsara. *If everything you do is for this life alone, you will not accomplish the Dharma. To practice the genuine Dharma, you have to counter attachment to samsaric perceptions.*

No need to meditate on emptiness if you have not countered attachment to the things you perceive. *One meditates on emptiness in order to release one's clinging, believing that things truly exist. Unless you are free from this, emptiness is no more than a word.*

No need to practice meditation if you do not turn your mind away from desire. *Great meditators who end up sidetracked by village ceremonies risk dying as ordinary men.*

No need for fine words if you have not assimilated the meaning yourself. *There are many who are fooled by smart talk about the view, so hit the crucial point of the natural state.*

No need to apply the instructions if you do not have devotion. *Any experiences, realization, or good qualities that occur depend on the teacher's blessing: without devotion the blessings can never possibly penetrate.*

9

Showing how to practice with determination and the great armor of diligence: five things one needs to do.

Son, there are five things you need to do.

You need to have fervent devotion to the teacher, for then the blessings of the lineage will automatically rub off on you. *The practice of the Secret Mantrayana is the path of devotion and blessings. The root and lineage teachers are of one essence. See the teacher as the Dharmakaya Buddha. That way the blessings of all the Buddhas will enter you.*

You need to accumulate exceptional merit, for then everything you wish for will work. *The wishes of someone who has merit will be accomplished. At all times offer the seven branches, backed by bodhichitta. That way you will necessarily acquire a good heart.*

You need to make your mind fit, for then extraordinary concentration will be born in your mind. *It is important to train perfectly in making the body and mind fit.*

You need to cultivate extraordinary concentration, for then the afflictive emotions will be overwhelmed. *Sustained calm crushes the afflictive emotions, profound insight eradicates their seeds.*

You need to be free of afflictive emotions, for then you will quickly attain enlightenment. *Besides your own mind divested of obscurations, there is no other enlightenment to be sought.*

10

Identifying counterfeit Dharma.

Son, there are five things that become lies.

As long as you delight in the things of this world, saying you are afraid of birth and death becomes a lie. *Unless you are truly free from attachment, it is impossible to gain liberation from birth and death.*

Unless you are afraid of birth and death, going for refuge becomes a lie. *The words alone will not help.*

Unless you are rid of desire, saying you are a great meditator becomes a lie. *Attachment to anything, inside or out, is a cage imprisoning you. Whether one is shackled with a golden chain or bound with a rope, it is the same.*

Unless you have understood the law of karma, saying you have realized the view becomes a lie. *You have to master the essential point that emptiness manifests as cause and effect.*

Unless you have abandoned the abyss of existence, saying you are a Buddha becomes a lie. *Without getting rid of the cause, the five poisonous emotions, you will never close off the abyss of samsara, their result. So be diligent in applying the antidote, the three trainings.*

II

Practicing over a long period with determination, the armor of diligence, and daring.

Son, there are five things that are true.

It is true to say that without meditating one will never become a Buddha. *If you do not put the path into practice, even the Buddha catching you with his hand cannot help you. This very universe rests on the palm of the Buddha Vairochana-Himasagara.*

It is true to say that if you do not break the samaya, you will not go to hell. *Always take your own mind as witness and never part from mindfulness and vigilance.*

It is true to say that if you separate skillful means and wisdom, you will fall to the Shravaka level. *One who trains in the Great Vehicle must never separate skillful means and wisdom. Train in the path of the six transcendent perfections.*

It is true to say that if you do not know how to unite view and conduct, you are on the wrong path. *Take heed that the view does not slide toward action, and that action does not slide toward the view.*

It is true to say that the mind is by nature perfectly pure and clear, unstained by defects. *Mind is intrinsically radiant and has never been con-*

taminated by adventitious impurities, so its natural expression is the great purity. This is the very reason exerting oneself on the path is meaningful. If it were intrinsically impure, there would be no transforming it into something pure, and there would therefore be no point in striving on the path.

12

Son, there are five things that are pointless: *you might do them but the result will be wrong.*

There is no point in following a master who does not have the nectar of the teachings. *It is important to check first whether he is authentic.*

There is no point in accepting a disciple who is not a proper vessel. *Even if he follows you like your shadow, do not give him instruction. It will benefit neither you nor him.*

There is no point in making a connection with someone who will not keep the samaya. *The fault of his breaking the samaya will rub off on you, and he will not benefit either.*

There is no point in performing positive actions that are mixed with negative ones. *The preparation and conclusion must not be mixed with negative action. It is the nature of mixed actions that they mature as happiness and suffering separately.*

There is no point in knowing the teachings if you do not act accordingly. *It is important, rather, to integrate everything you know with your being and to put it into practice.*

13

Putting the instructions into practice over a long period with determination, armor, and daring.

Son, there are eight instructions.

As you practice, cross the pass of attachment and aversion. *Begin by falling upon those bandits, the eight ordinary concerns.*

When you are studying the texts, don the armor of forbearance. *Earnestly put up with physical hardships and your inner fears regarding the profound meaning.*

When you are staying in sacred sites and secluded places, do not let your mind hanker after food and wealth. *It is important to have few desires and be content with what you have.*

When you want the profound teachings, follow a master well-versed in them. *Do not relegate the instructions to superficial knowledge: clear up all your doubts about them.*

When you meet a truly knowledgeable master, do all you can to please him and never upset him. *By doing so, you will gain all the qualities of his knowledge. Always be careful in your behavior.*

When the Dharma gets difficult, stamp on your faint-heartedness. *With no concern for body and life, serve the Teacher and act with one taste.*

When your family disowns you, cut all attachment in your mind. *Treat friends and enemies equally and let attachment and aversion be liberated by themselves.*

When you are straying into ordinary thoughts, bring your consciousness back to the essence. *If the mind strays onto the object, afflictive emotions will grow, so tether them with the rope of faith, diligence, mindfulness, and vigilance. Develop determination and endurance. Use the antidote of primal wisdom to let deluded thoughts be liberated by themselves. This is a crucial point.*

14

How to practice by applying whatever is necessary in the particular situation.

Son, there are thirty-four pieces of advice.

If you are distracted outwardly by crowds and bustle, your virtuous activities will be dispersed. If you are distracted inwardly by thoughts, afflictive emotions will rise up. If you are otherwise distracted by your own magical powers and giving blessings, your own life will be threatened. For this reason, as they are a source of obstacles, give up distractions.

When you are struck by death's poison, nothing will be of any use. There is no time to tarry: quickly, meditate!

Do not be concerned with how you live *in this life, subduing enemies and protecting your kin;* be concerned with how you will die.

Taking the example of a young maiden's bangles, practice alone without the luxury of attendants. *In particular, avoid bad company.*

As attachment to family is your own mind's deluded perception, cast it aside.

Do not indulge *in physical activities, talking, and thinking:* too much of these gives rise to adverse circumstances.

There is no need to be concerned with trying to please people. You will be much happier having no one for company. *Thus attachment and aversion will not arise. So,*

With no one to keep you company, there is no attachment or aversion.

Since sentient beings' desires are never satisfied, it is impossible to make everyone happy—*even the Buddha could not do so*—so stop trying to please people.

Here is a metaphor for being without thoughts related to attachment and aversion: stay alone like a corpse.

Avoiding the abodes of attachment and aversion and thus being free from clinging and desire, do not enter a pit of thorns: stay in a place where you will be happy.

Until now you have surrendered your bodies and lives to attachment and aversion. Enough with the past, now stop such surrender. *Now surrender your body and life to the Dharma.*

Since all beings are endowed with the buddha-nature, do not consider people as enemies and friends; maintain primal wisdom. *Apply yourself eagerly to sameness.*

Do not look to fame *or to experiencing any other of the eight ordinary concerns;* watch your own mind.

Practice the ascetic discipline of guarding the mind. Unless you are diligent *in this,* you will go down. *Even a single instant of negative thought creates the cause for being thrown into the lower realms.*

From time without beginning, your belief in the reality of things has fettered you in samsara. So now give up your wandering ways of the past.

Of the seven noble riches, the foremost, the source of them all, is being content. Go to the island in the ocean that has the riches you desire.

Without the capacity to be content, even a king is no better off than a beggar. Be satisfied with simply enough food and other necessities to stay alive. If you reach this island, you will never return.

If you have property, give it to your father. *If you please your teacher by offering him everything you have, he will give you all the profound instructions.*

If you make your old father happy, he will give you his heartfelt advice.

The teacher too speaks to his son straight from the heart. *To a suitable vessel he gives the instructions in their entirety.*

The disciple should guard them like his own heart and put them into practice. So once you have found a gem, do not throw it away.

Turn *the mind back from the deluded perceptions that are samsara and* correct yourself. *Travel the highway to enlightenment.*

When your vajra brothers and sisters are assembled, think of yourself as the least important of them all. When your brothers and sisters are all together, listen to what they say and carry it out.

If you fear *your practice* is being scattered, fence it in. *Rely on mindfulness and vigilance and never be without them.*

If you fear you are running after *the objects of the six senses,* hold yourself with the hook: *employ the watchman that is mindfulness.*

*Know that all perceptions are dharmakaya, and with that confidence—as though you had landed on an island of gold and jewels—*make your view stand firmly on its own.

Do not be ashamed in front of the deity, the teacher, or your own mind. Observe discipline without hypocrisy.

Give generously and impartially, *and stop expecting anything in return or any karmic reward.*

Patiently bear with adversity, *providing help in return for harm.*

Put up with suffering when you are listening and reflecting: *readily accept such things as illness, pain, hunger, and thirst for the sake of the Dharma, and take others' suffering upon yourself.*

Do not cast your meditation into the mouth of fame, *with hopes and so on of distinction and renown.*

Your conduct should be such that you are not carried away by the demons *of the eight ordinary concerns. It is important to match it with your progress.*

If you chase after the things you perceive, the demons that are the five poisonous thoughts will arise and you will be beguiled by the demon of appearances. *It is important, therefore, that the mind does not chase after the object.*

15

Six instructions for warding off defects.

Son, do not discredit the house of your forefathers. *Do not bring shame on your own root teacher, nor on the teachers of the lineage.*

Do not taint your siblings and relatives. *Avoid conflicts that prevent you from keeping the samaya with your brothers and sisters—those who have the same teacher as you and those who have entered the Vajrayana.*

Do not throw dust on other relatives, close or distant. *Never speak harshly to others who practice the Dharma.*

Without paying taxes to the king you cannot hope to be his subject. *If you do not please the teacher, his compassion and blessings will not flow.*

Do not race downhill *toward negative actions.*

Do not be clever in wrong ways *such as craft and pretence.*

16

An instruction on ten good and bad situations that do no harm—if one can cope with them.

Son, there are ten things that do no harm.

Here "if you can cope" implies a choice: if you can cope, take it on; if you cannot cope, do not take it on. "Do no harm" means: if a particular situation does no harm, use it; if it is harmful, don't.

So when you are able to take all adverse situations on the path without their affecting you adversely, if you can cope with the place, there is no harm in staying in your own country.

If you can cope with those with whom you are connected, *and do not develop attachment to friends and hatred for enemies,* there is no harm in not leaving your family.

If you can cope with the question of clothing, *and have completely given up such things as worrying about how attractive you are or being embarrassed,* there is no harm even in going naked.

If you can cope with the problem of attachment and aversion *and are able to take joy and sorrow on the path as one even taste,* however you conduct yourself outwardly, you will not come to any harm.

When you realize your own mind as being the teacher, all notions of difference are liberated by themselves. Thus, if you know how to handle the teacher, there is no harm in discontinuing respect.

In realizing that there are no such things as the names of samsara and nirvana and that everything one perceives is self-arisen primal wisdom, if you can cope with samsara, even if you do not practice, you will not come to any harm.

If you can cope with the lower realms *by liberating the mind and appearances into the absolute nature, so that there is no trace of the habitual tendencies,* you will not come to any harm even if you perform negative actions. *If it is for the sake of others, whatever one does is permissible.*

The absolute nature is free from effort and activity;
The essential nature appears in different ways
Yet the natural expression is free and nondual.
When you know your own mind to be samsara and nirvana,
Beyond the observance of all samayas to be kept,

you can cope with the hells, and there is no harm in not keeping the samayas even if you have entered the door of the secret mantras.

If you are confident in the view *that is beyond intellect and free from activity, and recognize that activities are delusion,* there is no harm in taking things easy and sleeping.

If you can cope with the problem of residence *and are not attached to the quality of your dwelling,* it does not matter where you live.

If you can cope with the problem of food *and are free from dualistic concepts of food being good or bad, pure or polluted,* it does not matter what you eat.

If you can cope with the problem of the body *and have severed the ties of self-love,* even if you do not steer clear of contagious diseases, you will come to no harm.

17

Examining and deriding one's own faults and those of Dharma practitioners in general.

Son, there are eighteen objects of derision.

These are, in general, derisory behavior, erroneous practices, foolishness, and breaches of samaya; and there are eight things that prevent such faults from occurring:

> *someone good-natured who is competent to guide one;*
> *a good friend who is clever at leading one;*
> *a concern for future lives that stems from remembering death;*
> *careful avoidance of negative deeds stemming from the conviction*
> *that happiness and suffering are the result of actions;*

a sense of shame in one's own eyes;
a sense of decency in others' regard;
great determination;
and reliability, as in someone whose word can be trusted and who
does not break his promise.

From the eight faults that are the opposite of these come derisory behavior and the rest.

An object of derision here is an object of scornful laughter or of contempt, something to be ashamed of both from the conventional point of view and from that of the holy Dharma.

In the beginning when faith is born, one is ready to leap in the air. *When one receives the teachings, one does all sorts of things such as tearing one's hair out and weeping.*

Later, torn by doubts, one fills desolate valleys with one's footprints. *Without having cleared up one's doubts about the instructions, one grows hesitant and wanders all over the place.*

In the end, having completely lost faith, one becomes a mooring stone on the bottom of hell. *In the end one develops wrong views with regard to the Dharma and the teacher.*

These are the three faults in not having firm faith.

In the beginning, having found the master, one talks about all the teachings he has transmitted. *Having entrusted body and soul to him, one proclaims the secret teachings for all to hear, saying, "These are the most profound of my teacher's words."*

Later, one tires of the master and criticizes him. *One regrets everything one offered before, and one spreads rumors, claiming he has hidden defects.*

In the end, one abandons the teacher and considers him as one's greatest enemy. *One makes new acquaintances and follows other teachers.*

These are the three faults of following the teacher in the wrong way.

In the beginning, when one achieves a degree of concentration, one thinks, "There is no practitioner as good as I am." *Priding oneself on some small experience one has in sustained calm, one gets the idea there is no greater meditator or better practitioner than oneself.*

Later, one gets tired of meditating and resembles an inmate in an open prison. *In the hermitage one becomes bored during the day and fearful at night; at sunset one is glad to eat and sleep.*

In the end, one gives up meditation and loiters in the villages. *If one does not integrate the Dharma with one's being, one ends up performing village ceremonies or working as a hired laborer, a servant, and so forth.*

These are the three faults of failing to go through the practice properly.

In the beginning when experiences occur, one brags about them *like someone deranged. One is contemptuous of relative truth.*

Later one gives up meditation and, as an expert in letters, takes to giving teachings. *Like someone who shows others the way when he himself has no idea which road to take, one explains the teachings to others without having any understanding or realization oneself.*

In the end when one abandons one's body, one dies in a completely ordinary state. *Like an ordinary being one dies without having really set out on the path.*

These are the three faults of not obtaining any stability in the experience of the practice.

In the beginning, one develops but a faint conviction in one's realization of the view. *Having merely gained a vague and general understanding, one prides oneself on one's superb realization. One looks down on others.*

Later, torn by doubts, one lies about one's knowledge and questions others. *Pretending to be knowledgeable when in fact one knows nothing, one pesters others with questions.*

In the end, far from having the view, one is completely dominated by errors and obscurations. *Having fallen under the influence of eternalistic and nihilistic views like those of the Tirthikas, one never realizes evenness, the union state free from elaboration.*

These are the three faults of not gaining the confidence of realization.

When the result is lost in error, the windows of liberation are shuttered. *By failing to unite skillful means and wisdom, one misses the crucial point of the path and closes the door to nirvana, the result.*

By blocking the windows of liberation, one will never interrupt the stream of birth and death. *Because of one's belief that everything that appears is real and the notion of one's body and mind as "I," one is fettered by karma and afflictive emotions, and there is no liberation.*

Unless one interrupts the stream of birth and death, one is powerless to choose where one will be reborn. *On account of one's actions and afflictive emotions, one cannot but take rebirth in existence.*

These are the three faults or objects of derision where the result is utterly wrong.

Therefore, recognize these faults that come from not blending your mind and the Dharma, and do your best to avoid them.

18

Clarifying errors and obscurations: fifteen ways in which the practice goes wrong.

Having turned away from the holy Dharma, one follows ordinary, worldly ways while retaining the appearance of Buddhadharma.

Son, there are fifteen ways in which the practice goes wrong.

The view rushes into uncertainty. *One repeats others' words without having transformed one's own being.*

The meditation gets lost in idiot meditation. *Without profound insight one does not destroy the foundation, afflictive emotions: experiences and realization cannot take birth.*

The action strays into wild, inappropriate conduct. *Acting in ways contrary to the Dharma, one behaves like a madman. One has not recognized the crucial point of accumulation and purification.*

The samaya gets lost in being undervalued. *Without knowing the precepts to be observed, one disdains the samaya, thinking there is no harm in spoiling it up to a point.*

The master is treated as one of one's own. *Thinking of him as an uncle, one fails to develop faith or respect.*

The disciple attends teachings unwillingly. *If you listen to keep others happy or for fear of people criticizing, you will never understand the teachings.*

The practice is left for when one has the leisure. *By falling under the power of sleep and indolence, one will never obtain the result.*

One's experiences are ghost sightings. *Like a clairvoyant, one sees spirits and thinks of them more and more.*

The result is the achievement of worldly fame. *The attachment and aversion of the eight ordinary concerns increase and one is no different from ordinary people.*

One receives the instructions inauthentically. *Without serving the teacher or putting the teachings into practice, one relies merely on having the texts and receiving the transmission. Thus one does not throw oneself with real diligence into experiencing the practice.*

Having obtained a human body in Jambudvipa, one returns empty-handed, *like coming back empty-handed from an island of jewels. From the bed of a Dharma practitioner they remove the corpse of an ordinary person. There was no point in obtaining a human body.*

At death, one dies with regrets. *At that time, even if you regret, you will have run out of means.*

The Dharma practitioner is betrayed by his own name. *Unless you have practiced the Dharma, being called a practitioner does not help. If you act contrary to the Dharma, though you may be called a "spiritual friend," you will have become a counselor in evil.*

One listens to empty sounds. *Like listening to a melodious song of praise, nothing will come from listening to the dry leaves of flattery and praise. One risks pointlessly wasting one's human life.*

If one acts contrary to the Dharma, after death one cannot but go to the hells.

The root and source of all these is attachment and clinging to the things of this life, so recognize them as faults and get rid of them.

19

Showing, by means of twenty-six kinds of folly, where indulging in negative actions will lead.

Taking twenty-six examples of folly in ordinary life,
Son, there are twenty-six kinds of folly *in the holy Dharma.*

It is foolish not to fear an army whose arrival is inevitable, *that is, to have no fear of death.*

It is foolish not to repay a debt you have definitely incurred, *that is, not to purify your karmic debts, negative actions, and obscurations.*

It is foolish to run toward an enemy who will surely take you captive, *that is, to cling to samsara unafraid.*

It is foolish to enjoy carrying a greater load than you can bear, *that is, to not shy away from the ripened effect of negative actions.*

It is foolish to be eager to go somewhere unpleasant, *that is, to take pleasure in doing negative actions.*

It is foolish to leap into an abyss where you are certain to die, *that is, to jump into the three lower realms.*

It is foolish to sow buckwheat and hope to grow barley, *that is, to hope that negative actions will result in happiness.*

It is foolish to expect the sun to shine into a north-facing cave, *that is, to expect the teacher's blessings to happen when you have no devotion.*

It is foolish to place your hope and trust in someone who is obviously going to deceive you, *that is, to be attached to the good things of this life.*

It is foolish for someone of humble origins to vie with one of royal blood, *like a common subject contending with a prince; that is, to hope to develop noble qualities when one is just an ordinary person.*

It is foolish to hope to be rich when you possess nothing, *that is, to hope to be other people's master when you have no qualities yourself.*

It is foolish for a cripple to try to ride a horse, *that is, to make a promise you cannot keep.*

It is foolish to say you have completed a task without having done any work, *that is, to disdain skillful means when you have not realized the natural state.*

It is foolish, when you have still not recovered from an illness, to get fed up with the doctor and to take a liking to someone who has prepared a vial of poison; *that is, to have no respect for the doctor who cures the disease of the five poisons while relishing the company of those who indulge in negative actions.*

It is foolish for a merchant with nothing to sell to be a hearty eater, *that is, to teach others when you have not realized the meaning yourself.*

It is foolish to run off without listening to your father's advice, *that is, to take the wrong direction without listening to the teacher's instructions.*

It is foolish for a daughter to ignore her mother's advice, *that is, to prefer the pleasures of the senses in this life to what is beneficial for future lives.*

It is foolish, having left the house naked and then found clothes, to return home again without them; *that is, having learned the Dharma, to get rich instead of practicing.*

It is foolish to take off your boots when there is no river; *that is, to interrupt the practice of Dharma when you do not have the confidence of realization.*

It is foolish to drink salty water that will never quench your thirst, *that is, to have desires and never know contentment.*

It is foolish to be oblivious of the inside when the outside has collapsed; *your body is old yet your mind is still full of attachment and aversion.*

It is foolish to be clever at counseling others while giving yourself the wrong advice. *You do not practice what you preach.*

It is foolish to scale a fortress without a ladder, *that is, to boast of heading for liberation without completing the accumulations.*

It is foolish for children to not want to do a job they will definitely have to do; *that is, for beginners to put off virtuous activities until later.*

It is foolish not to be worried about crossing an unfordable river, *that is, to be unconcerned by birth, old age, sickness, and death.*

It is foolish to look elsewhere when *the Buddha's wisdom* is already within you.

The above can all be summarized as five faults: hankering after the things of this life; wanting to have the result without the cause; not listening to the words of the teacher; pledging yourself to the holy Dharma but then following ordinary ways; and not practicing what you preach.

20

Nine pieces of personal advice for softening one's being.

This is personal advice because it consists of oral instructions spoken directly—advice to be kept in the heart.

Son, there are nine pieces of personal advice.

If you want to compete, take on the Buddha. *Look at the Capable One's life and train yourself following in his footsteps.*

If you want to backbite, slander the yidam. *All the time, without fail, be diligent in the approach and accomplishment practices.*

If you have to be mean, be so with the instructions. *If you keep them secret and practice them, blessings, experience, and realization will swiftly come.*

If you are going to be unkind, be unkind to your negative actions. *Do not look back at negative actions and friends who act negatively.*

By all means be munificent—with the teacher. *It is more beneficial than making offerings to the Buddhas of the three times.*

If you want to give someone the cold shoulder, make it samsara. *Investigate your mind minutely; be diligent in the methods that will prevent your taking birth in samsara in the future.*

If you are going to enumerate faults, list your own defects. *Depart from the land of your hidden defects.*

When you have the victory, give it to others. *Ultimately it will be for your own good.*

As for the sutras and tantras, tease them out like wool. *Seeking the teachings impartially and integrating them with your mind, correct your practice and your own mind. This is very important.*

21

Nine pieces of heartfelt advice for keeping a low profile.

Son, there are nine pieces of heartfelt advice.

Be a child of the mountains. *For the great meditator who never leaves the mountains, good qualities grow day by day, month by month.*

Eat the food of famine-time. *Do not let food, clothes, and conversation get the upper hand.*

Do the things that please the enemy. *If you do not cast your ordinary ways to the wind, you will never destroy the castle of desire and hatred.*

Wear clothes that no one wants. *Without any attachment it is easy to practice.*

Flee the crowds, alone. *Your virtuous activities will presently increase, there will be no obstacles, and you will get food and provisions as well.*

Be without a handle for your relations. *Unless you give up your longing and affection, you will not be able to cut your ties. Do not let people take your nose rope.*

Tie your fickleness down with a rope. *The human mind, like water, goes wherever it is led, so tether your mind with the rope of mindfulness.*

Abandon havens of delight. *Do not be attached to the pleasures of samsara. If you do not forsake them, you will never stop the constant stream of negative actions, misery, and bad talk.*

Focus your mind on space. *It is important to thoroughly familiarize yourself with the two kinds of no-self.*

22

Instructions, through five beatitudes, on taking good and bad circumstances equally.

Son, there are five beatitudes.

Blessed are they who recognize samsara for what it is: a poisonous tree of suffering. *Having recognized that its very nature is suffering, they avoid it.*

Blessed are they who see those that give rise to afflictive emotions as spiritual friends. *When they see an enemy, for example, he is a master making them develop patience.*

Blessed are they who correctly view the master who has trained in the three wisdoms. *By seeing the teacher as the Buddha and his instructions as nectar, they will be set on the path to lasting liberation.*

Blessed are they who see everything—outer and inner things and circumstances—as being without origin. *By doing so they will realize the wisdom mind of the Buddha.*

Blessed are they who postpone all activities and set out on the unmistaken path. *In short, if they give up all the activities of this life and put the perfect instructions into practice, the sun of happiness is certain to rise in their minds.*

23

Avoiding the twenty causes of breaking the samaya, the samaya being a distinguishing point between sutra and tantra.

Son, there are twenty things that lead to breaches of samaya.

Apart from in exceptional circumstances, to be *deliberately* secretive about your teacher while extolling your own virtues leads to a breach of samaya.

Unless it is to get rid of or to acquire, to view an erudite scholar and an uneducated person as equals leads to a breach of samaya.

Competition, *with self-seeking and hostile motives,* between patrons and disciples leads to a breach of samaya.

To have the intention of offering *the teacher your wealth, property, and so forth that are yours to dispose of* and to put off doing so leads to a breach of samaya.

Receiving as many teachings as you can possibly hear *without considering whether or not there are conflicts and suchlike in the lineage* leads to a breach of samaya. *An alternative version appears in the Commentary: "To receive the teachings unworthily . . ." Any teachings you receive must be with the prior approval of the teacher.*

Using pressure or complaint to insist on getting the instructions *prematurely* leads to a breach of samaya.

Using lies and cunning to deceive your teacher and fellow disciples leads to a breach of samaya.

To put the blame on the master for wrong *that is not your own doing* leads to a breach of samaya.

In a spirit of competition, to treat the master as a rival leads to a breach of samaya.

To abuse the master's confidence, *divulging secrets he has entrusted you with or keeping your own defects secret from the teacher,* leads to a breach of samaya.

To scorn his kindness, *rather than repaying it when you are able,* leads to a breach of samaya.

To be intent on looking after your own interests *by being utterly self-centered, self-seeking, and proud* leads to a breach of samaya.

To steal instructions and books—*writing them down secretly without asking your teacher or fellow disciples or, worse still, obtaining them by actually stealing the texts*—leads to a breach of samaya.

To secretly enumerate the master's faults—*the hidden defects of the teacher and his retinue*—leads to a breach of samaya.

To block another's aspiration, *discouraging someone who has faith,* leads to a breach of samaya.

To make an outer show of the inner practices, *performing the secret activities prematurely,* leads to a breach of samaya.

To be jealous of vajra brothers and sisters—*one's general brothers and sisters and closest vajra siblings*—leads to a breach of samaya.

To act indiscriminately without a teacher or instructions, *practicing just as one pleases without having obtained the teachings or, if you have obtained them, without approval,* leads to a breach of samaya.

To masquerade as a teacher, *giving clever explanations of one's own invention with no aural lineage and without knowing anything oneself,* leads to a breach of samaya.

If the Buddha taught that one should not, with animosity or attachment, look down on even the Tirthikas, this is no less applicable in the case of the others. For this reason, to criticize teachings and those who practice them leads to a breach of samaya.

To exhibit the instructions to unsuitable vessels, *giving the secret teachings literally to those in the lesser vehicles and the like,* leads to a breach of samaya.

Furthermore, having learned the different categories of root and branch samayas that have to be kept, the causes that lead to their degenerating, the disadvantages of their degenerating, and the benefits of keeping them, you should maintain constant diligence with mindfulness and carefulness.

This completes these instructions, which are like a mother who guides and cares for her child. Through them a faithful vessel will be inspired to practice the Dharma and, relying on the superior training in discipline in accordance with the general pitakas, will keep it as the basis of his practice and thereby transform his being.

This was the second section from the *Eighty Chapters of Personal Advice*, the instruction on perfect discipline, the basis.

III

Concentration

The next seventeen chapters comprise the instructions on the superior training of the mind, the perfect means.

24

Showing how the four blessings help one's meditation.

The combination of the teacher's blessings, the student's devotion, and the profundity of the instructions makes experience grow swiftly.

Son, there are four practices that confer blessing.

When you know your mind to be the absolute nature, all objects are liberated in the absolute nature and you will be unaffected by external circumstances. This is the blessing of yourself, as exemplified by the sole of a shoe.

Once all phenomena are recognized as the naturally arisen primal wisdom, they are beyond adventitious conceptual characteristics. This is the blessing of perceptions, as exemplified by a mountain torrent in spate.

With one-pointed concentration, there is no interruption in the flow. This is the blessing of the mind, as exemplified by the middle of a great river.

Like the black jackal, whose eyes see as well by night as by day, one is introduced to the nonduality of perceiver and perceived. This is the blessing of nonduality, as exemplified by a jackal.

Now, by recognizing that appearances are the mind, the mind is empty, emptiness is nondual, and nonduality is self-liberating, one clears away all misconceptions about the outer, inner, secret, and absolute.

However, this alone is not much help if you have not liberated your own mind into the absolute nature, just as ice, despite being water, does not function as water unless you melt it. So it is important to meditate with intense devotion.

Although a yogi currently on the path has truly realized the absolute nature of his mind, he has not yet liberated all phenomena in the absolute nature, and so qualities such as the twelve hundred qualities do not manifestly appear. Nevertheless, through gradual habituation to that realization, all phenomena are liberated or dissolved into the absolute nature, and at that time all the qualities up to the level of ultimate Buddhahood become manifest.

This is why it is taught that while we are ordinary beings, as at present, our realization can both increase and decline. From the attainment of the first level onwards, realization increases but does not decline. On the level of Buddhahood it does neither.

25

Showing, by means of illustrations, how using things as the path helps the meditation.

Son, there are four instructions for using things as the path.
As it is said in the Six Prerequisites for Concentration:

On account of material possessions one suffers.
To own nothing is supreme bliss.
By abandoning all its food,
The pelican becomes ever happier.

Accordingly, make freedom from attachment the path, as exemplified by the pelican carrying fish.

Since afflictive emotions can arise as primal wisdom, make the five poisons the path, as exemplified by the recitation of mantras over poison.

If we recognize the eight consciousnesses as unborn, we cut the root of existence, the notion of a self. Make the unborn nature of the eight consciousnesses the path, as exemplified by cutting a fruit tree at the roots.

As the unborn absolute nature is unaffected by relative phenomena, make the great purity the path, as exemplified by the lotus growing from the mud.

26

Showing by means of illustrations how knowledge helps the meditation.

Son, here are instructions on four things to be known.
All phenomena in samsara and nirvana are devoid of true existence. Know freedom from attachment, as illustrated by the magician.
As phenomena and their nature are not two separate things, know indivisibility, as illustrated by sandalwood or the musk deer.
Since there is no relying on conditioned phenomena with characteristics, know that relatives deceive, as illustrated by being let down by a friend.
Since the absolute nature has been present in you from the beginning, know inseparability, as illustrated by a sesame seed or the flame of a lamp. *When one knows this, the bonds of belief in true existence and dualistic concepts are loosened by themselves, and immaculate wisdom is born in one's mind.*

27

Showing by means of illustrations how the crucial instructions help the meditation.

Son, there are four crucial instructions.
Although the creative power of the empty absolute nature appears multifariously, from the moment phenomena manifest they have no inherent existence: appearance and emptiness are united. You need the crucial instruction that shows how to make a clear-cut decision regarding the unobstructed nature of appearances, as illustrated by a clean silver mirror.
When one is not bound by clinging to what is not two as being two, phenomenal characteristics are freed by themselves. You need the crucial instruction on not being bound by characteristics, as illustrated by a prisoner who has been released.
Although there is not even an atom to meditate upon with regard to the unborn nature of your own mind, do not be distracted for an instant. Be free from mental activity and conceptualization. This is the crucial instruction you need on not being distracted from the unborn nature, as illustrated by shooting an arrow straight at the target.
With the realization of the triple space, do not move from the inseparability of the absolute space and awareness. You need the crucial instruction on

resting in one-pointed concentration, as illustrated by an ophthalmic surgeon.

By this means deluded perceptions, being groundless, are cleared away and phenomenal characteristics fall apart by themselves.

28

Personal advice on how to cut conceptual constructs regarding mental and extramental phenomena.

Son, there are four "cuts."

Whatever dualistic thoughts arise, there are none that are anything other than the absolute nature. Cut the stream of the arising of dualistic thoughts and the following after them, taking the example of a tortoise placed on a silver platter.

Whatever appears, nothing has moved from the absolute nature. Decide that nothing is extraneous to the absolute nature, taking the example of gold jewelry.

The whole variety of joys and sorrows is one within the state of awareness. Decide on its indivisibility, taking the example of molasses and its sweet taste.

All of samsara and nirvana arises from the creative display of the spontaneous primal wisdom. Decide that it is naturally manifesting awareness, taking the example of the moon in the sky and its reflection in water.

29

Showing how dealing properly with samsara and nirvana helps the meditation.

Son, there are four views.

The essential nature being union, its display is arrayed as an ornament. View thoughts and appearances as the ornament of the absolute nature, taking the example of a rainbow adorning the sky.

When one knows thoughts to be the absolute nature, attachment and aversion are put to death. View thoughts as the absolute nature, taking the example of tempering and honing a sword.

There are no traces accumulated as habitual tendencies. View thoughts as leaving no trace, taking the example of birds flying in the sky.

Phenomena are freed in the absolute nature. View existence as untrue, taking the example of waking from a dream.

30

Explaining the actual method of resting in meditation.

Son, there are four kinds of meditation.

Bringing together everything that favors concentration and mastering the crucial point of how to rest in meditation, diligently meditate with increasing habituation, taking the example of the waxing moon.

This is the view of the Prajnaparamita (the Mother of the Victorious Ones), the sphere of the inexpressible, inconceivable, supreme primal wisdom. Meditate on thoughts and appearances as the inexpressible great bliss, taking the example of having your mouth full of water.

Meditate that fame and the like—*that is, the thoughts of the eight ordinary concerns*—are not ultimately true, taking the example of mist, which does not truly exist.

Meditate on the uncontrived nature as empty, taking the example of water and bubbles; *the nature of the mind is empty like space.*

31

Showing how conduct should be endowed with experience and realization.

Son, there are four kinds of conduct.

In your conduct, turn your back on worldly ways: consider the examples of a bride and a madman. *In other words, make sure you are conscientious and considerate of others' opinions, like an anxious newly wed bride; do not act contrary to the Dharma like a madman who does whatever occurs to him.*

In your conduct, *the multifarious phenomenal perceptions* should not move from the absolute nature: take the example of fish in the ocean.

In your conduct, whatever appears—*the five poisonous emotions and so forth*—should be primal wisdom: take the example of fire raging through a forest.

In your conduct, the many should have the single taste—*phenomena and their nature or appearance and emptiness being inseparable:* take the example of salt dissolving in water.

32

Showing different kinds of experience.

Son, there are four kinds of experience.

The experience of no clinging to thoughts, as illustrated by a small child and a mirror: *although there are perceptions, there is no clinging.*

The experience of wisdom taking birth where it has not previously arisen, as illustrated by a poor woman finding treasure: *experience and realization are newly born.*

The experience of neither apprehension nor esteem, as illustrated by a swallow *entering the nest* and a lion: *one has gained decisive confidence.*

The experience of being unafraid of philosophical views, as illustrated by the lion who is not scared of the fox: *there is no fear of the view and action of lower vehicles.*

33

The signs that arise from experience.

Son, there are four kinds of signs.

When experience and realization bloom within, this is the sign of awareness shining within, as illustrated by a butter lamp inside a vase. *For this there are four ways in which objects of knowledge are freed in their own nature.*

1. *They are self-freeing, like iron cutting iron.*
2. *Appearances and the mind being inseparable, they are freed through one single thing, like fire lighting a fire.*
3. *By knowing one's own nature, they are freed into the fundamental reality, like space mixing with space.*
4. *Appearances are recognized as being manifestations of the mind, like a mother and child meeting.*

When there is no effort, this is the sign of the mind not getting involved in the pleasures of the senses, as illustrated by a king seated on his throne.

When one curtails one's plans because there is no time to waste, or decides clearly that all phenomena are unborn, this is the sign of focusing the mind on the unborn nature, as illustrated by a sick person and a cemetery.

The sign of having stamped on the afflictive emotions, as illustrated by the pigeon and the hawk—*the thing to be rejected and the antidote.*

34

Showing that without experience and realization one is powerless not to be reborn in samsara.

Son, there are four instructions related to optical illusions, *with examples of being fooled by illusions.*

As in the example of perceiving a mirage as water, *believing there is something when there is nothing,* if you do not know that the pleasures of the senses are a delusion, you will wander.

As in the example of perceiving a rope as a snake, *thinking it is, even though it is not,* if you do not know that you are being fooled, you will wander.

As in the example of the parrot eating poison *(and, by thus imitating the peacock, causing its own death), if you behave as if you have attained realization even though you have not and* you cling to things thinking that they truly exist, you will wander.

Believing in existence where there is no existence, one is helplessly confused by attachment and aversion. As in the example of the child and the empty fist *tricking it into thinking it contains a treat,* if you are fooled by your perceptions, you will wander in samsara.

35

Son, there are ten ways of failing the Buddhas *in one's commitment, which must accord with one's level.*

The way to avoid failing in your commitment is to take the Buddhas of the three times as your witnesses; for the fault in breaking a promise knows no bounds, whereas if you do not break it, inconceivable good qualities will be yours: you will become the foremost child of all the Buddhas of the past, present, and future. Therefore, within each six-hour period of the day take a reckoning, and if you have broken your promise, make your confession and renew the promise with a firm vow.

Recognizing that all happiness and suffering is the manifestation of your own previous actions, even if the whole world rises up in enmity against you, do not stray from the absolute nature. If you do, you will be betraying the Buddhas of the three times.

Constantly supported by mindfulness and vigilance, whatever you do, do not wander from the continuum of the unborn absolute nature. If you do, you will be betraying the Buddhas of the three times.

Whatever happens to you, apply the antidote, refresh yourself with faith, assimilate the instructions, be unhypocritical in discipline, and have confidence in the law of actions and their results. By these means, even if your life is at stake, never lose sight of the Dharma. If you do, you will be betraying the Buddhas of the three times.

Keeping in mind the related benefits and risks, and remembering kindness, do not spoil even an atom's worth of your samaya with the sublime teacher. If you do, you will be betraying the Buddhas of the three times.

Remembering death and reflecting on the defects of samsara, rather than now accomplishing fame *and other goals related to the eight ordinary concerns* in this life, put all your efforts into the task of training in the mind *turned toward enlightenment.* If you involve yourself in the affairs of this life and are not diligent in the mind training, you will be betraying the Buddhas of the three times.

As it is said in all the sutras and tantras, see the noble teachers as Vajrasattva in person and have devotion. If you do not, you will be betraying the Buddhas of the three times.

Recognizing that everything that appears is the mind, that the mind itself is empty, and that the inseparable union of clarity and emptiness is primal wisdom, know that everything outside and inside is the mind, and do not have attachment or aversion. If you do, you will be betraying the Buddhas of the three times.

Acknowledging beings as your mothers, remembering their kindness, and wishing to repay that kindness, cultivate great compassion and work for the sake of sentient beings. If you *depart from bodhichitta and* strive for your own sake alone, you will be betraying the Buddhas of the three times.

All dualistic concepts on account of clinging to everything outside and inside as truly existing are the work of demons, so know that there is no duality of subject and object. If you fail to do so, you will be betraying the Buddhas of the three times.

With this body as a support, be careful—*that is, maintain mindfulness in the four kinds of conduct, guarding the body and so forth*—as you seek the fruit of Buddhahood. If you fail to do so, you will be betraying the Buddhas of the three times.

36

Using instructions to meditate without distraction.

Son, there are four ways not to be distracted.
Master the crucial point of the methods for settling in concentration, following the examples given in the Six Prerequisites for Concentration.
Do not be distracted from the expanse of the mind free of grasping, like a straight arrow.
Without any mental grasping at the unborn nature, do not be distracted from the absolute space, which is free from thoughts, like a *champion* athlete *or like a painter of sacred art mixing his colors.*
As no phenomena are extraneous to the absolute nature, do not be distracted from *their being indivisible, or from* the expanse of evenness, like a hooked fish.
With the view free from extreme beliefs and your meditation free from intellectual fabrication, do not be distracted from the state beyond all thought, as if you were removing a thorn.

37

Meditation using the instructions on the method of "resting."

Son, there are four instructions on the method.
To let go of the subject inside that apprehends the objects of the six consciousnesses there is the instruction on the state of mind devoid of all ordinary perception and thought, like a dry skull.
Now for the actual instruction on the method of "resting," which is sixfold:

1. *Leave things effortlessly in the expanse free from references.*
2. *Leave everything without contrivance in the uncompounded absolute space.*
3. *Though everything arises in your own mind, leave it without any notion of "I" or self.*
4. *Leave everything without conceptualization in the uncontrived expanse.*

5. *Leave things just as they are in the expanse free of subject and object.*

6. *Leave things in the ineffable unborn expanse.*

The instruction on the mind that, watching, sees nothing, like someone who has eaten poison.

The example is that of the falling lines that appear to the eyes of someone who has eaten a poisonous plant. Its meaning is that by recognizing that the apparent objects of the six consciousnesses are devoid of reality one reverses the belief in true existence.

The actual instruction concerns the primordial unborn nature and comprises six points:

1. *The absolute nature is primordially unstained by clinging.*
2. *The realization is naturally free from craving.*
3. *The way of arising is spontaneous and free from grasping.*
4. *The experience is naturally present and not something that is made.*
5. *The natural state is unborn and devoid of self.*
6. *The display arises spontaneously and is not something to be sought.*

For outer appearances not to be spoiled by inner clinging, there is the instruction on the mind free from judgments, like an infant.

The actual instruction:

1. *The absolute nature is the uncontrived mind.*
2. *The view is the mind without thoughts.*
3. *The primal wisdom is the mind without concepts.*
4. *The meditation is the undistracted mind.*
5. *The essential nature of the mind is unwavering.*
6. *The samaya of the mind is the knowledge that nothing transcends the mind.*
7. *The activity of the mind is not to give up.*

The instruction on leaving the mind as it is, as if stunned, like someone whose heart has been removed. *The example is that of someone whose heart has been taken out: there is no hope of revival and the continuous stream of thoughts is cut. The instruction on "leaving as it is, as if stunned" is that by leaving everything as it is in the uncontrived natural state—without a subject that leaves, without an owner, as if stunned—one will settle at ease, free of grasping and effort, in the arising of the multifarious phenomena. In this natural state of the inseparability of the two truths, leave things in uncontrived simplicity, a state of clear, empty awareness that is not produced by effort through different causes and conditions.*

38

The instruction on how to rest in the natural flow.

Son, there are four ways to stay.

Stay without thought in the clarity that is not acquired and can *never be lost, for the Buddha's wisdom has been present within you from the very beginning.*

Stay without thinking in the bliss that is not to be evoked and cannot slip away, *for the mind from the very beginning is not caught and is not fettered.*

Stay in vivid clarity, undistracted in the state beyond distraction, *for distracting objects have never been extraneous to the absolute nature.*

How does one stay like that? *There are six ways to be without contrivance:*

1. *If you look for mind, it is empty.*
2. *Block it and you will spoil it.*
3. *Contrive it and you will adulterate it.*
4. *Meditate and you will be bound.*
5. *Look at it and it will disappear.*
6. *Effort will obscure it.*

Therefore, do not seek, do not block, do not contrive, do not meditate, do not look, do not make effort: leave it just as it naturally is.

There being nothing in the mind for it to act on, nor anything to do through the path of action, nor anything that is accomplished, remain unhurried, with nothing to do, perfectly poised, *the practice neither overtaut nor slack, like the string of a bent bow.*

39

Unobstructed natural arising, the crucial point of the mind.

Son, there are six crucial points of the mind to be understood.

Awareness, the fourth moment beyond the three—that directly experienced, uncontrived state that is not adulterated by the notions of subject and object—is the simplicity of the dharmakaya. So recognize the mind with this instruction— the natural dissolution of concepts: relaxation is the crucial point of the mind, exemplified by someone who has completed a task.

Being free from the clinging to the true existence of things, one has no concerns, thinking of things as good or bad: freedom from concern is the crucial point of the mind, exemplified by someone who has recovered from an illness.

As there is not a single thing that has not been pure and perfect since the very beginning, be free of the dualistic fixation of blocking some things and encouraging others. Freedom from hesitation is the crucial point of the mind, exemplified by a madman jumping off a cliff.

Everything that appears is liberated as primal wisdom, so the view is free from duality, the meditation is free from fixation, the action is free from effort, and the result is free from aspiration. Freedom from expectation and apprehension is the crucial point of the mind, exemplified by one's *having* met a person *one had been looking* for.

Uttering the specific language of Ati overawes those in the lesser vehicles. Freedom from fear is the crucial point of the mind, exemplified by a lion walking among other savage beasts.

The natural state is naturally radiant; no veils obscure it. Clarity with absence of thoughts is the crucial point of the mind, exemplified by the flame of a lamp filled with sesame oil.

40

Showing that the view, meditation, action, and result are innate and not extraneous.

Son, there are four things you need not seek.

Since the wisdom of the absolute nature free of intellect dwells in you innately, there is no need to look for it anew using one-sided views that are the product of the intellect. Having the view that has no dualistic fixation, do not seek one that has; take the example of the sun: it does not have to look for its rays.

Regarding the uncontrived natural flow, there is no need to meditate on it with dualistic fixation as if it were something new for you. Having the meditation that has no object on which to focus, do not seek one that has; take the example of a wish-fulfilling gem: it does not have to look for the things one wants.

Since things to be rejected and antidotes—afflictive emotions and primal wisdom, for instance—have the same taste, there is no duality of deed and doer. Having the action free of adoption and rejection, do not seek one to adopt and reject; take the example of a person: he does not have to look for himself.

The result, the primordial state of Buddhahood, dwells within you. Having the result free of hope and fear, do not look for one with hope and fear; take the example of a monarch: he does not have to reassert his royalty—*a king presiding on his throne depends on no one else.*

Thus, since all phenomena in samsara and nirvana are by nature inseparable, do not move from the evenness of the absolute nature that is beyond hope and fear, concept and effort.

These chapters on the superior training of the mind have been arranged in a different order in the Commentary as follows. After the thirtieth chapter come chapters 36 to 39, at which point one jumps to chapter 77 in the section on the training in wisdom. Next, one returns to chapters 31 to 35, followed by chapter 40. Here, however, I have followed the exact order of the root text.

To sum up, I have used these chapters to give an explanation to suit readers' individual capacities, so that relying on the superior training in concentration according to the Prajnaparamita, *the* Epitome, *and the* Magical Display, *they practice the view and meditation on the path in much the same way as one brings up a small child—in stages—combining skillful means and wisdom like a bird flying in the sky. This completes the instruction.*

This was the third section from the *Eighty Chapters of Personal Advice,* the instruction on one-pointed concentration, the means.

Wisdom

The following thirty-eight chapters contain the instructions on the superior training of wisdom, the perfect essence.

41

Twelve points that explain the view.

The realization referred to in the Later Mind Section is like a slash with a very sharp blade: with the wisdom devoid of the three concepts, all afflictive emotions and discursive thoughts are severed at the root. The way this happens is that since all phenomena of the ground, path, and result—samsara and nirvana— arise as the play of one's own unborn mind, they are free from ontological extremes, from good and bad, like space. The mind is by nature unborn, its display is unobstructed, its essential characteristic is absence of duality, and so on. In introducing this, the All-Accomplishing King states,

> Because all things are subsumed in the root, the mind,
> It is the root that has to be taught.

Son, there are twelve points.

The unborn ultimate nature of your own mind is not concealed anywhere and yet nobody can see it as a concrete object with characteristics.

Though it has never stopped being yours since the very beginning, hitherto you have not recognized it as your nature.

Since nothing exists as such inherently, when things are examined nothing is seen. *However, when unexamined, they seem to exist: thus all the phenomena of samsara and nirvana* appear in every possible way, *unobstructedly.*

Though in fact there is nothing, deluded appearances appear in all their variety, but *since they do not intrinsically exist in any way,* there is nothing real.

Though you have wandered for kalpas *in existence,* you have never lost or been parted *from the buddha-nature, sugatagarbha.*

Though *the ultimate nature* appears *in* a variety of ways *as samsara and nirvana,* there has *never* been any change *in what it is.*

Without having *as much as* a part of the *minutest* atom *of solid existence,* it pervades everything *like space.*

Within emptiness, *which is like space,* the various *phenomena that arise through the interdependent process of cause and effect* appear *unobstructedly.*

The mind is like an unbroken horse: if you are tense and agitated, you cannot control it; if you relax, you can control it. Therefore, when it is not held or tied, it stays wherever it is.

By uniting sustained calm and profound insight, one travels through the space *of the absolute nature* unsupported, *like a soaring garuda.*

From the absolute nature that is not anything, anything can arise, so everything possible is accomplished without effort.

Without *the mind having color, shape,* form, or characteristics, *which*ever way one views it *and meditates on it, in that way* it appears.

To sum up, this is an introduction to the nature of the mind. As it is unborn, there is no real basis to it. As its display is unobstructed, it arises in various ways. As it is ultimately free of duality, there is nothing to cling to as true. When the conceptual mind is liberated in its essence, nothing ever moves from the dharmata.

42

Twelve kinds of confidence confirming the view.

From having seen the ultimate truth in its full nakedness, the mind is free of doubt.

Son, there are twelve kinds of confidence:

The confidence that *just as* the whole of existence *is created and destroyed* in space, *everything in samsara and nirvana* is one and the same *in thatness* and therefore has no intrinsic nature.

The confidence that since the root *of all things* is subsumed in the mind, Buddhahood is not *to be sought* elsewhere.

The confidence that since the mind *by nature* has no birth *and no cessation*, it is uncompounded.

The confidence that since everything that appears is delusory, in truth enemies and friends do not exist *inherently as different entities.*

The confidence that since all actions *based on delusion* are suffering— *that is, they are the cause of suffering*—in truth, *in terms of the ultimate nature*, there is nothing to be done.

The confidence that since *the unborn absolute space* is the nature of all *phenomena, the nature* is nondual.

The confidence that there is no traveling *the path*, for realizing *the unborn nature of your mind* is Buddhahood.

The confidence that the mind cannot be troubled by attachment and aversion, for everything that appears is untrue *like a magical illusion.*

The confidence that *although mind and appearances are many, they have one taste, and that therefore the thoughts related to the five poisons such as* attachment and aversion are *intrinsically* unborn.

The confidence that objects *such as friends and enemies* that arouse *afflictive emotions, apart from simply being labels assigned by the ordinary mind, do not have any essential existence of their own; they* all dissolve in the mind.

The confidence that as *the nature of mind* is the source of everything *in samsara and nirvana*, it is the Absolute Space—the Mother.

The confidence that *the natural state of the mind* is the great immensity, *for, like space,* it is the place where everything dwells.

43

An instruction on seeing the absolute nature in nine ways.

Son, there are nine things *that, as a yogi on the path,* one sees.
One sees that everything *in samsara and nirvana* is empty.
One sees that the root *of all phenomena* is the mind.
One sees that the nature *of one's own mind* is unborn.
One sees that *since the seventeen kinds of perception and so forth are unobstructed in the way they arise*, one's situation is unpredictable.
One sees that the nature *of all phenomena* is devoid of true existence.

One sees that *despite the multifariousness of appearances and perceptions,* the natural state *of the absolute space* does not change.

One sees that *since it is spontaneously arisen and free of causes and conditions,* the way-it-is is devoid of duality.

One sees that *while it displays multifariously because of conditions,* the ground nature itself does not tend toward any particular direction.

One sees that the fundamental nature is devoid of concepts, *for there are no thoughts of ontological extremes.*

44

Seeing seven aspects of sublimity.

The meditator is free, for his mind has no owner and no responsibility.
Son, there are seven sublime things.

To be free from intellectual meditation is the sublime "leaving things as they are": *Do not try to fixate on existence and nonexistence, appearance and emptiness, and so on.*

To be free of *the ordinary mind's dualistic* references *with regard to the absolute nature, which is beyond all reference,* is the sublime reference.

Neither thought nor no-thought transcends the intellect, and intellectual activity obscures freedom from intellect; thus, not to meditate on absence of thoughts is the sublime absence of thought.

Not to use any *object of knowledge* as a support is the sublime support.

Not to meditate on anything, *such as the union of appearances and emptiness, making it a mental object,* is the sublime meditation.

To remain undistracted, with no *deliberate* attempt to stop the movements *of the mind and mental factors,* is the sublime concentration.

When the mind is not involved with any *of the objects of the eight consciousnesses,* this is the sublime absorption.

In short, all these amount to leaving things as they are, unadulterated by dualistic fixation and contrivance.

45

An instruction on perceiving in a nondualistic way but without denying the six sense organs being distinct and different.

Son, there are six wisdom sense organs *that arise from certainty concerning the absolute nature.*

*When one knows that perceived forms are unborn, one does not grasp
at them, and therefore* one sees the forms of mind's projection with the
wisdom eye.

One understands the meaning of emptiness—*the absolute nature*—
with the wisdom ear.

One senses *the nature* as unborn with the wisdom nose.

One tastes *multifariousness* in a nondualistic way with the wisdom
tongue.

One touches *the truth*, the absolute nature, with the wisdom body.

One knows that all that arises as the mind's projection arises in the *unborn* nature of the mind with the wisdom mind.

46

*Using the above modes of perception to perceive in a nondualistic way without
denying things being distinct and different.*

*If your own mind is free in the absolute nature, everything that appears
outside arises as the absolute nature.*

Son, there are six wisdom objects.

The absolute nature seen as clarity and emptiness inseparable is the
wisdom form.

Sound understood as spontaneously arisen, *like the voice heard in an
echo that does not belong to anyone*, is the wisdom sound.

The *teacher's* instruction imbibed to satiety is the wisdom fragrance.

The experience of *all phenomena* as unborn is the wisdom flavor.

The great bliss—*the absolute nature*—touched is the wisdom texture.

The recognition *of the natural state, the dharmata*, is the wisdom phenomenon.

47

Upon investigation, things are seen to be nonexistent in six ways.

Son, there are six authentic experiences.

Since all phenomena have no true existence as such, to not see them at all
is authentic sight.

*Since there is no duality of a hearer and something to be heard regarding
the absolute nature,* to not hear anything is authentic hearing.

A NECKLACE OF JEWELS

There being in fact no duality of someone who senses and something to be sensed, to not sense anything is the authentic perception.

Similarly, to not taste anything is the authentic taste.

Not mentally touching anything, *true or false or whatever,* is the authentic contact.

Not being aware of any *characteristics in the whole of phenomena* is the authentic awareness.

48

Explaining six kinds of effortlessness, there being nothing in the absolute nature to adopt or reject.

If one knows how to leave all phenomena without deliberate action, one is liberated in the basic natural state:
Son, there are six declarations on effortlessness.

Because in the space of one's unborn mind there is not the duality of a viewer and something to be viewed, one settles in the view *without contrivance or modification, affirmation or negation, and one's mind remains* in total rest without any concept of vastness or constraint.

The meditation is the utter peace *of the absolute nature,* radiance from the depth, *free of grasping and devoid of rough edges—thoughts related to outer and inner phenomena.*

The action, *uncontrived and natural,* is joyful spontaneity, without *the effort of* adoption *or abstention.*

Since the mode of being of things is actualized, there is no hope *of achieving* the result or fear *of not achieving it*; there is all-pervading peace: *dualistic concepts of subject and object dissolve by themselves.*

It is the universal evenness *in the continuum of the absolute nature: things are* beyond all distinctions of quality or magnitude.

It is the utmost ease where the mind has no sorrow, *for samsara, without being rejected, is primordially free, beyond suffering.*

49

An instruction on sixteen metaphoric practices.

Son, there are sixteen metaphoric practices.
Always strip *the awareness* naked *so that it is unobscured by characteristics.*

407

Always perform the great ablution *of emptiness as the antidote for the belief in substantial existence and for clinging to true existence.*

Take the sun and the moon—*emptiness and compassion*—in your hand.

Whirl the wheel *of view and meditation.*

Gaze in the *magical* mirror *of your mind.*

Cure the sickness caused by the poison *of the afflictive emotions.*

Untie the rope binding you—*that of the three poisons or of subject and object.*

Flee *the company of evildoers: they are like* savage beasts of prey.

Having recognized the spontaneously arisen primal wisdom, reside in the crystal vase *of awareness—emptiness and clarity inseparable.*

Climb the jewel stairs *from the bottom to the top, practicing the ten Dharma activities and so on with faith, diligence, mindfulness, vigilance, and carefulness.*

Cut the tree *of belief in a self* at the root.

Sleep in the openness of space, *uncircumscribed awareness.*

Let your own thought-movements commit suicide.

Hasten to the golden isle *where everything that appears and is perceived arises as the absolute nature.*

Anoint your body with the balm *of concentration to allay the fever of desire and hatred.*

Pick sky flowers: *in truth they do not exist; phenomena are but names.*

50

There being nothing to adopt or reject, the view is free of affirmation or negation.

Son, there are five views.

All thoughts that arise are the unborn absolute nature, so do not get angry at thoughts. *The primal wisdom of no-thought is not to be meditated on separately.*

Primal wisdom or dharmata is not to be sought on some far shore rid of afflictive emotions and thoughts, so do not be attached to the absolute nature. *As long as you have attachment you create the cause for wandering in samsara.*

Knowing all phenomena to be equal, do not be proud of *your* concentration.

Everything unwanted and all wrong thoughts are a display of your own mind, so do not be resentful of anything wrong.

Since you yourself possess the spontaneously arisen primal wisdom, do not be confused with regard to wisdom. *Recognize it.*

51

Explaining ten aspects of complete confidence in the natural state.

Since all the dualistic perceptions of happiness, suffering, and so forth are freed in the absolute space, one cannot be benefited or harmed by anything:

Son, there are ten aspects to complete confidence.

The self-arisen primal wisdom or bodhichitta has no cause or conditions and is therefore unchanging in the past, present, and future.

Everything possible may pour down like rain *but bodhichitta, the kingly doer-of-all, will never get wet or stained.*

Similarly, the three worlds may overflow like a river, *but it will not be carried away.*

Even though the six mental states may blaze like fire, *it will not be consumed.*

The one thousand million worlds may be buffeted as if by the wind, *but it will remain unmoved.*

The three poisons may gather like darkness, *but it will not grope in confusion.*

The thousand million worlds may be filled by the sun, *but this will never illuminate the primal wisdom.*

Whole continents may be plunged into darkness, *but it can never be eclipsed by ignorance.*

Birth and death may be distinct, *but it cannot die.*

One may have karmic tendencies, *but from the very beginning the nature has never been affected, so there is nothing to discard now.*

Phenomenal existence may be turned upside down, *but the nature will not be destroyed or separated.*

These are the vajra words on the wisdom—the total confidence and conviction—that cannot be crushed by anything.

52

An instruction that matches examples and their meanings to show how the absolute nature permeates everything.

Son, there are four examples and their meanings.

Take the example of a Sugata's body: whichever way one looks at it, it is beautiful. *Similarly, everything a realized being does, since it is permeated with the realization of the* unborn nature, is bliss, *for he does not have ordinary attachment and aversion.*

Take the example of a smile and a scowl: two expressions but no more than *one* face. *Similarly,* everything that appears, everything that exists—*all the manifestation of samsara or nirvana*—does so within the unborn absolute nature.

Take the example of a blind person: it makes no difference whether one smiles at him or not. *Similarly, since everything that arises unobstructedly from the unborn absolute space is inseparable from it and has the same taste,* in the absolute nature there is nothing to be adopted or rejected.

Take the example of the trunk of a plantain tree: it has no core. *Similarly,* phenomenal existence has no essence, *for when examined using such logical arguments as "Neither one nor many," there is nothing to be found.*

53

When the four ontological extremes dissolve by themselves, it is shown that phenomena are the mind's projections and do not have to be abandoned.

Son, there are four dissolutions of extremes.

As regards all the phenomena of samsara and nirvana, in the absolute truth they are unborn, so they are beyond the extreme of existence.

In relative truth, *the appearance aspect that is the interdependent gathering of causes and conditions,* they are unceasing, so they are beyond the extreme of nonexistence.

Ultimately, the two truths, or appearance and emptiness, do not exist as distinct phenomena: *there is no basis for such distinctions, they are inseparable—in other words,* they are not two, so they are beyond the extreme of both existence and nonexistence.

Intellectually apprehended, "neither" arises as "both," so phenomena are beyond the extreme of neither existence nor nonexistence.

Regarding this there are four faults that occur if one asserts that the two truths are one and the same:

1. *it would follow that ordinary beings who see compounded phenomena could see the absolute truth;*

2. it would follow that the absolute truth could be an objective condition for afflictive emotions arising;
3. it would follow that there was no distinction between relative and absolute; and
4. it would follow that the absolute truth would not depend on listening to the teachings and reflecting on them.

And there are four faults that occur if one asserts that they are different, for it would then follow that:

1. the mind that had realized the absolute could not dispel the belief that relative phenomena truly exist;
2. absolute truth would not be the ultimate nature of relative phenomena;
3. the absence of intrinsic existence in relative phenomena would not be the absolute truth; and
4. sublime beings would see them separately and would be bound and liberated at one and the same time.

In our tradition there are none of these faults because we make no assertions at all about the two truths being either single or different. We establish two truths in relation to the conditions, deluded or nondeluded, of a single mind: in the deluded state the absolute truth does not appear to the relative, deluded mind, while in the nondeluded state the delusory relative does not appear to the mind that has realized the absolute truth. Thus the two truths are like light and darkness. On the one hand, they have one and the same nature but different aspects; on the other hand, their differences disallow their being one and the same. Both of these are explained in the Commentary.

54

Four ultimate aspects that decisively establish the ultimate path.

Son, there are four ultimates.
Having recognized all outer and inner phenomena to be your own mind, *like the things that appear in a dream,* to know that the mind is empty and immaterial is the ultimate reach of the view.
As exemplified by a person in a magical illusion, while not blocking the

five senses, to be free from notions of subject and object is the ultimate reach of meditation.

As exemplified by the accumulation of merit and wisdom by a great emanation, to know how to act uniting view and action is the ultimate reach of action.

As exemplified by an illusory being enjoying riches in a dream, to be free of the belief that there is any truth in phenomenal existence is the ultimate reach of experience and realization.

55

An instruction on the five dharmakaya aspects of the mind, with illustrations.

Son, there are five dharmakaya aspects of the mind, *the unobstructed, all-pervading primal wisdom or absolute nature, emptiness and clarity inseparable.*

The unmoving dharmakaya, *the absence of movement in the absolute nature, the naked state of awareness and emptiness inseparable,* illustrated by the oceanic deep.

The unchanging dharmakaya, *the absolute nature in which there is no change,* illustrated by Mount Meru.

The uninterrupted dharmakaya, *the continuous state of the absolute nature or radiant clarity,* illustrated by a great river.

The undimming dharmakaya, *the primal wisdom that neither grows brighter nor grows dimmer,* illustrated by the sun.

The thought-free dharmakaya, *clear awareness devoid of thought,* illustrated by the reflection of the moon in water.

56

An instruction using the symbolic language of the secret mantras.

Son, there are six primal wisdoms related to the mind.

The fresh nature, unadulterated *by thoughts,* is free of the duality *of subject and object; it* is the wisdom of coalescence.

The mind neither reaching out *toward the object* nor withdrawing, there is the wisdom of one taste *with regard to the manifold perceptions and thoughts.*

With no adoption or rejection *with regard to anything in samsara and nirvana*, there is the wisdom with no hope or fear.

Putting the seal *of the unborn absolute nature* on the perceptions *of the multifarious phenomena*, there is the spontaneously arisen wisdom.

The nature of mind beyond all ontological extremes, the union of appearances and emptiness, of awareness and emptiness, is the wisdom of union.

The eight consciousnesses and their objects having been empty from the very beginning, there is outer emptiness and inner emptiness: this is the wisdom of emptiness.

57

Introducing the nature of the mind.

Son, there are seven ways in which the nature of the mind is introduced.

The Great Space *says:*

> Its nature is not definitely any one thing:
> Whichever way one looks at it, in that way it appears.

Even a single object, on account of one's own mind, appears in various ways. For this reason, the outer object is devoid of intrinsic existence, and thus, the object is introduced as being the mind's projection.

The multifarious manifesting aspects of one's own mind arise unobstructedly like reflections: their nature is never anything other than emptiness. Thus, the mind's projection is introduced as a reflection.

The appearances of spontaneously arisen primal wisdom arise without bias, and thus, appearances are introduced as infinite.

By means of the pith instruction of the triple space, the consciousness is introduced as being without support.

By realizing the nature of one's own mind, awareness is introduced as being self-cognizing.

The objects that appear to the eight consciousnesses have never in fact come into existence, so the object is introduced as being unborn.

The ultimate unborn nature is devoid of dualistic characteristics, so the unborn is introduced as being free of conceptual constructions.

58

Placing a seal by introducing the ultimate nature of things that appear.

Son, there are six ways of introducing the ultimate nature of everything that arises, *everything being one in the absolute nature so that there is nothing to be adopted or rejected.*

From the creativity of the nature of one's own mind the seventeen kinds of perceptions and appearances—the six kinds of perceptions of the beings in the six realms, the two Tirthika views of eternalism and nihilism, and the nine different viewpoints of the nine vehicles—arise indeterminately, so do not value existence *by considering anything to be truly existent.*

Everything is the play of the absolute nature, so since you perceive things, good and bad, do not prize nonexistence.

Since phenomena do not fall into ontological extremes, do not reconcile them in *a conceptual* inseparability.

Do not differentiate things *as good or bad.*

Do not conceive of anything *as existent, nonexistent, or whatever by intellectual analysis.*

Do not be distracted from the radiant deep—*ultimate reality.*

59

Introducing the ultimate nature of things that appear.

Son, there are eight introductions.

The mind is perfectly clear, *like space, uncompounded awareness.*

The movements *of thoughts* subside by themselves *like ripples subsiding back into the water.*

Thoughts are levelled instantly, *the protuberance-like thoughts born from circumstances subsiding naturally the moment they arise.*

Awareness is naturally pure, *for it is unobscured by the eight consciousnesses.*

It is not perceptible, *for there is nothing that one can grasp with certainty and say, "This is it."*

The object is naturally empty, *because what appears has no intrinsic existence.*

Like a dream, it is there but it does not exist.

Like the moon reflected in water, it does not exist and yet it is there.

60

Nine sayings introducing the unborn nature of things that appear.

Phenomena lack true origin, they are deceptive appearances: without considering them to be real, without clinging to their existence,
Son, the unborn nature is introduced in nine ways.
All phenomena that arise interdependently, when investigated with reasoning directed at their ultimate status, have no inherent birth, so what is born is unborn, *like the horses and oxen in a magical illusion.*
What *is uncompounded and* has not been born *through causes and conditions* is unborn, *like space.*
Compounded phenomena do not exist as such, so what will never be born is unborn, *like the son of a barren woman.*
Forms and suchlike have no intrinsic existence, so what appears is unborn, *like a dream.*
There is nothing that can produce emptiness, so emptiness is unborn, *like the horn of a rabbit.*
Since it cannot be grasped with certainty—one cannot say, "This is it"— awareness is unborn, *like the eight consciousnesses of a person in an illusion.*
Since the unborn—or emptiness—is not one-sided, it has the potential to appear in every possible way: the unborn appears, *like an optical illusion.*
Since it is beyond intellectual investigation and has been unborn from the very beginning, the unborn is primordially nonexistent, *like space, which has always been so.*
The unborn is not affected by the concepts of the eight extremes—existence, nonexistence, and so forth—just as one cannot say, "Space is this (or that)," so the unborn is free from extremes.

61

An instruction with four similes introducing the ultimate nature of things that appear.

Son, there are four similes, *conventional examples used to signify the absolute nature.*
All phenomena arise from the state of inseparability of mind's triple space; there they dwell and into it they dissolve; they have never moved from it. So all intellectual assertions of tenets such as "they exist" or "they do not exist" are reduced to nothing. Therefore, taking the example of a mountain, *which is*

unmoved by circumstances, stamp your being with the view free from assertions.

Since there is neither meditation nor anything to be meditated upon, there is no intentional movement: taking the example of a king seated on his throne, stamp your being with the meditation free of effort.

Everything is the play of the absolute nature, and no phenomena are excluded, so taking the example of someone who has arrived on a golden island, stamp your being with the action free from dualistic perception, *where there is nothing to adopt and nothing to abandon.*

In the absolute nature, the basic way of being, which is naked and all-penetrating, freedom and nonfreedom are meaningless: there is no other result to be sought. Taking the example of a knot in a snake, stamp your being with the sole result in which there is freedom from hope and fear.

62

Five instructions on the ultimate nature of appearances.

Son, there are five instructions.

Ultimately, objects of knowledge, subject and object, are not born from causes and conditions; they do not depend on anything else; they are not the product of alteration; they are intrinsically unborn from the very beginning. Therefore, know that form and consciousness are unborn.

Without clinging, be aware of what you perceive, *the objects of the eight consciousnesses.*

Remain without being distracted by the eight *ordinary* concerns— *praise, criticism, and so forth.*

With the view able to stand up to circumstances, the meditation immune to distraction, the action resistant to going off course, and with confidence in the result, remain without the consciousness being carried away by circumstances.

Seal the mind *with the realization that your own mind is unborn.*

63

The view of the one absolute nature without distinct aspects.

Son, there are five experiences of wisdom *that indicate that one has gone to the heart of the view and meditation.*

The Six Points of Meditation *states,*

> Whatever dualistic thoughts may arise,
> If you recognize that very thought as the absolute nature,
> There is no need to meditate on any other dharmadhatu.

Accordingly, thoughts are the absolute nature, *they dissolve in the absolute nature devoid of dualistic thoughts of subject and object.*
All the characteristics *of both* samsara and nirvana are freed by themselves *in the nondual expanse of evenness.*
Looking directly confirms *the recognition of the absolute nature in all perceptions, like meeting an old acquaintance.*
Deluded clinging *to friends, enemies, and so forth* stops by itself.
The duality *of blocking impure perceptions and developing pure perceptions* vanishes by itself.

64

A brief explanation of the way in which the indivisible absolute nature arises.

Son, there are four ways in which the nondual absolute nature arises.
In the absolute nature, *the fundamental view of evenness,* there is no good or bad; this is the all-penetrating primal wisdom.
By dwelling naturally without seeking anything—*which is the meditation of the all-penetrating wisdom*—one remains in the state without conceptual constructs.
Not adulterating or fabricating—*which is the spontaneous action*—is the great impartiality.
The result of actualizing the absolute nature is that, as the ultimate nature of the mind arises spontaneously, primal wisdom unfolds in the expanse.

65

Six ways in which the indivisible absolute nature arises.

Son, there are six ways in which the nondual absolute nature arises.
Since *the nature of mind, which is spontaneously arisen primal wisdom,* arises in the state free of contrivance from the very beginning, it is fresh.

Since everything is complete within the mind, it is spontaneous.

Since there is no blocking or encouraging, it is great primal wisdom.

Since there is no *dualistic* division into samsara and nirvana, *good and bad*, it is the nondual vajra.

Since mind is Buddha from the very beginning *without depending on causes and conditions*, it is the self-born vajra.

Since it is not caught by enemies *or by good or bad circumstances*, it is the great evenness.

66

Four ways in which indivisible absolute nature arises.

Son, there are four ways of arising without duality.

With the mind's concepts of past, present, and future severed, and the mind left in the natural flow, it is clear and uncontrived, the natural radiance devoid of thoughts, *like an immaculate crystal*.

Without any concepts whatsoever, it is the mirror of awareness, *like an untarnished mirror*.

It is the *realization of the radiant primal wisdom*, self-cognizing awareness, *like a wishing-gem that naturally produces everything one could desire*.

In the spontaneously arisen primal wisdom, there is no "other-elimination," so everything arising by itself, it is the unpremeditated wisdom.

67

Some instructions on the indivisible absolute nature.

Son, there are four instructions.

The absolute nature has no bias, so in completely pervading all ten directions it is the great pervasion.

Since it is without an outer gate and inner sanctum—*or periphery and center*—it is the bodhichitta free of partiality.

As anything arises *from that bodhichitta*, it is the great unpredictability.

Since it is neither lit nor dimmed *by circumstances, the absolute nature* is the *perfectly* pure enlightened state.

68

An instruction on seeing the unborn absolute nature by means of eight kinds of natural dissolution.

Son, there are eight kinds of natural dissolution.

When one knows that the objects that appear have no true existence, one's belief in true existence naturally dissolves: the moment one rests with the mind undeluded in the direct perception of the absolute nature, everything that arises as the object of the six consciousnesses is ascertained as being appearance and emptiness inseparable, like a magical illusion or a dream. Thus,

Forms seen by the eye—*whether beautiful or ugly*—dissolve as they are seen. *How does this happen?* They dissolve in the sphere of the unborn, *which is the intrinsic nature of both object and consciousness.*

In the same way, sounds heard by the ear—*pleasant, unpleasant, and so forth*—fade away as they are heard; they fade away in the expanse of the unborn.

Odors smelled by the nose—*fragrant, foul, and so on*—dissolve as they are smelt; they fade away in the sphere of the unborn.

Tastes savored by the tongue—*sweet, sour, and so on*—dissolve as they are tasted; they fade away in the expanse of the unborn.

Sensations felt by the body—*smooth, rough, and so on*—dissolve as they are felt; they fade away in the expanse of the unborn.

Perceptions too—*the seventeen kinds of perceptions and others*—dissolve by themselves; they fade away in the sphere of the unborn, *appearance and emptiness inseparable.*

Words uttered—*whether of the Dharma or not*—dissolve by themselves; they dissolve in the expanse of the unborn, *sound and emptiness inseparable.*

Thoughts too—*whether virtuous or not*—are free in themselves; they dissolve into the sphere of the unborn, *naturally pure awareness.*

69

Seeing how having the four stainless things prevents one going astray.

Son, there are four things that are stainless.

To recognize the unborn *absolute nature* in everything that appears, *the whole of phenomenal existence, illustrated by the eight similes of illusion,* is the stainless wisdom of the view.

Taking the unborn *nature* as the path *at all times* is the stainless path *of meditation.*

When one settles in the natural flow, in the unborn nature, an incapacity to express *this nature* is the stainless experience.

Not to stray from the unborn nature into ordinary thoughts *related to past, present, and future* is the stainless result.

70

Showing that the practitioner's insight will not find anything else other than the unborn nature.

Son, there are five things you will not find.

When one investigates using the "neither one nor many" reasoning, there is no finding an object outside: *things are like the bits of hair that appear to someone with an ophthalmic condition.*

Since there is neither a seeker nor anything to be sought, there is no finding a mind inside. *That would be like space looking for space.*

When divided and subdivided into its limbs, digits, and so forth, there is no finding a body in between. *It is like the core of the plantain tree.*

As there exists neither a place in which to circle nor anyone to go around in it, there is no finding the sentient being you do not want to be. *Beings are like a crowd in a dream.*

Apart from your own unborn mind, there exists no other Buddha, so there is no finding the Buddha you would like to be.

71

How there is nothing to be found by someone on the path besides the absolute nature.

Son, there are five instances where there is nothing to be found.

From the beginning the nature of all phenomena, outer and inner, has never been anything but emptiness. Whatever appears *as an object outside* is an appearance of something that does not exist. *So even if you look for it,* you will never find it *in the past, present, or future:* there is nothing to be found.

Awareness, *your own mind inside,* is awareness and emptiness inseparable, so you will not find it: there is nothing to be found.

The body *composed of the six elements* has no essence, so you will not find it: there is nothing to be found.

Deluded beings *also* are, *in truth,* unborn, so you will not find them: there is nothing to be found.

As for the undeluded Buddha state, it is your own mind, so you will not find it *anywhere else*: there is nothing to be found.

72

A detailed explanation of how the absolute nature arises nondually.

Son, there are five things to take as the path, *leaving the mind without contrivance in its own state.*

There is nothing whatsoever to focus on regarding the absolute nature, so do not conceive of its being anything.

Do not indulge in any object *outside—forms, sounds, and suchlike.*

Mind is the Buddha, right now, so do not entertain any hope whatsoever—*such as a desire to obtain the qualities of the path and the result.*

Nothing that you perceive, suffering or bliss, afflictive emotions or primal wisdom, is extraneous to your own mind, so do not regard anything as a defect.

Give up thinking about past, present, and future, mulling over one's memories, and so on: "force"—*meaning leave*—the mind into its natural state.

73

An instruction on how the way-it-is endowed with triple emptiness arises by itself.

Son, emptiness is threefold, *the fundamental nature of all phenomena, for which from the very beginning there is no birth, no cessation, and no dwelling.*

Being intrinsically unborn from the beginning, phenomena outside are not born: they are empty.

Mind being without foundation or root, the mind inside is empty: it is not born.

The aggregates "in between" are empty: they do not dwell. *Form that appears is like foam; feeling experienced is like the plantain tree; perception is like a mirage; conditioning factors are like the plantain; consciousness is like a magical illusion.*

74

Sealing phenomenal existence by taking groundlessness as the path.

Son, there are three things to take as the path.

Take as the path the absence of any ground *acting as a support for,* or root *that gives rise to, anything in samsara and nirvana.*

Stay without giving importance to things—*as true or untrue, to be hoped for or feared, and so on.*

Apply the seal *of the unborn to phenomenal existence.*

75

Severing ties—outer, inner, and in-between.

If you do not cut outer and inner ties before putting the instructions into practice, the practice will degenerate into a mere attempt to impress others.

Son, there are four ties to be severed.

Sever outer ties *such as distracting circumstances—crowds and bustle.*

Sever inner ties *such as enemies and friends—objects that arouse attachment and aversion.*

Sever "in-between" ties *such as the things you cling to that concern this life.*

Moreover, having first gained a deep conviction concerning the teachings you have heard, having then cut through your intellectual doubts and having ultimately destroyed misconceptions regarding the view, meditation, and action, rely constantly on lonely places.

76

This chapter has two parts: the eight activities to be performed and how the teacher remedies faults in one's meditation and confers happiness and blessings.

i) The eight activities to be performed.

Son, there are eight activities to be performed.

At times such as the beginning of a practice, meditate on the three protections—*outer, inner, and secret.*

Make provision, *gathering everything you will need in order to practice.*

Simplify—*that is, remain in the natural state: leave your body, speech, and mind just as they are.*

Make offerings *to the teacher and the Three Jewels.*

Regarding the actions you have committed in the past, confess your negative actions *with the four powers.*

Pray *that experience and realization may be born in your being.*

Sit *on a comfortable seat in a secluded place,*

And perform the yogic exercises, *controlling body and speech.*

ii) How the teacher remedies faults in one's meditation and confers happiness and blessings.

In the Commentary, this section appears after the seventy-ninth chapter, but here we shall follow the order in the original text.

Visualize *your root teacher seated on a lotus and moon throne on the crown of your head.* Begin by *arousing bodhichitta and* performing the seven branches.

Next examine samsara. *Reflect on the nature of impermanence, suffering, and so on.*

Then recall the intermediate states. *There are six intermediate states. In the natural intermediate state one recognizes the absolute nature that one had not recognized, like an orphan meeting its mother. In the intermediate state between birth and death one recognizes the primal wisdom as if one held up a torch in a dark cave. In the intermediate state of dream one recognizes everything that appears as the mind, just as on an island of sages one would not find other beings even if one looked. In the intermediate state of concentration one makes clear what is not clear, like a model looking in a mirror. In the intermediate state of becoming one connects with one's remaining stock of positive actions, like inserting a pipe into a broken irrigation channel. In the intermediate state of the radiant absolute nature, primal wisdom appears all-penetrating, like a shooting star in the sky. The crucial points on these are condensed in the teacher's pith instructions. Put them into practice.*

77

Using seven concentrations to meditate.

Son, there are seven concentrations *in which one does not move away from the view and meditation.*

The concentration of the emptiness of the inner, *that is, the conscious-nesses of the sense organs, the eye being devoid of eyeness, and so forth.*

The concentration of the emptiness of the outer, *that is, the six objects, form being devoid of formness, and so forth.*

The concentration of the emptiness of both inner and outer, *compounded phenomena, the container and contents.*

The concentration of the emptiness of the *uncompounded* absolute.

The concentration of the lion's imposing demeanor, *which overawes deluded perceptions.*

The concentration of clear wisdom, *the natural state free from the duality of subject and object.*

The vajralike concentration, *indestructible and inseparable.*

78

Six preparatory branches of the practice.

Son, there are six preparatory practices.
Sit on a comfortable seat *as is proper for practicing concentration.*
Then visualize the channels *and wheels in the body, the container.*
Expel the *poisonous* energies *that are contained.*
Perform the *physical* yogic exercises, *filling with the upper and lower energies and dispelling obstacles.*
Rid yourself of other *pointless thoughts,* mental turbidity.
Bring the mind into the one-pointed concentration *of bliss, clarity, voidness, and the like.*

79

The five-limbed main practice of the yogi on the path.

Son, there are five branches in the main practice, *branches for practicing the actual path.*
Drop *ordinary* activities, put them off—*such things as business and farming the land: there will never come a time when they are finished.*
Once you leave them aside, virtuous activities will blossom and your body, speech, and mind will be extremely happy.
As a result, inner concentration will grow and various experiences occur: the mirror of awareness will shine within.

At that time the Sugatas will bestow their splendor. *The Buddhas, Bo-dhisattvas, and Vidyadharas will bless you, the guardians of virtue will protect you, and because of the majesty you will have gained, hindrances, negative forces, and obstacle makers will be unable to do you any harm.*

It will be impossible for conditioned thoughts *such as the five or three poisonous emotions* to arise.

In short, if you give up all ordinary activities, by practicing the profound path with no conflict between your mind and the three trainings you will temporarily and ultimately master infinite qualities, accomplishing your own and others' welfare according to your wishes.

These chapters on the superior training in wisdom have been arranged in a different order in the Commentary, which explains the text as follows. After the forty-second chapter it jumps straight to chapter 48. It then continues from chapter 50 to 54. After that come chapters 63 and 69. Next, chapters 43 to 47, after which come chapters 68, 70, 71, 49, and 55 to 59. Then chapters 60 to 67, leaving out chapter 63, which came earlier. Next, chapters 72 to 79, omitting chapter 77, which came in the section on the training of the mind. Here, however, I have followed the order in the root text.

To sum up, by using these chapters to realize the meaning of the Later Mind Section of the Great Perfection, one achieves certainty through "clearly distinguishing," and complete confidence. As if vanquishing an adversary with a razor-sharp blade, this is the path that eradicates samsara and establishes the unborn nature with certainty.

This concludes the instruction on this section, which I have explained to suit those with keen intelligence.

This was the fourth section from the *Eighty Chapters of Personal Advice,* the instruction on stainless wisdom, the essence.

V

Conclusion

80

A concluding instruction on examining the disciple and how the disciple should practice.

Son, there are three points in conclusion.

i) The defects of disciples to whom the instructions should not be given.

Recognize defects in disciples who might be liberated by these profound instructions: do not give the instructions to improper vessels whose natural disposition is unsuitable, *being bad-tempered, ungrateful, and so on;* who are inconstant *and have fickle minds;* who find fault *in their own teacher,* in the Dharma, and in individuals; and who, *having received the profound instructions,* will not put them into practice. *Even if you do give them the instructions, you will not do them any good, and divulging the secret teachings will result in criticism and retribution.*

ii) Suitable vessels to whom the teachings may be given.

To those who are good-natured—*who acknowledge what is done for them, are grateful for kindness, and so on;* who are stable *(their faith and suchlike never change);* who have very pure perception *with regard to the Dharma, people, and so forth;* and who are assiduous in the practice, *ac-*

complishing what they have heard—to them you can give the instructions. *By doing so you will ensure that they hold the lineage of the teachings and serve the doctrine, fulfilling the aims of many—themselves and others.*

iii) *As for how disciples who are suitable vessels should put the instructions they have been given into practice:*

They should see the teacher as the Buddha. *As a result they will receive the blessings of the lineage.* They should keep the instructions in their hearts. *If they are able to keep them secret and to practice them, the two accomplishments will come without effort.* Befriending solitude, *far from crowds and bustle,* they should practice. As a result, experience and realization will bloom and they will become the snow lion's cubs.

This completes the explanation of the instructions on how to recognize suitable disciples and on how to give rise to excellent qualities in one's being.

This was the fifth section from the *Eighty Chapters of Personal Advice,* the instruction on the vessel and a related teaching.

COLOPHON

This is the essence of the heart of Deshek Gyawopa, the Lord who attained the summit of the view.

It covers the Three Pitakas and follows the texts of Epitome, Magic, and Mind.

It is an instruction that within a single lifetime liberates those with faith, diligence, and wisdom.

Written down by Khyungpo Yamarwa exactly as the Lord spoke it, it is the culmination and quintessence of his profound teachings.

The Eighty Chapters of Personal Advice
By the glorious heruka, Zurchungpa,
Who bestows the fruit of complete liberation
On all who hear his name or even think of him,
Is the sublime and extraordinary jewel of the Ancient
    Translation lineage,

A treasure of the profound tantras, commentaries, and
    pith instructions,
An event as rare in the three times as the udumbara lotus
That I have come upon through no effort of my own.
Such is my delight and joy that I have written these
    notes.
If I have made the slightest error therein,
I confess it to the teacher and supreme deities.
Through the merit may the great enlightenment be
    swiftly attained.
In all our lives may we never be parted from the sublime
    tradition
Of the glorious Zur,
And by correctly holding, preserving, and spreading it,
May we achieve both aims—our own and others'.

• • •

*Using as a basis the text and structural outline transmit-
ted to me by the Vajradhara Khyentse Wangpo, I, the kusali Jamyang Lodrö Gyamtso Drayang, wrote these few
notes to make it clearer, thinking that they might be useful
for people of limited intellect like myself. They follow the
explanation given in the detailed commentary* The Lamp
of Shining Jewels. *I wrote them at Demchok Tashi Gempel at an auspicious time in the month of Kartika in the
Wood Mouse Year (1924). As a result of this, long may the
sublime doctrine of the secret and ultimate essence endure.*
    Sarwada mangalam bhavantu.

Notes

1. See Dudjom Rinpoche, *The Nyingma School of Tibetan Buddhism: Its Fundamentals and History*, 2 vols., translated by Gyurme Dorje and Matthew Kapstein (Boston: Wisdom Publications, 1991).

2. *Epitome, Magic,* and *Mind* (Tib. *mdo sgyu sems gsum*). These are the abbreviated titles of the root tantras of the three inner tantras: Mahayoga, Anuyoga, and Atiyoga. They refer to the *Epitome of Essential Meaning* (*mdo dgongs pa 'dus pa*), the root tantra of Anuyoga; the *Net of the Magical Display* (*sgyu 'phrul drva ba*), the root tantra of Mahayoga; and the Eighteen Tantras of the Mind Section (*sems sde bco brgyad*) of Atiyoga.

3. The Sanskrit *ratna* (lit. "jewel"), used with reference to the Three Jewels (Skt. *Triratna*, i.e., Buddha, Dharma, and Sangha), was translated into Tibetan as *dkon mchog*, meaning "rare and supreme." In the Vajrayana the teacher is often referred to as the Fourth Jewel.

4. Pronounced *bey* by Tibetans.

5. In this translation of the Commentary, Zurchungpa's root text appears in bold typeface, Shechen Gyaltsap's introduction, notes, and structural outline in italics, and Khyentse Rinpoche's commentary in normal lightface roman type. In the earlier parts of the book the different elements (root text, notes, and commentary) mostly appear separately, but in the later chapters they are largely intermingled.

6. The Tibetan verb *spel ba* includes among its many meanings: to thread (a necklace) and to compose (a literary work).

7. Ngok Loden Sherab (rngog blo ldan shes rab) (1059–1109) was one of the principal translators and masters of the New Translation tradition.

8. Tib. *ma chags mi chags chags pa med.*

9. Tib. *chags thogs: chags,* "to be stuck on something"; *thogs,* "to be prevented from moving forward."

10. The great translator Rinchen Zangpo (958–1055).

11. The title, derived from an Indian word, given to Tibetan translators of Sanskrit texts.

12. Samsaric action, any action performed with a samsaric goal in mind.

13. A full account of Zurchungpa's life is given in H. H. Dudjom Rinpoche's *History of the Nyingma School* (part 2 of Dudjom Rinpoche, Jikdrel Yeshe Dorje, *The Nyingma School of Tibetan Buddhism*, vol. 1, translated by Gyurme Dorje and Matthew Kapstein [Boston: Wisdom Publications, 1991], pp. 635–645).

14. Trak Gyawo was originally Zurpoche's hermitage, which he bequeathed to Zurchungpa, who meditated there for a total of fourteen years, and it was there that he finally passed away.

15. The Sanskrit word *dharma* (Tib. *chos*) has a wide range of meanings, including: (to name only a few): a thing, phenomenon, characteristic, attribute, mental object, topic, teaching, scripture, religion, law, custom, usage. In this book "Dharma" (in uppercase) refers exclusively to the second of the Three Jewels, the Buddha's teaching and Buddhist path.

16. I.e., the scriptures (or Dharma of transmission, Tib. *lung*) are not the Dharma of realization (Tib. *rtogs*).

17. "Our Teacher" probably refers in this case to the Buddha Shakyamuni, though of course it could equally well refer to one's own lama.

18. Tib. *rnam dkar gyi chos*, lit. "the perfectly white (or virtuous) Dharma."

19. This note of Shechen Gyaltsap and the following line of root text were missing in the edition that Khyentse Rinpoche taught from, which reads, "One is like a blind person who goes into a temple: the sprout of enlightenment—devotion, diligence, and compassion—will not grow." We have therefore inserted the missing text here from the more reliable woodblock edition.

20. I.e., do not let others lead you (by the nose); practice the Dharma to find happiness and freedom by yourself.

21. The traditional retreat that the Sangha observes during the three summer months.

22. See Bibliography.

23. Tib. *mkha' spyod*.

24. Lobpön Pawo is usually identified as Ashvagosha.

25. The story of Shabkar Tsogdruk Rangdrol's life has been translated as *The Life of Shabkar: The Autobiography of a Tibetan Yogin,* translated by Matthieu Ricard (Albany: SUNY Press, 1994; Ithaca: Snow Lion Publications, 2001).

26. The Tibetan word *zhen log* indicates a feeling of disgust or aversion,

feeling sick of or fed up with something, a distinct lack of desire, such as that felt by a jaundiced patient presented with greasy food. The words from which it is derived in Tibetan signify simply "the opposite of attachment."

27. See the story of Sunakshatra in Patrul Rinpoche, *The Words of My Perfect Teacher*, translated by the Padmakara Translation Group, 2nd ed. (Walnut Creek, Calif.: Altamira Press, 1998; Boston: Shambhala, 1998), p. 147.

28. Lit. "making the supports of the Three Jewels," i.e., making statues and paintings (supports of the Buddha's body), printing the scriptures (supports of the Buddha's speech), building stupas (supports of the Buddha's mind), and so on.

29. Zangdopelri (*zangs bdog dpal ri*), the Buddhafield of Padmasambhava.

30. Tib. *'bri gang med pa*, lit. "it does not diminish or become fuller."

31. Tib. *gsal 'grib med pa*, lit. "it does not grow brighter or dimmer."

32. The eight great chariots refer to the eight lineages of accomplishment, Tib. *sgrub brgyud shing rta chen po brgyad*, described in Dudjom Rinpoche's *History* (in vol. 1 of *The Nyingma School of Tibetan Buddhism*, pp. 852–853) as the Nyingmapa, Kadampa, Path and Fruit, Marpa Kagyupa, Shangpa Kagyupa, Kalachakra, Padampa Sangye's lineage of Pacification and Object of Cutting, and the Oddiyana Tradition of Service and Attainment.

33. Nagarjuna's *Letter to a Friend* (*Suhrillekha*), v. 23.

34. I.e., one who does not fade after a promising start.

35. As the Buddha's attendant, Ananda never had time to actually practice in retreat, and at the time of the First Council he had still not attained the state of Arhat. He was therefore not eligible to attend the Council, where the whole of the Buddha's teachings were to be recited and verified, even though he had heard all the Buddha's words and was obviously a priceless repository of these teachings. His presence at the Council was essential, so he was urged to meditate. As a result of the blessings he had received during all his time in the Buddha's presence, he attained Arhathood in a single night. He then proceeded to join the Council and to recite the sutras in their entirety to the assembly.

36. Mipham Jamyang Namgyal Gyatso (1846–1912) recognized Dilgo Khyentse Rinpoche as an incarnation and bestowed on him the empowerment of Manjushri.

37. Yamantaka is the wrathful form of Manjushri.

38. It should be remembered that when Khyentse Rinpoche gave this teaching he was addressing an audience of retreatants on whom he had just bestowed a number of empowerments.

39. Tib. *yin pa*, lit. "it is . . ."

40. Alternative translation: "rely on the teacher as your wisdom eye for a long time, without separating from him."

41. Tib. *rgya gad zer*, scolding in the sense of telling you that practicing the Dharma is a waste of time and that you should be doing something more worthwhile.

42. Implicit in the Tibetan here is the notion of *offering* to superior beings above and *giving* to lesser beings below. See Glossary, "offering and giving" and "four guests."

43. *The Way of the Bodhisattva*, VI, 2.

44. Do Khyentse Yeshe Dorje (1800–?) and Jamyang Khyentse Wangpo (1820–1892). It is impossible to measure the beneficial extent of these two great masters' activities.

45. Tib. *mkhas grub*, lit. "learned and accomplished." Siddhas are scholars who are not only fully versed in the teachings but have practiced them and attained a high level of realization.

46. One should not try to observe precepts that one cannot possibly keep. Giving one's limbs, for example, is only possible for a Bodhisattva who is on the Bodhisattva levels. Certain Vajrayana samayas can only be kept by practitioners who have attained full realization.

47. I.e., the five poisons as they are experienced by ordinary beings, as opposed to the way in which they are experienced by Vajrayana practitioners who, rather than giving up the five poisons, experience them as the five wisdoms.

48. Tib. *kun gzhi*; Skt. *alaya*.

49. Tib. *zung 'jug rdo rje'i sku*, the union of the dharmakaya and rupakaya.

50. According to the Khenpo Ngawang Pelzang in his *Guide to "The Words of My Perfect Teacher*," carefulness (Tib. *bag yod pa*) means exercising the utmost prudence in doing what is right and avoiding what is wrong.

51. Tib. *dgos med nga*, lit. "five things one does not need," in contrast to the five things in chapter 9 that one does need, *dgos yod lnga*.

52. "Fine words" here means saying things like "Everything is empty, everything is awareness" without having true realization. According to Khyentse Rinpoche's commentary, this line in the root text can also be translated, "No point in sweet words if you are self-centered."

53. "Illuminates the white path," i.e., opens the door to the Dharma.

54. Tib. *las kyi dbang mo*, the dakini Mahakarmendrani, who transmitted the Vajrakilaya teachings to Prabhahasti.

55. Tib. *go cha*; can refer to armorlike diligence or to the armor of patience.

56. Our universe is said to be located in the pistil of the thirteenth lotus flower, level with Buddha Vairochana-Himasagara's heart.

57. A Khampa (Eastern Tibetan) term of affectionate respect, used in this case by the old hunter for his teacher.

58. The Copper-Colored Mountain, the Buddhafield of Guru Rinpoche.

59. Compassion (Tib. *thugs rje*) in this context refers not only to compassion in its usual sense (Tib. *snying rje*) but also to the inseparability of the essential nature (*ngo bo*) and the natural expression (*rang bzhin*), the union of appearance and emptiness.

60. I.e., to sculpt statues, paint thangkas, print books, build stupas, and so forth.

61. Tib. *go cha*, in this case, seems to refer to the armor of both diligence and patience.

62. *The Way of the Bodhisattva*, VI, 2.

63. Alternative translation: "To have no one for company is great bliss."

64. Tib. *drang por srong*, "to correct." An alternative translation, which matches the imagery in Shechen Gyaltsap's note, would be, "keep to the straight."

65. The practice of giving one's own happiness to others and taking their suffering upon oneself (Tib. *gtong len*) is mentioned in numerous Bodhisattvayana texts, and described in particular in Atisha's *Seven-Point Mind Training*, on which a commentary by Dilgo Khyentse Rinpoche has been published in *Enlightened Courage* (Peyzac-le-Moustier: Editions Padmakara, 1992; Ithaca: Snow Lion Publications, 1994, 2006); in volume 1 of *The Collected Works of Dilgo Khyentse*.

66. The case against the common misconception that eating meat is acceptable is presented by Patrul Rinpoche in *The Words of My Perfect Teacher*. It is explained in detail by Shabkar Tsogdruk Rangdrol in *Food for Bodhisattvas* (Boston: Shambhala Publications, 2004).

67. Lit. "the bones of your father and forefathers," i.e., your family line.

68. Tibetan families are very conscious of the fact that a murder, for example, committed within the family (by another member of the family) taints all its members.

69. I.e., to be protected by the king and enjoy the advantages of being his subject.

70. The word "cope" (Tib. *theg pa*) is used here with the meaning "to deal successfully with something." It carries the sense that one's progress in the practice is not affected by things and situations that might normally distract one or hinder one's practice. The ten maxims in this chapter all use the same vocabulary in the Tibetan but have necessitated slight variations in their translation.

71. For a disciple who has true realization of the view, failure to make an outward show of devotion will have no adverse effects.

72. For example, by buying animals that are due to be slaughtered or buying a fisherman's catch and returning the fish to the water.

73. This statement can be understood in two ways. If an ordinary being has no fear of the hells, then failure to keep the samaya will make no difference. On a higher level, for a practitioner who has recognized the absolute nature and is therefore beyond any notion of samayas to be kept or not kept, the concept of hell no longer exists and not keeping the samaya in a literal sense is permissible.

74. "Polluted," Tib. *rme*, includes the notion of food that has been tainted by the person preparing it or that is considered "unclean" with regard to custom or religion.

75. Tib. *blo snying brang*, lit. "mind, heart, and chest."

76. Lit. "a prisoner without a yoke," i.e., someone in a prison with few constraints and hardships.

77. Tib. *log chos*, lit. "wrong paths."

78. Lit. "paternal uncle or maternal uncle" (Tib. *a khu'am a zhang*).

79. Lit. "the stone does not meet the bone of experience." Without smashing a bone with a stone (an image of diligence), the marrow of experience cannot be extracted.

80. Jambudvipa, the name of our world according to the ancient Buddhist cosmology.

81. I.e., Gampopa, Milarepa's foremost disciple.

82. I.e., there is no sign of accomplishment at death.

83. Tib. *sdig pa'i bshes gnyen*, the opposite of the Tibetan *dge ba'i bshes gnyen* (or "spiritual friend"); literally, a friend in evil as opposed to a friend in virtue.

84. *Letter to a Friend*, v. 86.

85. Readers in the Southern Hemisphere will, of course, need to read "south-facing" in this example.

86. A mill that has wooden wheels instead of proper millstones and is therefore useless for grinding grain.

87. The Tibetan phrase *gyong bcag pa* is used for softening leather. It therefore here means improving or training oneself.

88. "Meanness" here means small-minded and malicious as well as stingy.

89. "Do not look back": rather than looking back as one would usually do when one bids one's friends farewell, one should leave directly without looking back.

90. Lit. "make food, clothes, and conversation be the three losers."

91. In other words, if you are a failure in worldly terms.

92. Yaks in Tibet have their noses pierced (like bulls in the West) and a rope passed through the hole.

93. Tib. *skye med*, see Glossary, "unborn."

94. On the sutra path there are precepts and vows, but no samayas as there are in the Mantrayana.

95. Lit. "from the depth of your heart."

96. To inspire someone else to view a scholar and an uneducated person as equals is also a breach of samaya.

97. Tib. *rang dbang yod*, possessions that one has full control over.

98. The commentary in question is referred to by Shechen Gyaltsap in his colophon and is entitled *The Lamp of Shining Jewels*. We have not been able to identify either this work or its author.

99. "General" may refer to Dharma students in general or to all sentient beings, who, according to Jigme Lingpa, are our general brothers and sisters (Tib. *spyi'i mched*) in that we all possess the buddha-nature. Our closest vajra siblings (*'dres pa'i mched*) are those with whom we have received empowerment from the same teacher in the same mandala.

100. Tib. *gdams ngag ngom logs su gtab*: like a child showing everyone the sweet he has just been given.

101. Lit. "just as they sound," i.e., without explaining the inner, symbolic meanings.

102. This saying is attributed to Drikung Kyobpa Rinpoche.

103. I.e., someone who has reached the path of seeing.

104. The same Tibetan word, *zang zing*, is used in the first three lines. It generally means things, material objects, but it is also used to mean meat or fish as food.

105. In other words, die alone in a remote place where there are no disturbances.

106. This is one of the four lines in *Parting from the Four Attachments* by Jetsun Trakpa Gyaltsen (1147–1216).

107. Mirrors in ancient India and Tibet consisted of a polished metal disk rather than glass back-coated with silver.

108. The "ornament space" (Tib. *rgyan gyi nam mkha'*), the blue sky, which is conventionally considered as a "thing," as opposed to space defined as the absence of anything.

109. Lit. "eye-opening doctor," one who removes cataracts.

110. In the first instruction the Tibetan word *bcad* (meaning "to cut") is used on its own and in its literal sense, but in the other three instructions it is employed in the compound word *thag bcad pa*, meaning "to decide."

111. Tib. *dpe'i ye shes* and *don gyi ye shes*, respectively.

112. The syllable *phat* used in practices such as the *Chö* and transference practices (see *The Words of My Perfect Teacher*), and in the *trekchö* practice of the Great Perfection.

113. Tib. *spyod pa*, action, activity, or conduct, the third point after view and meditation.

114. For fear, in traditional society at least, of upsetting her husband or her mother-in-law.

115. Lit. "a fistful of sweet-tasting dough," considered a treat by Tibetan children.

116. The *Six Prerequisites for Concentration* gives six examples: (1) give up expectation, like a courtesan whose client has not kept his appointment; (2) give up possessions, like a pelican (see page 194); (3) give up attachment to a household, like a snake seeking a quiet life in a hole someone else has made; (4) live in the forest, like a deer-stalker who finds the forest so peaceful that he gives up hunting; (5) concentrate like an arrow-maker, undistracted by the bustle around him; and (6) stay alone, like a single bangle on a young maiden's wrist (see also page 130–31).

117. The concentrations practiced even by non-Buddhists that result in rebirth in the form and formless realms.

118. Tib. *bzhag thabs: bzhag pa* means to settle, to leave things, let them be, and also to rest, i.e., to rest in meditation.

119. The sixth sensory experience is that of the mind, which is considered here to be the sixth "sense organ."

120. Tib. *ri bo cog bzhag.*

121. Tib. *cog bzhag hor rdol; hor rdol* implies a sudden absence of ordinary thoughts.

122. Tib. *thang nge shreng nge*, a term applied to a bamboo stick or a violin string that springs back to its original position when bent or plucked.

123. Tib. *tshogs chen 'dus pa*, an Anuyoga tantra.

124. Tib. *stod smad.*

125. Tib. *rdul phra rab*, lit."infinitesimal particle," the smallest possible particle according to some Buddhist philosophical schools, produced by dividing matter into fragments until no further reduction is possible. One infinitesimal particle multiplied by seven to the power of seven would give a dust particle just visible to the naked eye in a shaft of sunlight.

126. Tib. *yid bzhag*, lit. "intellectually leaving things as they are," to be distinguished from the fifth of the seven, "sublime meditation" (*sgom*).

127. I.e., not to use ordinary supports.

128. Tib. *bsam gtan.*

129. Tib. *ting nge 'dzin*.

130. Of the six sense organs, the body is the organ of touch.

131. I.e., the "object" of the wisdom mind (Tib. *shes rab kyi chos*). The meaning of "dharma" (*chos*) in this case is "something that can be known."

132. Awareness (Tib. *rigpa*).

133. Tib. *yang dag pa drug*, lit. "six authenticities." Having dealt with the six wisdom sense organs and their six wisdom objects, Zurchungpa now explains the authentic, ultimate, or perfect ways in which these objects are experienced.

134. In this section "taste" and "experience" translate the same Tibetan word, *myong ba*.

135. "Wheel" (Tib. *'khor lo*) is used here in the traditional Indian sense of a weapon.

136. Tib. *chos spyod bcu*. Copying the canonical texts, making offerings, giving generously, listening to the Dharma, memorizing the teachings, reading them, explaining them, reciting prayers and sutras, reflecting on the meaning of the Dharma, and meditating on it.

137. I.e., faith, diligence, mindfulness, vigilance, and carefulness.

138. This is one of the four lines in *Parting from the Four Attachments*.

139. In these last two sentences Khyentse Rinpoche also appears to be commenting on the root verse that follows: "Do not be proud of your concentration."

140. Tib. *phrag dog*, which, as one of the five poisons, is more usually translated as "jealousy."

141. Tib. *srid pa*, also translated as "existence," "samsara."

142. The Tibetan word *snying po* means heart, core, essence.

143. See Glossary.

144. Neither existence nor nonexistence, apprehended intellectually, comes to the same thing as both existence and nonexistence, so constituting a fourth extreme.

145. The triple space is explained in chapter 27.

146. Lit. "awareness (Tib. *rig pa*) is introduced as having no object."

147. The Nepalese edition has *skye med ye med* for the root text, while the woodblock gives *skye med skye med*, which would translate as "the unborn is unborn."

148. I.e., one cannot apply concepts such as existence or nonexistence to space.

149. It might be helpful here to bear in mind that the Tibetan word for space (*nam mkha'*) is also the word for sky.

150. "It" in this and the following five statements refers to the way in which the absolute nature arises.

151. Lit. "a mirror unstained by oxidation," mirrors in Tibet traditionally consisting of a polished metal plate.

152. "Other-elimination" (Tib. *gzhan sel*) refers to our ordinary tendency to establish the existence of something by eliminating everything else that is other than it. In the present case, primal wisdom is not the result of eliminating other things.

153. The Tibetan word *grol*, often translated as "liberate" or "free," can also be translated as "dissolve, subside, fade, etc." and needs to be understood in the particular context of mind teaching. When we say that forms "are liberated," it is not the forms themselves that are freed, as it were, from a state of imprisonment, but rather the mind's attachment and conceptual activity with regard to forms and other phenomena. For the meditator there are no concepts of subject, object, or action, and so when something is seen, any concept of that thing naturally dissolves as it is seen, like ripples dissolving back into the water. The meditator sees forms, but any concept of them dissolves with the sight of them. The same applies to the way the meditator experiences all other sensory events, including thoughts. "Freedom" thus encompasses and transcends everything: the meditator, the phenomena he perceives, and the very perception of them.

154. See page 273.

155. The same Tibetan word, *snang*, is used here for perception and appearance.

156. The Tibetan word for samsara is *'khor ba*, meaning to turn, circle, go around and around.

157. The Tibetan word *mthu* usually denotes power, including magical power and the ability to exorcise. As Shechen Gyaltsap notes, in this context (perhaps as dialect, or in an anachronistic usage) it means "leave."

158. Tib. *'du byed*, also called "volition."

159. This is the fourth "tie to be severed," the "severing" in this case appearing in Shechen Gyaltsap's note, which employs the Tibetan verb *bchad* (meaning "to cut") in three forms: *phug bcad*, to make a decision or become convinced; *the tshom bcad*, to clear one's doubts; and *sgro 'dogs bcad*, to destroy misconceptions. These three are respectively qualified as outer, inner, and ultimate (*don*), mirroring the first three ties to be severed above.

160. The commentary here applies to both place and seat. The seat should be sufficiently comfortable to enable one to stay in meditation for as long as possible.

161. Tib. *'khrul 'khor*, pronounced "trulkor."

162. I.e., the universe and the beings in it.

163. Tib. *sbyor ba drug*. The Tibetan word *sbyor ba* (pronounced "jorwa")

has a number of different meanings. In this case it means preparation (the preparation for the "main practice" in the chapter that follows), but the well-known *jorwa druk* of the Kalachakra tradition refers to six kinds of yoga.

164. *Chakras* (Skt.).

165. In the practice of the channels and energies (*rtsa lung*), one usually visualizes oneself as the deity, that is to say, as appearance and emptiness inseparable. Nevertheless, although one's body is empty, for the purposes of the practice it is still visualized with a shape, and is therefore delimited from the empty space outside the body. This limit (the "skin" of the deity's body) is referred to as the outer fence of voidness (*phyi'i stong ra*).

166. Lit. "protectors of the white side," i.e., Dharma protectors.

167. Zurchungpa was one of the four disciples of Lharje Zurpoche known as the four summits. He was the one who had arrived at the summit of the view. (See H. H. Dudjom Rinpoche's *History of the Nyingma School* [in *The Nyingma School of Tibetan Buddhism*, vol. 1], p. 622.)

168. Tib. *tshogs chen 'dus pa*.

169. This colophon by Khyungpo Yamarwa, who wrote down Zurchungpa's teaching, is followed by Shechen Gyaltsap Rinpoche's own colophon.

170. Dilgo Khyentse Rinpoche seems to be implying here that Jamyang Khyentse Wangpo (1820–1892), as well as receiving these teachings transmitted from master to disciple over the centuries, had also had a vision of Zurchungpa in which he received the transmission of this text directly.

171. Shechen Gyaltsap Rinpoche (1871–1926), who refers to himself by the Indian term *kusali*, meaning a beggar.

172. Shechen Gyaltsap Rinpoche's hermitage at Shechen Monastery.

173. The month of October-November, when the moon is in the lunar mansion of the Pleiades.

174. Here, in our translation of Shechen Gyaltsap's Annotated Edition, Zurchungpa's root text is shown in roman typeface and Shechen Gyaltsap's annotations in italics.

Bibliography

WORKS REFERRED TO IN THE TEXT

Eighteen Tantras of the Mind Section—*sems sde bco brgyad*, a collection of tantras of the Great Perfection.

Epitome of Essential Meaning—*mdo dgongs pa 'dus pa*, the root tantra of Anuyoga.

Four Themes of Gampopa—*dvags po'i chos bzhi*, a famous work by the Kagyu master Gampopa Sönam Rinchen condensing the Kadampa and Mahamudra teachings.

Great Space—*nam mkha' che*, a tantra.

Guhyagarbha Tantra—*rgyud gsang ba snying po*, *Tantra of the Secret Essence*, the root tantra of Mahayoga, also called the *Root Tantra of the Net of the Magical Display*.

The Hundred Verses of Advice—*zhal gdams ding ri brgya rtsa ma*, by Padampa Sangye (translated by the Padmakara Translation Group: *The Hundred Verses of Advice: Tibetan Buddhist Teachings on What Matters Most.* Boston: Shambhala, 2005; in volume 2 of *The Collected Works of Dilgo Khyentse*).

History of the Nyingma School—*rnying ma'i chos 'byung*, by Dudjom Rinpoche, Jikdrel Yeshe Dorje (translated by Gyurme Dorje and Matthew Kapstein in *The Nyingma School of Tibetan Buddhism*, vol. 1. Boston: Wisdom Publications, 1991).

Lamp of Shining Jewels—*rin po che gsal ba'i sgron me*, an unidentified commentary on Zurchung Sherab Trakpa's *Eighty Chapters of Personal Advice*.

Letter to a Friend—*Suhrillekha, bshes pa'i spring yig*, by Nagarjuna (translated by the Padmakara Translation Group: *Nagarjuna's Letter to a Friend*. Ithaca, N.Y.: Snow Lion Publications, 2005).

Net of the Magical Display—sgyu 'phrul drva ba, the root tantra of Mahayoga.

Ornament of the Sutras—Sutralankara, mdo sde rgyen, one of the five great treatises that Maitreya transmitted to Asanga (translated by L. Jamspal et al.: *The Universal Vehicle Discourse Literature*. New York: American Institute of Buddhist Studies, 2004).

Parting from the Four Attachments—zhen pa bzhi bral, an important instruction by the Sakya master Jetsun Trakpa Gyaltsen (1147–1216). (A commentary by Chogye Trichen Rinpoche on this instruction has been published as *Parting from the Four Attachments: Jetsun Drakpa Gyaltsen's Song of Experience on Mind Training and the View*. Ithaca, N.Y.: Snow Lion Publications, 2003.)

Six Points of Meditation—bsgom don drug pa.

Six Prerequisites for Concentration—Dhyanasaddharma-vyavasthana, bsam gtan gyi chos drug rnam par gzhag pa, a Madhyamika shastra by Avadhuti-pa.

Sutra in Repayment of Kindness—Mahopaya-kaushalyabuddha-pratyupakaraka-sutra, thabs mkhas pa chen po sangs rgyas drin lan bsab pa'i mdo. The teachings the Buddha gave his mother when he visited the Heaven of the Thirty-three, where she had been reborn.

Treasury of Knowledge—shes bya mdzod, by Jamgön Kongtrul Lodrö Thaye (1813–1899), an encyclopedic work that covers all the teachings of both the sutras and tantras. (A translation of the entire *Treasury* is being published by Snow Lion Publications.)

The Way of the Bodhisattva—Bodhicharyavatara, byang chub sems dpa'i spyod pa la 'jug pa, by Shantideva (translated by the Padmakara Translation Group: *The Way of the Bodhisattva*, Boston: Shambhala Publications, 1997, 2006).

The Words of My Perfect Teacher—kun bzang bla ma'i zhal lung, by Patrul Rinpoche (translated by the Padmakara Translation Group: *The Words of My Perfect Teacher*, 2nd edition. Walnut Creek, Calif.: AltaMira Press, 1998; Boston: Shambhala Publications, 1998).

RECOMMENDED READING

Patrul Rinpoche. *The Words of My Perfect Teacher*. Translated by the Padmakara Translation Group. 2nd ed. Walnut Creek, Calif.: AltaMira Press, 1998; Boston: Shambhala Publications, 1998.

Longchen Yeshe Dorje, Kangyur Rinpoche. *Treasury of Precious Qualities.* Translated by the Padmakara Translation Group. Boston: Shambhala Publications, 2001.

Gampopa. *The Jewel Ornament of Liberation.* Translated by Khenpo Konchog Gyaltsen Rinpoche. Ithaca, N.Y.: Snow Lion Publications, 1998.

Rigdzin Jigme Lingpa (1730–1798).

A Wondrous Ocean of Advice for the Practice of Retreat in Solitude

Rigdzen Jigme Lingpa

Commentary by Dilgo Khyentse Rinpoche

About Rigdzin Jigme Lingpa

RIGDZIN JIGME LINGPA (1730–1798) is regarded as one of the most important figures in the Nyingma lineage and an incarnation of both the great master Vimalamitra and the Dharma king Trisong Detsen. He was born in southern Tibet in humble, obscure surroundings. At the age of six, he was placed in the monastery of Palri in southern Tibet, where, after taking the vows of preliminary ordination, he received a basic monastic education. A visionary encounter with Manjushrimitra, one of the patriarchs of the Dzogchen lineage, proved a turning point in his life, and he decided to lay aside his monastic robe in preference for the white shawl and the long hair of a yogi.

At the age of twenty-eight he began a three-year retreat at Palri Monastery, during the course of which he experienced visions in which the important cycle of teachings and practices known as the Longchen Nyingthig cycle arose as a spiritual revelation (terma) within his wisdom mind. It was, however, during his second retreat, which he began at the age of thirty-one at the sacred cave of Samye Chimpu, that his most profound experiences began to manifest and he beheld the great fourteenth-century master Longchen Rabjam in three successive visions. In these visions, Longchenpa encouraged him to disclose his visionary teachings and teach them to others, and the minds of the two masters mingled ineffably so that the realization of Longchenpa arose instantaneously in the mind of Jigme Lingpa.

Later, after concluding this retreat, Jigme Lingpa began to expound the Longchen Nyingthig, transmitting it to his close disciples. The Longchen Nyingthig subsequently spread throughout Tibet and remains to this day one of the most important systems of meditative and yogic practice in the Nyingma school.

447

The latter part of Jigme Lingpa's life was spent at Tsering Jong, a small hermitage and meditation center where he lived in great simplicity, instructing his many disciples. Among his compassionate actions was a lifelong activity of saving the lives of animals by buying them from butchers and hunters and setting them free.

Due to his inner realization, Jigme Lingpa was able to assimilate and express the whole of the Buddhist doctrine without arduous study. He compiled the Nyingma tantras in twenty-five volumes and composed a history of them. He produced nine volumes of original treatises and discovered terma texts. Prominent among these are the Longchen Nyingthig, a collection of meditation instructions and ritual texts discovered as terma; the *Yönten Rinpoche Dzö;* and *Yeshe Lama.* The Longchen Nyingthig tradition has flourished up to the present day, universally renowned for the depth of its teachings and its accomplished masters.

The Commentary
Dilgo Khyentse Rinpoche

WHEN JIGME LINGPA was living in the solitary place of Tsering Jong—his main residence, near Chongye in southern Tibet—he had many disciples who had stayed in retreat for thirty years. It was for them and for future practitioners that he wrote this heartfelt advice, *A Wondrous Ocean of Advice for the Practice of Retreat in Solitude*.

As you read this precious text and my commentary on it, please do so with the perfect motivation of bodhichitta to establish all beings under the sky in the supreme level of the vajradharas and the profound view of the Mantrayana.

The root text begins with Jigme Lingpa's offering of praise and request for blessings:

> *Embodiment of all the glorious buddhas,*
> *Lord of Compassion, Padmasambhava,*
> *Remain upon the pinnacle of my diademed deep-blue locks[1]*
> *And bless my mind.*

Padmasambhava, also known as Guru Rinpoche, is glorious with regard to himself for having attained total realization, and glorious with regard to others for his boundless compassion. As he said:

> Who sees me sees all the buddhas.
> Who accomplishes me accomplishes all the buddhas.
> I am the essence of all the sugatas.

Guru Rinpoche is the embodiment of all the buddhas. Although all buddhas have the same compassion for all sentient beings, for us Guru Rinpoche is the kindest of all since he chose to manifest in this degenerate age for our sake. Visualize him above your head and supplicate him to bless you so that your mind may turn to the dharma, your dharma practice may progress on the path, your delusion may be dispelled through practicing the path, and delusion may arise as wisdom.

In this text, Jigme Lingpa has gathered crucial points from various spiritual instructions and revealed their essence in order to facilitate the practitioner's efforts to put them into practice. The text is part of a genre called "mountain dharma" (richö), intended for those who endeavor to put the teachings into practice in the solitude of the mountains. In the past, when people's minds were naturally inclined toward virtue and attuned to the dharma, those who longed for enlightenment would search for a qualified teacher and, having found him, would request and receive the entire teaching needed to travel the spiritual path.

They would then go to a solitary place and become "children of the mountains," wearing mist as their clothing and rocky caves as their hats. They would thoroughly renounce all preoccupation with wealth, fame, comforts, and worldly pleasures. With full confidence in what they were doing, they would endeavor in solitude and poverty. Free from distractions, they would prepare for death with the help of their ascetic mode of life. These teachings are still preserved today. If you take them to heart and practice them with complete dedication, you will deserve the name of dharma practitioner.

Since all actions unfailingly bear fruit, if you practice to the best of your abilities, then by virtue of your efforts and the authenticity of your intention, you will obtain results.

Jigme Lingpa attained full realization of the Great Perfection and conquered the everlasting citadel of awareness. He actualized the four dimensions (kayas) of buddhahood. In this text he is describing the way he himself followed the path so that we can benefit from his experience. Even if you cannot practice the entire range of teachings mentioned here, whatever you are able to apply will be of great benefit, just as gold is always valuable, even a tiny piece of it.

Listen, all of you who possess faith, who keep samaya, and who strive from the depths of your hearts for spiritual ideals. In cyclic

existence, without beginning or end, with your negative actions act-
ing as the cause, you have fallen under the influence of adverse condi-
tions. Everything you can think of [in samsara] is just an experience
of fear and suffering. Beings of the six realms must experience this
continually, like prisoners cast into a dark cell.

Fervent devotion is the gateway to the dharma and the most important quality to possess. Without it, there is no way to gain any genuine
understanding or realization of the dharma, no way to progress along
the path, and no way to overcome obstacles. Devotion is a practitioner's
true wealth, the hand that harvests all accomplishments, and the wheel
that speeds one to the goal. When your mind is uplifted and transformed
by hearing the life stories of buddhas and saints, you experience *clear
faith.* When you long to follow their example and achieve liberation, you
have *yearning faith.* When certainty is born as a result of your own spiritual practice, you achieve *confident faith.* Finally, when faith is so much a
part of your being that you could not renounce it even at the cost of
your life, then you have *irreversible faith.*

It is also essential to keep pure samaya, the sacred bond formed between disciple and teacher. Without keeping your samaya, there is no
way to attain the common and supreme accomplishments, or siddhis. In
the Vajrayana one speaks of one hundred thousand samayas. However,
if you consider your spiritual teacher to be a real buddha, value his
teachings like your own heart, and carry out his instructions to the letter,
then you possess the essence of all samayas.

Even if you have devotion and maintain pure samayas, worldly activities can considerably delay the progress of your practice. Therefore, it is
important for a practitioner to give up all gross and subtle distractions,
as well as all ties to worldly life, in order to be able to practice in the
suitable isolation of a retreat. There is a saying that goes: "Right where
you are, abandon gross worldly ties and cast off the subtle ones as well."

Bodhisattvas deliberately incarnate again and again in samsara for the
sake of sentient beings. On the other hand, ordinary beings are power-
lessly dragged back to samsara again and again by their negative karma
resulting from their concern with egoistic aims such as compulsive craving for pleasure, comfort, wealth, power, and fame.

Only a real buddha can know when the three worlds of samsara first
began. Those who wander in samsara must endure the heat and cold of

the hells, the hunger and thirst of tormented spirits, and the servitude of animals. Human beings suffer from birth, old age, sickness, and death; from not experiencing what they want and experiencing what they don't want; from encountering enemies and parting from friends. Demigods suffer from acute jealousy and strife, and gods suffer from falling into the lower realms after having mindlessly enjoyed a long heavenly life. In short, sentient beings are constantly plagued by suffering. When an enlightened being looks at samsara, he views it as a prison, a pit of live embers, or a nest of vipers. One cannot find any source of lasting happiness in it: it is truly a terrifying place!

Until now we have been wandering in samsara. Unless we remedy the cause of this by practicing the dharma, there is no way to escape it; we are like a bee imprisoned in a bottle, helplessly flying up and down. What did we do wrong to become prisoners of samsara? The answer is negative actions.

> At present, if you have any physical illness or mental disturbance, or are in an undesirable situation, you panic and are totally upset and paranoid about everything, like someone overcome by nausea. So how will it be when you experience the sufferings of the three lower realms? Alas! Now the only means of escape from these sufferings is to accomplish the ultimate goal of the supreme dharma; otherwise, there is no way out.

You can hardly bear light pain, such as the prick of a thorn or a mild burn from a spark. If something goes against your desires, if you lose money or find yourself in an unpleasant situation, you get upset. You suspect that everyone wants to harm you, and you become so obsessed with your problems that you even lose your appetite. If you can't bear even such insignificant sufferings, what will happen when you encounter the inconceivable sufferings of hell?

If someone speaks unkind words to you—even if it's no more than "You are a liar"—it pierces your mind like an arrow and you think, "How dare he say that to me! I'm not going to let him get away with that!" Even if you come down with a very benign illness, you feel so uneasy and rush to the doctor.

So the only way to put an end to samsara is to practice the dharma. The dharma is offered to you, ready to be used. Therefore, it is up to you whether or not you practice it; the teacher cannot practice it for you. If you practice with full dedication, you can achieve liberation in the span of this present life; if not, you can prepare the ground for achieving it within a few lifetimes, or at least you will acquire some affinity for the dharma that will eventually lead you along the path.

On retreat, you practice four sessions a day. Why do you do it? Because you are hoping to attain the level of Shakyamuni Buddha.

But if your way of acting, speaking, and thinking is not in harmony with the dharma, you will certainly fail to achieve buddhahood. *Buddha* means someone in whom all defects are exhausted and all virtues have blossomed. When you look within yourself, you find plenty of defects and very few good qualities. So, in order to achieve your goal, it is imperative that you eradicate your imperfections and try to develop good qualities, just like a king who establishes righteous laws in his country.

Your purpose in remaining in retreat is not to achieve fame, not to earn your living, not to achieve any other worldly goals: your reason is to accomplish the dharma.

Those who are strongly motivated to practice the dharma do not really need to receive a lot of instructions, just the essential ones. In this present dark age, there is no time for extensive learning such as studying the entire Tripitaka and the numerous commentaries upon it. Anyway, people nowadays lack the necessary intelligence and diligence for such study. Now is the time to practice the pith oral instructions of your guru, which are like butter churned from milk.

Samsara is beginningless and will continue forever if you don't escape from its spinning wheel by following the directives of an enlightened being. Its fundamental causes are ignorance and the mental obscurations that stem from it: desire, attachment, aversion, anger, lack of discernment, pride, jealousy, and miserliness. This host of mental distortions forms powerful habits and tendencies that keep on reappearing in our thoughts and behavior, just as a rolled piece of paper keeps on re-rolling itself, even when pressed flat.

If you practice the dharma, you must do it in with full dedication and honesty; otherwise:

> *You may say, "Everything is an illusion," and then spend your day riding horses, drinking beer, and enjoying entertainments. Come evening, you don your cotton shawl [to show that you are practicing*

tummo], practice breathing like the noisy emptying and filling of a
bellows, then play your bell and drum. You won't become enlightened
by acting like this.

Can we get enlightenment like that? Never! If those with the eye of wisdom were to witness such behavior, they would be shocked and consider us completely crazy.

How, then, do we attain buddhahood? When you establish the limits of your retreat with the signs of the four guardians of the world, you promise to remain inside these limits for the duration of the retreat, without seeing even your parents or relatives. You know that by this method you can liberate yourself from the ocean of suffering of the three worlds of samsara, and be able to carry your parents and all sentient beings across it.

But why have you not as yet become a buddha? What keeps you in samsara? The answer is clear:

The cause of wandering in samsara is ego-clinging.

Definitions of the notion of "self" and how the ignorant mind clings to it as a reality are the subject of many treatises too extensive to be explained in detail here. In essence, the real troublemaker and source of samsara is the notion of "I" that we attach to the body-mind-name complex. Because of this "I," we are habitually drawn toward pleasant feelings and repulsed by unpleasant feelings. Notions of friend and enemy, attachment and hatred, are born, and thus the wheel of suffering revolves. Everything is permeated by ignorance—the failure to recognize that all phenomena in general and the "I" in particular are devoid of inherent existence and are, by nature, sheer emptiness.

Our fundamental grasping is with reference to our body, mind, and name. Examination reveals that our body is merely a collection of flesh, blood, bones, and vital humors; our mind is a collection of thoughts; and our name is a collection of letters and sounds. None of these constitutes an autonomous entity.

When a traveler reaches a guesthouse at night, he starts making plans for the next day. Likewise, when the mind inhabits the body, it is continually making endless plans, conceiving endless desires, and hence experiencing endless suffering.

Nagarjuna writes in his Letter to a Friend:[2] *"'Desires bring destruction, like the kimba fruit,' the Munindra [the Buddha] said." They should be abandoned, as these chains bind all beings to the prison of samsara.*

Never satisfied, we wander in the world of attachments like hungry dogs. The more we have, the more we want and the more we are tormented. Fettered by incessant wants and needs, we do not find the leisure to practice the dharma.

As soon as we are born we want some food; we want to talk; we want to be comfortable. All these self-centered impulses result from self-clinging. The Buddha said that to indulge in desire and allow self-clinging to become habitual is like eating the kimba fruit, which tastes delicious at first but turns out to be a fatal poison. We continually entertain a host of thoughts and cravings; yet even if we were to possess all the riches of the billionfold universe, we would still think, "I need to get more." To always desire more than we have is a mara that inhabits our mind and ruins our happiness. If we can cease to identify with the ego, we are free; if we cannot, it chains us like iron shackles. All this clinging comes from the thought "I" or "me" and from attachment, aversion, pride, and all other thoughts that the ego engenders. As long as our identification with the ego persists, we cannot escape samsara. Yet, if we examine this ego, we easily find, in truth, that it is totally nonexistent.

In brief, regarding ego-clinging: in clinging to your country, house, wealth, and possessions, you postpone the practice of dharma.

If you see your house or valuable possessions such as gold and silver as good things that will bring you physical well-being and mental peace, then you will cling to them. You postpone the practice of dharma, thinking, "Oh, first I will do some business and put some money aside," or "First I shall finish all my worldly activities."

You praise your deity when you find a mere needle or some thread, and you get depressed if you lose even a pen or a shoelace [saying, "How terrible! What shall I do now? That was such a good pen!"]. These are all external forms of ego-clinging.

All four mains schools of Tibetan Buddhism equally follow the authentic teachings of Buddha Shakyamuni. Yet, you may have entered the door of the dharma and joined one of these schools, say the Nyingma tradition, and, without having gone into the depth of the teachings, you think, "This school has the blessing of Guru Rinpoche; it is really a very good one. The others—Gelug, Sakya, and Kagyu—are not as good." And you feel contempt and animosity toward those who are on the path of these other schools.

> *Seeing members of your own tradition as gods and those of other traditions as demons, and without examining your own qualities, you think, "Would I not be fit to take Shakyamuni Buddha's place?" All these are internal forms of ego-clinging.*

You may think, "I am a Nyingmapa, so it won't do any harm if I drink alcohol; it won't be a problem if I have girlfriends or boyfriends; it won't matter if I don't cut my hair; there's no need to renounce the world," and so on. You may look down on other schools and people who wear monastic robes. You may say, "Ah! Look at those guys! They look very nice on the outside, but there's nothing inside. They are hardly Buddhists at all."

You never objectively scrutinize the level of your practice, such as how much you have done and the level of understanding you have reached; but, swelling up with pride, you carelessly assume that you are a great practitioner. Even if the Buddha himself were here teaching, you would like to have a seat above him. Having developed a little interest in the dharma, or having performed a few good actions, you think, "There's no dharma practitioner like me in the world!"

> *Clinging to the visualization in the development stage as being solid, having partiality in the generation of the bodhichitta, practicing the completion stage within a conceptual framework—you say all things are empty and lack self-nature, yet cling to the nature of emptiness, like a beautiful woman attached to her own body, and perceive it with a very tight and unclear mind, thinking, "No one has reached my level of meditation, so I don't need to ask for advice or consult anyone." Thus your life will be wasted in futility. These are all secret forms of ego-clinging.*

When you meditate on kyerim, the development stage, instead of considering the deity as the display of wisdom—appearing yet void, void yet appearing—you cling to it as a solid reality. You meditate on the peaceful deities as beautiful women and handsome men; you meditate on the wrathful deities as angry persons. You constantly discriminate between people. You think that those who like you—your relatives and friends—are very good, and that those who displease you a little bit are enemies. This is the sign that you have not developed any bodhichitta.

During the practice of dzogrim, the completion stage, if you have a few spiritual experiences you immediately think that you have achieved a high level of realization, that you are the peer of past siddhas; and if no experience comes, you doubt the teachings and the teacher, and become lax in your practice.

You will, for instance, think, "Oh! tummo—that's very good for keeping warm." Or "If I dress only in a cotton shawl, everyone will think I am a great yogi."

How will you tame your ego if you think, "There is no good in virtue; nothing wrong with sin; there is no need to accumulate merit; there is no point in purifying myself. I just have to keep my mouth shut and look at the sky."

Even though your mouth is full of profound words about emptiness, if your mind is filled with grasping at solid reality, with attachment and aversion, you are deceiving yourself like an old woman who imagines that she is a young girl.

To realize emptiness, the essence of the teachings, it is necessary to release all attachments to the ego. In the beginning you are just like a coquettish girl who, looking in the mirror, meticulously washes her face, carefully applies makeup, and arranges her hair and thinks, "I look like a heavenly princess." You have strong attachments and clinging to your meditation, and no more than an intellectual understanding of emptiness. As soon as there is grasping, the ego is present. When such obscurations occur, there is mental darkness, or ignorance. As the great Sakya master Kunga Nyingpo was told by Manjushri in a vision, "When there is attachment, there is no view."

For example, you practice the dharma a little bit and think, "Could there be any practitioner as great as I?" Or you keep some kind of discipline and think, "Where in the world could there be a monk as perfect as I?" Or you remain for a few years in retreat and think, "Whose meditation and insight are equal to mine?" Holding such attitudes, neglecting to seek guidance from anyone, you would feel no need to ask for teachings even if the Buddha came to you in person. Thus, your whole life would become meaningless.

In summary, the only way to become a genuine practitioner is to discard all inner, outer, and secret forms of ego-clinging.

> *My frank advice is this: if you strongly renounce clinging to your country, wealth, and possessions, half of the dharma will already be accomplished.*

When the time is right to dispel the disciple's defects and obstacles, the guru may appear to be constantly angry and scolding. But actually he is like a kind parent who, by scolding his children, corrects their defects and thus helps them progress. When a mother roughly grabs her child to prevent him from hurting himself, her intention is to benefit him in the long run. It is with this intention that the "frank advice" in this text is given by Jigme Lingpa. By acknowledging the truth of his frankness deep within yourself, you will most certainly come to the conclusion: "Regarding the affairs of this life, if I can accomplish them, fine; if I can't, it doesn't matter. What I really want is to accomplish the dharma. Until now I thought that these objects of attachment were useful to me; now, whatever may happen, I don't want any of them." If you have such an attitude, then half your dharma practice has been completed.

Jigme Lingpa adds:

> *Initially, by entering the door of the absolute teaching and having the capacity to cast off ego-clinging like spit in the dust, I captured the citadel of the natural state. I began to gather an entourage of students, becoming a source of benefit to others, training disciples by means of my basic intention [of compassion], and giving teachings. I kept only some immediate necessities and just enough clothing to protect myself from the cold and didn't say, "I'll need this wealth for later," or "I'll need it if I'm sick or dying," or "I'll need it to perform ceremonies if I am sick," or "I must put something aside to be used for funeral offerings when I die."*
>
> *Thus I didn't concern myself with worrying about my future*

means of support, but mainly made offerings to the Three Jewels,
ransomed the lives of animals, served and respected the sangha, gave
charity to beggars, and so forth.

We can read in the detailed accounts of Jigme Lingpa's life how he always used whatever resources he had with great generosity. Whenever he went to holy places like Samye or Lhasa, he offered thousands and thousands of lamps and, along the way, he would buy animals to set them free and save their lives. He would make large donations and serve tea to the monastic communities as well as make other material gifts. And he never failed to give alms to any beggar.

The text continues:

I didn't waste the offerings of the living and [those made on behalf
of] the dead by giving them to unworthy causes, nor did I hoard them
like bees storing honey in a hive. Since I didn't carry great wealth
with me, I felt no embarrassment before those who came to see me.

Jigme Lingpa is explaining how he never carried or possessed more than the minimum necessities. All his direct disciples could testify to his detachment from wealth. Here he speaks to all of us, the disciples who want to follow in his footsteps.

We will all die, remember that.

You may think, "I want to take care of my friends, get rid of my enemies, amass a lot of money, become famous and conquer the world." But even if you become the owner of a valley full of gold, even if your fame and renown spread throughout the universe, still when death comes there will be nothing left of you but a corpse to take to the cemetery. Death is the best teacher for all dharma practitioners. Just ponder what your state of mind will be when your breath is about to cease.

I request you to remember this at all times and on all occasions. Especially when you are on retreat: from the very moment you get up in the morning always think, "Death, death." In doing so, you will arrive at the clear understanding that there is no truly beneficial activity other than the dharma; and you won't fail to devote yourself to study, pondering and meditating. This is the only way to achieve firm confidence in the face of death.

> *Since the dharma itself is free from partiality, try to have pure perception regarding everyone. If one examines all the traditions, each of them is indeed profound in its own way; but for me, the view of the Great Perfection was fine, and all the root downfalls were dissolved in space.*

There are many different dharma lineages. In Tibet, the Land of Snow, there are four main schools that adhere perfectly to the tradition of Buddha Shakyamuni. This tradition says in essence:

> Do no evil at all;
> Act in a perfectly virtuous way;
> Subdue your own mind:
> This is the Buddha's Teaching.

Look upon all those who have crossed the gateway of the Buddha's teaching as worthy of respect. Think, "He belongs to the sangha. May he gaze upon me with compassion." Indeed, if you are following and practicing the path of a particular tradition, there isn't the slightest reason to despise, treat with contempt, or wish to eliminate any other dharma tradition. In truth, if you endeavor with great diligence in the dharma tradition of your choice and attain its culminating point, you will simultaneously achieve the qualities of the other traditions. The goal to be reached is one and the same for all schools. Therefore, train your mind always to see the purity in everything. Never criticize the actions of holy beings, no matter who they are. In short, you must have confidence in your own tradition without the slightest animosity toward the others.

A yogi who has true inner experience will gaze upon everything in the spirit of these words of Jetsun Milarepa: "The outer world itself is my book; I have no need for books written with black ink." A time will come when everything that appears before you will serve as an illustration or confirmation of the teachings. When the mind is inwardly firm, all outer phenomena appear as your friends and you never feel uneasy or uncomfortable about anything. Everything will serve as an enhancement for your practice.

Jigme Lingpa is saying that he was able to enjoy the waves of blessings from all traditions because he didn't indulge in any sectarianism. Nor was he stained by any of the fourteen downfalls of the Mantrayana, such as criticizing other spiritual views or proclaiming secret teachings to crowds of people.

> *When laying the foundation of the preliminary practices, you should not forsake them by saying, "Everything is empty," thereby losing your actions in the view.*

If you merely talk about the view of emptiness but at the same time behave inconsiderately, it is said that your conduct has become lost in the view. If you believe that, since everything is empty by nature, it is all right to do whatever you want and it makes no difference whether your actions are virtuous or nonvirtuous, then your conduct has become "lost in the view." All the great teachers say just the opposite—that the more you understand the view of emptiness, the more aware and careful you are regarding the law of cause and effect. In the Great Perfection, everything is centered on the view, which is the true summit of the nine vehicles. It is crucial to understand what is the view and action and not to confuse them. Action or conduct relies upon body and speech, while view concerns the mind.

There is no danger in itself in having a high view. But if, consequently, your actions become too detached from the law of cause and effect, wrongdoings and faults will pour down like rain.

You must scrupulously observe the karmic law of cause and effect, even with regard to your smallest actions. The Buddha described the harmful consequences of nonvirtuous actions as well as the benefit of virtuous ones. Do your practice and actions agree with his teaching or not? If they don't, confess your faults and repair the damage they have caused, and, from now on, keep watch over your actions.

> *Then, for the actual practice, you should live in an uninhabited area without acquaintances, accompanied by your friend Awareness, and vow to maintain the flow of the uncontrived natural state.*

The mountains are places where no one lives. Why would you want to go there? Not for hunting wild animals, not for sightseeing or recreation, but for "mountain dharma." In such uninhabited regions, you have no relatives, friends, or enemies to deal with and no useless occupations to pursue. You are thus free to devote yourself completely to spiritual practice. When Jetsun Milarepa was dwelling alone in the cave of Trakar Taktso, he had practically no clothes and no food except the nettles he could find right at the entrance to his cave. There was nothing to disturb his meditation. In such a place of solitude, your friends are awareness and inner bliss, not people you are attached to.

Once you have reached a mountain solitude, you need only abide at all times in the simplicity of the mind's nature. If any gratifying event occurs—whether brought on by friends, wealth, respect, or fame—do not think, "Oh! Look what I have now!" and become elated by such vain things. Do not nourish any expectations, hoping to get something beyond what you already have.

If any difficult circumstances manifest—such as obstacles, natural calamities, illness, or any other hardship—you might become very discouraged, thinking, "Now I won't be able to continue." If you allow your legs to be shackled by such obstacles, you won't go far.

You will also entertain hopes, thinking, "When are spiritual experiences and realization going to come?" To have spiritual experiences and realization, you will have to endeavor for your entire life. They will certainly not come by trying for only a day or even a year. So don't have any impatient expectations regarding the fruit of practice. After meditating for quite some time, you may think, "Oh, I have had no sign, no visions, no experiences, no realization. Maybe there is no truth to all these teachings after all." Do not entertain such destructive doubts.

> If you hear good or bad news that stirs up hopes and fears, don't regard it as true. Neither reject nor accept it. Be like a dead person, to whom one can say anything.

Once someone is dead, he won't be happy if other people praise him, nor will he be angry if someone criticizes him. He has gone somewhere else in the six realms. After you have spent a number of years in retreat, people may think that you must have reached a high degree of realization. Others may say that you have just been wasting your time. Don't care what people say about you and your practice—just persevere.

All you should think is: "I must go to a solitary place to practice the dharma. If I die there, that's all right." Why should you think of anything else? This will become clear in your mind when you

> Think how difficult it is to attain a human form, how difficult it is to meet the dharma, and about the rarity of true teachers.

Look at the country where you are now. How many people have ever heard the term "the Three Jewels" or the sound of OM MANI PADME HUM? And how many have not? You can appreciate the rarity of hearing the dharma and the even greater rarity of meeting an authentic teacher. But even so-called dharma practitioners hardly know how to follow a spiritual teacher properly: they live with plenty of expectations, plenty of defects, and plenty of wild thoughts. Using your human life to achieve trivial aims is like storing garbage in a golden vase.

You can't practice the dharma by relying on your own ideas. You must have the guidance of a spiritual master—and not just any master, but an authentic one. Once you receive his teachings and start to practice them, you will encounter many obstacles—the tricks of the demon, Mara.

> Think about the many ways that Mara can enter.

When your mind drifts away from the dharma, that's the demon. A demon is not something with a large, open mouth and fiery eyes. If you have no confidence in the dharma, if you do not persevere in the dharma and only think about passing your whole life comfortably, you have a more dangerous demon right in your own mind. To rid your mind of it,

> Ponder the fact that everyone will die.

Are you sure you're going to live for ten more years? Forget it! You can't even guarantee that you will live for another five minutes. If you could be assured that you will have the leisure to complete all your work, and still have enough time left for the dharma, then it would be all right to wait a few years to practice; but if you wait you are just fooling yourself. Look at how many corpses are carried to the cemetery every day in just one large city. Still you ignore death. Don't be blind. Ponder again and again the suddenness with which death may strike.

Think about the suffering and oppression endured by worldly people.

See how they toil, working in the fields, taking care of their kin, avoiding or subduing their enemies. They work with all sorts of machines; they can't sleep well at night. Even before the sun rises they are worrying about how to earn their living. If they were to endure even one hundredth of such hardship for the sake of practicing the dharma, they would easily achieve liberation. As for you, cast away all samsaric activities and preoccupations. Drop the heavy ones right here and cast away the light ones as far as you can.

You should thus have the same revulsion for samsara that someone with liver disease has for greasy food. If you don't keep this in mind, then having good meals, a fine patron, warm clothes, a comfortable place, and pleasant conversations will only prepare you for worldly life; and before even beginning to practice the dharma you will have already created obstacles. Furthermore, it is said, "You may raise your eyebrows and speak in a spiritual way about high realization, but if you haven't subdued the demons of ego-clinging and attachment to pleasure, the signs will show in your behavior and can also be detected in your dreams." It is essential to understand this.

You may look very impressive, with your eyes constantly gazing into the sky like a great meditator, declaring, "My view is that of the Great Perfection"—but if you lack inner stability, you will stumble over the first obstacle in your way.

As it is said, "The sign of being wise is self-control; and the sign of a mature spiritual experience is the absence of conflicting emotions." This means that to the same degree that one becomes wise and learned, one also becomes serene, peaceful, and subdued—not a reckless person bursting with pride and arrogance. However much your practice progresses year after year, you will have no concern with comfort and discomfort; you'll have no pride at all. You will be always at peace, untroubled by outer events, with a humble mind, beyond hopes and doubts and indifferent to the eight worldly concerns: gain and loss, pleasure and pain, praise and blame, fame and obscurity. There is a saying that goes: "In spiritual practice the difficulty comes at the beginning; in worldly affairs they come at the end." This means that when you renounce worldly affairs and devote yourself entirely to practice, you may encounter some outer and inner obstacles; but the more you persevere, the more happiness you will find. Conversely, worldly activities can give you ephemeral and superficial satisfactions at the start, but soon you will meet with bitter disappointment.

You can estimate the progress of your practice from your dreams. It is said: "To have no more negative dreams is the sign of having fully mastered meditation, and to make no distinctions between this life and the next is the sign of having fully mastered the view." The perceptions of the waking state are related to this life, and the perceptions of the dream state are related to the state of transition between death and next life, the bardo. If your daytime practice, such as meditating on a deity or upon the view of the Great Perfection, comes into your dreams and you are thus able to establish a continuity of practice throughout the waking and dream states, you will be able to master the experiences that arise in the bardo. If, for instance, when dreaming of a great danger you remember the guru and he comes to help you in your dream, the same thing will happen when you encounter the terrifying experiences of the bardo.

It is said: "Accepting offerings from the salary of a high official or from powerful people brings negative results."

Beware of your craving for patrons and benefactors. Otherwise, even if you have enough support for practicing quietly, you will keep chasing after wealth like a stray dog busily running from one place to another in search of food scraps.

When you think of going somewhere, before you step out the door, check your attitude and motivation: are you going to do something truly worthwhile? If yes, continue; if not, stay where you are.

If you think carefully about the source of their wealth and possessions, how can they possibly benefit your spiritual practice?

In Tibet and other places, many practitioners need to receive support from benefactors or important people. Remember the saying: "Where

465

there is power, there is defilement." Such powerful and important people get their wealth either by imposing duties on people under them or by force. If you practice in a perfect way and your understanding increases steadily, then the defilements linked with the wealth you may have received from such people will fade away.

> It is also said: "To misuse offerings is a razor blade to the life force. Overindulging in food cuts the life-vein of liberation."
> Finally, this will be the weight that drags you to the depth of hell.
> So reflect on this well: rely only on alms for your sustenance, and give up flattering others.

You should give up cultivating recognition, thinking, "I have to find a way to get some money or get a good position." As the Buddha said, "Virtuous ones should live on alms." Furthermore, whatever patrons donate, if they give well, you should not think, "Oh, he is a very good person"; and if they don't give much, you should not think, "He is a no-good miser." Just go for alms, without entertaining any of these thoughts. This is the practice that equalizes all merits: practitioners gain merit by endeavoring in the dharma and the patron by helping them to do so.

> As the buddhas of the past have said: Take the proper amount of food, moderate the length of time you sleep, and maintain keen awareness.
> If you eat too much food, your mental defilements will automatically arise; if you don't have enough, you'll beat your drum, chant, and perform village rites and only make your head spin. Then you'll say, "If I don't do this, I won't have enough food," and you'll become more frantic than a street dog. So be careful to eat the correct amount. Alcohol is the source of all faults, so drink only a cupful, no more. If you are unable to go without meat, eat only a suitable amount and practice food yoga in my advice in "How to Carry On Daily Activities" (Spyod yul lam khyer).

All the great practitioners of the past who remained in mountain solitudes, like Jetsun Milarepa, of course ate food, but only the minimum necessary to sustain life. If you eat too much, your emotions will increase and you will be prone to sleep.

Don't eat too much and don't drink too much. Meat is obtained at the price of great suffering to living beings; it is best to avoid it. If you can't, be aware of how negative this is and do some prayers for the sake of the animal you are eating. As for other food, don't just gorge yourself, but consume the food as an offering made to the deities of the mandala of your body. Even if you are not a monk or a nun, don't take much alcohol since it will weaken your mindfulness and lead you to all kinds of negative actions. The Buddha said that a monk who drinks even a drop of alcohol may no longer be his follower. If you drink, you can't even accomplish the most basic activities of ordinary life, let alone practice the development and completion stages.

Rest your body according to your own needs, approximately three hours, but never sleep too much.

In all your activities, you must apply the understanding of meditation during the postmeditation periods and enrich your meditation with the experiences of daily life, so that both grow stronger and deeper together. If you forget all about your meditation as soon as you leave your seat, how can you expect to progress on the path? The key points of the Vajrayana are to keep the realization of the view in all your actions and to perceive all phenomena as the display of the deity, all sounds as mantras, and all thoughts as natural manifestations of awareness. Such understanding must not be hampered by ego-clinging.

> *In describing how to undertake daily spiritual practice, it is of course difficult to set a single standard, as there are beings of high, mediocre, and inferior capacities. However, I will use as an example my own three years and five months in Palgyi Riwo. During this retreat I awoke before dawn at the latest, rose very briskly, and expelled the stale breath nine times to separate the pure and impure essences of the wind element. After finishing the preliminary practices, I prayed so fervently that tears rolled from my eyes.*
>
> *Then, for one session lasting till midmorning, I meditated on the prana practice of the completion stage from the extraordinary Drolthig Nyengyu.[3] Initially, it was necessary to generate courage to bear the pains arising from the movements of prana; but after some time all the blockages were spontaneously released, and the prana resumed*

its natural flow. Controlling the thirty-two channels of the left and the thirty-two channels of the right [at the navel center], I was able to detect the seasonal change in the lengths of day and night.

Those who become experts in prana practice know when the sun and moon are going to rise or set simply by the changes that happen in their channels and energies. They can also blend the upper prana (the life force or vitalizing energy) and the lower prana (the descending, clearing energy). When these two unite, one can move the prana to wherever in the body one wishes.

The ascending and descending pranas united, and a large, round vessel like a gourd was actually visible to the eye.[4] This was the source from which my ordinary and extraordinary signs of the path were actualized.

Even if you turn a pot that has only a very narrow aperture upside down, the water will not flow out of it. Likewise, when someone has totally mastered the containment of inner energies as Jigme Lingpa did, he will not lose his vital fluids. Jigme Lingpa realized the essence of the Hinayana and Mahayana. We can see in his life story how earnestly and with what great perseverance he practiced, and how wondrous were his experiences and realization. He says:

So if you only hold the breath for a short time and have unclear visualization, it is important not to boast about your practice.

When practicing on the veins and energies, you first undergo a period of hardship, pain, and difficulties. Then comes a stage of great craving for bliss. Finally you become free from clinging and experience the unity of unchanging bliss and emptiness.

Unclear visualizations are not of much use, so you must concentrate one-pointedly and prevent your mind from being carried away by wandering thoughts.

At midmorning I took tea or soup, and then offered sur, the burnt offering. Following that, I began a session of the approach and accomplishment practices.[5]

At the time of mantra recitation and accomplishment of the development stage, when meditating upon a deity, you must first visualize clearly and correctly the form, color, and various aspects of the deity without any clinging to it. Not only should the visualization of every detail (face, arms, etc.) be clear, but you should also think that the form that you visualize is permeated by, and can fully manifest, the wisdom, compassion, and power of all the buddhas. In short, you must be convinced that there is no difference between your visualization and the actual deity. Your visualization is not simply a beautiful person with many ornaments or an angry-looking demon; rather, it is a manifestation of the fully enlightened buddhas.

> In the development stage, the nature of the deity is free from clinging; its expression, which is the deity's form, is luminous; and its compassion is the clear concentration on the radiation and reabsorption of light rays. Only by maintaining an awareness of these will the development and completion stages be perfected.

Inwardly you should meditate on the intimate union of appearances and emptiness. While visualizing the deity, you must perceive the whole phenomenal world as its manifestation and yet as being empty at the same time. Thus you will combine the development and completion stages. The development stage alone cannot lead you to the ultimate accomplishment.

With the mind, do the visualization of the development stage; with the speech, recite the mantras; and make your body a proper vessel for concentration by keeping your posture straight and well balanced. From time to time generate fervent devotion, thinking that your guru and Guru Padmasambhava are one. At other times focus your attention on the face, arms, and all the details of the deity's ornaments, dress, and so on; at other times concentrate again on the emanation and reabsorption of the light rays. Never stray into ordinary perception. If you just hold your rosary in your hand and recite the mantra with your mouth while your mind wanders here and there, filled with desires and aversions, that will be of no help at all.

> Some lazy practitioners these days practice without making any effort, like an old man counting mani. This is not the correct way.

Here reference is made to some laypeople in Tibet who recite the mani mantra out of habit, without much concentration, without having received any instructions, and without associating any specific meditation with it.

> Going through these various practices, I finished this second session just after midday.
>
> Then I offered water tormas, recited the Confession of Downfalls, the Spontaneous Accomplishment of Wishes, the All-Victorious Ushnisha, Supreme Body of Wisdom, and so forth, and concluded with dharanis, mantras, and prayers from the Daily Recitations.[6]
>
> Following this, if I had any writing to do, I quickly wrote about eight pages. Then, if I had nothing special in mind, I would meditate on the thögal practice. During lunch I blew many special mantras and dharanis on the meat, generated compassion, and offered prayers. Then I practiced food yoga by visualizing my aggregates and elements as deities and recited the sutra for purifying the offerings received.[7]

When performing the food offering according to the Vajrayana, you should visualize the deities of the peaceful and wrathful mandalas in the different centers of your body: the forty-two peaceful deities in your heart center, the fifty-eight wrathful ones in your forehead center, the assembly of the vidyadharas in your throat center, and so on. Eat the food the way you would perform a fire ceremony, imagining that your two hands are the ritual utensils used to offer the various ingredients. Furthermore, when you swallow the food, imagine that you are putting the offering into the fire (which here is the inner fire, or tummo). The quintessence of the food then becomes an offering to the deities of the aggregates, elements, and senses of the mandala of your body. After that, recite purifying sutras, mantras, and dharanis, and the names of the buddhas. Whatever residues are left should be given to the lower guests, the harmful spirits with whom one has karmic debts.

> Next, I did two or three hundred prostrations and recited prayers from the sutras and tantras.

During a prolonged retreat, it is very good for the body to do daily two or three hundred prostrations. You should also do many prayers of aspirations, such as the Prayer of Good Actions and Samantabhadra's Prayer.

> *Then I immediately sat down and practiced the meditation and reci-*
> *tation of my yidam intensively. Thus I was able to accomplish the*
> *practices of many classes of yidams. At dusk I performed a gana-*
> *chakra feast offering, offered tormas, and finished the concluding*
> *practices and the dissolution of the completion stage. Then I made*
> *strong prayers to be able to perceive luminosity and also offered pray-*
> *ers, such as the Spontaneous Accomplishment of Wishes, strongly*
> *and impartially for myself and all beings. After a session of prana*
> *meditation, I began sleep yoga.*

You should sleep lying on your right side in the lion posture while visualizing a red four-petaled lotus in your heart center. In the center of this lotus, see your root guru in the form of Guru Rinpoche. He emanates boundless rays of light that fill up the room and illuminate all the space in the ten directions. Then, when you feel that you are falling asleep, think that all the phenomena of the universe melt into light and dissolve into the guru in your heart center. Then your body also dissolves into light and melts into the guru, and the guru himself dissolves like a rainbow vanishing in the sky. Fall asleep while remaining in that state.

> *Whenever I woke up, I didn't drift into confusion but one-pointedly*
> *kept my attention focused, and by so doing was able to make progress*
> *in my practice.*
>
> *In brief, during these three years I always ate the same amount*
> *of food and wore only one cotton shawl. Not one word passed*
> *through the small inner door of my retreat, and when the retreat*
> *helpers came, they didn't go beyond that inner door. As I had a sense*
> *of renunciation and weariness with samsara and an acute awareness*
> *of the uncertainty of death, I didn't utter a word of gossip or mean-*
> *ingless talk.*
>
> *However, my disciples, when you do retreat, you might have put*
> *a sign by your door, but your thoughts just wander; if there is a noise*
> *outside, you act like a watchman, and you listen to any babble. If*
> *you meet someone at the inner door, you discuss the news of China,*

Tibet, Mongolia, and everywhere else. Your six senses wander around outside, and you lose all the power of your retreat. You follow after external objects and perceptions, your accomplishments vanish outside, and you invite obstacles inside. If you fall into these habits, the time of your retreat will pass without your mind improving by a fraction. Never leave retreat just as ordinary as you were before.

Even if you have spent many years in retreat, if you find that your mind has become even wilder than before and is not mingled with the dharma, you have just wasted your time.

You must not become overly tense (concentrating too forcefully) or too relaxed (falling asleep or becoming completely distracted from your meditation). Just remain in unaltered simplicity, the freshness of the present moment, the unchanging nature of mind, which is the real buddha.

You must develop determination so that whatever you are doing, the essential nature of your mind is ineffable, beyond the intellect, not too tight, not too loose; it is beyond meditation, yet without the slightest distraction. While in retreat, whether you are sick, in pain, or dying, practicing the development stage or completion stage, writing or reciting daily prayers—without changing, establishing, modifying, or spoiling this present awareness, you should never separate from it. Once you do separate from it, various thoughts may arise, and under their influence the pride of being the "great meditator" will increase.

You will think, "I know the dharma. I have met many lamas." You will expose the faults of your dharma friends, amass wealth, and create disturbing situations, passing your time doing many things without doing one properly. Brainless folk will say, "He is a person of great merit and immense benefit to beings." When you start eating the tsampa offered for tormas, it will be a sure sign that Mara has already possessed you.

As it is said:

Commit your mind to the dharma.
Commit the dharma to a frugal, humble life.
Commit this frugal, humble life to the thought of death.
Commit death *to* occur in a deserted place.

> *All dharma practitioners should take these four resolutions of the*
> *noble Kadampas as their crown jewel, and the obstacles (maras) will*
> *be unable to interrupt them.*

Discarding all other thoughts, you should be concerned only with the dharma. You do not need to think about wealth, fame, and power, but should cultivate humility. Do this not only for a few months of retreat but for the entire duration of your life, until the very moment of your death. When death comes, it is of no use to be among many worldly people; it is better to die in an empty cave, one-pointedly absorbed in your spiritual practice. With this frame of mind, the obstacles of Mara will have no place to grasp hold of you.

> *Furthermore, if you speak of your experiences, realizations, or*
> *dreams; talk about dharma news and the difficulties of your retreat*
> *practices; or mention the faults of those who belong to the same lin-*
> *eage and hold the same view as yourself to people who do not have*
> *the same samaya, for instance, then your accomplishments will van-*
> *ish and this behavior will only serve to expose your own flaws. So*
> *keep a low profile, be in harmony with everyone, wear tattered*
> *clothes, and do not be preoccupied with mundane concerns. In the*
> *depth of your being you should have no fear even of the Lord of*
> *Death.*

Don't lose what you have gained by complaining, "I stayed so long in retreat and never received any experience or realization; you can't expect any results from this practice!" Practice with great joy. At the same time, you should be completely free from hope and fear, thinking, "If death comes today, I am confident."

> *Externally, by appearing even more peaceful than the King of Swans,*
> *Yulkhor Sung,*[8] *you should be able to give other people a positive im-*
> *pression.*

If outwardly you are self-controlled and gentle, and inwardly you have strength and confidence in your practice, having transformed yourself, you will be able to transform others. You should be able to inspire people to think, "Oh, a dharma practitioner should be someone like him."

> *In brief, someone practicing dharma should rely only on himself and not take advice from anyone except a true teacher. Even parents' advice, however honest it may be, will not be right. Be like a wild animal escaping from a cage.*

You must constantly check whether or not you succeed in using the teaching to tame your conflicting emotions. If any practice has the opposite result, increasing your conflicting emotions and your selfishness, it is not suited for you, and you should give it up. Once you have started to practice, don't follow just anyone's advice. Be like a wild animal jumping out of a trap and running as far away as it can. You must be completely free from samsara, not half in and half out.

> *When you are practicing in retreat, never break your commitment; be like a stake driven into hard ground, firmly planted. If you receive bad news, or if bad circumstances arise, do not panic; you should be oblivious like a madman.*

Once you have begun the practice, be very strong and stable. You should possess such inner determination and strength that you won't break your promise to stay in retreat even at the cost of your life. If people criticize you, don't lose heart. If they praise you, don't get excited about it. Just be like a madman who doesn't care the least whether people say good or bad things. Don't let anything affect your determination.

> *When you are with many people, do not let your mindfulness stray toward ordinary things.*

When you find yourself in the midst of a large gathering, never lose your mindfulness. Preserve the state of uncontrived simplicity and remember the guru's instructions.

You should be like a mother who has been separated from her newborn baby. A woman who has just had a child is extremely loving and attentive to him; and if someone takes the child away from her even for a very short time, she can't stop thinking about him. In the same way, you should never part from mindfulness and vigilance.

You should train in perceiving all phenomenal existence as infinitely pure.

Don't make any distinction between pure and impure phenomena; just realize the infinite primordial purity of everything.

When you meditate on prana and the completion stage, you should never lose your concentration, just like someone threading a needle. Even if death should come upon you unexpectedly, then without any sadness or regret and with nothing left unfinished in your mind, you should be like an eagle soaring through the sky.

Even if death were to strike you today like lightning, you must be ready to die without sadness or regret, without any residue of clinging to what is left behind. Remaining in the recognition of the view, you should leave this life like an eagle soaring up into the blue sky.

When the eagle takes flight into the vast sky, it never thinks, "My wings won't be able to carry me; I won't be able to fly that far." Likewise, when dying, remember your guru and his instructions, and adhere to them with complete confidence.

If you have these seven essential points, you will reach the ultimate accomplishment of the Victorious Ones, the buddhas of the past, and my wish will be fulfilled. Thus, you will make this human life meaningful, and, entering the gate of the supreme dharma, you will achieve the final result.

Among all the offerings you can make to your teacher, there is none that will please him more than genuine spiritual practice. So, to fulfill his wishes and give meaning to this human life, enter the path of dharma and practice it according to the guru's instructions.

A la la ho!
I, the Dzogchenpa Longchen Namkhai Naljor, the Yogi of the Vast Space, wrote this heart-advice, based on my own experience, for the

powerful yogi practitioner Jalu Dorje, "Adamantine Rainbow Body," who became an excellent vessel for the Secret Mantra through his faith and devotion. I request you all to keep it by your pillow.

If you can practice according to these pith instructions, you will always remain in harmony with the dharma and become a perfectly pure practitioner. This is why Jigme Lingpa says at the end of this text to "keep it by your pillow," meaning to keep it near at hand and read it time and time again. Try to act in accordance with it daily, rejoice, and pray to the guru to be able to do even better the next day.

If you go against these instructions, realize your mistake, offer your confession, recite the hundred-syllable mantra of Vajrasattva, and vow that it will never happen again. Never part from this teaching. Think of it as a disciplinarian who keeps watch over your actions, and remember that it is the essence of all that is to be practiced.

Although Jigme Lingpa dissolved his physical body into the absolute expanse of dharmakaya, the spiritual instructions he left are equivalent to his actual presence for those who take them to heart. If you try to apply these teachings, even you do not succeed in the beginning, you certainly can succeed by persevering. There is nothing that cannot be mastered through hard work. So it is up to you to practice.

• • •

Dilgo Khyentse Rinpoche gave these teachings on three occasions: twice in France, for the benefit of those about to enter a three-year retreat, and once in Nepal, at Shechen Monastery, at the request of the practitioner Lobsang Dorje. The present transcript is based on the first version given in France, with the addition of a few excerpts from the teachings given in Nepal.

These teachings were translated by Matthieu Könchog Tenzin, transcribed by Patricia Deakins and originally edited by John Deweese, Nur Richard, and Shirin Gale. It was reedited for this edition by Kendra Crossen. The root text of Jigme Lingpa was translated by David Christensen and slightly edited for this edition.

Notes

1. *Deep-blue* refer to shiny black hair with a deep blue luster in it.

2. Tib. *bShes-pa'i springs-yig;* Skt. *Suhrllekha.* English translation: *Nagarjuna's Letter to a Friend,* translated by the Padmakara Translation Group (Ithaca, N.Y.: Snow Lion, 2006).

3. Drolthig Nyengu refers to a particular oral transmission that Jigme Lingpa held, which is related to the cycle of termas revealed by Trengpo Tertön Sherap Öser, 1518–1584). The monastery of Palri, in central Tibet, where Jigme Lingpa stayed as a novice, followed the tradition of Trengpo Tertön. Dilgo Khyentse Rinpoche had a few texts composed by Jigme Lingpa about the practice of the Drolthig cycle, for which there was no transmission and that are not included in Jigme Linpa's collected works.

4. This shows he had control of his vital essence and that his abdomen looked like a large, round vessel, a physical sign resulting from having done much of this prana practice.

5. These are related to various steps in progressing in the meditation on the wisdom deity while visualizing it and reciting its mantra. The first steps are like approaching someone whom we don't know well yet. After a while, through familiarization and recognizing that the wisdom deity is none other than our buddha-nature, all ordinary and extraordinary accomplishments can be achieved.

6. Water torma (*chu gtor*), the Confession of Downfalls (*ltung bshags*), the Spontaneous Accomplishments of Wishes (*bsam pa lhun grub,* a prayer addressed to Guru Padmasambhava), the All-Victorious Ushnisha (*gtsug gtor rnam rgyal,* a purification prayer), and the Supreme Body of Wisdom (*ye shes sku mchog*), a confession prayer recited to repair the transgressions of samayas.

7. The sutra for purifying the offerings received: *yon sbyong gi mdo.*

8. A bodhisattva who manifested in the animal realm.

The Root Text

Rigdzen Jigme Lingpa

Embodiment of all the glorious buddhas,
Lord of Compassion, Padmasambhava,
Remain upon the pinnacle of my diademed deep-blue locks
And bless my mind.

Listen, all of you who possess faith, who keep samaya, and who strive from the depths of your hearts for spiritual ideals. In cyclic existence, without beginning or end, with your negative actions acting as the cause, you have fallen under the influence of adverse conditions. Everything you can think of [in samsara] is just an experience of fear and suffering. Beings of the six realms must experience this continually, like prisoners cast into a dark cell.

At present, if you have any physical illness or mental disturbance, or are in an undesirable situation, then you panic and are totally upset and paranoid about everything, like a like someone overcome by nausea. So how will it be when you experience the sufferings of the three lower realms? Alas! Now the only means of escape from these sufferings is to accomplish the ultimate goal of the supreme dharma; otherwise, there is no way out.

You may say, "Everything is an illusion," and then spend your day riding horses, drinking beer, and enjoying entertainments. Come evening, you don your cotton shawl [to show that you are practicing *tummo*], practice breathing like the noisy emptying and filling of a bellows, then play your bell and drum. You won't become enlightened by acting like this.

The cause of wandering in samsara is ego-clinging. Nagarjuna writes in his *Letter to a Friend*: "'Desires bring destruction, like the kimba fruit,' the Munindra [the Buddha] said." They should be abandoned, as these chains bind all beings to the prison of samsara. In brief, regarding ego-clinging: in clinging to your country, house, wealth, and possessions, you postpone the practice of dharma.

You praise your deity when you find a mere needle or some thread, and you get depressed if you lose even a pen or a shoelace. These are all external forms of ego-clinging.

Seeing members of your own tradition as gods and those of other traditions as demons, and without examining your own qualities, you think, "Would I not be fit to take Shakyamuni Buddha's place?" All these are internal forms of ego-clinging.

Clinging to the visualization in the development stage as being solid, having partiality in the generation of the bodhichitta, practicing the completion stage within a conceptual framework—you say all things are empty and lack self-nature, yet cling to the nature of emptiness, like a beautiful woman attached to her own body, and perceive it with a very tight and unclear mind, thinking, "No one has reached my level of meditation, so I don't need to ask for advice or consult anyone." Thus your life will be wasted in futility. These are all secret forms of ego-clinging.

My frank advice is this: if you strongly renounce clinging to your country, wealth, and possessions, half of the dharma will already be accomplished.

Initially, by entering the door of the absolute teaching and having the capacity to cast off ego-clinging like spit in the dust, I captured the citadel of the natural state. I began to gather an entourage of students, becoming a source of benefit to others, training disciples by means of my basic intention [of compassion], and giving teachings. I kept only some immediate necessities and just enough clothing to protect myself from the cold and didn't say, "I'll need this wealth for later," or "I'll need it if I'm sick or dying," or "I'll need it to perform ceremonies if I am sick," or "I must put something aside to be used for funeral offerings when I die."

Thus I didn't concern myself with worrying about my future means of support, but mainly made offerings to the Three Jewels, ransomed the lives of animals, served and respected the sangha, gave charity to beggars, and so forth.

I didn't waste the offerings of the living and [those made on behalf of] the dead by giving them to unworthy causes, nor did I hoard them like bees storing honey in a hive. Since I didn't carry great wealth with me, I felt no embarrassment before those who came to see me.

We will all die, remember that.

Since the dharma itself is free from partiality, try to have pure perception regarding everyone. If one examines all the traditions, each of them is indeed profound in its own way; but for me, the view of the Great Perfection was fine, and all the root downfalls were dissolved in space.

When laying the foundation of the preliminary practices, you should not forsake them by saying, "Everything is empty," thereby losing your actions in the view.

Then, for the actual practice, you should live in an uninhabited area without acquaintances, accompanied by your friend Awareness, and vow to maintain the flow of the uncontrived natural state.

If you hear good or bad news that stirs up hopes and fears, don't regard it as true. Neither reject nor accept it. Be like a dead person, to whom one can say anything.

Think how difficult it is to attain a human form, how difficult it is to meet the dharma, and about the rarity of true teachers.

Think about the many ways that Mara can enter.

Ponder the fact that everyone will die.

Think about the suffering and oppression endured by worldly people.

You should thus have the same revulsion for samsara that someone with liver disease has for greasy food. If you don't keep this in mind, then having good meals, a fine patron, warm clothes, a comfortable place, and pleasant conversations will only prepare you for worldly life; and before even beginning to practice the dharma you will have already created obstacles. Furthermore, it is said, "You may raise your eyebrows and speak in a spiritual way about high realization, but if you haven't subdued the demons of ego-clinging and attachment to pleasure, the signs will show in your behavior and can also be detected in your dreams." It is essential to understand this.

It is said: "Accepting offerings from the salary of a high official or from powerful people brings negative results."

If you think carefully about the source of their wealth and possessions, how can they possibly benefit your spiritual practice?

It is also said: "To misuse offerings is a razor blade to the life force. Overindulging in food cuts the life-vein of liberation."

Finally, this will be the weight that drags you to the depth of hell. So reflect on this well: rely only on alms for your sustenance, and give up flattering others.

As the buddhas of the past have said: Take the proper amount of food, moderate the length of time you sleep, and maintain keen awareness

If you eat too much food, your mental defilements will automatically arise; if you don't have enough, you'll beat your drum, chant, and perform village rites and only make your head spin. Then you'll say, "If I don't do this, I won't have enough food," and you'll become more frantic than a street dog. So be careful to eat the correct amount. Alcohol is the source of all faults, so drink only a cupful, no more. If you are unable to go without meat, eat only a suitable amount and practice food yoga in my advice in "How to Carry On Daily Activities" (*Spyod yul lam khyer*).

In describing how to undertake daily spiritual practice, it is of course difficult to set a single standard, as there are beings of high, mediocre, and inferior capacities. However, I will use as an example my own three years and five months [1756–1759] in Palgyi Riwo. During this retreat I awoke before dawn at the latest, rose very briskly, and expelled the stale breath nine times to separate the pure and impure essences of the wind element. After finishing the preliminary practices, I prayed so fervently that tears rolled from my eyes.

Then, for one session lasting till midmorning, I meditated on the prana practice of the completion stage from the extraordinary Drolthig Nyengyu. Initially, it was necessary to generate courage to bear the pains arising from the movements of prana; but after some time all the blockages were spontaneously released, and the prana resumed its natural flow. Controlling the thirty-two channels of the left and the thirty-two channels of the right [at the navel center], I was able to detect the seasonal change in the lengths of day and night.

The ascending and descending pranas united, and a large, round vessel like a gourd was actually visible to the eye. This was the source from which my ordinary and extraordinary signs of the path were actualized.

So if you only hold the breath for a short time and have unclear visualization, it is important not to boast about your practice.

At midmorning I took tea or soup, and then offered sur, the burnt offering. Following that, I began a session of the approach and accomplishment practices.

In the development stage, the nature of the deity is free from clinging; its expression, which is the deity's form, is luminous; and its compassion is the clear concentration on the radiation and reabsorption of light rays. Only by maintaining an awareness of these will the development and completion stages be perfected.

Some lazy practitioners these days practice without making any effort, like old man counting mani. This is not the correct way.

Going through these various practices, I finished this second session just after midday.

Then I offered water tormas, recited the Confession of Downfalls, the Spontaneous Accomplishment of Wishes, the All-Victorious Ushnisha, Supreme Body of Wisdom, and so forth, and concluded with dharanis, mantras, and prayers from the Daily Recitations.

Following this, if I had any writing to do, I quickly wrote about eight pages. Then, if I had nothing special in mind, I would meditate on the thögal practice. During lunch I blew many special mantras and dharanis on the meat, generated compassion, and offered prayers. Then I practiced food yoga by visualizing my aggregates and elements as deities and recited the sutra for purifying the offerings received.

Next, I did two or three hundred prostrations and recited prayers from the sutras and tantras.

Then I immediately sat down and practiced the meditation and recitation of my yidam intensively. Thus I was able to accomplish the practices of many classes of yidams. At dusk I performed a ganachakra feast offering, offered tormas, and finished the concluding practices and the dissolution of the completion stage. Then I made strong prayers to be able to perceive luminosity and also offered prayers, such as the Spontaneous Accomplishment of Wishes, strongly and impartially for myself and all beings. After a session of prana meditation, I began sleep yoga.

Whenever I woke up, I didn't drift into confusion but one-pointedly kept my attention focused, and by so doing was able to make progress in my practice.

In brief, during these three years I always ate the same amount of food and wore only one cotton shawl. Not one word passed through the small inner door of my retreat, and when the retreat helpers came, they didn't go beyond that inner door. As I had a sense of renunciation and a weariness with samsara, and an acute awareness of the uncertainty of death, I didn't utter a word of gossip or meaningless talk.

However, my disciples, when you do retreat, you might have put a sign by your door, but your thoughts just wander; if there is a noise outside, you act like a watchman, and you listen to any babble. If you meet someone at the inner door, you discuss the news of China, Tibet, Mongolia, and everywhere else. Your six senses wander around outside, and you lose all the power of your retreat. You follow after external objects and perceptions, your accomplishments vanish outside, and you invite obstacles inside. If you fall into these habits, the time of your retreat will pass without your mind improving by a fraction. Never leave retreat just as ordinary as you were before.

You must develop determination so that whatever you are doing, the essential nature of your mind is ineffable, beyond the intellect, not too tight, not too loose; it is beyond meditation, yet without the slightest distraction. While in retreat, whether you are sick, in pain, or dying, practicing the development stage or completion stage, writing or reciting daily prayers—without changing, establishing, modifying, or spoiling this present awareness, you should never separate from it. Once you do separate from it, various thoughts may arise, and under their influence the pride of being the "great meditator" will increase.

You will think, "I know the dharma. I have met many lamas." You will expose the faults of your dharma friends, amass wealth, and create disturbing situations, passing your time doing many things without doing one properly. Brainless folk will say, "He is a person of great merit and immense benefit to beings." When you start eating the tsampa offered for tormas, it will be a sure sign that Mara has already possessed you.

As it is said:

> Commit your mind to the dharma.
> Commit the dharma to a frugal, humble life.

Commit this frugal, humble life to the thought of death.
Commit death to occur in a deserted place.

All dharma practitioners should take these four resolutions of the noble Kadampas as their crown jewel, and the obstacles (maras) will be unable to interrupt them.

Furthermore, if you speak of your experiences, realizations, or dreams; talk about dharma news and the difficulties of your retreat practices; or mention the faults of those who belong to the same lineage and hold the same view as yourself to people who do not have the same samaya, for instance, then your accomplishments will vanish and this behavior will only serve to expose your own flaws. So keep a low profile, be in harmony with everyone, wear tattered clothes, and do not be preoccupied with mundane concerns. In the depth of your being you should have no fear even of the Lord of Death.

Externally, by appearing even more peaceful than the King of Swans, Yulkhor Sung, you should be able to give other people a positive impression.

In brief, someone practicing dharma should rely only on himself and not take advice from anyone except a true teacher. Even parents' advice, however honest it may be, will not be right. Be like a wild animal escaping from a cage.

When you are practicing in retreat, never break your commitment; be like a stake driven into hard ground, firmly planted. If you receive bad news, or if bad circumstances arise, do not panic; you should be oblivious like a madman.

When you are with many people, do not let your mindfulness stray toward ordinary things.

You should train in perceiving all phenomenal existence as infinitely pure.

When you meditate on prana and the completion stage, you should never lose your concentration, just like someone threading a needle. Even if death should come upon you unexpectedly, then without any sadness or regret and with nothing left unfinished in your mind, you should be like an eagle soaring through the sky.

If you have these seven essential points, you will reach the ultimate accomplishment of the Victorious Ones, the buddhas of the past, and my wish will be fulfilled. Thus, you will make this human life meaningful, and, entering the gate of the supreme dharma, you will achieve the final result.

A la la ho!

I, the Dzogchenpa Longchen Namkhai Naljor, the Yogi of the Vast Space, wrote this heart-advice, based on my own experience, for the powerful yogi practitioner Jalu Dorje, "Adamantine Rainbow Body," who became an excellent vessel for the Secret Mantra through his faith and devotion. I request you all to keep it by your pillow.

• • •

The root text of Jigme Lingpa was translated by David Christensen and slightly edited for this edition.

PURE APPEARANCE

*Development and Completion Stages in
Vajrayana Practice*

TRANSLATED FROM THE TIBETAN
BY ANI JINBA PALMO

OM SVASTI

By the kindness of the infinite victorious ones and their
    descendants
And the blessings of the wondrous three roots,
May the unrivaled manifestation of the great treasure of
    wisdom and compassion [Khyentse], the exalted guru,
Who has emanated according to his intention,
The *fearless holder of the teachings* of the Uddiyana lord and of
    the sutras and tantras of the unbiased tradition,
Completely victorious in all directions,
Ever remain in the indestructible vajra realm,
And may your wish for peace and happiness be *spontaneously
    accomplished* without effort.

• • •

*For the sake of auspiciousness, the precious, supreme tulku
of the great Vajradhara, Kyabje Dilgo Khyentse, was
kindly given a name by the supreme lord of the victorious
ones, the refuge-protector, guide through samsara and nirvana [His Holiness the Dalai Lama], and offered an
adornment of robes at the Maratika rock cave of long life.
At that time, this was written and offered on the excellent
eighth day of the waxing part of the eleventh month of the
auspicious Wood Sow year [29 December 1995] with one-
pointed aspiration by Vagindra Dharmamati, the bewil-
dered monk called Sha[de-u] Trül[shik].* JAYANTU

Acknowledgments

DILGO KHYENTSE RINPOCHE journeyed three times to North America in order to teach the buddhadharma. His last journey was for the purpose of officiating at the cremation of his student, Vidyadhara the Venerable Chögyam Trungpa Rinpoche, which took place at Karme Chöling in Barnet, Vermont, on May 26, 1987. At that time, Khyentse Rinpoche kindly accepted our invitation to remain in North America to teach extensively throughout our sangha.

During these visits, he gave teachings to the public and to all members of our sangha. While this was a very sad and poignant time for us, Khyentse Rinpoche provide a truly endless stream of precious amrita, the deathless nectar of the buddhadharma, through his twice-daily teachings on a variety of topics. This volume is a record of his vajrayana talks given to the Karma Dzong community in Boulder, Colorado, June 17–20, 1987.

These teachings were orally translated by the Venerable Tulku Pema Wangyal. Khyentse Rinpoche spoke in a seamless stream of teachings for a minimum of 20–30 minutes before he would allow time for translation. While Tulku Rinpoche was remarkable in his steady, lucid, and mesmerizing recall of Khyentse Rinpoche's words, he strongly advised us to have the entire teaching retranslated before this could be published in English. Taking his counsel to heart, we were fortunate to find Ani Jinba Palmo, a long-time student of Khyentse Rinpoche, willing to take on this project.

Ani Jinba completed her draft in the summer of 1991 while in her native land of Holland. Members of the Vajravairochana Translation Committee did all the editorial work, and Ani Jinba was closely consulted in further refining her translation for publication. Sherab Chödzin and Scott Wellenbach were the main editors, assisted by Larry Mermelstein, who also handled the composition.

The dedication at the beginning of this book is actually a longevity supplication for Khyentse Rinpoche's *Yangsi*, "one who has come back into existence," which was composed by Trülshik Rinpoche, the most senior and accomplished disciple of Khyentse Rinpoche, as well as being the lama who identified the rebirth of his beloved master.

We are deeply indebted to Ani Jinba for her care with and understanding of both Khyentse Rinpoche's difficult dialect and the meaning of his teachings. We would also like to thank Hazel Bercholz for her design and advice with production.

We are most appreciative of the permission of Shechen Rabjam Rinpoche to make these teachings available to vajrayana practitioners, for whom they were meant. A portion of the proceeds from this publication will go toward fulfilling Khyentse Rinpoche's buddha activity, especially at his monastery of Shechen Tennyi Dargye Ling in Boudhnath, Kathmandu, Nepal.

The Four Abhishekas
and the Three Samadhis

THE FOUR ABHISHEKAS

THE OTHER DAY I explained the stages of the ordinary path of the buddhadharma to all the students. Now I shall explain the meaning of the extraordinary secret-mantra vajrayana.

In essence, the secret-mantra vajrayana can be understood in terms of ground, path, and fruition. Regarding the ground, the minds of all sentient beings are pervaded by the tathagatagarbha. In the seed of the mind abides the essence of buddhahood, beyond meeting and parting. Just as oil is present in a mustard seed, and rice and barley have the potential to ripen within their seeds, similarly all beings have the ground potential in them from the very beginning; it does not have to be created again. If someone has gold and buries it under the ground, he cannot use it. Similarly, even though we have the ground potential, if it is not realized, just having it will not help us. All the sutras and tantras taught by the Buddha are methods for realizing this ground potential. Summarizing all the Buddha's teachings, we can divide them into the vehicle of characteristics, which takes the cause as the path, and the secret-mantra vajrayana, which takes the fruition as the path.

What is "taking the cause as the path"? All sentient beings have the potential, the tathagatagarbha, within. Through the right method, this can gradually be ripened. Through the accumulation of conceptual merit and nonconceptual wisdom for three immeasurable kalpas with the support of the six paramitas, one will realize the ultimate result, which is buddhahood. That is the vehicle of characteristics, which takes the cause as the path.

What is the secret mantra, which takes the fruition as the path? The ground, the essence of dharmata, that intrinsic awareness that has the tathagatagarbha within it, contains the qualities of the three kayas from the very beginning. The fruits of bringing the Buddha's activities to the path and getting used to them are the Buddha's kayas and the manifestation of his buddhafields. By bringing this fruition of kayas and buddhafields to the path, superior individuals can accomplish the tathagatagarbha, the ultimate state of buddhahood, in one lifetime, and mediocre individuals can do so in three or seven lifetimes. That is how the secret-mantra vajrayana takes the fruition as the path.

In essence, the secret-mantra vehicle can be divided into three categories: the empowerment, which is the door; the development and completion stages, which bring liberation; and the samaya, which is like a harmonious friend. If one wants to enter a house or a big hotel, one has to enter via the door. Similarly, if one wants to enter the secret-mantra vehicle, first one needs the empowerment. Just by going ahead and practicing the vajrayana and looking at the texts of vajaryana instructions on the development and completion stages, one does not receive the empowerment. By studying the texts and reflecting on their meaning without the empowerment, it is not possible to attain the result of the ordinary and supreme siddhis. Therefore, in the secret-mantra vehicle, without the support of the empowerment there is no siddhi. One needs the empowerment. Practicing the development and completion stages when the empowerment has ripened one's mind constitutes practicing the path of the secret mantra.

What is the quality of empowerment? It is called the "ripening empowerment." What is being ripened? All sentient beings have the potential of the tathagatagarbha, which is the intrinsic nature of mind. The means of ripening that potential is the ripening empowerment. As long as one has not received that ripening empowerment, it is not possible to attain the ordinary and supreme siddhis, even though one has tathagatagarbha. By way of analogy, if one has sand, no matter how much one pounds that sand, one will never get oil. But if one pounds just one small white mustard seed, one will get oil. All beings are like mustard seeds in that they have tathagatagarbha, but if one has not received the empowerment, that potential—the oil—cannot manifest.

As the buddha Vajradhara said, "Those who have not received empowerment are not allowed even to see the secret-mantra texts." If one looks at the texts without having received the empowerment, one cannot attain the ordinary and supreme siddhis. Receiving the empowerment is like receiving a visa: it allows one to listen to, meditate on, and accomplish the secret-mantra teachings. If one receives the empowerment and does not break the samaya, even if one cannot practice the development and completion stages, just through having received the empowerment, karma and obscurations are purified, and the potential for the ordinary and supreme siddhis develops. Having received the empowerment is like being a king's son: since the son belongs to a royal family, whether he is good or bad, he will always be known as a prince. Similarly, someone who has received empowerment will be known as a son of the buddhas.

Within the empowerment, there is the preparation and the actual abhisheka. For the preparation one needs a mandala made of powdered sand or a painted mandala. Just by laying eyes on this mandala, even one's five heinous crimes would be purified. Those who have received empowerment will be able to purify all the evil deeds and obscurations they have accumulated until now. If one has received empowerment, does not break the samaya, and regards one's teacher as the main deity of the mandala, such as Vajradhara or Vajrasattva, through the confidence that one has received that empowerment from him, one will be reborn as a human or a god in one's next life. As Guru Rinpoche said, "If one receives an empowerment every year, and in a hundred years one receives a hundred empowerments, even if one is reborn as an animal, one will be a very powerful animal." If one receives one empowerment every year, through these empowerments one's merit and windhorse will increase and one's obscurations will be purified. When those who have received empowerments die, even if they are reborn as animals, they will be born as powerful animals, such as lions or elephants. They will never be born as weak and lowly animals. If one receives many empowerments now, even if one does not practice the development and completion stages, if one keeps samaya, at death one will be reborn in a place where the secret-mantra doctrine flourishes. Then again one can receive empowerments, practice the secret mantra, and attain the stage of bud-dhahood within seven lifetimes. Such are the qualities of empowerment.

The transmission of the empowerment requires a qualified master to bestow it and a qualified student to receive it. If the teacher who bestows it is not a qualified master and he gives the empowerment pretending to have the necessary qualities, master and student will both go to hell. What is a qualified master? He must have entered the mandala of the secret-mantra vajrayana and have confidence in the development and completion stages. If he has students, he must look after them with great compassion, thinking to free them from the lower realms of samsara and put them on the path of the secret mantra. If he is such an individual, he is qualified to bestow the empowerment.

If the student is not a qualified vessel, it is like having pure water but pouring it into a dirty container. In this way, the water is spoiled. Simi-larly, even if a qualified teacher bestows a proper abhisheka, if the stu-dent who receives the empowerment does not have devotion toward the secret mantra and the teacher and cannot keep the samaya, both the student and the master will go to the lower realms. So the empower-ment should only be given by a qualified master to a qualified student.

Within the empowerment there are the four abhishekas, each of which has a preliminary, a main part, and a conclusion. The stages of the four abhishekas should be completed in order. For example, if it is a major empowerment, first the master who bestows the empowerment should be qualified to practice the recitation of the yidam Vajrasattva or whichever yidam of the three roots is being bestowed. He should have attained the samadhi of the development and completion stages. The qualified disciple should supplicate the master to bestow the empower-ment. Then the master promises to do so. If such conditions are present, the empowerment can be given. If it is a major empowerment, it con-tains the preparation and the main part.

What is the preparation? For instance, if one is going to put good food in a container, first that container should be thoroughly cleaned and washed. If the food is put in such a container, it will not spoil. Simi-larly, the mind of the student should be purified so that he will be ready to receive the empowerment. That is like cleaning the container—it is the preparation.

The preparation has three parts: preparing the deity, preparing the student, and preparing the vase. As for the preparation of the deity, for instance, if one wants to invite a government minister, first one must send him an invitation for a certain time on a certain day and request him to do certain things. Similarly, one must inform the deity that at such and such a time he should bestow the empowerment to such and such a student in order to benefit that student. Doing so, the master performs the practice and recitation of the deity and asks permission to bestow the empowerment.

Now let us turn to the preparation of the vase. The main article used in the empowerment is the vase. The vase has to be consecrated; otherwise, it is not proper to give the empowerment. Consecrating the vase is called the preparation of the vase.

After the preparation of the vase, the students successively receive four different things. First they are given a toothstick for purifying obscurations of body. Then they are given the consecrated water for purifying obscurations of speech. Then they are given the five-colored protection cord to purify obscurations of the mind. Finally they are given kusha grass as a token of auspicious connection with the Buddha, who attained enlightenment on a seat of kusha grass. The preparation is conducted the day before the main abhisheka, and as a result of the preparation the students have indications in their dreams of whether or not they are ready to receive the empowerment. The master should explain to the students how precious it is to receive the Buddha's teachings and how extremely fortunate they are to enter the path of the secret mantra. Through his explaining that in the secret-mantra vajrayana, just by seeing the mandala, the womb of rebirth in the lower realms is shut and one's karmic obscurations are purified, the students will develop faith and confidence and look forward to receiving such a profound empowerment. These are the preparatory stages of the empowerment through which the students become suitable vessels.

The stages of the four abhishekas accord with the four classes of tantra of the secret mantra: kriya, upa, yoga, and anuttara. According to kriya tantra, which is the first vehicle of the secret mantra, the abhisheka is given as follows: One visualizes the deity inside the vase. From the deity's body descends amrita, which comes out of the vase. That is the water empowerment. As a sign of the qualities of the five buddhas, the crown empowerment is given. The water empowerment and the crown empowerment are kriya empowerments.

After that, according to upa tantra, besides the water empowerment and the crown empowerment, there is the vajra empowerment, which is the empowerment of the mind of all the buddhas, the essence of bliss and emptiness inseparable. With the words, "Since you have entered the secret mantrayana this will be your name," the students are given the name empowerment of Vairochana. The vajra and name empowerments are upa empowerments.

Then, in yoga tantra there are five empowerments related to the five buddha families. The ordinary five empowerments are the body, speech, mind, quality, and activity aspects of all the buddhas. The buddha of the body category is Vairochana, the buddha of the speech category is Amitabha, the buddha of the mind category is Akshobhya, the buddha of the quality category is Ratnasambhava, and the buddha of the activity category is Amoghasiddhi. To symbolize these five buddhas there are five empowerments. In connection with Akshobhya, one receives water from the vase, which is called the water empowerment of Akshobhya. In connection with Ratnasambhava, one receives the crown, which is called the crown empowerment of Ratnasambhava. In connection with Amitabha, lord of the speech of all the buddhas, one receives the vajra, which is called the vajra empowerment of Amitabha. In connection with Amoghasiddhi, one receives the bell, which is called the bell empowerment of Amoghasiddhi. In connection with Vairochana, one receives the vajra and bell and the secret-mantra name is bestowed; this is called the name empowerment of Vairochana. Besides these five, one receives the empowerment of secret transmission and the concluding completion empowerment. Those are the empowerments of yoga tantra. The above are called the three outer tantras.

Compared with anuttara tantra, the view, meditation, and action and the development and completion stages of these tantras are very limited and not as profound and vast as in anuttara tantra. The two can be compared to the inside and outside of a house: important people such as ministers and so forth stay inside the house, whereas less important people stay outside. Thus kriya, upa, and yoga tantras are called outer tantras. The inner, anuttara tantra consists of father, mother, and nondual tantras. The father tantras are the cycles of Yamantaka and Guhyasamaja, which mainly subdue anger. The mother tantras are the Chakrasamvara and Hevajra tantras. The nondual tantras, which are the unity of the father and mother tantras, are the Kalachakra tantras.

According to the Nyingma tradition of the secret mantra, the ground is mahayoga, the path is anuyoga, and the fruition is atiyoga. Though the names are slightly different, the meaning is the same. In mahayoga the main tantra is the *Guhyagarbha Tantra* [Tib. *Gyütrül Drawa Sangwa Nyingpo*, "Secret Essence of the Illusory Web"], which has the eight classes of auspicious connections of apparent existence and so forth. In anuyoga there is the Tsokchen Düpa empowerment, in which the nine yanas are complete. [These nine yanas differ somewhat from the usual classification. The first yana is the vehicle of celestial beings and humans, followed by the first eight yanas; atiyoga is not included here.] Atiyoga is divided into the outer section on mind [Tib. sem de], the inner section on space [Tib. long de], and the secret section on oral instructions [Tib. men-ngag de]. These are the inner tantras of the secret mantra, the anuttara tantras. The empowerments of the anuttara tantras have the four abhishekas: the vase abhisheka, the secret abhisheka, the prajna-jnana abhisheka, and the word abhisheka.

For the vase abhisheka, as taught in kriya and upa tantra, one visualizes the deity of the mandala inside the vase. By having one's limbs washed during the vase abhisheka, one receives the abhisheka related to the five buddhas. In the secret abhisheka, from the bodies of the deities comes forth bodhichitta, which mixes with the amrita in the skull cup. That is the secret abhisheka. In the prajna-jnana abhisheka, from the heart center of the deity radiates blissful light, which develops the samadhi of bliss and emptiness in one's being. Just as the petals of a flower open when hit by sunlight, the wisdom of bliss and emptiness develops in one's mind when one receives these light rays. That is the prajna-jnana abhisheka. The fourth abhisheka, the word initiation, introduces the student to the nature of mind as it is.

The vase abhisheka should be bestowed with the support of a mandala made of colored sand. If there is no colored-sand mandala, one can use a painting or drawing of the mandala. For the secret abhisheka, the vajra master should visualize his own body as the mandala deity, for example, Chakrasamvara, thinking that in the different places of the body are the dakas and dakinis of the twenty-four sacred places. Thus the abhisheka is bestowed with the support of the vajra master's body. The prajna-jnana abhisheka is bestowed with the support of the bliss of the consort. The word abhisheka is bestowed with the support of absolute wisdom.

What is purified by the vase empowerment? Mainly the obscurations of body are purified. Whatever mandala deity is practiced, the body blessing of that deity will enter one's body. In the secret empowerment, the speech obscurations are purified, and the speech blessings of the mandala deity enter one's speech. In the prajna-jnana abhisheka, one's mind obscurations are purified, and the mind blessings of the mandala deity enter one's mind. In the fourth abhisheka, one's obscurations of body, speech, and mind combined are purified, and the wisdom blessings, which are of the nature of the unity of the body, speech, and mind of the mandala deity, enter one's mind.

Within these empowerments there are many different categories. A very famous major empowerment of the profound tantras is the Kalachakra. According to the view of Kalachakra, there are seven outer empowerments. These seven outer empowerments are like a preparation. For instance, a newly born baby should just suck his mother's milk and not be given solid food. As he grows, he can gradually be given some fruit and sweets. If he is given solid food like rice and meat, he will not be able to digest it. That is like the seven outer stages of the vase empowerment. Subsequently, there are the three inner, worldly empowerments. These are for more advanced students and can be compared to giving grown children rice and meat. They are similar to the above-mentioned secret and prajna-jnana abhishekas. Then there is the empowerment that transcends the world, which is the fourth, or word, abhisheka. That is the empowerment to become Lord Kalachakra, which is only given to those who have the ability to explain the tantras of the secret mantra to others, and is kept secret from other people. So there are eleven empowerments: the seven outer empowerments, the three inner, worldly empowerments, and the empowerment transcending the world. Nowadays these empowerments can be bestowed by His Holiness the Dalai Lama and Lama Kalu Rinpoche.

According to the yoga tradition of the secret mantra, tantra is mahayoga, transmission is anuyoga, and fruition is atiyoga. The main tantra is the *Guhyagarbha Tantra*, which has a peaceful section and a wrathful section. There are forty-two peaceful deities and fifty-eight wrathful blood-drinking deities. The empowerments of these peaceful and wrathful deities are bestowed through the following eighteen abhishekas: the ten outer, beneficial abhishekas, the five inner, energizing abhishekas, and the three secret, profound abhishekas. The ten outer, beneficial abhishekas can be compared to the stages of the vase abhisheka as explained before. There are eighteen different empowerment substances given to the student. As to what is beneficial, for example, if a seed is put in the ground, rain helps the seed to grow. Similarly, initially when the ten outer empowerments are bestowed, they help the student to purify his obscurations and make him a suitable vessel for the empowerment. They prepare him to do the practice of the development and completion stages. That is the benefit of the ten outer abhishekas.

Now let us turn to the five inner, energizing abshishekas. When one plants barley or rice in the ground, that seed has the potential to sprout. In the *Guhyagarbha Tantra*, the five inner, energizing abhishekas are the potential for the seed to develop. What are these five inner, energizing abhishekas? For the student who is only able to practice for his own benefit, there is the empowerment to listen to all the tantras of the secret mantra and the empowerment to practice the samadhi of the development and completion stages. For the student who is able to benefit others, there are two activity empowerments for the pacifying, enriching, magnetizing, and destroying karmas, a minor and a major one. For the student who is able to benefit both himself and others, there is the empowerment that ripens the potential within the stream of being of all sentient beings, which is called the "limitless vajra king transmission."

These outer, beneficial and inner, energizing empowerments will ripen the potential of the empowerment within the stream of all sentient beings, but what is even more profound than those are the three profound, secret abhishekas. In India, if the student had not perfected the development stage of the vase abhisheka, the secret, prajna-jnana, and word abhishekas were not given. When the development stage of the vase abhisheka had been perfected, the secret, prajna-jnana, and word abhishekas were bestowed, and the student was able to practice the completion stages of that mandala: the yogas of chandali, dream, illusory body, bardo, and so forth. The three secret, profound abhishekas enable the student to practice those completion stages. So, according to the tradition of *Guhyagarbha*, there are eighteen empowerments: the ten outer, beneficial empowerments; the five inner, energizing empowerments; and the three secret, profound empowerments.

The transmission of anuyoga has the Tsokchen Dupa empowerment, which is an empowerment for the nine yanas. Bestowing this nine-yana empowerment requires ten outer abhishekas, which are like the vase empowerment. Then there are eleven inner abhishekas, which are the

same as the five inner, energizing empowerments. Then there are thirteen abhishekas that are similar to the three secret, profound empowerments. The Tsokchen Dupa empowerment also has two secret,
completion abhishekas, so altogether there are thirty-six abhishekas in
the inner anuyoga.

In dzogchen, atiyoga, there is a detailed vase abhisheka, a simple secret abhisheka, a very simple, and an extremely simple abhisheka. The
vase, secret, prajna-jnana, and word abhishekas are bestowed with the
support of these four abhishekas. In the tantras of the secret mantra,
these are called the abhishekas orally taught by the guru.

There is also an abhisheka called the empowerment of the yidam's
blessings. When the secret-mantra vajrayana doctrine first appeared in
Jambudvipa, King Ja from the west saw seven wondrous indications in
his dreams. The volumes of the tantras descended on the roof of his
palace, and when he opened them he could understand the meaning of
the chapter on "The Vision of Vajrasattva." After practicing it for six
months he had an actual vision of Vajrasattva, and at that time he understood the meaning of all the tantras. That is the empowerment of the
yidam's blessings.

Then there is the empowerment of the vajradakini's indication. What
is this empowerment? Great siddhas such as Tilopa, Saraha, and Nagarjuna went to the dakini land of Uddiyana and saw the treasure of tantric
books. When they left, they took all the volumes on Chakrasamvara and
others away with them. The dakinis miraculously pursued them to protect the books, but they could not affect them with their miracles, and
they realized that Saraha, Nagarjuna, and so forth were accomplished
masters who could hold and transmit the teachings of the secret-mantra
vajrayana. Then they gave permission and indications on how to give
the empowerments and teachings on the development and completion
stages to qualified students in Jambudvipa. That is the empowerment of
the dakini's indication.

Then there is the empowerment of the intrinsic nature. In regard to
the realization of the inner wisdom of empowerment, the meaning of
the fourth empowerment, it is said, "The supreme empowerment is
something we have by ourselves. If we did not have this supreme empowerment ourselves, it could not be conferred upon us, just as there is
no way of giving the empowerment of a pea to a grain of rice." When
one realizes the intrinsic nature of one's mind, one receives the abhi-

sheka of one's own intrinsic awareness. Thus the abhisheka of the secret mantra is received.

That was a summary of how the empowerments of the Sarma and Nyingma tantric traditions are given, and all these are elaborate empowerments. The four abridged empowerments can be given just with the support of a vase or a torma. Yesterday I gave the Secret Essence Vajrasattva [Tib. Sangthik Dorsem] abhisheka with the support of the vase only. In the empowerment of the Guru Ladrup, the four abhishekas are bestowed with the support of the torma only. Then there is the empowerment of the blessings of body, speech, and mind, which is like a permission, and the empowerment of the mantra while focusing the awareness. All these empowerments still exist without having been distorted.

All the special students gathered here probably have received the empowerment of Vajrayogini or Chakrasamvara from Trungpa Rinpoche and have confidence in that. Now you will receive the empowerments of the Embodiment of the Three Jewels [Tib. Könchok Chidu] and the Three Roots of the Heart Essence [Tib. Nyingthik Tsa Sum], both of which have the four levels of abhisheka. If you have understood the meaning of empowerment a little bit, when you receive it you will know the mantra and enter in clearly. During the empowerment you should think:

> This is the vase empowerment. The body blessings are entering my mind, and broken samaya related to body is being amended. This is the secret empowerment. The speech blessings are entering my speech, broken samaya related to speech is being amended, and I can attain the sambhogakaya. This is the prajnajnana empowerment. The mind blessings are entering my mind, broken samaya related to mind is being amended, and I can attain the nirmanakaya. This is the fourth empowerment. I am being introduced to the nature of my mind. All broken samayas related to body, speech, and mind are being amended simultaneously, and the guru's wisdom mind is mingling with my mind.

As the guru gives the student the various empowerment substances during the empowerment, if the student recognizes and has confidence in all these stages, it will be very beneficial. That was a brief explanation of empowerment.

THE DEVELOPMENT STAGE

When one's being has been ripened by the empowerment, one should practice the path of the development and completion stages. Generally, sentient beings in the three worlds of existence are caught up in the phenomena of birth, death, and the state in between. In the secret-mantra vajrayana, which deals with the fruition, phenomena of birth are the nirmanakaya, phenomena of death are the dharmakaya, and phenomena of the state in between are the sambhogakaya. One trains in these three states as the nature of the three buddha kayas.

In this world of existence there are the relative and the absolute truth, and all phenomena are understood in terms of these two truths. On the path of the secret mantra, the relative truth is the development stage and the absolute truth is the completion stage. Of those two, the more profound is the completion stage. But if the development stage is not practiced before the completion stage, the completion stage will not be beneficial. And if someone wanting to practice the secret mantra does not receive empowerment, he cannot practice the development stage. Once he has received empowerment, he can practice the development stages. The preparation for the development stage is empowerment. When one has properly practiced the development stage, one can receive the teachings on the completion stage. So the preparation for the completion stage is the development stage. When one has perfected the completion stage, one has accomplished the result.

The development stage deals with the relative truth, relative appearances, such as this world, the outer universe, the inner inhabitants, and the emotions. Sentient beings have perceptions of a place, a body, and an experience. Regarding the perceptions of a place, if it is the hell realm, beings perceive it as hot or cold. If it is the preta realm, they perceive ugly, barren places that are frightening. If it is the animal realm, they perceive the great ocean, water, grass, woods, and so forth. If it is the human realm, they perceive their different homes. If it is the asura realm, they perceive different palaces and wish-fulfilling trees. If it is the god realm, they perceive the wish-fulfilling tree on top of Mount Meru, the jewel ground, and so forth. That is the place.

Within those places are the bodies of the sentient beings of the six realms. If there were just a body without a mind, the body could not function. When body and mind are together, body and speech follow the mind like a servant, and in that way beings create karma. With the support of body and mind, beings perform positive and negative actions. That is called deluded perception.

How did these perceptions become deluded? The universe and its inhabitants do not really exist. They are like a rainbow in the sky, but we hold onto them as if they existed. Also, we hold onto death as something that does not exist and cling to the idea that this body will last a long time. Thus we hold onto what is impermanent as permanent and cling to an ego where there is no ego. To someone who is drunk with wine it seems as though the ground is turning around, but that is just his drunken perception. The ground is not turning. In the same way, we hold on to the appearances of the universe, its inhabitants, and emotions as things that exist, whereas in reality they do not exist. They are our delusion. The outer universe—Mount Meru, the continents, and subcontinents; its inhabitants—the beings of the six realms; and the five poisons—the conflicting emotions—should be purified through the development stage.

To purify these delusions through the development stage, first one should purify the universe. The universe is gradually formed as follows: at the bottom, there is space; upon that, wind; upon that, fire; upon that, water; upon that, the ground; and upon that, Mount Meru with the ocean. If there were no empty space, it would not be possible to create this. When the universe is destroyed, it dissolves again into empty space; it never goes beyond the nature of empty space. As their nature does not transcend that of empty space, the universe and its inhabitants are created from empty space, and from that arise enjoyment and happiness. Since empty space is infinitely vast, there is no chance of the universe not fitting into empty space or of space being jammed full with the appearances of the universe and its contents. If there were no space, the universe could not appear.

With the support of emptiness, the universe and its contents appear, but they cannot appear based just on emptiness. It is because of interdependent connection that we perceive the universe and its inhabitants, even though its nature is emptiness. For instance, in the summer the land is warm from the sun, there is cool rain, flowers grow, and everything seems pleasant. In the winter the land is frozen, there is cold wind, and everything seems unpleasant. All this is due to interdependent causes and conditions. Similarly, the formation and destruction of the universe and its contents is due to the interdependent connection of cause and condition. If there are no parents, there cannot be a child; in the same way, everything is dependent on cause and condition. If many causes and conditions come together, something is created.

When the five elements—earth, water, fire, wind, and space—come together, earth ripens, water dissolves, fire warms, wind moves, and the four seasons are formed in the universe. Similarly, in our body, flesh and bones are the earth element, blood and lymph are the water element, the warmth of our body is the fire element, the breath inside our body is the wind element, and the space in between is the space element. So the body is formed through the gathering of the five elements. In this body formed through the elements, there is a mind. When many instants gather, that mind perceives past, present, and future thoughts.

When all causes and conditions are destroyed, there will be absolutely nothing. When there is appearance, for someone who has realized emptiness, whatever he perceives dissolves into emptiness, like a rainbow dissolving into space. If one looks at a rainbow in the sky, one sees a beautiful appearance of five colors, but if one were to try to grasp it, or use it to wear or eat, that would be futile. It can be seen, but it is empty. Similarly, all the appearances of the universe and its contents are empty. There is nothing beyond emptiness.

THE THREE SAMADHIS

The Samadhi of Suchness

In the Nyingma tradition of the secret mantra, the meditation of the development stage is practiced by means of the three samadhis. When meditating on the three samadhis, one starts with the samadhi of suchness. The samadhi of suchness is of the nature of emptiness. As I said before, the universe, its contents, and the emotions are all based on emptiness. To explain the nature of form: if there is no dharmakaya of the buddha, there is no sambhogakaya or nirmanakaya. If the dharmakaya of the buddha, the stainless inconceivable dharmadhatu, is there, when the inconceivable buddha qualities are gathered, the sambhogakaya manifests from that dharmadhatu. When the compassion of the sambhogakaya is moved for the sake of sentient beings, the nirmanakaya manifests. In that way, suchness samadhi comes from emptiness, the dharmakaya.

Now we have a body and a mind, we are comfortable and happy, we have friends and enemies, and we cling to having all that. We think all of that exists and hold onto it, but it does not really exist, and that grasping is delusion. To destroy that clinging one should meditate on emptiness. According to the hinayana tradition, the Buddha Shakyamuni taught that all compounded things are impermanent. In that way, the nature of emptiness could be understood. In the mahayana tradition, all phenomena are understood in terms of the three doors of liberation: the nature is emptiness, the path is free of characteristics, and the fruition is beyond expectation. On the path of the secret-mantra vajrayana, when total emptiness is mentioned during the development stage, that is the samadhi of suchness.

Unless the emptiness nature of the mind is realized, we cannot really understand the completion stage, and yet the method for realizing this emptiness nature is the very practice of the completion stage itself. So how should we meditate on emptiness during the development stage? At the beginning of most development-stage practices, one recites the mantra OM MAHASHUNYATA-JNANA-VAJRA-SVABHAVA-ATMAKO 'HAM. If this mantra is not there, one can recite A at the time of developing the samadhi of suchness. As we recite that mantra at the beginning of the suchness samadhi, all phenomena—our perceptions of the universe and its inhabitants and all other experiences—become completely empty, like a rainbow fading in the sky. If you firmly apprehend that all this is empty, the mind will experience a glimpse of emptiness. Recognizing this experience is called the samadhi of suchness.

If we ask what is the form of that samadhi of suchness, the buddha's dharmakaya does not have a face, arms, substance, or characteristics. The buddha's dharmakaya pervades the whole of samsara and nirvana. There are no samsaric karma and defilements outside of the dharmakaya. There is no nirvanic kaya or jnana outside of the dharmakaya. There is no such thing as samsara's dharmakaya being bad and nirvana's dharmakaya being good. Taking empty space as an analogy, the sun and moon above are pervaded by space, and the earth below is pervaded by space. The universe and its contents are all pervaded by space. All places where beings stay are pervaded by space. In the same way, there is nothing in samsara or nirvana that is not pervaded by emptiness. Since mind is empty, to understand its nature, the nature of that emptiness should be recognized. If there is no dharmakaya buddha, we cannot see the sambhogakaya and the nirmanakaya. That is why we have to meditate on the samadhi of suchness.

What is the use of meditating on the universe and its contents as emptiness? According to the Nyingma tradition, the Early Translation School, each of the three samadhis has three stages: purity, perfection, and ripening. Regarding purity: When someone dies, the universe and its contents are perceived as empty. His life force is cut, his mind wanders in the bardo, and his corpse is cremated. Not even his name remains. Everything becomes empty. That is the emptiness we should train in. Getting used to that emptiness is the samadhi of suchness. If we get used to the phenomena of death through the samadhi of suchness, the wisdom of dharmakaya will be realized. When we are meditating on the completion stage, we should know that the completion stage is a method for realizing emptiness, the samadhi of suchness. As is said, "Whoever is capable of realizing shunyata is capable of everything." When emptiness is realized, there is nothing more to realize, and taking that emptiness nature as the path is the purity.

When we rest in the nature of that emptiness, the qualities of the buddha's dharmakaya are perfected. That is the perfection.

When meditating on emptiness while practicing the completion stage, one has experiences of bliss, clarity, and nonthought. That is the ripening. Of those three, the experience of nonthought is also the samadhi of suchness.

The samadhi of suchness is the main meditation throughout all levels. At the time of fruition, it is the dharmakaya, and at the impure stage it transforms the universe and its contents into emptiness. Of the phenomena of birth, death, and bardo, it is a way of purifying the phenomena of death. It is important to understand this vital point of the samadhi of suchness.

The All-Illuminating Samadhi

It is not possible to attain liberation through emptiness alone. The essence of emptiness is compassion, and that compassion is called the all-illuminating samadhi, something that appears outside. In emptiness, there is no such thing as something that appears and something that makes things appear. It is one emptiness. When compassion arises from that state, it is called the all-illuminating samadhi.

How does one practice the all-illuminating samadhi? First one should recite the shunyata mantra and think that everything—the universe and its contents—is empty. Within that emptiness nature, thinking that all phenomena of samsara and nirvana are empty, one should generate compassion toward all sentient beings who have not realized shunyata. Thinking that in order to guide all sentient beings toward the realization of emptiness one will practice the samadhi of the yidam deity is the all-illuminating samadhi. It is not possible for beginners to have nonconceptual compassion. They have to have the concept of benefiting sentient beings.

Compassion is the life force of the mahayana path. Whether it is the mahayana path of characteristics or the mahayana path of the secret-mantra vajrayana, if there is no bodhichitta, it cannot be called mahayana. The root of bodhichitta is compassion toward sentient beings. As the Buddha Shakyamuni said, "Someone who has a head has eyes, ears, a nose, a mouth, a tongue, and a whole body. If he has no head, the body will be useless, since it cannot function." Similarly, if those on the mahayana path have no compassion, it cannot be the real mahayana path. Generating compassion in one's being is called the all-illuminating samadhi. While all buddhas abide in the expanse of dharmadhatu, they look after all sentient beings by means of the unity of emptiness and compassion. They never abide in emptiness for their own benefit. When sentient beings fall into delusion, the qualities of the buddhas manifest through the power of compassion. Compassion should be brought forth like dawn appearing when the sky is grey at daybreak.

When meditating on compassion, what is being purified? At death, when body and mind separate, first, as the elements dissolve, our eyes stop seeing, our ears stop hearing, our mouth and nose stop breathing, and our body stops feeling. Everything stops. As everything stops, we arrive at the ground, emptiness. Having arrived at that emptiness nature, if we could remain in that state we would attain enlightenment. But we will not be able to remain in that emptiness. As soon as we arrive at that emptiness, we fall back into delusion.

When we get used to the dharmakaya samadhi of suchness, great compassion toward beings who have not realized the dharmakaya samadhi arises. Through this samadhi, we purify the bardo phenomenon of falling back into delusion from the ground nature.

The nonconceptual compassion of the buddhas pervades all beings.

When the buddhas manifest as the sambhogakaya, having manifested sambhogakaya buddhafields with the five perfect aspects—the perfect place, the perfect time, the perfect teaching, the perfect teacher, and the perfect students—there is no more passing into nirvana and dissolving of buddhafields. The sambhogakaya buddhafield emanations naturally manifest for the benefit of sentient beings—that is called compassion.

As for meditating on the completion stage, it is not sufficient to only meditate on emptiness. That emptiness must have a luminosity aspect, and that luminosity aspect is compassion. When the concept of benefiting beings arises in one's mind, that is the luminosity aspect, the compassion of one who is a practitioner on the path. When the phenomena of birth are purified, even if one has attained perfect enlightenment, emanations will manifest continuously. When buddhas pass into nirvana, as they abide in the dharmakaya expanse, they manifest emanations for the benefit of sentient beings. It never happens that the buddhas do not appear.

What is being purified by this samadhi? When body and mind separate and one arrives in the ground nature, there is the obscuration that leads one to fall back into delusion in the bardo. That is being purified. What is perfected? In that state, the sambhogakaya buddha qualities are perfected. What is ripened? In the completion stage, there are experiences of bliss, luminosity, and nonthought. That luminosity nature is being ripened. The completion stage is its ripening. When purity, perfection, and ripening are complete, that is the actual mahayana path as-it-is. That is called the all-illuminating samadhi or perfectly manifesting samadhi.

The Seed Samadhi

The third samadhi is called the seed samadhi. We should practice the seed samadhi in the state of the unity of emptiness and compassion. What is this seed samadhi? When practicing the development stage and creating the support of the buddha palace and the deities, the seed syllable from which all that manifests is called the seed samadhi. The union of emptiness and compassion, the nature of the mind, is a samadhi without form. In the seed samadhi, there is a form. Just as consciousness is the source of body and speech, through which we can experience the phenomenal world, similarly, the buddhas manifest through the seed syllable, which transforms into the buddhafields and the deities. So, it is called the seed samadhi because from it the palace and deities manifest.

What do we visualize in the seed samadhi? Emptiness, which clears away the phenomenal world, and compassion, which arises for all beings who have not realized emptiness, are inseparable. Going to the core of compassion, we come to emptiness. There is no compassion other than emptiness. This nondual essence of emptiness and compassion takes the form of a seed syllable. For instance, if one is meditating on a deity of the vajra family, one visualizes the syllable HUM. If one is meditating on a deity of the speech family, one visualizes the syllable AH. If one is meditating on a deity of the body family, one visualizes the syllable OM. That is called the seed samadhi. Though the form is the seed syllable, the essence is the wisdom of the knowledge, compassion, and power of the deity. It is not just a syllable like the ones we write down. It is not some solid syllable. It is the essence of the buddha's mind.

How do we meditate on this seed syllable? After having purified the universe and its contents into emptiness, one should think the syllable HUM arises in empty space, like the moon shining in the sky. If the deity is blue in color, the HUM is blue. If the deity is white in color, the HUM is white. The white HUM shining like a moon in the sky is called the seed samadhi.

Regarding falling into delusion during the bardo, when the phenomena of the bardo start, there is a mind. That mind is supported by the mental body of the bardo. The experience of that mental body is like when we dream and feel as if we are moving around from place to place, although the physical body is not doing anything. During the bardo, we have a similar experience. In order to purify the bardo phenomena we practice the seed samadhi.

What is the benefit of meditating on this seed samadhi? We can see this with reference to doing the practices of Chakrasamvara, Vajrayogini, Vajrasattva, and so forth. For instance, when we meditate on Chakrasamvara, we first visualize the syllable HUM. When we meditate on Vajrayogini, we first visualize the syllable VAM. When we meditate on Guru Rinpoche, we visualize the syllable HRIH. When we meditate on Vajrasattva, we visualize the syllable HUM. That visualization symbolizes consciousness. What does it purify? It purifies the obscurations of the consciousness wandering in the bardo. That is why we visualize the syllable HUM. It should be visualized the color of the deity we are meditating on. HUM is the essence of the wisdom mind of all the bud-dhas. What does it purify? The obscurations of the being wandering in the bardo, the obscurations leading to taking rebirth, are purified. What is it that purifies? The essence of the buddhas' wisdom mind does the purifying. The reason that this purification can occur is this: Just as when many syllables are gathered one can recite mantras with these syllables and point out the dharma and the phenomena of samsara and nirvana, so from the seed syllables of the buddhas, mandalas can emanate and gather.

The nature of HUM is the essence of the buddhas' life. Of the three buddha kayas, the seed syllable represents the nirmanakaya. The HUM emanates the support of the buddha palace and the deities; that is what makes it the seed samadhi. When the nirmanakayas of the thousand buddhas come to this world, first each displays a buddhafield in this uni-verse and then the buddha manifests. Let us take the pure land of Ami-tabha, the Sukhavati in the west. First, through the aspirations and samadhi of the buddha, the buddhafield Sukhavati manifests and then the buddha Amitabha comes. So, what manifests the buddhafields and buddhas is the seed samadhi, which symbolizes the nature of the nirma-nakaya buddhas.

What is being purified? The obscurations that make one take rebirth while wandering in the bardo are being purified. The essence of that which purifies is the syllable HUM. The HUM, visualized in empty space, is the lord of the wisdom of all buddhas. What is purified by that? The obscurations of beings in the bardo leading them to take rebirth are puri-fied. What qualities are perfected? The qualities of the nirmanakaya bud-dhas are perfected. What is ripened? When practicing the completion stage, when the inseparable essence of bliss and emptiness, the samadhi of the wisdom of nonthought, develops in one's mind, the absolute coemergent wisdom, the mahamudra, the dzogpa chenpo—that wisdom—is born. The seed samadhi is the seed of developing that wisdom. For this to ripen, certain conditions are necessary. When a seed is planted in the ground, three conditions are necessary for it to ripen: summer, good soil, and rain. If those three conditions are present there will be good fruit. Similarly, the prerequisite preparation for the completion stage is the development stage. The development stage prepares one for the completion stage. Thus, when one starts to practice the basic samadhi of the seed syllable, light radiates from the seed syllable and creates the vajra protection tent. Then gradually the different elements are created. On the layers of the elements, one visualizes the development process.

There are four ways that beings take birth in this world: through parents and from a womb; from an egg; from warmth and moisture; or miraculously, without the fluid and blood of parents, like the gods. In regard to the development stage, birth from an egg corresponds to a very elaborate development-stage process, in which one visualizes by means of the causal and the fruition heruka. In regard to birth from warmth and moisture, when these two come together, beings are created. This can occur in a forest during the summer: when it is hot and it rains, insects are born. In the development-stage process corresponding to birth from warmth and moisture, habits related to that kind of birth are purified. In birth from an egg, first the egg is born from the mother and then through the warmth of the mother the being is formed. In miraculous birth, as in the celestial realms, the consciousness enters a lotus flower and then the body is formed. In the development-stage process corresponding to birth from an egg, one visualizes the causal heruka and the fruition heruka. First the egg is born from the mother, and then the being is formed from the egg, like a double birth. When the elaborate explanation of that is given, we talk about the five phases of purifying and developing and the three vajra ritual visualizations. In the development-stage process corresponding to birth from warmth and moisture, the suchness samadhi, the all-illuminating samadhi, and the seed samadhi are perfected instantly. One does not need to visualize the causal heruka and the fruition heruka. In the development-stage process corresponding to miraculous birth, there are four levels of visualization, which are instantly remembered and perfected. Through these four levels of visualization, the support is gradually stabilized. That is the seed samadhi.

These three samadhis are the basis for practicing the samadhi of the development stage. Regarding the purpose of developing the support of the mandala and the deities: For instance, a man has a perception of his house and possessions and people around. Through meditation on the seed syllable and its manifestation of the buddha palace and the deities, these habitual tendencies can be purified. In order to purify these habitual tendencies toward existence, we visualize the syllable HUM from which light radiates, making offerings to the buddhas and bodhisattvas and then gathering back their body, speech, and mind blessings. Then the light radiates again, touching all sentient beings and purifying their karmic obscurations. Then again it dissolves back into the syllable.

Then the light rays emanate the syllable BHRUM. This syllable BHRUM is composed of five parts, symbolizing the five wisdoms of all the buddhas. The buddha palace is manifested by Ushnisha-chakravartin. When Ushnisha-chakravartin was a bodhisattva performing enlightened activities, he made the aspiration that when he attained perfect buddhahood, the wisdom of his mind would manifest as the fields and palaces of all the buddhas, which are in essence the nature of Vairochana. Our human palaces are made of earth and stone, but buddha palaces manifest from the play of wisdom. They are pervaded by wisdom, and there is nothing solid to them. The BHRUM is yellow in color and emanates the five colors. From the BHRUM, the syllables of the different elements emanate, such as E YAM RAM SUM and so forth, gradually building up the elements below the buddha palace.

On that foundation, we visualize the protection circle made of many different vajras of different sizes. Upon that, in some sadhanas we visualize the eight charnal grounds; in some sadhanas there are no charnel grounds. If there are eight charnel grounds, in some sadhanas they are inside, and in some sadhanas outside, the protection circle.

Within those eight charnel grounds we visualize a thirty-two-petaled lotus, which symbolizes the thirty-two major marks of a buddha. Upon the lotus is a green sun disk: because the lotus stalk is green and the sun is like crystal, it reflects the color green. Upon that is a multicolored vajra with twelve prongs, three in the east, three in the south, three in the west, and three in the north. There are also vajras with twenty prongs.

The center of the vajra is square, and within that square, one visualizes the buddha palace. If it is a peaceful buddha palace, as a sign of the five wisdoms there are the walls of five layers, as well as the corners, the roof, the pendants, the vajra on top, and so forth. If it is a wrathful buddha palace, it has walls of three layers, made of human heads. In the center of the buddha palace is a lotus and a sun or moon disk. If the deity is wrathful, it is a sun disk; if the deity is peaceful, it is a moon disk. Upon that appears the syllable HUM. From that, light rays radiate, which make offerings to the buddhas and gather their blessings back into the HUM. Again light rays emanate to all sentient beings, purify their obscurations, and are gathered back into the HUM. Then, if the sadhana goes through the five phases of purifying and developing, the HUM transforms into a five-pronged vajra, which transforms into the deity, such as Vajra-sattva, Chakrasamvara, Chemchok, and so on. From the deity's heart center radiate light rays, which transform into the retinue, such as the five buddhas, the ten wrathful ones, and so on. That is called the meditation on the deity mandala in the support of the buddha palace.

First the buddha palace is visualized from the outside toward the inside: the protection circle, the fire, the charnel grounds, and so on. The deity is visualized from the inside toward the outside: first the main deity and from that the retinue manifests.

What is purified by this manifestation? The habitual tendencies toward houses, land, and possessions that are part of human existence in this world are purified through meditation on the buddha palace. The habitual tendencies toward people, parents and children, are purified by meditation on the deities. When the buddhas miraculously manifest the pure lands, each buddha manifests his own buddhafield, with a buddha palace, a bodhi tree, a temple with monks, and his own students. For instance, Buddha Shakyamuni has his disciples Shariputra and Maudgal-yayana, the sixteen arhats, and so forth. If our mind becomes accustomed to the buddhas' actions now, that is dealing with the fruition. In that way, the obscurations of the three worlds of samsara, the universe and its contents, are purified.

In the completion stage, the body is most important: the body is the buddha palace, and the nadis and bindus are the deities. Through the habit of visualizing the deities, by the ripening of that potential, habitual tendencies toward samsara are exhausted. Bringing the nirmanakaya buddha's manifestations of buddhafields and buddha palaces to the path purifies the obscurations of habitual tendencies toward samsara. In the meditation on the mandala of the deity in the completion stage, oneself as the mandala deity is called the samayasattva.

In the development stage, from the heart center of the deity light rays radiate, and from the pure lands the buddhas and bodhisattvas are invited in the form of the same deity. That which is invited is the jnana-sattva. Then the jnanasattva dissolves into the visualized deity, and they become inseparable. Just as when we have invited an important guest, we offer him food and pay respect, similarly, at this point, from our heart center we emanate many offering goddesses who prostrate, make offerings, and sing verses of praise. That is the meditation of the development stage, using the body as the path, which purifies obscurations of the body.

Since we not only have a body, but also speech and mind, in order to purify obscurations of speech, in the heart center of the deity we visualize a seed syllable from which light rays radiate. They purify obscurations of speech. All these appearances manifest from emptiness and have no real existence. This is like when the buddhas manifest buddha fields and then pass into nirvana. For instance, when Buddha Shakyamuni taught King Indrabhuti the teachings of Guhyasamaja, he first manifested the complete mandala of Guhyasamaja and then taught the tantra. After he had taught the tantra, as the emanation dissolved, the Guhyasamaja mandala with the buddha palace dissolved back into emptiness. Similarly, what we have visualized should be dissolved. The reason why it should be dissolved is that once we are born we have to die, and this dissolving purifies that impure habitual pattern. Manifesting and dissolving the buddhafields corresponds to using the buddhas' activities to progress on the path.

What is the benefit of meditating on the yoga of the nadis, prana, and bindu in the completion stage? Our mind is able to realize the wisdom of emptiness. Realizing the wisdom of emptiness is a preliminary for ripening. Thus, the universe dissolves into the contents, the beings; the contents, the beings, dissolve into the palace; the palace dissolves into the retinue; the retinue dissolves into the main deity; the deity dissolves into the mantra; the mantra dissolves into the seed syllable at the heart center; the seed syllable dissolves into emptiness; and then one rests the mind in the state of emptiness. That is called the completion stage of the samadhi of suchness.

This has been a brief explanation of the development stage, using form as the path to purify the habitual tendencies of birth. When we actually start to practice a sadhana, we will be able to get the elaborate instructions from our own teacher and understand them.

In practicing the development stage, at the beginning we should always have the thought of bodhichitta; in the middle, we should do the main practice of the development stage with one-pointed concentration; and in the end we should dedicate the merit to all sentient beings. Thus applying the root of the mahayana path, the three excellences, the ordinary and supreme siddhis of the development stage, the root of the secret-mantra path, will be attained.

If we practice the development stage according to the Sarma, or New Translation School, the universe and its contents are purified into emptiness, and from the state of emptiness the seed syllable manifests. There is no mention of the three samadhis. The three samadhis are a speciality of the development stage according to the Nyingma tradition. Practicing in this way will be a great benefit to your mind.

TWO

The First Three Bardos

THIS MORNING I talked about the ripening empowerments and the development stage of the secret-mantra vajrayana path. This afternoon I shall give detailed instructions on the completion stage. As I told you before, the development stage is dealing with the relative truth of all phenomena. Working with the appearances of relative truth—the universe and its contents, the buddha palace, the deities, light rays radiating from the mantra, and so forth—is using the relative truth as the path.

The completion stage is dealing with the absolute truth of phenomena. What does dealing with the absolute truth mean? When the uncontrived innate nature, the intrinsic nature, is controlled by samadhi, that is called yoga. In that way, the uncontrived innate nature is brought to the path. To bring the uncontrived innate nature to the path, one should meditate according to the nature of the absolute truth. The development stage is the preparation for the completion stage. The completion stage consists of the six vajra yogas: chandali, illusory body, dream, luminosity, bardo, and transference.

In the Nyingma tradition of the secret mantra, there are six bardos. The teachings on these six bardos are not different from those on the six yoga of the completion stage. The six bardos are the bardo of this life, the bardo of dying, the bardo of dharmata, the bardo of becoming, the bardo of dream, and the bardo of meditation. *Bardo* means the intermediate state between two bodies, when one body is done with and the next one is not yet born. If one is going somewhere, the state after leaving one's country and before arriving at the place one is going to is also called bardo. It is a state in which one has no control.

THE BARDO OF THIS LIFE

The first bardo is the bardo of this life [Tib. kye-ne bardo], which is the state between birth from the mother's womb and the moment of death. One might think that this state is not the bardo, because it lasts a long time compared with the bardo after death, which may only last an instant. Beginning with the moment of birth from the mother's womb, one is pushed by the power of one's karma. If one has accumulated positive actions, one will have a long life without disease, and one's work will be successful. If one has accumulated negative actions, one will have a short life with many diseases, and one's work will not be successful. One will meet enemies, one's wealth will diminish, and one will experience much suffering. Everything happens according to the karma one has accumulated from past lives. One might want to be happy and comfortable, but one does not have the control necessary to avoid the suffering resulting from one's past actions.

How should we deal with the bardo of this life? With the support of the ripening empowerments and the liberating instructions on the development and completion stages that I explained before, we should use this life as path. When we are born, as a baby we suck our mother's milk and sit on her lap. As we grow up, we start to walk and talk and have concepts about beautiful and ugly, good and bad. As we grow older, about twenty or thirty years old, if we have harmful enemies, we want to repay that harm. If we have beneficial friends, we want to repay that benefit. If we have wealth, we want to hoard it. Whatever work we want to do—work in the fields, work as a businessman, as an artist, or whatever—we can train to do that. As our body is being trained to do that work, we have no concept of impermanence. Since we never think about death, we never think about the holy dharma. When we think about this worldly existence only, we are distracted by our actions. While we are distracted by worldly actions, death can suddenly come upon us. Whether we are good or bad, there is no way to escape death. Even if we are very wealthy, we will have to die and leave behind all our wealth. Even if we are young and beautiful, we have no power over death and will have to leave our body behind. At death we will have great regret. But that regret comes too late.

If we had any certainty about when death will come, for instance, if we knew for sure that we had another fifty years to live, we could plan to work for this life for twenty-five years and then practice the dharma for twenty-five years. But we will never have that certainty. If we consider how many of our friends and relatives have died at a young age from the time we were born until now, how many of them have died while working, how many of them have died in the middle of all sorts of projects, and how many of them have died at war, we can see that there is no certainty whatsoever about how long we will live. When we know that death will come, we realize that the only thing that can help us is the holy dharma.

When death comes, if we have understood the dharma, it will not cause us any suffering. For the true practitioner, death is a way to experience the dharmakaya. If a very wealthy man has to go somewhere distant, he does not have to worry, because he can stay comfortably anywhere and die in luxury. Similarly, if we have practiced the dharma, we have the confidence of our dharma practice, so there is nothing to worry about when death comes.

What is it that protects us from the fears of death? Practicing the development stage as I explained before, meditating on oneself as the yidam deity, by practicing the mudra yoga of the body in the development stage, the mantra yoga of the speech recitation, and the suchness yoga of the mind in the completion stage purifies our obscurations of body, speech, and mind. If we attain inseparability of our body, speech, and mind from those of the yidam, whether it be Chakrasamvara, Vajrayogini, or Vajrasattva, through the power of that attainment, when the suffering of death comes we will have the confidence that through meditating on our yidam, we will overcome that suffering. Thus there will be no fear of death.

If we do not practice the dharma, when the time of death comes, it will be like taking a hair out of butter: only the hair, no butter or oil, comes out. Similarly, when the time of death comes, we have to leave everything except for our mind and the positive and negative actions we have committed in this lifetime. We have to leave our body, our friends and relatives, and our wealth and possessions. If we exert ourselves in practicing the yoga of the deity, the mantra, and the dharmakaya, we will not have any fear of leaving all that. As the incomparable Takpo Rinpoche said:

The best practitioners will realize the dharmakaya state at death. Middle-level practitioners can use death as the path and avoid birth in samsara with the support of the instructions on ejecting consciousness. Lower-level practitioners will have the confidence that through their practice of the yidam deity they will not go to the lower realms.

Thus, in bringing the bardo of this life to the path by practicing the development and completion stages, one should first listen, reflect, and meditate on the teachings properly, and after having understood them, one should develop experience. One should remember that when the suffering of death comes, through the power of practicing the path, one does not have to be afraid of that suffering. If one acquires that confidence, one will know that the illusory perceptions of the bardo of this life are impermanent. If one brings that impermanence to the path, purifying impure perceptions through the yogas of the deity, mantra, and dharmakaya, when pure perceptions appear, one will not be controlled by the terrifying illusory perceptions of samsara. If one practices well meditating on one's yidam deity, when one thinks that the bardo of this life is over and death is about to come, one will have the confidence that, when the terrifying appearances manifest in the bardo, by supplicating one's yidam deity, one will have an actual vision of one's yidam deity and he will guide one to the buddhafield. If one has that confidence, one has perfected the bardo of this life.

The best way to perfect the bardo of this life is to attain the ordinary and supreme siddhis in this very body, actually have a vision of one's yidam deity, and become inseparable from the body, speech, and mind of one's yidam deity. But even if that is not the case, it is sufficient to have achieved the confidence mentioned above. So that is how one should deal with the bardo of this life.

THE BARDO OF DYING

After that, one arrives in the bardo of dying. The bardo of dying starts when one gets a terminal illness and ends when one's breath stops. At the time of death, the yogin will know that the time has come. There are two types of death: premature death, when one's life span has not been completed, and timely death, when one's life span has been exhausted. Premature death can be avoided through rituals and mantras to prolong life. Timely death cannot be avoided. Even Buddha Shakyamuni and great siddhas of the past had to go when their life spans had been exhausted. Very courageous beings and kings with great wealth all have to go when their life spans are exhausted. They have no control over death. Everyone has to listen to the Lord of Death; there is no way to avoid or deceive him.

What will we think when death comes? First, when we become ill with a terminal disease, we will think, "I have to leave my parents, children, friends, and relatives. I have so much wealth and so many possessions and I have to leave it all behind. I cannot finish my business, so my wealth will not increase, and my children will use it up and waste it. When I die, the pleasant experiences of this life will be over, my body will be cremated, and my consciousness will go to the bardo, where there is only suffering." Thus we will be very upset.

A good practitioner will not feel upset about leaving anything behind. Guru Rinpoche said that when the time of death has come, even the king of the gods, Indra, does not have the power to avoid it. Even the king of wealth, Jambhala, will have to leave behind all his wealth when his life span is exhausted. He has no way of avoiding death. That is how powerful the Lord of Death is.

When a practitioner becomes ill with a terminal disease, he should think:

I am not going to be able to recover. Until now I have been able to rely on my teacher. I have entered the path of the Buddha's doctrine and have practiced the instructions. What was the reason for all that? I have been very carefully prepared for the suffering of dying. Now that it has come, I need instructions, just as someone who is sick needs medicine and someone who is thirsty needs water. It is useless to be attached to anything in this life, such as children and relatives, friends, my home, possessions, and so forth. Being attached to them will only upset me when I have to leave them behind, and that will not help me on the path of liberation. Whatever possessions I have I should offer to the sangha and to my spiritual friends, as when a person leaving for a faraway place gets rid of whatever he has.

We should wait for death as if a guest were coming. It is like training a soldier: He is given food, drink, and clothing, but it is when the enemy arrives that he is needed. In the same way, the practice of the dharma is needed at the time of death. One thinks, "When I die, I should not die like an ordinary being, but I should go to the buddhafields, such as Sukhavati or the Copper-Colored Mountain." This is like a son returning to his father's home or a daughter returning to her mother's home: they will arrive there without any doubt.

We should think that our teacher abides inseparably from Guru Rinpoche or Amitabha in their buddhafields and we are returning to the buddhafields to join him. We should think that it is much better to join our teacher in the buddhafields than to stay in this world and experience happiness, illness, friends and enemies, and so forth, because in the buddhafields there is no attachment or hatred, and everyone is happy. Since the buddhafield is a very happy place, if we have received instructions on the bardo of dying, giving up all attachment to this life, we should make the wish to apply the instructions one-pointedly.

If we cannot remember the instructions because of illness, we should request a close vajra brother or sister to remind us of the instructions at the moment of death. The spiritual friend should tell us not to be afraid of appearances in the bardo. He should remind us that they are our own perceptions and that we must remember the guru's instructions. Applying the instructions at the moment of death is like an actress looking in a mirror to check her makeup: At the moment of death our practice instructions that are unclear should be brought to mind.

One-pointedly remembering our teacher, we should maintain the unaltered natural state of mind and regard it as inseparable from our teacher. In that way, the teacher is not outside of oneself, but inseparable from our own mind. Since oneself and one's mind are beyond union and separation, wishing never to be separate from our teacher even for an instant, if we are able to remain in the view, we should watch the unaltered nature of mind. If we cannot see the unaltered nature, we should remember Guru Rinpoche or Amitabha and think that they are the nature of our mind, inseparable from one's teacher.

When the signs of death appear, such as the breath stopping and the eyes turning upward, and relatives in the room start to talk a lot, we should visualize our root teacher in our heart center as Amitabha, the yidam Vajrayogini, or Chakrasamvara. We should one-pointedly concentrate on that and recite our mantra. If the elements dissolve while we are thinking of the yidam, while we are mentally reciting the mantra and supplicating him, it will be as when trying to remember something while going to sleep: When we wake up, we can still remember it. If we fall asleep in that state, thoughts will not cut what we are trying to remember. Thus if we one-pointedly supplicate the root teacher in the form of Amitabha in our heart center, beyond union or separation from the nature of our mind, thinking that death will not lead to suffering and one-pointedly concentrating on that, when the dissolution of the elements takes place and the appearances of the bardo of becoming manifest, we will think that is the display of the protector Amitabha, inseparable from our teacher.

At that moment we will receive an actual vision of the deity and he will take us to the buddhafields. In the bardo we do not have a solid body, but a mental body. Because of that, during the bardo it is possible to perceive the deity and the teacher. While we have this solid body, even though we supplicate the guru and the deity, we cannot actually see them.

If we can train in the practice of the bardo before death comes, when the time of death approaches it will be easy to apply the instructions. To fight the enemy during a war, one needs to be prepared. Once the war has started, there is no time to collect the necessary weapons to fight the enemy. In the same way, to prepare for the enemy of death it is essential to prepare for death during this lifetime by practicing the instructions. If we have the confidence that we have such-and-such a teacher and have practiced such-and-such instructions, when death comes there will be no fear. As is said, for the yogin death is a state of enlightenment. So this is the essential practice for bringing the bardo of dying to the path.

At the time of death there is a sound of "trrrrrr." What is this sound? At present, body and mind are comfortably together, like a man sitting relaxed in his house. But when death comes, the mind wanders into the bardo and the body is left behind. The connection between body and mind is cut. When the connection between body and mind is cut, the five elements of the body—earth, water, fire, wind, and space—dissolve into each other. There are many different experiences of dissolution of the elements, depending on the individual. The most common dissolution among beings is the threefold experience called appearance, increase, and attainment.

When the breath has stopped and it seems that we have died, the white essence at the crown of the head, obtained from our father, comes down. As it is descending from the forehead center to the heart center, we experience all appearances as white light. It is like when the moon rises in a very clear autumn sky and bright moonlight appears everywhere. Such a white light appears everywhere. At the same time the mind experiences a state of great bliss, without any suffering or illness. Also, with regard to the kleshas, all thoughts of anger dissolve into the mind and hatred does not rise anymore.

If the dying person is a practitioner who can bring this experience to the path, he should be able to recognize the essence of the buddha's nirmanakaya. How is this essence of the buddha's nirmanakaya brought to the path? The practitioner should recognize the white essence, which is the upaya aspect, as the nature of the buddha's nirmanakaya. When the mind remains in that state of bliss, it does not get lost in delusion. If we cannot recognize this experience as the nirmanakaya, we will just feel very comfortable, as though enjoying a very good sleep in a comfortable bed.

As the red rakta, obtained from our mother, ascends from the navel center to the heart center, everything appears like a bright red light. We cannot see anything but red. At the same time the klesha of passion stops. When everything appears as red light and thoughts of passion stop, the mind experiences an incredible luminosity. If we can recognize this experience of luminosity, we will recognize the red light as the essence of the buddha's sambhogakaya, and we will not be caught in delusion. If we cannot recognize this experience as the sambhogakaya, we will be caught in delusion.

When the white essence from the crown of the head and the red rakta from the navel center have dissolved into the heart center, the consciousness dissolves. Our ordinary consciousness, by seeing forms with the eyes, can recognize deities and demons, beautiful and ugly, and by hearing sounds with the ears, it can recognize pleasant and unpleasant sounds. As this consciousness dissolves, one experiences intense darkness. As when the sky is without sun and moon and a cloud brings a heavy rainfall, we are unable to see anything, not even our own body and possessions. The mind is without any thoughts.

If we can recognize this state as the essence of the buddha's dharmakaya, we will not fall into delusion. If we cannot recognize this state as the essence of the dharmakaya, we will be caught in delusion. At this time all thoughts of ignorance dissolve into the intrinsic nature. If we are able to remain in that state for a while, when that state of darkness is finished, all phenomena of samsara and nirvana will be pervaded by the intrinsic nature of emptiness. That emptiness is not realized through meditation, but through the separation of body and mind. At this point, there is no way for the mind to avoid the experience of emptiness.

When the experience of emptiness arises as the nature of mind, if the dying person is a practitioner of the great perfection or mahamudra, by recognizing that experience and resting in that state, he will be liberated, like a child getting on his mother's lap. In that state there is no more delusion; it is the buddha's dharmakaya. All phenomena of samsara and nirvana dissolve into the state of dharmata, and one attains perfect buddhahood. If the deceased, like an ordinary, worldly person, does not recognize the view of the intrinsic nature, he will not experience this state for more than a fraction of a second, and from that state of dharmata he will again fall into delusion.

Someone who has confidence in the view but was not able to be liberated in that instant will again wander in samsara. Again he will experience deluded appearances in the form of sounds, lights, and rays. The sounds will be like thousands of thunderclaps resounding simultaneously in a very frightening manner. This sound is so powerful that it can move mountains, toss the waves of the ocean into the sky, and cause a hurricane. When a thousand thunderclaps resound simultaneously, we can only try to block our ears to avoid the noise. At the time of this great noise, we should recognize that it is just a display of our own mind and not something from outside. For instance, ordinarily when there is the sound of thunder, there is the danger that we might be hit by lightning, and if someone shoots a gun, there is the danger that we might be hit. If we recognize that there is nothing to be afraid of because that sound is not outside oneself but is the sound of dharmata, it will change into the mantra of whatever yidam deity one has relied on, such as Chakrasamvara's mantra, OM HRIH HA HA HUM HUM PHAT, or Vajrayogini's mantra, OM VAM VAIROCHANA. . . . Once the sounds change into the mantra of our yidam deity, we cannot avoid remembering our yidam. Just by remembering our yidam deity, we will be liberated.

Then we will experience a very bright light. Like rolls of brocade being unrolled, that five-colored light—white, red, blue, green, and yellow—is so bright and intense that we cannot look at it. Wherever we look, above or below, it appears everywhere. Recognizing that this light is the radiance of the intrinsic nature of our mind, we recognize the luminosity aspect of the mind, and the rainbow light dissolves into our heart center. In that state of nonthought, the intrinsic nature, we attain buddhahood. If we do not recognize that the light is the radiance of the intrinsic nature and our mind is distracted by it, we will be caught in delusion and wander into the bardo of becoming.

Then we will experience rays which are extremely bright and sharp. The points of the rays are like sharp weapons that might harm us. If we think that these weaponlike rays are going to cut us, we become very frightened and fall into delusion. If we recognize that the rays do not really exist and are nothing but the radiance of the intrinsic nature and we are able to rest in the state of nonthought, mahamudra, the appearances of the rays will subside and we will attain enlightenment in the state of nonthought, the intrinsic nature. We will not be deluded by the sounds, lights, and rays of the bardo.

In order to be able to bring these experiences to the path, we should supplicate our yidam deity now, recite the mantra, and think that such-and-such appearances will manifest during the bardo. In order to get used to those appearances, whatever we do now, we should consider it to be the bardo. When there is thunder and lightning, we should think that it is the sound of the bardo, and at that time we should remember our yidam deity or teacher. If we get used to thinking that everything is the bardo, we will not need to try to imagine that. Whatever we do, we will just naturally think it is the bardo. If we think that the appearances of the bardo are just our own fabrications and do not exist as something outside of us, and that all the appearances of the bardo are like an illusion, a dream, and we get used to the fears of the bardo now, that will help us in the future, when the bardo actually manifests.

THE BARDO OF DHARMATA

In the dharmata there is no intermediate state. However, when someone falls into delusion from the state of dharmata, between not being deluded and being deluded, appearances manifest, and that is called the bardo, or intermediate state, of dharmata. To bring that to the path we should recognize that the three appearances of sounds, lights, and rays, and the three experiences of appearance, increase, and attainment are the expression of our own mind.

Emptiness, the nature of our mind, is beyond fear and that which fears. As the mind cannot be grasped or touched, it is like space. If we have that confidence in the view, the illusory appearances of the bardo are liberated in the state of dharmata. When they are liberated, we are liberated in the ground nature and will not again wander in samsara. The reason why we can be liberated in the bardo is that when body and mind are separated, we return to the ground from which we have been deluded from the very beginning. When we properly recognize that ground, we cannot help but be liberated. If the dead person wanders around without recognizing that he is in the bardo, he will be deceived by the appearances in the bardo and will not recognize them. Then he cannot help but fall into delusion.

To recognize that the bardo of the dharmata is the display of our own nature, we should practice the instructions of the great perfection and mahamudra now, and train in perceiving all forms as the yidam deity, all sounds as the yidam's mantra, and all thoughts as the yidam's mind, the wisdom nature of bliss and emptiness inseparable. We should think that this is the bardo and there is no need to be afraid. By getting used to that, we will remember it through our habitual tendencies. So those are the instructions for liberation in the bardo of dharmata. If we are liberated in the bardo of dharmata, we cannot fall into delusion again. That completes the instructions on the first three bardos.

THREE

The Second Three Bardos

THE ROOT OF DELUSION, which creates the three worlds of samsara, consists of the perceptions of birth, death, and the bardo. The three methods for freeing ourselves from these deluded perceptions are the development stage, the completion stage, and mahamudra and the great perfection. While purifying the delusions of birth, death, and the bardo, if we recognize the nature of birth, death, and the intermediate state as it is, as the three buddha kayas, there are no impurities.

Holding on to something that does not exist, believing in something that is not true, through our ignorance we are deceived by these deluded perceptions. If a very good magician displays different things, such as beautiful animals and so forth, when we see them we might think they are real animals, but they are not. Similarly, what we perceive is not true in reality, and so these appearances of birth, death, and the bardo cause an enormous amount of suffering. Someone who has realized emptiness will perceive the appearances of birth, death, and the bardo as an enormous amount of suffering, but someone who has realized emptiness will perceive them as a rainbow in the sky or a mirage. He will not see any real existence. If we understand the nature of emptiness, without any sense of real existence, there is no way that birth, death, and the bardo will not naturally appear as the three buddha kayas.

As for a method for making birth, death, and the bardo appear in that way, the Buddha explained the inconceivable teachings of the causal vehicle of characteristics and of the fruition vehicle of the secret-mantra vajrayana. Between those, it is the unsurpassed secret-mantra vajrayana

that is the best, most perfect, and quickest method. Regarding the unsurpassed secret-mantra vajrayana, there are four classes of tantras: kriya,
upa, yoga, and anuttara. Practicing anuttara tantra is the supreme path,
which is very easy. In order to practice that path, we first need to ripen
our being with the ripening empowerment. Then we need to exert ourselves in the development and completion stages. In the completion
stage there are six yogas, or six bardos. The practice of the six bardos is
a method for pointing out the delusions of the bardo as a display of the
three kayas. The instructions hidden by Padmasambhava and discovered
by Karma Lingpa, the profound teachings of Karling Shitro, are such a
method.

These six bardos are the bardo of this life, the bardo of dying, the
bardo of dharmata, the bardo of becoming, the bardo of dream, and
the bardo of meditation. Previously I explained the bardo of this life, the
bardo of dying, and the bardo of dharmata. Now I shall explain the bardo
of becoming, the bardo of dream, and the bardo of meditation.

Bardo means intermediate state, when a past action is over and the
next action has not started. The state in between those two is called
bardo. When one is caught in between those two actions, if one needs
to do something one cannot do it. Though one cannot do anything, one
cannot just sit around. This state of delusion causes great suffering. The
best-known meaning of the word *bardo*, explained in all the sutras and
tantras, is the intermediate state when one has left one's previous body
behind and has not yet found one's next body. On the secret-mantra
vajrayana path this state is explained in terms of the six bardos.

THE BARDO OF BECOMING

Regarding the bardo of becoming, if one has not been liberated in the
ground nature after death and one has not recognized the appearances
of the bardo of dhamata as a display of the three kayas, one will wander
into the bardo of becoming. What is this bardo of becoming? It is the
time when one has left one's previous body and not yet found a new
one.

While wandering in the bardo of becoming, we have a mental body.
It is like when we are dreaming and have the feeling that we have a
body, but it is the body of our habitual patterns. There is no substantial,

obstructing body like we have now. With the mind depending on that mental body, we wonder where to go and what to do. We are very restless, not sure about what to do or where to go, and everything appears very frightening. As our body is without the white and red essences, which we received from our parents, we cannot draw support from the sun or moon. There is no perception of the sun and moon; everything is perceived as before dawn. We are without our children, relatives, friends, and enemies. Everything becomes very frightening, and we feel like we are being pursued by executioners with many weapons, or carried here, there, and everywhere like dry leaves by a fierce wind. We can still think as though we had the five sense organs; we can see the gods and gurus above and our parents, children, and relatives below. We do not recognize that we have died. We have the feeling that we are being pursued by enemies on every side.

To recognize that the appearances of the bardo of becoming are our own deluded perceptions and that there are no outside enemies, we should think that the appearances of the bardo are nothing but a dream. It is like when we are sleeping comfortably in our bed and have a dream about being pursued, caught, beaten, and killed by many soldiers. All these perceptions are just a dream, and we are comfortably lying in our bed. Similarly, when deluded appearances arise, if we recognize the intrinsic nature we will recognize that all the appearances of the bardo are delusions. Though we may be frightened of deluded perceptions, there is no reason to be so. All we need to do is remain in the intrinsic nature and remember our teacher and the instructions. With that confidence, we will see the frightening appearances like someone awakening from sleep, and we will not follow them. Thinking that the frightening appearances are a display of our yidam, when we are pursued by murderers with weapons we should meditate on them as messengers emanated by our yidam. Whatever sounds of thunder and lightening we hear, we should think that it is all the display of our yidam and not be frightened. Thus remaining in the intrinsic nature, the best practitioners will be liberated at this stage. A middle-level practitioner, remembering his teacher and yidam deity, should ask them for protection against those frightening appearances. With the confidence that the frightening appearances are nothing but the display of the body, speech, and mind of our yidam deity, we do not need to be frightened.

It is similar to seeing a movie with wars and so forth: we know that it is just a projection on a screen. If we are not frightened of the appearances and see the innate essence of the unaltered intrinsic nature, the appearances will fade like a rainbow fading in the sky. When they fade, there is no more suffering or fear from the projections in the bardo. Just from thinking that we want to go to the buddhafields and receive instructions from our teacher, just from supplicating our teacher, he will appear and take us to the buddhafields. In that way, we will be protected from the fears of the bardo of becoming.

As for the length of the bardo of becoming, if we have to stay two weeks in the bardo of becoming, during the first week we will have perceptions of our previous life, and during the next week we will have perceptions of our next life. But all these appearances should be dealt with in the same manner. In essence, we should remember our teacher, regard the projections in the bardo as a display of our yidam's body, speech, and mind, and with firm confidence develop devotion. In that way we will be protected from the fears of samsara.

THE BARDO OF DREAM

The fifth bardo is the bardo of dream. We have different perceptions of this life and the next. Regarding the perceptions of this life, we think it is permanent and stable, that we can just stay around and have a long life. When the frightening projections of the bardo manifest, if we have experience in the instructions of bardo practice, what we perceive in this life and in the bardo will be the same. Even though we are in the bardo, we will immediately remember our teacher and meditate on the instructions. As many appearances as manifest in the bardo will all make us progress on the path. Knowing that the perceptions of this life are nothing but suffering and impermanence, we will give up the eight worldly actions, one-pointedly concentrate on our teacher and the instructions, and feel inspired to practice. If that is how we feel, we have been able to bring the projections of the bardo to the path. If we do not feel like that, it is a sign that we have not been able to bring the bardo projections to the path.

Milarepa said: "If one feels no difference between this life and the next, one has thoroughly understood the view. If one feels no difference between day and night, one has thoroughly understood meditation."

Now the appearances of this life and the appearances of the daytime seem the same. The projections in dreams and the projections in the bardo seem the same. While comfortably sleeping in one's bed without any illness, if one has good dreams about having great wealth, attaining what one wants, arriving where one wants to be, meeting, talking, and having a nice time with one's parents and relatives who have died, at that time one's mind feels happy. But when one wakes up it is like a mirage; there is nothing real about all these experiences. As there is nothing real about this, it is called the bardo of dream.

Bringing the dream bardo on the path, we will be able to mix together appearances of day and dream. If we are able to mix appearances of day and dream, the experiences of this life and the bardo will mix. As they mix, when the projections of the bardo meet with the habitual patterns from this life, we will not have frightening experiences in the bardo. To mix the experiences of daily life with those of the dream bardo, we should first recognize dreams as such. When we are dreaming now, we think the dream is real and do not recognize it as a dream. That is a sign of not recognizing dreams. When we have frightening experiences in dreams, such as being eaten by wild animals, if we have confidence that we are not really being eaten but that it is just a dream, the fear will subside. When we have a good dream, such as meeting our parents who have passed away and talking with them, if we recognize that it is a dream and that our parents have died and are not there but that in dreams such deluded experiences arise, we will be able to recognize the dream as a dream. That is using dream as the path.

We mundane people like to accumulate profit, respect, and fame, and do not like loss, slander, and disgrace. Not liking slander and disgrace is due to habitual patterns related to the clinging to the permanence of this life. If we are trained to see everything in this life as impermanent, even though we encounter disgrace in this life, we will know that it has no essence and we will have no attachments to this life. In order to recognize dream as dream we need to meditate on the instructions of our teacher.

How do we meditate on these instructions? When going to sleep at night, we should visualize oneself as a deity such as Vajrasattva and in his heart center, a four-petaled red lotus. In the center of that lotus we should visualize a white syllable A, very fine. While falling asleep, we should visualize that from the syllable A light radiates, filling our body and room, which becomes as bright as in daytime. We should one-pointedly concentrate on that. As we fall asleep, the universe and its contents dissolve into light, which dissolves into the A. Then the A dissolves into emptiness. Remaining in that state of emptiness, we will recognize dream as dream. If we do not recognize the dream as such, when we wake up from our sleep we can try to meditate on it again.

There are two types of recognition: dream and luminosity. If we are mainly trying to recognize dreams, we should visualize a red lotus in our throat center and the radiation of light. That is the instruction for dream yoga.

If we recognize a dream, even when it is a good dream, there is no liking or excitement: it is just a dream, nothing permanent. If it is a bad dream, where we are killed or beaten by enemies, we think that it is just a dream. We will gradually recognize one dream and then another, and in that way all dreams will be recognized. If we are confident that our mind can change dreams, as we recognize a dream containing impure perceptions such as going to one of the eighteen hell realms and being beaten or killed by executioners, we should think that it is just a dream and that we are experiencing the sufferings of hell and so forth in our dream. Since dreams are mind-made, the mind can change them into anything. We can change the hell realm of our dream into a buddhafield and the executioners into the deities of a mandala, such as that of the hundred peaceful and wrathful deities or of our yidam—Vajrayogini, Vajrasattva, Chakrasamvara, and so on. With the confidence and devoted feeling that we are in a buddhafield with deities, having faith in them and reciting their mantra, we can instantly change impure perceptions into pure ones. The reason impure perceptions in dreams can instantly change into pure perceptions is that dreams are not permanent or reliable, but are deluded perceptions.

Just as we can change impure dreams into pure ones, we can change daytime experiences of the universe and its contents into a mandala with deities. The daytime perceptions of the universe and its contents are also impermanent and unreliable, just like last night's dream, but we hold onto them as something permanent. The nature of emptiness can be transformed into anything. If we have confidence in the view of emptiness, the appearances of the universe can be transformed into a buddhafield and the contents into deities, with all forms as the form of the deity, all sounds as the mantra of the deity, and all thoughts as the wisdom mind of the deity.

In changing appearances through samadhi in this way, first we have the inclination to transform the appearances, and then when our samadhi is stabilized, we can actually transform them. The universe naturally changes into a buddhafield. Similarly, we can change impure dreams into pure ones. If we can recognize dreams and transform them, out of one dream we can make many, and out of many dreams we can make one. It is our mental body that experiences the dream, not the solid body. In our dream, wherever we wish to go, there we go. If we concentrate on wishing to go to buddhafields such as Sukhavati and the Copper-Colored Mountain, we will arrive there in our dream. Whether we arrive there or not, the dream is an illusion, and illusions have no essence. If we hold onto an illusion as real, that is our own clinging.

Thinking that dreams are emptiness, we can change them into pure lands, such as the western buddhafield Sukhavati. In that buddhafield one can meet the buddha Amitabha and receive his prophecy. Now we are still alive and this is just a dream, but by thinking that in the future, when we have died, we will go there and be born from a lotus flower, we can prepare for being born there. In such a way we can change our perceptions. With the support of the dream we can see how we can change perceptions. In that way we will develop confidence in being able to change our perceptions of this life.

It is possible to transform perceptions because all appearances of this life have the nature of emptiness, and emptiness can be changed into anything. When King Trisong Detsen's messengers went to Mangyul to invite Guru Rinpoche to come to Tibet, they offered him a mandala of gold coins and gold dust. Guru Rinpoche just threw the gold into the sky, offering it to the three jewels. The messengers felt sorry that the gold was wasted, so Guru Padmasambhava smiled and said, "You do not need to feel sorry about it. I can make as much gold as I want." As he looked at the earth, his gaze changed the mountains and rocks of Mangyul into gold. If one has realized emptiness, one is able to transform things in such a way.

Whatever we perceive in this life we will be able to change into anything we like. Whatever impure perceptions we have now are all an illusion. Thinking to cut the root of illusion and change it into emptiness. we should develop confidence that today's perceptions and last night's dream are an illusion. Again and again we should meditate on perceptions of daily life as the play of deity, mantra, and dharmakaya. Whatever we do during the daytime, we should think that it is a dream. If we feel happy because of meeting friends or relatives, we should think it is a dream. If we are joyful because of being in a beautiful garden, we should think it is a dream. Thus thinking that whatever happens and whatever we do is a dream, when dreaming at night we will also recognize that to be a dream. Knowing that it is a dream, we will know that we can transform it, and transforming it, we can change impure into pure. With that confidence, when we wake up from our sleep, we will know that it is easy to change our dream. The reason it is easy is that dreams are just a manifestation of prana-mind and do not really exist.

During the day, we perceive solid things and think they actually exist, like clinging to impurities in gold. Even though we are attached to those appearances, if with diligence we continue to think that all that is emptiness and we can change it, we will actually be able to transform those appearances. If we are able to change the appearances in our dream, we will be able to change the projections in the bardo. Then there will be no more difference between this life and the next, and we will have thoroughly understood the view. If we are able to transform in such a way, we have perfected the practice of the bardo of dream.

THE BARDO OF MEDITATION

The sixth bardo is the bardo of meditation, which means the meditation of inner samadhi. How does this meditation of inner samadhi relate to the bardo? If we practice samadhi now, that does not mean we have stabilized it. In between stabilizing samadhi and just practicing samadhi lie the obstacles to samadhi—drowsiness and wildness of thoughts. With drowsiness and wildness, it is not possible to develop true samadhi. If one is not controlled by drowsiness and wildness, one will be able to develop true samadhi.

What is drowsiness? When the mind is gathered too much inside, we start to feel sleepy, our five senses become numb, and if we want to visualize something, we cannot. What is wildness? When the mind is gathered too much inside, if we try to control the perceptions of the five senses, we cannot. We are unable to concentrate, the mind has many thoughts, and we are distracted by them. If we try to tame the mind with mindfulness and awareness, we cannot. Our prana becomes unbalanced and we have pain in the heart center. If we can get rid of the faults of drowsiness and wildness, we can develop genuine samadhi. If we get lost in drowsiness and wildness, it is not possible to develop true samadhi.

It is very important to be aware of and try to control our thoughts; otherwise, we will get completely lost in them and go crazy. It is important to control the movements of our mind and try to find clarity, so that the arising of thought will slow down. The moment in between these constant movements of the mind we call the bardo. We cannot expect clarity from the very beginning of our practice. It is important to know what is going on and to control speedy thoughts, but we should not be influenced by expectation and doubt. We should not fall into those extremes. We should depend on antidotes for drowsiness and wildness. Nobody is without drowsiness and wildness. Ordinary people are like that.

Until now we have spoiled our mind by following thoughts, following past habits, welcoming future thoughts about subduing enemies and supporting relatives, thinking that if we do such-and-such we will be happy for a long time and if we do not, things will be bad. Thinking a lot, we have hopes about accomplishing our plans and fears about not accomplishing them. Hoping to accomplish our plans, we exert ourself day and night, not even sleeping. If we cannot accomplish them, we are very upset. If we think about what we have done up to now, we may have accomplished certain work that is very good. It has made us happy and comfortable. Now we want to do such-and-such in order to accomplish such-and-such, and we make more plans, following our present thoughts. Just as the wind tosses the waves on the ocean and the ocean is never calm, with this wildness, the mind will never be calm.

To develop samadhi, we have to get rid of drowsiness and wildness. To get rid of drowsiness and wildness, we have to practice shamatha, or stillness of mind. If we do not develop stillness, we will not be able to get rid of drowsiness and wildness. For instance, if one burns a butter lamp in a very windy place with no protective glass cover, it will be blown out by the wind. With a protective glass cover, the wind will not be able to blow out the butter lamp. In the beginning, it is very difficult for us to train the mind and be aware of its movements. When we recognize them, we see that they are very strong. But we should not give up.

We should continue. For example, if one wants to tame a wild elephant one needs time to train it. One should train it in a very skillful manner and always find the middle way, not too vigorous and not too mild. If one controls an elephant with a hook, it can be led to do whatever one wants. It will sit, walk, and even make sounds according to what one wants. Similarly, when the mind is still, we should look up and be joyful and happy, and when it is wild, we should look down, remember the sufferings of samsara and impermanence, and arouse renunciation. We should feel how useless it is to waste our time by following these thoughts. The speed of the movement will slow down. Then we should continue the practice, trying to encourage ourselves.

When a skilled craftsman makes golden ornaments, he has to go through different processes. He heats the gold with various substances for a long time, burns it, and beats it to improve the quality of the gold. In the same way, if we tame our mind in the right way, we develop a special state of samadhi. Right now our mind is not capable of developing samadhi. Though we want the mind to be still, thinking many thoughts, it is like a restless monkey; it never stays still. In that way, we will never develop samadhi. If we cannot develop samadhi in our mind, we will not generate the qualities of stillness.

The mind can be compared with a crippled rider and prana with a blind wild horse. If a crippled rider mounts a blind wild horse, since the horse is blind he cannot see whether the road is good or bad and whether it is suitable to go on or not. He just goes ahead anywhere. Since he just goes anywhere, the rider will be thrown off the horse. Though the rider can see whether the road is good or bad, because he is crippled he cannot control the wild horse. He cannot control its direction. In the same way, we are caught up in deluded perceptions. Our prana is like the blind wild horse, followed by our mind, which is like the crippled rider. For instance, if we are attached to relatives, because of that attachment our mind will be very active. If we have anger toward enemies, our mind will be distracted figuring out how to get rid of our enemies. Due to the fault of distraction, thoughts of desire, hatred, and ignorance will automatically arise. But if the mind is bound by the ropes of mindfulness and awareness, like an elephant tied with a rope, it cannot go anywhere.

Thus, through mindfulness and awareness the mind can be controlled. What is mindfulness? When body, speech, and mind are under control, they are in harmony with samadhi. If not, they are not in harmony with samadhi. Now we are not able to recognize what the mind does, how it gets wild and drowsy. Without the antidotes of mindfulness and awareness there is no way to control the mind. Watching our mind, we will be able to discover the faults of the mind and apply the right antidotes. When the mind is drowsy, we will be able to recognize that fault and know how to get rid of that drowsiness through mindfulness. When the mind is wild, we will be able to recognize this and apply the right antidote to get rid of it, so that we can develop samadhi. Awareness keeps analyzing body and mind to see whether they are acting in harmony with the dharma; it is like a teacher.

If we have both mindfulness and awareness, when the mind is wild and distracted, thinking only about worldly things, we should think that worldly actions have no essence. We should think that until now we have been caught up in the suffering of samsara, and realize how useless everything is that we do in that regard. If the mind is spoiled by being caught up in that way, there will be no way to become free from the suffering of the three lower realms. If the mind is not spoiled, our bliss and happiness will increase, just like that of the exalted ones. Thinking of that, we should try to heal the mind. In the beginning, it is very difficult to control, but gradually, as we get used to doing so, it becomes easier.

When we practice peaceful samadhi, three experiences arise. The first one is the experience of movement, which is likened to a waterfall coming down a steep mountain. When water falls down a steep mountain, it cannot be stopped even with great force. When one first meditates on stillness (Skt. shamatha) and insight (vipashyana), it is extremely difficult to control the mind. It is not possible to control it for a minute or even a second. When one gets distracted, if one thinks that it is impossible to control one's mind and just gives up, that will not help.

If one wants to catch a monkey or a wild horse, one should first give it food and be gentle with it. In that way one can catch it. Once one gets hold of it, one can make it do whatever one wants. Similarly, if we try to catch the mind while it is wild, it is not possible to control it. Knowing that our mind is wild, we should develop renunciation and weariness when the mind is not weary. When we feel weary, tamed by that suffering, the mind will stay still. In that state of being tamed by suffering, we can develop stillness and insight. When we do not feel happy, according to the great beings from the past, that is the best time to develop samadhi. Practicing samadhi with great diligence, in the future we will attain happiness and, eventually, the fruition of nonreturning. Thus we should rejoice and cheer the mind; in that state we can develop samadhi.

The second experience is the experience of achievement. What is achieved? We achieve a level that is quite peaceful compared to what we have had before. Once we have understood that our mind is like a waterfall coming down a mountain, we will not make the mind tense up, and it will be easier to meditate on stillness and insight. The strength of the wildness will let up. Properly concentrating on a visualization, our mind will be a little more steady than before. Even though the mind may be wild or drowsy, the force of that is not as strong as before. The mind is stronger because it is more used to samadhi. As wild as a horse may be, once it has been tamed, if one restrains it with a bridle and saddle, it will go wherever we want. In the same way, we can stabilize our samadhi a little bit. That is called the experience of achievement, which is like an ocean not stirred up by the wind.

The third experience happens when we get used to samadhi. When a yogin preaches samadhi, even if one shows him a hundred entertaining things, his mind will not be distracted in the least. He can completely control his mind through samadhi. Supported by the qualities of samadhi, the mind does not move. Even if we practice samadhi for many months or years, the mind will not become drowsy, sleepy, or weary. Even if we try to make it wild using desirable things, the mind will not be disturbed, because it has become steady. It is like a mountain on a great plain covered with a forest of all sorts of trees. No matter how much wind and rain come, the mountain cannot be moved.

To continue the samadhi practice, when drowsiness arises, we cheer the mind. When wildness arises, we tame it with mindfulness and awareness. In that way, we attain stability. When we get used to this, instead of being how we are now—cherishing ourselves above everyone else—if we meditate on bodhichitta, consider all sentient beings as our parents, give up anger toward enemies and attachment to friends, we will cherish other sentient beings above ourselves. We will not feel anger or attachment to others, and we will also not have anger or attachment to ourselves. This will come gradually as we get used to the practice.

When we have stabilized the meditation, body and mind will be comfortable. It is like the blind wild horse being able to see and the crippled rider being able to use his legs. Thus the rider can guide the horse along the right roads and carefully avoid going to the wrong places. In the same way, if we have stabilized our samadhi, body and mind will be comfortable and we can stay in samadhi for many days and nights. Without feeling any discomfort, whatever conditions of cold or heat occur, we will not fall ill or die from them. When body and mind experience bliss through samadhi, we will be able to levitate, go to all sorts of places, and do all sorts of things. That stability is the result of the right practice of samadhi. If we do not stabilize samadhi, even if we sit on a steady piece of wood, we will not be able to stay there. If we stabilize our samadhi, we will not be controlled by drowsiness and wildness. We can meditate as long as we want, and body and mind will be blissful. That is the perfection of the bardo of meditation.

This has been an abridged explanation of the practice of the six bardos. In essence, no matter which of the six bardos one practices, the main benefit is that clinging to the illusory perceptions of samsara as real subsides. If the illusory perceptions of samsara arise as pure appearances, we have understood the practice. The nature of samsaric delusions is pure. Phenomena are primordially pure kaya and jnana. But just as someone with an eye defect looking at the moon cannot see that the moon is beautiful and full because it is far away, if we do not recognize that the nature of phenomena is pure, we hold on to what is pure as impure, and cling to the impure as real. That clinging to reality is a delusion. The root of attachment to worldly affairs comes from the clinging to their reality.

In the god realm there are miraculous things such as the wish-fulfilling tree, crops that need no cultivation, one's own body radiating light so that one does not need sunlight or moonlight, the ability to levitate into the sky, and so forth. Even though such miraculous things exist, if one is attached to them, being distracted by that attachment, one will wander in samsara and be unable to progress on the path of liberation. Being distracted in this way through one's whole life, when death comes, one will think that one has been distracted one's whole life and realize that great suffering is about to begin. For instance, a celestial being who knows he is going to die goes through extreme suffering; an ordinary being does not experience that much suffering. Why does he not experience as much suffering? Celestial beings have incredible comfort and luxury, to which they are very attached. When they find out that they are going to die within a week, and they know where they will be reborn, they experience unbearable suffering. If a human being who lives comfortably experiences suffering, he will suffer more intensely than someone who is always suffering.

Even though one suffers, if one understands the nature of emptiness, there is no reason to not want that suffering. Suffering is the cause of developing renunciation toward samsara and confidence in karma and its result. Knowing that all appearances are impermanent and understanding the nature of impermanence, one will understand the pure phenomena of kaya and jnana. Knowing the nature of appearances, one will understand that projections are impure and illusory. Having rejected illusions, one will recognize that the nature of illusion is pure.

If someone discovers gold that looks black because it is covered with a stain, a specialist would recognize that. He knows that if the gold is polished so that the stain is removed, it will be very valuable. If it is heated and beaten, the gold will have a very good quality. Similarly, knowing that impure illusions are a delusion, with the support of the antidote we can purify illusory projections, so that all delusions appear as wisdom. That is called delusion appearing as wisdom. When delusion appears as wisdom, wisdom is a phenomenon of the buddha's kaya and jnana, in which there is nothing but purity.

For this to appear, it is necessary to apply the essential points of the teachings. To apply the essential points, we should develop renunciation and weariness toward the three worlds of samsara and dedicate whatever positive actions of body, speech, and mind we accumulate to the welfare of all sentient beings, instead of keeping them for ourselves. Considering that there are no beings who have not been our parents and all of them are tormented by suffering, we should wish for them all to obtain the root of our positive actions and the power of samadhi, and develop great compassion. We should not have any pride or partiality about our practice. Even though we have not attained all the qualities of the path, if we are very diligent in the practice, eventually we will definitely attain all the qualities. Without diligence, we cannot attain these qualities. Practicing the dharma with diligence, we will develop faith and devotion, compassion, and all the qualities of the path.

If we continuously exert ourselves in worldly actions with body, speech, and mind, we can succeed in subduing enemies and supporting relatives and friends, if we wish to do so. We will be successful in all worldly matters. If sometimes we are ambitious and sometimes we give up, we will not be successful in our aim. Similarly, to practice the dharma, we should also continuously exert ourselves.

Even if we develop special experiences and realization, we should not be proud of that. If our samadhi is disturbed by drowsiness and wildness, we should remember death and impermanence and the suffering of samsara. In that way, we will develop courage and diligence. Thus we cannot help but perceive the sixth bardo as the pure appearances of the three kayas. When the sixth bardo appears as the three kayas, impure is perceived as pure and, enjoying the appearances of the three buddha kayas, there is no suffering. One will be liberated in the result of the secret-mantra vajrayana path.

This explanation of the six bardos is according to the Nyingma tradition of the secret mantra. The Sarma tradition also has the bardo of dying, the bardo of becoming, and the bardo of this life. For instance, the six yogas of Naropa consist of chandali, illusory body, dream, luminosity, transference, and bardo. If one applies the essential points of these practices, they are the same.

It is important to remind oneself how fortunate one is. Now we have obtained a precious human body and have been born in a place where the Buddha's doctrine is known. We follow special spiritual teachers and friends and practice the holy dharma. It is extremely fortunate that we can practice the dharma, and in a future birth we may not be so fortunate. So we should not waste this precious opportunity, but practice the dharma now. Once we have heard the dharma, we should try to understand it by reflecting on it. Then if we practice it, it is inevitable that the qualities of the dharma will develop in our mind. As is said, "As a sign of hearing many teachings, one should be able to control one's mind. As a sign of having done a lot of practice, one should not have kleshas."

All the instructions we have gone through are very important and precious. If you practice for one hour, you will be able to develop samadhi in that time. It will be very good if you can practice according to these instructions.

FOUR

Development Stage and Vajrasattva Practice

ALL OF US HAVE ENTERED the path of the buddhadharma and follow a qualified teacher. Not only do we follow a qualified teacher, we also have received the profound instructions, and we have practiced those instructions, which is extremely fortunate.

For practicing the dharma, there are the casual vehicle of characteristics and the fruition vehicle of the secret-mantra vajrayana. Now we are practicing the extraordinary teachings of the secret-mantra vajrayana. In the secret-mantra vajrayana, once one has been ripened through the abhisheka, it is very important to practice the development and completion stages. In particular, it is extremely important to practice the development stage properly, since it is the preparation for the completion stage. If one can properly concentrate on the visualization during the development stage, stillness is accomplished within that state.

The development stages of the Sarma and Nyingma traditions are slightly different. In the development stage of the Nyingma tradition, one creates the mandala with the support of the three samadhis and seals it with purity, completion, and ripening. The form of the deity is used to progress on the path. If one makes progress and removes obstructing forces with the support of clear visualization of form, there will be progress in the yoga of the mantra recitation. The development and completion stages are both included in the three samadhis [the completion stage corresponds to the samadhi of suchness]. Because of that, through the development stage one can attain not only the ordinary but also the supreme siddhis.

The development stage is based on the three samadhis. For instance, if we, depending on that basis, practice the sadhana of Vajrasattva, we recite the mantra OM MAHASHUNYATA-JNANA-VAJRA-SVABHAVA-ATMAKO 'HAM, which means: From the very beginning all phenomena of samsara and nirvana are the unborn state of emptiness. That is the samadhi of suchness. While one recites the shunyata mantra and rests in the non-conceptual state of emptiness, the appearances of the universe and its contents become emptiness. This samadhi of suchness uses the essence of the buddha's dharmakaya to progress on the path.

"The play of unceasing compassion is like a rainbow in the sky." That is the all-illuminating samadhi. As all phenomena of samsara and nirvana fade into emptiness like a rainbow, there is no way for the mind not to experience emptiness. As that experience of emptiness arises, we generate compassion toward all sentient beings who have not realized this nature of emptiness. "May all beings reach the state of the glorious Vajrasattva. To that end, may I practice the yoga of Vajrasattva." That is the all-illuminating samadhi, which relates to the buddha's sambhogakaya.

In the mahayana vehicle of characteristics, the paths of emptiness and compassion are to be practiced inseparably. Meditating on emptiness alone, one will not attain the result of buddhahood. Meditating on compassion alone, one cannot get beyond the worldly path. When one practices in a state of nondual emptiness and compassion, practice becomes the mahayana vehicle of characteristics. Both the secret-mantra vajrayana and the causal vehicle of characteristics come from this profound view. The nature of the samadhi of suchness is emptiness, and the nature of the all-illuminating samadhi is great compassion. When we practice these two inseparably as prajna and upaya, as it is said: "The display of wisdom beyond substance arises as the unchanging syllable HUM."

The essence of the buddha's wisdom mind has no existing substance such as that of a pillar or vase. Even though it has no existing substance, the seed samadhi makes it possible to show students that which cannot be shown, the inconceivable dharmadhatu beyond speech, thought, or expression. Just as the sky has no solidity and cannot be grasped as if it were a pillar or a vase, the seed samadhi is like the appearance of a rainbow in the sky. Meditating on the nondual nature of emptiness and compassion in the form of a white HUM rising in the sky like the moon is the seed samadhi. It manifests the buddha palace and the mandala of deities, using the buddha's nirmanakaya to progress on the path.

What is the purpose of these three samadhis? Sentient beings in the three worlds of samsara are deluded by obscurations of birth, death, and bardo. The samadhi of suchness purifies obscurations of death, the all-illuminating samadhi purifies obscurations of the bardo, and the seed samadhi purifies obscurations of birth. So the three samadhis purify obscurations of birth, death, and bardo. If one practices the completion stage, one will experience a state of bliss, luminosity, and nonthought. On the path, the samadhi of nonthought is the samadhi of suchness, the samadhi of luminosity is the all-illuminating samadhi, and the samadhi of bliss is the seed samadhi. Their fruition is the three buddha kayas.

From the syllable HUM gradually emanate various syllables that manifest the elements, the protection circle, and the buddha palace. In the center, on a lion throne, a lotus, and a sun-and-moon disk, the syllable HUM descends from the sky, radiating light rays that make offerings to the buddhas and bodhisattvas and gather back the blessings of their body, speech, and mind, which dissolve into the HUM. Again the light rays radiate to all beings of the three worlds, purify their karmic obscurations, and dissolve back into the HUM, which transforms into a five-pronged vajra. The syllable HUM is the speech aspect; the vajra into which it transforms is the mind aspect. Then the vajra transforms into Vajrasattva with consort, which is the body aspect. These three vajra aspects should be complete within the practice of the development stage. Having visualized oneself as the deity in the development stage, one invites the wisdom of the buddhas and bodhisattvas from Akanishtha in the form of the deity one has visualized.

At first, oneself as the deity is called the samayasattva. Why is it called the samayasattva? For instance, if one's teacher is in front of one, and one makes the vow to accomplish such-and-such a virtuous action or do such-and-such a practice, one should not break that promise or samaya. Breaking that promise creates a seed for going to hell. If one does not break that promise but lives up to it, one can attain the ordinary and supreme siddhis. Similarly, when one meditates on one's body, speech, and mind as the nature of Vajrasattva, since the buddha's body, speech, and mind are inseparable from one's own body, speech, and mind, one is blessed by the body, speech, and mind of all the buddhas. That is the promise of the buddhas; therefore that visualization is called the samayasattva.

Now we are obscured by karma and defilements, but when we purify impure perceptions and meditate on pure appearances, when the light rays emanate from the OM at one's forehead center, the AH at our throat center, and the HUM at our heart center, the jnanasattva is invited from the Akanishtha buddhafield. The buddhas invited from the Akanishtha buddhafield are called jnanasattvas (wisdom beings) because they have abandoned all their obscurations, are complete with all good qualities, and have perfected their wisdom. Therefore they are called jnanasattvas.

Why are both the samayasattva and jnanasattva called sattva? Because they have promised to send the blessings of their body, speech, and mind for the sake of all sentient beings, and bodhisattvas never break their promise. Since it is their mind promise they are called sattva. [The Tibetan translation of *sattva, sempa,* means "brave mind."]

When the jnanasattva is invited, dissolves into the samayasattva, and samayasattva and jnanasattva mix inseparably, it is like adding yeast to rice pulp so that it becomes beer, or putting gold on a clay statue of the Buddha so that it becomes valuable. When samaya and jnana have become inseparable, in order to bless one's skandhas and sense organs as the secret mandala of the three seats, one emanates from one's heart center light rays that invite the devas of abhisheka. The five buddhas with their consorts are invited and bestow the abhisheka and blessings. This is like consecrating the deities, the inseparable samaya- and jnanasattvas, so that their blessings become even stronger than before. From one's heart center emanate offering goddesses who prostrate to the deity, make offerings, and sing verses of praise. Then they dissolve back into oneself. After they dissolve back into oneself, one's sense of the development stage is stabilized. That is a brief explanation of the development stage. If one meditates on oneself as Vajrasattva, that is the way to proceed.

In order to attain the ordinary and supreme siddhis through the development stage, one should combine the development and completion stages so that they are nondual. For that, the following three factors are necessary: clearly visualizing the details, remembering their meaning (recollection of purity), and having confidence that one is the deity (pride of the deity).

CLEARLY VISUALIZING THE DETAILS

Regarding the first factor, how do we clearly visualize the details? If we have a clear and stable visualization of the buddha's form, and continue to train in that visualization, our mind will attain stillness. If we are to visualize Vajrasattva, first we should visualize ourselves as the form of Vajrasattva. Then we should concentrate on the face, and then just on the eyes, their color, the eyelashes, the eyebrows, the circle of hair between the eyebrows radiating five colored lights, the nose, the mouth, the red lips, the ears, the hair, the crown, the topknot, the radiance of the hair, and the jeweled earrings. When a skilled artist paints a buddha, he first paints the face: the nose, the eyes, the circle of hair between the eyebrows, the mouth, and the ears. When all the details of the face are finished, he paints the expression, very youthful and beautiful. Then he paints the chest, the lower body, the legs in vajra posture, the lower garment of different-colored silks, the silk blouse, the right hand holding a five-pronged vajra at the heart center, and the left hand holding a bell at the left hip. Thus a skilled artist paints all the details very clearly in the right proportions, without mixing them up.

Though the details of the form are visualized this way, their nature is not solid like that of earth or rock. They are also not something flat but like a rainbow appearing in the sky. All the details of the body are completely clear and distinct. Within the body there is no flesh, blood, and bones. Rather, it is like a pitched tent. Vajrasattva's form is very youthful and attractive, without any signs of aging or ugliness.

Having concentrated on visualizing all the details in this way, we can then concentrate on the entire form. Then again we can visualize all the details. After concentrating for a long time on the entire form, when the mind becomes dull and the visualization unclear, we can again visualize the details as I described before—the eyes, the nose, the mouth, the head ornament, the earrings, the vajra in the hand—concentrating on each detail. When we clearly visualize each detail, the nature of the form should be radiant, like the moon shining. Each detail is perfect in color, distinct, as though painted by a very skilled artist. The nature of the details is empty, without any solidity or characteristics. Appearance and emptiness are inseparable, like a crystal vase.

In the heart center of Vajrasattva is the jnanasattva. Generally, wrathful deities have a peaceful jnanasattva, and peaceful deities have a wrathful jnanasattva in their heart center. For instance, Vajrakilaya has a peaceful Vajrasattva in his heart center. Sometimes, the basis of manifestation of the main deity is the jnanasattva in the heart center. For example, in the heart center of the dakini Yeshe Tsogyal is Jetsun Tara or Vajravarahi. Sometimes there are three types of deities of the same family. According to the *Guhyagarbha Tantra* tradition, with oneself as Vajrasattva, the jnanasattva is a Vajrasattva the size of four finger-widths in height. That form is without any ornaments, naked, very beautiful and attractive, not holding any attributes. He holds one hand at his heart center and one down at the side of his body. That, visualized clearly, is called the jnanasattva. The outer form of Vajrasattva is the samayasattva. Taking a human being as an analogy, the jnanasattva is like the human being's consciousness.

All the details of the jnanasattva should be visualized very clearly. In the heart center of the jnanasattva is a moon disk the size of a pea. On top of the moon disk is a standing five-pronged white vajra, symbolizing the mind of all the tathagatas, the nature of bliss and emptiness. In the center of the vajra is the mind syllable of Vajrasattva, a white HUM, the same color as the deity, from which light and light rays radiate. One should one-pointedly concentrate on that visualization. That HUM is called the samadhisattva.

So there are three sattvas: the samayasattva, the jnanasattva, and the samadhisattva. Building up these three satvas is the ultimate development stage of the deity. One can visualize the deity as large as a mountain, with the buddha palace in equal proportions. One can also visualize the deity the size of one's body, or as small as a cubit, a hand-span or a grain, whichever is most comfortable. When one visualizes Vajrasattva for a long time, the practice of the development stage will become stable.

In order to progress in the practice, one should visualize Vajrasattva as standing, getting up, walking around, eating and drinking, and so forth, and then sitting down again. Sometimes one should visualize the deity as large as Mount Meru, with wild animals roaming around on him, resting on the nose of Vajrasattva, flying around him, and so on. But all that should not disturb the visualization of Vajrasattva. Sometimes one should visualize the deity as small as a mustard seed, with all the details very fine. Then again one should visualize Vajrasattva as vast as space, with billions of buddhafields manifesting from every pore of his body. The pores of his body do not become bigger, nor do the buddha-fields become smaller; they are exactly the size of the pores of the buddha. The size of the buddhafields does not differ from their own exact size of two or three hundred thousand miles across. In each buddhafield abides a buddha teaching the doctrine to limitless disciples, displaying various miracles such as flying back and forth through the sky, and practicing samadhi. All that is maintained in the visualization in each pore of Vajrasattva's body. Then again one can bring the visualization back to the size one finds comfortable.

After concentrating for a long time on the samadhis, if we get tired, sleepy, bored, or drowsy, we should fix our eyes on empty space so that Vajrasattva's form can become clear again. We should remember biographies of past saints who meditated on Vajrasattva and the fruition they achieved, and generate great joy. We should reflect on the meaning of the dharma. If we have too many thoughts and cannot visualize, we should concentrate one-pointedly on the visualization of the HUM in the heart center of Vajrasattva. That is stillness (Skt. shamatha) without characteristics.

If we wish to practice stillness with characteristics, we can draw a white syllable HUM on a piece of canvas or paper a cubit in size. Putting that right in front of you, concentrate one-pointedly on it, not letting thoughts follow anything else. If there is any noise or if there are people going or coming, do not look at them or talk to them, but just concentrate on the HUM. If we can look clearly at the HUM, when we close our eyes we will see the HUM very clearly. Similarly, we could put a painting of Vajrasattva in front of us and concentrate on that. After some time, we will be able to see it very vividly with our eyes closed. If we visualize such an image in our heart center, our wild thoughts will be pacified.

If we are neither drowsy nor wild, but in a state of clear visualization, we can stay without eating for a whole day. Meditating in this way, we will stabilize the practice. Even if our practice is not yet that steady and we do not get those signs of stability, just concentrating on the form of the Buddha has great benefit. For instance, if a child who is upset and crying sees an image of the Buddha and offers a flower that he has in his hand, through that action he makes a direct connection and in the future will follow the Buddha. Since the Buddha's activities are inconceivable, we should consider that just looking at the Buddha's form has great benefit.

As for Vajrasattva, sentient beings with karma and defilements, who have sins and obscurations, just by hearing his name and thinking about it, will be purified of those obscurations. All the infinite mandalas manifest from Vajrasattva. In the Sarma tradition, Kalachakra, Chakrasamvara, Hevajra, and so forth all manifest from Vajrasattva. In the Nyingma tradition, Yangdak Heruka, Vajrakilaya, and so forth all manifest from Vajrasattva. As Vajrasattva is the lord of all families, concentrating on the form of Vajrasattva alone is equal to concentrating on the forms of all the buddhas. That one-pointed concentration without the flaws of drowsiness and wildness will develop samadhi in one's mind. In the four great classes of tantra of the secret-mantra vajrayana there is no text without the name of Vajrasattva, so one should cultivate an attitude of great joy toward being able to do this practice. In that way one can develop the ability to practice samadhi. If the mind becomes too wild, we should concentrate again on the thangka. Then when we close our eyes, the image on the thangka should appear vividly.

In the same way, in visualizing our own body in that form, if we meditate for a long time, we will be able to visualize the details very clearly and feel the presence of the deity. In the first stage, that of visualization as a mental object, if we practice the development stage for a long time, first the mind will think that we are Vajrasattva—his body is colored white, he holds a vajra and bell, embraces his consort Vajratopa ("vajra pride"), also white in color, and so forth. All that will appear in the mind very vividly. That stage is called visualization as a mental object: at this stage, the object becomes vivid in one's mental state.

In the second stage, that of visualization as a sense object, having continued that training, one will actually transform into Vajrasattva and see and feel that very clearly. With the support of the confidence in oneself as Vajrasattva, the pride of the deity, concentrating on one's own body, one can actually transform into Vajrasattva.

In the last stage, that of visualization as a physical appearance, the body appears as the deity. If a teacher has mastered this practice, a student who has devotion will perceive the master as Vajrasattva. Physical forms actually appear as the deity. That is the fruition of the practice. Completing these three stages, one perfects the clear visualization of the details.

If one practices until one has perfected these stages, the merit of visualizing the buddha's form is immense. Accomplishing stillness is the perfect basis for samadhi. As for the benefit of reciting the secret mantra of

Vajrasattva, there is no difference between reciting the mantra with one's mouth and visualizing through the mind's samadhi. Thus one should consider the great benefit of this practice. That concludes the discussion of the first topic, clearly visualizing the details.

REMEMBERING THE MEANING OF THE DETAILS

Visualizing the deity's form alone is called the gross or ordinary development stage [without the three samadhis]. Through the color and attributes of the buddha, the inner, mind qualities are displayed externally in order to train sentient beings. Thus we perceive peaceful and wrathful appearances, which are not ordinary forms. Merely visualizing the form very clearly will not lead us to the state of liberation. In order to gain certainty that the forms we visualize are not ordinary forms, we should remember their meaning.

How do we remember their meaning? For instance, Vajrasattva has one face, which symbolizes that within the intrinsic nature of emptiness all phenomena of samsara and nirvana are one. There is not a samsaric emptiness and a nirvanic emptiness; they are one. The nature of samsaric emptiness is perfect with all the unconditioned qualities, and the nature of nirvanic emptiness also is perfect with all the unconditioned qualities. Vajrasattva has one face, symbolizing the nature of samsara and nirvana beyond accepting and rejecting.

Though having attained the state of fruition, the buddha kaya has both the dharmakaya and the rupakaya. At the time of persevering on the path of enlightenment, there are two kinds of accumulations: the accumulation of conceptual merit and the accumulation of nonconceptual merit. When first developing bodhichitta, there are two factors: the upaya of great compassion and the prajna of emptiness. That is what is symbolized by the two arms of Vajrasattva.

The white color of Vajrasattva symbolizes that his body, speech, and mind are completely free of any obscurations. For the sake of disciples, his body is beyond death and impermanence. He does not pass into nirvana like the buddhas, but always remains, free of birth and death, with a very youthful and beautiful body.

Symbolizing that he directly and indirectly performs peaceful activities such as turning the wheel of the dharma and wrathful, destroying activities to train beings, he has two legs. No matter how many actions the buddha displays in taking birth in the three worlds of existence for the sake of sentient beings—sometimes manifesting as a householder, sometimes as a monk, and sometimes as a wild animal, a bird, and so forth—he is not stained by any of the faults of the three worlds of samsara. He is not like the shravakas and pratyekabuddhas, who pass into nirvana aiming for their own enlightenment and cannot vastly benefit beings like the bodhisattvas. Symbolizing that he does not fall into the extreme of either samsara or nirvana, he has two legs and is seated in vajra posture.

His right hand holds a golden five-pronged vajra at his heart center. The upper five prongs symbolize the five buddhas and the lower five prongs symbolize their five consorts. The center of the vajra symbolizes that in whatever form the five buddhas and their consorts manifest, they are not different from the one essence of the wisdom display. So there is one center connecting them, From the point of view of the form aspect, the five-pronged vajra is very beautiful; from the point of view of the emptiness aspect, there is no attachment to worldly wealth—it symbolizes being without attachment. The five-pronged vajra appears as a symbol of nondual appearance and emptiness. Symbolizing the natural wisdom of Vajrasattva's mind, where appearances and emptiness are inseparable, and that samsara and nirvana do not go beyond the one essence of Vajrasattva, his right hand holds a vajra at his heart center.

His left hand holding a bell symbolizes the prajna aspect. The nature of prajna is emptiness. Compassion manifesting within the state of emptiness is like sound coming from a bell. The sound comes from the bell, but that sound has no concrete existence. Similarly, when from within the expanse of prajna, emptiness, the Buddha shows to sentient beings to be trained whichever of the three vehicles is effective for training them, there is no such concept as "I have accomplished the aim of teaching them the dharma," or "I have not accomplished the aim of teaching them the dharma." Regarding the teachings, there is no concept of time; teachers always teach for the benefit of beings. That is symbolized by the bell held in the left hand.

Who has this great compassion to teach the dharma to all beings? Vajrasattva has this great compassion. Explaining it from the aspect of the buddha's nature, he is without any manifesting characteristics and does not move from the expanse of dharmakaya. But in order to show a form to the beings to be trained, that dharmakaya has all the unconditioned qualities, such as the five wisdoms, the six paramitas, and so forth. These are symbolized by the thirteen jewel ornaments and the five silk garments. The five silk garments are the upper and lower garments and the ribbons around the crown. The thirteen jewel ornaments are the crown, the topknot, the earrings, the necklaces, the armlets, the bracelets, the anklets, and the apron. Ten of the thirteen ornaments symbolize the ten powers and three symbolize the three kayas.

Symbolizing that Vajrasattva's mind is unchanging within the wisdom state of nondual bliss-emptiness, he is in union with his consort. Symbolizing the wisdom emptiness of the consort, she is naked, without any clothes. Though she is naked, she is adorned with the five bone ornaments, symbolizing that she is beyond union with or separation from the five wisdoms. The right hand of the consort holds a hooked knife, the right arm embracing the neck of her consort, which symbolizes cutting the root of attachment to the three worlds of samsara. Her left hand holds a kapala filled with amrita; this symbolizes the enjoyment of continuous bliss-emptiness. Though prajna and upaya appear in the form of the principal deity and consort, in the ultimate nature there is no difference between them. To symbolize that, the deities kiss each other.

From their bodies radiate billions of light rays of the five wisdoms and the sixth, self-born wisdom, pervading the infinite buddhafields with light rays of body. All those buddhafields are just a display of Vajrasattva's form, which, like our karma body, is just a display of wisdom. His form abiding in that expanse of light rays is seated on a lotus, symbolizing that he is not touched by faults of body, speech, and mind. Symbolizing that he continuously looks after all sentient beings with great compassion, there is a moon disk on the lotus, upon which Vajrasattva sits. Symbolizing that Vajrasattva spontaneously perfects all unconditioned qualities, he manifests in sambhogakaya form. However his form appears, it is very beautiful and there is nothing ugly about it. Even if one were to look at his face for many days, one would never have enough of seeing it. He is without any signs of an ordinary worldly body; he is the lord of nondual appearance and emptiness.

This is the way one should remember the meaning of all the different details, such as the arms, the legs, and so forth. Vajrasattva has all these qualities of purity. One might think that if one visualizes oneself as Vajrasattva with these qualities, one will be able to obtain such qualities in the future, and that at the time of the ground these qualities are not there, at the time of the path they are neither there nor not there, and at the time of the result they are all there. But that is not the case. In the ground nature these unconditioned qualities are all perfectly present. On the path, from the point of view of appearance, all these unconditioned qualities manifest according to one's perception, and from the point of view of emptiness, the essence of these qualities is perfected. In the fruition, these unconditioned qualities are perfect in the way they appear and the way they are. In brief, one-pointedly visualizing oneself as Vajrasattva, the basis of manifestation of all the buddhas, one should think one really is Vajrasattva.

To illustrate the qualities of that buddha—the ten powers, the four fearlessnesses, the eighteen distinctive features, and all other unconditioned qualities—one visualizes the outer buddha palace, perfectly adorned and arranged. If one does not visualize the buddha palace, one can just visualize oneself as Vajrasattva in the center of the protection circle. That is easier to visualize and includes everything.

In brief, everything about Vajrasattva, up to the pores of his skin, illustrates his unconditioned qualities. As one maintains the pride that there is no ordinary conditioned body subject to suffering, the obscurations of one's ordinary conditioned body are purified, and the buddha wisdom is realized. If one can visualize like that, with the certainty that one has the unconditioned wisdom body of the buddha and no ordinary karmic body, one will develop the confidence that one will actually obtain that unconditioned wisdom body. That concludes the discussion of the second topic, remembering the meaning, or being aware, of the qualities and importance of the visualization.

PRIDE OF THE DEITY

The third topic is confidence that one is the deity, or maintaining the pride of the deity. We are not trying to fabricate something that is not there. We are just trying to see what is within our nature. Visualizing the earth as gold will not change the earth into gold. Though the meditator is an ordinary person, he has the potential of the tathagatagarbha, where all unconditioned qualities are primordially present, just as oil is present in a mustard seed. If one presses a small mustard seed, one will obtain oil. Similarly, through clearly visualizing the details, remembering their meaning, and maintaining the pride of the deity, we cannot help but actualize the qualities present in the tathagatagarbha. It is not as though now we are impure ordinary individuals deluded by karma and defilements, but in the future we might be transformed and be pure. From the point of view of the qualities of the ground, the victorious Vajrasattva has exhausted all faults and perfected all qualities. The nature of the wisdom mind of nondual bliss and emptiness of all the buddhas is the nature of our own tathagatagarbha. Because of that nature we should maintain the pride of the deity.

As explained during the discussion of remembering the meaning, the wisdom form of all the buddhas manifests in the form of Vajrasattva. All the parts of Vajrasattva—his face, arms, legs, and so forth, up to the pores of his skin—are pervaded with the buddhas' wisdom, which benefits sentient beings. If even one pore of the skin of Vajrasattva's body benefits sentient beings, visualizing our body, speech, and mind as Vajrasattva will have immense benefit. Though we are ordinary individuals and beginners, the qualities of Vajrasattva are present in the nature of our mind. So it is not as if we are trying to fabricate something we do not have. We are just trying to uncover the potential we have within. Thinking that we are actually Vajrasattva himself, we should maintain the pride of the deity.

We should mix the pride of the deity with remembering the meaning. If one has pure gold, it can be used if it is heated, mixed with other substances, and beaten. Similarly, as Vajrasattva is primordially present in the natural state of one's mind, the tathagatagarbha, if we meditate on Vajrasattva according to the various points of the development stage and the completion stage, remembering the meaning and maintaining the pride of the deity, there is no way that the qualities of the tathagatagarbha will not be realized. Not remembering the meaning during the visualizations of the development stage is like leaving a gold mine undiscovered. As no one knows it exists, no one will use it, so it will not have any benefit. If the gold is discovered by someone, it can be used. The way to use the tathagatagarbha is to practice the development stage.

Regarding the confidence that one is Vajrasattva oneself: The root of wandering in the three worlds of samsara is ego-clinging. If we meditate thinking that that ego is the deity, that is not impure pride, but becomes pure pride. Once this pure pride has arisen in the mind, there is no need to do anything special about impure pride, as it has been transformed into pure pride. That is the oral instruction of the profound method of the secret-mantra vajrayana. Stabilizing this pride will also help the visualization. If we think that we are visualizing ourselves as something we are not, we will not be very happy. If we think that we are visualizing ourselves as something we are, we will develop confidence. Continuing that meditation, we will develop all the qualities of the development stage. When we notice that these qualities are developing, we attain the certainty and confidence that we are actually like that.

What is the wisdom body of Vajrasattva like? That one body pervades all the buddhafields. In order for all the buddhafields to be displayed in one pore of his body, it is not necessary to make the pore bigger or the buddhafields smaller; they can both remain just as they are. For instance, when Milarepa got inside a wild yak's horn in Kungthang to avoid a hailstorm, the wild yak's horn did not get bigger and Milarepa did not shrink. But he was quite comfortable in that wild yak's horn. Similarly, within the body of Vajrasattva whole buddhafields can take form with everything manifest. If one is able to display such miracles, there is no reason to feel uncomfortable about countless buddhafields abiding in one pore of the body. When it is explained according to its appearance aspect, it is luminous like a rainbow; when it is explained according to its emptiness aspect, it is without substantial flesh and blood. Because the buddha's body is an unconditioned wisdom body, however beings visualize it in accordance with their interest and devotion, that is the way the form will actually appear. As soon as we think about that form, the blessings of the buddha's body will enter our mind. Thus we should maintain the pride of the deity.

While meditating on that samadhi, our mind might become drowsy or wild. If it becomes drowsy or spaced out, we should concentrate on the importance of the practice, the qualities of Vajrasattva, and the supreme and ordinary siddhis we can attain from meditating on Vajrasattva, and rejoice. If the mind becomes wild, we should concentrate on the form of the buddha. Even visualizing the buddha's form for just one second has immense benefit. If we are distracted by beautiful worldly forms and things, entertainment, and so forth, and feel like doing something else, we are wasting one's time, getting distracted from our own nature, and there is no benefit whatsoever. Concentrating on the form of Vajrasattva makes our wisdom mind, the potential within, unfold. We should try to get used to doing it for a long time. We should keep our mindfulness and awareness. Mindfulness means thinking that we are Vajrasattva and always maintaining that pride without forgetting it. Awareness is watching whether we are meditating on Vajrasattva's form and whether the qualities are developing in our being. We should check up on ourselves repeatedly and, if those qualities are not developing, we should train in the methods of developing them. If we practice for a long time in this way, our practice will become stabilized.

Mantra Recitation

When our practice has become stabilized, if we meditate on the emptiness aspect of the development stage for a long time and our mind becomes weary, to progress in the practice we should do the yoga of mantra recitation. What is this yoga of mantra recitation? In general, in ordinary individuals, body, speech, and mind are separate things. The body is a form made of flesh and blood, the speech is what speaks, and the mind is all the thoughts that arise. For instance, when we die and the mind has gone into the bardo, the physical body is cremated or thrown in the water, and there is nothing left of the speech. The body, speech, and mind of a buddha are not like that. The body alone can perform all activities of speech and mind, the speech alone can perform all activities of body and mind, and the mind alone can perform all activities of body and speech. Since his body, speech, and mind are inseparable, one of these aspects can perform the activities of the others. If a buddha can benefit more beings through his body, he will manifest his body. If he can benefit more beings with his speech, he will manifest his speech. If he can benefit more beings through the blessings of his mind, he will manifest his mind. Thus, visualizing his body is not different from visualizing his speech. His speech is the secret mantra.

For instance, now we do not actually see the form of Vajrasattva or recognize the ultimate Vajrasattva, the wisdom of awareness-emptiness. Even though we do not recognize that, the six-syllable mantra OM VAJRASATTVA HUM and the hundred-syllable mantra are the miraculously displayed form of Vajrasattva's speech. That mantra is a manifestation of Vajrasattva, and if we recite that mantra—for instance if we recite the hundred-syllable mantra 21 times without being distracted—our evil deeds will not increase and will gradually be exhausted. If with undistracted mind we recite 100 or 108 times the hundred-syllable mantra, even if we have broken samaya and committed the five heinous crimes, they will be purified. The six-syllable or the hundred-syllable secret mantras are blessed by Vajrasattva. If one gathers many medicines, blends them, and has them blessed by gurus, giving this blessed medicine to beings will remove their illness and obstacles, protect them, and prevent harm. In the same way, if one recites Vajrasattva's mantra, the deity manifests in the form of the mantra.

We should not think that if we are actually able to see the form of Vajrasattva that would be great, but just reciting his mantra is easy and therefore not as great. Because Vajrasattva actually manifests in his mantra, reciting the mantra with the visualization is of great benefit. Through the recitation, as our obscurations are gradually exhausted, the mantra will transform into the deity, and we will actually have a vision of Vajrasattva. He will give us prophecies, and we will attain the five types of higher perception and so forth. It is inevitable that such an accomplishment will naturally happen. The deity and the mantra are not separate things. Even though it is the speech of Vajrasattva, one should think that it is actually Vajrasattva.

If we pray to a wish-fulfilling jewel, food, clothes, and whatever wealth we want will naturally arise. Similarly, if we recite the mantra with one-pointed concentration and meditate on the samadhis, the supreme and ordinary siddhis can be attained through recitation of that mantra, even though when we look at the mantra it has no mind, and when it is written there is nothing but the shape of the drawn syllables.

The buddha has body, speech, and mind activities. Of those, his speech activity is the one that brings the most benefit to sentient beings. How is it that the speech activity is the one that is of greatest benefit? Our Buddha, Shakyamuni, manifested in this world with his body, but when he passed into nirvana his body disappeared, so we can no longer connect with his appearance aspect. But his speech is preserved in writings such as the sutras and tantras, so we can study his teachings. If we hear, contemplate, and meditate on those teachings, we will know what the Buddha said to accept and what to reject. If we know what to accept and what to reject, that knowledge is also the Buddha's activity. So speech is very important.

Even if they have not developed faith and devotion, when beings see the six-syllable mantra OM VAJRASATTVA HUM and when the thought of that arises in their mind, that is like planting a seed of enlightenment. It is inevitable that they will have a connection with Vajrasattva in the future. If we write the mantra on a rock or cloth or paper and leave it somewhere, some beings will make a connection just by seeing it. If they just think, "Oh, this may be a mantra written in Sanskrit or Tibetan," just by looking at it, they make a strong connection. It is because each syllable is not ordinary but completely blessed and because it manifests from the wisdom state of enlightened beings that it has such significant benefit. Beings that have no direct way to connect will naturally make a connection through mantras written on rocks or pieces of cloth or paper. In that way, a seed of enlightenment is planted, and it is inevitable that through that seed Vajrasattva will take care of them.

In the past there was a great Indian scholar named Vasubandhu, who used to recite 9,900,000 texts. Because he did not want to interrupt his recitations, at night he would sit naked in a tub filled with oil, to clarify his prana, and recite the texts. Once when he was sitting there reciting, there was a pigeon in his room. The pigeon did not know what the master was reciting, but heard the sound of the Buddha's teachings again and again. Though the pigeon could not arouse devotion, just through hearing the sounds, when the pigeon died he was reborn as a student of master Vasubandhu and became just as learned as the master. He was known as the pandita Sthiramati, and from birth he could remember all the sutras he had heard in his previous life. In the same way, if beings just hear the sound of Vajrasattva's mantra, it will have immense benefit in their next life.

When Vajrasattva's mantra is written on rocks or flags that hang in the air, the wind blows over those mantras. Then whoever is touched by that wind will make a strong connection with Vajrasattva and be saved from the three lower realms. So that is an important way to protect beings. It is a connection taking place in an indirect way. For instance, in building a fire, if we have coals that just need to be blown on, the fire will burn quite easily. In the same way, through the recitation of the mantra, our karma and obscurations will be purified. The power of it will be like having coals for the fire.

It is important to combine the visualization and recitation. Meditating on the form of Vajrasattva while reciting his mantra is much more beneficial. It is like when one wants to approach someone and calls his name again and again. If one does that, in the end that man will say, "What?" When sending a letter of request to a minister, if one sends it not only once but twice or three times, in the end that minister will send a reply. Similarly, when one constantly recites Vajrasattva's name, through the support of that recitation Vajrasattva will always look after us with compassion and give us special blessings.

Some sadhanas of other deities have sections on approaching, close approaching, accomplishment, and great accomplishment. Every sadhana has an approaching, accomplishment, and activity aspect. For the recitation of Vajrasattva's mantra, concentrating on the seed syllable HUM surrounded by the mantra and reciting OM VAJRASATTVA HUM or the hundred-syllable mantra while one-pointedly concentrating on the visualization of Vajrasattva's body, speech, and mind is the approaching aspect. The emanating of light rays from the mantra is the close-approaching aspect. When one attains the supreme and ordinary siddhis, one applies the activities. As one meditates on oneself as Vajrasattva with the seed syllable and the six-syllable mantra in the heart center turning clockwise, inconceivable light rays radiate and pervade limitless buddhafields. When the light rays touch the heart centers of the buddhas and bodhisattvas, they are very happy and send their body, speech, and mind blessings back with the light rays. It is like bees taking honey from flowers. As the light rays dissolve into one's body, speech, and mind, one's broken samayas of body, speech, and mind are purified. One obtains the body, speech, and mind blessings, and one's visualization of Vajrasattva becomes even more clear and stable than before.

Again from Vajrasattva's heart center radiate light rays, which pervade the beings of the six realms. The suffering of each realm, such as the heat and cold of the hell beings and the hunger and thirst of the pretas, is pacified. As the sun rising in the sky melts the frost with its warmth, all their impure perceptions are dispelled by the light rays emanating from the seed syllable and the mantra in the heart center of Vajrasattva. All phenomena should be considered as of the nature of the three vajras. All forms are Vajrasattva's buddha field and Vajrasattva's form. They appear but their nature is emptiness. All sounds are Vajrasattva's mantra. All thoughts are the wisdom of bliss and emptiness inseparable.

Visualizing the radiating light rays in this manner, one recites the six-syllable mantra OM VAJRASATTVA HUM. The six paramitas of Vajrasattva's mind are perfected. In reciting the hundred-syllable mantra one recites the syllables of the hundred peaceful and wrathful deities. Whatever deity of the secret-mantra vajrayana one practices, throughout the Sarma or Nyingma there is not a single one who is not connected with Vajrasattva. Therefore Vajrasattva is the lord of all the families and manifests all the buddhas. Within this practice the recitation, accomplishment, and activity are fulfilled. For instance, in the first stage, through emanating light rays and making offerings, we approach the buddhas' and bodhisattvas' blessings, which is the approaching aspect. The accomplishment aspect is gathering the blessings back into oneself through the light rays and becoming inseparable from Vajrasattva's body, speech, and mind. Then, emanating light rays to all beings and purifying them is the activity aspect. In the Vajrasattva practice, these three aspects are very simple, but they include everything.

After the buddhas have manifested their buddhafields, when their activities are completed, they remain in the dharmakaya state and their buddhafield dissolves. Similarly, one visualizes Vajrasattva's form, concentrates one-pointedly on the visualization, trains in the purity, perfection, and ripening, and exerts oneself in the recitation of the mantra. At the end of the session, the outer universe dissolves into the protection circle, that dissolves into the buddha palace, that dissolves into Vajrasattva, the consort dissolves into Vajrasattva, Vajrasattva dissolves into the mantra, the mantra dissolves HUM, and the HUM fades into space, like a rainbow. Then the mind has an experience of emptiness. One should rest for a while in that state.

That is the absolute Vajrasattva. It is the mind's aspect—appearance and emptiness both. When thoughts arise again, the universe becomes Vajrasattva's buddhafield, the contents become Vajrasattva's form, and all sounds become his mantra. Thus the purity is used to progress on the path.

The form is the mudra teaching of the development stage, the speech recitation is the mantra teaching, and the mind meditation is the teaching of the completion stage, the absolute teaching. As for the appearance aspect, one visualizes Vajrasattva's buddhafield and the form of the deity, which dissolves into the expanse of emptiness. When dissolving the form in the expanse of emptiness, it is the mind that dissolves it. Vajrasattva is not a form that can be touched with the hands; neither is it something that one cannot see. It is made by the mind, and after it has dissolved back into the mind, when one looks at that mind, it seems that something is there. If one asks a child whether there is a mind, he will say that there is. If one asks him to look at the nature of that mind and see whether it is white, yellow, red, blue, square, or round, he will not be able to find anything. Similarly, when Vajrasattva has dissolved into the state of emptiness, that illustrates the nature of appearance and emptiness inseparable.

The mind has an appearing aspect. Because inside the body there is a mind, we can see with our eyes, hear with our ears, remember with our mind, like good things, and dislike bad things. That thinking mind is like a rainbow in empty space: it cannot be touched with the hands nor seen with the eyes. Even a great scholar cannot explain how to meditate on the nature of that mind. The recognition of the nature of the mind, the nature of appearance and emptiness inseparable, in the development stage is called the yoga of luminosity.

We are not producing something that is not there. All we visualize and try to concentrate upon is within our nature. It unfolds from there. The nature of appearance is not ordinary but should be recognized as empty. From emptiness anything can manifest. We should be able to remember the instructions for the practice, work with the details, remember the meaning of them all, and have confidence that we ourselves have that potential within. External phenomena should be realized as nothing but a display of what is within.

We should have confidence that this practice is very important. The practice of Vajrasattva has such blessings that it naturally purifies all breaches of samaya and all subtle and gross obscurations. This samadhi-meditation should be combined with the three excellencies: the application of bodhichitta, the main practice beyond concepts, and the dedication of merit to all sentient beings, which is the basis of the mahayana vehicle. Just by remembering Vajrasattva's name, the door to rebirth in the lower realms is shut, broken samaya is purified, and body, speech, and mind accomplishments are attained. That concludes this brief instruction on the development stage.

FIVE

The Four Binding Forces

I N THE STAGES OF THE PATH of the mahayana secret-mantra vajra-yana, there are the development stage and the completion stage. It is important to start with the practice of the development stage. Just as a man has a body, speech, and mind, as well as activity that combines those three, within the development stage there are four binding forces. The practice of relating to our body as the form of the buddha deity to progress on the path is the binding force of appearance as the deity. Relating to our speech as the essence of the buddha's speech to progress on the path is the binding force of mantra recitation. Relating to our mind as the buddha's mind to progress on the path is the binding force of the unchanging view. Making our body, speech, and mind inseparable from the buddha's body, speech, and mind, we use buddha activity to progress on the path. This is the binding force of activity. These are the four binding forces, which are special instructions on the development stage by Guru Rinpoche.

THE BINDING FORCE OF
APPEARANCES AS THE DEITY

Let us discuss the first binding force, appearances as the deity. All phenomena, the universe and its contents, are formed through the five elements: earth, water, fire, wind, and space. Of these five elements, earth solidifies, water moistens, fire gives heat, wind moves, and space pervades. Those are the actions of the five elements.

The natures of the five elements are the five consorts of the buddhas. The nature of earth is Buddhalochana, the nature of water is Mamaki, the nature of fire is Pandaravasini, the nature of wind is Samayatara, and the nature of space is Dhatvishvari. The nature of the five buddha consorts is the way the five elements are. As for the way they appear: earth is solid, water is wet, fire is hot, wind moves, and space pervades.

Through our impure perception, the universe and its contents manifest from the five elements. When the universe is destroyed, it is also through the five elements. Recognizing the elements as the nature of the five buddha consorts, one meditates on the mandala as in the secret-mantra vajrayana path, with the elements and Mount Meru below and, on top of them, the buddha palace. There is nothing that is not made of the five elements, which should be recognized as a display of the five consorts.

Regarding the contents of the universe, sentient beings: all beings have the five skandhas, which are form, feeling, perception, formation, and consciousness. From the impure, samsaric point of view, these conditioned, fundamental skandhas are the basis of all karma and emotions; their nature is impure. When their purity is recognized according to the secret-mantra vajrayana path, they are the five buddhas. Form is Vairochana, feeling is Ratnasambhava, perception is Amitabha, formation is Amoghasiddhi, and consciousness is Akshobhya. The way they are is the five buddhas, and the way they appear is the five skandhas. According to the impure, samsaric outlook, these five skandhas are the basis of all karma and emotions and thus the basis of samsara. One recognizes their nature as the five buddhas during the development stage. In the elaborate development-stage practice, meditation on a single deity who embodies all the families, such as Vajrasattva, a deity who embodies all the tathagatas, is called a single mudra. The mudra's pure aspect is the five buddhas. From the perspective of what is to be purified and what purifies, one can practice according to the five buddha families.

Elaborating on those five buddha families, if the sattvas and so on are introduced, one can practice according to the forty-two peaceful deities. One can also practice according to the three families, corresponding to body, speech, and mind. Step by step, the practice can be made more elaborate, up to the hundred deities and, when each of their aspects is considered, one thousand deities can be emanated, and so forth. All these are a display of the five skandhas.

As one recognizes the five skandhas to be a display of the buddha families and purifies the karmic obscurations and defilements accumulated by the impure skandhas, one develops the support of pure buddha kayas and buddhafields. That is when body, speech, mind, quality, and activity appear as the five buddha families. What is called the nature of the deity—the essence of the deity—can appear as one family, five families, or as inconceivable emanations.

The five skandhas are the inner contents, sentient beings, and the five elements are the outer container, the universe. Making the connection between these two are the five sense organs—eyes, ears, nose, tongue, and body—and consciousness. The five sense organs have the five sense fields of form, sound, smell, taste, and touch. In the impure, samsaric mode, these five sense fields are perceived with the five sense organs: the eyes see form, the ears hear sound, the nose smells, the tongue tastes, and the body feels. In dependence on that, consciousness becomes attached to beautiful objects and generates aversion toward ugly objects, and in that way the karma of attachment and aversion is accumulated. If one speaks of their ultimate nature, consciousness is pure as the eight sattvas and their consorts, as in the *Shitro*, or the eight close disciples and the eight offering goddesses. From the perspective of the way things are, what makes a connection between the five skandhas and the five elements is the pure eight sattvas and their consorts. From the perspective of the way things appear, it is the impure sense organs.

When the sense organs perceive an object, kleshas develop. That is how they become the cause of wandering in samsara, accumulating karma of attachment and aversion. If one can meditate on all that as the nature of the deity, one will not be deluded. It is not that a yogin of the secret-mantra vajrayana does not see form or hear sound, but when he sees a form with his eyes, there is no attachment or aversion, and when he hears a sound with his ears, there is no hope or fear about pleasant or unpleasant. He has no clinging concerning it. In order to destroy clinging, one should visualize the form of the deity. When one visualizes the form of the deity, one should visualize the support of the buddha palace, the deity, and the protection circle. Just as we worldly people have a house to stay in, the deity has a buddha palace inside of which the mandala of the deity abides.

When the meditation of the development stage becomes stable, one can emanate many principal deities and their retinues. When the meditation is not yet stable, one should concentrate on the details of one deity, such as Vajrasattva. In essence, if we try to analyze the ceaseless appearing aspect with our awareness, it cannot transcend the expanse of emptiness endowed with all the supreme aspects. The outer five elements that we perceive can be crushed into dust, dust into atoms, atoms into atomlessness, and atomlessness into emptiness. If we analyze the wisdom of emptiness into outer and inner emptiness, there are the five consorts for the outer emptiness. As for the inner contents, sentient beings, in the *Guhyagarbha Tantra*, for instance, there are the container, the contents, and the mind stream. At the time of impure delusion, the outer container is the five elements. The inner contents, sentient beings, are the five skandhas. When sense objects are connected with that, the mind stream is the kleshas, the five poisons. In the pure aspect, the container, the five elements, is the five buddha consorts; and the contents, sentient beings, the five skandhas, are the five buddhas.

The sense organs meet objects, giving rise to consciousness and subsequently kleshas, the five poisons. In relative truth, they are perceived as impure by ordinary individuals, but a yogin will know how to use them. For instance, when someone who is skilled in searching for precious stones looks at the earth, he will know where there is gold underneath, unearth it, and use it for jewelry or other purposes. When the five elements and the five skandhas arise as a display of the five wisdoms, there are no more impure perceptions. In the secret-mantra vajrayana path, the relative truth is not rejected but perceived as the deities. Samsara and nirvana are realized as the same. In this indivisible truth of evenness and purity, there is no duality of rejecting the relative and accepting the absolute. The rejected and accepted truths are inseparable and appear as a play of the intrinsic nature.

To perceive that, one should visualize the support of the buddha palace with all the ornaments. Within that are the forms of the deities. The forms of all deities should not be visualized as something compounded of flesh and blood, nor something solid and obstructed like clay or golden statues. They should be visualized like a rainbow in space.

Though they are like a rainbow, they are not just a form without potential. Their form has potential, and without obstruction they can perform any activity that has to be performed. They are not concrete and unable to act, but the pores of their bodies and all the buddha palaces have the dynamic power of all the qualities of the enlightened state. They should be visualized as a play of omniscient wisdom; even just one pore of their bodies has the potential to perform body, speech, and mind activity, training those who need to be trained, expounding the dharma, and performing whatever other activity is beneficial.

One should visualize as I explained before, clearly visualizing the details, remembering their meaning, and maintaining the pride of the deity. All the substantial perceptions we have of the universe and its contents will appear as a pure play of the kaya and jnana of the buddhas. As that perception becomes stable, first the visualization is like a mental object; in the middle, it is like a sense object—one actually sees one's own body as the deity and all places as pure buddhafields; and finally one perceives physical appearance as the deity—when Guru Rinpoche gave the eight-logos empowerment to his twenty-five disciples, they actually perceived him as the deity. When these three stages of visualization are perfected, that is called the binding force of appearances as the deity.

The Tibetan expression for this is *kyepa lheser*. *Kye* means the outer container—the habitual patterns that make up the universe—which is seen as a buddhafield. The deluded habitual patterns that make up the contents, sentient beings, are seen as being of the nature of the deity. The five poisons, the emotions, are seen as the wisdom play of the deities, free from attachment and aversion. That is called *kyepa lheser*. When two pieces of wood are to be put together, one uses a nail to join them. Similarly, as one seals the impure perceptions of the universe, its contents, and emotions as the pure play of kaya and jnana, though one rejects impure perceptions until pure kaya and jnana arise, in fact they have always been inseparable.

It is not as if we are trying to fabricate something. We are just trying to recognize the nature of the universe and its contents, which is naturally pure. For instance, suppose we try to obtain a wish-fulfilling jewel from underground or from the depths of the ocean. When the jewel has been brought up, we can use it. As long as it is down in the ocean, we cannot use it. Thus, visualizing one's aggregates and skandhas as the wisdom form of the buddha is known as *kyepa lheser*, the nail [binding force] for giving birth to [developing] the deity.

THE BINDING FORCE OF MANTRA RECITATION

The second binding force is the recitation of the mantra, blessing speech as the speech of the buddha. Though the universe is formed by all the five elements, in that process wind is the most important. Also when the universe is destroyed, it is done by wind. When the bodies of sentient beings, who make up the contents, are formed, it is by the wind that the five elements are gathered and then scattered again. At the time of death, consciousness is pushed by wind and goes into the bardo, and the body is left behind. Wind has very powerful energy; it is because of that that there is communication between mind and object. When the eyes see form and the ears hear sound, one thinks that one sees and hears—there is communication between mind and object. This is caused by the power of wind. In the very beginning, when sentient beings fell into delusion out of the dharmata state of tathagatagarbha, this was caused by the movement of wind. Due to that movement, they fell into the delusion of holding onto an ego. So that wind is very powerful.

What are the characteristics of this wind? It is light and moving. This wind has two aspects: the impure wind, which is called the karmic wind, and the pure wisdom wind. In the case of the impure karmic wind, the mind is moved by the wind. Action and reaction is based on this wind. Speech is based on this wind. Though the sound of speech has no form or color, when one communicates one's thoughts to someone through speech, they know what one is thinking. This communication through speech is done through wind. There is nothing that is more powerful than wind. If one practices the yoga of wind, the root of samsaric delusion will be cut, and one will be able to attain the supreme and ordinary siddhis.

Where is this karmic wind? Within our body we have nadis that generate attachment and aversion. The right one, called the rasana, is red, and the left one, called the lalana, is white. The rasana and the lalana are the nadis of the duality of object and mind. When the wind moves into the rasana and lalana, it makes the mind move. Where is the pure wisdom wind? In between the rasana and the lalana is the central channel, the avadhuti, through which the wisdom prana circulates. All the sounds of the Buddha's teachings unfold from this wisdom energy channel. The channels of the Buddha's body contain the vowels and consonants, which are the basis of the 84,000 dharmas taught by the Buddha, based on that wind.

Regarding our body, whatever actions we perform are all based on this wind, energy. Without this pervading energy, we would be unable to do anything. The karmic wind contains the five elements: earth, water, fire, wind, and space. During meditation, the energy of the five elements has color and shape. The earth energy is yellow and shaped like a square, the fire energy is red and shaped like a triangle, the water energy is white and shaped like a circle, the wind energy is green and shaped like a triangle, and the space energy is blue and shaped like an octagon.

In the center of the body, between the heart and the lungs, is the life vein. When the energy (prana) is in that life vein, if that life vein is filled and not damaged, the person will have a long life. If the energy in that life vein escapes, it is inevitable that that person will die. That is called the life-holding prana. The energy that pervades our whole body, makes us able to move our limbs, enables our eyes to see forms, even if they are very far away, and enables us to hear sound, is called the pervading prana. The energy that runs through our mouth and nose is called the rising prana. The energy that circulates through our lower orifices is called the descending prana. Then there is the fire-balancing prana, which gives the body warmth. When the power of the fire-balancing prana degenerates, one cannot digest food and becomes ill.

These five energies are the basis of how things function. The inner division [that of the contents, or sentient beings] has ten categories: the five elements plus the rising prana, the descending prana, the life-holding prana, the fire-balancing prana, and the pervading prana. When the buddha's speech is used to progress on the path, these five energies transform into wisdom energy.

How can one use the buddhas' speech to progress on the path? In the secret-mantra vajrayana, when we recite mantras, the speech of the buddhas, those mantras stop the power of impure energy and increase the power of pure wisdom energy. What is such a mantra? There are three types of mantra: the infallible-cause root mantra, the condition-developing mantra, and the activity recitation mantra.

What is the infallible-cause root mantra? While visualizing the deity in the development stage, through the seed samadhi which, as I explained earlier, is done with the support of the seed syllable of the deity—for instance, the HUM of Vajrasattva and Vajrapani, the DHIH of Manjushri, the OM of Vairochana, the HRIH of Avalokiteshvara and Amitabha, and so forth—the form of the buddha is accomplished. That is the infallible-cause root mantra. When Guru Rinpoche came to train sentient beings in Jambudvipa, the buddha Amitabha emanated the nature of his great wisdom mind in the form of the syllable HRIH to Lake Dhanakosha, and from it a young boy with the major and minor signs manifested. That is the infallible-cause root mantra.

The condition-developing mantra is done while visualizing the buddha palace. These are mantras such as SPHARANA PHAT, SAMHARANA HUM, and so forth. Then the deity develops. For instance, from the seed syllable light rays radiate as one says SPHARANA PHAT. Then, as one says SAM-HARANA HUM, the light rays are gathered back and dissolve into the HUM. That transforms into a five-pronged white vajra. As one recites OM VAJ-RASATTVA AH, it becomes the form of Vajrasattva. All those recitations are called condition-developing mantras. They are the mantras used to generate [develop] the deity. These Sanskrit mantras are found in all sadhanas.

In the activity recitation mantra, one recites the mantra and through its power karma and defilements are exhausted, as though consumed by fire. According to the secret-mantra vajrayana, the buddha's wisdom appears in the form of the mantra. It is important to have confidence that the mantra has that dynamic power. For instance, the six syllables of the mantras OM VAJRASATTVA HUM or OM MANI PADME HUM perfect the six paramitas. They possess the inconceivable qualities of the six paramitas, which are blessed as the six syllables. Whoever recites these six syllables will shut the door to rebirth in the six realms of samsara. He will purify the obscurations of the six emotions and poisons and attain the state of the six buddhas. Thus inconceivable benefits arise from recitation of this mantra, which is a sign that the wisdom of the buddhas is present in it.

We beginners recite with the sense that the deity is the mantra. For instance, in the sadhana of Chakrasamvara, one needs to practice with the sense that the deity and the mantra are inseparable. As we practice in that way, though at present we are not able to have an actual vision of Chakrasamvara, hear his speech, or go to his buddhafield, Chakra-samvara's life essence appears in the form of the mantra OM HRIH HA HA HUM HUM PHAT, and if we have received the abhisheka, we are able to recite it. As we do the visualization with the support of the recitation, when through the dynamic power of the mantra our karmic obscurations and defilements are exhausted, the mantra transforms into the deity. It will transform into glorious Chakrasamvara, who will look after us. That is how one can attain siddhi. The mantra has inconceivable power. Of the buddha's body, speech, and mind, his speech is the most powerful and active. I explained the reason for this earlier.

Among the ways of reciting, there is what is known as mental recitation. We visualize ourselves as Chakrasamvara with the life-syllable HUM in his heart center and the mantra OM HRIH HA HA HUM HUM PHAT going around it. As we concentrate on the mantra going around the seed syllable, if we visualize each syllable as it goes around, even if we do not recite the mantra with the tongue, that is recitation. That is what we call mental recitation.

The recitation can also be combined with the breath. When we breathe in, we visualize the breath in the form of the syllable OM. While the breath stays inside, we visualize the syllable AH. When we breathe out, we visualize the syllable HUM. The essence of the buddha's body, speech, and mind, the nature of the three vajras, is primordially present. If we recognize that the nature of the buddha's body, speech, and mind is primordially present, when the breath comes in, there is the sound OM; when it stays inside, the sound AH; and when it goes out, the sound HUM. Concentrating one-pointedly in this way on the visualization as we breathe naturally, without altering it, is called the *dorje depa*, or vajra recitation. What does this vajra recitation mean? Visualizing the buddha's three vajras of body, speech, and mind in the form of the white syllable OM, the red syllable AH, and the dark blue syllable HUM; thinking that they are the mantra, and concentrating on the visualization—this mental visualization combined with breathing—is called the vajra recitation. The buddha's wisdom, the vajra mind, the nature of nondual wakefulness, appears as the three syllables, and the blessings of the buddha's body, speech, and mind enter the stream of one's being. When we have realized the nature of the way things are, breathing in while visualizing OM, keeping the breath inside the belly while visualizing AH, and exhaling while visualizing HUM come naturally. As when gold is polished its natural quality shines through even more, through this practice the qualities of the wisdom within will naturally manifest.

One can also combine the vajra recitation with the vase breathing. For vase breathing, one should understand these four instructions: inhaling, filling spreading, and shooting like an arrow. The great siddha

Naropa said that if one does not apply these four instructions in the right way, the practice may be dangerous. First, inhaling the breath through the nostrils, one should visualize the syllable oм. Second, after inhaling, one should suppress the upper breath and contract the lower breath, and so join the upper and lower breath. This is called the fierce vase breathing. One should concentrate one-pointedly below the navel. As breath and action are the same, wherever the mind's visualization is concentrated, there the breath is concentrated. If the joint [upper and lower] breath escapes upward, it will cause problems. It should be pressed down into the belly. One should one-pointedly concentrate on the navel center, and while the breath remains in the belly, one should visualize the syllable ah. One does the visualization one-pointedly as the belly is filled with air. When those two are mixed inseparably, that is called mingling the mind with the prana, which is the "filling" aspect of the instructions.

In that state, if one cannot hold the joint breath for a long time, through both nostrils one should take another short breath and press that down into the navel center. In that way one can hold it a bit longer. To mix the breath that was there and the newly inhaled breath, one should rotate the belly three times to the right, three times to the left, and three times in the center. In this way, one will be able to hold the breath a little longer. That is called "spreading."

When one cannot hold it any longer, one should exhale the breath through the two nostrils without leaving any behind. That is called "shooting like an arrow." This arrow shot should be visualized as of the nature of hum. The inhalation should be visualized as the syllable oм, and filling and spreading should be visualized as the syllable ah.

In that way, the vajra recitation can be combined with the vase breathing. If one meditates on the vajra recitation for a long time, for instance, if one holds the breath in the belly for an hour, two hours, or three hours, and then exhales, in the end one will be able to do one whole session with just one inhalation. In that way, one will develop the qualities of the energy.

To recite with speech, one uses the support of the tongue and the lips, uttering the sound of the mantra with the right pronunciation. That is called verbal recitation. There is no difference in the benefit of the three types of recitation [mental, verbal, and "blocking"]. The vajra recitation with the right visualization is especially effective in taming the prana and the mind. It can also prolong one's life and make the prana enter the avadhuti. Thus one should exert oneself in that recitation. As one does the recitation it is very important to know that the mantra and the deity are inseparable. As it is said, "The mantra is the form of the yogini; the yogini is the form of the mantra." Even if one does not actually realize one's yidam deity, when one has strong confidence that the mantra is the same as the deity, one will receive the blessings of the deity's wisdom nature. In the secret mantra, siddhi comes through confidence and devotion. If one has no confidence and devotion, but only an intellectual idea, one will not attain siddhi. If through devotion one thinks that one is actually the yogini, and if through devotion one thinks one's karmic obscurations and defilements are being purified, that will happen.

Within the recitation there are three stages: approaching, accomplishment, and application of the activities. What is approaching? First one should know the source and the history of the teachings on the deity whose sadhana one is going to practice. Then one should receive the empowerment. If one is going to do the practice after receiving the empowerment, one should have confidence that one can do the practice. Visualizing one's body as the deity, reciting the mantra with one's speech, and concentrating on the visualization with one's mind in samadhi is called approaching. When the visualization has become very clear, from one's heart center one emanates light rays making offerings to the buddhas and bodhisattvas. They purify the obscurations of beings and dissolve into one's heart center. Then one recites the mantra while visualizing that it circles from the mouths of the principal and consort through their secret centers. This is the accomplishment. Why is it called accomplishment? For instance, if one wants to deal with a government minister, one should first make contact with him. That is called *nyenpa*, or approaching. Then, when one knows the minister and is familiar with him, if one has anything to ask, one can do so. That is the *druppa*, or accomplishment. When one knows the minister very well, since he has a high poisition, he can give one a position, and through that power one can accomplish one's work. That is the *lejor*, or application of the activities.

Of the stages of approaching, accomplishment, and application of the activities, at first the most important is the approaching. When one has perfected the approaching stage, the accomplishment is the most important. When one has perfected both the approaching and the accomplishment stages, it will be easy to apply the activities. If one has not perfected the approaching and accomplishment stages, it is not suitable to practice the application of the activities. After perfecting the approaching and accomplishment stages, one can bestow the vajracharya empowerment, do the fire offering, perform consecrations, and so on. All that is called application of the activities. All such activity should be accomplished by means of the mantra.

If one recites the mantra one-pointedly with the confidence that the mantra and the deity are inseparable, one cannot help but attain siddhi. If one does not have strong confidence and one doubts whether there is benefit in reciting the mantra, or believes that there might be benefit later but not now, as a result of such doubts the blessings of the mantra will not be able to enter one's being.

There are different numbers of syllables in each mantra, symbolizing different things. For instance, the vajra-guru mantra has twelve syllables, which symbolize the twelve branches of the teachings. The six syllables of OM VAJRASATTVA HUM symbolize the six wisdoms, and the six syllables of OM MANI PADME HUM symbolize the six paramitas and the six wisdoms. Thus, one should one-pointedly concentrate on the visualization while reciting the mantra, and the prana and the mantra should be inseparable. When the breath is going in and out of the mouth and nostrils, there is the sound of reciting the mantra, and there is the one-pointed samadhi on the visualization with confidence that the mantra is the deity, then cause and condition are combined. It is like when hot sun rays are shining on dry grass and one puts a magnifying glass between them, causing the grass to ignite right away. In the same way, it is very important that the three factors just mentioned be inseparable.

If the mind is not one-pointedly concentrated on the visualization, even if we recite a lot of mantras, we will not attain the signs of the deity. If we do not have the confidence and faith that the mantra and the deity are inseparable, we cannot attain accomplishment in the secret mantra. Thus we should properly recite the mantra with the confidence and devotion that deity and mantra are inseparable. In that way, we should recite as many mantras as required, such as 400,000 or 1,200,000. We should recite the mantra 100,000 times for each syllable in the mantra and 100,000 extra times to make up for mistakes, which makes 1,300,000 mantras for the vajra-guru mantra of twelve syllables. Since OM VAJRA-SATTVA HUM has six syllables, we recite that mantra 700,000 times.

575

The recitation can be done according to time, number, or signs. Recitation according to time is when one makes a commitment to do the recitation for one month, six months, or some other length of time. Recitation according to number is when one recites the number of mantras mentioned in the text. Recitation according to signs is when one does the recitation until one attains the signs. When a superior practitioner attains accomplishment by being blessed as inseparable from the deity, it is not necessary to depend on time and numbers. When one does the recitation in this way, one's obscurations of deluded ordinary speech will be purified, and the blessings of the buddha's speech will enter one's stream of being. One will be able to control the mind with the prana, unlike the crippled rider who gets taken anywhere at all.

When we have perfected the mental and the verbal recitation, we should do the blocking recitation [cessation recitation]. Doing vase breathing and concentrating on the visualization of the mantra going around the seed syllable in the heart center is called the blocking recitation. When holding the vase breath, as a result of controlling the prana, the mind will not fall into delusion. If the blind wild horse is bound, it will not be able to go anywhere. Similarly, if the prana is bound, thoughts of duality are forcefully blocked. When we are tired of the visualization of the deity, we can do this recitation, if we do it one-pointedly. When we are tired of the recitation, we can concentrate on the visualization of the deity. We can alternate the two in this way. For instance, since our body and speech are mixed, we can explain our thoughts and understand what others say. If there were just the body without the speech and the mind, we would not be able to do that. It is very important to know that the deity and the mantra are inseparable. This is the binding force of the mantra recitation: our impure speech and the pure speech of the buddha are mixed together, so that the pure blessings of the buddha's speech purify the impure deluded speech.

THE BINDING FORCE OF
THE UNCHANGING VIEW

The third binding force is the binding force of the unchanging view (Tib. gongpa mi gyurwe ser), using the mind to progress on the path. What is this mind? All samsaric actions are performed by the mind, and all nirvanic actions are done by the mind. The mind is not just one mind; it can be analyzed into mind and the nature of mind. If we have positive thoughts such as faith, devotion, and compassion, that is the mind. If we have negative thoughts such as desire, hatred, and ignorance, that is also the mind.

What is the nature of the mind? Since we do not recognize the intrinsic nature of mind, we are caught in the delusions of the three worlds of samsara. The binding force of the unchanging view is to know the intrinsic nature of mind. To know the intrinsic nature of mind, one should first understand the mind. If one does not analyze and examine the mind, it seems to be something that is very active. If one really opens it up from within, the mind has no shape, no color, and no substance. It is something that does not exist, and its nature is emptiness. But it is not just emptiness; that emptiness is inseparable from luminosity.

It seems that inside our body there is a mind, and since within the body there is a mind, we can see with the eyes and hear with the ears. If there is something pleasant, the mind will like it; if there is something unpleasant, the mind will dislike it. That is the mind within the body. When body and mind are separated, that is called death. When we die, where does that mind go? It goes into the bardo. When the mind has gone into the bardo, the body is left behind. Inside that body which is left behind, there are eyes but they cannot see. There are ears, but they cannot hear. Though it may be treated nicely, it cannot like. Though it may be treated badly, it cannot dislike. The body could be compared to a hotel and the mind to a guest.

While the mind is in the body, the body can function. When body and mind have separated, it is like cutting the strings of a musical instrument—there will not be any musical sound. Similarly, when body and mind have separated, the speech will not bring forth any sound. One will not be able to talk.

How should we examine this mind? It is whatever is thinking all these different thoughts, such as thoughts of past, present, and future. Thoughts about this morning are past thoughts. What they are about has already gone. The thoughts about this evening are future thoughts, and we do not know when or how those future things will happen. As for present thoughts, for instance as I am teaching the dharma, concentrating on the sounds of the dharma is thought regarding the present. As all the students listen to the sound of the teacher teaching the dharma, reflecting on the meaning of the sound, that is the mind. Though it is the mind, it is the present mind.

If one wants to analyze it with awareness, we could examine, looking very closely, whether the mind is white, yellow, or red, whether it has a shape, and if that shape is square, round, or semicircular. If we think that the mind dwells in the body, we should examine where it dwells: in the flesh, the blood, the bones, the skin, the liver, the lungs? If it dwells in the body, we should be able to point out where it is. This would be similar to identifying a person by explaining where he is, whether he is young or old, and whether the person is a man or a woman. We feel that the mind is present somewhere in the body, but we cannot point out where it is. As we cannot determine where it is, we might think there is no mind. However, whatever we feel is the mind; it is the mind feeling the mind. There is nothing else that can feel.

Since the mind feels the mind, it does not find the mind. Not finding the mind is called emptiness. Is it like the emptiness of a container or empty space? If one throws dust into empty space, the space is not affected. If one lights a fire in empty space, the space does not burn. Similarly, if the mind had a shape or substance, that would be affected by dust or be burned by fire. But that is not so at all. Perhaps we should say that mind does not exist, but it is not like an empty container or empty space. Mind is something nonexisting that knows everything. That which knows everything, that knower, does it have eyes, ears, a nose, a tongue? That knower that knows what it did in the past, knows what to do in the future in order to be happy, and knows what will make it unhappy, that knower does not have eyes, ears, a nose, or a tongue. When we say that it does not exist, what thinks that it does not exist is called the luminosity aspect of the mind.

If we were to try to separate the emptiness and the luminosity aspects of the mind, it would not be possible. The emptiness of the mind is luminosity. How would we analyze that nature of inseparable emptiness and luminosity? Without following past thoughts, without inviting future thoughts, leaving the present mind unmanipulated, there is a mindfulness watching and seeing whether this unaltered mind is distracted or not. If that mindfulness is sustained without distraction, we will recognize the natural state of the mind (Tib. neluk). When we recognize this natural state of the mind and remain in that state of recognition for a long time without fabrication, that is called the nature of mind (Tib.

semnyi). Recognizing that nature of mind is the pointing out given by the gurus in mahamudra and ati. If we have not recognized this nature of mind, we can refer just to mind, by saying that when we are practicing the development stage it is the mind that meditates, and when reciting mantras it is the mind that meditates. If we do not eventually permeate the practice with that understanding of the nature of mind, there will be no benefit. If we have recognized the nature of the mind and practice the development stage within that state, there will really be accomplishment. If we recite the mantra within that nature, the blessings are much stronger. That is called the binding force of the unchanging view.

Even if a very skillful teacher tries to describe this binding force of the unchanging view, it is not possible to understand it. A devoted student who meditates for a long time with confidence and devotion will understand it through his own experience. If a teacher explains it and one just thinks that the nature of mind is like that, that will not help. First one should look and see whether the mind is empty. Starting from the nature of emptiness, look and see how the mind is. Though it is empty, is it just empty? Are emptiness and clarity inseparable? If one recognizes that they are inseparable, one should rest in the nature of that recognition.

The life of all of samsara and nirvana comes down to the nature of mind. On the secret-mantra vajrayana path, it is through confidence in and devotion to the guru that the nature of mind is recognized. And that nature of mind is the nature of the wisdom of the two knowledges, which is the wisdom of the vajrayana deities. If one recognizes that, like getting to know a friend on whom one can rely, it will be helpful. If one recognizes the nature of mind, the development and completion stages are all included in that. There is nothing that is not included in that. If one does not recognize the nature of mind, one will be deluded by the three worlds of samsara. If one does not recognize the nature of mind, the mind very actively accumulates the karma of attachment and aversion and is deluded by samsara. If a horse is bound by a rope, it can only go as far as the rope allows. Similarly, if one has recognized the nature of mind, the mind cannot be deluded. If it is not deluded, one will recognize the state of nondelusion. That state of nondelusion is called the binding force of the unchanging view.

All the great siddhas have had the power to make visible things invisible and manifest things that are invisible, fly in the sky, and go through rocks without obstruction. When we realize the nature of mind, the nature of emptiness, we realize that all phenomena are based on this powerful energy, so that we too can move freely through objects without any obstruction. We think that the sky is empty so we cannot walk in it, and that the earth is solid so we can walk on it, but all those concepts are made by the mind. If we would realize that in the nature of mind the earth is just as empty as the sky, we could remain in space like Milarepa and go through earth without obstruction. That is called the binding force of the unchanging view.

If we bring this binding force of the unchanging view into practice, the life force of meditating on the deity and reciting the mantra is captured. Through this binding force of the unchanging view, the deluded mind is cleared up and the undeluded nature of mind is understood. When the undeluded nature of mind binds deluded mind, even when there is movement, we recognize the emptiness nature of it, and the deluded mind comes back to its intrinsic nature. When a horse is controlled with a rope, it can only go as far as the rope allows. Similarly, when the nature of the mind has unfolded, the mind cannot fall into delusion. As the great siddhas said, if we take a pigeon out into the ocean on a boat and set it free, it will fly around the ocean, but as it will not find any trees or rocks to sit on, it will come back to the boat. Similarly, though the mind fabricates countless past, future, and present thoughts, it cannot help but come back in the end to its natural state of emptiness.

How do we know that this mind is empty? The mind of this morning is not there now; the present mind will not be there tonight. Who knows what tonight's mind will be? Trying to look at this mind, we have the feeling that there are thoughts about past, present, and future. If we analyze them with our awareness, the past thought is like a dead man, already gone. It has no form, color, or shape. We do not know what the future mind will think—positive or negative thoughts, who knows? Where is this present thinking mind? Looking inside and examining ourselves, we will not be able to find the mind. The nature of not finding it is empty. Resting in that nature without fabrication and recognizing the nature of that resting is called the binding force of the unchanging view.

The Binding Force of
Applying the Activities

Since body, speech, and mind are joined, one is able to perform useful actions, such as working in the fields, doing business, and so forth, which involve body, speech, and mind. If we perform harmful actions such as fighting a war and subduing enemies, those also involve body, speech, and mind. Similarly, when we meditate on our body as the deity with the binding force of appearances as the deity, recite the mantra with the binding force of sound as the mantra, and understand the nature of mind with the binding force of the unchanging view, that realization is the body, speech, and mind of whatever deity we are meditating on. When the body, speech, and mind are joined together, we can perform many activities to benefit beings. For instance, Buddha Shakyamuni manifested his body in Jambudvipa, his speech turned the wheel of the dharma, and his mind guided sentient beings on the path of liberation. Thus he performed the twelve acts. Guru Rinpoche displayed the twelve acts in twelve months.

Now, in meditating on ourselves as the deity, we use the acts of the Buddha to progress on the path. Using the Buddha's actions to progress on the path, we visualize ourselves as the deity with the seed syllable and the mantra in the heart center. Unfolding the binding force of the unchanging view through radiating light rays that purify obscurations and illness, increase life and merit, tame those who need to be tamed, and destroy enemies and obstacles, and doing the visualization in a state of samadhi, we combine the binding force of the unchanging view and samadhi. This is accomplished just by meditating in samadhi. That is called the power of interdependent connection.

When substance, mantra, and medicine are combined, there will naturally be inconceivable potential. [The reference here is to certain special medicines, such as an eye balm that allows one to see precious stones underground.] Just as Western gadgets are made from the potential of various substances, when performing pacifying, enriching, magnetizing, and destroying activities through fire offerings, purifications, or empowerments, if substance, mantra, and samadhi are combined, the benefit will be much greater. When an individual meditates on the body as the deity, speech as the mantra, and mind as the play of dharmata, if he performs a purification, cures a disease, removes a defilement, bestows a long-life empowerment, or does long-life practice, that is called the binding force of applying the activities. When buddha activity and one's actions of body, speech, and mind are inseparable, through pure buddha activity one's impure actions transform into pure activity. That is the fourth binding force. If we could practice this, it would be the infallible cause of attaining supreme siddhi, as Guru Rinpoche said. Thus, if we can apply the binding force of the unchanging view, there is no way that we will not attain liberation.

If you listen to these teachings I have given, understand them by reflecting on them, and integrate them with your practice, you will gradually attain the signs. Remember that.

PRIMORDIAL PURITY

Oral Instructions on the Three Words That Strike the Vital Point

TRANSLATED FROM THE TIBETAN
BY ANI JINBA PALMO

OM SVASTI

By the kindness of the infinite victorious ones and their
   descendents
And the blessings of the wondrous three roots,
May the unrivaled manifestation of the great treasure of
   wisdom and compassion [Khyentse], the exalted guru,
Who has emanated according to his intention,
The *fearless holder of the teachings* of the Uddiyana lord and of
   the sutras and tantras of the unbiased tradition,
Completely victorious in all directions,
Ever remain in the indestructible vajra realm,
And may your wish for peace and happiness be *spontaneously*
accomplished without effort.

•   •   •

For the sake of auspiciousness, the precious, supreme tulku
of the great Vajradhara, Kyabje Dilgo Khyentse, was
kindly given a name by the supreme lord of the victorious
ones, the refuge-protector, guide through samsara and nir-
vana [His Holiness the Dalai Lama], and offered an
adornment of robes at the Maratika rock cave of long life.
At that time, this was written and offered on the excellent
eighth day of the waxing part of the eleventh month of the
auspicious Wood Sow year [29 December 1995] with one-
pointed aspiration by Vagindra Dharmamati, the bewil-
dered monk called Sha[de-u] Trül[shik]. JAYANTU

Acknowledgments

Dilgo Khyentse Rinpoche came to North America three times during the course of his lifetime. On his third journey, in 1987, he presided over the cremation of the Vidyadhara Chögyam Trungpa Rinpoche and then offered a series of courses on the buddha dharma in three major Vajradhatu centers: Karme Chöling in Vermont, Karma Dzong Boulder in Colorado, and Karma Dzong Halifax in Nova Scotia. In the vajrayana sections of these seminars, Khyentse Rinpoche presented the essentials of the practice of the higher yanas. At Karme Chöling, he taught on ngöndro practice, taking as his focus the preliminaries for his own terma, the *Rangjung Pema Nyingthik*. In Boulder, his main emphasis was the form aspect of vajrayana practice, supplemented by teaching on the bardos, and he focused on key points of sadhana practice, with reference to the sadhana of Vajrasattva in particular. These talks were published in the first volume of this series, *Pure Appearance*, which is reprinted in the present volume of the *Collected Works*.

In Halifax, Khyentse Rinpoche emphasized the formless aspect of vajrayana practice, focusing on the practice of *trekchö*, "cutting through" to primordial purity. He based his teaching on the initial verses of *Three Words That Strike the Vital Point*, which is the posthumous instruction of Prahevajra, or Garap Dorje, to Manjushrimitra—two of the early atiyoga lineage holders—and on Paltrul Rinpoche's commentary. In these three talks, which were given on June 25–27, 1987, and are presented in this work, Khyentse Rinpoche described the view, meditation, and action of dzogchen. We are honored to be able to present these essential mind instructions of Khyentse Rinpoche to the vajrayana sangha of Vajradhatu and beyond.

The oral interpreter for Khyentse Rinpoche talks was Taklung Tsetrul Pema Wangyal Rinpoche, who cautioned that, due to the length of Khyentse Rinpoche's discourse and the subtlety of the subject matter, the instructions be retranslated prior to publication. We were fortunate that Ani Jinba Palmo, a long-time student of Khyentse Rinpoche experienced in translating for him, was willing to undertake the project. Working directly from tape and from a transcription of the Tibetan rendered by Lama Ugyen Shenpen, Ani Jinba retranslated the entirety of Khyentse Rinpoche's lectures. She was able to consult with Jigme Khyentse Rinpoche, who clarified many of the difficult points in the material, and we are deeply grateful to both of these skilled and learned students of Khyentse Rinpoche. We also wish to thank Matthieu Ricard, Khyentse Rinpoche's translator, who read through a portion of the initial draft and offered a number of valuable suggestions.

The production of *Primordial Purity* has been the responsibility of the Vajravairochana Translation Committee. Sherab Chödzin Kohn and Scott Wellenbach served as editors, working in consultation with Lama Ugyen Shenpen and Lama Chönam Wazi, while the copy-editing and composition was handled by Larry Mermelstein, executing the design of Hazel Bercholz.

A translation of the root verses of *The Three Words That Strike the Vital Point* has been appended to this work. Following the pioneering work of Tulku Thondup, a number of translations of this text have appeared in print and circulated privately. Erik Pema Kunsang's translation, originally published in *Crystal Cave*, is included here with his kind permission, as it was the rendering followed most closely by Ani Jinba, though his wording of certain terms has been amended slightly. Erik has made a few revisions since this was first published, and we are pleased to include these here.

The longevity supplication that appears at the beginning of the book was written by Trülshik Rinpoche on the occasion of Khyentse Rinpoche's tulku receiving a name and robes from His Holiness the Dalai Lama.

We deeply appreciate the permission of Shechen Rabjam Rinpoche to publish these talks, and a portion of the proceeds from this publication will be used to help support Shechen Monastery, Khyentse Rinpoche's seat in Boudhnath, Kathmandu, Nepal.

View

"IN ORDER TO LEAD to the state of perfect buddhahood all sentient beings whose number is as vast as the sky, may I listen to the profound, holy dharma." Thus we should arouse the supreme thought of enlightenment and listen to the dharma in such a way as to remember everything properly. With respect to the stages of the teachings, the supreme secret mantrayana is superior to the vehicle that examines characteristics. According to the Nyingma tradition, the teaching can be divided into nine yanas, the ninth of which is the atiyoga yana. The atiyoga yana can be divided into the outer division of mind (Tib. semde), the inner division of space (Tib. longde), and the secret division of key, or oral, instructions (Tib. men-ngag-de). The teachings I am going to give here belong to the secret division of key instructions. Within this, there are two sections: the path of *trekchö*, or "cutting through," which is for liberating students who are very diligent; and the path of *thögal*, or "direct crossing," which is for effortlessly liberating students who are lazy.

First I shall explain the stages of trekchö, of which there are two parts: the history of the lineage, an understanding of which helps to develop faith, and an elaborate explanation of the crucial points of view, meditation, and action.

LINEAGE HISTORY

To start with, in the explanation of the history of the lineage, which helps to develop faith, it is said, "Homage to the unequaled root guru, a treasury of compassion." As a field of refuge, because the guru is the embodiment of all refuges, he is called unequaled. As an object of offerings, he is also unequaled, because making offering to just one pore of the guru's skin is of greater worth and much more meritorious than making offerings to a thousand buddhas. As for the blessings of compassion, the guru's blessings are unequaled, for just practicing guru yoga and supplicating your guru will cause coemergent wisdom to arise in your mind effortlessly.

The love of the buddhas and bodhisattvas for sentient beings is like the love of a mother for her only child. During this age of the five corruptions, sentient beings are unable to see the Buddha's face or hear his speech. Out of great love for all beings and with the wisdom of the knowledge, love, and power of all the buddhas, for the sake of those to be tamed, the guru has taken human form—a vajra body with the six elements. As far as the quality aspect is concerned, he is not different from the buddhas. As far as the kindness and compassion aspect is concerned, he excels all the buddhas. The text says, "I prostrate to the kind root guru," who is the lord of compassion.

In the practice that I am explaining here, because the guru is the embodiment of all refuges, in paying homage to the guru, one pays homage to all the refuges there are. How can one recognize this guru? The teachers from dharmakaya Samantabhadra up to one's present root guru are all gurus. There are three lineages, according to the Old Translation School: the mind lineage of the victorious ones, the symbolic lineage of the vidyadharas, and the hearing lineage of superior individuals.

Mind Lineage of the Victorious Ones

Let us first consider the mind lineage of the victorious ones. All the dharmakaya buddhas have perfected the twenty-four qualities of freeing and ripening. They abide in equanimity throughout the three times, never interrupted, in the sphere of their own self-cognizing wisdom, the ocean of kaya and jnana of undefiled inner luminosity. All unconditioned dharma turns upon that unconditioned wisdom; therefore, it is called the wheel of dharma. These unconditioned teachings are not ordinary words that have come about through the efforts of ordinary individuals.

The mind lineage of the victorious ones passes from dharmakaya Samantabhadra down to the five sambhogakaya buddhas. One may ask what this mind lineage is. To describe dharmakaya Samantabhadra and the five families of victorious ones from the perspective of those to be trained: In the tradition of the New Translation School, the dharmakaya buddha Samantabhadra, the primordial buddha who is perfectly enlightened from the very beginning, is called Vajradhara or Vajradhara the sixth. As the lord of all the families, he is the lord of the five families, and so he is known as the sixth, Vajradhara, which refers to the dharmakaya. The nature of the dharmakaya can be understood in terms of the five wisdoms, which are connected with the five buddha families. The five victorious ones associated with those families are Akshobhya, Ratnasambhava, Amitabha, Amoghasiddhi, and Vairochana. Though there is this fivefold classification, there are essentially no differences of high and low or greater and lesser compassion between Samantabhadra and the five victorious ones. They are all buddhas. They can be compared to many forms reflecting in a crystal ball, which are all within the crystal ball.

Even though it is not understood through words, the unconditioned knowledge of the five victorious ones below is known by the widsom mind of dharmakaya Samantabhadra, by his self-cognizing wisdom. The unconditioned wisdom mind of dharmakaya Samantabhadra above is known by the five victorious ones. There are no differences between them in terms of these two knowledges or the qualities.

For example, if a hundred mirrors were hanging in a house with one person in it, there would be one hundred reflections of that person, and since they would all be reflections of that one person, they would all be the same. The mind lineage of the victorious ones is like that.

Symbolic Lineage of the Vidyadharas

The symbolic lineage of the vidyadharas passes from the five victorious ones down to the protectors of the three families, in particular to the Lord of Secret Vajrapani, and then to the five noble ones. According to dzogchen ("great perfection"), the lineage runs from the five victorious ones to Vajrasattva and then to Prahevajra (Tib. Garap Dorje). That is called the symbolic lineage of the vidyadharas.

About the meaning of *vidyadhara*: *Vidya*, or "awareness," means wisdom free from eternalism and nihilism. Those who always, beyond meditation and postmeditation, *hold* (Skt. *dhara*) awareness in their hands within the space of compassion are called *vidyadharas* ("awareness holders"). In regard to their primordial nature, all the holders of the lineage, from the five victorious ones, the Lord of Secret Vajrapani, Vajrasattva, and so on down to Prahevajra, are buddhas. As to their manifestation, they attained realization through nothing more than being shown a symbol.

What is this realization through being shown a symbol like? For example, when Guru Rinpoche, Padmakara, met Shri Simha, Shri Simha made the pointing mudra toward Guru Rinpoche's heart center and said KO HA A SHA SA MA HA DROL, which means "All that arises is liberated as it arises." Just through being shown that symbol and hearing those symbolic sounds, the minds of Shri Simha and Guru Rinpoche became inseparable. No actual words were necessary. Since in this lineage the transmission of realization takes place in this way, it is called the symbolic lineage of vidyadharas.

Hearing Lineage of Superior Individuals

The hearing lineage of superior individuals passes through Prahevajra, acharya Manjushrimitra, learned Jnanasutra, pandita Vimalamitra, and Uddiyana Padmakara and then to the lord [King Trisong Detsen], the subjects [the other disciples], and the companion [Yeshe Tsogyal]. Why is it called the hearing lineage of superior individuals? The abhishekas, transmissions, and teachings are given by means of words and writings; because this lineage passes through the words of one person and the hearing of another, it is called the hearing lineage of superior individuals.

The Three Words That Strike the Vital Point

These three lineages are condensed in the key instructions on the *Three Words That Strike the Vital Point,* which I shall be explaining here. From the perspective of the view of the key instructions on the *Three Words That Strike the Vital Point,* what is the mind lineage of the victorious ones? It is omniscient Longchen Rabjam ("Infinite Great Expanse"). Though Longchen Rabjam was a guru who was born in Tibet, his wisdom was equal to that of the Buddha. He attained the state of the exhaustion of samsara and nirvana.

The mahapandita Vimalamitra promised to take birth in Tibet once every hundred years in order to spread the dzogchen teachings. He manifested uninterruptedly in this fashion down to Jamyang Khyentse Wangpo [Khyentse I] and Jamyang Chökyi Lodrö [Khyentse II, Dzongsar Khyentse I] of the present age.

Among all these manifestations, one was a great master knowledgeable in all the different sciences existing in his time. This was Longchenpa, who possessed all the good qualities, such as exertion, intellectual understanding, the accomplishment of experiences and realization, and noble activities. He was unequaled in establishing the foundation of the dzogchen doctrine. He appeared to be the embodiment of all the qualities of the six ornaments and two supreme ones of Jambudvipa. Apart from his principal outer guru, the vidyadhara Kumaradza, he had about twenty other dzogchen teachers. However, in addition to that, since Longchen Rabjam's mind became inseparable from Samantabhadra, he is the mind lineage of the victorious ones.

Longchenpa had many incarnations who were born in Tibet. The supreme of them all was the omniscient Jigme Lingpa, who stayed in the charnel ground known as Tragmar Ke-u Tsang at the sacred place of Samye Chimphu for three years, one-pointedly practicing mantra recitation. While meditating on the dzogchen view, he had three visions of Longchen Rabjam. Subsequently, he received the blessings of his body, speech, and mind and was appointed a holder of the dzogchen teaching. Through that appointment, through the visions, and through merely hearing the words, "May the mind blessings of the lineage be transmitted; may they be transmitted!" and "May the lineage of spoken words be perfected; may it be perfected!" the minds of master and student became inseparable. This was how the mind terma of omniscient Jigme Lingpa—the dharma space treasure, the dzogchen *Heart Essence of the Great Expanse* or *Longchen Nyingthik* (Tib. klong chen snying thig), came to be spread throughout Jambudvipa. Since Jigme Lingpa was liberated through merely being shown a symbol by omniscient Longchen Rabjam, he is the symbolic lineage of the vidyadharas.

In regard to the hearing lineage of superior individuals, omniscient Jigme Lingpa had four disciples called the four Jigmes ("fearless ones") from Kham, as well as an inconceivable retinue of emanations of the lord, the subjects, and the companion. His extraordinary heart son was Jigme Gyalwe Nyugu, who was an emanation of noble Avalokiteshvara. To him, omniscient Jigme Lingpa gave the entire cycle of the ripening and freeing teachings of the *Heart Essence of the Great Expanse*. Jigme

Gyalwe Nyugu in turn gave this teaching to both Jamyang Khyentse Wangpo and Paltrul Chökyi Wangpo. In that way, the abhishekas, transmissions, and teachings of dzogchen passed from the mouth of one person to the ear of another. Hence, this is called the hearing lineage of superior individuals.

Paltrul Rinpoche, Chökyi Wangpo, held all three of these lineages. In the key instructions on the *Three Words That Strike the Vital Point,* which has few words but is profound in meaning, Paltrül Chökyi Wangpo conveys an understanding of all the fundamentals of the cutting-through, primordial-purity aspect of dzogchen (Tib. dzogchen kadak trekchö).

That is the historical background that authenticates this teaching by establishing that it includes the three lineages. Academic and intellectual understanding alone cannot incorporate the view, meditation, and action of dzogchen. This is because the view, meditation, and action of dzogchen can only be understood through the superior meditation of the buddhas. The superior meditation of the buddhas belongs to the sphere of their self-cognizing wisdom and not to the dry words of learned individuals. Thus, since it is said that the meaning of the tantras is seen through omniscience, those who explain such tantras as the Guhyagarbha, Hevajra, or Chakrasamvara should themselves have attained the level of a noble one. Having understood the view, meditation, and action of the tantras through the unconditioned knowledge of their self-cognizing wisdom, they are able to teach it to others. Even individuals who have perfected all the ten branches of knowledge cannot understand the tantras through the words alone. Since there is no difference between the subject matter of the tantras and the naked mind of the Buddha and since the tantras are bound by the six limits and the four ways, when investigating them, one must use one's own self-cognizing wisdom. Otherwise there is no benefit.

Let us take an example from the Kagyu lineage. The mahasiddha Tilopa said, "I, Tilo, do not have a human guru." Tilopa went to the dakini land of Uddiyana and actually received the secret dakini treasure from Vajrayogini, which he taught as a hearing lineage.

Among the eighty-four Indian mahasiddhas, Tilopa's realization is considered to be equal to space. Someone who has perfected the view, meditation, and action in that way is able to explain the tantras. Others cannot do so. Ordinary people like us cannot understand them. Gurus who hold the three lineages, have perfected the impartial view of dzogchen, have exhausted samsara and nirvana in the expanse of the dharmadhatu, and have mixed their mind with the mind lineage comprise an authentic lineage.

There is no teacher in this world superior to the Buddha. The outer form of the Buddha was the supreme nirmanakaya who performed the twelve acts in India. Though he was an emanation of buddha, not the actual dharmakaya buddha, his mind essence was the actual dharmakaya. The genuine understanding of his view, beyond meditation and postmeditation, is dzogchen. His teachings are absolutely unerring.

For example, the Buddha is referred to as omniscient. When one comes to understand the view, one sees that because there is nothing to be known beyond the Buddha's knowledge, he was said to be omniscient. The teaching of the ultimate view known by the Buddha is dzogchen. Therefore, whoever teaches it should be recognized as having realized the unerring view of the Buddha, free from delusion. This should not be someone without lineage or legitimate source. According to the investigations of the learned ones:

> All dharma is the Buddha's oral teachings and the
>   commentaries upon them.
> The commentaries come from proper contemplation of
>   the view.
> Due to that, the teachings of the Buddha Shakyamuni
> Will remain in this world for a long time.

As the teachings of the Victorious One and the authentic commentaries of his disciples were established through critical investigation of quotations, logic, and key instructions, they are unmistaken. Those who have directly seen the truth of the dharmata will not depend on inference, but will directly realize the Buddha's view. However, we cannot realize the Buddha's view directly, but through inference. The Buddha's view can be directly realized through all the teachings of the secret-mantra vajrayana, but among them, the heart advice for directly realizing the view of the Buddha is dzogchen.

Within dzogchen are found the outer division of mind, the inner division of space, and the secret division of key instructions. Among those, the division of key instructions is the one that is like the pure heart's blood. To teach according to that view is to follow the intention of the omniscient guru and his sons [Longchenpa, Jigme Lingpa, and Gyalwe

Nyugu]. In order to elucidate that, with this invocation, I have presented a brief history of this genuine lineage.

MEANING OF THE TEXT

Following the history of the lineage and the invocation, we turn to the actual meaning of the text. As it is said: "In explaining the actual meaning of a text, unless things are given names, everyone will be confused. Therefore a skilled master will indicate phenomena by name."

It is said that all phenomena, from the samsaric phenomena of skandhas, dhatus, and ayatanas up to the nirvanic phenomena of kaya and jnana, should be indicated by names and sounds. In doing this, there are two kinds of names: arbitrary and meaningful. Calling certain objects "pillar" or "vase," for instance, is something that cannot be explained. It is arbitrary; there is no reason. On the other hand, some names indicate the intended meaning. As instances of this second category, the names of omniscient Longchen Rabjam, the vidyadhara Jigme Lingpa, and Jigme Gyalwe Nyugu indicate the meaning of the view, meditation, and action of dzogchen. Here the meaning to be expressed and the words that express it—which are the teaching and the teachers of dzogchen, respectively—never depart from the nature of dzogchen. If teaching and teacher are connected, then when the teacher is authentic, the doctrine must also be regarded as authentic. If the teacher is not authentic, the teaching is also not authentic. When both teacher and teaching are authentic, what is to be expressed is based on the names of the teachers, and what expresses that, the names, includes the view, meditation, and action of dzogchen.

If one understands the meaning indicated, that is called understanding through the merging of sound and meaning, which first develops through hearing the teachings. What is this understanding through the merging of sound and meaning? For example, hearing the sound of the words "Longchen Rabjam" can directly point out the meaning of the dzogchen view. When that is pointed out, it is called understanding through the merging of sound and meaning. If one does not have that power of recognition, when the mind is not focused but one just hears the sound of a word through the ears, the meaning of the word does not settle in the mind. In order to point out the understanding through this merging of sound and meaning, the view, meditation, and action of dzogchen are taught. Here the indication is made with the key instructions on the *Three Words That Strike the Vital Point*.

One might ask what these words are in the key instructions on the *Three Worlds That Strike the Vital Point*. The sound and the word are the same. For example, the word "mother" can be understood as indicating someone who is very kind. If one says "mother," the meaning of what that word expresses is pointed out. What is known as "the three words" is like that.

What are the three words? "View," "meditation," and "action." What does it mean to "strike the vital point" with these three words? If one wants to kill a man and strikes his heart with a weapon, the man will not live another hour. He will die immediately. What vital point do these three words strike? Just as oil is present in a mustard seed, all of us, all sentient beings, have buddha nature. Though it is present, we do not recognize it, because our minds are obscured by delusions. When, as a result of the view, meditation, and action, we come to recognize these delusions, we can get rid of them in a moment. In one day sentient beings can be transformed into buddhas—that is the ultimate view, meditation, and action of dzogchen. Such a power of transformation is called "striking the vital point."

Let us say, for example, that one is ill. If there is a skillful doctor who accurately knows the point in our body where that disease resides—the spine, the flesh, the bones, or whatever—and draws it out of there, one will be immediately cured. In the same way, this view, meditation, and action can cut the life force of delusion in a moment. Thus they are said to strike the vital point.

Where did this view, meditation, and action originally come from? In order to spread the teachings of dzogchen in Jambudvipa, Vajrasattva himself manifested as a vidyadhara, Prahevajra, taking birth in the dakini land of Uddiyana as the son of a princess. Later, when the body of Prahevajra disappeared into a mass of stainless light, his disciple Manjushrimitra cried out in despair: "Alas, alas! Now that the guru is dissolving into light, who will dispel the darkness of the world?" When he uttered these words of longing, Prahevajra was moved by compassion to give him the key instructions on the *Three Words That Strike the Vital Point*. As soon as the key instructions on the *Three Words That Strike the Vital Point* fell into the hands of Manjushrimitra, though he had already understood the view, meditation, and action of dzogchen, the mind of guru and disciple became one. The mind lineage merged into one. To illustrate this, let us think of the analogy of a golden locket depicting a principal deity and the retinue: the gold pervades all of them.

The key instructions on the *Three Words That Strike the Vital Point* were taught by the dzogchen vidyadharas. Within the realm of human experience, these vidyadharas turned the wheel of dharma. When they manifested passing into nirvana, into the extraordinary luminous wisdom space of the buddhas, which is beyond human experience, at that moment they gave extraordinary instruction to an equally fortunate and worthy student, and the minds of guru and disciple became inseparable. So, in this way, when the vidyadhara Prahevajra manifested passing into nirvana and transmitted the wisdom of the mind lineage to his student, the student's realization became equal to that of the master.

That transmission is known as the final testament, and starting from dharmakaya Samantabhadra and continuing up to this point, that great potential (Tib. tsal) exists in the key instructions of dzogchen. The meaning of that is elaborately explained in the key instructions on the *Three Words That Strike the Vital Point*.

View

The first of the three words is "view." If one has not recognized the view, there can be no meditation or action. Those who have the view are like those who have the essence of wealth—lots of gold and diamonds. It is no problem for them to enjoy wealth in this world. But beggars who have no possessions can only imagine being rich. They cannot enjoy wealth. So unless we have realized the unerring view, we will not attain the state of omniscience. If you have no eyes, even if you have ears, tongue, nose, and the other senses, you are disabled. The view is like the eyes. If it is not realized without error, just imagining it will not enable one to progress on the path of liberation and omniscience.

The Buddha said:

> It is easy to progress through discipline,
> But that is not the view.
> Through discipline, one can attain a fortunate existence.
> Through the view, one can attain the supreme state.

That supreme state is the state of omniscient wisdom. To attain that is to understand the view. To make that view attainable, the Teacher, the perfect Buddha Bhagavat, introduced the different levels of the view, starting with the shravaka yana and progressing on up to the atiyoga yana. Even though the Buddha introduced all these levels, individuals should exercise discrimination concerning these views—whether they are vast or not, whether they are profound or not, whether they correspond to the ultimate state of buddhahood or not. If, discriminating in this way, one asks what the ultimate view is, the answer is the view of dzogchen. This ultimate view of dzogchen is the wisdom of the buddhas' meditation. As the Sakya Pandita said:

> This view of atiyoga is not the result of a vehicle.
> It is not a view to be ascertained through one's intelligence.

It is the result, the direct realization, of the buddhas' wisdom, known by the noble ones through their own self-cognizing wisdom. Therefore, it is known as "the sphere of one's own self-cognizing wisdom."

After the Bhagavat, the perfect Buddha Shakyamuni, had meditated and attained enlightenment under the bodhi tree, he said:

> I have discovered a nectarlike dharma
> That is profound, nonconceptual, and unconditioned.
> Since no one I show it to will be able to understand it,
> I will remain silent in the forest.

Realizing that it could not be expressed in words or speech, the Buddha showed the way of meditation, the view of which is what is established by dzogchen. It is said:

> This view of dzogchen is beyond words.
> It cannot be indicated through speech
> And transcends the sphere of mind and mental activity.

It cannot be expressed in words at all. This is not just true of dzogchen; it is said that even "the prajnaparamita is beyond speech, thought, and expression." It is impossible to indicate it through words.

Out of his skillful means and compassion, the Buddha taught the emptiness aspect of the view through the metaphor of the sky, the luminosity aspect through the metaphor of the sun and moon, and the aspect of pervading all of samsara and nirvana through the metaphor of sun rays and moon rays, thus illustrating each aspect with different analogies.

To summarize these metaphors, the view is an object of proper hearing and reflection. Through hearing, the view is understood; through reflection, it is experienced. And if one meditates, the view will unfold free of error. If one does not do that—if one just blindly thinks, "This is the view"—that is not enough. As the Buddha said:

> Just as gold must be burned, cut into, and rubbed,
> My teachings should be properly investigated.
> They should not be accepted merely out of respect.

The more one examines the Buddha's teachings through quotations and logic, the more profound and vast they become. One cannot help but develop a special trust and confidence in them. The views of other yanas, the non-Buddhist views and particularly the view of Christianity, no matter how elaborately they may be explained, do not become more profound and vast. Since the other views do not become more profound in this way, and since it is said that a view should be judged by its profundity, the teaching of dzogchen is the ultimate Buddhist view.

You might ask, "Do any of the eight lower vehicles teach a view other than that of dzogchen?" The answer is that none of them does. For example, let us start with the view of the first vehicle, the shravaka yana, about the truth of suffering, that it is based on impermanence. That impermanence is an aspect of emptiness. That feature of emptiness is taught on dzogchen—clear, in detail, and complete. The charge that the shravaka yana does not teach even a fraction of the principle of emptiness is not at all true. If it were true, the shravaka yana would not be able to eradicate the obscuration of the kleshas, which it can do.

If one has not realized the view of emptiness, then, as it is said:

> For whomever emptiness is possible
> Everything is possible.

Those people who are able to understand emptiness fully should receive extended teachings on emptiness. Those who can only understand a third of it should be taught only a third of it. Those who can understand only a small fraction of it should be taught only a small fraction. In this way they will gradually come to understand the ultimate view.

People come from the east, the south, the west, and the north. Some come by foot, others on horseback, some riding elephants, some by car, and others by plane. They all arrive at the same place but at different speeds. The speed depends on the view. If the nature of the view is correctly introduced, meditation and action will only assist the view. Once the view has been introduced, meditation and action will come along without much difficulty.

Certain sounds are able to indicate the meaning of the view of all the root and lineage gurus. Take for example the word *sang-gye*, which is the Tibetan translation of *buddha*. *Sang* means "awake"—awakened from the sleep of deluded ignorance. *Gye* means "blossom"—the lotus-like blossoming of the wisdom of the two knowledges of everything that can be known. These two words indicate, respectively, the qualities of abandoning and realization of the Buddha himself. Not only that, but bodhisattvas dwelling at the level of the tenth bhumi have these inconceivable qualities of omniscient wisdom. In sum, there are absolutely no buddha qualities that are not included within abandoning and realization.

Now in the same way, when explaining the view of dzogchen it is said:

> The view is Longchen Rabjam.

With regard to that, concerning what is being indicated, what is *long* ("expanse")? It is explained to be the view that leads to the exhaustion of the four visions, known as *longchen rabjam* ("infinite great expanse"). It is the ultimate realization of the true meaning of dzogchen. Concerning the name, the indication, the one who introduced the genuine realization of Samantabhadra, the wisdom of the 6,400,000 dzogchen tantras, is omniscient Longchen Rabjam. The name and the teaching have become one. When the person and the dharma are mixed as one, the person is dzogchen and the dharma is dzogchen.

Why is that teaching introduced? The vast meaning of the teachings is of the sphere of the minds of the noble ones and cannot be expressed by ordinary people. However, with the support of the guru's key instructions, it is possible to indicate it vaguely. As is said, "The best practice is to rely on the guru's transmission." Also, "The guru's key instructions are easy to practice and can be understood with little trouble." Thus one can attain buddhahood without difficulty. The easy way to realize the Buddha's view is to rely on the key instructions.

The key instructions on the *Three Words That Strike the Vital Point* begin, "The view is Longchen Rabjam." This view has to be understood. The guru referred to, who is indicating that, is omniscient Longchen Rabjam. As was said above, omniscient Longchen Rabjam fully understood the view of the teachings of the three divisions of dzogchen. For the sake of his students he composed the treatises of the *Seven Treasures* (Tib. dzö dun), the *Three Cycles of Relaxation* (Tib. ngalso korsum; also translated as *Kindly Bent to Ease Us*), and the *Three Cycles of Self-Liberation* (Tib. rangdröl korsum). These are teachings explained through words. This omniscient one transmitted his wisdom mind to Terchen Ratna Lingpa, Orgyen Terdak Lingpa, Lhatsun Namkha Jigme, Rigdzin Jigme Lingpa, Jamyang Khyentse Wangpo, Jamgön Lodrö Thaye, and Jamyang Chökyi Lodrö. Because he transmitted his mind blessings to all these great beings, they constitute the mind lineage of the victorious ones.

When he was taught the ultimate meaning of the mind lineage of the victorious ones, for example, the omniscient vidyadhara Jigme Lingpa had three visions of Longchen Rabjam. First, he received the blessings of his body; second, the blessings of his speech; and third, the blessings of his mind. Omniscient Longchen Rabjam transmitted these blessings of body, speech, and mind while in the form of an Indian pandita—very beautiful and peaceful, like a tathagata.

In Jigme Lingpa's first vision, Longchen Rabjam looked a little old. In his second vision, Longchen Rabjam handed him a book containing the hidden meaning of the *Seven Treasures*. As Longchen Rabjam was telling him what the book contained, he transmitted his mind stream to him. This shows what is meant by the "outer guru." As for the inner guru, after the third vision, Jigme Lingpa realized the self-manifesting impartial view of dzogchen—"Longchen Rabjam" was not just an outer pandita.

When the nature of inner awareness has been realized as Longchen Rabjam, if the awareness is strong, delusion will be exhausted and liberated into its ground. If you need to teach the realization of Longchen Rabjam in one sitting, on the spot, you can do so. If you can do that, that is called the absolute realization.

The view of dzogchen has to be explained through the aspect of what is to be indicated. Omniscient Jigme Lingpa said that when one's mind is in the right frame, the guru is not outside. For someone whose mind is in the right frame and has merged with the dharma, the master is not outside. However, the gurus who grant abhishekas, transmissions, and key instructions to people like us, whose faces we see and whose voices we hear, these masters that liberate us, are all outer masters, who serve as a means to communicate with the inner guru. These gurus confer abhishekas, transmissions, and key instructions, pointing out the liberating path of omniscience, so we should listen to what they say. If we hear, reflect on, and meditate on the teachings, there will be a time when we actually realize our intrinsic nature, the sugatagarbha.

When we have realized that, the guru who has taught us the dharma will not be outside us anymore, but inside. Where inside? The guru is the nature of our mind. Once we have realized the nature of our mind, it is no longer necessary to search for the guru outside. If the view of the mind is maintained beyond meditation and postmeditation, the guru is present beyond meeting and parting.

It is said that when the outer guru points out the key instructions, the gradual introduction to the vital points of view, meditation, and action of dzogchen takes place. From among those, to indicate the view that is to be realized, we should speak about what *longchen* ("great expanse") means. *Long* means something vast, like vast space. It is impossible to measure space in miles. Space is vast and its nature is empty. Because it is vast and empty, space is used to point to the view. Inside of it is the world with all its contents—mountains, islands, and so on. No matter how vast an array of the world and its contents is conceived of, it will never be impossible to fit it within space. What does it prove that the world and its contents—all the mountains, islands, and so on, no matter how numerous and vast they are—could never fill up space? It proves that space is not a substantial thing. Even the Buddha would not have been able to assert that.

So what does the world with all its contents have as its basis? Its basis is space, and it cannot have any basis other than space. Even though the world and its contents of lakes, islands, towns, people—whatever has form—are pervaded by space, if one were to ask if the nature of space and the nature of the world and its contents are the same, the answer would be that they are not the same at all. Without giving up its distinguishing characteristic, space is the basis of the world and its contents.

Without seeming to, the world and its contents have as their basis the same, empty space. Thinking like this, we should understand the word *longchen* to denote something vast. What is this *long?* According to dzogchen, it shows the emptiness aspect of the view—primordial purity.

What does *rabjam* ("infinite" or "universe") mean? It means a very large amount. How large? For example, if one were to try to count all the trees in all the forests of Jambudvipa, even spending one's whole life at it, one would not be able to finish the count. Similarly, all samsaric and nirvanic phenomena have as their basis the nature of primordially pure great emptiness, and all samsaric phenomena of skandhas, dhatus, ayatanas, karma, and kleshas and all nirvanic phenomena of kaya and jnana existing together are said to be *rabjam.*

What do samsaric and nirvanic phenomena have as their basis? All samsaric phenomena of karma and kleshas are based on the nature of primordially pure great emptiness. All nirvanic phenomena of inconceivable kaya and jnana are also based on primordially pure great emptiness. If one were to ask if the samsaric phenomena of karmic and emotional obscurations are the same as the primordially pure great emptiness, the answer would be that they are not. The reason why they are not the same is that the samsaric phenomena of karma and kleshas give rise to confusion and suffering. Through the kleshas, we produce the karma of passion, aggression, and ignorance and experience the sufferings of the six realms. In primordially pure great emptiness, even the name of suffering does not exist. Someone who has realized primordially pure great emptiness sees samsaric phenomena as projections without inherent existence, like a rainbow in the sky or like the water in a mirage.

In what sense are the nirvanic phenomena of kaya and jnana based on primordially pure great emptiness? Their natures are mixed as one. Kaya and jnana are spontaneously present in the nature of primordially pure great emptiness. Although kaya and jnana are spontaneously present, with regard to primordially pure great emptiness, to explain the qualities of the Buddha, for example, it is said that there are the thirty-two major and eighty minor marks. What are the thirty-two major marks? They are the circle of hair between the Buddha's eyebrows, the protuberance on the crown of his head (Skt. ushnisha), and so forth. Each of these qualities is inconceivable. Although they exist in primordially pure great emptiness, Buddha's ushnisha is not something raised up, and the circle of hair between his eyebrows is not something round and white. They do not exist as form or substance. The cause of the ushnisha on Buddha's head and the circle of hair between his eyebrows is the inconceivable treasure of merit that is naturally and spontaneously present in primordially pure great emptiness.

This is analogous to gold or diamonds. If one has a diamond, whether it is as big as a mountain or as small as a sesame seed, the preciousness of diamond is present within it. In the same way, the treasure of all the unconditioned qualities is naturally and spontaneously present.

When the sun shines in the sky, its rays pervade Jambudvipa. The sun does not need to think that it should try to pervade the earth with its rays. When the sun shines in the sky, its rays spontaneously pervade the earth. In the same way, if we realize the essential nature of primordially pure great emptiness, the inconceivable unconditioned phenomena of the buddhas are all naturally complete and perfect in that state. How is that so? They are in the nature of our minds right now, but we do not realize that. Not realizing the primordially pure great emptiness of the natural state of mind is called ignorance. Such ignorance is the root of the 84,000 kleshas.

According to dzogchen, there are two kinds of ignorance: coemergent ignorance and conceptual ignorance. What is coemergent ignorance? In the natural state of dzogchen, the confusion of the three worlds of samsara, which is like a stain, is called coemergent ignorance. When one has fully recognized that this coemergent ignorance is the expressive power (Tib. tsal) of primordially pure great emptiness, it is inevitable that this coemergent ignorance will be thoroughly purified.

Ignorance is like camphor, which is white and has a strong smell. Camphor is a good medicine for fever. If camphor is exposed to the air, it evaporates. Having evaporated into the air, it does not remain anywhere. Confusion is just like that.

What is the unconfused intrinsic nature (Skt. dharmata)? It is naturally present in one's own innature nature, not brought from elsewhere or touched up like something gilded by a skillful goldsmith. Effortlessly, the inconceivable qualities are naturally perfect.

The only difference between buddhas and sentient beings is whether these qualities are realized or not. In terms of how things are, there is no difference between buddhas and sentient beings. However, in terms of how things appear, sentient beings are confused and buddhas are not. So confusion is the only difference.

If two pieces of gold are to be used to make an ornament and one is stained and the other is not, the stained piece cannot be fully valued and used in the ornament until it has been purified. Once the stain has been removed and it looks like gold again, it is ready for use in the ornament. All the while, however, both pieces are made of the same gold.

The nature of samsaric and nirvanic phenomena is similar. Primordial purity is the emptiness aspect, and rabjam ("infinite") is the appearance aspect of samsara and nirvana. What is the basis of samsaric and nirvanic phenomena? It is spontaneous presence, according to dzogchen. If one asks whether spontaneous presence in dzogchen and primordial purity are different, they are not. The nature of spontaneous presence is primordial purity.

Do these appearances of spontaneously present kaya and jnana affect the primordial purity? They do not. Because primordially pure emptiness is the inconceivable wisdom of the vast dharmadhatu, all the inconceivable qualities of unconditioned spontaneous presence are there in the nature of that primordially pure great emptiness—they are spontaneously present there.

When pointing this out to students, the appearance aspect must be distinguished from the emptiness aspect. From the point of view of the actual primordially pure great emptiness, spontaneous presence does not have to be looked for elsewhere. It is not something different. Spontaneous presence exists in the nature of primordial purity. Once the view of spontaneous presence and its qualities are manifest, there is no need to search for primordially pure great emptiness elsewhere.

The Madhyamaka Tradition and Longchen Rabjam

The pinnacle of all the views of the causal vehicle that examines characteristics is the prasangika madhyamaka. There is a slight difference in the prasangika madhyamaka taught by Nagarjuna and that taught by Chandrakirti. What is this difference? Glorious Chandrakirti stressed mainly the emptiness aspect, teaching the view of dharmadhatu in which everything is realized to be of the nature of emptiness. Emptiness is established through the sevenfold analysis of a chariot. Though Chandrakirti accurately understood Nagarjuna's view, which is extensively and clearly expounded in the *Root Stanzas on Madhyamaka* (Tib. uma tsawa sherap; Skt. Mula-madhyamaka-karika) and the other five texts in the Collection of Reasonings (Tib. riktsok), his own view emphasized the emptiness aspect, whereas Nagarjuna's stressed the union of appearance and emptiness. Even thought Nagarjuna taught the union of appearance and emptiness, that does not deny the emptiness referred to in Chandrakirti's teachings. Chandrakirti's emphasis on emptiness and Nagarjuna's emphasis on appearance, taken together, are the inseparability of appearance and emptiness.

Thus, the view of glorious Chandrakirti and the view of glorious protector Nagarjuna in his *Root Stanzas on Madhyamaka* and the other five texts in his Collection of Reasonings cover the second turning of the Buddha's three turnings of the wheel of dharma—the one known as "no characteristics"—which teaches the nature of emptiness, the path of signlessness, and the result of wishlessness. This is the ultimate meaning of the *Prajnaparamita in One Hundred Thousand Verses* (Tib. sherap kyi pharöl tu chinpa tongtrak gyapa; Skt. Shatasahasrika-prajnaparamita), which is found in the great Kanjur (Tib. bka' 'gyur), the collection of texts containing the teachings of the Victorious One.

Noble Nagarjuna was like a second buddha come to this world. He composed commentaries explaining all the Buddha's views. The six ornaments and the two supreme ones of the sacred land of India accept that there is no difference between Nagarjuna's commentaries and the Buddha's teachings. This is because Nagarjuna's commentaries cover all three turnings of the wheel as well as the secret-mantra vajrayana. The commentaries constituting his Collection of Talks (Tib. tamtsok) deal with the first turning of the wheel—the teachings on the four truths. His *Root Stanzas on Madhyamaka* and the other five texts in the Collection of Reasonings deal with the second turning—the teaching of no characteristics. His Collection of Praises (Tib. tö-tsok) deals with the last turning—the teachings on the absolute truth. After that, in order to elucidate fully the doctrine of the secret-mantra vajrayana, he wrote *The Clear Vision of the Five Buddhas* (Tib. rig-nge gongsal), a commentary on *The Secret Gathering* (Tib. sangwa dupa; Skt. Guhyasamaja). All of Buddha's teachings are covered in Nagarjuna's commentaries.

Similarly, in the writings of omniscient Longchen Rabjam, such as the *Seven Treasures,* all the teachings can be found without error. The *Seven Treasures* explain everything from the 84,000 components of the dharma and the 360 non-Buddhist wrong views up to the nonduality of primordial purity and spontaneous presence of dzogchen.

Though the doctrines of the 360 non-Buddhist schools lie outside of the buddhadharma, if we do not know their views we will not be able to recognize the faults of the non-Buddhist views and the qualities of the Buddhist views. By examining the faults of non-Buddhist views—that the eternalist view has such-and-such defects and that the nihilist view has such-and-such defects—we will come to think that the philosophical system of madhyamaka is correct and does not fall into any extreme. We will come to understand the ultimate true meaning of madhyamaka. When we understand the true meaning of madhyamaka, we cannot help but understand the view of dzogchen.

Among the great gurus of the Nyingma secret-mantra teaching in Tibet, there was Rongzom Pandita, who was recognized by Lord Atisha to be an incarnation of the omniscient Indian mahasiddha Krishnacharya. He mainly practiced and taught primordially pure great emptiness, and his teachings are largely on that aspect. When we say "Rong Long," we are referring to omniscient Rongzom Pandita and Longchen Rabjam. These two are like the sun and moon in the sky of the teachings of the Nyingma, the Old Translation School.

Longchen Rabjam mainly taught the union of appearance and emptiness. The view of Longchen Rabjam's *Seven Treasures* and the teachings of noble Nagarjuna on both the three turnings of the wheel and the sutras and tantras are inseparable. Because of this inseparability, we find this praise in the supplication to Longchenpa:

Your mind has the compassion, learning, and realization
Of the six ornaments and two supreme ones of Jambudvipa.

The person known as Longchen Rabjam was born in Tibet and studied the sutras, tantras, and sciences. He received direct transmission from noble Sarasvati and exalted Tara, and was able to revitalize the teachings of dzogchen. He was an incarnation of Vimalamitra. Here, the ultimate view of dzogchen is introduced through the name Longchen Rabjam. By *longchen,* we should understand "primordial purity," and by *rabjam,* "spontaneous presence." Thus when the text says that "The view is Longchen Rabjam," the dzogchen view is being introduced, which should be understood as the union of primordial purity and spontaneous presence. Once the natural state of the union of primordial purity and spontaneous presence has been understood, when this union of primordial purity and spontaneous presence is practiced, one cannot help but also practice the inseparability of the Buddha's dharmakaya and rupakaya.

Meditation

The ultimate view pointed out by the words of the guru is Longchen Rabjam. That view is not something outside. If that view were outside, it would not be able to cut the life force of delusion within. Practicing the essence of one's intrinsic nature within, the sugatagarbha, is what is called meditation. What is meditation like? Emptiness, that nature free of any concept of phenomena—one's self-cognizing wisdom—is called knowledge. Once we have realized the intrinsic nature of emptiness through this knowledge, we do not have to look for compassion elsewhere. Great compassion is present in the nature of emptiness.

We may generate compassion toward a being who is suffering, but that kind of compassion is only aroused when we see suffering. When we do not see suffering, that compassion is not aroused, and so it is not actually ultimate compassion. Ultimate compassion is self-existent and all-pervasive.

Once we realize emptiness and are aware that sentient beings have not realized it, we will naturally feel compassion for all beings all the time, while meditating or not, in a continuous flow. Great compassion will manifest, and when it does so, it is not merely out of sadness.

Recognizing that sentient beings are confused, we will know how to remove this bewilderment in whatever way is effective. Compassion such as this and knowledge only differ with respect to their names; their nature is essentially the same.

This knowledge and love are like the life force of the view of emptiness. If one needs to emanate for the sake of sentient beings or explain the intrinsic nature of sugatagarbha—whatever is necessary—it comes from this knowledge and love. Since it does not come from the state of great emptiness alone, the text says:

> The meditation is Khyentse Öser ("light rays of knowledge and love").

When the view of the natural state of nondual emptiness and compassion has been introduced and the meditator starts to become accustomed to it, then one has the first actual realization of emptiness. This is similar to the causal vehicle that examines characteristics. When you realize the truth of the path of seeing, you are beginning to realize the intrinsic nature of sugatagarbha. From then on, that realization will grow.

Action

With that realization, absolute bodhichitta develops in one's being. When that has developed, one knows that the minds of sentient beings and buddhas are one. When meditators who have realized this are pervaded with loving compassion and want to lead all sentient beings who have not realized it to the state of buddhahood, then anything whatsoever that they do—even just opening or closing their eyes or stretching and bending their arms—benefits sentient beings. It is not as though sometimes they benefit sentient beings and sometimes not. The benefit for sentient beings is naturally and spontaneously accomplished. It is never too early or too late to benefit beings. It is not like that at all. Because in that state all bodhisattva action is complete, the text says:

The action is Gyalwe Nyugu ("the sprout of the victorious ones").

In the beginning, this view, meditation, and action should be introduced; in the middle, they should be practiced; and in the end, the fruit of that practice is that you have control over body, speech, and mind. Though view, meditation, and action are different names, in essence they are one. They cannot be separated in anyone's being.

If you realize emptiness, there is absolutely no doubt that you can attain buddhahood in one lifetime. What teaching has a view that is so utterly beyond doubt? It is the teaching of dzogchen.

How is the whole of existence reduced to dust just by realizing a fraction of the dzogchen view? When you realize emptiness, you care less about the eight worldly concerns. There is not much hope and fear. If you realize just a fraction of the view of emptiness, your mind will not be moved by worldly distractions, which are like waves on the ocean. You must gradually grow accustomed to that nature which absolutely cannot be moved.

For example, it is said that bodhisattvas who have attained the first bhumi, if they so wish, can attain buddhahood in seven days. Or they can choose to attain buddhahood when samsara is emptied. When you begin to realize the ultimate view of emptiness, you can choose like that. Then, when the view of emptiness is fully realized, though you actually see the truth of suffering of samsaric deluded appearances, they are just empty projections. By way of an analogy, consider a rainbow: whether it appears in the sky or does not appear, you will have no thoughts of liking or disliking. Whatever appearances of samsara or nirvana arise— bad or good—you will feel at ease.

Remaining comfortably in that state is called being carefree and at ease in the view of dzogchen. You will feel amused within. In that state, you will realize that the appearance of relatively true delusions and the appearance of undeluded ultimate reality are amusing.

The Scholar's Way and the Hermit's Way

The three phases just discussed are the "three words" in the key instructions on the *Three Words That Strike the Vital Point*. As for the method of realizing the view, in the tradition of the causal vehicle of characteristics, as was explained above, scholars received the view of the Buddha's teaching and analyzed it logically. They understood it through quotations and logic. Once that had been understood, the view of the ultimate nature had to be realized, and so the Buddha gave this instruction:

> Having accepted my teachings, after hearing them and
>   reflecting on them,
> You should apply meditation.

In the beginning, you should listen to what you have not heard. In the middle, you should reflect on the meaning of what you have heard so that it can be understood. In the end, you should practice the meaning of what you have reflected on through meditation.

However, unlike in the vehicle of characteristics, you cannot gain certainty in the dzogchen view through the complexities of quotations and logic. There are two ways to gain certainty in the dzogchen view: the scholar's way of analytical meditation and the hermit's way of leaving things as they are.

In the scholar's way, one gains certainty in the meaning of the dzogchen teaching through quotations, logic, and key instructions, some of which are explained extensively and some of which are explained profoundly in Longchenpa's *Seven Treasures*. That is the scholar's way of analytical meditation.

For the hermit's way of leaving things as they are, there are key instructions on dzogchen, such as those in *Vimalamitra's Heart Essence* (Tib. bima nyingthik) and *Dakini's Heart Essence* (Tib. khandro nyingthik). So that these meditation instructions may be practiced, words of living experience are given. As it is said, "Even if one may have no knowledge of the five sciences, if these instructions are applied with blind faith, one will gain accomplishment." Since dzogchen is the most profound and vast teaching, one should have confidence that it can instantly remove all the confused appearances of conflicting emotions. If the authentic guru is recognized as the Buddha, the dharmakaya itself, one will realize the view of dzogchen. That is called the hermit's way of leaving things as they are.

In this age of the five corruptions, people have short lives and much disease. Their exertion is weak. They are very distracted and attached to the things of this life. Therefore, this heart of the ultimate key instructions, *Three Words That Strike the Vital Point*, which is like nectar that can revive the gods, is taught. The meaning is experienced through meditation practice, so it is unnecessary to analyze all the different extreme views.

View

When practicing meditation, we should become accustomed to the meaning of the view. Where is this view? At the moment our deluded mind probably is not in possession of the view. The unerring ultimate view is not something far away and spectacular that we need to look for outside, like embarking in a boat across the ocean after one has already exhausted all the land on Jambudvipa. That would be the approach of the causal vehicle of characteristics. When recognized within our present state of delusion, the view is naturally in the state of primordially pure great emptiness.

For example, in the sand of the Ganges River, sand and gold are mixed. Someone who knows the value of gold will get it by removing the sand and obtaining the precious substance. But when ordinary people look at it, they will just see the sand and the gold as the same. How do we separate the gold from the sand? We should leave the mind in its natural, uncontrived flow. If we look at the nature of that uncontrived state, we find it is disturbed by many thought waves. We are carried away by these waves of confusion: we follow after previous habits, stimulate thoughts of the future, and lose present awareness. What are these waves of confusion? They are the expressive power of the view. They are not separate from the view.

How does one stop these waves of confusion? This can be compared to the adjustment of an engine by someone who knows the key points of how an engine works. If the engine needs power or if we need it to run very quickly, a skilled person who knows how to tune the engine can give it the power of a thousand people. Similarly, in regard to the waves of confusion, if we know the key point of view, there is no need to stretch the extremes of lots of intellectual studies and texts. There is no need to accumulate merit and purify obscurations in order to realize the view. It will be realized within that state.

We must recognize that these waves of confusion obscure the view. Even in the case of strong waves of confusion, such as hatred arising so strongly that we would give up our life to accomplish its goal or desire arising so strongly that we would give all our wealth without holding any back in order to acquire the sought after object, confusion can only control us because we do not investigate it. If we know how to investigate these waves of confusion, we see that they are nothing but a rainbow in the sky or a mirage on the plains. Through analytical meditation over a considerable period of time, we would come to understand that this confusion, which is nothing but a rainbow or a mirage, in the beginning has no origin, in the middle has no location, and in the end has no cessation. It is devoid of the eight extremes of concept.

On the other hand, in order to realize the view through meditation based on the experience of the key instructions, not much is needed. Why is that? While engulfed in these waves of confusion, if one strongly shouts PHAT while focusing on the uncontrived nature of mind, those thoughts will be scattered. If a heap of sand as large as Mount Meru were to be hit by a whirlwind, it would not take long to scatter the sand. Shouting PHAT is like that.

What is this sound of PHAT? It is the self-resounding wisdom of inseparable prajna and upaya. It is like a sharp instrument that cuts all the trees. What does it cut? The past confusion is followed by the next con-fusion, and the following confusion is added to the previous one in an uninterrupted chain. It is like beads strung on a mala: if the string is cut, then all the beads will be scattered. Similarly, if one shouts PHAT at con-fused thoughts, all those confused thoughts will be cut and scattered. Then, looking at the naked state, one will recognize that though one's mind has no shape, color, or substance whatsoever, all the six sense per-ceptions naturally manifest continuously from its nature. Resting in that naked state is the sense of "The view is Longchen Rabjam."

Why should we utter this forceful, short, and sharp sound of PHAT to cut the waves of confusion? We are deceived by the lies of relative truth, and those lies can be cut by PHAT, since it is self-resounding wisdom. When we have recognized its nature, we will think, "Oh! This is what the uncontrived dharmata is like!" Phenomena arising from this nature—thoughts—are like the play of a child. The view of uncontrived dharmata is like the thinking of an old man: We think, "What is called 'confusion' is just this." It is resolved. This resolution is called the view. That is the first point of the three words striking the vital point.

To introduce the natural state of the view through the experience of meditation, one should not follow after thoughts of the past nor stimu-late thoughts of the future, but rest directly in the present mind without altering it. Without worrying about whether one's thoughts are thoughts of faith, devotion, and compassion or passion, aggression, and ignorance, one should leave the mind in its natural flow (Tib. rangbap su shak).

Muddy water, if it is stirred up further, cannot become clear. If the water is left as it is, however, the dirt will settle and the water will be clear. In parallel fashion, it is said: "Uncontrived mind is fully awake; contrived mind is not fully awake." One should rest directly in the na-ture of mind without fabricating anything. As the Kagyupas say, "This meditator who rests simply (directly) without altering it (uncontrived)." When the mind rests directly and uncontrived, even though the essence of the natural state of mind cannot be recognized in the sense of your being able to say, "This is it!"—though it is free of such a reference point—as long as you do not get distracted as ordinary people do, you will be able to recognize the nature of the natural flow. If one rests un-contrived in that state of recognition, it will naturally become stronger, and the strength of deluded thoughts will inevitably diminish. Then, with faith and devotion to the root and lineage gurus, the natural state of mind will be realized. This is called recognizing one's nature.

What is this recognition of one's nature? The view that is within us has been introduced to us. It is not as though through the blessings of the guru the view has been brought into us from somewhere else. It is not that we have received something we did not have before. Recognizing this gem that exists in us is like finding a hidden treasure that belongs to us under the floor of our own home. It will make us confident that our poverty has been overcome. Resting in that state of recognizing our nature summarizes the dzogchen view. So we should rest uncontrived in that state.

TWO

Meditation

THE VEHICLE OF CHARACTERISTICS is concerned with the cause of realization. Taking the cause of attaining the state of buddhahood as the path and expecting a result at some later time is called the vehicle of characteristics. In the secret-mantra vajrayana, which takes the result, or fruition, as the path, the result—all the phenomena of the kaya and jnana of the buddhas—is perfect from the very beginning within the intrinsic nature of the sugatagarbha. The secret-mantra vajrayana takes things as they are as the path. When we introduce all the teachings of the secret mantra, there is nothing that is not included within these two: the upaya of unchanging great bliss and prajna endowed with all the supreme aspects.

Between those, the vehicle that focuses on the upaya of the wisdom of great bliss, emphasizing taking the appearances of relative truth as the path while introducing the secret-mantra vajrayana path of abhisheka, samaya, accomplishment, activity, and liturgical practice, is the foundation of mahayoga.

Taking emptiness endowed with all the supreme aspects as the path is anuyoga. Emptiness endowed with all the supreme aspects primordially abides beyond speech, concepts, and expression. If emptiness is not realized through the upaya of bliss, it cannot be realized otherwise in the context of anuyoga. Therefore, through the syllable HAM melting at the mahasukha chakra at the crown of the head as the body, bliss as the speech, and nonthought as the mind, body, speech, and mind are brought to the path as vajra nature. This is the transmission of anuyoga, which is like the life-tree of the secret-mantra path.

Practicing mahayoga and anuyoga together—literally taking as the path the meditation of the noble buddhas, which is beyond the sphere of mental effort—is the fruition of atiyoga. The Tibetan translation of *atiyoga* means "ultimate yoga." Among all the yogas, the supreme one, the highest, is atiyoga. In atiyoga, the empty nature of mind as such is the dharmakaya, its inherent luminosity is the sambhogakaya, and its unceasing compassion is the nirmanakaya. Trekchö practice emphasizes primordially pure emptiness, while thogal practice emphasizes spontaneous presence. If we unify these two, the four kayas and five wisdoms will manifest.

Initially, however, it is very important to introduce the view of primordial purity, free from the very beginning. That is why we are emphasizing primordial purity. There are many ways to realize this primordial purity, such as the view that cuts the continuity of the city, the meditation on the self-liberation of samsara and nirvana, the action of the primordial freedom of peace and existence, and the result of the self-liberating three kayas.

When he was teaching primarily the view of primordial purity, Prahevajra assumed a body of light and gave the acharya Manjushrimitra a testament summarizing all the vital points of the key instructions concerning the primordial purity of dzogchen: recognizing one's nature is the view, deciding on one thing is the meditation, and having confidence in liberation is the action. These constitute the *Three Words That Strike the Vital Point*, which is a marvelous way of attaining the sublime state of the three kayas easily.

In the key instructions on the *Three Words That Strike the Vital Point*, the view, which is introduced first by saying "The view is Longchen Rabjam," is regarded as the object. The cognizing subject comes up in the second point explaining meditation: "The meditation is Khyentse Öser." This is regarded as the subject.

What is *khyen*? Khyen is the unceasing knowledge aspect of wisdom. It is one's own awareness, the intrinsic nature of primordially pure emptiness as it is. Realizing that is called possessing the essential nature of emptiness and compassion. Because the nature of emptiness is inseparable from compassion, when the nature of emptiness—the unceasing knowledge aspect—is realized, a great loving compassion naturally manifests without having to be sought. The key point here is that emptiness and compassion are indivisible in our basic nature. Even in the causal vehicle of characteristics, the mahayana, the understanding that the upaya of great compassion and the prajna of emptiness are indivisible is taught as the ultimate view. Throughout the nine yanas there is not one stage in which upaya and prajna are not distinguished. Realization of the nonconceptual nature of the view is known as the sphere of one's self-cognizing wisdom. And this aspect of one's self-cognizing wisdom is called the unceasing knowledge aspect. In the special vocabulary of dzogchen, it is called the self-existing lamp of prajna. That is the unceasing knowledge aspect of wisdom.

This unceasing knowledge aspect of wisdom is of two sorts: knowledge of things as they are (Tib. chi tawa khyenpa) and knowledge of things as they appear (Tib. chi nyepa khyenpa). In knowledge of things as they are, emptiness is realized as it is. In knowledge of things as they appear, the causes, conditions, and results—whether simultaneous or not, whether deluded or not—of all phenomena of samsara, nirvana, and the path—from form up to omniscience—which arise from the self-expressive power of emptiness, are perfectly distinguished. When we say, "I pay homage to the omniscient one, the perfect buddha bhagavat," the reference is to the wisdom of the two knowledges. This is because the qualities of the Buddha are nothing more than the two knowledges.

When we have that knowledge, we do not have to search elsewhere for great loving compassion. It is naturally there already. When the expressive power of knowledge has unfolded, it is like the sun shining on this world. One does not have to try to find sunbeams somewhere else; they naturally illuminate Jambudvipa. Though knowledge and love appear to be different, their nature, like that of fire and heat, is spontaneously present from the very beginning.

How is this indicated? When the omniscient vidyadhara Jigme Lingpa began practicing at Palri Tsechok Ling, the Palri Tsogyal tulku named him Pema Wangchen Khyentse Öser. During his three years of practice in the charnel ground of Samye Chimphu, omniscient Jigme Lingpa had three visions of the omniscient dharmaraja Longchen Rabjam, who gave him direct transmission. Through the vision of his form, Longchen Rabjam conferred the blessings of his body. By giving Jigme Lingpa a book that contained the *Seven Treasures* in a hidden way and asking Jigme Lingpa to elucidate it, Longchen Rabjam conferred upon him the blessings of his speech and gave him permission to compose commentaries. By mixing their minds inseparably, Longchen Rabjam conferred the blessings of his mind. That is how vidyadhara Jigme Lingpa was perfected by the symbolic lineage of the vidyadharas.

Based on this perfection conferred by the symbolic lineage, Jigme Lingpa composed the root text and commentary called *The Treasury of Qualities* (Tib. yönten dzö). This explains topics concerning the view, meditation, and action of the Old Translation School that were not thoroughly explained in the *Seven Treasures* or the *Three Cycles on Relaxation*. It takes the approach that all phenomena of the ground and path are one.

There are three texts that were widely famed in the snowy land of Tibet as the three chariots of the teaching of dzogchen: *Dakini's Heart Essence*, which Guru Rinpoche Padmakara gave to the dakini Yeshe Tsogyal in the dakini feast hall at Shotö Tidro; *Vimalamitra's Heart Essence*, which contains the 190 key instructions on dzogchen given by pandita Vimalamitra chiefly to Neten Dangma Lhüngyal, Nyangben Tingdzin Sangpo, and the dharmaraja Trisong Detsen; and the *Profound Inner Essence* (Tib. zabmo yangtik), which distills the essence of the two "inner essence" texts* as well as the seventeen tantras and four profound volumes and was composed by the omniscient Longchen Rabjam through the special transmissions of pandita Vimalamitra and the acharya Padmakara and his consort. These are the three Nyingthiks.

When the great translator Vairochana went to India at the age of fifteen, he received direct transmission from the wisdom forms of the vidyadhara Shri Simha and the acharya Manjushrimitra. He received completely all the abhishekas, transmissions, and key instructions of the seventeen tantras. His mind was equal event to that of the great acharya Guru Rinpoche. It was due to the compassion of the great, praiseworthy translator Vairochana that the outer semde, the inner longde, and the secret men-ngag-de came to the snowy land of Tibet. All these teachings are summarized in a unified fashion in the commentary called the *Wisdom Guru* (Tib. yeshe lama). That is why it is part of the symbolic lineage of the vidyadharas.

What is the essential nature indicated by the great vidyadhara? Earlier we explained "The view is Longchen Rabjam"—recognizing one's own

---

*These are the *Dakini Inner Essence* (Tib. khandro yangtik), which is Longchenpa's elaboration of the *Dakini Heart Essence*; and the *Guru Inner Essence* (Tib. lama yangtik), which is Longchenpa's elaboration of *Vimalamitra's Heart Essence*.

nature. We also mentioned that in meditation one should decide on one thing. Now, if one does not have trust and a special confidence in deciding on one thing, one will not be able to do it. Deciding on one thing in dzogchen meditation is called Khyentse Öser. From the outer guru we receive the abhishekas, transmissions, and key instructions. Based on having been introduced to our wisdom mind, the ultimate view comes forth from within. The highest view of primordial purity, the self-manifesting impartial view of dzogchen, is realized. We will have the realization that samsara and nirvana are like the back and front of our hand. All deluded samsaric phenomena only exist because we do not investigate and analyze them. When we do investigate them, the lie of their vivid presence collapses. We do not need to look elsewhere for the nirvanic phenomena of kaya and jnana. They are complete in our own nature. As it is said: "The self-existing luminous youthful vase body is inseparable from the first buddha Khyentse Öser, i.e., resting in the heart essence." That is the meditation of deciding on one point. Resting in that state of meditation is called the yoga of resting like a flowing river.

When the view of dzogchen has been completely realized, there is no longer any difference between meditation and postmeditation. All phenomena appear as the play of wisdom. Beginners like us interested in the supreme yana cannot understand this yoga of resting like a flowing river. When it has been recognized, as Milarepa said:

> When meditating on mahamudra,
> Maintain it without fluctuation.

If sometimes we practice with diligence and at other times just take it easy, we will not be able to develop confidence in our meditation on the view. What must we do to develop this confidence? We must understand that day and night, throughout the entire dimension of our lives, there is no difference between the meditation experience and the postmeditation experience.

Initially we identify the fresh and naked state of uncontrived awareness through conditioned mindfulness. However, if we leave the awareness as it is, at some point innate mindfulness, a natural state of awareness, will arise without our having to manipulate it through a conditioned mindfulness. Through that innate mindfulness, the yoga of resting like a flowing river is maintained constantly, day and night, during deep sleep, in dreams—all the time. In order to recognize that, one should leave the mind uncontrived in the natural state. This unaltered stage of mind is free from the very beginning. This is the view of primordial purity. While one is maintaining that unaltered nature, lots of thought projections will arise. These thoughts might be positive, such as faith, devotion, and renunciation; or negative, such as passion, aggression, and ignorance. However, both these types of thoughts are projected from the same basis, the intrinsic nature of sugatagarbha. It is not that there is a bad place from which negative thoughts arise and a good place from which positive thoughts arise.

Where does the root of our confusion come from? The Buddha Bhagavat said that there are two ways of relating with thought projections in meditation: that of the dog and that of the lion. If a dog is hit by a stone, it does not check to see who threw the stone, but runs after the stone. In this way, it will be hit by many stones and never find out where they are coming from. When a lion is hit by a stone, it pays no heed to the stone, but looks and finds out who threw it. Because of that, the lion is only hit once.

So when thought projections appear and we follow along with them, many thoughts will appear like ripples on the surface of the water, and we will be carried away by them. That confusion is called the confusion of looking outside. Proceeding in that way, we cannot trace the source of our thoughts. Therefore, we should look within, like an actress looking in a mirror. Though there is a display of thoughts, if we trace them to their origin, we will find that they manifest from wisdom. When we have identified that wisdom, we will not be carried away by thoughts. It is like when a tree is cut off at the root: its branches, leaves, and flowers dry up automatically.

Where is that wisdom? Though there may be many thoughts of attachment or aversion, their nature is empty. When we experience intense pleasure and feel so happy it is unbearable and so excited we cannot sleep, if we look at the nature of that happiness, we will see that it is empty. The wisdom of that emptiness is the nature of primordial purity. That is what we should look at. When we get very angry and think we want to kill our enemy even at the cost of our life, when our face turns red from unbearable anger and we think about getting hold of a weapon, if instead of indulging in this anger, we look at its nature, we will see that it is empty. Once we recognize this empty nature, it is inevitable that the anger will naturally dissolve, like ice melting into water.

Are the thought projections and the awareness the same? They are not the same, because projections move and awareness does not. Are they completely different? No, because whatever is projected from the awareness arises from the state of awareness. This can be compared to asking whether water and ice are the same. Are they the same? Ice is hard. People and horses can walk on it. Water is liquid and moist. If we try to walk on it, our legs get wet. It is not firm. Are ice and water different, then? One cannot say they are entirely different, because when ice melts it becomes water. Similarly, it is unacceptable to say that projections and awareness are the same. Projections move; self-cognizing awareness does not. But one cannot say they are different either, because the projections, or expressive power, of the awareness manifest from the awareness itself.

Relying on the vital point that they are not different and not letting the projections wander, if the mind then apprehends the natural face of awareness, the essence of the intrinsic nature will become manifest.

According to the causal vehicle of characteristics, when emotions arise, one should apply an antidote. When passion arises, one should meditate on ugliness. When ignorance arises, one should meditate on dependent origination. When anger arises, one should meditate on patience. What is to be abandoned and the antidote are like two armies meeting in battle. This is what is called regarding emotions as enemies. Regarding the emotions as negative and applying an antidote, one constantly struggles to conquer them.

In the bodhisattva yana, emotions are brought to the path and transformed into emptiness. If emotions occur, we definitely have attachment or aversion to the five sense objects, regarding them as good or bad. If we look to see if that attachment or aversion is in the outer object, the inner senses, or the consciousness in between, we will definitely come to understand that the emotion by nature is without origin, location, or cessation. When that has become clear, the wisdom of emptiness is resolved. By resting in that state, the emotion will be liberated.

In the secret-mantra vajrayana, emotions are transmuted on the path. How so? In the foundation of mahayoga, it is like a skilled doctor transforming poison into medicine, which is called the supreme art of extracting the essences. In mahayoga, emotions are brought to the path by way of liberation through union. In the anuyoga of scriptures, emotions are transformed into bliss, luminosity, and the wisdom of nonthought. All the emotions are transformed into emptiness. Both the form and the nature of the emotions are transmuted into the state of dharmata. In dzogchen, when emotions arise, they should not be rejected and no anti-dote should be applied.

As you maintain effortless, natural mindfulness, relaxation will come automatically. By way of analogy, the surface of the ocean may be tubulent with many waves, but seven fathoms down it is completely still, like milk that has turned to curd. In the same way, no matter how turbulent the waves of thought projections become, once one determines that the nature of the thoughts is empty, it is inevitable that the power of thoughts will be naturally pacified. If one rests in that stage of tranquillity, there is no longer any need for an antidote for each emotion. Becoming accustomed to that state in which there is no longer any need for support is "the meditation is Khyentse Öser."

In the dzogchen texts, one finds such phrases as "practice the yoga of space" and "the great meditation of no meditation." What do these phrases mean? According to the other yanas, the object of meditation and the mind that meditates are two different things. According to dzogchen, what is to be meditated on and the meditator are of one taste. This is the meaning of "When the mind dwells in its own state, that is called seeing one's mind." When one sees that, sees what is present in oneself, how does one practice the yoga of space? When space is used as the object of meditation, since the characteristic of space is to be empty from the very beginning, there are no reference points such as visualizing A or HUM. There is nothing to be grasped.

The same is true in recognizing the intrinsic nature. When the primordially unchanging mother luminosity is present as the ground, if one has just a bit of understanding of path luminosity, as the experience of that path luminosity becomes more and more intense and stable, the ground luminosity can be identified.

At present, the ground luminosity is not entirely manifest in our mind. It is inconceivable wisdom, and if that complete realization of the Buddha were manifest in our mind, confusion would have been purified as groundless, like the liberation of Samantabhadra with six special qualities.

In the causal vehicle of characteristics, however, in the path of unification, the appearance of heat is an indication of the realization of emptiness. It can be likened to rubbing two sticks together to produce a fire.

From the heat produced by rubbing the sticks, a fire will be kindled. Similarly, emptiness must first be recognized through the samadhi in which heat arises. By way of contrast, in the meditation of resting in the inconceivable intrinsic nature, as was mentioned above, even when thoughts of passion and aggression arise, one should not follow these thoughts or try to stop them. One should leave them in the natural flow without any alteration. Even though thoughts arise, they are like the movement of waves on the ocean. They come from the ocean and dissolve into the ocean. Since the expressive power of thought arises from the state of dharmata, if it is left unaltered in the natural flow, when it dissolves, it dissolves into the state of dharmata. As it is said, "In the space between the incidental occurrences of thought, the wisdom of nonthought arises, and they are freed."

When the previous thought has passed and the next thought has not yet occurred, in between these two is the essence of the present naked awareness, the awareness of the first instant, which is called the naked dharmata. When mentally analyzing the nature of the thought, we find that previously there was no origin of the thought and no thought originating. We find that at present there is no location and nothing to locate. In the future there will be no destination and nothing to go to it.

If we examine whether this is so or not, analyzing in the manner of madhyamaka the nature of thoughts arising from the intrinsic nature of the mind, we can look at this morning's past thought, this evening's future thought, and the present thought. We find that a past thought and a present thought cannot be together. In order for them to meet, the past thought would have to be present or the present thought would have to be past. Since the past is already over and is not an actual thing, and the present thought can be recognized, there is absolutely no way for the two to meet.

In regard to the meeting of present and future thoughts, it is just as impossible for a future thought to have arisen as for there to be a horn on a rabbit, a flower in the sky, or a child of a barren woman. And, as the present thought has arisen in the mind, the characteristics of the present and future contradict each other. These two cannot meet. It might perhaps seem that they meet, but this is like making ourselves see two moons by looking at the moon in the sky and pressing on our eye with our finger. Though there is only one moon up there, when we press on our eye it seems as if there are two. If we do not investigate and analyze phenomena, we think they exist, just as we might think two moons exist. Through attachment to this naive belief, the power of the past thought seems to connect it to the present thought, and the power of the present thought seems to connect it to the future thought. However, if we precisely analyze past, present, and future thoughts, we see that sixty split-second thoughts arise and cease in the time it takes to snap our fingers. It is said that sixty segments of a mushroom can be pierced with a needle in the time of a finger snap. Thoughts arise in our mind that quickly.

How can we realize this trick? If the mind is left to its natural flow without any alteration, the present thought will not stay very long. When the present thought occurs, if we think it should not occur and try to stop it, that will block the expressive power of awareness. When the expressive power of awareness is blocked, the natural flow of energy is obstructed, and this causes obstacles such as depression and so forth. So when the present thought first arises and we recognize it, we should rest in the natural flow of that recognition without any alteration. It is like ripples in water: as soon as they arise, they disappear without a trace, which is the characteristic of thoughts. There is absolutely nothing solid, true, or imperishable about a thought. If we watch as the present thought falls apart, at the point where the future thought has not yet arisen and the present thought has dissolved and become past, we will see the nature of mind.

What is the nature of mind like? It has no color, shape, or substance, no matter how much we may look for them. It is not semicircular or circular or spherical. It is not male or female. It has no form, such as that of a horse, elephant, or mountain. It is radiant emptiness. If one mentally investigates that radiant emptiness without the grasping of thinking, "It is empty," it will be like someone who has achieved stability in resting in the intrinsic nature beyond meeting or parting. It is not as though one does not see forms with one's eyes or hear sounds with one's ears. One does, but the forms seen by the eyes and the sounds heard by the ears do not disturb one's inner samadhi. It is the same when a beginner looks at that state of emptiness with undistracted mind. One's eyes will see forms, one's ears will hear sounds, and one will feel all kinds of sensations. And though there will be attachment to beautiful things and aversion to ugly things, pleasure in pleasant sounds and displeasure in unpleasant sounds, excitement when happy thoughts occur and worry when unpleasant thoughts occur, when these reactions occur there will be no grasping. When there is no grasping, everything that arises has the radiant aspect of knowing everything and being aware of everything.

If we were practicing a worldly form of shamatha, we would close our eyes, hold our breath, and rein in our mind. However, in meditation on the intrinsic nature, the six sense consciousness do not have to be blocked. Just leaving those consciousnesses as they are without following them is all right. Though one might try to distinguish the unceasing and vivid six sense consciousnesses from their empty nature, it cannot be done. Because their nature is emptiness, there will be a vivid awareness of the dharmata. Those consciousnesses are vivid because they have the knowledge aspect of knowing all and being aware of all. The nature of dharmata endowed with this knowledge aspect is called "mother luminosity present as the ground." Here one sees a glimpse of its essence, which is primordial purity, and of its nature, which is spontaneous presence.

The Buddha Bhagavat said that even bodhisattvas approaching the end of the tenth bhumi could only see the buddha nature as through the eye of a needle. If bodhisattvas approaching the end of the tenth bhumi can only see that much of the buddha nature, how can we beginners see it at all?

The methods of the secret-mantra vajrayana are very profound, and the blessings of the guru are very great. If we have particular confidence in and devotion to our guru, when the guru's blessings enter our minds, we cannot help but have some semblance of the experience of the intrinsic nature arise in our beings. By way of analogy, if one has seen a picture of the moon and knows what it looks like, when one sees the moon in the sky, there is no need to be told what it is again. One recognizes it. The fraction of the intrinsic nature we can experience now is like the picture of the moon. Even though it is only a glimpse, if we are asked if we have seen the intrinsic nature, we can say that we have. It is like a person who has only drunk one mouthful of the ocean: one can still say one has drunk from the ocean.

Such a glimpse is not arrived at by intellectual study, but through experience. When this glimpse is left without any alteration, it will become prolonged and more stable, and the power of thoughts will inevitably diminish. It is like hot and cold. When the body is warmed by fire, feelings of cold subside automatically. When the body feels cold, feelings of heat subside automatically.

Otherwise, if seeing the intrinsic nature did not diminish the power of thoughts automatically, we would need an antidote for each thought. We would have to think like this: "There is a thought. I shouldn't let myself be carried away by it. It has no origin and no cessation. It is empty." Thinking like that is trying to *make* thoughts empty; it is straying into superimposing the concept of emptiness. There is no need to do so: thoughts are empty from the very beginning. Once we have recognized the source of this primordial emptiness, when we have even a fraction of the experience of that recognition, that is the mixing of mother and child luminosity. The nature of the primordially unchanging mother luminosity, which abides as the ground, is spontaneously present in oneself. It is like a great ocean. Though spontaneously present, it is obscured by the expressive power of thoughts.

When we meditate now, we think of meditation as akin to looking far away into deep space some time in the distant future, and we imagine that ordinary people like us are at present so tossed about by thoughts that there is no meditation whatsoever, as is said in the traditions of other vehicles. But it is not like that. If we maintain the natural flow of the intrinsic nature without being controlled by its expressive power—the projecting and dissolving of thoughts—we cannot help but have a glimpse of the mother luminosity present as the ground. Once we experience and recognize that nature, we cannot help but develop confidence in that awareness, sugatagarbha. Once that confidence unfolds in our being, it becomes increasingly clear and stable.

When a child meets its mother—this is even true of animals—the child is able to recognize its mother even among thousands of others, because mother and child have come together as the result of a karmic connection from previous lives. In the same way, if we experience a glimpse of the child luminosity, it is inevitable that the mother luminosity present as the ground will manifest and that the two will mix equally in one taste. By way of analogy, this can be compared to all the rivers flowing throughout different places in Jambudvipa: in the end they come together in the great ocean. When the experience of recognition is mixed with the mother luminosity present as the ground, that is called the meeting of mother and child luminosity. And this meeting of mother and child is called "the mind's essence." It is also known as the introduction to the dissolving of mind. That introduction to the dissolving of mind, the nature that is encountered when the past thought has dissolved and before the next thought has had time to occur, is the wisdom of nonthought.

Once we have had a glimpse of the wisdom of nonthought, confidence arises. And as the sages of the past said, "When confidence is born from within, the one that has given rise to it and the object are gone." That is very profound. What does it mean? When we are certain that this is the dharmata, the buddha nature, when we are confident that we have had a glimpse of recognition and hold on to that glimpse without letting go, the experience will arise again and again. As that experience becomes prolonged and more stable, the previous confidence will disappear without any basis. It is like lighting a fire by rubbing two pieces of wood together: once the fire has started, those two pieces of wood will be consumed. In just that way, the previous confidence vanishes naturally. When that previous confidence has disappeared, a greater confidence will unfold in your being, which is a sign that your confidence has become deeper.

Meditating is like having to travel to many distant countries. If we have not seen lots of easy roads, difficult roads, oceans, mountains, rocks, and so forth, that is a sign we have not traveled very far. If we rest in the nature of the mind without altering it, sometimes we have good experiences. We think we have recognized mind's nature and would like to remain in that state for a long time. We think that even if we were deprived of food and clothing, we would be able to meditate. But sometimes we have bad experiences. Lots of emotions disturb us, like waves on the ocean. We think that though we have meditated for many years, our practice still does not have as much as a sesame seed's essence to it, and we are just incapable of practicing properly.

When tranquillity, bliss, and clarity occur, we should not regard them as anything special. When we are drowsy or distracted, we should not feel beaten or weary. We should remain without feeling high or low. If we rest in the nature of dharmata, without feeling high or low, we will gradually grow accustomed to it. As a result of that, thought projections will no longer be able to shake that experience of mind.

It is like an old man watching a child at play: whether the child plays good games or bad games, the old man just sees it as play, without any reference point. He does not consider it good play or bad play. Similarly, whether happy thoughts or unhappy thoughts arise in the mind, we should recognize them to be of the nature of the natural flow of dharmata and leave them in that natural flow. Through confidence in the natural flow, we will not be moved. No matter how many externally caused thoughts arise, we will not be moved. When that happens, it is called being carefree and at ease. It is called carefree because we are without the narrow-mindedness of thinking "I can't meditate" or "I am so drowsy and distracted."

We should continually look at that nature, as it is said:

> Whether eating or sleeping, going or staying,
> Whatever one does, there is nothing more than this
> Even in the teachings of the buddhas of the three times.

By maintaining that state of recognition, we will arrive at certainty. Then the expressive power of thought will be unable to stop it.

To begin with, while practicing the preliminaries, we should arouse renunciation, weariness with samsara, faith, and devotion again and again. At first, devotion and renunciation have to be contrived. We should continue meditating until sincere devotion and renunciation have arisen in our being. But at the point of meditating on the main practice of dzogchen, it is of no use to think that we should have thoughts of faith, devotion, compassion, and so forth—signs of the mahayana path—and try to produce them. Why not? Cultivating such things arouses the expressive power of awareness and obscures the ground nature. When thoughts and emotions occur, we should not stop them, thinking that thoughts should not occur and that we should be without attachment and aversion while meditating. Positive and negative thoughts manifest as virtue and evil, but their nature is the same—the expressive power of dharmata. If that expressive power of intrinsic awareness is left in its natural flow, it will have no more strength, and the basis out of which the expressive power manifests will be very strong.

If we create a lot of movement in the expressive power, the ground is lost. Though the ground remains unaltered, it is obscured by confusion at present. Therefore, when yogins rest directly and without any alteration within the self-recognition of the nature of thoughts, they will know the ground. It will become increasingly easier to identify that experience of the innate and uncontrived ground. We may think that we are presently unable to remain in the yoga of resting like a flowing river, but this is not something that takes a long time to achieve. It takes many months or years to manifest signs of accomplishment when meditating on the pranas and nadis or on a yidam. But if a highly realized guru introduces us to the naked experience of dzogchen, we can connect with it right where we are, right in the moment.

However, we do not believe in this introduction. Just as the eye does not see its eyelash because it is so near, we do not believe how easy it is to recognize the intrinsic nature. When, through the guru's key instructions, we do believe it, that is deciding on one thing. Once this is stabilized, we will understand the intrinsic nature of awareness and have no more doubt.

In general, the so-called mind, due to the six sense consciousness, spontaneously has past, present, and future thoughts. But their nature is empty and their quality is radiant. Though their nature is empty, attachment to emptiness makes it small emptiness. Though their quality is radiant, attachment to radiance makes it small radiance. Once the nature of the awareness is recognized as it is, the confidence will arise that the earlier recognition of emptiness is like something that can be peeled away. The vastness of the radiant quality depends on whether there is grasping or not. That is why it is said, "When there is grasping, there is no view."

If nongrasping is something produced by the mind, it is artificial nongrasping. But when the very nature of the dharmata manifests out of itself, we are no longer excited by experiences. For example, if a dzogchen yogin resting in the intrinsic nature has a vision of the thousand buddhas telling him or her that they will attain buddhahood in such and such a pure land, that yogin will not be especially happy. It is not that there is a lack of devotion toward those buddhas, but that since all the buddhas are a display of one's own awareness and not outside of it, once one has recognized awareness, the wisdom that is present as the ground of the three kayas, there is nothing wondrous about having an outer vision of the thousand buddhas giving a prophecy.

If one is without grasping, as it is said, "Even if surrounded by a hundred murderers, one will have no fear." But we have not been able to understand this through actual experience. How can we understand this through experience? Through the preliminary mind training, we look for the origin, location, and destination of the mind. Once the mind has been introduced as without origin, without location, and without cessation, we cannot help but attain the state of the exhaustion of the dharmata.

Now the guru gives us experiential instruction on meditation, and some students do the practice merely thinking that thoughts are without origin and without cessation. No one in this way actually develops confidence from within. Thinking that thoughts neither originate, cease, nor stay is just an understanding of what is written in the books about no origin, no cessation, and no location. Those students have not yet realized no origin, no cessation, and no location through experience. The realization of no origin, no cessation, and no location through experience was pointed to by Aryadeva when he said, "Even though some doubt might arise in one's mind, wondering if all phenomena really are empty, one cannot help but completely let go of the confusion of dualistic existence."

Once one has found emptiness, it is like the summertime, when the earth becomes warm and all the orchards and forests start to grow naturally without effort. When the nature of awareness has been identified, there is no longer any difference between meditation and the postmeditation experience, and so it is said:

Not having meditated and not having been separated from it,
One is inseparable from the nature of no meditation.

Does the ultimate dzogchen meditation have a view of fabricating, such as trying to overcome drowsiness and distraction during shamatha and vipashyana practice? It does not. The absence of such fabrication is the meaning of "not having meditated." "Not having been separated from it" means that nonmeditation is not like falling asleep. Maintaining the yoga of a flowing river with effortless mindfulness settled in its natural state, we will not have as much as a sesame seed of distraction. Once one no longer becomes distracted, it is as the Bhagavat, the perfect Buddha, said:

When one has become unbiased in regard to meditation and
postmeditation, one is like an elephant:
When the elephant goes, it rests in the natural state.
When it stays, it rests in the natural state.

As there is not the slightest wavering from that natural state, there is nothing to meditate on and no meditation. "Not having been separated from it" means remaining in that nature of nothing to meditate on and no meditation. What one is not separate from is the view of the intrinsic nature. That is called the great meditation that is no meditation. When one rests in the ultimate unfabricated nature, the dharmata, there is nothing special to meditate on and no meditation. Subject and object are mixed as one taste, which is meditation on what is called the luminous depths of great primordial purity. When one is beyond meeting with or parting from that state, there is no more certainty about something to be meditated on and someone meditating. This is from the perspective of the ultimate nature of the way things are. But in regard to the way things appear, if beginners do not cut the root of basic confusion, just talking about not having meditated and not having been separated from it is of no help.

In order to cut the root of basic confusion, one should rest in the natural state without altering it. Once one is resting in the genuine natural state, one should neither follow one's thoughts nor search for an antidote for them. If the intrinsic nature is left in its natural state, as it is said, "When water is not stirred, it will become clear." Just as dirty water, if not stirred, will become clear, if the nature of mind is left unaltered, as it is, deluded thoughts will automatically clear up. The natural flow of the intrinsic nature will come automatically.

That is why this meditation is also called oceanlike natural contemplation. Though many phenomena such as mountains, rocks, fruit trees, forests, galaxies, and stars reflect in the ocean, their appearance does not make the ocean any more crowded; and the absence of their reflection does not make it any more spacious. Whether they appear or not does not benefit or harm the ocean. In the same way, when one rests in the state of vaguely recognizing the natural flow of the intrinsic nature, even if appearances of the six senses arise within that state of recognition, since they are not followed up by thoughts of attachment and aversion, there is no harm. As the six sense consciousness arise without cessation, there is no benefit. Since in that sense it is like an ocean, this meditation is also called oceanlike natural contemplation.

Unlike practice with the body such as prostrations and practice with speech such as reciting mantras, in which every day there is some result that can be counted in numbers, just resting in the natural flow of the intrinsic nature produces no apparent result. Though nothing may be perceived, the mind has to continue its effort for a long time. When diligence of body, speech, and mind are compared, diligence of mind is the most difficult. To have diligence of mind, one has to control one's mind. In order to do that, since natural mindfulness like a flowing river does not occur at present, we must artificially put the mind in its natural state through conditioned mindfulness. If we sustain that for a long time, we will automatically come to know the nature of the mind. Remaining in that recognition, the mind will spontaneously become more clear.

When consciousness is left unaltered in its natural state, for beginners the radiant view of spacelike primordial purity spoken of in the dzogchen texts will not manifest right away. Though it is not manifest, awareness is there. It is in the sphere of deluded thoughts, like gold in the sand. If one does not follow deluded thoughts but remains properly in the natural flow without thoughts arising and tends one's mindfulness like a herdsman, awareness is right there.

If there are many clouds in the sky and a strong wind clears them away, the sky will be radiant blue. In the same way, by leaving the mind in the uncontrived natural flow and not following thoughts, we rest at ease in the nature of dharmata. Because we are relaxed, we will gradually be able to distinguish mind from awareness. When we can distinguish those two, we will be able to recognize the nature of awareness and rest in that state of recognition without altering anything.

Sometimes we will recognize the nature of awareness and sometimes not. When we recognize the nature of awareness, we think to ourselves, "I had such a good meditation!" and we are happy. When we have not been able to identify the nature of awareness, we think that we do not know how to meditate and feel terrible. That is not the way to proceed. Even though we may not recognize the nature of awareness, the innate unaltered mind is there. Deciding on that nature and leaving it as it is, we should rest without altering anything.

Even though we may actually recognize the nature of awareness, we should not hold on to that mindfulness tightly, thinking, "I have indeed recognized it." If we do hold on to it tightly, it will be like when a thread is twisted too taut: one cannot sew with it, because it knots up. In the same way, if one is too tense, one's mindfulness will be obscured. If mindfulness is not grasped too tightly but left in the natural flow, sometimes it will be clear and sometimes not. But we should not get caught up in whether it is clear or not. If genuine mindfulness is left without being altered, gradually we will come to know, through our own experience, "This is awareness, and this is ignorance; this is mind, and this is wisdom."

In the view of dzogchen, there are what are called "decision" (Tib. lada) and "differentiation" (Tib. shen-je). "Decision" means resting in the natural state without any doubts about whether "my mind is right" or "my mind is not right." Directly deciding without any artificial concepts about earlier or later, one should decide on the unaltered intrinsic nature, thinking, "This is it." With confidence like that, it will naturally be right. That is called "decision."

"Differentiation" is when, in that state, awareness manifests and mind does not. It is good to differentiate mind and awareness through experience. But matters will only be obscured by reading many commentaries and then trying to fabricate experience on that basis, wondering when such a high, skylike view of primordial purity is going to manifest and what it will be like. As it is said, "The altered mind is not buddhahood." One should not try to cultivate anything at all. Reading books can give us a good comprehension of view, meditation, and action, but when resting in meditation, we should not add concepts based on our book learning. If one puts patches on new clothes, they look old and not very nice. In the same way, if we alter the mind a lot by trying to add concepts, it is like patching new cloth. The natural state of mind will be obscured.

In brief, we should leave the nature of mind unaltered. As it is said, "A great meditator leaves everything as it is, unaltered." If we leave things unaltered, the intrinsic nature of mind will naturally manifest. When it manifests and is recognized through experience, we do not need to make a deliberate effort. It will not take long for it to manifest of its own accord.

When that unaltered nature becomes stronger, even though thoughts may arise, they will be merely like drawings on water. Thoughts will arise, but the mind will not be moved. When there is no movement, it is called "mountainlike natural contemplation." Imagine a huge mountain in the center of a great plain, very firm and stable; wind and water cannot move it. In the same way, when we are introduced to the view of the intrinsic nature, if we remain in the confidence, then confused thoughts of the three times will definitely not be able to cause any agitation. Maintaining that view is called meditation.

Though view and meditation can be distinguished as distinct aspects, their nature is not different. There is absolutely no meditation other than the view. Meditation in this case does not mean meditating with a deliberate reference point. This is nonconceptual meditation. Nonconceptual meditation is without mind-made effort.

The nature of the natural flow of meditation should be recognized. When we rest in meditation within that and meditation has found its natural place, like a horse tied by a halter, it cannot go very far but will stay where it is. Thus, if one recognizes the intrinsic nature from which the expressive power arises, the expressive power will neither benefit nor harm. It will be self-arising and self-liberating. When the child luminosity experienced on the path recognizes the mother luminosity present as the ground and the two meet, there will be no mistake or confusion whatsoever about whether they have recognized each other or not. There will also be no mistake or confusion about identifying the natural flow of the intrinsic nature and maintaining it. The four places to get lost and the four places to err mentioned in the teachings are all due to attachment to the expressive power of thought—expectations about emptiness, expectations about bliss, feeling happy when they arise and disappointed when they do not. Resting at ease in the unaltered state, which is the intrinsic nature, is meditation.

While maintaining the yoga of resting like a flowing river, in the beginning when resting in that effortless state for a long time, we will become drowsy and distracted and will not have any stability in our samadhi. In order to avoid that, it is helpful to train in many short sessions. If the mind is trained gradually in short sessions, it will become good and clear. When the mind has gained stability in the nature of dharmata, it becomes unchanging. At present, the characteristic of the mind's manifestation is that it always changes. When one lets the mind remain unaltered in its natural flow, if the thought waves begin to toss about and one becomes very agitated, as we said above when discussing recognizing one's nature, one should focus the awareness one-pointedly and forcefully shout the sound PHAT. The turbulent thought waves will be dispersed. If they are not dispersed by our shouting it just once, we should shout it again, and that will disperse them.

This can be compared to threshing grain. When the grain is beaten, the husk comes off and the actual grain is revealed. As we look at that nature which has been revealed by the dispersal of the thought waves—the naked intrinsic nature—and maintain that clarity without altering it, the natural flow will manifest from within. Since beginners will be unable to sustain meditation without effort, when looking at that arising they should again and again arouse renunciation of samsara, trust in karma and its result and, in particular, sincere devotion to the guru who introduced their mind to them as the intrinsic nature. If one can supplicate the guru, the power of his or her blessing will be like that of a forest fire fanned by a windstorm.

It is difficult to meditate on the effortless nature in places where there is a lot of distraction. Practicing in solitary places and giving up the eight worldly concerns, we should meditate one-pointedly. In that way, we will come to understand our own nature.

The three important stages in the practice of dzogchen are recognizing, perfecting one's skill, and gaining stability. In recognizing, as we said above, one distinguishes mind from awareness and recognizes the nature of awareness. In addition, one should perfect one's skill in that recognition. If one just recognizes the awareness without perfecting the skill, the awareness cannot work as an antidote for one's deluded thoughts. A young prince cannot rule his kingdom until he has grown up, so just recognizing him will not be of much help. When the skill is perfected, the mind will no longer be drowsy and distracted, and it can be controlled. If one practices with the right effort, the result of that effort will come about. When that occurs, one will be able to maintain the practice correctly.

Practicing the dharma is a little difficult in the beginning. But beginning with hardship, one ends with happiness. Why is the beginning difficult? Hearing, reflecting, and meditating to develop experience and realization require effort. Without effort, nothing can be accomplished. Therefore, at the beginning we have to be very diligent and undergo hardship. Later, things will be easier. One's practice will become more stable, one's confidence will progress, and mindfulness and awareness will come naturally. If one does not cultivate anything now, one will not even develop renunciation toward samsara or trust in karma and its result.

When arousing devotion toward one's guru, one should trust that the guru is the dharmakaya. Seeing the guru as the dharmakaya means regarding the guru as the inconceivable dharmadhatu wisdom. The form of the guru is the relative aspect. Since the dharmakaya pervades the whole of samsara and nirvana, whenever one remembers the guru, the guru is present in one's mind, beyond meeting or parting.

If one recognizes this presence, that will help. If one lacks the devotion that has the conviction that one's guru is the Buddha, that will not help. Only through devotion can one remove all obstacles and strengthen one's practice. When effortless devotion develops in one's being, just through remembering the guru's name or seeing the guru in one's dreams, ordinary thoughts will naturally stop. Merely thinking about one's guru with inner confidence will advance one's practice.

A fruit may have a lot of skin, but if we peel away the layers one by one, we will gradually get to the inner essence. One cannot get to the inner essence by peeling off only the first layer. In the same way, one does not come to the inner essence of the mind right away. But by working through the range of changing circumstances, such as gain and loss, good and bad situations, the mind will become stable. In a yogin's meditation, many experiences, such as bliss, clarity, and nonthought, will arise. If one becomes attached to any of these experiences, one only gets more caught up in samsara. But if one is not attached to experience, one will be able to attain stability.

If dirty water is boiled a long time, one will not get sick from drinking it. It will taste good and sweet, and one will be able to gain sustenance from drinking it. Thus sometimes in a yogin's meditation, through favorable circumstances, faith, devotion, and compassion may arise; sometimes, through favorable circumstances, lust, hatred, and stupidity may arise; sometimes one may be drowsy, and sometimes excited. Under all these circumstances one should make a great effort to arouse devotion toward one's guru. When continuous mindfulness of the natural flow of the intrinsic nature is maintained and completely integrated in the mind, the natural flow of the intrinsic nature will truly manifest.

We may speak of the yogin's meditation being destroyed. This means that the shell of experience has been stripped off and the yogin can see the essence of the intrinsic nature directly. If one cannot strip away the shell of experience, one cannot recognize the essential nature as it is. To strip away the shell, it is important to be without hope or fear.

If one fabricates mental reference points such as "My meditation is empty; this must be emptiness," or "This is clarity, it must be clarity," the nature of dharmata will be obscured. One should not try to fabricate anything, whether the natural flow appears or not. If one just decides on one thing and leaves it like that, it will come.

It is difficult to have natural, effortless mindfulness, and one should be very diligent for a long time, maintaining the unaltered intrinsic nature by resting in the state that is like a flowing river. As Milarepa said:

> When I go, that is brought to the path.
> The six senses are self-liberated as I go.
> When I stay, I stay at rest without altering anything.
> When I drink, I drink the water of mindfulness and awareness.
> I am drinking constantly.

Without that kind of an approach, we might give up meditation on the effortless nature of the mind, thinking it might be better to work on the development stage; and when we cannot complete the development stage, we might think it would be better to work on the completion stage. It is not that those teachings are not profound, but if we try to master the techniques of many different instructions, we will not gain stability in even one of them. However, if we decide on one thing, both the development and completion stages will be accomplished. Through deciding on one thing, every practice will be accomplished.

In the beginning, through tightening the mind a little bit by constantly maintaining unaltered mindfulness, we will learn the nature of mindfulness. The omniscient Longchen Rabjam mentioned six types of mindfulness in the *Treasury of Key Instructions* (Tib. men-ngag dzö). When at the beginning ordinary people keep watch on whether they are distracted or not, that is conditioned mindfulness. When, through constantly practicing conditioned mindfulness, awareness manifests again and again and we become accustomed to conditioned mindfulness, the intrinsic state of mindfulness will come naturally.

What is the intrinsic state of mindfulness? No matter what occurs—whether attachment and aversion, experiences of bliss, clarity, and non-thought, or nothing at all, and we are just relaxed—we watch the nature of mind. The nature of our awareness has a liberating aspect, and when that liberating aspect has been recognized, we can no longer be deceived by the expressive power of thought.

If we do not recognize this liberating aspect, we will be tricked by the expressive power of thought. If we try to make discriminations without having recognized this liberating aspect, we are just fabricating things. With a fabricating mind, there is absolutely no way to attain buddhahood. If we recognize the liberating aspect, decide on that one thing, and rest in that nature, all expressive power will dissolve into the ground luminosity of the intrinsic nature.

Display (Tib. rölpa) is the outer object, which causes attachment and hatred; expressive power is the energy that is present as soon as it arises. These two are gross and subtle, respectively. As it is said:

> If one does not distinguish the expressive power and what manifests from it,
> How can one know the nature of awakened mind?

The distinction between the expressive power and what manifests from it is very subtle and very difficult to realize. Knowing its nature, ascertaining that the source of the expressive power is the intrinsic nature, and maintaining that state without altering it—that is the vital point of "The meditation is Khyentse Öser." There is no need to look for any meditation other than this.

As was said above, deciding on the view and maintaining the meditation, we will recognize, perfect the skill, and gain stability. After gaining stability, everything is liberated by that universal antidote, the unaltered state of the intrinsic nature. Maintaining that again and again, there will be no difference between meditation and postmeditation, good and bad, subtle and gross. It is very important to rest in that state without altering anything.

THREE

Action

THE KEY INSTRUCTIONS on the *Three Words That Strike the Vital Point*, which is from the dzogchen tradition, were given by the vidyadhara Prahevajra to the acharya Manjushrimitra as a testament that condenses the entire meaning of primordial purity, trekchö, into the crucial points of view, meditation, and action. We have gone through the view, which is recognizing one's nature, and through the meditation, which is deciding on one point. Now I shall explain the action, which is gaining confidence in liberation.

What is it that indicates gaining confidence in liberation? "The action is Gyalwe Nyugu" indicates that. To summarize the essence of dzogchen: when the ultimate thought of enlightenment (Skt. bodhichitta) is brought to the path, the source of delusion collapses. The ultimate thought of enlightenment, the wisdom of the meditation of the buddhas and bodhisattvas, when taught through words and syllables, is dzogchen. When someone has realized the view of dzogchen and has perfected the meditation on that basis, then the precious thought of enlightenment develops in their mind, and at that point whatever actions of body, speech, and mind are performed, there is not even one that will be but for the benefit of sentient beings.

This can be compared to adding medicine to water. If one adds medicine to water, all of the water turns into medicine. If one were to add poison to the water, all of it would turn to poison. Whoever drinks the medicinal water or washes with it will derive only benefit from it. It cannot cause trouble at all. In the same way, once we have experienced the ultimate thought of enlightenment, we will spontaneously benefit beings without having to try to do so. Thus, since the omniscient vidya-dhara Jigme Lingpa perfected the self-manifesting, impartial view of dzogchen, the teaching of the Longchen Nyingthik that came forth from the expressive power of his awareness brings incomparable benefit to beings. This is because of the power of his aspiration to maintain the nonconceptual ultimate thought of enlightenment in solidary places.

Though this great omniscient teacher had an inconceivable number of disciples, as numerous as the stars in the sky or the trees on the earth, his extraordinary heart sons were the four fearless (Tib. jigme) ones from Kham, one of which was Jigme Gyalwe Nyugu, who was an emanation of Avalokiteshvara. He received the abhishekas, transmissions, key instructions, and explanations of the dzogchen *Heart Essence of the Great Expanse* from the omniscient Jigme Lingpa.

When he was about to go back to his homeland, the great omniscient one said: "It seems that in your uncivilized country, where people only eat meat and drink blood and do nothing but rob and steal, you will have some disciples. You should benefit them through the *Heart Essence of Luminosity* (Tib. ösel nyingthik) teachings."

Saying that, he entrusted them to him. Due to that, of all the ominiscient one's disciples, Jigme Gyalwe Nyugu became the best known. His benefit of the teachings and beings was inconceivable and, in particular, he transmitted his realization to his own two extraordinary disciples, Jamyang Khyentse Wangpo and Paltrul Chökyi Wangpo, both of whom spread the study and practice of the teachings. To this day, among all the different schools of Tibetan Buddhism there is none that is not linked to Jamyang Khyentse Wangpo.

This is all due to the power of the ultimate thought of enlightenment. According to the key instructions of dzogchen, to develop the potential of the ultimate thought of enlightenment in one's being, one needs to gain confidence in liberation. Without confidence in the view and meditation, even if one has the intention to help others, one will be fettered by distraction, stuck in the sphere of the eight worldly concerns, and enslaved by passion and aggression. If one has perfected the view and meditation of dzogchen, even if outwardly one does not benefit beings in an elaborate way, by giving teachings to a great number of people and so forth, through the self-existing compassion that resides in the depths of one's heart, one cannot help but naturally guide all beings on the path

of liberation through seeing, hearing, remembering, and feeling. Therefore, one should gain confidence in the view and meditation.

What is this confidence in the view and meditation like? One should
be able to naturally liberate all deluded samsaric perceptions. The liberating vital point comes down to view and meditation. When we gain
ultimate confidence in the view and meditation, all karmic and emotional confusion is liberated. This is analogous to clouds in the sky. No
matter how dense the clouds are, when a strong wind arises, the sky will
become absolutely clear. Clouds are impermanent; the sky is always
there. When clouds gather, the sky does not disappear, and when there
are no clouds, the sky does not actually become any more brilliant. We
should know that vital point of liberation.

In all dzogchen instructions, there are three points: decision (Tib.
lada), differentiation (Tib. shen-je), and self-liberation (Tib. rangdröl).
"Decision" means deciding on the view, and "differentiation" means
gaining confidence in the meditation that distinguishes mind and awareness. Relying on the power of confidence in the view and meditation is
like knowing how to turn on an engine: one can automatically accomplish any task, no matter how difficult. It is very important to know this
secret way to liberate.

In regard to liberation, in the ordinary vehicles, that which is to be
rejected and its antidote are opposed. What is to be rejected is regarded
as the enemy. The antidote, which is something other than that, something opposed to that, is what liberates. In dzogchen, however, among
the vital points of the key instructions is that of the self-liberation of what
is to be rejected. What is self-liberation? That which is to be rejected is
incidental; it is not at all present in the original basis. What is to be rejected is karma and kleshas. If karma and kleshas were present in the
original basis, its nature would not be primordially pure. At present,
being deluded, we hold on to what does not exist, which is like an illusion or mirage—just a magic trick. When those who have realized the
intrinsic nature see it, unlike deluded beings of the three worlds, they
are not confused by it at all.

The reason for calling delusion incidental is that delusion appears,
though there is no basis for it. When the natural state of the basis, which
is devoid of delusion, is realized, delusion is without a basis or root.
Though when there are clouds in the sky, it is not clear, and when there
are no clouds, it is very bright, the sky itself is unchanging. Similarly, in

regard to the ground, path, and fruition: respectively, the obscurations of karma and kleshas are seen to be present; they are seen as a mixture, sometimes present and sometimes not; but the ultimate nature is not bound by obscurations. The source of not being bound comes down to the view of emptiness. If one can get a grip on the view of emptiness, it is inevitable that the basis of delusion will be liberated.

Up to atiyoga, that which is to be rejected is regarded as the enemy, and the antidote to it is regarded as a friend. When two things are in battle and fighting, this can only produce more fighting. In that way, when what is to be rejected and the antidote to it are opposed to one another, the root of the obscurations constituting what is to be rejected cannot be overcome. On the other hand, if one realizes the nature of dharmata, the natural state that is devoid of anything to be rejected, one sees that the nature of what is to be rejected is also emptiness.

If there were no karma and kleshas to give up, the Buddha could not have taught the 84,000 dharmas. As everyone would have been awakened and would have realized the dharmakaya, there would have been no reason to turn the wheel of dharma. There would also have been no way to do so. The gradual teaching the Buddha provided by turning the wheel of dharma is there thanks to what is to be rejected. Because of that, there is something to work with. What is to be rejected should not be regarded as an enemy but as a friend. Once we have captured the life force of what is to be rejected from within, it is inevitable that the basis of delusion will be purified. That is because the nature of the karma and kleshas to be given up is emptiness. Therefore we should know the vital point of emptiness.

What is the vital point of emptiness? As was discussed above, through recognizing our nature and deciding on one thing, we will come to know the vital point of what is to be rejected. Regarding karmic and emotional obscurations in one's being, if we search for an antidote elsewhere, taking the approach that obscurations are to be dealt with in a manner that resembles smashing a vase with a hammer, of course it will be difficult. But when the obscuration to be rejected arises, if along with it we arouse confidence in self-manifesting awareness, it is impossible for the basis of what is to be rejected not be liberated.

Lacking confidence in such liberation, even if we were to remain in a mountain retreat for many months or years and practice diligently in body and speech, we would be completely unable to uproot the poisonous tree of emotions within. If we are unable to uproot that tree, it will not be possible to get out of the three worlds of samsara. If we know and grow accustomed to the vital point of liberation and gain confidence in the intrinsic nature, whether we are going or staying—no matter what we are doing—our emotions will be liberated as they occur. Though outwardly you may not be famous, inwardly it will come spontaneously. Even though passion and aggression arise, if we recognize that their nature is emptiness and rest in that emptiness, there will be no passion and aggression toward the object at all.

When we teach beginners the basic nature of things, as described above, it may often seem to them nothing but a nihilistic view. So how should we deal with this vital point of liberation now? Having maintained the experience of the unaltered natural state of mind for a long time and having distinguished mind from awareness, as discussed above, we will have the experience of "This must be dzogchen, the view of the intrinsic nature," which is like meeting someone we know.

Due to the impurity of incidental obscurations of the mind—what is to be rejected—when things we like happen, we become attached to them: for example, a thought of intense joy arising from obtaining high rank, experiencing worldly entertainment, or meeting our parents, relatives, husband or wife, or others who are close to us whom we have not seen for a long time. As soon as that thought of joy arises, we become attached to it. If we reject that, thinking we should not have attachment and that all conditioned existence is impermanent, we will wind up with a fight between that which is to be rejected and the antidote to it. That will not help. But if we look at the nature of that intense joy without altering it, we will arrive at the wisdom of emptiness endowed with all the supreme aspects. The reason we will arrive there is that even though we become attached to this intense joy and feel ecstatic, its nature is nothing other than emptiness.

To use another example, if we see an enemy, someone we do not like, we will become angry when we look at that enemy. We may become so angry that we feel like eating his or her heart raw, and, since the specific characteristic of anger is to kill or fight, if we pursue that anger, we would accumulate that karma. Nevertheless, if we look at the nature of anger as soon as it arises, we will see that it is emptiness.

From among the bliss, luminosity, and nonthought that arise in the mind, because we develop intense passion for an object we want, the nonconceptual wisdom of bliss-emptiness is present right there. If we recognize this nonconceptual wisdom of bliss-emptiness, our mind cannot help but relax, and it will not be fettered by passion and intense joy. We will not be tense at all. If we recognize the nature of aggression as the mirrorlike wisdom of luminosity and emptiness, since aggression is empty, we will not be controlled by it and will not think that we must subdue or kill our opponent even at the cost of our life. All that will relax and fall apart.

Though the sky may be filled with clouds, as many clouds as there are can vanish in a few minutes, leaving a clear sky. Thus though we may think that feelings of passion and aggression are to be rejected, there is no need to do so. If we recognize the very nature of passion and aggression, that itself is the antidote. If we recognize the nature of that antidote, the awareness of bliss-emptiness and luminosity-emptiness, and that awareness is left naked, we see that there has never been any passion or aggression in the nature of the awareness. There is no basis to give rise to passion or aggression. That is called the state of dharmata, where mind is groundless and without any expressive power. This is what the omniscient vidyadhara Jigme Lingpa was talking about when, in relation to an incident in the later part of his life, which appears in his biography, he said, "This samsaric mind is beyond meeting or parting from the three doors of liberation."

Since it is like space, the vital point of liberating that nature is the antidote to attachment and anger. Since it is right there with the klesha, what is to be rejected, there is no need for some antidote. When what is to be rejected is liberated by itself, by what is to be rejected, that is called self-liberation. Confidence in liberation means that through confidence in the view and meditation, when what is to be rejected occurs, we will observe its nature and know that it is inseparable, beyond meeting or parting, from the intrinsic nature of emptiness. Through that emptiness, what is to be rejected is spontaneously liberated. When it is liberated, no karma is produced.

Someone who achieves the realization of emptiness does not produce karma. Because of their confidence in the view of dharmata, great gurus such as Tilopa in no way incurred the fault of taking life when killing fish. Tilopa clearly demonstrated that to his disciple Naropa when he subsequently snapped his fingers and brought the fish back to life. Since the object to be killed and the killing mind have both been purified in the one great intrinsic nature of primordial purity, there is absolutely no vestige of an ordinary thought of aggression. Once there is no longer any ordinary thought of aggression, the karma of something rejected is not accumulated. If that karma is not accumulated, the confused, conditioned karmic three realms of samsara become groundless and without any expressive power.

Therefore, if thoughts of attachment or aggression come up while we are practicing, just as soon as they arise, we should remember the view of deciding on one thing, which we were introduced to earlier on. If we remember our experience of the view, passion and aggression cannot help but be spontaneously liberated. When we develop anger toward an enemy and are determined not to give up until we kill our foe—even if we have reached the point where we are holding a weapon in our hand—if we recognize the luminosity-emptiness wisdom of awareness in that state of anger, that intense anger toward our enemy will be interrupted and relaxed. Once it is relaxed, we will not carry out that act of hatred.

This can be compared to the traceless flight of a bird. When a bird flies through the sky, one cannot point to any trace of where it has been. In the same way, when a thought of passion or aggression occurs, if we have the confidence of self-liberation, it will disappear without leaving a trace and will be utterly incapable of producing any karma.

For example, if one sows a seed in a field and does not water it, even if it is left there for many years, no sprout will grow. In the same way, if we do not produce a karmic reaction, nothing will happen, since the three realms of samsara are an illusion produced by karma, phenomena generated by karma. If we recognize that nature, we will see that we have been totally deluded in countless lives up to this point. If we realize the view of shunyata, confusion is instantly destroyed without difficulty. Confusion is self-liberated.

Otherwise, if we think that the quality of confusion is like being covered by a cloth and that it is to be removed through purification, we will have to be accumulating merit and purifying obscurations for a long time. But if we have confidence in the view, confusion will inevitably be self-liberated.

The lower yanas, those below dzogchen, do not realize that when thoughts of passion and aggression occur, the antidote comes from the expressive power of those thoughts. They maintain that the Buddha did not teach that. That is why, in those lower yanas, not knowing that the antidote for what is to be rejected is already there, one looks for it somewhere else. In dzogchen, when thoughts of passion and aggression occur in one's mind, if one looks at their nature and knows the vital point of the great self-liberation in the dharmata, the basis of all delusion is inevitably liberated.

In the special terminology of dzogchen, thoughts, karma, and emotions are said to be incidental. Merely recognizing anger as the wisdom of luminosity-emptiness and passion as the wisdom of bliss-emptiness is not enough. That recognition has to be continually sustained. If we do not sustain it, we cannot get at the root of our confusion. It will be like an illness that recurs again and again. When we recognize it and maintain that state of recognition, the view of the intrinsic nature becomes stronger. Like washing a cloth and getting it spotlessly clean, it will be primordially free and pure.

First we should recognize what is to be rejected. Upon recognizing it, we should know that the wisdom of luminosity-emptiness and the wisdom of bliss-emptiness are in between occurrences of what is to be rejected. Through the power of resting in the state of both luminosity-emptiness and bliss-emptiness, what is to be rejected will be naturally pacified and liberated. Once it has been naturally pacified and liberated, when one rests in that state that has been experienced previously, what is to be rejected will not be able to increase. In that way, all thought will be spontaneously liberated.

Once liberated, we will see that confusion, other than being labeled "confusion," is nothing whatsoever. As it is said:

This great ignorance concept
Is what makes us fall into the ocean of samsara.

Thus, ignorance's magic trick is thought. In the beginning we should look at the mind and understand that mind is without origin, cessation, or location. Why should we do that? Because we will automatically be liberated.

Mahamudra begins with pointing out the mind, which brings an understanding of awareness. Though that is understood, in the mahamudra tradition one must meditate diligently on the three points of stillness, movement, and awareness for a long time. If one is able to do that, one will inevitably recognize the nature of self-liberating awareness. In dzog-chen, we rely on the view of differentiating mind and awareness. If one can maintain recognition of that for a long time, one will inevitably arrive at the basis.

As far as the terminology is concerned, in mahamudra this is called bringing mind to the path, and in dzogchen it is called bringing wisdom to the path. However, if the source of the wisdom in regard to bringing wisdom to the path is not pointed out, there can be no liberation. If there can be no liberation, it is not the correct view of dzogchen.

In summary, in regard to liberation, what is to be rejected and the antidote to it do not have to be opposed. What is to be rejected is liberated by itself. Passion is liberated by itself. Aggression is liberated by itself. Ignorance is liberated by itself. In the beginning that self-liberation will be somewhat fabricated. But if one really gains confidence in the view of the intrinsic nature, the mind does not need to fabricate anything. It is liberated from the very beginning.

At present, we are confused about phenomena. Though they are liberated, we cannot recognize this, and so we hold on to them. It like someone with jaundice who sees a white conch as yellow. It is very important to recognize this.

To achieve this liberation, in the beginning when a deluded thought comes up, we should recognize it. When that recognition is sealed with the view that has been pointed out, the thought will be liberated as groundless and rootless. When it is liberated, there should be no trace left behind. If there is a trace, karma will again be produced. If there is no trace left, that is the sign that the thought has been liberated.

In some teachings it is said that all one needs to do is recognize thoughts. But merely recognizing them is not enough. That recognition has to be liberated. Of course, for a beginner it is enough just to recognize thoughts. Lacking that recognition, if one only looks outward, when positive and negative thoughts arise, one will not recognize them. But to go further, if that recognition is sealed with the view of the intrinsic nature, the thoughts will vanish. But even though they have vanished, if one is not able to be free of any trace left behind by those thoughts, karma will be produced. If there is no trace left, the thought is liberated.

As for how this liberation happens, pandita Vimalamitra spoke of three ways. In the beginning, the liberation of thoughts by recognizing them is like meeting an old friend. In the middle, the self-liberation of thoughts by themselves is like the freeing of a knot in a snake. In the end, the liberation of thoughts as they occur, with neither harm nor benefit, is like a thief entering an empty house.

When we recognize a thought, that recognition alone will not liberate it. It is not that we should not recognize it; it must be recognized. But then when recognizing it, without grasping at the thought, the basis from which it arises—the unaltered natural state of mind pointed out by our teacher—should also be recognized. When we look at that recognition, the strength of the thought is broken, and the recognition of the intrinsic nature becomes stronger. Then no reaction can be produced. Once we cease producing a reaction, since thoughts in themselves are self-arising and self-liberating, we will find the source of that liberation. Being taken in by a thought is like being afraid of a man wearing a lion's mask. But if we know that the nature of thoughts is emptiness, like realizing that it is only a man wearing a mask, the strength of the thought will be broken and we will naturally relax.

We are not wandering in the three worlds of samsara just through one thought alone. There is a continuous stream of thoughts. Take for example thoughts of harming an enemy. First we think that our enemy has harmed us in such and such a way or rebuked us with such and such words. Then we think that we should retaliate in a corresponding way. Then we think about doing this. Then we actually start the harmful action. Just the first thought of harming our enemy cannot accumulate karma. But when many thoughts follow one after another and are not liberated, just liberating one thought will not help. All the following thoughts must also be liberated.

If the first thought is liberated, it is inevitable that the subsequent ones will be liberated as well. So first we should recognize the thought, and upon recognizing it, it should be liberated without a trace.

Recall meeting an old friend, someone we know well, whom we have stayed with for a long time, a person that we would recognize among thousands of other people the moment we saw their face. Not only would we recognize such a person, but we would walk with them and spend time with them. In the same way, first the thought is recognized, and then the nature of recognition should be liberated in the view of the dharmata that was pointed out by our guru. When it has been liberated, it is free of basis and root, without leaving a trace. And just as we are not satisfied by merely seeing the face of old friends, but as soon as we recognize them we also speak with them, ask them how things are, relax with them, and thus feel good about having met them, so, in the same way, along with recognition there must be simultaneous liberation.

In the middle, the self-liberation of thoughts is like the knot in a snake freeing itself. First the thought is recognized. As that recognition takes place, the view introduced to us by our teacher becomes stronger while the thought becomes weaker. Afterward, if thoughts leave a trace, though a little bit of effort is needed, beginners must recognize that. Becoming accustomed to this liberation by recognition can be compared to the freeing of a snake knot. If a knot is tied using the body of a snake, it does not have to be untied by someone. The snake's body itself is the antidote and can untie itself.

When recognition of the thought is sealed with the view of the intrinsic nature, there is no need for what is to be rejected and the antidote to struggle with each other. What is to be rejected is itself the antidote and will liberate itself. Like the knot in the snake untying by itself, it is not necessary to look for some other antidote. The antidote is liberated by the antidote itself. What is to be rejected is liberated by itself.

When we become accustomed to that, first we recognize the thought. Then, without trying to perfect the skill of recognition, it should be sealed with the view of the intrinsic nature. We do not need to make any more effort, thinking, "It has been sealed and liberated without a trace." When we seal the thought as soon as it is recognized with the view of the intrinsic nature, the force of the thought is broken, and it naturally relaxes. The present thought has no more power, and the next thought cannot yet be thought. When the next thought is not thought, there will be no trace left behind. And if there is no trace left behind, it is impossible for karma to be accumulated.

When we gain confidence in the view of the intrinsic nature without distraction or confusion, the arising of a deluded thought is like a thief entering an empty house. The house has nothing to lose, and the thief has nothing to gain. Whether the thief comes into the house or not, there is neither benefit nor harm. In the same way, thoughts will arise like reflections; but the moment they occur, the view of the intrinsic nature is right there. Since the view of the intrinsic nature is stronger than the thought, the thought will automatically be groundless and rootless. When that happens, there is also no trace left behind. If we can maintain the continuity of that state in which no trace is left, that is what is known as liberation. It is like a drawing mode on the surface of water: there is no need to find something to erase it. Before the end of the drawing has been completed, the beginning has already disappeared.

If it is not like that, we are not yet able to liberate. We should look at our minds and see if thoughts of passion and aggression occur. When they occur, we should see whether they are sealed with the view we have experienced. If they are sealed, we should see whether they are liberated without leaving a trace, without producing a reaction.

We should investigate our minds in detail. What is called "thought" can be either gross or subtle. When a gross thought arises from within and we look at its face, we recognize whether we feel happy or angry. That is a gross thought. In addition to gross thoughts, many thoughts will unfold like drawings on the surface of water; they are neither beneficial nor harmful. As they unfold, we may think that our mind is not distracted, that there is no trace left behind, and that we have recognized the thoughts; but the subtle thoughts occur in a hidden fashion, and karma is accumulated. It is like an ant's nest underneath us—lots of thoughts come up from underneath, and we cannot help but become confused. If we cannot liberate the undercurrent, many thoughts will amass together and produce a reaction. But if we know how to avoid producing a reaction, even if thoughts occur, there is neither benefit nor harm. That is how we can avoid accumulating karma through thoughts.

The characteristic of thoughts is that the way they manifest is uncertain. They do appear. Thoughts of attachment and aversion will definitely appear. If we use those thoughts as an antidote, as soon as they appear they will be liberated. If we seal thoughts with the view of the intrinsic nature, they will inevitably be liberated.

However, if we do not thoroughly understand the view of the intrinsic nature but get lost in the sidetrack of thinking that we do, there will be a lot of unnoticed thought activity and, though we may think that our mind is not distracted and that there are no traces of thoughts left behind, actually we are automatically accumulating a lot of karma. It is not the body and speech that accumulate karma, but the mind. Unless there really is no trace left behind, the mind will not stop producing reactions.

Once we are no longer producing reactions, thoughts are like designs drawn on water, which disappear as they are drawn. If it is like that, though the thought occurs, there is neither benefit nor harm.

The occurrence of thoughts happens the same way for yogins and worldly people. Even a yogin who has actually realized the ultimate nature will not be completely free of thoughts. Someone who had no thoughts at all would be inanimate, like a rock or a piece of wood. Even though yogins have thoughts, they remain unaffected. But worldly people get caught in their thoughts. That is how they get confused. That is what is meant when it is said that the yogin's mind surpasses the worldly mind. Even though a yogin has thoughts, they are like many images reflecting on the ocean. The reflections of trees, forests, rocks, mountains, stars, and planets do not change the nature of the ocean. The ocean does not have to expand or shrink in order to reflect these images. In the same way, though a lot of thoughts, both positive and negative, manifest in the yogin's mind, they do not leave a trace and are recognized and liberated. There is no confusion.

When an ordinary person has thoughts, it is like erecting houses and planting trees in a small space—every house and tree makes the space more crowded, and less of it is available for use. When ordinary people have many thoughts, they are carried away by them. Enslaved by their thoughts, they have lots of troubles and are very busy in this life. In future lives, they will also experience lots of happiness and suffering. Therefore, it is said that if one cannot liberate thoughts, one should cut the trace of the habitual patterns of past thoughts, not stimulate thoughts of the future, and not let the present awareness wander free. Once thoughts are liberated, all this is not necessary. If thoughts do not affect us, liberation or nonliberation is utterly not at issue. What is called "liberation" is when a thought leaves no trace and so no positive or negative karma is accumulated.

If we do not know this vital point of liberation and cannot apply the method of liberation, even if the mind is without thoughts and remains pitch black for a long time, that is not the dzogchen view. If the mind remains in a dull state of nonthought for a long time, we might remain for an entire intermediate eon in the realm of the formless gods. Even so, this is only like passing out from being drunk—it will not sever the root of existence. Later, when the power of this shamatha is exhausted, we will again be deluded in the three realms of samsara. This is because we are not able to liberate our thoughts.

If thoughts are not liberated, we cannot cut the root of delusion. It is like being unable to cut the root of a poisonous tree. When a yogin has attained liberation, whether the mind is still or not it is liberated. This is conviction in self-liberation. This liberation needs no further antidotes. That which is to be rejected is already self-liberated. If one knows the crucial point of self-liberation, that is how thoughts are liberated.

The key instructions of dzogchen mention four ways of liberation: primordial liberation, naked liberation, self-liberation, and liberation upon occurrence. In all four of these ways of liberation, we must recognize that thoughts arise from the state of dharmata. If that recognition is then sealed with the view of the intrinsic nature, all the key points of the way of liberation are complete right there. But if we merely maintain the still mind of shamatha, we are like the gods of the higher realms, who are unable to eradicate the conflicting emotions.

Within both shamatha and vipashyana meditation there are many distractions. When mind remains still without moving, it is called shamatha, or tranquillity. When the nature of one's awareness is recognized in that state, it is tranquillity, but not the tranquillity in which thoughts do not occur. Though thoughts occur, if the nature of awareness is not obscured, it is still tranquillity. When thoughts occur and awareness is not lost, tranquillity is automatically present. If the nature of awareness is as if held in the palm of the hand, thought occurrence will neither benefit nor harm, and there will be absolutely no grasping at the experience of tranquillity. That is called the view without grasping. It is referred to in the saying, "If there is grasping, that is not the view." That grasping should be destroyed from within.

With regard to the nature of mind: bliss, luminosity, and nonthought exist in our deluded mind now. When the nature of awareness has been understood, they exist there too. Though the terms we use are the same in both cases, there is a difference in meaning. The bliss, luminosity, and nonthought in the realization of awareness are superior. Though bliss, luminosity, and nonthought may be experienced by the mind, without the vital point of liberation, that is not the dzogchen view. When awareness recognizes bliss, luminosity, and nonthought, the vital point of liberation is there. In this bliss, luminosity, and nonthought, bliss is liberated as it is, and luminosity is also liberated as it is.

Liberation while resting in the state of nonthought is the essence of the natural state of awareness. Once you hold the essence of the natural state of awareness in the palm of your hand, in that recognition of naked awareness it is impossible for thoughts not to be liberated. It is like when two countries are at war. When the cause of the war, the person who started it, has been captured by the other country, the war will end. In the same way, when the crucial point of the self-liberating nature of awareness, self-liberating within the intrinsic nature of mind, is captured, mind can no longer be moved by confusion. It is liberated. That liberation is not something new. Rather, it is of the nature of the great primordial liberation, free from the very beginning. For someone who has the technique of liberation, whatever thoughts arise are the display of wisdom. In this regard, it is said that all phenomena are the display of wisdom.

Once a yogin has understood the nature of that great wisdom, even though he may not be visualizing his body as the deity, no matter what he does or says, his body is the deity. This is due to his confidence in the view of the dharmata, which is the binding force of the unchanging view during the development stage. Even though he may not recite lots of mantras, mind dwelling in the intrinsic nature is the ultimate of all mantras, inexpressible wisdom. When that wisdom is recognized, the power of recitation is complete.

Someone who has attained direct realization of the intrinsic nature has tremendous power. When the Indian mahasiddhas performed miracles, such as burning down a whole forest just by showing the threatening mudra, this was not due to the power of the mudra but to that of the inner view of the intrinsic nature. When one has realized all phenomena as emptiness through the inner view, one has mastered the ability to transform substance into nothingness and nothingness into substance, as needed. Without confidence in the inner view, it will be difficult to make substantial phenomena nonexistent or vice versa. For example, if we wish to destroy a house, we generally have to do a lot of work using weapons or tools. But if we have confidence in the view of dharmata, then meditation on deities, recitation of mantra, the power of destroying mantras, and the force of miracles will come spontaneously. No other tools will be necessary.

This is like a field that is having a good crop: one need not make any special effort for the sheaves; they will come along naturally with the grain. In the same way, if we have well understood the view of the intrinsic nature, sugatagarbha, the ocean of unconditioned phenomena will be spontaneously accomplished, faith and devotion will arise, and we will see our teacher as the Buddha. Due to the power of that, we will be able to attain all the supreme and ordinary siddhis. Guru Rinpoche and the vidyadhara Shri Simha, for instance, gained mastery over the expressive power of awareness and perfected the inner view of dharmata. For them the whole of samsara and nirvana became a display of the intrinsic nature. That display can be whatever one wants it to be. Sentient beings can be transformed into buddhas; impurity can be transformed into purity.

When the buddha qualities are explained in the causal vehicle of characteristics, it is said that if bodhisattvas who have attained the ten powers want to remain, they can do so for as many eons as they like without aging. If they do not want to remain, they can pass away immediately. When one has command of the inner samadhi, that is called having command of the ten powers. This has nothing to do with a transmission of outer powers. As one maintains that nature over and over again, the view of the dharmata is free, and all confusion is purified as groundless. That is condensing a hundred crucial points into one.

Once one has gained confidence in the view of dharmata in that way, buddha qualities will be spontaneously present without effort. When the sun shines, it is not necessary to do something extra to make the rays shine as well.

For a yogin who has confidence in the view of the dharmata or a bodhisattva who has attained the first bhumi through the path of the causal vehicle of characteristics—someone who has directly realized the view of emptiness—if on his right side there is a person venerating him and making pleasing offerings of brocade clothing and so forth, and on his left side there is an enemy who is attacking him and cutting his flesh to pieces, he will not feel attachment to one nor aversion to the other, but will treat them both equally. He can do this because he has attained confidence in the view of dharmata.

In the Jataka tales it is told that when the kind Bhagavat was the sage Kshantivadin he did not feel any suffering when all his limbs were cut off. Eventually, even his head was to be cut off. In general, someone who was going to have their head cut off would become angry, but not Kshantivadin. Instead, he made the aspiration, "Though now you have cut off all my limbs, in the future, when I attain perfect buddhahood, may I cut off all your obscurations of karma and klesha." No anger arose in him in the beginning. None arose in the middle. None arose in the end. In the language of dzogchen, we would say that he was able to liberate and, because of his aspiration, the one harming him became his disciple. As it is said:

With whoever harms us we should make a positive connection.
I take refuge in that source of happiness.

Whoever relates with a person who has actually realized the view of dharmata will become their disciple. Whether they venerate that yogin with faith and devotion or make a negative connection by beating or killing the yogin, in the future they will all become the yogin's disciples without the slightest distinction. This is because the yogin has no concept whatsoever of benefit or harm. Having realized the view of emptiness, which is like space, yogins have no aversion to those who harm them and no attachment to those who benefit them.

In any number of sutras or tantras, it is explained that the view of equanimity is extremely profound. According to the causal vehicle of characteristics, though the ultimate view of equanimity arises for a bodhisattva on the eighth bhumi through personal experience, even one at that level cannot manifest, develop, and perfect it.

Now in the secret-mantra vajrayana path, the view of the mahayoga yana is discussed in terms of the inseparability of purity-equanimity and truth. Purity is equanimity, and equanimity is the absolute truth. When explaining the dharma of dzogchen, it is called the dharma beyond positive and negative and cause and effect. When it is seen that positive and negative are equal in being emptiness, the view of equanimity has been understood.

That is the true view.

When we have perfected it, then what is called liberation does not involve a liberator and something that is to be newly liberated. That is confidence in the intrinsic nature.

Having attained such confidence in the view of inner equanimity, which is known as gaining confidence in liberation, whatever we do with body and speech is sealed with that view. If sandalwood or musk has been put in a box, even when they have been removed, the box will be permeated with their strong odor. In the same way, when body, speech, and mind are sealed with the view of equanimity, whatever we do with body, speech, and mind is the display of wisdom, which is free of delusion. Therefore, that ultimate, primordially pure natural state, the great primordial purity liberated from the very beginning, is known as gaining confidence in liberation.

SUMMARY: INSEPARABILITY OF VIEW, MEDITATION, AND ACTION

We have been looking at the vital points of view, meditation, and action. At the time of teaching, view, meditation, and action are presented as three things, but in essence they are one. When the view is perfected, meditation and action will also naturally be perfected. When meditation is perfected, the view and action will manifest spontaneously. In the ordinary sutras and tantras, the view—the object to be known—is understood by the knowing mind. In that approach, one needs to make a lot of effort in understanding quotations, logic, and key instructions. The dzogchen view, which is present in us from the very beginning, can be introduced to us by a master who possesses the blessings of the mind lineage. When a rich parent gives a child his inheritance, the child will recognize the wealth as his own. In the same way, the view that has been introduced to us is something we have ourselves, not something from outside. Meditation is resting in the nature of that view; there is no meditation other than that view.

According to the language of the ordinary yanas, it sounds as if the view is understood through inference, and meditation is actual experience. But it does not have to be like that. The view must be actually realized, and meditation is not inference. It is resting in the intrinsic nature. Meditation does not involve the analysis of what is meditated upon and the one meditating on it, nor of drowsiness and excitement, distraction and confusion. It is free from an object of meditation and meditating. That is the great meditation of no meditation. Once we have gained confidence in the view and meditation, though they are indeed something we explicitly practice during practice sessions, in postmeditation we should also apply the view and meditation that we have practiced during the sessions. Practice in postmeditation should not be something different.

To say more about the inseparability of view, meditation, and action: In the beginning, the view is introduced, the view of the nondual nature of primordial purity and spontaneous accomplishment. When maintaining that through meditation, if the view is regarded as the object and meditation as the subject, then omniscient wisdom and loving compassion will naturally come from the expressive power of primordial purity and spontaneous accomplishment. That expressive power is not something separate from the view. If one has confidence in the view of primordial purity, then knowledge will come naturally. And once one has confidence in the view of knowledge, no additional meditation on loving compassion is needed. It will come spontaneously.

Knowledge and compassion are not two different things, because the expressive power of knowledge is reflected as compassion, and the source of compassion is knowledge. The knowledge we are talking about is not just conventional knowledge, but actual knowledge of the nature of dharmata.

When the buddhas comprehend the nature of dharmata, the 84,000 dharmas are expressed from that intrinsic nature. When the nature of dharmata is realized and the dharmas are expressed, the wisdom of the buddhas, madhyamaka, the view, is reflected from that expressive power. When one understands the view of dharmata, it is not necessary to hear and reflect again. As it comes from within, one does not need to train in it again. It will naturally manifest in the expanse of knowledge, like a river rising during the monsoon rains. It does not manifest just for the sake of skill and fame. It inevitably benefits the teaching and beings. That is what is called spontaneous compassion.

The Buddha knows all sentient beings are deluded, and though he does not have any fixed concept of taking on this suffering of beings—conceptual sadness would be an example of this—his compassion naturally manifests wherever the violent karma and defilements of sentient beings are erupting. This happens without any specific focusing on his part. It happens naturally, just as all rivers flow into the ocean and not somewhere else. When these qualities of knowledge, compassion, and power develop, bodhisattva activity will be spontaneously complete.

What is bodhisattva activity? Accomplishing the benefit of beings in an unsurpassed way without the slightest concept of benefit for oneself. When one has actually realized the view of the intrinsic nature, there is absolutely no holding on to the distinction of self and other. Any sense of possessiveness related to oneself falls away. Through great compassion toward others, oneself and others become equal. There is absolutely no difference.

As an analogy, think of the mountains, rocks, trees, forests, and so on—all the things that take form on the earth: the earth does not foster good things and reject bad things. It treats them all equally. In the same way, bodhisattva activity pervades everywhere, and it is impossible for this pervasive quality to be in vain. It is like during the monsoon rains, when plants even grow from cracks in rocks, and inevitably trees and forests will fill the rocks and mountains and naturally break through them. The natural effect of bodhisattva activity can be compared to this.

When view, meditation, and action are taught, they have to be explained separately. When the view is taught—that the intrinsic nature is like space—one might think that dzogchen does not have the view, meditation, and action referred to in the other vehicles. If we teach just the view of emptiness to adherents of the gradual path, they will be inclined to think that the view is that of a blank emptiness. For that reason, view, meditation, and action are described from many different perspectives. Ati dzogchen does not denigrate or deny the gradual vehicles. Ultimately, the understanding of all the gradual vehicles boils down to the ati dzogchen view. The view, meditation, and action of other vehicles are guides to dzogchen.

By way of analogy, if you want to travel to an eastern country, all the roads to the east will lead there. Similarly, the view, meditation, and action of all the nine yanas are ways to reach the dzogchen view. They do not contradict dzogchen. If one actually realizes the dzogchen view, one will not give up the other eight vehicles, because the qualities of all nine vehicles are naturally present in the view of dzogchen. Whatever the quality of the vehicle—for example, in the shravaka yana, trying to achieve liberation for oneself; or in the bodhisattva yana, realizing that the two obscurations are veiling the dharmata and achieving liberation for the sake of others—all lead to the realization of dzogchen.

Though view, meditation, and action take many forms, all are of one taste. Realizing that view of one taste is like putting a single bridge across a hundred rivers. When one has perfected dzogchen, all the qualities of the view, meditation, and action of all nine yanas are fulfilled and complete. Someone who has actually realized dzogchen can explain all the stages of the nine yanas. One will naturally have the ability to know all the crucial points of the entire progression of the nine vehicles.

In Tibet there were eight important schools known as the eight chariots of the practice lineage. All had abhishekas, commentaries, and key instructions. All these different views lead to the ultimate pointing out, the view of dzogchen, atiyoga. The pointing out of the ultimate, the fourth abhisheka, is considered the ultimate of all empowerments. There are ten categories of subject matter in tantra: the view of suchness, determinate conduct, mandala array, graded levels of abhisheka, samaya that is not to be transgressed, display of enlightened activity, fulfillment of aspiration, offerings that bring fulfillment of the goal, unwavering contemplation, and mantra recitation. But if one gains confidence in the view of dharmata, all these will be manifest within that. They will all be present and do not have to be looked for elsewhere. Therefore, even though the words of the instructions that we have been discussing are few, they contain all the essential points.

What these few words teach is dzogchen's view of primordial purity. Even if one were to hear and contemplate all the 84,000 dharmas, one would find that ultimately there is nothing that needs to be introduced beyond the *Three Words That Strike the Vital Point*. Even if one were to compare these three words to the teachings of a hundred learned teachers and a thousand siddhas, one would find that there is nothing they can teach beyond this. When we have understood the meaning of this teaching, which condenses all the crucial points into one and cannot be excelled by anything else, we will find that, as it says in the secret-mantra vajrayana, "This is the advice for attaining buddhahood in one lifetime."

Omniscient Longchen Rabjam understood the entire meaning of the three divisions and nine spaces of dzogchen and became inseparable from Samantabhadra. If we were actually to meet Longchen Rabjam and receive teachings from him, he could not teach us anything beyond the *Three Words That Strike the Vital Point*. The vidyadhara Jigme Lingpa, Jigme Gyalwe Nyugu, and all the vidyadharas and gurus of the three lineages could not possibly teach us anything beyond this instruction.

There are many detailed teachings to guide us in this view, such as those related to the preparatory practice and the main practice. They are all steps leading to this profound view. When one practices in accord with these instructions, which are the essence of the 84,000 dharmas, even if one only has a glimpse of the view through one's own experience, one's emotions and attachment to this life will naturally be liberated.

In this degenerate age, when people's life span is short, their intelligence is dull, and their exertion is minimal, encountering such extraordinary teaching, which enables one to attain liberation in one lifetime, is like finding lion's milk. All the previous lineage teachers down to me have not only expounded the words but have also had the actual experience of this dzogchen view. If one were to hold a medicinal root in the palm of one's hand, one would be able to see clearly its size, shape, structure, and color. In the same way, the lineage masters gained confidence through their own experience and taught from that realization.

Paltrul Rinpoche's key instructions on the *Three Words That Strike the Vital Point* is brief in words but profound in meaning. This explanation I have given corresponds with what I have received and what I have understood. If you practice accordingly, you cannot help but be liberated. It will not be enough, however, just to practice for one or two days. In such a short time, we cannot break through our confusion. Even though you cannot spend your whole life continuously practicing in solitary retreat, please do as much practice as you can every day. As it is said, "A collection of drops can become an ocean." Since the teaching becomes more and more profound through continuous practice, confusion will naturally be purified, and all good qualities will spontaneously unfold. Those are the key instructions of the gurus of the three lineages.

These instructions should not be openly discussed or given to the public without careful consideration. Considering this difficult time and our short life span, I have spoken these profound words for the sake of those with the right karma and fortune. I have given these teachings with the motivation that beings in this degenerate age who are interested in such a practice might be able to dispel the confusion of samsara. If it is practiced properly, it will definitely be of benefit. As it is beneficial, if we begin to develop some experience in our being, we will understand the importance of this teaching and know why I spoke of it as including all the crucial points. There is a saying that as a sign of knowledge, we are tamed and, as a sign of having practiced, we have no conflicting emotions. The bonds of conflicting emotions will be cut and, through the guru's kindness, we will recognize all the important instructions.

The dharma is something we have to become accustomed to repeatedly. Merely hearing the sound of the dharma can close the gates to the three lower realms, but just that will not bring liberation. We should hear the dharma again and again. As it is Repa Shiwa Ö said:

Even one word of teaching can lead to buddhahood in one
   lifetime.
Training again and again is the basis of virtuous action.
Studying many books is the cause of arrogance.
Just receiving one word of pith instruction from a realized guru
   is the basis of enlightenment.

Through one word of instruction, liberation can be attained. Attaining liberation through one word, we will understand the meaning of the
dharma. The Buddha Shakyamuni accumulated merit for three measureless eons, attained enlightenment, and turned the wheel of the dharma
solely for the sake of sentient beings. If we understand that vital point,
the vision of the Buddha will be fulfilled and the benefit of sentient beings will be accomplished. It is necessary to hear the teachings and reflect
on them for a long time with great exertion. Without exertion, it is impossible to develop qualities in our being.

If we make an effort toward the dharma, we will realize its profound
importance more and more. Otherwise, we will just think, "Oh, that is
the dharma," and not gain any confidence in it. But if we continue making an effort for a long time, our confidence will be strong. Just to receive one verse of dharma, a bodhisattva abiding on the bhumis would
arouse the courage to cross the three worlds, even if they were engulfed
in flames. When we have understood its importance, we will be able to
give up our body, life, and happiness for the sake of the dharma. Seeing
them to be of no more value than a mustard seed, we will think, "I can
get them at any time, so I can let them go," which is a sign of confidence
in the dharma. It is very important to keep practicing until we develop
special confidence in the view and meditation. The reason it is so important I have explained according to what I know. If each of you will take
the time to practice properly, you will realize the primordial purity of
trekchö, the view of dzogchen.

The Special Teaching
of Khepa Shri Gyalpo

THREE WORDS THAT
STRIKE THE VITAL POINT

Homage to the guru.

The view is Longchen Rabjam (Infinite Great Expanse).
The meditation is Khyentse Öser (Light Rays of Knowledge
and Love).
The action is Gyalwey Nyugu (Son of the Victorious Ones).
For the one who practices in this way,
There is no doubt about enlightenment in one lifetime.
But even if not, there is still happiness—a la la.

The view, Longchen Rabjam, is as follows:
To hit the vital point with the three lines,
First, let your mind rest loosely.
Without projecting, without concentrating—without
thoughts.
While relaxed and remaining evenly in that state
Suddenly exclaim a mind-shattering PHAT.
Forceful, short and sharp—emaho!
Nothing whatsoever—totally disengaged.
Disengaged but utterly open.
A total openness which is indescribable.

Recognize this as the dharmakaya awareness.
To recognize your nature, that is the first vital point.

After this, whether you are thinking or still,
Whether you are angry or attached, happy or sad,
At all times and on all occasions
Acknowledge the recognized dharmakaya
And let the child luminosity unite with the already known
    mother.
Rest in the state of inexpressible awareness.
Destroy again and again stillness, bliss, clarity, and thinking.
Let the syllable of knowledge and means suddenly strike down.
No difference between meditation and postmeditation.
No division between sessions and breaks.
Rest continuously in the undivided state.
However, as long as you have not attained stability,
It is essential to practice giving up distractions.
Divide your meditation into sessions.
At all times and in all situations
Maintain the single continuity of dharmakaya.
Resolve that there is nothing other than this.
To decide on one thing, that is the second vital point.

At this time, your likes and dislikes, joys and sorrows,
And all your passing thoughts without exception
Leave no trace in the state of recognition.
By recognizing dharmakaya in what is liberated,
As in the analogy of drawing on water,
There is unceasing self-occurring self-liberation.
Whatever occurs is fresh food for the empty awareness.
Whatever is thought is an expression of the dharmakaya king.
Traceless and naturally free—a la la.
The way thoughts occur is the same as before,
But the way they are freed is the most special key point.
Without this, meditation is but the path of confusion.
Possessing it is the uncultivated state of dharmakaya.
To gain confidence in liberation, that is the third vital point.

This view endowed with three vital points,
And the meditation of combined knowledge and compassion,
Is aided by the general action of the sons of the victorious ones.
Even if the victorious ones of the three times were to confer
    together,
They would have no oral instructions superior to this.

The dharmakaya treasure revealer of awareness-display
Discovered this as a treasure from the expanse of knowledge.
It is unlike extracts of earth and stone.
It is the testament of Garab Dorje.
It is the heart essence of the three lineages.
It is entrusted with secrecy to heart disciples.
It is the profound meaning and words from the heart.
It is words from the heart, the essential meaning.
Do not let the essential meaning fade away.
Do not let the instruction dissipate.

This was the special teaching of Khepa Shri Gyalpo.

• • •

*In accordance with oral teachings from Kyabje Dilgo Khyen-
tse and Tulku Pema Wangyal, and later numerous times
from Kyabje Tulku Urgyen and Chökyi Nyima Rinpoche,
this was translated at Samye Chimphu in 1987 by Erik
Pema Kunsang.*

THE LAMP THAT DISPELS DARKNESS

Instructions That Point Directly to the
Nature of the Mind According to the
Tradition of the Old Meditators

JAMGÖN MIPHAM RINPOCHE

COMMENTARY BY DILGO KHYENTSE RINPOCHE

About Jamgön Mipham Rinpoche

JAMGÖN MIPHAM RINPOCHE (1846–1912) was one of the most brilliant scholars and luminaries of Tibetan Buddhism in modern times. In addition to having the experiences and realizations of a great bodhisattva and Vajrayana yogi, he wrote many outstanding treatises on a wide range of subjects, clarifying with great conviction the philosophical view and practice of the Nyingma tradition. A number of his works have been translated into Western languages.

Mipham Rinpoche shaped the general academic curriculum at the Shri Singha College at Dzogchen Monastery in Eastern Tibet, and it became the basis of how the Nyingma tradition is studied today. He was an important member of the Rime, or nonsectarian movement. When Dilgo Khyentse Rinpoche was born, Mipham Rinpoche blessed him and gave him the name Tashi Paljor, as well as a special transmission of Manjushri. Mipham Rinpoche had many students who became important teachers, including Shechen Gyaltsap Pema Namgyal, Katok Situ, Adzom Drukpa, Khenpo Kunpel, and the Third Dodrupchen.

The Commentary

Dilgo Khyentse Rinpoche

BEFORE WE BEGIN to study these teachings, it is essential that we understand that, as it is often said, "The foundation practice (ngön-dro) is even more profound than the main practice." The reason for this is that there will be no result if we do not investigate in depth the various stages of the foundation practice and do not practice it so that each stage becomes a true part of our being. If we hastily jump to the main practice, our meditative experience will not progress and realization will not be accomplished.

It is essential to study and practice texts such as *The Words of My Perfect Teacher*[1] or any other detailed explanation related to this foundation practice before going on to the main practice. So clearly keep in mind how indispensable this practice is.

Though there are many teachings on the main practice, the one that will be taught here is a short text by Lama Mipham Rinpoche, who was Manjushri in human form. It is a teaching on the nature of the mind known as *The Instructions That Point Directly to the Nature of the Mind According to the Tradition of the Old Meditators*. The specific name of this instruction is *The Lamp That Dispels Darkness*. These instructions contain the whole of the Great Perfection practice and expound its essence in just a few pages, in a way that is easy to understand even without having studied extensively. They are presented in a direct, naked way, called *martri* in Tibetan, which means "red instructions," because they show the essential points of practice as if someone had opened his chest and shown the red of his heart.

The text begins with homage to the teacher as being inseparable from

Manjushri. Generally it is important to study all the basic scriptures and the commentaries on them in a gradual way, while applying intelligence to comprehend their meaning. Then it is necessary to receive the pith instructions that distill the quintessence of the teachings in such a way that we can directly put them into practice. Therefore, in general we first listen to the teachings, then reflect upon them again and again, and finally experience them through meditation.

However, without necessarily undertaking extensive studies, we may also simply rely upon the pith instructions given by an authentic master, since these instructions gather the essence of all these teachings in a way that is easy to understand and put into practice. Through these teachings we can realize the nature of mind, according to the pith instructions of the Great Perfection, and thus travel the path to its ultimate end and achieve the level of a vidyadhara, an awareness-holder.

What is it that we call mind? Mind is that which conceives and remembers all sorts of things. When we enter a temple and see the sacred objects, we feel great devotion and are inspired to take refuge. If we enter an ordinary room and see the various objects in it, we think about how they can be used. We discriminate between them, perceiving some as good and some as bad. This whole collection of thoughts is called the mind. Yet we ordinary beings are not aware of the true nature of this mind. To recognize its nature is the point of the Great Perfection practice.

What is the support of the mind? The mind is supported by the body—a collection of many internal parts (flesh, bones, and organs) within an outer envelope (the skin). This body is set in motion by the various energies, or pranas.

The Tibetan word for "body," *lus*, carries the sense of "something left behind," because the body is what is left behind at the time of death. After we die, driven by the positive and negative actions committed in the past, our consciousness will wander in the bardo, the intermediate state between death and the next birth. There is no way for the consciousness to take the physical body along with it after death.

When body and mind are together, one has the ability to see, to hear, to feel, to like what is pleasant, and to dislike what is unpleasant. In brief, the body is like a vessel and the mind is like its content.

Once the body and mind come together in a living being, speech can occur naturally. By assembling the various parts of a lute—the wood, the different strings, the bits of wood to tie the strings—we can play music. Likewise, when the elements of the body and mind come together, then the faculty of speech can function. When the body and mind go their separate ways at the time of death, the speech faculty vanishes into space. But while we are alive, they function together and must be harmoniously coordinated to perform any action. For instance, if the mind conceives faith in the teacher and the Three Jewels, then speech will follow through the recitation of prayers and praises, and the body will follow by showing respect, doing prostrations, and so forth.

There are various types of bodies throughout the various realms of samsara. Our gross human body made of flesh and bones becomes a corpse that is scattered at the time of death. When the ordinary body is sleeping comfortably, there is a subtle "dream body" that can travel to the four directions of the world and perform all kinds of dream actions. This kind of body is a manifestation of one's karmic tendencies. Likewise, in the bardo after death, there is a "mental body," which, though not material, still provides a support for consciousness.

The combination of body, speech, and mind is powerful: it can lead us to enlightenment or to the hell realms. Among the three, the mind is like a king and the other two are like his servants. This is obvious at the time of death when the mind continues—carrying the load of karmic seeds engendered by past positive and negative actions—but the body is left behind as a corpse. Though a corpse has eyes, it cannot see, and even if you wrap it in brocades and speak nice words to it, it doesn't care and won't be pleased. If you beat it with sticks and stones and burn it, it is not displeased and won't suffer. Therefore, it is the all-powerful mind that empowers the body. When body, speech, and mind are combined during our lifetime, the mind is supported by a basic consciousness imprinted with all the karmic residues of past good and bad actions, which remain there just like a letter of debt.

Let us look a little more into that mind. There are past thoughts—like those we had this morning, which no longer exist. There are future thoughts—like those we will have tonight, which are not yet born and are unpredictable. At this very moment, while listening to the teachings and trying to focus one-pointedly, there are present thoughts. If examined, past thoughts are like a dead corpse; they have ceased to exist. Future thoughts are unborn; they do not yet exist. Present thoughts seem to have some sort of existence, but how could there be a present thought in the middle of nowhere, without being supported by either the past or the future, neither of which exists in the present?

In order to try to recognize the nature of mind, we must first leave the mind in a very relaxed, open, and uncontrived state. Certain activities force the mind to focus on something, thus diverting it from its natural condition. For example, in the practice of the development stage, we train to concentrate the mind upon a deity and its attributes. Likewise, when reciting the mantra of Manjushri, OM A RA PA TSA NA DHIH, we concentrate upon reciting all the syllables and remembering the benefit of the mantra. In both these examples, the mind is maintained in a state of concentration that is somehow artificial.

By contrast, in the uncontrived state there is no effort to focus the mind on any concrete support. Simply let it rest, and try to be aware of the present mind, fresh and uncontrived. Although we speak of a "present mind," it is not a graspable entity. If we search for the mind in the head, chest, heart, or other parts of the body, and try to identify whether it has any shape or color, the more we look, the more we realize that we cannot find anything that can be defined as "the" mind.

Is the mind nothing at all, then? This cannot be said either. The mind is constantly aware of outer and inner phenomena. It reacts to external conditions. If it sees an image of the Buddha, it will conceive faith and be inspired to take refuge and ask for blessings. If someone creates a disturbance or causes irritation, faith will be lost immediately and turn into anger. The mind is constantly changing.

The right way to investigate the nature of mind is not to perpetuate past thoughts, not to invite the arising of future thoughts, and to remain in the present in a balanced state. The mind should be neither distracted by outer objects nor excessively withdrawn into a state of apathy. Let it rest in a relaxed and open state.

Remain in such a state, without trying to conceive thoughts of devotion and compassion, without being distracted by outer events or invaded by anger and attachment—simply allow the mind to remain as it is, yet fully aware. This is called mindfulness. Just as a young child cannot be left alone but needs the constant attention of his parents so he won't get lost, mindfulness is necessary so that the mind won't get lost in distraction. To cultivate mindfulness is very important in order to progress in recognizing the nature of mind.

Mindfulness is not something that is acquired right away; persever-ance is needed. We must be mindful in all circumstances, not just while resting in the state of meditative evenness. While eating, walking, and so on, it is important to be constantly alert and vigilant in watching the condition of the mind.

When beginners try to remain in a state of evenness, they will first reach a state where there are neither positive thoughts (such as devotion, faith, and compassion) nor negative thoughts (such as anger and crav-ing). This is just a foggy dullness, an amorphous state where there are neither good nor bad, virtuous nor unvirtuous thoughts. Such a state, which is devoid of natural brightness or lucidity, is called *nag thom me wa* in Tibetan, which means something like "dark torpor" or "opaque confusion." It is just an amorphous state about which nothing much can be said. One cannot say that "it is like this" or "it is like that," because it is devoid of vipashyana, the superior insight that brings a deeper, clearer understanding of the nature of mind. The limited, indescribable state of simply dwelling in complete quiescence or stillness is plain shamatha.

Mental darkness is caused by the eighty-four thousand obscuring emotions that completely envelop the mind. These emotions arise from the basic consciousness, which is synonymous with ignorance. *Marigpa* is "basic ignorance" or "not-knowing": that is, not seeing, not hearing, and above all not knowing what is the path to enlightenment. This amorphous state of the mind cannot be easily defined, because it has no clear characteristics. There is the feeling that there is "something," but it cannot be said that it is here or there in the body—in the eyes, the lungs, the heart, or the brain—or anywhere else. Basically it is just com-plete dullness or mental darkness, which is neither virtue nor nonvirtue. It is *lung ma ten* or "undetermined," something that cannot be defined through reasoning.

How does that mental darkness first occur? Every sentient being has the buddha-nature, or tathagatagarbha. Fundamentally, there is no such thing as "ignorance" or "unknowing" or "unawareness." Where does the concept of subject and object come from, then? It appears when the phenomenal manifestation first arises out of the primordial ground of the buddha-nature. Perceiving this manifestation as being something other than oneself—other that the primordial nature of mind—is the very root of ignorance and mental darkness. Yet that delusion does not *belong* to the buddha-nature, just as stains on a piece of gold, which mask its true quality, do not belong to the gold itself. Likewise, the obscurations of ignorance are temporarily attached to the buddha-nature but don't belong to it.

What obscures the buddha-nature is the amorphous consciousness—an incidental veil extraneous to the buddha-nature. That is the first thing the mind comes up against when it tries to look at its own nature. Beginners encounter this state of mental darkness because the lucidity of awareness beyond concepts has not yet arisen to illuminate the darkness. Therefore, the amorphous consciousness is not genuine, true meditation. As the Prayer of Samantabhadra[2] describes:

> The vacant state of not thinking of anything
> Is itself the cause of ignorance and confusion.

This dull state is the source of delusion. How, then, is the true nature of mind to be discovered? By letting the mind look at itself, letting it rest in a state of simplicity, and watching its nature. The mind is not something that can be looked at with the eyes or grasped with the hands. The mind has to look at itself. What we need to do is not to analyze this mental darkness discursively; rather we have to first let the mind rest in a state of complete naturalness or simplicity, just as it is, without falling into distraction. A state will be soon attained that is free from obvious movements of the mind such as aversion for enemies, unpleasant feelings, or attraction toward pleasant things. This state is also free from the opaque dullness that one experienced before. It is a state that is lucid, clear, and spacious, like the experience of looking into the vast sky.

There is a feeling of both immensity and clarity, a state of openness that allows awareness to unfold, just as physical space allows mountains and continents and the whole universe to manifest. It is an awareness that has no inside and outside, that is all-encompassing and transparent like the sky. The quality of space is total openness; if space were solid, then when we spoke to someone, the words would not reach that person, neither would there be a way to move within space nor for phenomena to appear.

Such a state is recognized only through one's own experience; it cannot be described. What is actually looked at (the state of open awareness) and what looks at it (awareness itself) are not two different things, one looking at the other. It is simply a state of sheer awareness of natural clarity.

In the previous state of dullness, one remains in a state of confusion and doubt, thinking, "Is that the nature of the mind, or is it something else?" But when we experience awareness, there is no more hesitation. There is an unmistakable understanding and recognition of what the teacher indicated to be the nature of mind. We may think, "This is it." There will be a clear-cut conviction that there is nothing other than that to be found.

Nonetheless, this is still not something that can be expressed; one can try to say something about it, but it cannot be defined in words, because by nature it is indescribable and beyond all conceptual limitations such as "It exists" or "It does not exist." It is not an object like a pot, which has a certain shape, color, and size. Neither is it pure nothingness, a blank state devoid of any quality.

Can it be said, then, that it is something existing and nonexisting at the same time? Or that it is neither existing nor nonexisting? These are just more incorrect concepts. No matter how much we try, we cannot describe awareness in words.

When recognition of awareness arises, it is not as though it has been given to us by our spiritual teacher, nor is it something that was not there before and is now born in our mind. Rather, awareness is the natural continuity of something that has been present forever, the pure, void, primordial clarity of mind. Why is it called rigpa? It is rigpa because it has a faculty of being "aware" of everything, as opposed to marigpa, "unawareness," "basic ignorance," which does not know anything.

Awareness is different from deluded mind in that awareness is totally free from clinging. The recognition of awareness corresponds to the first of the three precepts in the *Tsik Sum Ne Dek* (Three Words That Strike the Vital Point):[3] "To be introduced to one's own nature." Why were we dwelling in a state of mental darkness before? Because the clarity of wisdom was lacking. Now there is a clear awareness that illuminates everything like the sun rising at dawn and shedding light on the whole world.

The state of opacity gradually becomes clearer and clearer, just as, at the moment of dawn, there is first a faint light and then the sky becomes brighter and brighter. This is why in the beginning stages of meditation we meet and deal only with this mental opacity, but that should not cause us to abandon meditation. We should keep meditating on that obscure state, which is like a veil, since at the core of its many layers the true nature of awareness is to be found.

But divesting awareness of its veils of deluded mind is not something that can be done by force, like peeling the skin off a fruit. Awareness will appear of its own accord when the right conditions are present. When it arises, there is complete certainty that one has correctly recognized what the teacher indicated and what is mentioned in profound teachings on the Great Perfection such Longchen Rabjam's *Choying Dzö* (Treasure of the Absolute Expanse). When an egg hatches and breaks open, we clearly see the qualities of the baby bird, the color of its feathers, and other features. Likewise, when awareness is no longer encased within the eggshell of deluded mind, unobstructed awareness is revealed. By continuously blending luminous emptiness with awareness, it will be possible to have a direct experience of this naked awareness.

The next instruction is "the pith instruction for cutting through the net of samsaric existence." Our buddha-nature is not given to us through the blessings of the teacher or as a siddhi by the yidam deity. Even when we are completely deluded, the nature of this primordial purity remains unchanged throughout the three times—past, present, and future.

At the beginning, buddha-nature is primordially pure but not recognized; when we are practicing the path, part of it is recognized but not yet fully actualized; and at the time of the ultimate fruit, when all obscurations have been discarded and all qualities acquired, it will be fully realized as it is. Although there is a process of recognition, the nature itself never changes. This is why the great teacher Karma Chagme said when he realized this nature, "But I've known that nature forever! It seems my teacher and spiritual friends were hiding the fact that this was it." So, besides recognizing the primordial nature of mind, there is nothing to be known about the mind and nothing else to fabricate.

We have said that mental darkness cannot be described because it has no shape, color, or location. Because it is devoid of characteristics, we cannot say that this state exists, nor that it is completely nonexistent, since there is a basic consciousness within it. It is simply a state of indetermination that we cannot qualify in any way. The nature of awareness is also something that cannot be described, but it is not the same kind of indescribability. As has been said:

The nature is not existent—the Victorious Ones didn't see it.
It is not nonexisting—it is the ground of both samsara and
   nirvana.
It is the middle path, which unites all opposites.

Awareness cannot be expressed or described, but at the same time it
is associated with a clear-cut confidence that this absolute nature of mind
is the true meaning of the fourth empowerment. It is a state free from
any doubt and hesitation. There is a great difference in the ineffability of
the dark, amorphous state that cannot be described and the state of pure
awareness, which is also beyond description. The difference is as great
as that between a blind person and a sighted one. The blindness is like
the basic consciousness, alaya, which is the support of all past tendencies
of samsara and nirvana. The sightedness is the dharmakaya, the "ultimate dimension" of awakening, which is unconditioned and free from
all limitation. This great difference is explained in numerous pith instructions.

In many instructions the Tibetan term *thamal gyi shepa*, "ordinary
mind," is used. In this case, *thamal shepa* means an uncontrived state of
simplicity in which past thoughts are not continued, future thoughts are
not invited, and present awareness is neither distracted by outer phenomena nor withdrawn in dull slackness. That is the "good" or positive
ordinary consciousness, the seed of buddhahood. But we also speak of
"ordinary mind" in the sense of the mind that has not been trained in
the Dharma and is filled with thoughts of attachment and revulsion. This
is the "bad" or negative ordinary mind, which needs to be discarded.

The positive ordinary state of mind is not the fruit of intellectual activity. Its aspects of natural awareness and clarity need to be recognized
through experience and realization, not through fabrication. We should
not declare that the mind is empty or conceive this notion in a forced
manner. Nor should we try to make the mind clear and luminous by
force. These qualities are a pure, natural state without any intellectual
contrivance. With dualistic clinging—a meditation split into a meditator
and an object of meditation—there is no Great Perfection. If the natural
simplicity of mind is realized, this is the Great Perfection, a state completely devoid of concepts of meditator and meditation. In truth there is
nothing to meditate upon. "Meditation" should be a state in which we
do not exert the intellect in identifying experiences as "This is such" and

"This is not such." This is the positive absence of intellectual activity. The negative one is a state of torpor in which one is unable to use one's intellect.

When it is said that the natural state is inexpressible, this refers to the indescribable wisdom beyond the intellect, the prajnaparamita. This is the positive inexpressibility. Inexpressibility does not refer to the state of someone who cannot speak because he is completely drunk or in a deep sleep. These are the negative inexpressibilities.

Thus, these two expressions refer to both a correct state to be embraced and a wrong state to be avoided. It is very important not to confuse them. Otherwise, one may come to think and say, as some people do, that the Great Perfection is simply a blank, quiet state devoid of any thought. To say this is a sign that we have failed to properly listen to the teachings, ponder them, and integrate them into our being through meditation. If this profound teaching is truly practiced, we will have complete confidence that there is none superior. This is why Jigme Lingpa says in the *Dorje Tsig Kang* (Adamantine Root Verses):[4] "Even if a thousand buddhas and great siddhas were in front of me, I would have no doubts to be clarified." Through realization, there will be a direct experience of this very profound meaning.

Those who cling to either the lucid or the void aspect of the mind are caught in dualistic attachment to subject and object. There cannot be realization with clinging. As Manjushri said in a vision that appeared to the glorious Sakyapa teacher Trakpa Gyaltsen, "Where there is clinging, there is no view."

Clinging to either the lucid or the void aspect of mind should be dissolved by looking at the mind that clings, examining it to see if it has any location in the body—in the head, the heart, and so forth—or whether it has any color or shape. The more you look, the less you can find it.

When the experience of emptiness predominates, you feel as if you could pass through rocks, or that you have no solid body, that the whole material world has melted into space. Instead of clinging to such an experience, look at the mind that clings and establish again that it has no shape and no location. Otherwise, if the mind is allowed to become entangled in dualistic clinging, it will become like the hairs of a yak—so entangled with one another that it is impossible to separate them. Even if you have long been striving to stabilize your mind in quietness through shamatha practice, you will end up completely stuck in dualistic concepts.

Whenever you cling to a meditative experience, when it inevitably fades away you feel as if your meditation has faltered, that you have lost some clarity or experience of emptiness, and that your efforts have been unsuccessful. This is a false perception. Furthermore, when you experience some clarity and try to analyze it, or when you have a feeling of emptiness and try to immobilize the mind in this blank state, mistaking it for what the teacher has said about emptiness, then you are stuck just like a horse tied to a pole firmly driven into the hard ground.

If the peg of intellectual fabrication is lifted and your awareness is allowed to appear simply as it is—naked, free, and vivid—the experience of clarity and emptiness will become much vaster. As is said in the instructions of the Longchen Nyingthig, the clarity will be such that we will feel able to see the entire universe. The experience of emptiness will be such that we will perceive continents and mountains as being immaterial. We will feel capable of easily leaving a footprint or handprint in solid stone. This is a state with no periphery or center, very open, vast, and completely free of clinging. It is the natural condition of phenomena. In it there is also a sense of complete certainty and a clear-cut confidence brought about by the limpidity of this state of mind. This is awareness.

Awareness basically means freedom from clinging. If there is clinging, it is not awareness; it is the ordinary mind. Awareness is the arising of naked wisdom devoid of the husk of ordinary meditative experiences. View, meditation, and action, the development and completion stages— everything is included within the realization of this naked wisdom.

When clinging to the luminous and void aspects of mind is completely destroyed, this corresponds to the second sentence of the "Three Words That Strike the Vital Point," which says, "Decide on a single point." Here, this is called "the pith instruction for cutting through the net of samsaric existence." A fish caught in a net can't go anywhere, but if the net is cut with a knife, the fish can freely swim anywhere it likes in the vast ocean. Likewise, awareness is enveloped by many conceptual and discursive thoughts, but if these thoughts are destroyed over and over again, awareness will be laid bare.

When the husk is removed from a grain of rice, it becomes edible, and when the husk is removed from a grain of barley, good tsampa can be made from it. Likewise, awareness must be divested of the discursive mind and the husk of meditative experiences.

There is no need to seek out experiences of clarity or emptiness. Leave the mind in its natural condition, in utter simplicity. If it is allowed to remain in natural awareness, then, whenever an attractive object arises before the mind, there will first be a thought of attraction, but that thought will be liberated as it arises and leave no karmic traces. The same is true of thoughts of revulsion. If awareness comes simultaneously with these thoughts, they will not engender compulsive attraction or repulsion. Entangling desire will give way to bliss-void, anger to luminosity-void, and neutral thoughts to awareness-void. If one recognizes awareness, even if thoughts of attachment or repulsion arise, awareness will remain clear and distinct in the midst of thoughts, just as a drop of mercury that has fallen into the dust doesn't blend with it but remains bright and pure.

Awareness will become clearer and clearer of its own accord; we don't have to force it to become so. In the practice of the Great Perfection, we first recognize the primordial nature of mind, and then become more and more experienced in recognizing it, eventually achieving complete stability in its realization. Those are the three graded stages in the practice.

The first stage, recognizing the nature, corresponds to "cutting through the net of samsaric existence." It is recognizing the difference between deluded mind and pure awareness. But it is not enough to recognize awareness. We need to become *experienced* in recognizing it, the second stage. Otherwise we are like a young prince, the son of a universal monarch, who is indeed of royal lineage but has not yet developed the skill to govern the kingdom and is unable to perform all the activities of a great king. If we simply recognize awareness without developing the skill to its ultimate point, there is a danger of falling under the power of strong tendencies that have been accumulated over many lifetimes. So do not be satisfied by a mere glimpse of awareness, but allow its presence to become permanent, the third stage.

This is achieved through mindfulness and vigilance. At the beginning, vigilance means paying constant attention to your state of mind, examining whether the mind is distracted from the recognition of awareness. This is a somewhat fabricated or contrived mindfulness. Genuine mindfulness will develop gradually. In his *Men-ngak Dzö* (Treasure of Pith

Instructions), Longchen Rabjam discusses six ways of "using mindfulness as a spy": During your session, use mindfulness as a spy to check whether (1) you are becoming preoccupied by details of mundane life, (2) you are distracted because of laziness, (3) your mind is going astray and becoming obscured, (4) you have gotten carried away by deluded thoughts, (5) you have strayed into mental chatter, or (6) your mind is still in a completely ordinary state.

When we reach the point where, whenever a thought of desire or aversion arises, awareness is there at the same time, without our having to purposefully arouse it, that is uncontrived, genuine mindfulness. At this stage, all thoughts will be liberated as they arise.

Some people might imagine that a yogi of the Great Perfection has no thoughts at all, just like the earth or a stone, but this is not the case Thoughts will continue to arise just as before; the difference is that they are immediately liberated upon arising and therefore do not accumulate karma. When a thought is not liberated as it arises, then that first thought leads to a second thought, the second to a third, and then action and karma will result. This is the very process of delusion. It is therefore very important to maintain the recognition of awareness without distraction. To do that, train in maintaining mindfulness over a long period of time. It is not sufficient to think, "I'll practice for a while—a few months or a few years." Be like Jetsun Milarepa, who declared that he would practice until his face fell on the ground, which means until the very moment of his death.

Just as many flowers bloom in the summer meadow, many experiences arise in the mind of the meditator who strives in the practice.

Sometimes a state of gloom or meditational darkness is experienced. If you feel resigned to such a state, thinking, "I'll just relax in this absence of discursive thoughts since I can't realize the Great Perfection anyway," your meditation will stagnate. At other times, freedom from thoughts will be associated with a very clear insight, as in vipashyana practice—a very open, transparent, and all-encompassing mental stillness. It may be thought that this is the ultimate realization, like that achieved by Longchenpa or Jigme Lingpa. This mistaken conclusion will not be fruitful.

Sometimes there are experiences of total happiness or bliss, a feeling that one could meditate for months, day and night without interruption, and that no emotion whatsoever—whether desire or revulsion—could disturb such bliss. But a meditator whose bliss is tainted with clinging is just like a fly that has fallen into honey. At other times, however, one may experience more freedom from clinging.

Sometimes there will be experiences of clarity, of sharp acumen. When reading the scriptures, you have a sense of great understanding. But these experiences are usually still pervaded by clinging. At other times, there will be experiences of lucidity, with no obscuration of any kind, free from clinging.

Sometimes the mind will become so wild that you feel depressed, thinking, "I've been practicing meditation for so many years, yet my mind is still as wild as that of someone who hasn't done any practice." At other times, a completely dull and clouded feeling will arise, like the heavy torpor of someone drunk with beer.

At other times, you will dwell in very soft, even, and pleasant states. Sometimes subtle thoughts will move ceaselessly like ripples on the water, sometimes they will become wild and violent like waves. Sometimes you will suddenly feel great anger at someone and think, "Oh, now I must go beat him up." Sometimes desire will oppress you. All of these experiences will thoroughly disrupt your meditation.

Why is that so? For countless ages different karmas have accumulated that manifest as energies (pranas) that are closely linked with the mind. Karmic energy is like a blind horse, and the mind rides it like a lame person. Without a rider, the blind horse might jump in the water or fall off a cliff. The horse needs a rider to lead it safely around. Similarly, without a horse, the lame rider cannot go anywhere. Thus, the horse and rider each need the other in order to function.

It is these waves of karmic energy that create the ever-changing experiences in meditation. When you travel in an airplane, you can see all sorts of landscapes below—lakes, mountains, lush forests, deserts, cold and warm places. Likewise, during meditation, experiences of all kinds pass before your mind's eye. At that time, the most important thing is to avoid any kind of clinging. Don't proudly think that these are "good" experiences and "Now I have realized the Great Perfection!" Neither should you be discouraged by "bad" periods of practice and feel like giving up meditation altogether, telling yourself, "I'll never succeed."

Let the mind remain in its completely natural, uncontrived state. Be like a newborn baby in its cradle. Even if surrounded by threatening armies wielding swords, the baby has no fear. In brief, there should be no modification of the natural state.

There are five stages in the quieting of thoughts. First, one experiences *ceaseless movement*, then *attainment*, followed by *familiarization* and *stability*, and finally *ultimate reach*. The first stage is like water falling off a cliff, the second like a mountain stream rushing through a gorge, the third like a wide river flowing leisurely, and the fourth like a calm ocean. The fifth is like a flame burning bright and clear in the absence of wind.

In the first stage, mind is constantly in motion, not stopping even for a second and creating a great inner tumult. At that time, persevere; do not feel discouraged or give up the meditation. Persevere how? By being neither too tense nor too loose. This is a vital point of meditation. If your mindfulness has become slack, revive it by becoming more brisk and alert. If mindfulness returns, do not maintain it by force, but simply rest within awareness. Meditation must be like the strings of a lute, which give their best sound when neither too tight nor too loose.

In addition, don't disassociate meditation from the postmeditation period. The understanding gained in meditation should shed light on the path of action in postmeditation, and the experiences of postmeditation should enrich meditation and make it progress. These two will thus constantly reinforce each other. If the insights that you gain through today's meditation are maintained in all actions, speech, and thoughts, then tomorrow's meditation will improve. Without letting the mind wander in the ordinary state during postmeditation, persevere in blending meditation and nonmeditation until there is no difference between them.

Then the time will arrive when you are able to clearly distinguish between deluded mind and awareness, and a state is reached that is completely free from doubt and hesitation about the nature of awareness. That is what is called *lada* in Tibetan, the unerring certainty that "This is it!"

Following this, when experiences of bliss, clarity and absence of thought arise, be skillful in not confusing the basic consciousness (alaya) with the dharmakaya, ordinary mind with awareness, intellect with wisdom, and so forth. There are ten such things not to be confused, as is explained in the commentaries of Jigme Lingpa's *Yonten Rinpoche Dzö* (Treasury of Precious Qualities).[5] Without these clear distinctions, it will be impossible to recognize naked awareness as it is. Ordinary mind is what entangles beings in samsara, and awareness is what liberates them;

the basic consciousness, the alaya, is the support of all the samsaric tendencies (the dull, indeterminate state of mental darkness mentioned earlier), while the dharmakaya is pure awareness divested of all obscuration, a clear, void, unchanging realization that is like the sky. If there is clinging, that is intellect; if there is no clinging, that is wisdom.

To progress, we need the constant guidance of a qualified teacher. As we report to him the progress of our meditation and describe our experiences, he may say, "You should relax more," or on the contrary, "Be more vigilant." It is important at this time to rely upon a teacher's instructions. When the great Gampopa had many spiritual experiences, he explained them to Jetsun Milarepa and was thus able to avoid deviations and continue to progress.

Once you've been introduced to this nature of the mind, you should achieve stability and confidence in recognizing it, so that the mind remains in that state of simplicity without wavering. If we allow water to remain still without agitating it, it becomes limpid and transparent; but if we stir it up with a stick, mud rises and the water becomes turbid. Likewise, leave the mind in a state of natural clarity, without interference, so that awareness remains limpid.

Between meditation sessions, it is beneficial to read commentaries that explain the difference between mind and awareness, and other crucial points of the practice. But at the time of meditation, you should remain in complete simplicity, filled with confidence in your teacher. If good experiences occur, don't be satisfied with them but strive even more in your practice. If bad or weak experiences occur, don't be discouraged and tempted to give up, but keep up a regular practice.

While resting in evenness during meditation, do not entertain thoughts such as "The teaching says that awareness is like this, but it's not like that for me," or "This must be such-and-such experience that I have read about." These thoughts will only obscure your meditation. In brief, while meditating don't examine the various aspects of practice or recall the intellectual learning you've gotten from books. If you simply maintain a steady mindfulness, the natural condition of awareness, then the tranquil state of shamatha and the clear insight of vipashyana will continually be combined.

When firmness and stability in practice are attained, there is no longer any separation between shamatha and vipashyana. Until then, we need to practice by stages—first shamatha, quieting the mind, and then applying vipashyana, the widened perspective or deeper insight that dissolves the clinging to the calm of shamatha. In the Great Perfection, the equivalent of shamatha is to remain in the state of simplicity, undisturbed by the arising of thoughts, while the equivalent of vipashyana is the spontaneous liberation of thoughts upon their arising. It is impossible to avoid accumulating karma if we merely dwell in the tranquillity of shamatha, because without the immediate liberation of thoughts that comes with vipashyana, the chain of deluded thoughts will not be broken.

The essential union of shamatha and vipashyana is the pith instruction of remaining in skylike equanimity. The sky is unchanging and doesn't care whether or not it contains worlds and continents. No matter how many world-systems there are, the sky is never filled up with them, nor would it become vaster if there were none at all. Likewise, once all experiences and thoughts are liberated as we experience them, the realization of the great equal taste is attained—a state devoid of efforts to generate devotion and compassion or eliminate negative emotions. That is the third pith instruction, on abiding in spacelike equanimity.

Having clearly recognized the distinction between mind and awareness, and having understood how to meditate, then, as Saraha said, "Give up the thinker and the objects of thoughts, and just remain like a young child, without any concepts." In the practice of the development stage, there are objects to concentrate on—such as the form and attributes of the deity and all the details of the mandala—and there is also a discursive mind that focuses upon these details. This is not the ultimate way to look at the natural state of the mind.

To discover this natural state, remain in a state free from all concepts, just like a very young child who is not yet used to the sophisticated adult way of thinking. Although a newborn infant can see with his eyes, he does not discriminate between beautiful and ugly forms, trying to attract what is beautiful or repulse what is considered ugly. He hasn't yet learned to react in terms of conceptual thoughts. This is the way to remain in the state of complete relaxation and simplicity.

In order to realize this, it is necessary to receive the pith instructions of a qualified spiritual teacher. The recognition of the nature of the mind is the meaning of the fourth initiation, which gives direct access to the ultimate nature of mind. This cannot be received without a qualified teacher. To what will this enlightened teacher introduce you? To the in-herent buddha-nature, the tathagatagarbha, the uncontrived awareness. Even though we have had it since the beginning, we do not realize it. It is through the instructions of the teacher who points toward this nature that we recognize it and become free from all doubt and misconceptions. Someone who is very clever at finding gems and precious stones knows how to recognize the presence of a hidden gold mine. He will tell others, "Here you can find gold," and by digging there they are sure to find it.

When we say that the primordial awareness is inherent or coemergent with mind, it means it has always been there from the very beginning. There was never any separation from that buddha-nature. Without trying to alter this nature in any way, let it arise by itself. This is why it is said that there are no other practices to be done besides practicing on the mind, and why the eighty-four thousand sections of the Buddha's teaching are all aimed at the recognition of the nature of mind.

The absolute nature that has always accompanied the mind as a shadow accompanies the body is what we call the absolute, primordial, and continuous luminosity. If we simply let the mind rest in the natural state and have the insight to distinguish the deluded mind from pure awareness, this is the vital point that gathers together all other instructions, just like one hundred rivers passing under a single bridge.

If, at all times and in all circumstances, we are able to preserve this primordial simplicity, then there should be no difference between meditation, considered to be worthwhile, and postmeditation, considered ordinary or useless.

When we are experienced in preserving the continuity of awareness, it will continue even in deep sleep. The state of sleep, which normally is obscure and dull, will become more and more aware, lucid, and luminous, until there is no more distinction between waking and sleeping. The realization of luminosity will persist throughout day and night. If there is no longer any difference between awareness in the daytime and in deep sleep, that is the sign that meditation has reached perfection.

Deep sleep resembles the onset of death, dreaming resembles the bardo, and the waking state corresponds to being alive. Continuously, day after day and night after night, we go through the cycle of sleep, dream, and waking. If, through practice, the recognition of the simplicity of awareness is maintained throughout both dreams and deep sleep, we will be ready to practice at the time of death and in the bardo. When frightening dreams occur, we will have no fear, because we'll recognize them as dreams and illusions. We may also have very good dreams, such as traveling to buddhafields, meeting with the buddhas and receiving their teachings, and being able to direct the course of our dreams at will.

If such a level of practice has been achieved, then after death, in the actual bardo, whatever experiences arise will be recognized as being of the same nature as dreams and illusions. Instead of being frightened, we will remember the teacher and his instructions, and liberation will be possible. In brief, if we can recognize the state of luminosity in deep sleep, that signifies that meditation has become firm and reached its ultimate level. This is the sign of a perfectly correct path. For instance, in practicing the inner heat (tummo), one becomes able to bring all the energies to the central channel. In meditating upon the illusory body, as a sign of accomplishment one will be able to pass through rocks. All these signs do not need to be cultivated or sought after; they will come naturally once the true nature of mind has been realized.

Expressions of such realization will also be natural. Faith and devotion will follow, because devotion leads to realization, and realization increases devotion even more. When Gampopa asked Milarepa, "When should I work to benefit beings?" Milarepa told him: "A day will come when you will see the naked state of awareness, and you will see me, your old father, as the Buddha in person. When you have such devotion, it will be the time to start helping beings."

There will also be an experience of much greater compassion because the essence of emptiness is compassion. Once emptiness is realized, great compassion arises naturally. The two cannot be separated.

Unimpeded intelligence will also arise naturally. Consider as an example the omniscient Jigme Lingpa. Even though he didn't do any formal study of scriptures besides the *Getsul Karika* (Precepts of the Novice Monks), natural wisdom surged in his being through his inner realization of the nature of mind, and he became capable of mastering and explaining the most difficult points and treatises of the Buddha's teachings.

With this practice on the nature of the mind, there is no need to undergo great hardships like those encountered when practicing tummo or performing yogic exercises. These hardships are unnecessary here. Neither is it necessary to do greatly elaborate sadhanas and mantra recitations, nor to gather all sorts of ingredients and substances for the mandala and the offerings.

In brief, it is through one's own experience arising from practice that the truth of these teachings will be recognized or not. When the nature of mind is truly seen, all obscuring conceptual thoughts as well as habitual tendencies accumulated over countless lifetimes will be cleared away. That is the meaning of the Tibetan word *sang*, which is the same word as in *sang gye* ("buddha"). *Sang* ("cleared") refers to the fact that all obscurations, gross and subtle, have been cleared. *Gye* ("developed" or "grown") refers to the fact that all the qualities of enlightenment have been fully developed. As the scriptures say, "The darkness of obscurations has been cleared and the lotus of qualities has fully bloomed." Buddhahood endowed with the twofold wisdom will be achieved—the wisdom that knows the nature of everything, and the wisdom that knows all phenomena, no matter how many there are. These two wisdoms will arise effortlessly and one will achieve buddhahood, capturing the primordial citadel and becoming one with the primordial Buddha Samantabhadra, in whom the three kayas, or dimensions of awakening, are naturally present.

Thus Lama Mipham has given this very direct instruction on the nature of the mind. If you devote yourself to such a practice with great endeavor, in a solitary mountain retreat, by first completing the five hundred thousand accumulations of the preliminary practice and constantly seeking to recognize the nature of mind according to this instruction, there is no doubt that realization will arise from within.

• • •

These teachings were given at Shechen Monastery in Nepal in 1989. They were translated orally by Matthieu Könchog Tenzin and transcribed and edited by Könchog Tashi and Daniel Staffler. Further editing was done by Kendra Crossen for the present edition.

NOTES

1. Patrul Rinpoche, *The Words of My Perfect Teacher*, rev. ed., translated by the Padmakara Translation Group (Boston: Shambhala Publications, 1998).

2. The Prayer of Samantabhadra (kun bzang smon lam) comes from the Northern Termas revealed by Rigdzin Gödem (rig'dzin rgod kyi ldem 'phru can; 1337–1408), also known as Tertön Ngodrup Gyaltsen (gter ston dngos grub rgyal mtshan).

3. *Tsig Sum Ney Dek* (Three Words That Strike the Vital Point) is a profound teaching on the nature of mind and the ways to deal with the arising of thoughts, according to the Great Perfection. It was written in the form of detailed meditative instructions by famed master and hermit Patrul Rinpoche (1808–1887) and based upon a most essential teaching spoken by Garab Dorje to Shri Singha, two founding masters of the Dzogchen lineage. (For Khyentse Rinpoche's commentary on this teaching, see *Primordial Purity* in this volume.)

4. Found in the cycle of the Longchen Nyingthig.

5. The famous exposition of the path of the nine vehicles according to the Nyingma tradition, written by Jigme Lingpa after having a vision of Longchen Rabjam.

The Root Text

THE LAMP THAT DISPELS DARKNESS

AN INSTRUCTION THAT POINTS DIRECTLY TO THE NATURE OF MIND IN THE TRADITION OF THE OLD MEDITATORS

Jamgön Mipham Rinpoche

Homage to the guru and Manjushri Jnanasattva.

Without the need for lengthy study, thought, and meditation,
But by remaining in the nature of mind,
An ordinary town yogi can reach an awareness-holder's stage
    with minor hardship—
This is the power of the most profound of paths.

When your attention is allowed to settle naturally, without thinking of anything, and you just rest in that state, you experience a neutral and indifferent state of mind that is vacant and blank.

As long as an insight of clear and decisive knowing is not present, this is what past teachers called "unknowing" (marigpa). Since you cannot define it by "It's like this" or "This is it," such a state of mind is also called "undetermined" (lungmaten). Since you are also unable to describe such a state, it is labeled "ordinary indifference" (thamal tang nyom). In fact, you have settled into alaya's ordinary, amorphous state.

Nonconceptual awareness ought to be developed through settling the mind, but without insight into the very nature of mind, this is not genuine meditation training. It is what the *Aspiration of Samantabhadra* says:

The vacant state of not thinking of anything
Is itself the cause of ignorance and confusion.

When your mind does experience this vacant state, devoid of both mental constructs and clarity, look effortlessly into the nature of that which notices this state.

When you do so, there is a pure awareness (rigpa), devoid of concepts, that is totally open, free from inside and outside, like a clear, luminous sky. This pure awareness is not a duality of experienced and experiencer, yet it is possible to have the clear conviction that it is your true nature and "none other than this."

As this state cannot be expressed precisely with concepts or words, once you experience such conviction, it can appropriately be called "beyond extremes," "indescribable, "innate luminosity," "open presence," or "pure awareness." When the awareness of knowing the nature of your own mind has dawned, the darkness of the amorphous state is cleared and, just as when the interior of a house becomes visible at daybreak, you have found certainty in the nature of mind.

This is known as the "instruction to break open the eggshell of ignorance."

With this realization you understand that the timeless presence of this nature is not formed from causes and conditions, that it does not change throughout the three times, and that one cannot find anything else, not even so much as an atom, that could be called "mind."

The previous vacant state was indescribable simply because you had failed to clearly ascertain its nature. Pure awareness is also indescribable, but you have now apprehended its nature through direct experience, beyond any doubt. There is a great difference in the ineffability of each, much like the difference between being blind and having sight. This also explains the essential distinction between the basic consciousness (alaya) and the nondual realization of the dharmakaya, the ultimate dimension of awakening.

For this same reason, "ordinary mind," "mental nondoing," "ineffability," and other terms all have both a deluded and a wisdom aspect. So when you comprehend this crucial point, you can realize the profound dharma.

When about to settle in the natural way of mind-essence, some people merely try to stay conscious and aware. Then they rest in this state of mental consciousness with the feeling: "Ah, how clear!" Other people fixate on a state of utter void as if their mind had gone blank. Both of these cases, however, are simply aspects of consciousness clinging to a dualistic experience. Whenever this duality occurs—between the clarity and the one perceiving clarity, the emptiness and the one perceiving emptiness—look into the nature of this stream of rigidly fixated mindfulness. By doing so, you pull up the stake to which the dualistic mind, which holds to a perceiver and something perceived, is tethered, and make room for the naked, wide-open natural state of awareness—a luminous emptiness without center or edge.

To apprehend in a nondual way this luminous and open, natural state is the essence of awareness. It is the dawn of naked wisdom, free from the veils of fixated experience.

This was the *instruction on cutting through the net of samsaric existence*.

With this spontaneous self-cognizance of your innate nature, recognize the awareness that is free from the various veils of assumptions and temporary experiences—just as rice is free from its husk.

It's not enough just to recognize this nature of awareness; you must stabilize a steady familiarity with this state. So it is important to sustain, without distraction, a constant remembrance of settling into the natural state.

As you continue to practice in this way, sometimes there is a dull and absent-minded state of unknowing.

Sometimes there is a thought-free state of openness revealing the brilliance of vipashyana.

Sometimes there is an experience of bliss with attachment, sometimes an experience of bliss without attachment.

Sometimes there are various experiences of clarity with fixation, sometimes a flawless brilliance free from fixation.

Sometimes there are unpleasant and grueling experiences, sometimes pleasant and smooth experiences.

Sometimes there is a strong turbulence of discursive thought that carries you away and disperses the meditation, sometimes a torpid state of dullness without any clarity.

These and other types of unpredictable experiences are thought states cultivated since beginningless time, the countless waves of karmic wind. They are like the changing scenery during a long journey in the mountains, sometimes pleasant, sometimes steep and frightening. Therefore, maintain the natural state without attaching special importance to whatever arises.

Don't become discouraged by the experience of turbulence that may accompany a multitude of thoughts blazing up like a fire when you are not yet fully trained in this practice. Instead, maintain unbroken practice by keeping a balance between being tight and loose. That way, the feeling of attainment and other experiences will gradually occur.

Usually, at this point, you will gain confidence in the difference between knowing and unknowing, the ground consciousness and dharmakaya, mental consciousness and pure awareness, as recognized in your own experience through the oral instructions of the teacher.

When maintaining this recognition—like water that clears when left unstirred—let your consciousness settle in itself, as its nature of awareness is naturally present. This instruction should be regarded as the chief point.

Don't get involved in speculations about what to accept or reject, like, "Is my meditation object consciousness or awareness?" Nor should you rely on theoretical book knowledge, which only increases thought activity. These involvements may somewhat obscure your shamatha and vipashyana.

At some point you will reach a more stable familiarity with shamatha and vipashyana as a natural unity—shamatha being an ongoing steadiness in remembering to settle in the natural state, and vipashyana the recognition of your essence as natural cognizance.

Attaining this stability, in which the shamatha of primordially abiding in the natural state and the vipashyana of natural luminosity are basically indivisible—that is the dawn of self-existing awareness, the realization of the Great Perfection.

This was the *instruction on abiding in spacelike equanimity*.

The glorious Saraha said:

Completely abandoning the thinker and what is thought,
Remain like a thought-free child.

This was the method of resting, and

If you apply yourself to the teacher's words and endeavor,

then, when you have obtained the instruction that brings you face to face with awareness (rigpa),

The coemergent will dawn without a doubt.

Thus dawns the self-existing awareness that is rigpa—the nature of your mind, which is primordially coemergent with your mind. This nature (dharmata) of all things (dharmas) is also the original and ultimate luminosity.

This being so, the settling in naturalness and the manner of sustaining the rigpa of recognizing one's natural face, the mind-essence or nature of mind, is an instruction that condenses a hundred vital points into one.

Moreover, this is what you should sustain continuously.

Mark the degree of progress in this practice through the luminosity at night.

Understand that the sign of being on the correct path is a spontaneous increase in faith, compassion, and intelligence.

Experience within yourself the ease of this practice and the lessening of hardship.

Be certain of its depth and swiftness, because your realization corresponds to that produced with the greatest effort on other paths.

This is the fruition to be attained by training in your mind's luminous wakefulness:

As the obscuration of thoughts and habitual tendencies naturally clears (*bud*) and the twofold wisdom effortlessly unfolds (*dha*), you capture the primordial citadel and spontaneously accomplish the three kayas.

Profound. Secret. Sealed.

• • •

On the auspicious twelfth day of the second month in the
year of the Fire Horse (April 6, 1906), Mipham Jampal
Dorje wrote this practical guidance with comprehensible

dharma terms, a profound instruction in accord with the experience of all the Old Meditators, for the benefit of town yogis who do not especially wish to exert themselves in general studies and reflections, yet still desire to train in mind-essence.

May it be virtuous.

• • •

This translation by Erik Pema Kunsang first appeared in Crystal Cave *(Rangjung Yeshe Publications, 1990). The current, revised version was made at Rangjung Yeshe Gomdé, U.S.A., in 2004, and edited by Michael Tweed. ©2004 by Rangjung Yeshe Publications, www.rangjung.-com. Modifications were made by Matthieu Ricard for the sake of harmonizing the terminology with Khyentse Rin-poche's commentary.*

SELECTED VERSE

The Ultimate Teacher, the Absolute

The ultimate teacher, the absolute, is never separate from us,
Yet immature beings, not recognizing this, look outside and
   seek him far away.
Sole father, with your immense love you have shown me my
   own wealth;
I, who was a pauper, constantly feel your presence in the depth
   of my heart.

Wisdom teacher pervading all the world and beings, samsara
   and nirvana,
You show how all phenomena can arise as teachings,
Convincing me that everything is the absolute teacher;
I long for ultimate realization and feel your presence in the
   depth of my heart.

To Ugyen Shenpen

First, the outer guru reveals the Dharma.
The key point is to turn the mind toward Dharma.

In the middle, through the inner guru of hearing and
    contemplating,
The key point is to apply Dharma as a perfect path.

Finally, through the secret guru of one's mind,
The key point is to liberate confused thoughts into space.

By merging the guru of the beginning, middle, and end,
The key point is that confusion dawn as wisdom.

So that the precious guru of sign, meaning, and symbol
Remain inseparable from oneself, faith and yearning are
    essential.

If you are unsparing in your appreciation, faith, and longing,
Wherever you dwell in the three levels, you will meet the
    guru's blessings.

If you do not find conviction in trust, faith, and devotion,
Even if your father were the guru, what good would it do?

Do not be attached to the form body as the ultimate guru.
The true meaning, the guru of the dharmakaya, pervades
    samsara and nirvana.

If through the confusion of not recognizing your nature you
    do not see the guru,
With the golden scalpel of oral instructions, open your eyes of
    utter faith.
Look! There is no meeting or parting!

By the force of that, the undefiled virtues accumulate
In abundance, like the joyous rain clouds of spring.
There is no doubt that you will attain conviction
In the source of blessings, siddhi, and buddha activity.

With these words, the pith of the authentic speech
Of the genuine learned and accomplished ones,
Arising as an offering of the profound essence,
Mangala[1] instructs Ugyen, who is endowed with devotion and faith.

• • •

This poem was composed by Dilgo Khyentse Rinpoche for Lama Ugyen Shenpen. It was translated from the Tibetan by Nelson Dudley, Lama Ugyen Shenpen, and the Nalanda Translation Committee. Lama Ugyen Shenpen (1941–1994) was a close student and attendant of Dilgo Khyentse Rinpoche, who brought him to America in 1976. Lama Ugyen stayed to serve Trungpa Rinpoche, Sakyong Mipham Rinpoche, and the entire Vajradhatu/Shambhala sangha for the remainder of his life. He was the main adviser to the Nalanda Translation Committee and provided invaluable guidance and perspective for, in particular, the vajrayana practice of the community.

Mixing Dharma with Your Mind

HRIH, quintessence of the infinite conquerors' wisdom,
No sooner alights on the pistil-cup of a thousand-petaled lotus
In the middle of Uddiyana's limpid Sindhu Lake than it
    becomes
The accomplished, self-arisen adamantine master—may he
    guide us!

To you, my student, living far across the ocean, so difficult to
    reach,
But who, like a water lily in the early morning sun
Turning to me your thousand petals of devotion and love,
Has become rich with the honey of understanding.

Here, in a land of rock and snow mountains, forests, rivers,
    and dense thickets,
Its hill slopes beautiful with hamlets, fields of grain, and
    flowers,
A kingdom wearing a shawl of white clouds,
At the Royal Palace of Great Bliss
In the Dharma Sanctuary garden,² this old man
Upon his divine drum slowly sounds the lines of this letter.

Of those who just this once have obtained the nectar of the
    sacred Dharma,
Some proclaim the scriptures and reasoning of their extensive
    study;
But far rarer than they, like stars in the daytime,
Are those who experience the holy Dharma mixing with the
    stream of their mind.

Especially these days, increasing disputes are such
That what little remains of the teachings is just a semblance;
Since that has happened because of our own behavior, we
    sentient beings

706

Must stay careful, mindful, and vigilant—that is most
important.

Human life is shorter than a sheep's tail;
To act according to Dharma is rarer than precious gold.
Even casually playing around, you amass negative actions,
emotions, and evils.
The key point is to develop disillusionment in your mind.

There are many ways to practice, but their innermost essence
Is to recognize the fundamental nature of your mind;
It is easy, effective, and the very life-force of the Dharma—
Yet rare are those who can work with their minds and keep
at it.

The beginningless propensities for obscuration have been with
you so long;
But if you recognize their essence, they are just the mind's
display—
Thoughts arising from the unborn, nondwelling, unceasing
ultimate nature
And dissolving there . . . look at that hidden deception!

Sustaining it is hard at first, but when you get used to the
radiance of thoughts,
Their arising and being freed in the ultimate nature becomes
simultaneous,
And you will be like an old man watching what children are
doing,
Ever carefree and relaxed, maintaining it with ease.

From the Lord of Uddiyana, our only refuge particularly in this
dark age,
The guru is inseparable; seeing him as the Buddha in person,
Activate that devotion insistently like a nursing calf,
And it is natural that the blessings of the mind lineage will
arise.

Train in seeing joy and sorrow, whichever arises, without any
    clinging,
As illusion, and everything as a reminder of renunciation,
    disillusionment,
And compassion; exchanging your happiness for suffering,
Learn to take everything as the support of Dharma.

The time will come when whatever happens, seemingly good
    or bad,
Brings your Dharma practice to mind all by itself:
That will be the moment your realization has progressed
In accordance with what is considered "mixing the Dharma
    with your mind."

I have seen the garden of the nonsectarian teachings with my
    own eyes;
Heard the profound and secret nectar from all the guides;
And whatever I know, I have strung together as this garland of
    words of instruction—
May it lead your mind to liberation.

· · ·

This poem was included in a letter by Dilgo Khyentse Rinpoche
to his disciple and former attendant Ugyen Shenpen (see page
705), who was living in the United States.

Brilliant Moon in the Sky, Ocean of Dharma on the Ground

As old man Brilliant Moon travels in the sky,
Prince Ocean of Dharma remains on the ground;
Though in the illusion of circumstance, there seems to be great
  distance between,
In the mind's heart-realm of one flavor, separations do not
  exist.

Brilliant Moon's light-garland streams from heaven's height;
From the moment it touches Ocean of Dharma on the ground,
It becomes activity for the welfare of others, dispelling the
  torment of the dark age.
Since in the absolute meaning there is no separation, this self-
  expression of auspicious coincidence occurs.

The only father Padma Drime's[3] shoot of wisdom
Blossoms by design in Ocean of Dharma's pond,
Brilliant Moon pours on the amrita of truth—
There is no other way for us to meet again and again.

From cool Ocean of Dharma, rivers in the four directions,
East, west, south, north, temporarily flow,
But since they are one in the great ocean of buddha-activity for
  the welfare of the teachings and beings,
The prince enters the one realm of Brilliant Moon.

Little teardrops trickle from the corners of the eyes of the only
  son,
And a vivid sadness arises in the old father's mind-moon—
This is the fruition of our mutual prayer not to be separated
  throughout our lives;
Having confidence in this, we rest in uncontrived innate space.

Our sublime guides are like the sun, moon, and garlands of
constellations,
And we are supreme among the fortunate ones who have
taken over their action.
The benefit to beings of the Rime teachings is inexhaustible;
This is the offering from the feast of meeting the only father
guru.

The dark clouds of these degenerate times are blacker than the
cosmic darkness.
Yet the force of the aspiration to buddha-activity is a powerful
wind to disperse them.
When it is aroused, it is the time when Brilliant Moon's true
meaning dawns,
And when Ocean of Dharma spreads, unfolding the treasure of
true joy and delight.

In the space where thoughts of sadness are groundless and
rootless,
One meets one's own mind as the sparkling smile of primordial
buddha.
The laughing dance of the little boy with cheerfulness and
insight
Liberates happiness and sorrow in the dharmakaya space of
equal flavor.

It is not far, being self-abiding innate wisdom,
It is not near, being beyond seer and seen;
Being beyond speech, thought, expression, it pervades all.
In the carefree state beyond reference point, there is nothing
whatever to be done.

If one decides to act, for as long as there is sky,
In time and space, the teachings' benefit to beings cannot be
exhausted.
It is the buddha-activity of Manjushri, Samantabhadra, and the
Lotus-Born One—
Taking up this burden brings us great satisfaction.

For us yogins, actions and projections without reference point
  have dissolved;
In the state of relaxation, whatever we do arises as an
  ornament.
Though born in the dank womb of a grim and horrific dark
  age,
We cannot help but sing the thunderous song of delight.

Since this singer's voice is not melodious, it might irritate your
  ear.
Yet, since it expresses the true, undeceiving meaning, it is as if
  the words were written in melted gold,
Giving greater joy to the mind than a hundred thousand songs
  from one's lover.
They should please you and make you smile broadly!

This is the disjointed song of a madman, inimical to the
  learned.
Being no doha[4] of a siddha, who will pay attention?
Though I know the way things are, I am driven by the strong
  wind of thoughts.
This is written on an airplane, created by fingers moving with
  the gait of an insect.

When I look at the sky, it symbolizes the completely perfect
  view
On the path of the limitless dharmadhatu.
Through this realm of space beyond cares, containing all
  without partiality,
Through this vast all-pervading space, the meteor flies.

When I look at space it reminds me of the experience of
  uncontrived meditation.
The rainbow clouds, the sun, and the moon wander regardless
  of day and night.
It is the symbol of vast space, without increase or decrease—
One enjoys the carefree meditation state of one's own innate
  mind.

The boundless arrangement of earth's mountains, plains, and
    oceans
Symbolizes the action of bodhichitta for the welfare of others.
It is buddha-activity that puts whatever arises uninhibitedly to
    the benefit of all,
Existing spontaneously as long as there is sky.

Sky, ocean, earth and sun and moon
All are of the nature of the four elements and their
    configurations.
Thus ground, path, and fruition are inseparable in the
    dharmadhatu ocean;
Relaxed and refreshed, may I sit, sleep, and act.

This song of the journey is a haphazard little one;
In the sky the clouds haphazardly move about,
The gadgetry of the white metal wing acts haphazardly.
I offer this as an old man's haphazard footprint.

With a happy face and white hair, smiling,
The old man totters along, supported;
One-pointedly wishing that we meet again soon,
This is respectfully presented by Mangalam,[5] who travels on
    the rays of the sun.

• • •

This poem was written in 1976 toward the end of Khyentse Rinpoche's visit to the United States. He wrote the poem to Chögyam Trungpa Rinpoche on the airplane after their parting at
the Oakland Airport in California. The poem's basic metaphor
plays on their personal names: one of Khyentse Rinpoche's
names was Rabsel Dawa, which means "Brilliant Moon";
"Ocean of Dharma" is the translation of Trungpa Rinpoche's
name, Chökyi Gyamtso.

The Source of All Phenomena

The source of all phenomena of samsara and nirvana
Is the nature of mind—void, luminous,
All-encompassing, vast as the sky.

When in that state of skylike vastness,
Relax into its openness; stay in that very openness,
Merge with that skylike state:
Naturally, it will become more and more relaxed.
Excellent!

If you become accomplished
In this method of integrating mind with view,
Your realization will naturally become vast.
And just as the sun shines freely throughout space,
Your compassion cannot fail to shine on all unrealized beings.

Notes

1. Mangala is a name used by Dilgo Khyentse Rinpoche.

2. Khyentse Rinpoche uses the Sanskrit equivalent of the place name, Rajakoti Mahasukha Dharmadipa, to refer to Dechen Chöling, the palace of the Queen Mother of Bhutan.

3. "Padma Drime" refers to Jamgön Kongtrul of Shechen, who was a teacher of both Khyentse Rinpoche and Trungpa Rinpoche.

4. Doha: song of realization.

5. Mangala: See note 1.

GLOSSARY

The spelling and style of foreign terms may vary among the texts included in the three volumes of the *Collected Works of Dilgo Khyentse*, as the texts were originally prepared by different translators and publishing houses. In these cases, variations are indicated in the glossary for each volume.

Abhidharma (Skt.): One of the three pitakas constituting the Pali canon, the scriptures of Theravada Buddhism; the branch of the Buddha's teachings that deals mainly with psychology and logic.

abhisheka (Skt.): *See* empowerment.

absolute nature (Tib. chonyid; Skt. dharmata): The true nature of phenomena, which is emptiness. Also, ultimate reality, ultimate nature.

absolute truth: The ultimate nature of the mind and the true status of phenomena, which can only be known by primal wisdom, beyond all conceptual constructs and duality. *See also* relative truth.

accomplishment (Skt. siddhi): (1) Tib. dngos grub: the result (and goal) of spiritual practice. Common accomplishments include supernatural powers, which a bodhisattva may use to benefit beings. The principal goal, however, is the supreme accomplishment, which is enlightenment. (2) Tib. sgrub pa: in the context of the recitation of mantras, *see* approach and accomplishment.

acharya (Skt.): (1) An accomplished master of meditation practice and study. (2) An official position in a monastery. (3) A preceptor, scholar, or teacher.

afflictive emotions (Skt. klesha): Mental factors (sometimes rendered as "poisons") that influence thoughts and actions and produce suffering. *See also* three poisons; five poisons.

aggregate (Skt. skandha): One of five psychophysical components into which a person can be analyzed, which together produce the illusion of a self: form, feeling, perception, conditioning factors, and consciousness.

Akshobhya: One of the five buddhas and lord of the vajra family. *See also* buddha families, five.

alaya (Skt): Basic consciousness. *See* ground-of-all.

Amitabha (Skt.): The Buddha of Infinite Light; the buddha of the lotus family.

Amoghasiddhi: One of the five buddhas and lord of the karma family. *See also* buddha families, five.

amrita (Skt.; Tib. dutsi): The ambrosia of the gods, which confers immortality or other powers. A symbol of wisdom used in development-stage practice, both as a material offering and in the visualizations of the offering stage (and sometimes in the ganachakra ritual). *Dutsi* also refers to an herbal medicine made during Tibetan Buddhist ceremonies known as drubchens.

Ananda: A cousin of the Buddha who became his attendant. Since he was able to remember everything he had heard the Buddha say, he ensured the preservation of the Sutra teachings by reciting the sutras in their entirety at the First Council, held after the Buddha's passing.

Ancient Tradition (Tib. Nyingma): The teachings of the Secret Mantrayana propagated in Tibet by the great masters Vimalamitra and Padmasambhava in the eighth century C.E. Sometimes called the Ancient Translation, Old Translation, or Early Translation school. Followers of this tradition are called Nyingmapas.

Ancient Translations (Tib. Ngagyur): The first teachings translated from Sanskrit and propagated in Tibet, those of the Ancient Tradition (Nyingma), as distinct from the teachings of the New Tradition (Sarma), which were translated and propagated from the tenth century onward.

anuyoga: *See* nine vehicles.

approach and accomplishment: Two steps in practices involving the recitation of a mantra. In the first, practitioners approach the deity that they are visualizing by reciting the deity's mantra. In the second, they identify themselves with the deity. *See also* deity.

arhat (Skt.): Literally, "one who has vanquished the enemy" (the enemy being afflictive emotions): a practitioner of the Basic Vehicle who has attained the cessation of suffering (nirvana), but not the perfect buddhahood of the Great Vehicle.

Aryadeva (second century): The most famous disciple of Nagarjuna, whose teachings he commented upon in several treatises on Madhyamika philosophy. *See also* Middle Way.

Asanga (fourth century): The founder of the Yogachara school and author of many important treatises, in particular the five teachings he received from Maitreya.

asura (Skt.): Also called demigod or jealous god: a class of beings whose jealous nature spoils their enjoyment of their fortunate rebirth in the higher realms and involves them in constant conflict with the gods in the god realms.

ati: *See* Atiyoga.

Atisha (982–1054): Also known as Atisha Dipamkara or Jowo Atisha. This great Indian master and scholar, one of the main teachers at the famous university of Vikramashila, was a strict follower of the monastic rule. Although he was an accomplished master of the tantras, the last ten years of his life that he spent in Tibet were mainly devoted to propagating the teachings on refuge and bodhichitta, and to contributing to the translation of Buddhist texts. His disciples founded the Kadam school.

Atiyoga (Skt.; Tib. Dzogchen): The highest of the three inner yogas, the summit of the nine vehicles according to the classification of the Nyingma School. *See also* Great Perfection.

avadhuti (Skt.): Central channel. *See* channel.

Avalokiteshvara (Skt.; Tib. Chenrezi): The Bodhisattva of Compassion, who is the essence of the speech of all the buddhas.

awareness (Tib. rigpa; Skt. vidya): The original state of the mind: fresh, vast, luminous, and beyond thought.

awareness-holder: *See* vidyadhara.

bardo (Tib.): *See* intermediate state.

Basic Vehicle (Skt. Hinayana): Literally, "lesser vehicle" (in relation to the Mahayana, or Great Vehicle); the vehicle of the shravakas and pratyekabuddhas.

bhumi (Skt.): One of the levels or stages of awakening of the bodhisattvas.

bindu: *See* essence.

bodhichitta (Skt.): Literally, "mind of enlightenment." On the relative level, it is the wish to attain buddhahood for the sake of all beings, as well as the practice of the path of love, compassion, the six transcendent perfections, and so on, necessary for achieving that goal. On the absolute level, it is the direct insight into the ultimate nature.

bodhisattva (Skt.): A follower of the Great Vehicle whose aim is enlightenment for all beings.

Brahma (Skt.): The principal god in the world of form.

Buddha/buddha (Skt.): (1) Buddha Shakyamuni, the universal historical Buddha of our time, the fourth of the thousand buddhas of the present

kalpa, who lived around the fifth century B.C.E. (2) One who has dispelled
the darkness of the two obscurations and developed the two kinds of
omniscience (knowing the nature of phenomena and knowing the multiplicity of phenomena).

buddhadharma: *See* Dharma.

buddha families, five: The five buddha families—tathagata (or buddha),
vajra, ratna, padma, and karma—represent five aspects of the innate
qualities of our enlightened essence. Each is presided over by a buddha:
Vairochana, Akshobhya, Ratnasambhava, Amitabha, and Amoghasiddhi,
respectively.

buddhafield: A dimension or world manifested through the enlightened
aspirations of a buddha or bodhisattva, in which beings may abide and
progress toward enlightenment without ever falling back into lower
states of existence. In fact, any place perceived as the pure manifestation
of spontaneous wisdom is a pure land.

buddha-nature (Skt. tathagatagarbha): The essence of buddhahood, or the
buddha potential. The luminous and empty nature of the mind, which
is present, albeit veiled, in all sentient beings. When the obscuring veils
are removed and it is revealed, it is tathagata, or buddhahood. Every
sentient being has the potential to actualize this buddha-nature by attaining perfect knowledge of the nature of mind.

Capable One (Skt. muni): An epithet of Buddha Shakyamuni, often translated as "Mighty One."

Causal Vehicle of Characteristics: The vehicle that teaches the path as the
cause for attaining enlightenment. It includes the vehicles of the shravakas, pratyekabuddhas, and bodhisattvas (that is, those bodhisattvas practicing the Sutra path and not that of the Mantras). It is distinct from the
Resultant Vehicle of the Mantras, or Secret Mantrayana, which takes the
result (enlightenment) as the path.

channels (Skt. nadi): Subtle veins in which the subtle energy (Tib. lung; Skt.
prana) circulates. The left and right principal channels run from the nostrils to just below the navel, where they join the central channel (Skt.
avadhuti). *See also* energy.

channels and energies (exercises of): Exercises combining visualization,
concentration, and physical movements, in which the flow of subtle
energies through the subtle channels is controlled and directed. These
practices should only be attempted with the proper transmission and
guidance, after completing the preliminary practice and achieving some
stability in the generation phase.

Chenrezi: *See* Avalokiteshvara.

circumambulation: An act of veneration that consists of walking clockwise, concentratedly and with awareness, around a sacred object such as a temple, stupa, or holy mountain, or the residence and even the person of a spiritual master.

concentration (Skt. dhyana): Meditative absorption, a state of mind without any distraction, essential for all meditative practices, the result of which depends on the motivation and view of the meditator.

completion stage: *See* perfection stage.

crown protuberance (Skt. ushnisha): A prominence on the head, one of the thirty-two major marks of a buddha.

dakini (Skt.; Tib. khandroma, "moving through space": The feminine principle associated with wisdom and with the enlightened activities of the lama. There are ordinary dakinis, who are beings with a certain degree of spiritual power, and wisdom dakinis, who are fully realized.

deity (Tib. lha; Skt. deva): A buddha or wisdom deity, or sometimes a wealth deity or Dharma protector, as distinct from a nonenlightened god in the world of desire, the world of form, or the world of formlessness. *See also* gods.

demon (Skt. mara): In the context of Buddhist meditation and practice, a demon is any factor, on the physical or mental plane, that obstructs enlightenment. *See also* four demons.

dependent origination: A fundamental element of Buddhist teaching, according to which phenomena are understood not as discretely existent entities but as the coincidence of interdependent conditions.

deva: *See* gods.

development and completion: The two principal phases of tantric practice. The development stage (Tib. kyerim), sometimes called the creation stage or the generation stage, involves meditation on sights, sounds, and thoughts as deities, mantras, and wisdom, respectively. The completion stage (Tib. dzogrim) refers to the dissolution of visualized forms into an experience of emptiness. It also denotes the meditation on the subtle channels, energies, and essential substances of the body. "Development and completion" may also refer to the first two inner tantras, Mahayoga and Anuyoga.

dharani (Skt.): A mantra that has been blessed by a buddha or bodhisattva and has the power to help beings. Several of the sutras contain dharanis, often quite long.

Dharma (Skt.; Tib. Chö): The Buddha's doctrine; the teachings transmitted in the scriptures and the qualities of realization attained through their practice. The Sanskrit word *dharma* has ten principal meanings, including "anything that can be known." Vasubandhu defines the Dharma, in its Buddhist sense, as the "protective dharma": "It corrects every one of the enemies, the afflictive emotions; and it protects us from the lower realms. These two characteristics are absent from other spiritual traditions."

dharmadhatu (Skt.): Absolute expanse, absolute dimension, or basic space. One of many terms expressing the true nature of reality, with slightly different applications in different contexts. The term is a synonym for *emptiness* and is often paired with *jnana*, primordial wisdom.

dharmakaya (Skt., "dharma body"): The emptiness aspect of buddhahood; also translated as "body of truth," or "absolute dimension."

Dharma protector (Skt. dharmapala): The Dharma protectors fulfill the enlightened activities of the lama in protecting the teaching from being diluted and its transmission from being disturbed or distorted. Protectors are sometimes emanations of buddhas or bodhisattvas, or sometimes spirits, gods, or demons who have been subjugated by a great spiritual master and bound under oath.

dharmata: *See* absolute nature.

duality: The mental state that conceives of subject and object, of an "I" that perceives and a phenomenon that is perceived.

Dzogchen / Dzogpa Chenpo / dzokpa chenpo: *See* Great Perfection.

dzogrim: *See* development and completion.

eight freedoms: The eight states of freedom from the eight unfavorable conditions, which are essential in order to hear and practice the Buddha's teachings.

eight incompatible propensities: Eight propensities that prevent one from practicing the Dharma and thus making effective use of a precious human body: (1) excessive attachment to family, worldly commitments, success, and so forth, (2) a basically bad character, (3) a lack of fear or dissatisfaction with regard to the sufferings of samsara, (4) a complete absence of faith, (5) a propensity for harmful or negative actions, (6) a lack of interest in the Dharma, (7) the fact of having broken one's vows, and (8) the fact of having broken the Vajrayana samayas.

eight intrusive circumstances: Eight circumstances that prevent one from practicing the Dharma and thus making effective use of a precious human body: (1) being overwhelmed by the five poisons, (2) being extremely stupid, (3) having a false teacher who has wrong views, (4) being lazy, (5) being overwhelmed by the results of one's previous bad karma, (6) being someone's servant and thus lacking the autonomy to practice, (7) following the Dharma merely in order to be fed and clothed, and to avoid other difficulties in life, and (8) taking up the Dharma only in order to win wealth and prestige.

eight logos (Tib. sgrub pa bka' brgyad): Also known as the eight sadhana teachings. The eight principal herukas or yidams and their corresponding practices of the mahayoga yana within the Nyingma lineage.

eight ordinary/worldly concerns: The normal preoccupations of unrealized people without a clear spiritual perspective: gain and loss, pleasure and pain, praise and criticism, fame and infamy.

eight unfavorable conditions: The eight conditions in which sentient beings lack the opportunity to hear and practice the Buddha's teachings: being born (1) in the hell realm, (2) as a preta, (3) as an animal, or (4) as a long-lived god; or as a human being but (5) in a world where no buddha has appeared, or (6) in a barbaric region where the Buddha's doctrine is unknown, or (7) as someone holding wrong views, or (8) as someone mute or mentally deficient.

empowerment (Skt. abhisheka): Literally, "transfer of power." The authorization to hear, study, and practice the teachings of the Vajrayana; this takes place in a ceremony which may be extremely elaborate or utterly simple.

emptiness (Skt. shunyata): The absence of true existence in all phenomena.

energy (Tib. lung; Skt. prana, vayu): Literally "wind," described as "light and mobile": any one of a number of subtle energies that regulate the functions of the body and influence the mind, which is said to ride or be carried on the *lung* like a rider on a horse. Mastery of these subtle energies in the perfection phase greatly enhances the practitioner's realization. *See also* channels and energies.

enlightenment (Tib. byang chub; Skt. bodhi): Purification (byang) of all obscurations and realization (chub) of all qualities.

essence (Tib. thigle; Skt. bindu): Literally, "drop." The essence or seed of great bliss; in the channels there are different kinds, pure or degenerate. The term *thigle* has a number of different meanings according to the context and type of practice.

eternalism: The belief in an eternally existing entity such as a soul. This is one of the extreme views refuted by the proponents of the Middle Way.

evenness (Skt. samata): Sameness, equality: all things equally have the nature of emptiness.

five aggregates: *See* aggregate.

five circumstantial advantages: The last five of the ten advantages: (1) a buddha has appeared in this world, (2) he has taught the doctrine, (3) his teaching has endured until now, (4) there are spiritual friends who can teach it, and (5) one has been accepted as a disciple by such a teacher.

five individual advantages: The first five of the ten advantages: (1) to be born a human, (2) in a region where the Buddha's doctrine is taught, (3) with all one's sense organs complete, (4) with a propensity for positive deeds, and (5) with faith in the Dharma.

five paths: Five successive stages in the path to enlightenment: the paths of accumulating, joining, seeing, meditation, and the path beyond learning.

five poisons: The five principal afflictive emotions: (1) bewilderment, ignorance, or confusion, (2) attachment or desire, (3) aversion, hatred, or anger, (4) jealousy, and (5) pride.

five sciences: The traditional sciences of language, logic, philosophy, medicine, and arts.

five wisdoms: Five aspects of the wisdom of buddhahood: the wisdom of the absolute space, mirrorlike wisdom, the wisdom of equality, discriminating wisdom, and all-accomplishing wisdom.

four boundless qualities: Unlimited love, compassion, joy, and equanimity.

four demons: The demon of the aggregates, the demon of afflictive emotions, the demon of the Lord of Death, and the demon of the sons of the gods (or demon of distraction). *See also* demon.

Four Great Kings: The protectors of the four directions, who dwell in the first of the six god realms of the world of desire.

four guests: (1) The buddhas and bodhisattvas, (2) the Dharma protectors, (3) the beings of the six realms, and (4) those with whom we have karmic debts. *See also* offering and giving.

four kayas: The three kayas plus the svabhavikakaya, the kaya of the nature as it is, representing the inseparability of the first three kayas.

Gampopa (1079–1153): Gampopa Sonam Rinchen, also known as Dagpo Rinpoche, was the most famous disciple of Milarepa and the founder of the Kagyu monastic order.

gandharva (Skt.): Literally, "smell eater." A spirit that feeds on smells. Also, a being in the intermediate state (bardo) who inhabits a mental body and therefore feeds not on solid food but on odors.

Garab Dorje (Tib.; Skt. Prahevajra): A nirmanakaya or manifested body of the Buddha, appearing as the first human master of the Dzogchen (Ati) teachings; he gave these teachings to Manjushrimitra and Shri Singha.

garuda (Skt.): A mythical bird symbolizing primordial wisdom, of great size and able to fly as soon as it is hatched. The five colors in which it is sometimes represented symbolize the five wisdoms. The enemy of the nagas, it is depicted with a snake in its beak, symbolizing consuming the afflictive emotions.

Gelug: One of the schools of the New Tradition, founded by Je Tsongkhapa (1357–1419). The adherents of this school are called Gelugpas.

generation phase (Skt. utpattikrama): The meditation associated with sadhana practice in which one purifies oneself of one's habitual clingings by meditating on forms, sounds, and thoughts as having the nature of deities, mantras, and wisdom. See also perfection phase.

geshe (Tib.): Spiritual friend. The usual term for a Kadam teacher, later used as the title for a doctor of philosophy in the Gelug school.

gods (Tib. lha; Skt. deva): A class of beings who, as a result of accumulating positive actions in previous lives, experience immense happiness and comfort, and may therefore be wrongly considered an ideal state to which one should aspire. Those in the worlds of form and formlessness experience an extended form of the meditation they practiced (without the aim of achieving liberation from samsara) in their previous life. Gods such as Indra in the world of desire have, as a result of their merit, a certain power to affect the lives of other beings, and they are therefore worshiped, for example, by Hindus. The same Tibetan and Sanskrit term is also used to refer to enlightened beings, in which case it is more usually translated as "deity."

Great Perfection (Tib. dzogpa chenpo /dzogchen): Another name for Atiyoga. Perfection means that the mind, in its nature, naturally contains all the qualities of the three bodies: its nature is emptiness, the dharmakaya; its natural expression is clarity, the sambhogakaya; and its compassion is all-encompassing, the nirmanakaya. Great means that this perfection is the natural condition of all things.

Great Vehicle (Skt. mahayana): The vehicle of the bodhisattvas, referred to as great because it aims at full buddhahood for the sake of all beings.

ground-of-all (Tib. kunzhi; Skt. alaya): The ground consciousness in which the habitual tendencies are stored. It is the basis for the other consciousnesses. In certain teachings, *kunzhi* (kun gzhi) is used to signify the original nature, the primordial purity.

Guru Rinpoche: The name by which Padmasambhava is most commonly known in Tibet.

habitual tendencies (Skt. vasana): Habitual patterns of thought, speech, or action created by one's attitudes and deeds in past lives.

Heaven of the Thirty-three: The second of the six gods' realms in the world of desire. The abode of Indra and his thirty-two ministers.

hell: One of the six realms, in which great suffering is undergone, mainly in the form of intense heat or cold. Beings in the hell realm mostly experience the effects of actions rather than creating new causes.

heruka (Skt): A wrathful male deity.

Indra (Skt.): The king of the gods, ruler of the god realm known as the Heaven of the Thirty-three.

intermediate state (Tib. bardo): The term used for various states of consciousness in life; it most often refers to the state between death and rebirth.

Jambudvipa (Skt.; Tib. Dzambuling): In Buddhist cosmology, the southern continent or "land of Jambu," which is the terrestrial world in which we live.

Jamgön Kongtrul Lodrö Thaye (1813–1899): Also known as Jamgön Kongtrul the Great. An important teacher of the nonsectarian movement (Rime), responsible, with Jamyang KhyentseWangpo, for compiling several great collections of teachings and practices from all traditions, including the *Treasury of Rediscovered Teachings*.

Jetsun Milarepa (1040–1123): Tibet's great yogi and poet, whose biography and spiritual songs are among the best loved works in Tibetan Buddhism. One of the foremost disciples of Marpa, he is among the great masters at the origin of the Kagyu school.

Jigme Gyalwa'i Nyugu (nineteenth century): One of Jigme Lingpa's four principal disciples, and the root teacher of Patrul Rinpoche.

Jigme Lingpa (1729–1798): The discoverer of the Longchen Nyingthig teachings, revealed to him in a vision he had of Longchenpa. He is considered to be a combined emanation of Vimalamitra and King Trisong Detsen. Patrul Rinpoche is often considered to be the emanation of Jigme Lingpa's speech.

jnana (Skt.; Tib. yeshe): Primal or primordial wisdom.

jnanasattva (Skt.; Tib. yeshe sempa): Literally, "wisdom-being." One of the components or "beings" in Vajrayana development-stage practice. *Jnanasattva* denotes the true nature of the deity, an aspect of enlightenment— in contrast to the form of the deity that the practitioner is visualizing (samayasattva), with which it is often invited to merge. The jnanasattva, while retaining this status, is also visualized in many practices as another deity in the heart center of the samayasattva.

Kadam (Tib.): The first of the schools of the New Tradition,which followed the teachings of Atisha. It stressed compassion, study, and pure discipline. Its teachings were continued by all the other schools, in particular the Gelug, which is also known as the New Kadam school.

Kagyu: One of the schools of the New Tradition, which followed the teachings brought to Tibet from India by Marpa the Translator in the eleventh century and transmitted to Milarepa. The Kagyu school has a number of branches. Adherents of the schools are called Kagyupas.

Kalachakra (Skt.): Literally, "wheel of time." The title of a tantra (the *Kalachakra Tantra*) and a Vajrayana system taught by Buddha Shakyamuni. It shows the interrelationship between the phenomenal world, the physical body, and the mind.

kalpa (Skt.): A unit of time of inconceivable length, used in Buddhist cosmology to describe the cycles of formation and destruction of a universe, and the ages of increase and decrease within them.

Kangyur (Tib.): Literally, "translated word." The Tibetan translations of the original canonical works that recorded the Buddha's teachings of the Tripitaka and the tantras. The Kangyur consists of more than one hundred volumes.

karma (Skt.): Although this term simply means "action," it has come to be widely used to signify the result produced by past actions, often with the implication of destiny or fate, beyond one's control. In the Buddhist teachings, the principle of karma covers the whole process of actions leading to results in future lives, which is definitely within one's control. *See also* law of cause and effect.

karmic energy (Tib. las kyi rlung): The subtle energy determined by one's karma, in contrast to the energy connected with wisdom (ye shes kyi rlung).

karmic obscurations (obscurations of past actions): Obscurations created by negative actions. *See also* obscurations.

kaya: *See* three kayas; four kayas.

klesha (Skt.): *See* afflictive emotions.

kriya: *See* nine vehicles.

kyerim: *See* development and completion

lama (Tib.; Skt. guru): (1) A spiritual teacher, explained as the contraction of *bla na med pa* ("nothing superior"). (2) Loosely, a Buddhist monk or a yogi in general.

law of cause and effect: The process by which every action inevitably produces a corresponding effect. *See also* karma.

Lesser Vehicle: *See* Basic Vehicle.

liberation: (1) thar pa: freedom from samsara, as either an arhat or a buddha; (2) bsgral las byed pa: a practice performed by a fully realized being in order to liberate the consciousness of a malignant being into a buddhafield.

Lilavajra (eighth century): One of the most important Vidyadharas of the Kriya and Yoga tantras, and a major holder of the transmission of the *Guhyagarbha Tantra* in the Mahayoga lineage.

Longchenpa (1308–1363): One of the most influential spiritual masters and scholars of the Nyingma school, also known as the Omniscient Sovereign or King of Dharma. He wrote more than two hundred and fifty treatises covering almost all of Buddhist theory and practice up to the Great Perfection, including the *Seven Treasures*, the *Nyingthig Yabzhi*, the *Trilogy of Rest*, the *Trilogy of Natural Freedom*, the *Trilogy of Dispelling Darkness*, and the *Miscellaneous Writings*.

Lotus-Born One: *See* Padmasambhava.

lower realms: The hells, the preta realm, and the animal realm.

Madhyamika/Madhyamaka (Skt.): The Middle Way philosophical doctrine propounded by Nagarjuna and his followers. The Madhyamaka avoids the extremes of existence and nonexistence.

Mahamudra (Skt.): Literally, "Great Seal," meaning that the seal of the absolute nature is on everything, that all phenomena belong to the wisdom mandala. The term is used to denote the teaching, the meditation practice, or the supreme accomplishment.

Mahayana (Skt.): *See* Great Vehicle.

Mahayoga (Skt.): The first of the three higher yogas according to the classification of the Dharma into nine vehicles. In this yoga, the main emphasis is on the generation phase.

Maitreya: The buddha to come, the fifth in this present kalpa. He is one of the eight principal bodhisattva disciples of Buddha Shakyamuni.

mala (Skt.): A rosary used for counting the number of recitations or prostrations performed by a practitioner.

mandala (Skt.): Center and surrounding. A symbolic graphic representation of a tantric deity's realm of existence.

mani (Skt.): The mantra of Avalokiteshvara, OM MANI PADME HUM.

Manjushri (Skt.): A bodhisattva of the tenth or highest level, one of Buddha Shakyamuni's eight principal bodhisattva disciples. He embodies the knowledge and wisdom of all the buddhas and is usually depicted holding the sword of wisdom in his right hand and a book resting on a lotus in his left.

Manjushrimitra (Skt.): One of the patriarchs of the Dzogchen (Ati) lineage, the main student of Garab Dorje.

mantra (Skt.): A manifestation of supreme enlightenment in the form of sound; syllables which, in the sadhanas of the Secret Mantrayana, protect the mind of the practitioner from ordinary perceptions and invoke the wisdom deities.

Mantrayana: *See* Secret Mantrayana.

mara: *See* demon.

Marpa (1012–1097): A great Tibetan master and translator who was a disciple of Drogmi, Naropa, Maitripa, and other great siddhas. He brought many tantras from India to Tibet and translated them. These teachings were passed down through Milarepa and his other disciples, and are the basis of the teachings of the Kagyu lineage.

merit (Skt. punya): The first of the two accumulations."Merit" is also sometimes used loosely to translate the Tibetan terms *dge ba* (virtue, positive action) and *dge rtsa* (sources of good for the future).

Middle Way (Skt. Madhyamaka): A teaching on emptiness first expounded by Nagarjuna and considered to be the basis of the Secret Mantrayana."Middle" in this context means that it is beyond the extreme points of view of nihilism and eternalism. *See also* Madhyamika/Madhyamaka.

Milarepa: *See* Jetsun Milarepa.

Mount Meru: Literally, "supreme mountain" in Sanskrit. The four-sided mountain in the form of an inverted pyramid that is the center of our universe according to Buddhist cosmology.

mudra (Skt.): Sacred gesture; symbolic hand gesture.

nadi: *See* channels.

Nagarjuna (first–second century): A great Indian master who expounded the teachings of the Middle Way and composed numerous philosophical and medical treatises.

nagas (Skt.): Serpentlike beings (classed in the animal realm) living in the water or under the earth and endowed with magical powers and wealth. The most powerful ones have several heads.

Nalanda: The birthplace near Rajagriha of the Buddha's disciple Shariputra, which much later, starting in the time of the Gupta kings (fifth century), became one of the great centers of learning in Buddhist India. It was destroyed around 1200 C.E.

Naropa (1016–1100): An Indian pandita and siddha, the disciple of Tilopa and teacher of Marpa the Translator.

negative action: Harmful action, unwholesome act, evil. A physical, verbal, or mental action that produces suffering.

neither one nor many: One of the four great arguments used by the Madhyamaka school in investigating the nature of phenomena. It demonstrates that no phenomenon can truly exist either as a single, discrete thing or as a plurality.

New Tradition (Tib. Sarma): The tradition of the tantras that were translated and propagated from the tenth century onward by Rinchen Zangpo and others. It designates all the schools of Tibetan Buddhism except for the Nyingma, or Ancient Tradition.

New Translations: *See* New Tradition.

nihilism: The view that denies the existence of past and future lives, the principle of cause and effect, and so on. One of the extreme views refuted by the proponents of the Middle Way.

nine vehicles: The three vehicles of the Sutrayana (those of the shravakas, pratyekabuddhas, and bodhisattvas) and the six vehicles of the Vajrayana (Kriyatantra, Upatantra, Yogatantra, Mahayoga, Anuyoga, and Atiyoga).

nirmanakaya (Skt.): Literally, "body of manifestation." The aspect of buddhahood that manifests out of compassion to help ordinary beings.

nirvana (Skt.): Literally, "beyond suffering." While nirvana can be loosely understood as the goal of Buddhist practice, the opposite of samsara, the term is understood differently by the different vehicles: the nirvana of the Basic Vehicle, the peace of cessation that an arhat attains, is very different from a buddha's nirvana, the state of perfect enlightenment that transcends both samsara and nirvana.

no-self (Skt. anatman, nairatmya): Egolessness; the absence of independent or intrinsic existence, either of oneself or of external phenomena.

Nyingma: *See* Ancient Tradition.

obscurations (Skt. avarana): Factors that veil our buddha-nature. *See also* two obscurations.

obscurations of afflictive emotions. Thoughts of hatred, attachment,and so on that prevent one from attaining liberation. *See* obscurations.

offering and giving: The distinction is usually made, particularly in such practices as the incense offering (Tib. sang) and burnt offerings (Tib. sur), between *offering* to sublime beings "above," such as the buddhas and bodhisattvas, and *giving* (as part of the practice of generosity) to ordinary beings "below," including animals and spirits. *See also* four guests.

Padampa Sangye (eleventh–twelfth century): An Indian siddha who established the teachings of the Shijepa school and who traveled to Tibet several times. He was the teacher of Machik Labdrön, to whom he transmitted the Chö teachings.

Padmakara: *See* Padmasambhava.

Padmasambhava: The Lotus-Born Teacher from Oddiyana, often called Guru Rinpoche. During the reign of King Trisong Detsen, this great master subjugated the evil forces hostile to the propagation of Buddhism in Tibet, spread the Buddhist teaching of Vajrayana in that country, and hid innumerable spiritual treasures for the benefit of future generations. He is venerated as the Second Buddha, whose coming was predicted by the first one, Buddha Shakyamuni, to give the special teachings of Vajrayana.

pandita (Skt.): A scholar, someone learned in the five sciences. The term is particularly used to refer to Indian scholars.

paramita: *See* transcendent perfection.

path of seeing: The third of the five paths; the stage at which a bodhisattva in meditation gains a genuine experience of emptiness.

paths of accumulating and joining: The first two of the five paths that prepare the bodhisattva for attaining the path of seeing.

Patrul Rinpoche (1808–1887): Orgyen Jigme Chökyi Wangpo, a major holder of the Longchen Nyingthig teachings and exponent of Shantideva's *Bodhicharyavatara* (*The Way of the Bodhisattva*), famed for his simple lifestyle. He is the author of *The Words of My Perfect Teacher* and is often considered to be the emanation of Jigme Lingpa's speech.

perfection phase (Tib. dzogrim; Skt. sampannakrama): Also known as the completion stage. (1) "With characteristics" (Tib. mtshan bcas): meditation on the channels and energies of the body visualized as a vajra body. (2) "Without characteristics" (Tib. mtshan med): the meditation phase during which the forms visualized in the generation phase are dissolved and one remains in the experience of emptiness.

pitaka (Skt.): Literally, "basket." A collection of scriptures, originally in the form of palm-leaf folios stored in baskets. The Buddha's teachings are generally divided into three pitakas (Tripitaka): Vinaya, Sutra, and Abhidharma.

pith instructions (Skt. upadesha): Instructions that explain the most profound points of the teachings in a condensed and direct way for the purposes of practice.

positive action: A beneficial act or virtue; a physical, verbal, or mental action that produces happiness.

prana (Skt.): *See* energy.

Pratimoksha (Skt.): Literally, "individual liberation." The collective term for the different forms of Buddhist ordination and their respective vows, as laid down in the Vinaya.

pratyekabuddha (Skt.): A follower of the Basic Vehicle who attains liberation (the cessation of suffering) without the help of a spiritual teacher.

precious human body: Rebirth as a human being free from the eight unfavorable conditions and possessing the ten advantages. This is the only situation in which it is possible to hear and practice the Buddha's teachings properly. According to the Omniscient Longchenpa, the precious human body requires sixteen further conditions in order to be fully effective, namely freedom from the eight intrusive circumstances and eight incompatible propensities.

preliminary practice (Tib. ngöndro): The traditional preparation a practitioner needs to complete before beginning the main practice of the Mantrayana. It comprises five principal sections—refuge, bodhichitta, purification (meditation on Vajrasattva), offering of the mandala, and guru yoga—each performed one hundred thousand times.

pretas (Skt.): Also known as hungry ghosts or hungry spirits. A class of beings whose attachment and miserliness in previous lives result in constant hunger and the frustration of their desires.

primal wisdom (Tib. yeshe; Skt. jnana): The knowing (shes pa) that has always been present since the beginning (ye nas); awareness; clarity-emptiness, naturally dwelling in all beings. Often translated as "primordial wisdom."

primordial wisdom: *See* primal wisdom

profound insight (Tib. lhakthong; Skt. vipashyana): The perception, through wisdom, of the true nature of things.

protectors: *See* Dharma protectors.

pure perception: The perception of all the world and its contents as a pure buddhafield, as the display of kayas and wisdoms.

refuge: (1) Tib. skyabs yul: the object in which one takes refuge; (2) skyabs 'gro: the practice of taking refuge.

relative truth: Literally, "all-concealing truth" (Tib. kun rdzob bden pa): the apparent truth perceived and taken as real by the deluded mind. This apparent or relative truth conceals the true nature of phenomena. *See also* absolute truth.

rigpa: *See* awareness.

Rime (Tib.): A nonsectarian movement begun during the nineteenth century whose essence was to collect and preserve, in a spirit of impartiality, all the spiritual lineages of Tibetan Buddhism.

Rinchen Zangpo (958–1055): The most famous translator of the second propagation of Buddhism in Tibet, when the New Tradition began.

ringsel (Tib.): Pearl-like relics found in the bodily remains or ashes of someone who has attained a high degree of realization during his or her lifetime.

rishi (Skt.): A sage, hermit, or saint; particularly, the famous sages of Indian myth, who had enormous longevity and magical powers.

rupakaya (Skt.): The "body of form," which includes the sambhogakaya and nirmanakaya together.

sadhana (Skt.): The method for accomplishing the level of a particular deity, for example, the lama, yidam, or dakini.

Sakya (Tib.): One of the schools of the New Tradition, founded by Khön Könchok Gyalpo (1034–1102).

Sakya Pandita: An important Sakya master (1182–1251), known in Tibetan as Kunga Gyaltsen.

samadhi (Skt.): Meditative absorption of different degrees. Generally translated as "concentration."

samadhisattva (Skt., "concentration-being"): One of the three components or "beings" in the Vajrayana development-stage practice. *Samadhisattva* refers to the seed syllable or symbolic implement (e.g., a vajra), visualized at the heart center of the jnanasattva particularly for the purposes of the mantra recitation stage of a deity practice.

Samantabhadra (Skt.; Tib. Kuntu Zangpo): (1) The original buddha (Adibuddha), the source of the lineage of the tantra transmissions of the Nyingma school; he who has never fallen into delusion, the dharmakaya buddha, represented as a naked figure, deep blue like the sky, in union with Samantabhadri, as a symbol of awareness-emptiness, the pure, absolute nature, ever present and unobstructed. (2) The bodhisattva Samantabhadra, one of the eight principal bodhisattva disciples of Buddha Shakyamuni, renowned for the way in which, through the power of his concentration, he miraculously multiplied the offerings he made.

samaya (Skt.): Literally, "promise." The sacred links between the teacher and disciple, and also between disciples, in the Vajrayana; literally, "promise" in Tibetan (dam tshig). The Sanskrit word *samaya* can mean agreement, engagement, convention, precept, or boundary. Although there are many detailed obligations, the most essential samaya is to consider the teacher's body, speech, and mind as pure.

sambhogakaya (Skt.): Literally, "body of perfect enjoyment": the spontaneously luminous aspect of buddhahood, only perceptible to highly realized beings.

samsara (Skt.): Literally, "wheel," and therefore also translated as "cyclic existence." Tthe endless round of birth, death, and rebirth in which beings suffer as a result of their actions and afflictive emotions.

Samye (Tib.): Literally, "inconceivable." The first monastery in Tibet, in the Tsangpo Valley southeast of Lhasa, built during the time of King Trisong Detsen.

Sangha (Skt.): The community of Buddhist practitioners.

Saraha: An Indian mahasiddha, author of three cycles of dohas (songs of realization).

Sarma: *See* New Tradition.

Secret Mantrayana: A branch of the Great Vehicle that uses the special techniques of the tantras to pursue the path of enlightenment for all beings more rapidly. Synonymous with Vajrayana.

seven branches: A form of prayer in seven parts: prostration, offering, confession, rejoicing, requesting the teachers to turn the wheel of Dharma, requesting them not to pass into nirvana, and dedication of merit.

seven noble riches: Faith, discipline, generosity, learning, a sense of decency, a sense of shame, and wisdom.

seven-point posture of Vairochana: The seven points of the ideal meditation posture: legs crossed in the vajra posture, back straight, hands in the gesture of meditation, eyes gazing along the nose, chin slightly tucked in, shoulders well apart "like a vulture's wings," and the tip of the tongue touching the palate.

shamatha: *See* sustained calm.

Shantarakshita: Also called the Bodhisattva Abbot. A great Indian pandita of the Mahayana school who was abbot of the Buddhist university of Nalanda and author of a number of philosophical commentaries, such as the *Madhyamakalankara* (Adornment of the Middle Way). He was invited to Tibet by King Trisong Detsen to consecrate the site of the first Tibetan monastery at Samye and to ordain the first Tibetan monks.

Shariputra: One of the two foremost shravaka disciples of Buddha Shakyamuni.

shravaka (Skt.): Literally, "one who listens." A follower of the Basic Vehicle (shravakayana), whose goal is to attain liberation for himself as an arhat.

Shri Simha / Shri Singha: The chief disciple and successor of Manjushrimitra in the lineage of the Dzogchen teachings.

siddha (Skt.): Literally, "one who has attained the accomplishments." Someone who has attained the fruit of the practice of the Secret Mantrayana.

siddhi (Skt.): *See* accomplishment.

six consciousnesses / six sense consciousnesses: The consciousnesses related to vision, hearing, smell, taste, touch, and mentation.

six realms of existence: Six modes of existence caused and dominated by particular mental poisons: the hells (anger) and the realms of the pretas (miserliness), animals (bewilderment or ignorance), humans (desire), asuras (jealousy), and gods (pride). These correspond to deluded perceptions produced by beings' karma and apprehended as real.

six sense organs: The eye, ear, nose, tongue, body, and mind.

six transcendent perfections (Skt. paramita): Transcendent generosity, discipline, patience, diligence, concentration, and wisdom.

skandha: *See* aggregate.

skillful means (Skt. upaya): Spontaneous, altruistic activity born from wisdom.

Songtsen Gampo (617–698): The first of Tibet's three great religious kings. It was during his time that the first Buddhist temples were built.

spiritual friend (Skt. kalyanamitra): A synonym for *spiritual teacher.*

stupa (Skt.): Literally "support of offering." A symbolic representation of the Buddha's mind. The most typical Buddhist monument, which often has a wide square base, a rounded midsection, and a tall conical upper section topped by a sun and a moon. Stupas frequently contain the relics of enlightened beings. They vary in size from tiny clay models to the vast stupas at Borobodur in Indonesia and Baudha in Nepal.

Sugata (Skt.): Literally, "one who has gone to bliss": an epithet of a buddha.

sugatagarbha (Skt.): *See* buddha-nature.

supreme accomplishment: *See* accomplishment.

sustained calm (Tib. shine; Skt. shamatha): The basis of all concentrations; a calm, undistracted state of unwavering concentration.

sutra (Skt.): (1) A scripture containing the teachings of the Buddha. (2) The Sutra teachings are the exoteric teachings of Buddhism belonging to Hinayana and Mahayana, in contrast to the esoteric Tantra teachings. They are causal teachings that regard the path as the cause of enlightenment.

Sutrapitaka: One of the Three Pitakas (or Tripitaka), dealing with meditation.

tantra (Skt.): Any one of the texts on which the Vajrayana teachings are based. The tantras reveal the continuity between the original purity of the nature of mind and the result of the path, which is the realization of that nature.

Tathagata (Skt.): Literally, "one who has gone to thusness": an epithet of a buddha.

tathagatagarbha: *See* buddha-nature.

ten advantages: The ten conditions that enable one to hear and practice the Buddha's teachings. They are divided into five individual advantages and five circumstantial advantages.

terma (Tib.): Literally, "treasure." Transmission through concealed treasures, hidden mainly by Guru Rinpoche and Yeshe Tsogyal, to be discovered at the proper time by a tertön, a treasure revealer, for the benefit of future disciples. Terma is one of the two chief traditions of the Nyingma school, the other being Kama. Concealed treasure are of various kinds, including texts, ritual objects, relics, and "mind treasures."

thögal (Tib.): *See* trekchö and thögal.

Three Jewels (Skt. triratna): The Buddha, Dharma, and Sangha.

three kayas (Skt. trikaya, "three bodies"): The three aspects of buddhahood: dharmakaya, sambhogakaya, and nirmanakaya. *See those entries in the glossary; see also* four kayas; rupakaya; svabhavikakaya.

three kinds of suffering: The three fundamental types of suffering to which beings in samsara are subject: the suffering of change, suffering upon suffering, and the suffering of everything composite (or all-pervading suffering in the making).

Three Pitakas: *See* Tripitaka.

three poisons: The three afflictive emotions of bewilderment, attachment, and aversion. *See also* five poisons.

three seats: The aggregates and elements, ayatanas (the sense organs and their corresponding sense objects), and limbs of one's body, whose true nature, according to the pure perception of the Mantrayana, is the mandala of the male and female tathagatas, the male and female bodhisattvas, and other deities.

three sweet foods: Sugar, molasses, and honey.

three trainings (Skt. trishiksha): The threefold training in discipline, concentration, and wisdom.

three vehicles (Skt. triyana): The vehicles of the shravakas, pratyekabuddhas, and bodhisattvas.

three ways of pleasing the teacher: (1) Making material offerings, (2) helping him through physical, verbal, or mental tasks, and (3) practicing what he teaches.

three white foods: Milk, butter, and curd (yogurt), which are traditionally considered to be very pure foods.

three worlds: The world of desire, the world of form, and the world of formlessness. Alternatively: the world of gods above the earth, that of humans on the earth, and that of the nagas under the earth.

Tilopa: One of the eighty-four mahasiddhas of India; teacher of Naropa.

Tirthika (Skt.): A proponent of extreme philosophical views such as nihilism and eternalism. This term is often used to imply non-Buddhist religious traditions in India.

toothstick: A stick from the neem tree used in India as a toothbrush. In Tibetan Buddhism it symbolizes purification of speech, and a similar stick is thrown by the recipients of an empowerment onto a drawing of a four-petaled lotus with a circle in the center, to determine, depending on where the stick falls, to which of the five families the disciple belongs.

torma (Tib.): A ritual cake of varying shape and composition, used in practices and rituals of the Vajrayana. Depending on the circumstances, it is considered an offering, a representation or mandala of the meditational deity, or even a kind of symbolic weapon in ceremonies to remove obstacles from the path.

Trakpa Gyaltsen (1147–1216): One of the five great scholars of the Sakya School, who are known as the Sakya Gongma.

transcendent perfection (Skt. paramita): A practice of a bodhisattva combining skillful means and wisdom, the compassionate motivation of attaining enlightenment for the sake of all beings, and the view of emptiness. *See* six transcendent perfections.

trekchö and thögal (Tib.): The practices of cutting through the solidity of clinging and of direct vision, relating respectively to primordial purity and spontaneous accomplishment.

Tripitaka: The three collections of the Buddha's teachings: Vinaya, Sutra, and Abhidharma. The Vajrayana teachings are sometimes considered to be a fourth pitaka. *See also* pitaka.

Trisong Detsen (790–844): The thirty-eighth king of Tibet, second of the three great religious kings. It was due to his efforts that the great masters came from India and established Buddhism firmly in Tibet.

tummo (Tib.): The practice of inner heat, which raises the body temperature through yogic techniques associated with the subtle body of energy channels, energy-winds, and energy-drops. It is taught to advanced practitioners in the Vajrayana path.

Tushita Heaven: *Tushita* is literally "the Joyous" in Sanskrit. One of the realms of the gods in the world of desire, in which Buddha Shakyamuni took a final rebirth before appearing in this world. The future buddha, Maitreya, is currently in the Tushita Heaven teaching the Mahayana.

two accumulations: The accumulation of merit and the accumulation of wisdom (Tib. yeshe).

two obscurations: The obscurations of afflictive emotions and conceptual obscurations. *See also* obscurations.

two truths: The absolute and relative truths.

Uddiyana/Oddiyana (Tib.): In Tibetan Buddhist literature, a land described as being ruled by several kings, each of whom were named Indrabhuti. Oddiyana is said to be a seat of Vajrayana practice situated possibly in the geographical area of northwestern Pakistan (one of many possible locations). A number of Vajrayana practitioners are said to have stayed and practiced there. The first Vajrayana teachings were supposedly given there by Shakyamuni Buddha, at the request of King Indrabodhi.

unborn: Not produced by anything, having no origin, that which has not come into existence. As Dilgo Khyentse Rinpoche explains, "By 'unborn' we mean that this absolute nature is not something that has come into existence at one point and may cease to exist at another. It is completely beyond coming into existence and ceasing to exist."

universal monarch (Skt. chakravartin): A king ruling over a world system; an emperor.

upaya: *See* skillful means.

ushnisha: *See* crown protuberance.

Vairochana: One of the five tathagatas and lord of the buddha family

Vairotsana: Tibet's greatest translator and one of the first seven monks to

GLOSSARY

be ordained in Tibet. He was one of the principal disciples of Padmasambhava and of Shri Singha.

Vaishravana: One of the Four Great Kings (whose god realm is the first in
the world of desire); guardian of the north and god of wealth.

vajra (Skt.; Tib. dorje): Also diamond, adamantine thunderbolt: a symbol of
unchanging and indestructible wisdom capable of penetrating through
everything; a ritual instrument symbolizing compassion, skillful means,
or awareness, and always associated with the bell, the symbol of wisdom
or emptiness.

vajra brothers and sisters: Students of the same teacher, or with whom one
has received Vajrayana teachings.

Vajradhara (Skt.): Literally, "vajra holder." In the New Tradition, Vajradhara is the primordial buddha, source of all the tantras. In the Ancient
Tradition, Vajradhara represents the principle of the teacher as enlightened holder of the Vajrayana teachings.

Vajrasattva (Skt.): The buddha who embodies the forty-two peaceful and
fifty-eight wrathful deities. The practice of Vajrasattva and recitation of
his mantra are particularly effective for purifying negative actions. In the
lineage of the Great Perfection he is the sambhogakaya buddha.

Vajrayana (Skt.): Also called the Diamond Vehicle or Mantrayana. A collection of teachings and practices based on the tantras, scriptures that discourse on the primordial purity of the mind. The six classes of Vajrayana
tantras convey this teaching in an increasingly direct and profound way.
The gateway to the Vajrayana is the empowerment, which is given by
the spiritual master. *See also* Secret Mantrayana.

vase empowerment: The first of the four empowerments. Receiving this
empowerment purifies the defilements of the body, enables one to meditate on the generation phase, and sows the seed for obtaining the vajra
body and the nirmanakaya.

vehicle (Skt. yana):. The means for traveling the path to enlightenment.

Vehicle of Characteristics: *See* Causal Vehicle of Characteristics.

Victorious One: (Skt. jina): A general epithet for a buddha.

Vidyadhara (Skt.; Tib. Rigdzin): Literally, "knowledge holder." One who
through profound means holds the deities, mantras, and the wisdom of
great bliss.

vihara (Skt.): A Buddhist monastery; a temple, dwelling place for monks, or
sanctuary.

Vikramashila: One of the most famous Buddhist universities of India,
destroyed in the twelfth century.

Vimalamitra: A great Indian master who held an important place in the lineages of the Great Perfection. He went to Tibet in the eighth century, where he taught extensively, and composed and translated numerous Sanskrit texts. The quintessence of his teaching is known as the Vima Nyingthig.

Vinaya (Skt.): One of the three pitakas; the section of the Buddha's teaching that deals with discipline, and in particular with the vows of monastic ordination.

vipashyana: *See* profound insight.

virtuous activities: The practice of Dharma in general, The term often refers to activities such as prostrations, circumambulation, and recitations of the scriptures.

wisdom: *See* primal wisdom.

wish-fulfilling jewel / wishing gem (Tib. yishin norbu; Skt. chintamani): A fabulous jewel found in the realms of the gods or nagas that fulfills all wishes.

world of desire (Skt. kamaloka, kamadhatu): The first of the three worlds, comprising the hells, and the realms of the pretas, animals, humans, asuras, and the six classes of kamaloka gods (Four Great Kings, Heaven of the Thirty-three, Heaven Free of Conflict, the Joyous Realm, Enjoying Magical Creations, and Mastery over Others' Creations).

world of form (Skt. rupadhatu): The second of the three worlds, including the twelve realms of the four concentrations and the five pure abodes.

world of formlessness: (Skt. arupadhatu): The third of the three worlds, at the peak of existence. It includes the spheres of infinite space, infinite consciousness, utter nothingness, and neither existence nor nonexistence.

wrong view (Skt. mithyadrishti): A false belief, particularly a view that will lead one to courses of action that bring more suffering.

yidam (Tib.; Skt. ishtadevata): A deity representing enlightenment, in a male or female, peaceful or wrathful form, that corresponds to the practitioner's individual nature. The yidam is the source of accomplishments.

yoga (Skt., "union"): The Tibetan term for yoga means "union with the natural state," a reference to spiritual practice.

yogi/yogin (Skt.): A person practicing a spiritual path.

SOURCES AND CREDITS

Dilgo Khyentse Rinpoche to Vajrayana practitioners at Karma Dzong, Boulder, Colorado, in June 1987. Translated from the Tibetan by Ani Jinba Palmo (Halifax, NS: Vajravairochana Translation Committee, 2002). © 1992, 2002 by Shechen Tennyi Dargyeling, Inc. Dedication translated by the Nalanda Translation Committee, © 1996 by the Nalanda Translation Committee.

A Wondrous Ocean of Advice for the Practice of Retreat in Solitude. Commentary by Dilgo Khyentse Rinpoche, translated from the Tibetan by Matthieu Könchog Tenzin. © 2010 by Shechen Publications, www .shechen.org. Root text (*ri chos zhal gdam ngo mtshar rgya mtsho*) by Jigme Lingpa, translated by David Christensen. (For further details of the translation and editing, see the colophon on page 485.)

Zurchungpa's Testament: A Commentary on Zurchung Sherab Trakpa's Eighty Chapters of Personal Advice, by Dilgo Khyentse Rinpoche, translated and edited by the Padmakara Translation Group (Ithaca, N.Y.: Snow Lion Publications, 2006). © 2006 by the Padmakara Translation Group. Reprinted by arrangement with Snow Lion Publications, Ithaca, N.Y., www.snowlionpub.com.

SELECTED VERSE

"Brilliant Moon in the Sky, Ocean of Dharma on the Ground" © 1977 by Dilgo Khyentse Rinpoche, translation © 1977 by Chögyam Trungpa. Used by special permission of Diana J. Mukpo and the Nalanda Translation Committee.

"Mixing Dharma with Your Mind" © 1977 by Dilgo Khyentse Rinpoche, translation © Padmakara Translation Group and Nelson Dudley.

"The Source of All Phenomena" is no. 86 in vol. 3 of the Tibetan edition of Khyentse Rinpoche's collected works, *skyabs rje dil mgo mkhyen brtse rin po che'i bka' bum* (Shechen Publications, 1995). The English version of this poem first appeared in *Journey to Enlightenment* by Matthieu Ricard (New York; Aperture, 1996; reprinted in paperback as *The Spirit of Tibet*), translated from the Tibetan by the Padmakara Translation Group, © 1996 by Shechen Publications, www.shechen.org.

ABOUT THE DILGO
KHYENTSE FELLOWSHIP
AND SHECHEN

DILGO KHYENTSE FELLOWSHIP is a nonprofit organization dedicated to continuing the spiritual and cultural legacy of Dilgo Khyentse Rinpoche. With its affiliated Shechen branches throughout the world, it preserves and promotes the unique heritage of the Tibetan Buddhist people.

Under the guidance of Rabjam Rinpoche, Shechen offers an authentic education in Buddhist philosophy, meditation, and sacred arts to over a thousand children, monks, and nuns. Facilities include monasteries, a nunnery, philosophical colleges, and retreat centers throughout Nepal, India, Bhutan, and Tibet.

The Shechen Institute of Traditional Tibetan Art (also known as the Tsering Art School) trains students in the traditional painting and crafts of eastern Tibet. Shechen Archives preserves rare Tibetan books, photographs, and artworks, and Shechen Publications reprints and publishes extant texts and translations.

The charitable activities of Dilgo Khyentse Rinpoche are advanced through humanitarian projects administered by Karuna-Shechen, including Shechen Medical Clinics and social outreach programs in Nepal and India.

The work of the Dilgo Khyentse Fellowship is supported by private donations, sponsorship programs, and foundations. For more information, please visit www.shechen.org.

INDEX

Page references to illustrations are in italic type.

Abhidharma, 28, 715
abhisheka. *See* empowerment(s)
absolute nature, 225–32, 234–35, 715
  analysis and, 274, 285
  aspects, lack of, 279–80, 349, 416–17
  concentration and, 192–94
  direct perception of, 283
  examples of, 260–62, 277–78, 345,
    409–10
  great pervasion of, 282–83, 350, 418
  nine ways of seeing, 245–46, 342,
    404–5
  nondual arising of, 280, 282–83, 288–
    90, 349–50, 352, 417–18, 421
  recognizing, 222, 280, 299
  remaining in, 199–200, 213–14, 223–25
  sixteen metaphoric practices on,
    254–56
  two accumulations and, 157
  See also dharmata
absolute truth, 194, 291, 518, 658, 715
absorption, sublime, 248
accomplishment (siddhi), 313, 574, 715
  bardo of this life and, 521
  empowerment and, 494–95
  mantra and, 559, 572
  supreme, 475, 582
  time needed for, 632
  view, role in, 657
accomplishment stage, 172, 477n5, 716
  mantra and, 574–75
  sadhanas, aspect of, 469, 482, 561–62

accumulations, two, 101–2, 157, 267,
  493–94, 552
action(s), 234–35, 295, 340, 400–401
  awareness of, 73
  distracting, 132
  samsaric, 31, 430n12
  spontaneous, 233, 252–53
  view and, 116, 267
activities, binding force of, 564, 581–82
Adamantine Root Verses (Jigme Lingpa),
  681
advice, meaning of, 171
afflictive emotions, 95, 128, 289, 715
  bodhichitta and, 259
  causes of, 129
  concentration and, 108–9, 189
  at death, 525
  dispelling, 208, 209–10
  emptiness of, 74, 118, 308–9
  food and, 467
  freedom from, 313
  ignorance and, 676
  incidental, 649
  practice, results from, 474
  profound insight and, 156
  purifying, 565, 566
  as spiritual friends, 178–79
  views, variance through yanas,
    624–25
  as wisdom, 205, 257
  See also five poisons; three poisons

INDEX

pointless activities for, 102–5, 120–22, 148, 324, 325, 370–71, 373
pretense in, 166–68
proper practice, 171–78, 174, 331, 384–85
rarity and preciousness of, 60, 91–92, 463, 480, 543
suitability for, 68
ten activities of, 255, 437n136
timeliness in, 80–90, 322–23, 368–69
translation of, 28–30
unconditioned, 592–93
urgency of practicing, 34
vehicles of, 28, 48, 93–94, 219, 493–94, 529–30, 591, 609
worldly concerns and, 70, 110, 130–42, 307, 309, 465
"wrong," 155–62, 329, 381–82
youth and, 89
See also Buddhism; instructions (Dharma)
dharmadhatu, 279, 506, 509, 545, 608, 720
dharmakaya, 38, 101, 139, 194, 240, 720
alaya and, 680, 686, 694
at death, 520, 525–26
five wisdoms and, 593
guru as, 638–39
mind and, 268–69
phenomena and, 246
rupakaya and, 552, 611
samadhi of suchness and, 506, 507–8
as teacher, 77
See also kayas
Dharma practitioners
capacity of, 117
diligence of, 170
inauthentic, 160–61
lazy, 469–70, 591
perfectly pure, 476
qualities of, 473–75, 484
teaching prematurely, 153–54, 167–68
See also disciples
Dharma protectors, 308, 720
dharmata, 214, 243, 250, 607, 647, 715
at death, 526, 527–28
exhaustion of, 633

luminosity in, 628
thoughts in, 626
three kayas in, 494
view of, 616, 657–58, 660, 662
See also absolute nature
Dhatvishvari, 565
Dilgo Khyentse Rinpoche, i, xxv–xxix, 486, 584, 668, 700
diligence, 82, 101, 128, 638
in concentration, 301, 306
death and, 90
in Dharma, 69–73, 542
emptiness and, 119
faith and, 41, 43
in meditation, 203
of mind, 635
in mindfulness, 640
need for, 81, 105–9, 324, 371
disciples, 68
capacity of, 78–79, 501
suitability of, 137, 159, 311–13, 355, 426–27
worthiness of, 120–21
See also Dharma practitioners
discipline, 26, 35, 36, 139–40, 309, 322–33, 327–28, 377–78
foundation of, 80
thirteen instructions on, 90–102, 323, 369–70
dissolution, natural, 283–84, 350–51, 419, 438n153
doha, 710, 713n4
Do Khyentse Yeshe Dorje, 86
Dordogne, France, xviii, xxviii, 10
doubt, 75, 150–51, 270, 462
dreams
appearance as, 274, 276
bardo experience and, 511
bardo of, 299–300
body in, 674
conduct in, 67
continuity of awareness in, 689–90
existence as, 202
progress, signs of in, 465, 480
recognizing, 533–36
sentient beings in, 286
dream yoga, 534

meditation on, 103–4
of meditative experiences, 306
outer and inner, 271, 286–87
patience and, 124
posture as aid in realizing, 297
samadhi and, 506–8, 510–13, 545
signs of realization of, 625–26
threefold, 290–92, 352, 421
understanding through yanas, 507,
602–3
vital point of, 645
without grasping, 627–28
See also under appearance; bliss; clarity; compassion; karma; mind;
phenomena
enemies, 56, 127–28
concept of, 134
helping, 178–79, 294
inherent existence, lack of, 244, 245
pleasing, 175–76
energy (prana), 297, 304–5, 538, 553, 576,
685, 721
in completion stage, 516
mantra and, 575
practices using, 467–68, 481–82
types of, 570
vajra recitation and, 573–74
enlightenment, 283, 721
ground of, 119–20
meditation and, 113
mind and, 229–30
presence of, 289
striving for, 101
See also buddhahood
Epitome of Essential Meaning, 25, 236, 314,
355
equal taste. *See* one taste
equanimity, 657–58
abiding in spacelike, 682–88, 695–96
essence (bindu), 515, 516, 531, 721
at death, 524–25
eternalism, 222, 273, 721
evenness, 235, 281–82, 721
mindfulness of, 221
and purity, union of, 117, 118
remaining in, 253, 676
resting in, 229, 687
of samsara and nirvana, 280

evil spirits. *See* demons
excellencies, three, 563
exchange (of self and other), 140
exertion, 664. *See also* diligence; effort
existence
absolute nature and, 260
belief in, 135, 225
as dream, waking from, 202
freedom from, 262–63
illusory, 210–12
of perceptions and appearances,
273–74
root of, 193–94
Expanse Section, 239
expectation, freedom from, 233–34
extremes
four, 262–66, 270, 273–74, 346, 410–11
freedom from, 221–22, 246, 277

faith, 35, 82, 214–15, 319–21
Dharma, as prerequisite for, 37, 363
discouraging another's, 183
karma and, 46–49
lack of, 40–42, 57–58, 150–51, 319, 363
meaning of, 39
objects worthy of, 80–81
six virtues of, 42–45, 319, 364
ten causes of, 45–55, 320, 364
types of, 39–40, 451
fame, 134, 141, 158–59
death and, 32, 49–50
from Dharma practice, 161
family, 32–33, 59, 83, 131, 145, 176–77
father tantras, 498
faults, 148, 150, 182, 319
examining, 174
five, 171
from lack of faith, 40–42
See also defects; folly, twenty-six
kinds
fear, 234, 531–32
fickleness, 177
fire ceremonies, 470
five paths, 191, 289
five poisons, 74, 98, 193, 722. *See also* afflictive emotions
fixation, freedom from, 233

purifying, 563
undervaluing, 157
samayasattva, 515, 546, 547, 549
Samayatara, 565
sambhogakaya, 101, 510, 525, 554, 731.
 See also kayas
sameness, 134, 375, 721. See also evenness
samsara, 138, 163, 173–74, 178, 210, 261,
 731
 as absolute nature, 146
 appearance in, 240–42, 245
 basis of, 606–8
 dharmakaya and, 507
 Dzogchen view of, 622
 existence of, 262, 286
 fear in, 33–34
 four root sufferings of, 44
 freedom from, 60
 illusion of, 77–78
 as mind's play, 216–17
 primordial freedom of, 253
 purity of, 541, 542
 rebirth and, 87–88, 135, 210
 revulsion toward, 215–16, 298, 464
 suffering of, 31, 52, 100, 450, 451–52,
 453, 478
 wisdom and, 200–202, 335–36, 392–93
samsaric existence, cutting the net,
 679–82, 694–95
Samye Chimpu (cave), 447, 595, 620
Samye (monastery), 29, 92–93, 731
Sangha, 38, 731
Sanskrit, 28
Saraha, 78, 171, 502, 688, 696, 731
Sarma. See New Tradition
sattvas, three, 549. See also jnanasattva;
 samadhisattva; samayasattva
scriptures, 38, 54
secret abhisheka, 499, 500
Secret Essence Vajrasattva abhisheka,
 503
secret-mantra vajrayana. See Vajrayana
Secret Mantrayana. See Vajrayana
secret transmission empowerment, 498
sectarianism, 93–94, 456, 460, 461
seed syllables, 510–11, 570–71

seeing, path of, 191, 435n103, 612, 728
self, notion of, 193–94, 224. See also ego-
 clinging
self-awareness, 223
self-deception, 60–61, 457
senses
 attachment to, 69, 103
 in development stage, 566
 emptiness of, 302
 nature of mind meditation and, 628
 six wisdom, 248–51, 343–44, 405–7
 as wisdom, 233
sentient beings
 benefiting, 74–75, 509, 510, 612, 642–
 44, 660–61, 664
 cherishing above self, 540
 purifying, 565, 566, 567
 trying to please, 132–33
 unborn nature of, 286, 287
seven branches, 107, 298, 731
seven noble riches, 135–36, 731
Seven Treasures (Longchenpa), 604, 609,
 610, 614, 620, 621
Shabkar Tsogdruk Rangdrol, 54
shamatha. See sustained calm
Shantarakshita, 29, 732
Shariputra, 61–62, 515, 732
Shechen Gyaltsap Pema Gyurmed
 Namgyal, xxvi, 25, 315, 358, 439n171
Shechen Monastery (Nepal), xxviii
Shechen Monastery (Tibet), xxvi, xxviii
Shechen Rabjam Rinpoche (seventh),
 xxvii, xxviii, xxix
shravakas, 27, 28, 116–17, 119, 602, 732
Shri Simha, 594, 621, 657, 732
sickness, 43–44
siddhas, 69, 656, 732
sight, authentic, 250–51
silence, benefits of, 132
simplicity, 252, 281, 290, 472, 677, 683,
 688
single taste. See one taste
Six Points of Meditation, 279–80
Six Prerequisites for Concentration, 192,
 220, 436n116
six-syllable mantra (Vajrasattva), 558,
 559, 560, 561